Clinical Textbook of Addictive Disorders

The Guilford Substance Abuse Series

EDITORS

HOWARD T. BLANE, Ph.D.
Research Institute on Alcoholism, Buffalo

THOMAS R. KOSTEN, M.D.
Yale University School of Medicine, New Haven

CLINICAL TEXTBOOK OF ADDICTIVE DISORDERS
Richard J. Frances and Sheldon I. Miller, Editors

DRINKING AND DRIVING:
ADVANCES IN RESEARCH AND PREVENTION
R. Jean Wilson and Robert E. Mann, Editors

ADDICTION AND THE VULNERABLE SELF:
MODIFIED DYNAMIC GROUP THERAPY FOR SUBSTANCE ABUSERS
Edward J. Khantzian, Kurt S. Halliday, and William E. McAuliffe

ALCOHOL AND THE FAMILY:
RESEARCH AND CLINICAL PERSPECTIVES
R. Lorraine Collins, Kenneth E. Leonard, and John S. Searles, Editors

CHILDREN OF ALCOHOLICS: CRITICAL PERSPECTIVES
Michael Windle and John S. Searles, Editors

GROUP PSYCHOTHERAPY WITH ADULT CHILDREN OF
ALCOHOLICS: TREATMENT TECHNIQUES AND
COUNTERTRANSFERENCE CONSIDERATIONS
Marsha Vannicelli

PSYCHOLOGICAL THEORIES OF DRINKING AND ALCOHOLISM
Howard T. Blane and Kenneth E. Leonard, Editors

ALCOHOL AND BIOLOGICAL MEMBRANES
Walter A. Hunt

ALCOHOL PROBLEMS IN WOMEN:
ANTECEDENTS, CONSEQUENCES, AND INTERVENTION
Sharon C. Wilsnack and Linda J. Beckman, Editors

DRINKING AND CRIME: PERSPECTIVES ON THE
RELATIONSHIPS BETWEEN ALCOHOL CONSUMPTION
AND CRIMINAL BEHAVIOR
James J. Collins, Jr., Editor

Clinical Textbook of Addictive Disorders

Edited by

RICHARD J. FRANCES, M.D.
*University of Medicine and Dentistry
of New Jersey*

SHELDON I. MILLER, M.D.
Northwestern University School of Medicine

Foreword by Melvin Sabshin, M.D.

THE GUILFORD PRESS
New York   London

© 1991 The Guilford Press
A Division of Guilford Publications, Inc.
72 Spring Street, New York, NY 10012

Printed in the United States of America.

This book is printed on acid-free paper.

Last digit is print number: 9 8 7 6 5 4 3

Library of Congress Cataloging-in-Publication Data

Clinical textbook of addictive disorders / edited by Richard J.
  Frances, Sheldon I. Miller; foreword by Melvin Sabshin.
        p.   cm. — (The Guilford substance abuse series)
    Includes bibliographical references.
    Includes Index.
    ISBN 0-89862-552-1
    1. Substance abuse. 2. Alcoholism. I. Frances, Richard J.
  II. Miller, Sheldon I.   III. Series.
    [DNLM: 1. Substance Dependence—therapy.   WM 270 C6416]
  RC564.C55   1991
  616.86—dc20
  DNLM/DLC
  for Library of Congress   90-13816
                                                          CIP

Marsha, Jenny, Avram, and David
Sarah, Lynne, and David

We love you!

Contributors

ROBERT C. ABRAMS, M.D.   Associate Professor of Clinical Psychiatry, Cornell University Medical College–New York Hospital, Westchester Division, White Plains, New York

GEORGE ALEXOPOULOS, M.D.   Associate Professor of Clinical Psychiatry, Cornell University Medical College–New York Hospital, Westchester Division, White Plains, New York

ARTHUR I. ALTERMAN, Ph.D.   Veterans Affairs Medical Center, Philadelphia, Pennsylvania; Professor of Psychiatry, University of Pennsylvania School of Medicine, Philadelphia, Pennsylvania

RICARDO CASTANEDA, M.D.   Assistant Professor of Psychiatry, Director, Alcoholism Inpatient Service, Division of Alcoholism and Drug Abuse, New York University Medical Center, New York, New York

BEVERLY R. DELANEY, M.D.   Instructor of Clinical Psychiatry, New Jersey Medical School, University of Medicine and Dentistry of New Jersey, Newark, New Jersey

STEPHEN L. DILTS, M.D.   Associate Professor of Psychiatry, University of Colorado Health Sciences Center, Denver, Colorado; Associate Director of Psychiatric Services, Denver General Hospital, Denver, Colorado

LANCE M. DODES, M.D.   Clinical Instructor of Psychiatry, Mount Auburn Hospital, Cambridge, Massachusetts

DENNIS M. DONOVAN, Ph.D.   Chief, Inpatient Addictions Treatment Center, Veterans Affairs Medical Center, Seattle, Washington; Associate Professor, Department of Psychiatry and Behavioral Sciences, University of Washington School of Medicine, Seattle, Washington

ROBERT L. DuPONT, M.D.   President, Institute for Behavior & Health, Inc., Rockville, Maryland; Clinical Professor of Psychiatry, Georgetown University School of Medicine, Washington, D.C.

RICHARD J. FRANCES, M.D.   Professor of Clinical Psychiatry, Vice Chairman of Department of Psychiatry, New Jersey Medical School, University of Medicine and Dentistry of New Jersey, Newark, New Jersey

HUGO FRANCO, M.D.   Clinical Assistant Professor of Psychiatry, Director, Dual Diagnosis Service, Division of Alcoholism and Drug Abuse, New York University Medical Center, New York, New York

MARC GALANTER, M.D.   Professor of Psychiatry, Director, Division of Alcoholism and Drug Abuse, New York University Medical Center, New York, New York

DONALD W. GOODWIN, M.D.   Professor and Chairman, Department of Psychiatry, University of Kansas Medical Center, Kansas City, Kansas

DEBORAH L. HALLER, Ph.D. Associate Chairman, Division of Substance Abuse Medicine, Assistant Professor of Psychiatry and Medicine, Medical College of Virginia Hospitals, Virginia Commonwealth University, Richmond, Virginia

ANTHONY W. HEATH, Ph.D. Associate Professor, Department of Human and Family Resources, Northern Illinois University, DeKalb, Illinois

PAULA L. HOFFMAN, Ph.D. Chief, Section on Receptor Mechanisms, Laboratory of Physiologic and Pharmacologic Studies, National Institute on Alcohol Abuse and Alcoholism, Bethesda, Maryland

NORMAN HYMOWITZ, Ph.D. Professor of Clinical Psychiatry, Department of Psychiatry, New Jersey Medical School, University of Medicine and Dentistry of New Jersey, Newark, New Jersey

PATRICIA G. ISBELL, M.D. Fellow in Child Psychiatry, University of Miami, Miami, Florida

YIFRAH KAMINER, M.D. Clinical Associate Professor of Psychiatry and Human Behavior, Department of Psychiatry, Brown University, Providence, Rhode Island; Director, Abuse Intervention Center, Bradley Hospital, East Providence, Rhode Island

LORI D. KARAN, M.D. Medical Director of Inpatient Services, Division of Substance Abuse Medicine, Assistant Professor of Medicine and Psychiatry, Medical College of Virginia Hospitals, Virginia Commonwealth University, Richmond, Virginia

STEVEN E. KELLER, Ph.D. Associate Professor of Psychiatry, Associate Professor of Neuroscience, New Jersey Medical School, University of Medicine and Dentistry of New Jersey, Newark, New Jersey

EDWARD J. KHANTZIAN, M.D. Associate Professor of Psychiatry, Harvard Medical School at The Cambridge Hospital, Cambridge, Massachusetts

PRISCILLA W. MACKAY, Ph.D. Staff Psychologist, Veterans Affairs Medical Center, Seattle, Washington; Acting Instructor, Department of Psychiatry and Behavioral Sciences, University of Washington School of Medicine, Seattle, Washington

G. ALAN MARLATT, Ph.D. Director, The Addictive Behaviors Research Center, Professor, Department of Psychology, University of Washington, Seattle, Washington

A. THOMAS McLELLAN, Ph.D. Veterans Affairs Medical Center, Philadelphia, Pennsylvania; Clinical Professor of Psychiatry, University of Pennsylvania School of Medicine, Philadelphia, Pennsylvania

ADA C. MEZZICH, Ph.D. Adjunct Assistant Professor of Psychiatry, University of Pittsburgh School of Medicine, Western Psychiatric Institute and Clinic, Pittsburgh, Pennsylvania

NORMAN S. MILLER, M.D. Assistant Professor of Psychiatry, Cornell University Medical College, Assistant Attending Psychiatrist, New York Hospital–Cornell Medical Center, Westchester Division, White Plains, New York

SHELDON I. MILLER, M.D.   Lizzie Gilman Professor and Chairman, Department of Psychiatry and Behavioral Science, Northwestern University School of Medicine, Chicago, Illinois

ROBERT B. MILLMAN, M.D.   Saul P. Steinberg Distinguished Professor of Psychiatry and Public Health, Cornell University Medical College, New York, New York

STEVEN M. MIRIN, M.D.   General Director and Acting Psychiatrist in Chief, McLean Hospital, Belmont, Massachusetts; Associate Professor of Psychiatry, Harvard Medical School, Boston, Massachusetts

EDGAR P. NACE, M.D.   Chief of Service, Substance Abuse Programs, Timberlawn Psychiatric Hospital, Dallas, Texas; Associate Professor of Clinical Psychiatry, Southwestern Medical School, Dallas, Texas

CHARLES P. O'BRIEN, M.D., Ph.D.   Veterans Affairs Medical Center, Philadelphia, Pennsylvania; Professor of Psychiatry, University of Pennsylvania School of Medicine, Philadelphia, Pennsylvania

PEGGY J. OTT, Ph.D.   Staff Psychologist/Senior Clinician, University of Pittsburgh School of Medicine, Western Psychiatric Institute and Clinic, Pittsburgh, Pennsylvania

MELVIN SABSHIN, M.D.   Medical Director, American Psychiatric Association, Washington, D.C.

KEITH E. SAYLOR, Ph.D.   Director of Research, Institute for Behavior & Health, Inc., Rockville, Maryland

STEVEN J. SCHLEIFER, M.D.   Associate Professor of Psychiatry, Director of Consultation–Liaison Psychiatry, New Jersey Medical School, University of Medicine and Dentistry of New Jersey, Newark, New Jersey

SIDNEY H. SCHNOLL, M.D., Ph.D.   Chairman, Division of Substance Abuse Medicine, Professor of Medicine and Psychiatry, Medical College of Virginia Hospitals, Virginia Commonwealth University, Richmond, Virginia

M. DUNCAN STANTON, Ph.D.   Professor and Director, Division of Family Programs, Department of Psychiatry, University of Rochester Medical Center, Rochester, New York

BORIS TABAKOFF, Ph.D.   Scientific Director, Division of Intramural Clinical and Biological Research, National Institute on Alcohol Abuse and Alcoholism, Bethesda, Maryland

RALPH E. TARTER, Ph.D.   Professor of Psychiatry and Neurology, University of Pittsburgh School of Medicine, Western Psychiatric Institute and Clinic, Pittsburgh, Pennsylvania

HUBERT H. THOMASON, JR., M.D.   Assistant Clinical Professor of Psychiatry, University of Colorado Health Sciences Center, Denver, Colorado; Medical Director, Substance Treatment Services, Denver General Hospital, Denver, Colorado

SUSAN TROSS, Ph.D.   Assistant Professor of Psychiatry, New Jersey Medical School, University of Medicine and Dentistry of New Jersey, Newark, New Jersey

CARLTON E. TURNER, Ph.D., D.Sc.   President, Princeton Diagnostic Laboratories of America, South Plainfield, New Jersey

KARL VEREBEY, Ph.D.   Chief Toxicologist, The City of New York, Department of Health, Bureau of Laboratories, New York, New York

JULIA K. WARNOCK, M.D., Ph.D.   Assistant Professor of Psychiatry, University of Kansas Medical Center, Kansas City, Kansas

CAROL J. WEISS, M.D.   Instructor of Psychiatry and Public Health, Cornell University Medical College, New York, New York

ROGER D. WEISS, M.D.   Clinical Director, Alcohol and Drug Abuse Program, McLean Hospital, Belmont, Massachusetts; Assistant Professor of Psychiatry, Harvard Medical School, Boston, Massachusetts

JOSEPH WESTERMEYER, M.D., Ph.D.   Professor and Chairman, Department of Psychiatry, University of Oklahoma Health Sciences Center, Oklahoma City, Oklahoma

Foreword

I am honored to introduce this excellent new *Clinical Textbook of Addictive Disorders,* edited by Drs. Frances and Miller and a prestigious editorial board. For almost three decades after World War II, American psychiatry's involvement in addictive disorders waned. During the past 10 years, however, there has been a dramatic change. Perhaps in no period since Dr. Benjamin Rush focused his considerable energies on the treatment of alcoholism has there been such significant attention paid by psychiatrists to the importance of developing scientific knowledge about diagnostic issues, treatment outcome, and the interrelationship between biological and psychosocial issues in addiction. This textbook reflects all of these changes. It begins with an overview that places addictions in a historical context; it goes on to describe the consequences of addiction to each drug, diagnostic issues, and problems with special populations; and then reviews the differential therapeutics of addiction treatment with descriptions of each modality.

Perhaps no area in psychiatric education needs greater emphasis and expansion than the treatment of addictive disorders. In addition to being of use to medical students, psychiatric residents, and psychiatrists, the book will serve as an educational vehicle for addiction professionals including psychologists, social workers, addiction counselors, and nurses. Moreover, teachers, lawyers, and law enforcement personnel are vitally concerned with the problems of addiction and should find the book useful.

It has been a pleasure to work closely with Drs. Frances and Miller, who in the past decade have played an important role in alerting the American Psychiatric Association (APA) to the importance of the rapid developments in addiction psychiatry, in their roles as chairpersons of the APA's Committee on Alcoholism. Dr. Richard Frances is interested in diagnostic issues and differential therapeutics, especially in the area of addictive disorders. He has played a national leadership role as founding president of the American Academy of Psychiatrists in Alcoholism and Addictions, and was important in helping to create the new Council on Addiction Psychiatry within the APA. Dr. Frances developed and led an inpatient alcohol treatment program at New York Hospital for 10 years, which is an important training ground for psychiatric residents; he has also pursued strong interests in education as director of residency training at New Jersey Medical School. He has written extensively in almost every area of addiction treatment and is the author (with J. E. Franklin) of *A Concise Guide to Treatment of Alcoholism and Addictions.*

Dr. Sheldon Miller, Lizzie Gilman Professor and Chairman of the Department of Psychiatry and Behavioral Science, Northwestern University School of

Medicine, is past president of the American Academy of Psychiatrists in Alcoholism and Addictions, and is a prominent leader in the addiction field who has himself played an important role as a researcher, teacher, and clinician. He is currently founding and editing a journal, under the auspices of The American Psychiatric Press, Inc., entitled the *American Journal of Addictions*. This major undertaking under his stewardship will reflect the importance of addictions as a re-emerging area of major concern for all psychiatrists.

The editors have done an excellent job in organizing the textbook, bringing together scholarly reviews and clinical wisdom. It is clear that we are still at an early stage in terms of knowing the best treatment or combination of treatment for patients with addictive disorders, especially those with comorbidity. It is essential, on scientific and clinical grounds, that we tailor treatments to fit patients' needs. There is no doubt that much research is needed to provide greater empirical evidence for our diagnostic and treatment approaches.

The book begins with an introductory chapter by the editors, which describes the widening scope of addiction treatment and lists some of the trends taking place in the field. A historical and cultural perspective on addiction treatment is eloquently described by Dr. Westermeyer. The second section, describing the signs, symptoms, clinical course, pharmacological treatment, and pathogenesis of addiction to each psychoactive substance, has been developed by experts on those topics. The third section is devoted to diagnostic methods. I was particularly pleased with the chapters in the section on special populations, including the one on comorbidity by Drs. Mirin and Weiss, which describes the latest psychiatric knowledge of the interaction between addictive disorders and other psychiatric disorders. Indeed, I believe that this type of interest in comorbidity will become the modal pattern in American psychiatry. Dr. Kaminer's scholarly review of adolescent psychiatry, and Drs. Abrams and Alexopoulos's chapter on geriatric addictions, are both well-written scientific reviews of their fields. The selection of authors for the section that describes treatment modalities and differential therapeutics is also outstanding. The Philadelphia group, led by Dr. O'Brien, has been especially important in articulating the differential therapeutics of addictions, and the introductory chapter by members of this group is a useful guide to treatment choices based on scientific outcome studies. Drs. Dodes and Khantzian point to the importance of understanding psychodynamic issues in approaching psychiatric treatment of addicted patients. Finally, a section that includes chapters by Dr. Goodwin's group and that of Dr. Tabakoff emphasizes the clinical relevance of research findings on familial alcoholism and other important biological developments.

The book includes chapters by many nationally eminent addictions experts, including Drs. Millman, Galanter, Mirin, O'Brien, Schnoll, Marlatt, Goodwin, Khantzian, and Tabakoff (among others), but it also includes younger coauthors who are especially dedicated to furthering the leading edge of the field. The book uses recent references, is clearly written, and avoids overinclusive details.

In summary, this is a timely textbook, long awaited by both psychiatric generalists and addiction psychiatrists who are interested in learning more about the theoretical underpinnings, the empirical evidence, and practical know-how of conducting addiction treatment. I am confident that several decades from now, this book will be remembered as part of the particular turning point in American psychiatry when addictive disorders became central to the field.

MELVIN SABSHIN, M.D.

Preface

We set out to bring together the most prestigious internationally prominent clinicians, educators, and researchers in the addiction field as chapter authors and editorial board participants in this *Clinical Textbook of Addictive Disorders*. We wanted an authoritative, rich, and convenient source of information that would be useful to all categories of health care clinicians, especially psychiatrists, other physicians, psychologists, social workers, nurses, certified addiction counselors, psychiatric residents, and students in each of these fields. Patients, families, and many allied helping professionals (such as the clergy, educators, lawyers, and police officers) are also in need of the best information about treatment of addictive disorders. Advances in diagnosis, epidemiology, understanding of the addictive process, heredity, pathophysiology, complications, and treatment outcome studies have led to a deepening understanding of addictive disorders and have expanded the armamentarium of treatment choices employed by professionals. In each chapter, we have asked distinguished authors to describe and update their area and to state clearly when they are expressing their own opinions. These are sometimes divergent and are not in all cases those of the editorial board or ourselves, but do reflect the state of a rapidly developing field that is full of controversy.

We have been eclectic clinicians in the trenches, who have led large treatment programs at the New Jersey Medical School, St. Barnabas Hospital, the New York Hospital, Sheppard Pratt Hospital, the U.S. Navy, and the U.S. Public Health Service. We have worked with thousands of inpatients, thousands of outpatients, and hundreds of psychiatric residents, using team approaches in inpatient, outpatient, and organized outpatient treatment settings. We have been teachers and researchers with a keen interest in the treatment outcome literature. In the process of founding the American Academy of Psychiatrists in Alcoholism and Addictions, which is currently a national organization with approximately 1,000 members, we have been in close communication with eminent therapists about their treatment practices. We are gratified by the public and professional reawakening regarding the critical need to prevent, diagnose, and treat alcohol and drug addiction. At the same time, increasing costs have led to the importance of choosing wisely among treatment settings and formats, in order to maximize cost-effectiveness and to extend the benefits of treatment most widely.

Even though there has been a growth in psychiatric residency curriculums and the creation of 44 university-based psychiatric fellowships, there is still a major shortage of well-trained addictions experts, and there is a greater need than ever for psychiatric generalists to become more expert in the field (Galanter, 1989; Miller & Frances, 1986).

We have asked our authors to focus on the most clinically relevant material as concisely and clearly as possible. They have in most instances reviewed and summarized, and avoided extensive detailed presentation of research data. By outlining chapters for authors in advance of the book, we were able to achieve consistency within sections of the book and to reduce redundancy. We were delighted to find that some of our best researchers are also delightfully good teachers and writers. Our internationally famous editorial board made excellent comments and added to the quality of our reviews.

Many have labored long to pull the latest information together in this textbook. Our scholarly, careful, and hard-working authors were diligent, accommodating, wise, and tolerant of the need for revisions, which were inevitable when two editors, an editorial board, and a publisher are as careful as we were. Our publisher, Seymour Weingarten, had many keen insights and useful suggestions that have enriched the book and made it more pleasant to read.

We are very grateful to Roberta Shepherd and Chanda Johnson, who prepared the manuscript. Many of our teachers, colleagues, and students have given important advice on this project, and we will only be able to name a few: John Franklin, M.D., Allen Frances, M.D., Howard Gilman, M.D., Donna Holmes, Ph.D., Jacob Lindenthal, Ph.D., William Layman, M.D., Marc Galanter, M.D., Steven Schleifer, M.D., and Alice Condé. We are grateful to all the members of the American Academy of Psychiatrists in Alcoholism and Addictions who have contributed to educating us about their treatment practices. We would like to also thank our wives, Marsha and Sarah, for their suggestions and patience with us, and we hope that our children, Jenny, Avram, and David, and Lynne and David, will enjoy reading it.

Finally, the ultimate test of the value of our authors' contributions is in whether this volume will lead to better patient care through providing the necessary skills, attitudes, and knowledge about addictions to our clinician readers. No patient population is more interesting, challenging, or rewarding to work with, nor currently more underdiagnosed and undertreated.

RICHARD J. FRANCES, M.D.
SHELDON I. MILLER, M.D.

References

Galanter, M. (1989). *Postgraduate medical fellowships in alcoholism and drug abuse*. New York: Center for Medical Fellowship in Alcoholism and Drug Abuse, New York University.

Miller, S. I., & Frances, R. J. (1986). Psychiatrists and the treatment of addictions: Perceptions and practices. *American Journal of Alcohol and Drug Abuse, 12*(3), 187–197.

Contents

PART IV.   EMERGING TREATMENT ISSUES
FOR SPECIAL POPULATIONS

PART V.   TREATMENT SELECTION AND MODALITIES

PART VI.   TREATMENT IMPLICATIONS OF NEW
ALCOHOL RESEARCH FINDINGS

Clinical Textbook of Addictive Disorders

PART ONE

OVERVIEW AND HISTORICAL CONTEXT

1

Addiction Treatment: The Widening Scope

RICHARD J. FRANCES
SHELDON I. MILLER

If they have to get addicted, I would rather have them addicted to psychotherapy than to drugs—Semrad (1983, p. 179)

Magnitude of the Problem

President Bush has reflected the public's view that drug abuse is the number one problem in the United States, and the sheer availability of treatment for addictive disorders has markedly increased in recent years. However, considerable evidence exists that addictions remain markedly underdiagnosed and undertreated in a variety of clinical settings. Fewer than 10% of addicted people either are in self-help groups or receive professional treatment; very few receive psychiatric evaluation; and the field's major challenge is helping substance abusers to accept and continue treatment (Frances, Miller, & Galanter, 1989). Although everyone talks about the need for increased treatment slots because of intravenous drug use and the risks of spread of human immunodeficiency virus (HIV) infection (Schleifer et al., 1989), there has not been a major increase in treatment availability in some of the communities showing greatest need, such as those that serve the inner-city poor. Addicted patients in emergency rooms, general hospital beds, and physicians' offices are often not diagnosed, confronted, or treated.

Addictive disorders pose a dangerous threat to our nation's health, play a major role in crime and in corruption, and lead to enormous direct and indirect costs. Both cheap and highly available, alcohol, tobacco, and illegal drugs are used, are abused, and lead to dependence. The lifetime incidence of alcohol and drug abuse approaches one-fifth of the population, and this abuse has devastating effects on families and significant others (Helzer & Pryzbeck, 1988). In 1988, 13 million Americans were diagnosed as alcoholics, and 14.5 million had used illegal drugs (Office of the President, 1989). Victims of accidents, homicide, and family violence add to the numbers who are adversely affected by addictive disorders. Harwood, Napolitano, Kristiansen, and Collins (1984) reported projections that the direct and indirect costs of alcoholism

3

would reach $89.5 billion and those of drug abuse would reach $46.9 billion by 1990, and that the costs of both forms of abuse would rise to $150 billion by 1995. These projections were based on 1983 dollars and did not take inflation into account. A recent U. S. Chamber of Commerce estimate of $110 billion for illegal drug sales would make addiction the most profitable U.S. industry and a major drain on the nation's economy (Office of the President, 1989). Holder (1987) found that untreated alcoholics had twice the general health care costs of nonalcoholics and that there were significant cost reductions in the 24 months after alcohol treatment.

It has been estimated that more than two-thirds of hospitalized alcoholics have additional psychiatric disorders and that 15% of alcoholics will die of suicide (Frances & Allen, 1985; Frances, Franklin, & Flavin, 1987). Half of 40,000 annual car deaths; three-fourths of robberies and felony assaults by young people; and half of homicides, accidents, and burns are also substance-related. Drug-related gunfights and drive-by shootings, both of which are on the increase, kill bystanders and terrorize neighborhoods. Physical complications of addictive disorders, including cirrhosis, cancer, hepatitis, organic brain diseases, ulcers, impotence, infertility, fetal alcohol and addiction syndromes, HIV transmission, heart disease, pneumonia, and tuberculosis, are major contributors to morbidity and mortality. Half of all acquired immune deficiency syndrome (AIDS) deaths relate to intravenous drug use, which is the largest source of new HIV infection (Schilling et al., 1989).

The use of illegal drugs in the United States went from practically being nonexistent in the 1950s to including approximately one-third of Americans in 1985. By 1982, 20 million Americans had tried cocaine; it was recently estimated that there are 6 million current regular cocaine users, with an increased number who are becoming dependent. In the 3 years from 1985 to 1988, drug-related hospital admissions more than doubled. The 200,000 babies born to mothers who use drugs are at greater risk of low birth weight, perinatal complications, mental and physical complications, prematurity, child abuse, and infant mortality than are the babies of non-drug-using mothers. (Office of the President, 1989).

The effects of drugs on drug-exporting countries in Central and South America, and in Southeast and West Asia, have been devastating and have led to serious social, health, economic, and political upheaval. The resulting corruption, violence, international tension, and economic drain have threatened regional and global peace and stability and have made drugs a major preoccupation of American foreign policy. New forms of drug administration and packaging, such as smokeable "crack" cocaine or "ice" amphetamines, threaten to reverse trends in the direction of reduced illegal drug use and to lead to greater severity of consequences of dependence.

However, the trend toward lowered illegal drug use, with an estimated 37% drop from 1985 to 1989, may indicate that some drug battles were beginning to be won before President Bush launched his assault on drugs late in 1989. The battle to inform the public, which has had the greatest effect in reducing casual middle-class use of marijuana and cocaine, is succeeding, as evidenced by reports that drugs are seen in many surveys as the leading threat to the nation, outweighing fears of war. The White House drug control strategy (Office of the President, 1989) in fact sets attainable, realistic goals. For example, a 2-year goal of 10% reduction and a 10-year goal of 50% reduction in people reporting illegal drug use are in the direction of current trends. There also seems to be acceptance that the aim is for containment and decrease of the problem; it is recognized that elimination of addictive disorders is unlikely in a society as free as ours. The strategy has been criticized as relying too heavily on interdiction rather than treatment, avoiding the problems of alcohol and tobacco, and potentially further stigmatizing or scapegoating addicted patients. It is an evolving process and will be further refined as results are studied.

The myths, misinformation, and misunderstanding regarding addicted patients lead to avoidance of important issues and to stigmatization, which further contribute to denial, neglect, fear, and suffering. Addicts' behavior is labeled as entirely willful rather than as part of an illness that is treatable. The recent emphasis on toughness of laws increases the dangers of scapegoating addicts for all of society's problems, rather than seeing that any of us and our families can need rescuing from an addictive disorder.

The frustration with inadequate anti drug campaigns has led a growing group of well-intentioned political and professional leaders to raise a dialogue for legalization of drugs, in an effort to remove the profit motive for drug promotion. Legalization is opposed by most clinicians in the addiction field, who feel that availability, use, abuse, and dependence would be increased in ways that would dangerously exacerbate the problem—results that followed the termination of Prohibition in the 1930s. The direct consequences of increased cocaine use, for example, would be more widespread psychiatric and medical complications of addiction and an increased number of babies born affected by their mothers' cocaine use. The corrupting effects of cocaine on personality would still be present even if the drugs were made legally available. With legalization, incentive for drug treatment might decline, and greater numbers would be trapped in an addictive cycle. In all probability, a vastly increased number of people would become addicted to stimulants and opioids. Fortunately, America is not ready for legalization of drugs; the idea is impractical on clinical as well as political and moral grounds. At the same time, however, the dialogue had helped to point out that efforts at stopping drugs from coming into the country alone, or current means of treatment and prevention, may not be sufficient to reduce the problem in major ways. While efforts in many directions are needed, considerable attention should be paid to research in order to find new and effective means of addressing prevention and treatment.

Keeping an Open Mind

Patients with addictive disorders are a heterogeneous and complicated group. The stereotypes about treatment of patients with addictions are filled with striking paradoxes and can lead to stigmatization, which may in turn result in underfunding of treatment and research. Addicts are described as among the hardest patients to treat, the most ungrateful, the angriest, the most sociopathic, and the most dependent and in need of support; yet in the hands of therapists with proper skills and attitudes, they may have greater possibilities of rehabilitation and recovery than many other categories of psychiatric patients. They are among the most appreciative of the sobriety that recovery and treatment provide, and often among the most ridden with guilt and shame about the effects of addictive behavior. Afflicted with the acute and chronic effects of psychoactive substances on brain function, they may initially require the most support and yet may be in need of the greatest confrontation and even coercion, especially in regard to denial of the addiction.

The same patients who are the most dependent on substances are the least able to allow themselves to depend on others, and yet ultimately may come to rely on self-help and to benefit greatly from groups. Having dependency needs gratified by human contact rather than drugs, which is captured in the Semrad quotation at the beginning of this chapter, is a major theme of this book. A long-term goal of learning to take and give to others maturely is present in many treatments. Addicted patients are both the biggest risk takers and the most frightened. They have the greatest and most unrealistic of high expectations, while also frequently being easily disappointed and feeling helpless and hopeless.

In the state of active addiction, these patients are among the most likely to seek drugs to change their mood, but in recovery they may be among the most frightened of even taking medications prescribed by physicians. They range from the most hopeless, frightened, selfish, aggressive, and disheveled, to paradoxically having the highest expectations; showing considerable bravery in facing the challenges of recovery; being the most generous with their time and efforts in helping fellow patients; and, surprisingly, sometimes being among the most prestigious, fastidious, and compulsive of people. Addicts can seem to be both the toughest and the most vulnerable, the most ashamed and the proudest, the most lying and denying and the most honest in facing the truth.

Addicts have defied description in terms of one cluster of traits or personality style; they encompass a wide range of patients, some with additional psychiatric problems. The problem of whether certain temperaments, which may be biologically determined, may predispose individuals to one or another form of addictive disorder is a promising hypothesis currently being studied (Cloninger, Dinwiddie, & Reich, 1989). However, the specific way in which genetics translate to alcoholism or any other addiction has not yet been determined. The question of what is inherited, and how that inheritance interacts with the environment to lead to addictive disorders in certain people, remains unanswered (see Goodwin & Warnock, Chapter 21, this volume).

Patients with addictive disorders in fact come in all shapes, colors, and sizes, accompanied with the whole array of *Diagnostic and Statistical Manual*

(DSM) diagnoses. Each patient thus presents a unique set of challenges to the therapist, as well as sharing common human problems with fellow addicts and psychiatric patients (Allen & Frances, 1986). In addition to reading textbooks such as this one, students of addictive disorders need to watch their patients carefully and listen to them closely. A good deal of psychotherapy and rehabilitation involves helping the addicted patient solve life problems once the drugs have been removed. Whether these problems have been there earlier or are caused by the addictive process, drug effects, or medical complications, they cannot be dealt with while substance use continues; the more they are coped with in a drug-free state, the smaller the chance for a relapse becomes. It is odd but true that patients are sometimes frightened of becoming addicted to Twelve-Step programs or to psychotherapy, when these are far preferable to psychoactive substances. The same addicts who are great believers in magic are also the most mistrustful. Working through a patient's mistrust of medication, individual therapy, and group treatments is a challenge in which the therapist's dependability, integrity, good judgment, and flexibility are constantly tested. In evaluating each patient and struggling with making the diagnosis, tailoring treatment plans, and making adjustments in treatment-resistant cases, we recommend keeping an open mind; clinical experience and good judgment should be combined with an up-to-date knowledge of the treatment literature and new techniques (Frances, 1988).

Trends in Addiction Treatment

The futurist Alvin Toffler, in his book *The Third Wave*, has talked about the revolutionary societal and power changes that are taking place in the postindividual revolution (Toffler, 1980). These changes affect society as a whole and the health care system, and lead to changing patterns of alcoholism and drug abuse and their treatment. These power shifts also affect health care delivery. Toffler describes (1) changes in the power structure brought about by the threat of violence affecting governmental, military, and police power; (2) changes in financial power; and (3) the enormous revolution of knowledge, information, and education.

Toffler's observations about societal change have implications for addiction treatment. Each of these changing cultural areas has had an effect on the addiction field, and in turn has been affected by the powerful influence of addictions on our culture. Violence and the threat of violence, the corrupting influence of drugs within our own country, and the international repercussions of governments literally fighting wars with drug lords have all had important police, military, political, and governmental effects. For instance, the U.S. invasion of Panama in late 1989 was in part a response to illegal drug traffic.

The country is beginning to mobilize in what will be a long fight to regain control over our nation's streets, and this leads to creation of powerful political forces on both sides that will inevitably affect treatment and treatment resources. Few politicians can avoid the issue of drug abuse, especially in relation to crime. The question of whether to invest more in instruments of force or instruments of treatment and prevention has important health policy implications. In addition, there is rising governmental pressure for civil commitment and coercive efforts to force treatment for drug abusers who use illegal drugs, commit crime, are hazardous to others, and are severely in need of care.

Major changes in our economy, sources of wealth, and finances also have major effects on addiction treatment. The vast wealth of drug cartels, and the financial incentives (both real and illusory) for young people in urban ghettos to get involved with illegal drug sales, are powerful factors in the intractability of the drug problem. In addition, the legal promotion of cigarettes and smokeless tobacco, and the large financial stake for promoting these products within and outside of our borders, have led to fights against labeling and limitations of sales; these factors also pose a challenge to any treatment and prevention efforts.

The costliness of substance problems to industry is vast, and accidents such as the *Exxon Valdez* oil spill have generated a need for greater action. Corporations' awareness of the cost-effectiveness of promoting prevention and treatment programs, including wellness, fitness, and employee assistance programs, has been a major factor in promoting treatment. More than 10,000 corporations have employee assistance programs, and these have been well received by management and labor (Frances & Franklin, 1987). However, spiraling costs of health care have alarmed the corporate world along with third-party payers, and will lead to pressures to contain costs in order to avoid disaster. In desperation, the carriers as well as the employers are beginning to consider rationing treatment, even though they realize the potential dangers of doing so.

Changing social patterns, such as increases in wealth for some, increased leisure time, and more complicated family arrangements, have contributed to a culture that seeks excitement, escape, and release; these changes have thus fueled experimentation with, use of, and addiction to substances. At the other end of the spectrum, disadvantaged urban centers with high unemployment, high dropout rates in schools, inadequate social services, and breakdown of the family system have all contributed to an atmosphere ripe for drug addiction as either an emotional escape or a perceived economic way to escape conditions of poverty. With astronomical and quick tax-free profits, and few or no captial expenses necessary, the drug trade beckons those with ambition, regardless of lack of education, skills, or training. Advances in medicine and pharmacology have also contributed to a "feel good" culture in which people use both illegal and legal drugs to seek relief from pain, anxiety, and depression and to attain a desired state of feeling.

The third major shift in power has been caused by a revolution in the development of new information, information processing, and technology. On the downside, these changes have led to the development of new abusable drugs, increases in marketing and availability of drugs, new forms of packaging and administering drugs, more sophisticated methods of escaping police detection, and increased communication among criminals (providing for a global network of operations for drug cartels).

On the positive side, the information revolution has also led to greater public awareness of drug problems and their consequences, as a result of the efforts of the mass media. This is fostering research toward an understanding of addictive disorders, as well as greater public education regarding them. We are obtaining data more rapidly about the scope of the problem, its changing nature, epidemiology and patterns of use and abuse, comorbidity, and differential therapeutics. Over the last few years, we have seen the greatest expansion of research funds in drugs and alcohol since the founding of the Alcohol, Drug Abuse, and Mental Health Administration (ADAMHA). There is an increasing effort to train health care professionals of every discipline, together with a general societal awakening about the importance of the problem.

The rapid growth of information and technology affects the knowledge base of clinicians, patients, and their families, and results in better targeting of resources to problems. Treatment outcome research is likely to yield a better knowledge of differential therapeutics, and systems will be refined in carefully tailored treatment programs so that the right treatment or combination of treatments is given to the right patient in an efficient and flexible manner. Treatments need to be custom-made and not mass-produced; this will become possible with more sophisticated means of gathering history, making the right diagnoses, and developing treatments targeted to specific symptom patterns and subpopulations (Hester & Miller, 1989). This movement will be fueled not only by treatment considerations but also by third-party insurers, who question the use of a single treatment for all suffering from addictive disorders, regardless of their diversity. Since information will be more widely available, patients, families, and referral services will be increasingly sophisticated and will require a more open and direct relationship with treatment staff. Community, family, and patient advocacy groups will have closer communication with the treatment team, and care will be increasingly consumer-directed.

Costs need to be considered in each decision. Care must be taken not to spend all resources on expensive procedures such as inpatient treatment unless necessary, and to make sure that resources are available for important outpatient treatment and aftercare. Families or corporations should not be pushed into feeling guilty by treatment centers' requests that blank checks be written for unproven treatments. Unless efforts to contain spiraling costs become successful, a major breakdown of support for addiction treatment in particular and the health care system in general is likely to occur (Mezachow, Miller, Seixas, & Frances, 1987).

For many years, advertising and the mass media have directly and indirectly promoted addictive behavior. In recent years public health programs, public messages, statements by important public figures, and mass media coverage have led to changing public attitudes about drug and alcohol abuse, and this trend is likely to continue. Greater awareness of the social costs of the problem has also led to awareness of the special needs of subpopulations and increasing subspecialization within the addiction field. Programs for minorities, women, adolescents, geriatric patients, cultural and ethnic groups, the mentally retarded, and the physically handicapped have highlighted the need for customized care (Frances & Strauser, 1988). In populations with major medical complications, especially the large numbers of HIV-infected addicts and their families, there will be an increasing need for sophisticated medical services. Community supports are especially hard to develop for this population, which has not been as well organized or mobilized to fight the spread of AIDS as has been the case in the gay community (see Schleifer, Delaney, Tross, & Keller, Chapter 13, this volume).

Increased research on genetics; new drugs to block craving; the ability to treat psychiatric and medical complications in a sophisticated way; greater involvement of families in treatment; drugs that block effects of substances; drugs to treat withdrawal and prolonged abstinence syndromes, as well as psychiatric complications; and the application of new technologies such as cerebral blood flow scanners and positron emission tomography—all these developments are also likely to have treatment and research implications. The development of animal models may lead to important pharmacological developments as well as to better understanding of the mechanism, etiology, and pathophysiology of addictions (Frances & Franklin, 1988).

Perhaps the most important opportunities for clinical research are likely to come from those who work most closely with patients; these individuals see the specific clinical problems that subpopulations bring and can raise research questions devoted to answering those questions. These problems are likely to lead to new treatment approaches that are more relevant to clinical care than questions raised centrally by those who are far away from patient care. There will be a need to gather opinions from those directly in the field, whose enormous practical wisdom must be tested in rigorous controlled treatment outcome studies. In order to be most effective, treatment programs must also be organized so that those who care for patients have major input in their design and implementation, which will need to be customized to patient needs and to local cultural conditions. The days in which patients can be treated in "cookie cutter" programs are numbered.

Whether we look at changes in the threat of violence, the world of finance, or the development of information or technology, we see that they have effects both in promoting and in fighting the spread of addictive disorders, as well as important effects on shaping treatment and prevention stragegies. The rapid pace of societal change will necessitate major changes in approaching addiction treatment.

In summary, the major trends are as follows:

• Increased knowledge and information about etiology, pathophysiology, epidemiology, clinical course, and treatment of addictive disorders.

- Use of structured interviews, laboratory tests, and computer-ratable instruments to help us better screen, diagnose, and refer patients, and to customize addiction treatment.
- Increased subspecialization, and greater numbers of addiction experts.
- Increased differential therapeutics, targeting treatment for psychiatric and medical comorbidity.
- A widening distribution of knowledge shared by patients and their families.
- More universally available treatment.
- Increased partnership among the medical community, lay advocacy groups, and Twelve-Step self-help programs.
- New and better treatment methods.
- More use of outpatient and organized outpatient treatment programs to contain costs by limiting inpatient care.
- An increased knowledge of changing trends and fads in abuse with more rapid epidemiological study.
- A continued increase in public concern and awareness.
- Greater efforts at prevention at the family, school, mass media, and medical screening levels.
- An increased use of team approaches, requiring close communication among disciplines.
- An increase in managed care with groups of providers such as health maintenance organizations, which are showing increasing concern for the costs of treatment.
- An increase in basic and clinical research.
- An increase in peer review, quality assurance, and efforts to remove abuses in the field (such as overfilling hospital beds).

There are likely to be conflicts within some of these trends, such as a consolidation of growth and power in hospital chains at a time when programs will need to be tailored more closely to subpopulations and local conditions. The changes provide opportunities to reverse recent declines in the image of psychiatry, to spread information, and to make innovations in treatment more rapidly. Unlike the area of psychoanalysis, in which the doctor must go through special experiences in order to achieve a special understanding that would be difficult to communicate on a mass scale, knowledge about alcohol and drug treatment is openly accessible and less arcane. Increasingly, well-informed patients and their families will play a greater role in participating in the process of treatment planning.

Trends in Diagnosis

Considerable progress on nosology has occurred with the revised third edition of the DSM (DSM-III-R) and work on the fourth edition (DSM-IV). The criteria developed for the DSM-III-R are measurable and reliable, and have proven valid in field trials. The concept of psychoactive substance dependency was broadened in the DSM-III-R to include psychosocial criteria as well as tolerance and withdrawal, and the concept of abuse was narrowed to a residual category of those who have major problems with substances but do not meet at least three operational criteria. The concept of a general dependent syndrome with interchangeable items for most drugs was built in, and the ability to diagnose moderate, mild, and severe addictive disorders has also proven to have clinical validity (Rounsaville & Kranzler, 1989).

Whereas in the creation of the DSM-III-R a group of experts developed clinical criteria in large part on the basis of their own clinical experience, the DSM-IV process is relying on greater empirical data and field study. The process for developing DSM-IV criteria has involved a work group and advisors, who initially conducted extensive literature reviews of studies using DSM-III-R criteria. Unanswered diagnostic problems are leading to reanalysis of unpublished data and to field trials. The substance disorders work group is examining the following key areas that could affect typology: whether to include a subtype of familial alcohol or substance abuse or dependence, with diagnostic and treatment implications; ways of dealing with "dual diagnosis"; the question of whether to combine amphetamines and other stimulants and cocaine into one category; and the various implications of the concept of the protracted abstinence syndrome. In addition, the questions of how to set points of addiction disorders to describe where use leaves off and abuse begins; at what point to apply the label "dependence"; and how to note severity of dependence are hotly debated. The importance of agreed-upon criteria for subtypes of psychiatric substance disorders for any research on treatment outcome is obvious. The problem of not having clear biological markers or easy-to-apply ways of telling when alcohol use has led to abuse and when it has led to dependence leads to problems in matching data sets when doing research, as well as in helping patients to accept their diagnosis and get treatment.

Until a greater etiological understanding of the sources of addictive disorders with a clear pathophysiological basis is understood, our diagnostic system must rely on keen observation and description, careful listening to patients, and careful history taking from patients and their relatives. The use of toxicology, the use of laboratory evidence on complications of addiction, and (in future) the development of better biological markers are all aids in making the correct diagnosis. Unfortunately, there are too many false positives and false negatives for any of the biological markers to be applied in a way that has current major clinical application. Markers of recent heavy alcohol use, such as carbohydrate-deficient transferrin (Stibler, Borg, & Joustin, 1986) and serum γ-glutamyltransferase, show promise for use as screening devices and aids in early detection of relapse in relapse prevention aftercare programs.

Models of Addictive Disorders and Their Treatment

The addiction field has not yet arrived at clear etiological models of the addictive disorders including their causes, pathophysiology, clinical course, and epidemiological patterns. Nor has it developed treatments that perfectly fit these models. Even with advances in nosology, addictive disorders are complex to describe and are affected by a number of etiological dimensions, and no single explanatory means of subtyping has yet been proven. Subtyping by familial versus nonfamilial occurrence (Goodwin, Schulsinger, Hermansen, Guze, & Winokur, 1973; Frances, Bucky, & Alexopoulos, 1984), primary versus secondary status (Schuckit, 1985), comorbidity (including associated character disorders), temperament, severity, drug category, and other characteristics all have their value, but at present all are still at best descriptive. Achieving an understanding of addictive disorders at the biological level has been the goal of studies in the following areas: possible genetic markers; possible family linkages; effects on neurotransmitters, receptors, peptides, and endorphins; effects on the cell membrane that could contribute to the development of tolerance and withdrawal; animal models; brain imaging and cerebral blood flow; and computerized electroencephalography (Sullivan, 1990). A widening biological understanding of addictive disorders has important implications for a variety of treatment approaches, especially psychopharmacological approaches that treat effects of intoxication, withdrawal, and psychiatric comorbidity.

Unfortunately, at this writing there is no proven biological treatment for alcoholism. Each promising drug that has been tested in the hope it would reduce relapse by intervening in the basic disease process has failed. The most recent example is the use of lithium in the treatment of depression-free alcoholism, which has been reported in a large multicenter Veterans Affairs (VA) study to be ineffective (Dorus et al., 1989). We continue to hope for breakthroughs, and the research continues. Current groups of drugs under consideration include the tricyclic antidepressants. There is also interest in the effect of serotonin uptake inhibitors, both tricyclics and others. For the moment, only Antabuse remains as a symptomatic adjunct to a comprehensive biopsychosocial approach to alcoholism. In addition, heroin competitors and narcotic blockers remain available for treatment of narcotic addiction. Current research on cocaine treatment includes interesting and promising data on the use of tricyclic antidepressants (Gawin, Kleber, & Byck, 1989). With increasing understanding of the biology of the central nervous system and the role of the various neurotransmitter systems, it is hoped that specific treatment approaches will be developed (see Tabakoff & Hoffman, Chapter 22, this volume).

At the psychological level, a variety of etiological models have implications for treatment approaches. The application of psychodynamic principles to addictive disorders rests on an understanding of the effects of child development interacting with temperament; knowledge of areas of conflict; an understanding of unconscious phenomena, defenses, and object relations, with an emphasis on transference and countertransference issues; and use of an ego-psychological model. Early psychodynamic theorists hypothesized major instinctive fixation at an oral level of functioning, and connected addictive behavior with defenses against homosexuality and masturbation (Lorand, 1948). Modern psychodynamic theorists have emphasized a self-medication hypothesis, self-care, and the use of substances to regulate affect (see Dodes & Khantzian, Chapter 17, this volume). Psychodynamic principles are the basis for exploratory treatments that use individual psychotherapy to help patients better understand their conflicts, feelings, and patterns of dealing with situations, and to help them seek meaningful interaction and dependency with people rather than with drugs (Khantzian, 1986; Silber, 1974; Krystal, 1982; Frances, Khantzian, & Tamerin, 1989).

Cognitive and behavioral therapists (Miller & Hester, 1980), have applied principles of learning, conditioning, and cognitive theories to treatment of addictive disorders. Approaches that include education, behavioral therapy, and cognitive treatments have been growing in sophistication and lend themselves to research. Cognitive treatments focus on cognitive distortions found in the thought patterns, intellectual outlook, and emotional attitude of addicted patients, and focus on helping the patients make specific changes in these areas that can add to self-fulfillment and improve interpersonal relationships. Treatment of depression and anxiety through correction of cognitive distortions and poor self-evaluation is aimed at helping patients modify the tendency to view themselves as helpless, hopeless losers through designing tasks that help the patients correct distortions in interpretation of experience. In addition to this cognitive approach, behavioral interventions encompass solving problems through building specific skills (such as in social skills training), relapse prevention, self-monitoring, relaxation, and contingency contracting, all of which are being tested through research (see Mackay, Donovan, & Marlatt, Chapter 20, this volume).

Approaches that recognize the importance of cultural and social issues have theoretical underpinnings in general systems theory; sociocultural models; family therapy theory; use of spirituality and religion; and social models of control through interdiction, limitation of availability, social policies, laws, and calls to community and public involvement (see Galanter, Castaneda, & Franco, Chapter 19, and Heath & Stanton, Chapter 18, this volume). Community action programs to limit use of nicotine in public places, organized efforts to reduce drunk driving through use of designated drivers, and laws that raise the legal drinking age are examples of social policies aimed at prevention and treatment.

Treatment approaches such as rehabilitation programs, the Twelve-Step self-help movement, and organized outpatient programs tend to borrow from a number of the theoretical models described above. The best programs tailor the model of treatment to individual needs of patients and are flexible in using models to their maximal effectiveness (Frances & Franklin, 1989). The ultimate test of any of the theories described above remains clinical effectiveness. At our current state of knowledge, therapists should be trained to incorporate a variety of these modalities in their work, because no single one has proven to be explanatory or to meet all of the complex problems presented by patients (Hester & Miller, 1989). As this book is being written, there are multicenter treatment studies underway that hope to shed light on the questions of what treatment is best for whom and what are the characteristics upon which treatment choices should be based.

Given this wide range of theoretical models, an armamentarium of treatment approaches, and a limited budget, what are therapists, patients, families, and administrators to do? Which treatment or combination of treatments is likely to be most effective for a given patient? What is the best setting, and what is the best use of limited treatment resources? Who is best equipped to treat this patient, and how focused or diffuse should the treatment be? This volume is devoted to helping clinicians, patients, and their families answer these questions as best we can (see Alterman, O'Brien, & McLellan, Chapter 16).

The clinician who is treating addicted patients must become familiar with a variety of models of addictive disorders. The clinician must expand his or her skills in a range of treatment approaches and combinations of these approaches to best serve patients. Experienced addiction clinicians use their knowledge of psychodynamics, educate patients, incorporate beneficial cognitive and behavioral tools, work together with self-help groups, stay apprised of new biological findings, consult on developing public policy, and work toward tailoring approaches to cultural subpopulations and those with additional comorbidity.

In summary, differential therapeutics includes choices of individual, family, group, and biological approaches, based on a variety of models of addictive behavior. The psychiatrist has an important leadership role in flexibility tailoring treatment to patients' needs, evaluating indications for making sure each patient is getting the right treatment or right combination of treatments, and keeping up with advances in treatment outcome research. In order for these treatments to be effective, the patient must remain abstinent while in treatment, with the exception of use of methadone replacement when appropriate.

Unfortunately, in spite of growing attention to addictive disorders, there remains a national shortage of psychiatrists well trained in the addictions. An effort to increase the number of university-based fellowships has led to the creation of 44 such fellowships nationally. Clinical training in addiction psychiatry needs to be strengthened at every level of psychiatric training, with high-quality rotations in substance abuse and supervised clinical experience. Similar efforts need to be mounted in addiction medicine and other primary care specialties, as well as in allied health care professions such as nursing, social work, psychology, and counseling, which must also provide more specialized addiction training.

Establishing a Treatment Alliance

A crucial part of intervention is motivating patients for treatment. In no other illness is it as difficult to get patients to accept the problem, nor is the need for a treatment alliance more important. Motivation is a two-way street that also requires readiness on the part of clinicians to diagnose and work through patients' resistances. When we consider the magnitude of the national problem and the prevalence of the disease of addiction, the relatively low rates of patients who agree to go to Twelve-Step and professional programs are largely due to the remarkable power of defensive denial in addicted patients, and the need for a crisis to lead them to treatment. Addictive disorders contribute to denial, lying, and organicity within a patient, which have an infectious quality leading to denial, neglect, enabling, and sometimes corruption of relationships with family members, social agencies, and physicians. The patient's inability to accept strong dependency needs, and difficulty in agreeing to transfer those dependency needs onto something other than the self, leads to resistance to both Twelve-Step self-help groups and other forms of treatment.

Denial of the effects of substance use on relationships at work, at school, in the family, and with the law, as well as of medical complications, needs careful exploration; attention must be paid to early signs and symptoms of problems. At work, personality conflicts, lateness in getting projects done, and absences will occur long before the patient has lost a job. At home, sexual problems, problems in communication, conflicts with children, and quarreling will occur long before spouse and child abuse and neglect or other major family problems lead to divorce. Increases in numbers of traffic violations and accidents are likely to occur before an arrest for driving while intoxicated. Blackouts, gastritis, tolerance, and subtle signs of withdrawal are likely to occur before severe tremors, early morning drinking, ulcers, cirrhosis, and pancreatitis. (For a description of assessment tools that provide comprehensive questionnaires for diagnostic purposes, see Tarter, Ott, & Mezzich, Chapter 11, this volume.)

More often than not, the patient, family, and therapists struggle with the stigma of an addictive disorder and are reluctant both to admit to its impact on so many areas of functioning and to agree to a program of abstinence, which is the goal of treatment recommended by most clinicians. Frequently, feelings of helplessness and hopelessness about achieving a stable, substance-free recovery are a result of associated depression, anxiety, and previous failed efforts at cutting down. One valuable means of confronting hopelessness is providing exposure to the life histories of recovering addicts and pointing to periods in the patient's own life where abstinence was accompanied by improved functioning.

The challenge of forming a therapeutic alliance with treatment-resistant addicted patients is formidable and perhaps increased by typical transferences to authority figures, based on the patients' frequently having had parents with substance problems. When a patient has been the victim of parental inconsistency and neglect as the result of a familial alcohol or drug problem, it is not surprising that he or she has difficulty trusting nurses, teachers, or anyone in an authority position and may trust siblings or peers more. The patient may evoke in the therapist reactions of fear, disgust, and frustration, making the therapist feel the way the patient does and causing the therapist to avoid closeness (Frances, Khantzian, & Tamerin, 1989). Frequently, self-destructiveness and masochism are expressed in negating treatment. The therapist requires considerable knowledge, skill, and the ability to be in touch with his or her own feelings to form an alliance in which the patient's negative feelings and attitudes can be expressed and the therapist is not frightened off by the patient's anger (Silber, 1974). Staff "burnout" is often the result of therapists' difficulty in dealing with countertransference reactions that interfere with patient care.

It is generally agreed that treatment of patients with addictive disorders requires a caring relationship; greater activity on the part of the therapist than for many other disorders; a degree of therapeutic zeal, with guards against overidentification; and a high degree of empathy. The therapist must guard against overidentification with the patient's helplessness, hopelessness, and low self-esteem, which are commonly present in the early stages of treatment. Considerable confrontation of defenses, especially denial, and the ability to provide support are also valuable. It should be emphasized that confrontation may be a new way of conducting therapy for some therapists, who are used to more supportive and nurturing roles with other psychiatric patients. Experience with successful treatment of patients leads to the development of informed optimism on the part of the therapist. The ability to tolerate one's own anxiety, depression, and pain as well as that of patients is likewise needed; the therapist should thus have considerable self-knowledge. Flexibility, persistence, patience, the capacity to listen, honesty, integrity, and wisdom are other essential qualities for an effective therapist with addicted patients (Frances & Franklin, 1989).

Treatment outcome is not negatively affected by the use of coercion in leading to initiation of treatment. In our culture, most patients seek treatment for alcoholism because of the threat of losing their jobs. Confrontation by family members, friends, health professionals, and the law is a powerful motivator that leads people to seek help. The initial task in helping a patient make a diagnosis and accepting help may be assisted by having family members, friends, employer, probation officer, teacher, or others involved in the process of confrontation. Formal interventions commonly practiced to force patients to accept inpatient rehabilitation are described by Johnson (1980); they involve a number of important people in the patient's life confronting the addicted individual in an organized way, with the help of a therapist. The intervention is designed to create a crisis in the patient's life in which either treatment is accepted or a major loss of status, job, or family tie is a threat. The effectiveness and possible adverse consequences of such interventions have not been well studied. Frequently, it is possible to achieve the same results with escalating forms of confrontation and intervention, without some of the possible dangers of exacerbating alienation that can occur when interventions are not tactfully done. Perhaps the most important thing to note, however, is this: Whether intervention is the best approach or not, waiting for a patient to reach "bottom" is no longer an appropriate requirement for entering treatment.

Generally, it is best to get the patient's cooperation in agreeing to an optimal treatment plan for that patient. However, a patient may not agree and yet may be willing to meet the therapist part way. Frequently, less restrictive forms of treatment can be attempted within a treatment contract that involves the patient's agreeing to more intensive or less personally acceptable forms of treatment if the agreed-on approach is not successful. Patients will vary in what forms of treatment they will accept. For example, a treatment-resistant patient may agree to accept going to Twelve-Step meetings only if an initial attempt at individual treatment is unsuccessful. The therapist should make a clinical judgment before agreeing to a contract as to what is minimally needed to assure a reasonable shot at success. In our experience, one area that cannot be compromised is the need for an abstinence goal to be set at the beginning of treatment, and an unswerving attention to the possibility and dangers of relapse.

In the initial phases of evaluating patients with substance abuse, it is frequently valuable to get information from family members and significant others, and helpful to involve them in the treatment. The support of interested others is very helpful in achieving compliance. In summary, considerable knowledge and the right attitudes are required of the therapist in developing a therapeutic alliance, especially with treatment-resistant addicted patients. A sophisticated knowledge of possible blocks to treatment (including comorbidity), skill in tactfully confronting denial, and an empathic and flexible attitude are helpful.

Overview of This Book

The object of this book is to help the clinician to build an updated practical knowledge base about addictive disorders, and then to provide an armamentarium of treatment approaches and clinical strategies for treatment selection and implementation. Basic information about the effects of specific substances is given; then the addiction process as a whole and alternative treatments that cut across substances are described. Unlike many drug abuse textbooks, which are organized around each substance, this book discusses treatment across substances. This general approach is useful because many of the principles and treatment techniques can be applied to a variety of addictions, and because a high percentage of addicted patients have multiple-substance dependence. No treatment is best for everyone, and the test of any treatment for any patient is effectiveness. This volume reflects both reviews of the treatment outcome literature and the clinical wisdom of our chapter authors in matching the right combination of treatment approaches. Clearly, treatment programs will bene-fit from increasing their therapeutic options, flexibility, use of the latest re-search information, treatment targeting, and attention to cost-effectiveness.

Here is a brief summary of what lies ahead. In order to frame our current state of the art in treating addictions, Westermeyer (Chapter 2) presents a rich cultural-anthropological perspective on the history of addictive disorders and their treatment. His chapter emphasizes that culture and society greatly affect the definition, incidence, expression, course, and treatment of addictions, and that they have complex interactions with biological and psychological factors.

In the "Psychoactive Substance Disorders" section, each class of substance is accorded a chapter that describes definitions, diagnostic features, clinical features, course, differential diagnosis, pathophysiology (where known), in-toxication, overdose, withdrawal, detoxification, emergency treatment, neuro-psychological findings, and (in some instances) pharmacological treatment strategies. Nace and Isbell (Chapter 3) provide an excellent review of the latest information on alcoholism. Weiss and Millman (Chapter 7) provide a rich clinical description of the effects of hallucinogens, phencyclidine (PCP), mari-juana, and inhalants—drugs that continue to be used beginning in adolescence, even though their use and abuse have recently declined. In the chapter on sedatives (Chapter 4), DuPont and Saylor discuss their opinion that fear of abuse of benzodiazepines by substance abusers can lead to underutilization of useful medications for treating anxiety disorders. Karan, Haller, and Schnoll (Chapter 6) give a full description of the patterns of use and clinical course of cocaine addiction. Hymowitz, in his chapter on tobacco dependence (Chapter 8), includes a section on treatment that is especially useful because of his expertise in that area, as well as the relative neglect of treatment strategies for tobacco dependence elsewhere in the text. Thomason and Dilts (Chapter 5) include pharmacological, behavioral, and therapeutic community approaches to opioid dependence. Each chapter author is an expert on the substance discussed in his or her chapter. A concluding chapter by N. S. Miller (Chapter 9) focuses on multiple-substance dependence.

The section on "Diagnostic Instruments" includes a chapter by Verebey and Turner (Chapter 10) that comprehensively describes the use of laboratory testing and toxicology in the diagnosis of substance use disorders, with atten-tion to their forensic implications. Tarter et al. (Chapter 11) provide a clinical-ly useful description of how to employ diagnostic instruments and assessment. The value of psychometric and neuropsychological testing is discussed from research and clinical perspectives.

The section on "Emerging Treatment Issues for Special Populations" presents the latest findings on mentally ill chemically abusers (Mirin & Weiss, Chapter 12), those with AIDS and addictions (Schleifer et al., Chapter 13) child and adolescent substance abusers (Kaminer, Chapter 14), and geriatric substance abusers (Abrams & Alexopoulos, Chapter 15). The topics of AIDS and addictions and of dual-diagnosis patients are currently receiving heavy research attention, which is well described in these two chapters. Comorbid psychiatric disorders may be the results of substance disorders; may serve as risk factors for substance disorders; and may interact in complex ways that can modify the clinical course, expression, and treatment response of addictive disorders. Treatments need to address comorbid disorders in order to have maximal effectiveness. Kaminer points out that substance abuse research in the child and adolescent population has been relatively deficient, in spite of recent attention to the issues related to children of alcoholics. Similarly, the elderly substance-abusing patient has been often overlooked in research, and Abrams and Alexopoulos provide a state-of-the-art description of clinical issues in this population.

The section on "Treatment Selection and Modalities" is introduced by a chapter on differential therapeutics and treatment selection by Alterman et al. (Chapter 16), which describes an overview of integration of modalities and evaluations of treatment outcome research. The pioneering work in this area is being done by this Philadelphia VA Hospital group. Dodes and Khantzian (Chapter 17) discuss individual psychotherapy of addictive patients from a psychodynamic perspective. They have many useful insights and hypotheses about the use of substances for self-medication, the value of emphasis in treatment of self-care and affect regulation, and the usefulness of psychodynamic models in understanding important issues faced by addicted patients. Heath and Stanton (Chapter 18) provide a scholarly review of the family therapy research, with a thorough knowledge of the value of system approaches. Galanter et al. (Chapter 19) describe group therapy approaches and self-help groups (Twelve-Step organizations and others). Mackay et al. (Chapter 20) discuss cognitive and behavioral treatment and review the value of education, relapse prevention, social skills training, excercise, and counseling. Perhaps the most promising area of recent treatment outcome research has been in the area of cognitive and behavioral treatment approaches that lend themselves to controlled treatment outcome studies. This whole section on treatment selection demonstrates the rapid progress and the potential applicability of clinical research in addiction treatment.

The section on "Treatment Implications of New Alcohol Research Findings" targets alcohol and reminds us of the importance of a strong scientific underpinning for meaningful advances in the treatment field. Goodwin's pioneering work in the area of familial versus nonfamilial alcoholism is brought up to date by Goodwin and Warnock in Chapter 21. Tabakoff and Hoffman (Chapter 22) present the latest clinical implications of neuroscience advances regarding alcohol's effects on membranes, neurotransmitters, receptors, and brain mechanisms, and discuss these in relation to tolerance and withdrawal. New specific and effective pharmacotherapies will depend on better understanding of the variety of harmful effects of alcohol.

In summary, while we have seen trends toward subspecialization even within the addiction field, it becomes equally important for the clinician to have a wide base of knowledge of both addictive disorders and general psychiatry, in order to maximize availability of treatment options. In this volume, we have chosen to focus only on addictions to psychoactive substances and have chosen not to grapple with the question of whether some eating disorders, gambling, or other compulsive behaviors fit within the realm of addiction. In the interest of saving space, we have also tried to focus on information that has the greatest clinical usefulness and practicality, and have limited the size of our bibliographies and depth of reporting of research findings.

Finally, we are heartened by the vigorous growth of psychiatrists' interest in the addiction field and by the kind of therapeutic, teaching, and research zeal demonstrated by so many of our chapter authors.

References

Allen, M. H. & Frances, R. J. (1986). Varieties of psychopathology found in patients with addictive disorders: A review. In R. E. Meyer (Ed.), *Psychopathology and addictive disorders* (pp. 17–38). New York: Guilford Press.

Cloninger, C. R., Dinwiddie, S. H., & Reich, T. R. (1989). Epidemiology and genetics of alcoholism. In A. Tasman, R. J. Hales, & A. Frances (Eds.), *Review of psychiatry* (Vol. 8, pp. 293–308). Washington, DC: American Psychiatric Press.

Dorus, W., Ostrow, D. G., Anton, R., Cushman, P., Collins, J. F., Schaefer, M., Charles, H. L., Desai, P., Hayashida, M., Malkerneker, V., Willenbring, M., Fiscella, R., & Sather, M. R. (1989). Lithium treatment of depressed and nondepressed alcoholics. *Journal of the American Medical Association, 262*(12), 1646–1652.

Frances, R. J. (1988). Update of alcohol and drug disorder treatment. *Journal of Clinical Psychiatry, 49* (9), 13–17.

Frances, R. J., & Allen, M. (1985). The interaction of substance-use disorders with nonpsychotic psychiatric disorders. In R. Michels (Ed.), *Psychiatry* (Vol. 1, pp. 1–13). New York: Basic Books.

Frances, R. J., Bucky, S., & Alexopoulos, G. S. (1984). Outcome study of familial and nonfamilial alcoholism. *American Journal of Psychiatry, 141*(11), 1469–1471.

Frances, R. J., & Franklin, J. E. (1987). Primary prevention of alcoholism and drug abuse. In S. Talbott & J. Barter (eds.), *Primary prevention in psychiatry* (pp. 153–184). Washington, DC: American Psychiatric Press.

Frances, R. J., & Franklin, J. E. (1988). Alcohol and other psychoactive substance use disorders. In J. A. Talbotts, R. E. Hales, & S. C. Yudofsky (Eds.), *Textbook of psychiatry* (pp. 313–357). Washington, DC: American Psychiatric Press.

Frances, R. J. & Franklin, J. E. (1989). *A concise guide to treatment of alcoholism and addictions.* Washington, DC: American Psychiatric Press.

Frances, R. J., Franklin, J. E., & Flavin, D. K. (1987). Suicide and alcoholism. *American Journal of Drug and Alcohol Abuse, 13*(3), 327–341.

Frances, R. J., Khantzian, E. J., & Tamerin, J. S. (1989). Psychodynamic psychotherapy. In M. Galanter & T. B. Karasu (Eds.), *Treatments of psychiatric disorders* (Vol. II, pp. 1103–1111). Washington, DC: American Psychiatric Press.

Frances, R. J., Miller, S. I., & Galanter, M. (1989). Psychosocial treatment of addictions. In A. Tasman, R. J. Hales, & A. Frances (Eds.), *Review of psychiatry* (Vol. 8, pp. 341–359). Washington, DC: American Psychiatric Press.

Frances, R. J., & Strauser, W. (1988). Psychosocial aspects of alcohol abuse. In J. G. Howells (Ed.), *Modern perspectives in psychosocial pathology* (Vol. 11, pp. 113–134). New York: Brunner/Mazel.

Gawin, F. H., Kleber, H. D., & Byck, R. (1989). Desipramine facilitation of initial cocaine abstinence. *Archives of General Psychiatry, 46,* 117–121.

Goodwin, D., Shulsinger, F., Hermansen, L., Guze, S. B., & Winokur, G. (1973). Alcohol problems in adoptees raised apart from alcoholic biological parents. *Archives of General Psychiatry, 28,* 238–242.

Harwood, H. J., Napolitano, D. M., Kristiansen, P. L., & Collins, J. J. (1984). *Economic costs to society of alcohol and drug abuse and mental illness: 1980* (Publication No. RTI/2734/00-001FR). Research Triangle Park, NC: Research Triangle Institute.

Helzer, J. E., & Pryzbeck, F. R. (1988). The co-occurrence of alcoholism with other psychiatric disorders in the general population and its impact on treatment. *Journal of Studies on Alcohol, 49*(3), 219–224.

Hester, R. K., & Miller, W. R. (1989). *Handbook of alcoholism treatment approaches: Effective alternatives.* New York: Pergamon Press.

Holder, M. D. (1987). Alcoholism treatment and potential health care cost saving. *Medical Care, 25*(1), 52–71.

Johnson, V. (1980). *I'll quit tomorrow.* New York: Harper & Row.

Khantzian, E. (1986). A contemporary psychodynamic approach to drug abuse treatment. *American Journal of Drug and Alcohol Abuse, 12*(3), 213–223.

Krystal, H. (1982). Alexithymia and the effectiveness of psychoanalytic treatment. *International Journal of Psychoanalytic Psychotherapy, 9,* 353–338.

Lorand, S. (1948). A summary of psychoanalytic literature on problems of alcoholism: Bibliography. *Yearbook of Psychoanalysis, 1,* 359–378.

Mezachow, J., Miller, S. I., Seixas, F., & Frances, R. J. (1987). The impact of cost containment on alcohol and drug treatment. *Hospital and Community Psychiatry, 38*(5), 506–511.

Miller, W. R., & Hester, R. K. (1980). Treating the problem drinker: Modern approaches. In W. R. Miller (Ed.), *The addictive behaviors: Treatment of alcoholism, drug abuse, smoking and obesity* (pp. 111–141). Oxford: Pergamon Press.

Office of the President. (1989, September). *National drug control strategy.* Washington, DC: U.S. Government Printing Office.

Rounsaville, B., & Kranzler, H. (1989). The DSM-III-R diagnosis of alcoholism. In A. Tasman, R. J. Hales, & A. Frances (Eds.), *Review of psychiatry* (Vol. 8, pp. 322–340). Washington, DC: American Psychiatric Press.

Semrad, E. (1983). *The heart of a therapist* (S. Rako & H. Mazer, Eds.). New York: Jason Aronson.

Schilling, R. F., Schinke, S. P., Nichols, S., Zayas, L., Miller, S. O., Orlandi, M. A., & Botvin, G. J. (1989). Developing strategies for AIDS prevention research with black and Hispanic drug users. *Public Health Reports, 104*(17), 1–12.

Schleifer, S., Keller, S., Lombardo, J., Franklin, J., LaFarge, S., & Miller, S. (1989). HIV-1 antibody reactivity in inner-city alcoholics. *Journal of the American Medical Association, 262,*(19), 2680–2681.

Schuckit, M. A. (1985). The clinical implications of primary diagnostic groups among alcoholics. *Archives of General Psychiatry, 42* 1043–1049.

Silber, A. (1974). Rationale for the technique of psychotherapy with alcoholics. *International Journal of Psychoanalytic Psychotherapy, 3,* 28–47.

Stibler, H., Borg, S., & Joustin, M. (1986). Micro anion exchange chromatography of carbohydrate-deficient transferrin in relation to alcohol consumption (Swedish Patent 8400587-5). *Alcoholism: Clinical and Experimental Research, 10*(5), 535–544.

Sullivan, D. (1990). *Seventh special report to the U.S. Congress on alcohol and health.* Rockville, MD: National Institute on Alcohol Abuse and Alcoholism.

Toffler, A. (1980). *The third wave.* New York: Bantam Books.

2

Historical and Social Context of Psychoactive Substance Disorders

JOSEPH WESTERMEYER

Introduction

Historical and social factors are key to the understanding of psychoactive substance use disorders. These factors affect the rates of substance disorders in the community, the types of substances abused, the characteristics of abusers, the course of these disorders, and the efficacy of treatment. Knowledge of these background features helps in understanding the genesis of these disorders, their treatment outcome, and preventive approaches.

Psychoactive substances subserve several human functions that can enhance individual as well as social existence. On the individual level, desirable ends include the following: relief of adverse mental and emotional states (e.g., anticipatory anxiety before battle, social phobia at a party); relief of physical symptoms (e.g., pain, diarrhea); stimulation to function despite fatigue or boredom; and "time out" from day-to-day existence through altered states of consciousness. Socially, alcohol and drugs are used in numerous rituals and ceremonies, from alcohol in Jewish Passover rites and the Roman Catholic Mass, to peyote in the Native American Church and the serving of opium at certain Hindu marriages. To a certain extent, the history of human civilization parallels the development of psychoactive substances.

Paradoxically, these substances that bless and benefit our existence also torment and decivilize us. Individuals, societies, and cultures began learning this disturbing truth at least a few and possibly several millenia ago. We continue to rediscover this harsh reality today and tomorrow, as though each new generation and nation must learn afresh for itself. As our societies become more complex, so too do our psychoactive substances, our means of consuming them, and the problems associated with them. Preventive and treatment efforts, also age-old and wrought at great cost, are our forebears' gifts to us for dealing with psychoactive substance use gone astray.

History and Origins

Prehistory

Methods for the study of psychoactive substance use disorders through time and space include the archeological record, anthropological studies of preliterate societies, and the historical record. Archeological data document the importance of alcohol commerce in late prehistorical and early historical times, both in the Mediterranean (where wine vessels have been discovered in numerous shipwrecks) and in China (where wine vessels have been found in burial sites). Poppy seed caches have been recorded in a prehistoric site in northern Turkey. Incised poppy capsules have been noted in the prehistoric headdresses of Cretan goddesses or priestesses, indicating an early awareness of opium harvest methods. Availability of carbohydrate in excess of dietary needs, fostered by neolithic farming technology and animal husbandry, probably permitted sporadic cases of alcohol abuse (Westermeyer, 1988).

Anthropological studies of preliterate societies have shown the almost universal use of psychoactive substances. Tribal and peasant societies of North and South America focused on the development of stimulant drugs (e.g., coca leaf, tobacco leaf, coffee bean) and numerous hallucinogenic drugs (e.g., peyote). Hallucinogens in particular were used for ritual purposes, and stimulant drugs were used for secular purposes such as hard labor or long hunts. New World peoples discovered diverse modes of administration, such as chewing, nasal insufflation or "snuffing," pulmonary inhalation or "smoking," and rectal clysis (DuToit, 1977; Furst & Coe, 1977). African and Middle Eastern ethnic groups produced a smaller number of stimulants, such as qat, and hallucinogens, such as cannabis (Getahun & Krikorias, 1973; Kennedy, Teague, & Fairbanks, 1980). Groups across Africa and the Eurasian land mass specialized in obtaining alcohol from numerous sources, such as honey, grains, tubers, fruits, and mammalian milk (Wolcott, 1974). Certain drugs were also used across vast distances, such as opium across Asia (Westermeyer, 1983) and the stimulant sedative combination betel–areca across South Asia to Oceania (Ahluwalia & Ponnampalam, 1968; Burton-Bradley, 1977). Of interest is the fact that Old World peoples primarily consumed drugs by ingestion prior to Columbus's travel to the New World; nasal insufflation, smoking, and clysis were not known.

Early History

Historical records of alcohol, opium, and other psychoactive substances appear with the earliest Egyptian and Chinese writings. Opium was described as an ingested medication in these first documents, especially for medicinal purposes. Mayan, Aztec, and Incan statues and glyphs indicated drug use for ritual reasons (DuToit, 1977; Furst & Coe, 1977; Waddell, 1976). Medieval accounts recorded traditional alcohol and drug use. Travelers of that era often viewed use patterns in other areas as unusual, aberrant, or problematic; examples include reports of Scandinavian "beserker" drinkers by the English, and reports by Crusaders of Islamic military units or "assassins" intoxicated on cannabis. Along with animal sacrifice and the serving of meat (Smith, 1968), the provision of alcohol, betel, opium, tobacco, or other psychoactive substances came to represent hospitality or to have cultural, ritual, or religious symbolism (Bacon, 1951). Affiliation with specific ethnic groups, social classes, sects, and castes came to be associated with consumption of specific psychoactive substances. For example, one group in India consumed alcohol but not cannabis, whereas an adjacent group consumed cannabis but not alcohol (Carstairs, 1954). Culture change may be signaled by altered patterns of psychoactive usage (Caetano, 1987). Religious as well as ethnic identity may be tied to alcohol or drug consumption. For example, wine is a traditional aspect of Jewish, Catholic, and certain other Christian rituals and ceremonies, whereas Islam and fundamentalist Christian sects prohibit alcohol drinking. In addition to distinguishing people from one another, substance use may serve to maintain cooperation and communication across ethnic groups, as Heath (1971) observed in Bolivia.

Culture and Social Change

In recent centuries, political, commercial, and technical advances have modified the types, supply, cost, and availability of psychoactive substance, along with modes of administration (Westermeyer, 1987, 1989). International commerce, built on cheaper and more efficient transportation, and increasing income have fostered drug production and distribution. Increasing disposable income has often resulted in greater recreational intoxication (Caetano, Suzman, Rosen, & Voorhees-Rosen, 1983). Development of parenteral injection for medical purposes was readily adapted to recreational drug self-administration in the mid-1800s, within several years of its invention. Purification and modification of plant compounds (e.g., cocaine from the coca leaf, morphine and heroin from opium, hashish oil from the cannabis plant) produced substances that were both more potent and more easily smuggled and sold illicitly. Laboratory synthesis has led to new drugs (e.g., the stimulant amphetamines, the sedative barbiturates and benzodiazepines, the opioid fentanyl, the hallucinogen phencyclidine) that are more potent and often cheaper than purified plant compounds.

Historical and cultural factors may theoretically affect the pharmacokinetics and pharmacodynamics of psychoactive substance, just as the pharmacology of these substances may affect their historical and traditional use. A case in point is the flushing reaction observed among a greater-than-expected number of Asians and Native Americans (but neither universal in these peoples, nor limited to them). Absence of alcohol among the northern Asian peoples who subsequently peopled much of East Asia and the Americas is a likely explanation, but the exact reason is unknown. Of interest to epidemiologists, the flushing reaction has been promulgated as a reason for two opposite phenomena: first, the low rates of alcoholism among Asian peoples, who presumably find the reaction adversive and hence drink little (although rates are increasing across much of Asia; see Sargent, 1972); and second, the high rates of alcoholism among Native American peoples, who presumably must "drink through" their flushing reaction to enjoy other alcohol effects. Flushing may also be more or less desirable, depending upon how the culture values this biological effect. Among many East and Southeast Asian peoples influenced by Buddhist precepts, flushing is viewed as the emergence of cupidity or rage and the loss of control. Native Americans do not have the same attitude toward flushing. Modal differences in alcohol metabolism have also been observed among ethnic groups, and these differences have supported arguments in favor of biological causation. However, the intraethnic differences in alcohol metabolism greatly exceed the interethnic differences (Fenna, Mix, Schaefer, & Gilbert, 1971). Large sample sizes can also lead to the so-called "Meehl effect," in which small and unimportant but statistically significant differences frequently result. Despite some minimal pharmacokinetic differences among people of different races, the observed differences appear to be more due to pharmacodynamics. That is, the influence of people vis-à-vis the drug (i.e., their traditions, taboos, expectations, patterns of use) appears to exert greater influence than the drug vis-à-vis the people (e.g., rates of absorption and catabolism, flushing reactions). It may be that both pharmacodynamic and pharmacokinetic factors are simultaneously in operation, but in ways not yet well understood.

As psychoactive substance use phased into substance abuse in many advanced civilizations, social and cultural means evolved to control usage. One method was law and law enforcement. Aztecs utilized this method in pre-Columbian times to limit the frequency and amount of drinking (Paredes, 1975). Later, in the post-Columbian period, England countered its "gin epidemic" (Rodin, 1981; Thurn, 1978) with a tax on imported gin, and its later "opium epidemic" (Berridge, 1978; Kramer, 1979) with prescribing laws. Another method has been religious stricture. Early in the Buddhist religious movement, abstinence from alcohol was recommended as a means of quitting earthly bondage in order to achieve contentment in this life and eternal *nirvana* after death. Islam became the second great religion to adopt abstinence from alcohol, reportedly when a town was sacked as a result of a drunken nighttime guard. The gin epidemic in England spawned several abstinence-oriented Christian sects, despite the earlier status of wine as a Christian sacramental substance. The Church of Jesus Christ of Latter-Day Saints (the group popularly known as the Mormans) forbids any use of psychoactive substances, including caffeine and nicotine.

In addition to religion as a preventive measure, religion has also served as a therapy for psychoactive substance abuse. Native Americans and Latin Americans, plagued with high rates of alcoholism, have joined fundamentalist Christian sects as a means of garnering social support while resisting peer pressures to drink (Hippler, 1973; Kearny, 1970). Many Native Americans have joined the Native American Church, in which peyote is a sacramental substance but alcohol is proscribed (Albaugh & Anderson, 1974). Although peyote is generally safe under these ceremonial circumstances (Bergman, 1971), peyote abuse has been reported anecdotally (LaBarre, 1941).

Patterns of Psychoactive Substance Use

Traditional patterns of psychoactive substance use in most societies were episodic, coming at times of personal celebrations (e.g., birth, marriage), rituals (e.g., arrivals, departures, changes in status), and seasonal celebrations (e.g., harvest, New Year). Exceptions to this pattern were daily or at least occasional use of alcohol as a foodstuff, and use of various stimulants (e.g., betel–areca, tea and coffee, coca leaf) in association with long, hard labor (e.g., paddy rice or taro farming, silver mining). Daily beer or wine drinking was limited to Europe, especially the para-Mediterranean wine countries and central grain–beer countries. Such daily or "titer" use is not without its problems, even when socially sanctioned. Although binge-type alcohol problems (e.g., delirium tremens, fights, falls) were and are rare, hepatic cirrhosis and other organ damage may result from daily use of more than 2 to 4 ounces of alcohol, depending on body weight (Bonfiglio, Falli, & Pacine, 1977; Karayannis & Kelepouris, 1967). Daily use of stimulants, especially if heavy or addictive, can lead to biomedical or psychosocial problems, such as oral cancers in the case of betel–areca chewing, or psychobehavioral changes in the case of coca leaf chewing (Burton-Bradley, 1977; Negrete, 1978).

Socially sanctioned, episodic psychoactive substance use may involve even heavy use and marked intoxication or drunkenness (Bunzel, 1940; Carpenter, 1959). In a low-technology environment, this pattern caused few problems, although psychotomimetic drugs such as cannabis could cause toxic psychosis (Chopra & Smith, 1974; Thacore, 1973). In a high-technology environment, with motor vehicles and industrial machinery, intoxication even at mild traditional levels is life-threatening (Stull, 1972; Westermeyer & Brantner, 1972).

Among other consequence of technology and advanced civilization are widespread substance abuse epidemics, or long-lasting endemics. In the pre-Columbian era, sporadic cases of acute and chronic substance abuse problems had been known for at least a millenium, and possibly two millenia. However, relatively sudden, massive substance abuse increases appeared early in the post-Columbian era. One of these was the English gin epidemic (Rodin, 1981; Thurn, 1978), which began in the late 1600s and continued for several decades. Transatlantic intercontinental trade and the beginnings of the Industrial Revolution were the immediate causes. At about the same time, opium epidemics broke out in several Oriental countries. The origins of these were somewhat different. The post-Columbian spread of tobacco smoking to Asia introduced the inhabitants to inhalation as a new mode of drug administration. This new route of administration applied to an old drug, opium, produced a combination more addictive than the old opium-eating tradition. Governmental pressures against tobacco smoking (which was viewed as wasteful and associated with seditious elements) probably accelerated the popularity of opium smoking. Subsequently, European colonialism and international trade contributed to the import of Indian opium to several East Asian countries (Westermeyer, 1983). Opium epidemics also occurred in Europe and North

America (Kramer, 1979). Although East Asia has largely controlled its opium problem, opiate endemics continue in Southeast and South Asia, the Middle East, most of Europe, and much of North America.

Historical Models of Substance Use

Although ceremonial alcohol use is widely appreciated, not so well known is the ceremonial use of drugs. Peyote buttons are a sacramental substance in the Native American Church (Bergman, 1971). Hallucinogen use for religious purposes still occurs among many South American ethnic groups (DuToit, 1977). Supernatural sanctions, both prescribing use within certain bounds and proscribing use outside these bounds, inveigh against abuse of these substances by devotees (Bacon, 1951; Paredes, 1975). Thus, ceremonial or religious use tends to be relatively safe. Examples of abuse do occur, however, such as the occasional Catholic priest who becomes alcoholic beginning with abuse of sacramental wine, or the rare abuse of peyote as cited above.

Secular but social use of alcohol and drugs occurs in numerous quasi-ritual contexts (Negrete, 1978; Burton-Bradley, 1977; Paredes, 1975). Drinking may occur at annual events, such as New Year or harvest ceremonies (e.g., Thanksgiving in the United States). Weddings, births, funerals, and other family rituals are occasions for alcohol or drug use in many cultures. Marking of friendships, business arrangements, or intergroup competitions can virtually require substance use in some groups. For example, the *dutsen* in German-speaking Central Europe is a brief ritual in which friends or associates agree to address each other by the informal *du* ("thou") rather than by the formal *Sie* ("you"). Participants, holding an alcoholic beverage in their right hands, link their right arms, toast each other, and drink with arms linked. The use of betel–areca, pulque or beer, coca leaf, and other intoxicants has accompanied group work tasks, such as harvests or community *corvée* obligations (forced labor for, say, the lord of the manor). Although substance use may be heavy at ceremonial events, even involving intoxication, the social control of the group over dosage and the brief duration of use augurs against chronic abuse (although problems related to acute abuse may occur). Problems can develop if the group's central rationale for existence rests on substance use; this phenomenon has been described for some habitués of opium dens, cocktail lounges, ethnic bars, and street drinking groups. In these latter instances, group norms for alcohol or drug use may foster substance abuse rather than prevent it (Csikszentmihalyi, 1968; Dumont, 1967; Westermeyer, 1974).

Medicinal reasons for substance use have prevailed in one place or another with virtually all psychoactive substances, including alcohol, opium, cannabis, tobacco, the stimulants, and the hallucinogens (Berridge, 1978). Insofar as substances are prescribed or administered solely by healers or physicians, abuse is rare or absent. For example, the prescribing of oral opium by Chinese physicians over many centuries had few or no adverse social consequences. On the other hand, self-prescribing for medicinal purposes carries risks. For example, certain Northern Europeans, Southeast Asians, and others use alcohol for insomnia, colds, pain, and other maladies—a practice that can and does lead to chronic alcohol abuse. Self-prescribing of opium by poppy farmers similarly antedates opium addiction in a majority of cases (Westermeyer, 1983). Thus, professional control over medicinal use has been relatively benign, whereas individual control over medicinal use of psychoactive compounds has often been problematic.

Dietary use of substances falls into two general categories: (1) the use of alcohol as a source of calories, and (2) the use of cannabis and other herbal intoxicants to enhance taste. Fermentation of grains, tubers, and fruits into alcohol has been a convenient way of storing calories that would otherwise deteriorate. Unique tastes and eating experiences associated with beverage alcohol (e.g., various wines) have further fostered their use, expecially at ritual, ceremonial, or social meals. Cannabis has also been used from the Middle East to the Malay Archipelago as a means of enhancing soups, teas, pastries, and other sweets. Opium and other substances have been served at South Asian ceremonies (e.g., weddings) as a postprandial "dessert."

Recreational use can presumably occur in either social or individual settings. Much substance use today occurs in recreational or "party" settings that have some psychosocial rationales (e.g., social "time out," meeting friends), but minimal or no ritual or ceremonial aspects. So-called recreational substance use in these social contexts may in fact be quasi-medicinal (i.e., to reduce symptoms associated with social phobia, low self-esteem, boredom, or chronic dysphoria). Even solitary psychoactive substance use can be recreational (i.e., to induce relaxation) or medicinal (i.e., to relieve loneliness, insomnia, or pain).

Other purposes exist, but are not as widespread as those described above. In the 19th century, young European women took belladonna before social events in order to give themselves a ruddy, blushing complexion. A particular substance or pattern of use can represent a social or ethnic identity (Caetano, 1987; Carstairs, 1954; Ogan, 1966). Children may inhale household or industrial solvents as a means of mimicking adult intoxication (Kaufman, 1975). Intoxication may simply serve as a means for continuing social behaviors, such as fights or homicide, that previously existed without intoxication (Levy & Kunitz, 1969). Particular patterns of production or use may represent rebellion by disenfranchised groups (Cameron, 1968; Connell, 1961; Levinson, 1974; Lurie, 1972).

History of Substance Abuse Treatment

Historical and literary accounts have long documented individual attempts to draw back from the abyss of alcohol and drug abuse. At various times autobiographical, biographical, journalistic, and anecdotal, these descriptions list centuries-old methods still employed today in lay and professional settings. Modalities include gradual decrease in dosage; symptomatic use of nonaddicting medications; isolation from the substance; relocation away from fellow users; religious conversion; group support; asylum in a supportive and nondemanding environment; and treatment with a variety of shamanistic, spiritual, dietary, herbal, and medicinal methods (Albaugh & Anderson, 1974; Hippler, 1973; Westermeyer, 1973, 1983).

Beginning with Galenic medicine, a key strategy has been to identify certain syndromes as having their etiology in alcohol and drug abuse. Once the etiology is determined, the specific treatment (i.e., cessation of substance abuse) can be prescribed. Examples of such substance-associated disorders include delirium tremens (i.e., alcohol withdrawal) and withdrawal seizures; morphinism (i.e., opioid withdrawal); cannabis-induced acute psychosis; stimulant psychosis; and various fetal effects, such as fetal alcohol syndrome. Thus, description of pathophysiological and psychopathological processes, together with diagnostic labeling, has been a crucial historical step in the development of modern assessment and treatment for substance use disorders (Rodin, 1981; Thacore, 1973; Westermeyer, 1983).

Modern treatment approaches have their origins in methods developed by Benjamin Rush, a physician from the Revolutionary War era who is often credited as the father of American psychiatry. Rush developed a categorization of drinkers and alcoholics. He further prescribed treatment that consisted of a period of "asylum" from responsibilities and access to alcohol, to take place in a family-like setting, in a milieu of respect, consideration, and social support. As Rush's concepts were extrapolated to the growing American society, large state-supported institutions were developed—although some smaller, private asylums or sanitoria for alcoholics have persisted up to the current time.

Medical treatments can interact with cultural factors. For example, disulfiram can act as an excuse for Native American alcoholics to resist peer pressures to drink (Savard, 1968). Ethnic similarity between patients and staff appears to be more critical to the treatment process than in other medical or psychiatric conditions (Shore & Von Fumetti, 1972). Strong ethnic affiliation may be associated with more optimal treatment outcomes, although ethnic affiliation may change as a result of treatment (Westermeyer & Neider, 1985).

On a federal level, treatment for drug abuse (largely opioid dependence) began with the Harrison Act of 1914, which outlawed nonmedical use of opiate drugs. For a time, heroin maintenance was prescribed and dispensed in several clinics around the country. Although research studies were not conducted, case reports from these clinics indicated that many patients were able to resume stable lives while receiving maintenance doses of heroin. These clinics were phased out, largely because of moral, political, and religious opposition. Two long-term prison-like hospitals for opiate addicts were established (one in Kentucky and one in Texas). Research in these institutions contributed greatly to our understanding of opiate addiction (and alcoholism, which was also studied), but the demonstrated inefficacy of prison treatment led to their demise as treatment facilities. These legal and medical approaches beginning in 1914 were effective in reducing opiate dependence in the societal mainstream. However, certain occupational, geographical, and ethnic groups continued to use drugs that were made illicit by the Harrison Act. These included seamen, musicians, certain minority groups, and inhabitants of areas involved in smuggling (e.g., San Antonio, Texas; Louisiana seaports; New York City).

Following World War II, medical and social leaders were more aware of widespread mental disabilities in the country, because of the high rate of psychiatric disorders among inductees and veterans. This led to the establishment of the National Institute of Mental Health (NIMH), which had divisions of alcoholism and drug abuse. By the 1970s, it became apparent that substance use disorders were widely prevalent. Numerous indices of alcohol abuse and alcoholism had been increasing since World War II, including hepatic cirrhosis and violence-related mortality. Endemic abuse of cocaine and opiates exploded into an epidemic in the late 1960s, followed by the appearance of stimulant and hallucinogen abuse. It was evident that neither the alcohol epidemic nor the drug epidemic was being adequately addressed by NIMH. This led to the formation of the National Institute on Alcohol Abuse and Alcoholism (NIAAA) and the National Institute on Drug Abuse (NIDA), both of which have equal status with NIMH under the Alcohol, Drug Abuse, and Mental Health Administration (ADAMHA). Located within the Department of Health and Human Services, ADAMHA has fostered the development of substance abuse research, training, clinical services, and prevention. Governmental support for these efforts has come largely from elected officials who have personally experienced psychoactive substance use disorders, either in themselves or in their families. For example, most of the last several presidents have had a spouse, parent, sibling, or offspring with a substance disorder.

Social and Self-Help Movements

Abstinence-oriented social movements first appeared among orgnized religions. Certain South Asian sects, arising from early Persian religions and Hinduism, abstained from alcohol. Buddhist clergy were forbidden to drink alcoholic beverages, and pious Buddhist laity were urged to refrain from drinking or at least to drink moderately. Early on, Moslems were urged not to drink; tradition has it that Mohammed himself established abstinence for his followers. Abstinence-oriented Christian sects evolved in England and then in Central Europe at about the time of the gin epidemic.

Religiomania has long served as a cure for dipsomania and narcotomania. Opium addicts in Asia have hied themselves to monasteries in the hope that clerical asceticism would cure them, which it sometimes did (Westermeyer, 1973, 1983). Many Latin Americans and Native Americans with high rates of alcoholism, have abandoned Catholicism and Anglicanism in favor of abstinence-prescribing fundamentalist Christian sects (Hippler, 1973; Kearny, 1970) and the Native American Church (Albaugh & Anderson, 1974). Children raised in these sects are taught the importance of lifelong abstinence from alcohol and other drugs of abuse. Despite this childhood socialization, those leaving these sects as adults can develop substance use disorders. Thus, the anti-substance-disorder effects of various religions appear to persist only so long as one is actively affiliated with the group.

Abstinent societies not tied to specific religions began to appear in the 18th and 19th centuries. Examples include the Anti-Opium Society in China and the Women's Christian Temperance Union in the United States. These groups engaged in political action, public education, social pressure against addiction or alcoholism, and support for abstinence. These led eventually to "prohibition" movements that sought legal strictures against the production, sale, and/or consumption of psychoactive substances outside of religious or medical contexts. In Asia these movements began against tobacco (which was viewed in the 1600s and 1700s as a habit associated with political sedition) and then later changed to oppose primarily opium. In Northern Europe and the United States, prohibition laws first involved opiates and cannabis, but later expanded to include alcohol. As Moslem peoples emerged from colonial regimes, their nations passed antialcohol legislation that ranged from mild strictures for Moslems alone, to harsh measures against all inhabitants of the country.

Numerous self-help groups in the United States were founded during the Depression era. Many more were begun after World War II. These groups involved individuals who banded together to meet their common financial, social, or personal needs (Lieberman & Borman, 1976). One of these movements was Alcoholics Anonymous (AA), one of whose founders was an alcoholic physician (W. W., 1949). Like other movements of its era (such as Recovery for the mentally ill), AA differed in several important aspects from earlier abstinence-oriented groups. These differences were as follows:

- Individuals could remain in their homes, families, and jobs, rather than joining a separate sect or going off to a retreat, asylum, or monastery.
- Considerable structure was involved, with specific meetings and phased "step" recovery activities.
- The concept of a recovery process over time was introduced; this had biological, psychological, social, and spiritual dimensions.
- Organization was kept predominantly atomistic (i.e., on the local, small-group level) rather than hierarchical (i.e., on a regional or national level).
- Membership required self-identity as an alcoholic (i.e., supportive or concerned persons were excluded).

Like earlier movements, AA also emphasized the importance of abstinence from all psychoactive substances (although tobacco and coffee are notably present at most AA meetings today); reliance on a superior spiritual force (the "Higher Power"); and social affiliation or "fellowship" for mutual support. Although first established in the United States, AA has spread to many other parts of the world over the last 50 years. It has also led to similar groups whose identity centers on other drugs and even other problems: Narcotics Anonymous, Cocaine Anonymous, Overeaters Anonymous, Gamblers Anonymous, and Emotions Anonymous (formerly Neurotics Anonymous). Groups for those personally affected by alcoholism have also appeared, such as Alateen for the teenaged offspring of alcoholic parents and Al-Anon for the spouses, parents, and other concerned associates of alcoholic persons. Over the last several years, the Adult Children of Alcoholics and Addicts (ACOAA) has also evolved to meet the needs of those distressed or maladaptive adults raised by alcoholic parents. Mothers Against Drunk Drivers (MADD) was originally formed to meet the support needs of parents whose children had been killed by drunken auto drivers. MADD has since expanded its activities as a "watchdog" group that follows the records of legislators and judges in regard to alcohol-related legal offenses. Social and cultural composition of the self-help group appears to be an important factor in effecting theraputic outcomes (Jilek-Aall, 1978).

Factors Affecting Alcohol–Drug Epidemics

Numerous factors contribute to the development of substance abuse epidemics. One of the first of these, the gin epidemic in late 17th- and 18th-century England, was fostered by the following factors:

- English merchant ships returning empty from trips to North America loaded on gin as ballast in the Caribbean before returning across the Atlantic to England.
- Gin was derived from sugar cane grown with slave labor; with no import tax, calories of gin were literally cheaper than calories of bread in London.
- The beginnings of the Industrial Revolution had given rise to repressive social conditions and a loss of traditional rural values, fostering widespread drunkenness with inexpensive gin.
- Although traditions and social controls existed for the drinking of mead and ale, these traditions and controls did not extend to gin drinking, with the result that daily excessive gin drinking appeared.

During this period, numerous sequelae of alcoholism were first recognized, including the description of the fetal alcohol syndrome (Rodin, 1981). The gin epidemic raged for several decades, perhaps as long as a century. It eventually receded under such pressures as an import tax on gin, antialcohol propaganda in the literature and art of the day, and evolution of abstinence-oriented Protestant sects for the working classes.

The opium epidemic in many countries of East and Southeast Asia began about the same time as the European alcohol epidemic. Several factors, some similar to the European situation but some different, contributed to the opium epidemic. These were as follows:

- Tobacco smoking had been introduced to Asia from the New World; it became a popular pastime in smoking houses that were frequented by the artisans, artists, adventurists, and literati of the day.
- As European and New World concepts and artifacts flooded into Asia, tobacco-smoking houses were viewed as places of culture change and even political sedition; they were gradually outlawed.
- Opium eating, which had never been a significant social problem, was combined with this new technology (i.e., drug consumption by volatilization and inhalation); opium smoking thus became widespread.
- Political corruption, government inefficiency, and absence of statecraft skills to deal with widespread drug abuse, abetted by the political and economic imperialism of European powers, led to centuries of wide-spread opium addiction among various Asian nations. Some countries have reversed the problem in this century (e.g., Japan, Korea, China, Manchuria), and others have not (e.g., Thailand, Laos, Burma, Pakistan, Afghanistan, Iran).

Trends in Problems across Time and Space

The appearance of new drugs (or reappearance of old ones in new forms) exposes social groups to agents against which they have no "immunity." That is, the community or nation has no tradition for problem-free or as least controlled use of the substance. Users themselves may not perceive the actual risks associated with the new psychoactive substance. This can also occur when the group has familiarity with the substance, but in a different form. For example, traditions may exist for wine, but not beer or distilled alcohol; pipe smoking may be limited by customs that do not extend to cigarette smoking.

Symbolic aspects of certain drugs or modes of drug administration may displace the issue from psychoactive substance use per se, to associated issues of ethnic identity, culture change, political upheaval, class struggle, or in-tergenerational conflict (Ogan, 1966; Robbins, 1973). Examples include the following: the use of cannabis by one caste or ethnic group and the use of alcohol by an adjacent but different group (Carstairs, 1954); cannabis and hallucinogen use as antiauthority symbols in the late 1960s and 1970s; and illicit raising of poppy as a cash crop and opium smuggling by ethnic minorities in Asia (Westermeyer, 1983).

As drug use has spread in the last few centuries, drug production and commerce has become an important economic resource in many areas (Westermeyer, 1989). Early examples in the 1800s were the British trading companies and large areas of India, which depended for their wealth on opium sales to China. Numerous backward areas in the world today maintain their participation in national and world markets through their participation in illicit drug production and sales: Afghanistan, Burma, Laos, Mexico, Pakinstan, and Thailand in opium and heroin; the Caribbean nations and Mexico in cannabis production and cocaine commerce; and several South and Central American countries in cocaine production and commerce. Several states in the United States count cannabis as a major, albeit illicit, cash crop: North Carolina, Tennessee, Kentucky, Kansas, Nebraska, New Mexico, California, and Hawaii (Culhane, 1989).

Government instability, corruption, or inefficiency can cause or result from drug production, export, and/or smuggling today. For example, Iran had become largely free of illicit drug use and production until the political disruption and war of the last several years. Other unstable countries in South Asia, the Middle East, Africa, and Latin America have become producers, transshippers, or importers of illicit drugs. Breakdown of traditional Islam has led to increased alcohol abuse in some Moslem countries, contributing to a backlash of Islamic fundamentalism. Likewise, in the United States and Latin America, widespread alcoholism predates the shift to Christian fundamentalism.

Industrialization and technological advances have fostered a redefinition of substance abuse (Stull, 1972). An intoxicated or "hung-over" (withdrawing) ox-cart driver can effect limited damage, other than to cart, ox, and self. The alcohol- or drug-affected driver of a modern high-speed bus, captain of an oil supertanker, or pilot of a jet transport can kill scores of people and destroy equipment and material worth millions of dollars. Handicraft artisans under the influence of drugs or alcohol can do little damage, whereas workers in a factory can harm themselves or others as well as destroying expensive machinery and bringing production to a halt.

Since World War II, and especially since the 1960s, adolescent-onset substance abuse has escalated from rare sporadic cases to a high prevalence in many communities (Cameron, 1968; Coombs & Globetti, 1986). Several factors appear to foster it: widespread parental substance abuse, societal neglect of adolescents, poverty, rapid social changes, and political upheaval. Whatever the cause, the consequences are remarkably similar: undermining of normal adolescent psychosocial development, poor socialization of children to assume adult roles, lack of job skills, emotional immaturity, increased rates of adolescent psychiatric morbidity, and increased adolescent mortality (i.e., suicide, accidents, homicide).

Trends in Treatment and Prevention

From the time of Benjamin Rush, two central treatment methods were established, based on the psychiatric treatment methods of the late 1700s. One of these, as noted earlier, was "asylum" in a supportive environment away from drink and companion drinkers. The other was "moral treatment," consisting of a civil, respectful consideration for the recovering person. Both methods persist today and remain as two standard treatment strategies (although neither has been validated by research). They were not and are not inevitably successful, however. Nor were these methods readily available to the increasing numbers of alcoholics and addicts generated in the 1800s and 1900s. Thus, other methods have been tried.

One of these methods was the substitution of one drug for another. For example, laudanum (combined alcohol and opiates) was once prescribed for alcoholism. Morphine and later heroin were recommended for opium addiction during the mid-1800s. This approach is not extinct, as exemplified by the frequent recommendation in the 1970s that alcoholics substitute cannabis smoking for alcohol. Currently methadone is used for chronic opiate addicts who have failed three or more attempts at drug-free treatment. Despite adversive selection factors, methadone maintenance patients tend to do well as long as they comply with treatment. Following the original method of Dole and Nyswander (1965), methadone maintenance should be accompanied by an active, well-staffed psychosocial treatment program that has both individual and group therapies.

Detoxification became prevalent in the mid-1900s. Public detoxification facilities, established first in Eastern Europe, spread throughout the world. For many patients, this resource offers an entree into recovery. For others, "revolving door" detoxification may actually produce lifelong institutionalization on the installment plan (Gallant et al., 1973). The problem of the treatment-resistant public inebriate exists today in all parts of the United States. The so-called "Minnesota model" of treatment developed from several sources: a state hospital program (at Wilmar) and a later private program (at Hazelden), supplemented by the first day program for alcoholism (at the Minneapolis Veterans Administration Hospital). The characteristics of this "model" have varied over time as treatment has evolved and changed, and definitions still differ from one person to the next. However, characteristics often ascribed to the model include the following:

1. A period of residential or inpatient care, ranging from a few weeks to several months.
2. Focus on the psychoactive substance use disorder, with little or no consideration of associated psychiatric conditions or individual psychosocial factors.
3. Heavy emphasis on AA concepts, resources, and precepts, such as the "Twelve Steps" of recovery.
4. Referral to AA or another self-help group upon discharge from residential or inpatient care, with minimal or no ongoing professional treatment.
5. Minimal or no family therapy or counseling (although family orientation to AA principles and Al-Anon may take place).

6. Negative attitudes toward ongoing psychotherapies and pharmaco-therapies for substance use disorder or associated psychiatric disorder.

At the time of its evolution in the 1950s and 1960s, this model served to bridge the formerly separate hospital programs and self-help groups—a laudable achievement. However, if it is applied rigidly in light of current knowledge, some patients (who might otherwise be helped) will fail in or drop out of treatment. Nowadays, many treatment programs employ aspects of the old "Minnesota model," integrating them flexibly with newer methods in a more individualized and patient-centered manner.

The workplace has been a locus of prevention, early recognition, referral for treatment, and rehabilitation. Following World War II, Hudolin and coworkers in Yugoslavia established factory-based and farm commune-based recovery groups, with ties to treatment facilities. Over the last two decades, alcoholism counselors have worked in similar "employee assistance programs" in the United States.

More sophisticated methods of pharmacotherapy have appeared in the 1900s, although these remain few by comparison with other areas of medicine. Safe detoxification is possible through increased basic and clinical appreciation of withdrawal syndromes. Disulfiram, naltrexone, and methadone may be prescribed as maintenance drugs in the early difficult months and years of recovery. Medications currently being investigated for use in selected cases include buspirone, calcium channel blockers, fluoxetine, tegretol, and tricy-clics.

Several new diagnostic and treatment methods are currently being tried in an attempt to improve clinical outcomes. One of these is the recognition of comorbid conditions accompanying substance abuse, in which concurrent or modified treatment may improve success. For example, concurrent treatment for affective disorders, anxiety disorders, eating disorders, and pathological gambling is being attempted. For chronic conditions—such as mild mental retardation, borderline intelligence, organic brain syndrome, or chronic schizophrenia—substance abuse treatment, rehabilitation, and self-help pro-cedures may need to be modified. Intensive outpatient programs, conducted during the day, evening, or weekend, may assist certain patients to recover when other measures fail. These intensive outpatient programs are modeled after similar psychiatric programs. Much of the treatment time is spent in groups of various sizes, although individual and family sessions may occur as well. Staff is typically multidisciplinary, with counselors, nurses, occupational and recreational therapists, psychologists, psychiatrists, and social workers. Matching of patients to specific treatment modalities or therapists may be effective, but further research is needed to develop this approach. Monitoring of recovery in several contexts and by several sources, such as at work, by licensing agencies or unions, in the family, and with medical resources, appears to enhance outcome.

Preventive techniques first applied to the gin epidemic are still useful today: control over hours and location of sales; taxes or duties to increase cost; changing of public attitudes via the mass media; education; and abstinence-oriented religion (Popham, Schmidt, & DeLint, 1975; Lowinger, 1977; Smart, Murray, & Arif, 1988). The prolonged Asian opium epidemic demonstrated that laws alone are ineffective unless accompanied by socially integrated treatment; recovery programs; compulsory abstinence in identified cases; police pressure against drug production, commerce, and consumption; and follow-up monitoring (Westermeyer, 1976). Experience with antialcohol "prohibition" laws in Europe and North America has demonstrated the futility of outlawing substance use that was supported by many citizens. Adverse results from the Prohibition era in the United States included increased criminality associated with bootlegging alcohol, lack of quality control (e.g., methanol and lead contaminants), and development of unhealthy drinking patterns (e.g., surreptitious, rapid, without food, in a deviant setting). Public interest groups such as MADD may aid in reducing certain alcohol- and drug-related problems. Much work still remains to be done in this area. Despite expenditures of over $8 billion by the United States since 1970 to reduce drug availability, the government is still unable to prevent the import and production of illicit drugs. Mortality from hepatic cirrhosis, alcohol-related accidents, and suicide continue at an unprecedented level among young American males.

References

Ahluwalia, H. S., & Ponnampalam, J. T. (1968). The socioeconomic aspects of betel-nut chewing. *Journal of Tropical Medical Hygiene, 71,* 48–50.

Albaugh, B. J., & Anderson, P. O. (1974). Peyote in the treatment of alcoholism among American Indians. *American Journal of Psychiatry, 131,* 1247–1250.

Bacon, S. D. (1951). Studies of drinking in Jewish culture: I. General introduction. *Quarterly Journal of Studies on Alcohol, 12,* 444–450.

Bergman, R. L. (1971). Navaho peyote use: Its apparent safety. *American Journal of Psychiatry, 128,* 695–699.

Berridge, V. (1978). Working class opium eating in the nineteenth century: Establishing the factors. *British Journal of Addiction, 73,* 363–374.

Bonfiglio, G., Falli, S., & Pacine, A. (1977). Alcoholism in Italy: An outline highlighting some special features. *British Journal of Addiction, 73,* 3–12.

Bunzel, R. (1940). Role of alcoholism in two Central American cultures. *Psychiatry, 3,* 361–387.

Burton-Bradley, B. C. (1977). Some implications of betel chewing. *Medical Journal of Australia, 2,* 744–746.

Caetano, R. (1987). Acculturation and drinking patterns among U.S. Hispanics. *British Journal of Addiction, 82,* 789–799.

Caetano, R., Suzman, R. M., Rosen, D. H., & Vorhees-Rosen, D. J. (1983). The Shetland Islands: Longitudinal changes in alcohol consumption in a changing environment. *British Journal of Addiction, 78,* 21–36.

Cameron, D. C. (1968). Youth and drugs: A world view. *Journal of the American Medical Association, 206,* 1267–1271.

Carpenter, E. S. (1959). Alcohol in the Iroquois dream quest. *American Journal of Psychiatry, 116,* 158–151.

Carstairs, G. M. (1954). Daru and bhang: Cultural factors in the choice of intoxicant. *Quarterly Journal of Studies on Alcohol, 15,* 220–237.

Chopra, G. S., & Smith, J. W. (1974). Psychotic reactions following cannabis use in East Indians. *Archives of General Psychiatry, 30,* 24–27.

Connell, K. H. (1961). Illicit distribution: An Irish peasant industry. *Historical Studies of Ireland, 3,* 58–91.

Coombs, D. W., & Globetti, G. (1986). Alcohol use and alcoholism in Latin America: Changing patterns and sociocultural explanations. *International Journal of the Addictions, 21,* 59–81.

Culhane, C. (1989). Pot harvest gains across country. *The United States Journal, 13,*(8), 14.

Czikszentmihalyi, M. (1968). A cross-cultural comparison of some structural characteristics of group drinking. *Human Development, 11,* 210–216.

Dole, V. P., & Nyswander, M. E. (1965). A medical treatment of diacetylmorphine (heroin) addiction. *Journal of the American Medical Association, 193,* 646–650.

Dumont, M. (1967). Tavern culture: The sustenance of homeless men. *American Journal of Orthopsychiatry, 37,* 938–945.

DuToit, B. M. (1977). *Drugs, rituals and altered states of consciousness.* Rotterdam: Balkema.

Fenna, D. L., Mix, O., Schaefer, J., & Gilbert, A. L. (1971). Ethanol metabolism in various racial groups. *Canadian Medical Association Journal, 105,* 472–475.

Furst, P. T., & Coe, M. D. (1977). Ritual enemas. *Natural History, 86,* 88–89.

Gallant, D. M., Bishop, M. P., Mouledoux, A., Faulkner, M. A., Brisolara, A., & Swanson, W. A. (1973). The revolving door alcoholic. *Archives of General Psychiatry, 28,* 633–635.

Getahun, A., & Krikorias, A. D. (1973). Chat: Coffee's rival from Hirar, Ethiopia. *Economic Botany, 27,* 353–389.

Heath, D. (1971). Peasants, revolution, and drinking: Interethnic drinking patterns in two Bolivian communities. *Human Organization, 30,* 179–186.

Hippler, A. E. (1973). Fundamentalist Christianity: An Alaskan Athabascan technique for overcoming alcohol abuse. *Transcultural Psychiatric Research Review, 10,* 173–179.

Jilek-Aall, L. M. (1978). Alcohol and the Indian–white relationship: A study of the function of Alcoholics Anonymous among Coast Salish Indians. *Confinia Psychiatrica, 21,* 195–233.

Karayannis, A. D., & Kelepouris, M. B. (1967). Impressions of the drinking habits and alcohol problem in modern Greece. *British Journal of Addiction, 62,* 71–73.

Kaufman, A. (1975). Gasoline sniffing among children in a Pueblo Indian village. *Pediatrics, 51,* 1060–1063.

Kearny, M. (1970). Drunkenness and religious conversion in a Mexican village. *Quarterly Journal of Studies on Alcohol, 31,* 248–249.

Kennedy, J. G., Teague, J., & Fairbanks, L. (1980). Quat use in North Yemen and the problem of addiction: A study in medical anthropology. *Culture, Medicine and Psychiatry, 4,* 311–344.

Kramer, J. C. (1979). Opium rampant: Medical use, misuse and abuse in Britain and the west in the 17th and 18th centuries. *British Journal of Addiction, 74,* 377–389.

LaBarre, W. (1941). A cultist drug addiction in an Indian alcoholic. *Bulletin of the Menninger Clinic, 5,* 40–56.

Levinson, D. (1974). The etiology of skid rows in the United States. *International Journal of Social Psychiatry, 20,* 25–33.

Levy, J. E., & Kunitz, S. J. (1969). Notes on some White Mountain Apache social pathologies. *Plateau, 42,* 11–19.

Lieberman, M. A., & Borman, L. D. (1976). Self-help groups. *Journal of Applied Behavioral Science, 12,* 261–403.

Lowinger, P. (1977). The solution to narcotic addiction in the People's Republic of China. *American Journal of Drug and Alcohol Abuse, 4,* 165–178.

Lurie, N. O. (1972). Indian drinking patterns. *American Journal of Orthopsychiatry, 42,* 554.

Negrete, J. C. (1978). Coca leaf chewing: A public health assessment. *British Journal of Addiction, 73,* 283–290.

Ogan, E. (1966). Drinking behavior and race relations. *American Anthropologist, 68,* 181–188.

Paredes, A. (1975). Social control of drinking among the Aztec Indians of Mesoamerica. *Quarterly Journal of Studies on Alcohol, 36,* 1139–1153.

Popham, R. E., Schmidt, W., & DeLint, J. (1975). The prevention of alcoholism: Epidemiological studies of the effects of government control measures. *British Journal of Addiction, 70,* 125–144.

Robbins, R. H. (1973). Alcohol and the identity strugle: Some effects of economic change on interpersonal relations. *American Anthropologist, 75,* 99–122.

Rodin, A. E. (1981). Infants and gin mania in 18th-century London. *Journal of the American Medical Association, 245,* 1237–1239.

Sargent, M. J. (1972). Changes in Japanese drinking patterns. *Quarterly Journal of Studies on Alcohol, 28,* 709–722.

Savard, R. J. (1968). Effects of disulfiram therapy on relationships within the Navajo drinking group. *Quarterly Journal of Studies on Alcohol, 29,* 909–916.

Shore, J. H., & Von Fumetti, B. (1972). Three alcohol programs for American Indians. *American Journal of Psychiatry, 128,* 1450–1454.

Smart, R., Murray, G. F., & Arif, A. (1988). Drug abuse and prevention programs in 29 countries. *International Journal of the Addictions, 23,* 1–17.

Smith, W. R. (1968). Sacrifice among the Seminites. In W. A. Lessa & E. Z. Vogt (Eds.), *Reader in comparative religion* (pp. 39–48). New York: Harper & Row.

Stull, D. D. (1972). Victims of modernization: Accident rates and Papago Indian adjustment. *Human Organization, 31,* 227–240.

Thacore, V. R. (1973). Bhang psychosis. *British Journal of Psychiatry, 123,* 225–229.

Thurn, R. J. (1978). The gin plague. *Minnesota Medicine, 61,* 241–243.

W. W. (1949). The severity of alcoholics. *American Journal of Psychiatry, 106,* 370–375.

Waddell, J. (1976). The place of the cactus wine ritual in the Papago Indian ecosystem. In A. Bihari (Ed.), *Realm of the extra human: Ideas and actions* (pp. 213–228). The Hague: Mouton.

Westermeyer, J. (1973). Folk treatments for opium addiction in Laos. *British Journal of Addiction, 68,* 345–349.

Westermeyer, J. (1974). Opium dens: A social resource for addicts in Laos. *Archives of General Psychiatry, 31,* 237–240.

Westermeyer, J. (1976). The pro-heroin effects of anti-opium laws. *Archives of General Psychiatry, 33,* 1135–1139.

Westermeyer, J. (1983). *Poppies, pipes and people.* Berkeley: University of California Press.

Westermeyer, J. (1987). Cultural patterns of drug and alcohol use: An analysis of host and agent in the cultural environment. *United Nations Bulletin on Narcotics, 39,* 11–27.

Westermeyer, J. (1988). The pursuit of intoxication: Our 100 century-old romance with psychoactive substances. *American Journal of Drug and Alcohol Abuse, 14,* 175–187.

Westermeyer, J. (1989). Monitoring recovery from substance abuse: Rationales, methods and challenges. *Advances in Alcohol and Substance Abuse, 8,* 93–105.

Westermeyer, J., & Brantner, J. (1972). Violent death and alcohol use among the Chippewa in Minnesota. *Minnesota Medicine, 55,* 749–752.

Westermeyer, J., & Neider, J. (1985). Cultural affiliation among American Indian alcoholics: Correlation and change over a ten year period. *Journal of Operational Psychiatry, 16,* 17–28.

Wolcott, H. F. (1974). *African beer garden of Bulawayo: Integrated drinking in a segregated society.* New Brunswick, NJ: Rutgers Center of Alcohol Studies.

PART TWO

PSYCHOACTIVE SUBSTANCE DISORDERS

3

Alcohol

EDGAR P. NACE
PATRICIA G. ISBELL

Prior to the repopularization of the disease concept of alcoholism by Alcoholics Anonymous (AA) in the 1940s, alcoholism was viewed from a moral and legal perspective. In 1956, the American Medical Association acknowledged alcoholism as a disease. A few years earlier, the World Health Organization (1952) defined alcoholism as follows: "Alcoholism may be characterized as a chronic behavioral disorder manifested by repeated drinking of alcohol beverages in excess of dietary and social uses of the community and to the extent that it interferes with the drinker's health or his social and economic functioning" (p.32). In the 1960s, Jellinek's (1960) significant work served as a major factor in changing professional and public attitudes of alcoholism as a moral failure. A decade later, the National Council on Alcoholism (NCA) published its criteria for the diagnosis of alcoholism (NCA Criteria Committee, 1972). In contrast to criteria provided by the American Psychiatric Association (APA), which emphasized identification of advanced drinking, the NCA criteria attempted to identify early and late signs and symptoms of the illness. In subsequent revisions of the *Diagnostic and Statistical Manual* (DSM), the criteria included social consequences (APA, 1980, 1987). There continues to be substantial debate regarding the best definition. The following definition is used by many in the field and is a useful overall construct: Alcoholism exists when an individual continues to use alcohol despite significant impairment in social and physical functioning. The impairments in social functioning may include significant difficulties in employment, in marital and family relationships, and in legal problems secondary to alcohol use, such as charges of driving while intoxicated. The impairments in physical health frequently include liver damage, central and peripheral nervous system dysfunction, and hematological abnormalities.

Diagnosis

The symptoms associated with alcohol dependence are far-ranging and involve biological, psychological, and social domains. The presenting symptoms vary from patient to patient, and such heterogeneity may mislead the clinician.

Medical problems, job loss, marital strife, and arrests for drunk driving may have similar diagnostic impact. The number of symptoms of abuse determines the diagnosis rather than any specific category of symptoms. In Vaillant's (1983) study of 400 males, criteria for psychological dependence correlated .87 with a scale measuring social consequences of drinking.

In assessing a patient for alcoholism, problems related to the drinker, the family, and the community should be considered (Moser, 1980). Problems for the drinker may include declining job performance, joblessness, divorce, arrests (especially for driving while intoxicated and public intoxication), accidents, withdrawal symptoms, broken relationships, and associated medical illness (e.g., gastritis, anemia, pancreatitis, cirrhosis). Assessment of family functioning may reveal marital discord, spouse abuse, child abuse, financial problems, depression or anxiety syndromes, child neglect, child developmental problems, school dropout, and delinquency. At the community level, manifestations may include violence, accidents, property damage, economic costs of welfare or health services, and decreased work productivity.

Numerous scales and tests have been constructed to facilitate the diagnosis of alcoholism. The Michigan Alcoholism Screening Test (MAST; Selzer, 1971) and the criteria established by the NCA are two well-known examples. A modification of the MAST, the Self-Administered Alcoholism Screening Test (SASSI), has proven effective in general medical settings with a reported sensitivity of 95% and a specificity of 98% (Davis, Hunt, Morse, & O'Brien, 1987).

A useful interview device is the CAGE questionnaire (Ewing, 1984). "CAGE" is a mnemonic device (Cut down: "Has anyone ever recommended that you *cut* back or stop drinking?" Annoyed: "Have you ever felt *annoyed* or angry if someone comments on your drinking?" Guilt: "Have there been times when you've felt *guilty* about or regretted things that occurred because of drinking?" Eye-opener: "Have you ever used alcohol to help you get started in the morning, to steady your nerves?"). Positive answers to three of these four questions strongly suggest alcoholism.

More recently, the revised third edition of the DSM (DSM-III-R; APA, 1987) lists nine criteria, three of which must be met for the diagnosis of alcohol dependence. These criteria rely less on the classic concepts of addiction, such as tolerance and withdrawal symptoms, and place more emphasis on the salience of alcohol use and the degree of involvement with alcohol. This conceptual advance avoids reliance on criteria that may not emerge until middle or late stages of the disease. The main symptoms characteristic of alcohol and other types of drug dependence are briefly listed (see Table 3.1).

Criteria 1 and 2 refer to "loss of control" as described by Jellinek (1960). Loss of control has two aspects: the inability to regulate intake (see criterion 1) and the inability to stay stopped (criterion 2). Criteria 3, 4, and 5 reflect the salience or importance of usage to the alcoholic as reflected in time taken up (3), or by the priority of usage over important social or occupational functions (4 and 5). Criterion 6 expresses the profound dependence on the substance

TABLE 3.1. DSM-III-R Criteria for Psychoactive Substance Dependence

---

A. At least three of the following:

(1) substance often taken in larger amounts or over a longer period than the person intended

(2) persistent desire or one or more unsuccessful efforts to cut down or control substance use

(3) a great deal of time spent in activities necessary to get the substance (e.g., theft), taking the substance (e.g., chain smoking), or recovering from its effects

(4) frequent intoxication or withdrawal symptoms when expected to fulfill major role obligations at work, school, or home (e.g., does not go to work because hung over, goes to school or work "high," intoxicated while taking care of his or her children), or when substance use is physically hazardous (e.g., drive when intoxicated)

(5) important social, occupational, or recreational activities given up or reduced because of substance use

(6) continued substance use despite knowledge of having a persistent or recurrent social, psychological, or physical problem that is caused or exacerbated by the use of the substance (e.g., keeps using heroin despite family arguments about it, cocaine-induced depression, or having an ulcer made worse by drinking)

(7) marked tolerance: need for markedly increased amounts of the substance (i.e., at least a 50% increase) in order to achieve intoxication or desired effect, or markedly diminished effect with continued use of the same amount

Note: The following items may not apply to cannabis, hallucinogens, or phencyclidine (PCP):

(8) characteristic withdrawal symptoms (see specific withdrawal syndromes under Psychoactive Substance-induced Organic Mental Disorders)

(9) substance often taken to relieve or avoid withdrawal symptoms

B. Some symptoms of the disturbance have persisted for at least one month, or have occurred repeatedly over a longer period of time.

Criteria for Severity of Psychoactive Substance Dependence:

Mild: Few, if any, symptoms in excess of those required to make the diagnosis, and the symptoms result in no more than mild impairment in occupational functioning or in usual social activities or relationships with others.

Moderate: Symptoms or functional impairment between "mild" and "severe."

Severe: Many symptoms in excess of those required to make the diagnosis, and the symptoms markedly interfere with occupational functioning or with usual social activities or relationships with others.

In Partial Remission: During the past six months, some use of the substance and some symptoms of dependence.

In Full Remission: During the past six months, either no use of the substance, or use of the substance and no symptoms of dependence.

Note. From the *Diagnostic and Statistical Manual of Mental Disorders* (3rd ed., rev., pp. 167–168) by the American Psychiatric Association, 1987, Washington, DC: Author. Copyright 1987 by the American Psychiatric Association. Reprinted by permission.

combined with denial, so that drinking continues in the face of obvious adverse consequences. Criteria 7, 8, and 9 address tolerance and subsequent withdrawal symptoms.

In addition to broadening diagnostic criteria, DSM-III-R distinguishes degree of dependence as mild, moderate, or severe (see bottom portion of Table 3.1). The degree of dependence is also considered by the category of alcohol abuse. The alcohol abuser—that is, one not yet dependent but using alcohol in a pathological way—would meet the criteria listed in Table 3.2.

The line between abuse and dependence is often a fine one. The abuser may be so categorized because he or she minimizes the effects of alcohol. Abuse may form a continuum and be hard to separate from the "mild" dependence category.

Another aspect of the DSM-III-R criteria that should be noted is that quantity of alcohol drunk is not mentioned. For the most part this is appropriate, because the context and consequences of alcohol use shape the clinical syndrome. Nevertheless, one should attempt to ascertain quantity as part of the diagnostic assessment.

Several studies document that quantity and frequency of drinking are related, and in turn are associated with pathological patterns of use. For example, Fillmore (1974) reported a positive correlation (.43) between frequency of drinking and amount consumed per occasion. In a study of English students (Orford, Waller, & Peto, 1974), the correlation between frequency of drinking and amount consumed per drinking day was .50 for males and .60 for females. Quantity of alcohol drunk is associated with both loss of control and alcohol dependence symptoms. A contrast of males who reported having 60–120 drinks per month with those reporting in excess of 120 drinks per month is instructive (Clark & Midanik, 1982). (A drink is a 12-ounce beer, a 4-ounce glass of wine, or 1 ounce of 100 proof whiskey.) Of the 60- to 120-drink group, 9% met criteria for alcohol dependence and 17% for loss of control. For those drinking in excess of 120 drinks per month, the comparable percentages were 39% and 38%, respectively. For women who had 60–120 drinks per month, 11% qualified for alcohol dependence and 20% for loss of control. Of women drinking in excess of 120 drinks per month, 52% met criteria for both alcohol dependence and loss of control (Clark & Midanik, 1982).

Medical data obtained from a physical examination and the laboratory

TABLE 3.2. DSM-III-R Criteria for Psychoactive Substance Abuse

---

A. A maladaptive pattern of psychoactive substance use indicated by at least one of the following:

    (1) continued use despite knowledge of having a persistent or recurrent social, occupational, psychological, or physical problem that is caused or exacerbated by use of the psychoactive substance

    (2) recurrent use in situations in which use is physically hazardous (e.g., driving while intoxicated)

B. Some symptoms of the disturbance have persisted for at least one month, or have occurred repeatedly over a longer period of time.

C. Never met the criteria for Psychoactive Substance Dependence for this substance.

Note. From the *Diagnostic and Statistical Manual of Mental Disorders* (3rd ed., rev., p. 169) by the American Psychiatric Association, 1987, Washington, DC: Author. Copyright 1987 by the American Psychiatric Association. Reprinted by permission.

are useful in diagnosing alcoholism. The types of possible medical findings are reviewed in another section of this chapter. Unfortunately, most of these develop after at least 5 years of alcoholism, and therefore reflect middle to late stages of the disease. Even so, such medical findings can be persuasive in confronting the denial of a chronic alcoholic.

Several commonly ordered laboratory tests are useful for detecting heavy drinking. Serum γ-glutamyltransferase (GGT) has been established as a sensitive test of early liver dysfunction. The GGT is elevated in 70% of alcoholics and heavy drinkers (Kristenson, Trell, Fex, & Hood, 1980). In a study of patients admitted for alcoholism treatment at the Mayo Clinic, 63% had an elevated GGT, and 48% an elevated serum glutamic-oxaloacetic transferase (SGOT) (Morse & Hurt, 1979).

Another useful screening test is an increased erythrocyte mean corpuscular volume (MCV), which was elevated in 26% of the patients in the Mayo Clinic study. In both male and female alcoholics, the combination of elevated GGT and MCV identified 90% of alcoholic patients (Skinner, 1981). Other tests that may be elevated are triglycerides, serum alkaline phosphatase, serum bilirubin, and uric acid. However, because the number of false negatives is sizeable, laboratory tests cannot be relied upon alone. A careful history (including history from significant others), physical examination, and consideration of the DSM-III-R criteria constitute the data base, in addition to laboratory data, upon which alcoholism is diagnosed.

Establishing the diagnosis of alcoholism is one matter, but presenting it to the patient is another. A few points should be made regarding the presentation:

1. Confront the denial; use the words "alcoholism" or "alcohol dependence."
2. Provide an explanation of why the diagnosis applies; have facts at hand.
3. Explain old prejudices and stereotypes of alcoholism.
4. Emphasize that alcoholism is a disease; be sensitive to guilt and shame, and explain that people do not intend to become alcoholic and it usually occurs without a person's being aware of it.
5. Instill hope; results of treatment are excellent if the patient is willing to try.
6. Have an outline of treatment recommendations and options prepared.

When the clinician is alert to the possibility of alcoholism in a patient, understands the protean manifestations of the disease, and applies diagnostic criteria, the possibility of misdiagnosis is greatly reduced.

Comorbidity

Over the past decade, compelling data on the high comorbidity of alcoholism with other psychiatric disorders have become available. Epidemiologic Catchment Area (ECA) data (Helzer & Pryzbeck, 1988) indicate that 44% of male alcoholics and 65% of female alcoholics have a lifetime diagnosis of an additional psychiatric disorder. Each of the psychiatric disorders studied is more likely to occur in the alcoholic population than in the general population. Within the general population, about 34% are found to have a diagnosable psychiatric illness at some time in their lives; one-third of these will have a second disorder as well. The vulnerability of the alcoholic to a "dual" diagnosis is highlighted by the fact that nearly half (47%) meet criteria for a second disorder.

Drug Abuse/Dependence

A major form of comorbidity is alcoholism with drug abuse/dependence. Within the general population, 3.5% of people who are not alcoholic meet criteria for a diagnosis of alcohol abuse/dependence. In contrast, 18% of the population with a diagnosis of alcohol abuse/dependence also meet criteria for drug abuse/dependence (Helzer & Pryzbeck, 1988). In a clinical sample of over 500 patients, the overlap of alcohol abuse/dependence and drug abuse/dependence was 38% (Ross, Glaser, & Germanson, 1988).

The more serious the drug abuse disorder, the more likely it is that alcohol abuse/dependence will be found. For example, the ECA data indicate that if no drug abuse problem exists the rate of alcohol abuse/dependence is 11% (compared to 13% for the total population). When only tetrahydrocannabinol (THC; the "active ingredient" in marijuana) abuse/dependence is present the prevalence of alcohol abuse/dependence rose to 36%. With the "harder" drugs, the rates of alcohol abuse/dependence rise: amphetamine (62%), opioids (67%), barbiturates (71%), and cocaine (84%) (Helzer & Pryzbeck, 1988).

Anxiety Disorders

Anxiety disorders are the most common psychiatric disorder found in the general population. The 1-month prevalence rate is 7.3%, and the lifetime prevalence rate is 14.6%. Alcohol abuse/dependence has a 1-month prevalence rate of 2.8%, and a liftime rate of 13.3% (Regier et al., 1988).

Given these two commonly occurring disorders, it is not surprising to find considerable comorbidity. A diagnosis of generalized anxiety was made in 26% of patients presenting to a large substance abuse program, although nearly 52% met criteria for a lifetime diagnosis of generalized anxiety disorder (Ross et al., 1988).

The same treatment center has reported the rate of phobic disorders among alcoholics to be 30% (Ross et al., 1988); by sex, phobic disorders are reported as occurring in 44% of women and 20% of men (Hesselbrock,

Meyer, & Keener, 1985). Among these disorders the most common is agoraphobia, followed by simple phobia, social phobia, and agoraphobia with panic attacks (Ross et al., 1988).

Panic disorder is also found at considerably greater rates in the alcoholic population. In the general population, the lifetime prevalence of panic disorder is 2% for females and 1% for men. In treatment programs, the disorder is found in approximately 9% of patients (Ross et al., 1988). Female alcoholics are three times more likely to have panic disorder than male alcoholics (Helzer & Pryzbeck, 1988).

Obsessive–compulsive disorder is found in about 2.5% of the adult population, according to ECA lifetime prevalence data (Regier et al., 1988). This disorder may have been overlooked in earlier studies of anxiety and alcoholism, but recent data indicate an increased comorbidity in alcoholic patients.

The available data indicate that generalized anxiety disorder is the only anxiety disorder for which alcoholism is more likely than not to precede the development of symptoms. At least 51% of patients with a lifetime history of alcoholism and generalized anxiety disorder were determined to have the alcoholism at least 1 year prior to the anxiety disorder. For other anxiety disorders, it is more common for the disorder to be primary in onset. For example, in dual-disorder patients, alcohol abuse/dependence preceded panic disorder in only 23% of cases; in phobic patients, it did so in 32%; and in obsessive–compulsive patients, it did so in 39%. Similarly, alcoholism has been noted commonly to follow the onset of post traumatic stress disorder.

Affective Disorders

Depression has long been linked with alcoholism, but the nature of this linkage is only gradually being understood. ECA data (Helzer & Pryzbeck, 1988) indicate that major depression and dysthymia occur between 1.5 and 2 times more commonly in alcoholics. In male alcoholics major depression has a 5% lifetime prevalence rate, compared to 3% for the total male population. Female alcoholics, however, have a prevalence rate of major depression of 19%, compared to 7% in the total female population.

Clinic samples report higher rates of depression in alcoholics. In a combined outpatient and inpatient sample using the National Institute of Mental Health Diagnostic Interview Schedule, major depression was found in nearly 23% of alcoholics and dysthymia in 13%. If both alcoholism and drug abuse were present, the respective rates increased to 36% and 23% (Ross et al., 1988).

There is a strong sex difference in order of onset. In males alcoholism proceeds depression in 78% of cases. For women the reverse is true: Depression is the antecedent diagnosis in 66% of cases (Helzer & Pryzbeck, 1988).

Mania

The recent ECA data have revealed considerable comorbidity between alcoholism and bipolar affective disorder. Mania occurs in the population at a lifetime prevalence rate of 0.3% in men and 0.4% in females. However, the alcoholic woman has a 10-fold increased risk of mania (4% of alcoholic women also have a history of mania), and the alcoholic male has a risk three times greater (1%). Approximately 2–3% of hospitalized alcoholics are found to have bipolar disorder (Hesselbrock et al., 1985; Ross et al., 1988).

Schizophrenia

The difficult clinical course of the patient with both schizophrenia and alcoholism has become increasingly apparent as knowledge of this form of comorbidity develops. Drug abuse is known to be common in the schizophrenic population, but only recently has the magnitude of comorbidity with alcoholism been determined. According to ECA data (Helzer & Pryzbeck, 1988), the alcoholic individual is four times more likely to have schizophrenia than the nonalcoholic. In a large clinical sample of alcoholics, 8% were also schizophrenic and at least 50% had developed alcoholism after the onset of schizophrenia (Ross et al., 1988).

Personality Disorders

The assumption that alcoholism and personality disorders are linked in some fashion has a long history. Earlier editions of the DSM (DSM-I and DSM-II) classified alcoholism along with personality disorders. By 1980, with publication of DSM-III, substance use disorders (including alcoholism) were understood as entities independent of the personality disorders. However, the comorbidity of alcoholism and personality disorders is extensive, and our knowledge of comorbidity has been improved by the use of standardized diagnostic instruments.

Generally, antisocial personality disorder (APD) is the most prevalent personality disorder associated with alcoholism when samples from public treatment centers are studied, and borderline personality disorder (BPD) is the most common in studies from private treatment facilities. In a sample of alcoholics consecutively admitted to a private psychiatric hospital, 13% were found to have BPD according to conservative diagnostic criteria (Nace, Saxon, & Shore, 1983). In a more recent private psychiatric hospital sample, 57% of substance-abusing patients met DSM-III-R criteria for a personality disorder; in this latter sample, BPD was the most commonly occurring personality disorder (Nace, Davis, & Gaspari, 1991).

Personality disorder occurs more commonly in alcoholics than in the general population. A prospective long-term study of a nonclinical sample (Drake & Vaillant, 1985) determined that by age 47, 23% of males met criteria for a personality disorder. However, the alcoholic males in the sample met criteria for a personality disorder in 37% of cases. Personality disorders are more common in alcoholics than among general psychiatric patients. In a review of over 2,400 psychiatric patients (Koenigsberg, Kaplan, Gilmore, & Cooper, 1985), 36% were found to have a personality disorder. The alcoholics in this clinical sample, however, had a personality disorder in 48% of cases. In this sample, BPD was most common personality disorder (43%), followed by APD (21%) and mixed personality disorder (17%). In a review of alcoholism and APD, a positive association was found in 11 of 14 studies (Grande, Wolfe, Schubert, Patterson, & Brocco, 1984). Estimates of APD in clinical samples vary from 20% to 49% in males and from 5% to 20% in females (Schuckit, 1973). ECA study data document APD in 15% of alcoholic men and 4% of alcoholic women. These prevalences exceed the rate of APD in the total population by 4 times for men and 12 times for women (Helzer & Pryzbeck 1988).

Ethnicity and Alcoholism

Cultural attitudes exert a powerful influence on drinking behaviors and response to treatment. It has been shown that although cultural approval may increase the accessibility of alcohol, ritualistic use of the drug by the culture may help to inhibit abuse or dependence (Westermeyer, 1986). The lower rates of drinking problems among American Italians and Jews have been explained by the traditional use of wine in these groups; integration of drinking into family life; and, in the Jewish drinkers, the religious significance attached to alcohol (Snyder, 1958). However, even ethnic groups with ritualistic use patterns do not consistently show low incidences of alcoholism or of alcoholic complications. For example, French and Italian people have high cirrhosis death rates in association with alcohol use.

Many Native American tribal groups have high rates of alcohol-related problems (Westermeyer, 1986). Traditionally, Apaches had relatively few problems with alcoholism, but more recently they have developed higher rates of drinking problems. Westermeyer (1986) has noted increasing rates of alcoholism and medical complications secondary to alcohol as Native American tribes have moved from their native lands to "integrated" towns.

The most significant epidemiological data on alcohol use among African-Americans relate to the high number of deaths related to alcoholic cirrhosis (Nace, 1984) and to the high rates of homicide in association with alcohol use. Williams (1986) has reported that the literature does not accurately reflect the high prevalence and incidence of alcoholism among African-Americans.

A finding that may be linked to the lower level of alcoholism among Orientals is that as many as 50% of Orientals do not possess ALDH-1, one of four clinically significant isoenzymes of aldehyde dehydrogenase (ALDH). The higher rate of facial flushing is probably a result of acetaldehyde accumulation due to the absence of this isoenzyme. Sue (1987) has cautioned that although many consider Asian-Americans to be at low risk for developing alcoholism, there are subgroups with patterns of high rates of alcohol consumption that require further investigation.

Mexican-Americans make up the largest subgroup among the Hispanic population in the United States and have been studied the most frequently in regard to manifestation and treatment of alcoholism. However, as is the case with African-Americans, there are still relatively few data. Available data do show a greater prevalence of heavy drinking and alcohol-related problems than in the general population (Nace, 1984).

Finally, Babor and Mendelson's (1986) findings show the importance of ethnotherapy, a treatment technique that employs ethnic identity as a medium of intervention, in the treatment of alcoholism.

Pharmacology of Alcohol

In this section, ethyl alcohol, the hydrophilic molecule itself, is considered. Its small size and chemical simplicity enable it to affect almost all cells of the body, especially those cells in the central nervous system (CNS). As previously noted, ethyl alcohol is a CNS depressant that affects all levels of the brain, beginning with depression of the reticular activating system and the cortex.

Alcohol is absorbed primarily from the stomach and the proximal portion of the small intestine. Approximately 95% of alcohol is metabolized by the liver, at a rate of approximately one drink per hour (the usual drink contains 8 to 10 g of absolute alcohol). The remainder is excreted directly through the lungs, urine, and perspiration. Factors that affect the absorption of alcohol include high alcohol concentration, which reduces the rate of absorption, most likely secondary to pylorospasm. Ingestion of food decreases alcohol absorption by retarding gastric emptying. The presence of drugs such as antidepressants also delays gastric emptying.

The principal route of metabolism of alcohol is through the alcohol dehydrogenase (ADH) pathway. The major product is the extremely toxic substance acetaldehyde. Acetaldehyde is further broken down to acetic acid via the enzyme ALDH, and subsequently goes through the citric acid cycle to become carbon dioxide and water. Both ADH and ALDH possess several distinct isoenzymes that may have an impact on the genetic predisposition to alcoholism, as noted above in the discussion of Asian-Americans and alcohol. Another pathway for oxidation, the microsomal ethanol-oxidizing system (MEOS), is induced by chronic ingestion of alcohol. The increase in the activity of this MEOS pathway can increase the rate of elimination by 50–70%. This MEOS may be responsible for the increased metabolic tolerance seen in chronic alcoholics for other hypnotic–sedative drugs as well as for alcohol.

The specific mechanism of alcohol on the CNS remains under investigation. The theory that alcohol may produce a morphine-like substance in the brains of certain individuals has had a significant impact on the field, leading to a greater focus on the neurochemical changes in the brain that may result from alcohol ingestion. The effect of alcohol on neurotransmitters such as dopamine or serotonin may produce morphine-like compounds called tetrahydropapaverolines and tetrahydrocarbolines (Davis & Walsh, 1970). In their *in vitro* experiments, Davis and Walsh reported the conversion of dopamine to tetrahydropapaveroline instead of to norepinephrine. In the *in vivo* work of Myers (1983), tetrahydroisoquinolines were injected into the brains of previously abstinent rats, resulting in an increased preference for alcohol. There are also animal data suggesting that opiate antagonists such as naltrexone will suppress alcohol consumption (Altschuler, Philips, & Feinhandler, 1980). At this time, these findings are of theoretical interest; however, they might merit a trial in human subjects.

Another neurochemical theory of physical dependence on ethanol, which involves norepinephrine metabolism, has been studied by Tabakoff, Sutker, and Randall (1983). Tabakoff and colleagues have shown that adaption to chronic ethanol exposure results in a subsequent "rebound" phenomenon of norepinephrine turnover.

Another neurochemical theory of addiction involves the γ-aminobutryic acid (GABA) system. Suzdak, Glowa, and Crawley (1986) have reported that an imidazobenzodiazepine, RO 15-4513, acts as a selective benzodiazepine antagonist of alcohol, blocking the effects of alcohol on the GABA-stimulated chloride channel. Further animal studies by Samson, Toliver, and Pfeffer (1987) have demonstrated that administration of RO 15-4513 results in a dose-dependent suppression of ethanol intake. The specificity of this drug has come into question (Suzdak, Glowa, & Crawley, 1987), since it has also been found to have some partial inverse antagonist effects.

Clinical Features

Alcohol Intoxication

The most frequent alcohol-induced organic mental disorder, alcohol intoxication, is characterized by an alteration in behavior with varying stages, depending on the amount of alcohol used and upon individual variation and tolerance. The maladaptive behavior effects most commonly seen are impaired judgment, mood lability, disinhibition of aggressive impulses, and social or occupational dysfunction. At lower levels of alcohol ingestion, stimulant properties predominate. This may be related to a direct stimulant effect or to a selective depression of inhibitory neurons at relatively low blood alcohol concentrations. A blood alcohol level of 30 mg% will produce a euphoric effect in most individuals who do not have an established tolerance. At 50 mg%, the CNS depressant effects of alcohol become prominent, with associated motor coordination problems and some cognitive deficits. In the United States, the legal level of intoxication is 100 mg%. There is evidence that even at blood alcohol levels of 15 mg%, present after approximately one drink, there is significant impairment in the ability to operate a motor vehicle (Moskowitz, Burns, & Williams, 1985). At levels greater than 250 mg%, significant confusion and a decreased state of consciousness may occur. Alcoholic coma may occur at this level, and at greater than 400 mg%, death may result. Secondary to an established high tolerance, some chronic heavy drinkers may not show these effects even at higher blood levels.

Alcohol Idiosyncratic Intoxication

Alcohol idiosyncratic intoxication, a rare condition, is characterized by assaultive, violent behavior occurring within minutes after ingestion of quantities of alcohol not sufficient to cause intoxication in most people (APA, 1987). There continues to be controversy as to whether this phenomenon exists, since it has never been clearly documented under experimental conditions.

Uncomplicated Alcohol Withdrawal

On another spectrum are the withdrawal syndromes that occur upon the cessation of alcohol use or upon decreased use following chronic intake. In the alcohol-dependent person, symptoms of withdrawal typically begin 4 to 6 hours after the last drink, peak at 24 to 48 hours, and may last up to 5 days. These symptoms represent autonomic nervous system hyperactivity resulting as a rebound phenomenon from the depressant effect of alcohol. The characteristic symptoms include tremulousness, anxiety, increased heart rate, increased blood pressure, sweating, nausea, hyperreflexia, and insomnia. These symptoms vary in intensity, based on the severity of the alcoholism and the general physical condition of the patient. An alcohol withdrawal seizure is most likely to occur 7 to 48 hours after the last drink and is grand mal in type. The most reliable predictors of a withdrawal seizure are a history of previous seizures and photophobia during the withdrawal period. Sixteen percent of alcoholic patients will have alcohol withdrawal seizures, and one-third of this subgroup will progress to delirium tremens. Hypomagnesemia, respiratory alkalosis, and hypoglycemia have been shown to be associated with withdrawal seizures.

Alcohol Withdrawal Delirium

Further along on the withdrawal continuum is alcohol withdrawal delirium or delirium tremens. This is a much less common syndrome; however, it carries a mortality rate of 10–15% if untreated. Onset is usually 48 to 72 hours after the last drink and rarely begins beyond 7 days. This very serious disorder is made even more life-threatening when there is concurrent liver failure, infection, or trauma present. Characteristic signs and symptoms include disorientation, fluctuating consciousness, vivid hallucinations, agitation, and mild hyperpyrexia. This delirium usually runs its course in 48 to 72 hours and requires close medical observation and treatment.

Alcoholic Hallucinosis

Alcoholic hallucinosis is another syndrome related to the cessation or reduction in heavy consumption of alcohol. It is most typically associated with vivid auditory hallucinations, but without the marked clouding of sensorium that is present in alcohol withdrawal delirium. The hallucinations, which may be auditory or visual, usually develop within 48 hours after cessation of or reduction in heavy ingestion of alcohol. It is usually limited to 1 week in duration and must be distinguished from other mental disorders.

Alcohol Amnestic Disorder

Alcohol amnestic disorder constitutes a continuum involving Wernicke's acute encephalopathy, the amnestic disorder per se (commonly known as Korsakoff's psychosis), and cerebellar degeneration. The etiology is based on nutritional factors, specifically on the thiamine deficiency present with chronic alcohol use. Other factors, such as familial transketolase deficiency, may also be important in the pathogenesis of this syndrome in a subgroup of individuals. Wernicke's acute encephalopathy, with the triad of confusion, bilateral gaze nystagmus and bilateral paralysis of the lateral rectus ocular muscles, and ataxia, may clear with vigorous thiamine replacement. Treatment with thiamine will usually reverse the ocular symptoms in 1 to 6 hours. Recovery of cognitive and cerebellar function is less predictable and frequently incomplete.

The disorder in memory that may persist, Korsakoff's, is best correlated with lesions in the diencephalon, especially the dorsomedial nucleus. The memory defect, categorized by anterograde and retrograde amnesia, is classically a more severe anterograde amnesia, where new information is not transferred from short- to long-term memory. In contrast to other dementias, intellectual function is typically preserved. In a review of the Wernicke–Korsakoff syndrome, McEvoy (1982) points out that 20% of these patients show complete recovery over a period of months to years, 60% show some improvement, and 20% show minimal improvement. Previously believed to be a distinct clinical entity, alcoholic cerebellar degeneration may be indistinguishable clinically and pathophysiologically from the cerebellar dysfunction seen with Wernicke–Korsakoff syndrome.

Alcoholic amnestic disorder should not be confused with "blackouts," which are typically periods of retrograde amnesia during periods of intoxication. Blackouts, caused by high blood alcohol levels, may occur in nonalcoholics, as well as at any time in the course of alcoholism.

Dementia Associated with Alcoholism

The second most common adult dementia after Alzheimer's disease is the dementia associated with chronic alcohol use. Eckardt and Martin (1986) report that approximately 9% of alcoholics acquire this condition. This dementia in large part is secondary to the direct neurotoxic effects of alcohol on the brain.

Neuropsychological Findings

The neuropsychological deficits found in alcoholics are largely related to nondominant-hemisphere functions. The following areas are commonly impaired: new learning, visuospatial function, abstract thinking, and psychomotor skills. These cognitive deficits and occasionally cortical atrophy will improve with abstinence, as evidenced by computed tomography studies. Although neurotoxic effects of alcohol are well recognized in the development of cognitive impairment, there is evidence that genetic, metabolic, and environmental variables may also play important roles. Not all alcoholics show impairment on neuropsychological, neurophysiological, or structural measures. The subjects who show the most impairment on neuropsychological measures tend to be over 40 years of age. Porjesz and Begleiter (1985) have reported that among some subjects in their sample, the male offspring of male alcoholics have an increase in the P3 wave of evoked potentials. This indicates the possibility of a marker and suggests that there may be neuropsychological deficits prior to the onset of alcoholism.

Medical Complications of Alcoholism

Nervous System

Ethanol damages the CNS and peripheral nervous system by altering neurotransmitter levels, cell membrane fluidity, and function.

Alcoholic dementia and the Wernicke–Korsakoff syndrome have already been discussed. Hepatic encephalopathy occurs in the setting of severe liver failure due to either severe alcoholic hepatitis or cirrhosis. Early manifestations of encephalopathy include inappropriate behavior, agitation, depression, apathy, and sleep disturbance. Confusion, disorientation, and depressed mental status develop in the advanced stages of encephalopathy. Physical examination may demonstrate asterixis, tremor, rigidity, hyperreflexia, and fetor hepaticas. Treatment requires the elimination of the offending condition, dietary protein restriction, and removal of nitrogenous waste from the gut with osmotic laxatives and antibiotics (lactulose, neomycin).

Alcoholic peripheral neuropathy is the result of alcohol toxicity and B vitamin deficiency. Pain, paresthesias, and weakness of alcoholic peripheral neuropathy begin in the lower extremities. Advanced neuropathy can assume the classic stocking–glove distribution similar to that seen in diabetic neuropathy. Involvement of the motor nerves results in muscular atrophy and weakness. Physical findings include stocking–glove anesthesia, decreased deep tendon reflexes, dorsal column dysfunction, hyperhidrosis, and postural orthostasis. Treatment consists of abstinence and B vitamin supplements. Phenytoin, carbamazepine, tricyclic antidepressants, and nerve blocks all have been used with variable success (Adams & Victor, 1981).

Tobacco–alcohol amblyopia, central pontine myelinosis, and Marchiafava–Bignami disease are discussed in another section.

Liver

The spectrum of alcoholic liver disease includes steatosis, hepatitis, and cirrhosis. Although fewer than one-third of alcoholics will develop cirrhosis, alcohol is the leading cause of cirrhosis and cirrhosis-related deaths in Western societies (Lieber & Leo, 1982). The risk of cirrhosis is increased with a daily consumption of as little as 20 g of alcohol in females and 40 g in males.

Hepatic steatosis, or fatty liver, is a common, reversible condition that does not progress to cirrhosis (Lieber & Leo, 1982). Signs and symptoms of alcoholic steatosis include nausea, vomiting, hepatomegaly, right upper quadrant pain, and tenderness. Ascites and jaundice are uncommon. Laboratory data may reveal mild elevation of transaminases, alkaline phosphatase, or bilirubin. Clinically, fatty liver may mimic or coexist with alcoholic hepatitis. Symptoms of alcoholic fatty liver should resolve within 2 weeks of abstinence.

Alcoholic hepatitis frequently coexists with fatty liver and cirrhosis. Symptoms include anorexia, nausea, vomiting, fever, chills, and abdominal pain. Hepatomegaly and right upper quadrant tenderness are common. Transaminase levels rarely exceed 500 I.U., with a typical ratio of aspartate aminotransferase to alanine aminotransferase of 2 : 1 to 5 : 1. Liver biopsy can be helpful in distinguishing fatty liver from mild hepatitis. Ascites, encephalopathy, high bilirubin levels, and prolongation of the prothrombin time are poor prognostic indicators that portend an increased mortality. Treatment consists of abstinence and nutritional support. Treatment with steroids, propylthiouracil, and colchicine has yielded mixed results. Histological recovery from alcoholic hepatitis can require from 6 weeks to 6 months. Of patients with alcoholic hepatitis who continue to drink, 50% will develop cirrhosis (Galambos, 1985).

Gastrointestinal Tract and Pancreas

Parotid gland enlargement occurs in approximately 50% of alcoholics with cirrhosis. Vitamin deficiencies are primarily responsible for the development of reversible stomatitis, glossitis, and cheilitis. Alcohol is directly toxic to the stomach. High intragastric concentrations of alcohol impair gastric emptying. The net result of these factors is the formation of gastritis, which in its most severe form may become hemorrhagic. Epigastric pain, nausea, and vomiting following an alcoholic binge suggest the diagnosis of acute gastritis. These symptoms resolve quickly over 1 to 2 days with abstinence and antacid therapy. Upper gastrointestinal hemmorhage in the alcoholic is usually due to a gastritis or peptic ulcer. While less common, esophagitis, Mallory–Weiss tear, and esophageal varices are all important causes of upper gastrointestinal hemorrhage that must be excluded.

Diarrhea and malabsorption are common problems, which result from an increase in intestinal transit time; a decrease in villous height and number; and disruption of the active transport processes for water, sodium, glucose, and amino acids.

Pancreatic disease is clinically apparent in only 5–10% of alcoholics. Metabolic, genetic, and dietary factors may also contribute to the expression of pancreatic damage. The actual mechanism by which alcohol injures the pancreatic acinus is unclear. During acute pancreatitis, intense pancreatic inflammation results from intracellular activation and release of proteolytic enzymes. Autodigestion of the pancreas produces interstitial edema, necrosis and hemorrhage. The end result of acute alcoholic pancreatitis may be chronic pancreatitis. Acute pancreatitis presents as a dull, steady, epigastric pain that may radiate to the back. Bending or sitting may partially relieve the pain, confirming its retroperitoneal origin. Pain may be precipitated or aggravated by meals, and relieved by meals or by vomiting. The serum amylase is the most sensitive test for acute pancreatitis. An amylase level 1.5 to 2 times the upper limit of normal has a sensitivity of 95% and specificity of 98% for the diagnosis of acute pancreatitis. The management of acute pancreatitis includes intravenous fluids, nasogastric suction, and parenteral analgesics. Uncomplicated pancreatitis will usually resolve in 2 to 4 days with these supportive measures. Severe pancreatitis may lead to shock, renal failure, coagulopathy, adult respiratory distress syndrome, pancreatic abscess, and pancreatic pseudocyst. The mortality of severe pancreatitis with complications may exceed 30% (Ranson, 1984). Cessation of alcohol intake may diminish the pancreatic pain, but does not necessarily halt the progression of pancreatic exocrine and endocrine dysfunction.

Nutrition

Alcohol interferes with normal nutrition by several mechanisms. Ethanol can suppress appetite through its effect on the CNS. Gastric, hepatic, and pancreatic disease may further decrease enteral intake and contribute to maldigestion or malabsorption. Signs of malnutrition include thinning of the hair, ecchymosis, glossitis, abdominal distention, peripheral edema, hypocalcemic tetany, and neuropathy. Alcoholics are especially susceptible to deficiencies of thiamine, folate, B vitamins, and ascorbic acid. Nutritional management consists of abstinence and institution of a well-balanced diet plus multivitamins. Specific vitamin therapy may be indicated for treatment of a defined deficiency.

Fetal Effects

The fetus is most vulnerable to the effects of alcohol during the first trimester. The fetal effects of maternal alcohol abuse range from spontaneous abortion and intrauterine growth retardation to the fetal alcohol syndrome (FAS). Neurological features of the FAS range from mild CNS dysfunction (attention deficit disorders and hyperactivity) to severe mental retardation. Commonly recognized somatic abnormalities include short palpebral fissures, midfacial hypoplasia, absence of the philtrum, and a thin upper lip. Alcohol should be avoided during pregnancy.

Cardiovascular Effects

Alcohol is a common cause of dilated cardiomyopathy. The diagnosis is confirmed by echocardiography, which will demonstrate enlargement of all four cardiac chambers with systolic dysfunction. This finding is in contrast to wet beriberi, where cardiac output is increased and high-output congestive heart failure predominates. Transient atrial and ventricular arrhythmias ("holiday heart syndrome") may follow a weekend of binge drinking, even in the absence of clinically demonstrable myocardial damage. Damage may be irreversible once the signs and symptoms of congestive heart failure develop.

High-density lipoproteins (HDLs) are elevated in moderate drinkers. This elevation is primarily through an increase in the HDL-3 fraction, whereas epidemiological studies have associated increases in the HDL-2 fraction with a lower incidence of coronary artery disease in the general population (Haskell, Camargo, & Williams, 1984). Alcohol can raise both the pulse and blood pressure, acutely decreasing exercise tolerance in patients with known ischemic heart disease (Potter & Beevers, 1984). Alcoholism should be considered in the differential diagnosis of new-onset or poorly controlled angina or hypertension. The risk of hemorrhagic stroke is more than doubled for light drinkers compared to nondrinkers, and nearly tripled for heavy drinkers (Donahue, Abbott, Reed, & Yano, 1986).

Hematology

Alcohol interferes with the oral intake and intestinal uptake of vitamins and minerals essential for normal hematopoiesis, and may be intrinsically toxic to the bone marrow (Herbert, 1980).

Anemia can result from hemorrhage, hemolysis, or bone marrow hypoplasia. Marrow hypoplasia can result from the toxic effect of alcohol on the bone marrow of folate deficiency. The bone marrow changes of megaloblastosis secondary to folate deficiency are reversible with 1 day of folate supplementation. Macrocytosis can also occur in the absense of folate deficiency, although the mechanism in unknown.

Leukopenia is less common, resulting from the same mechanisms of toxic and nutritional factors already enumerated. Hypersplenism, an irreversible complication, may also contribute to leukopenia, thrombocytopenia, and anemia. Bone marrow recovery with resolution of leukopenia usually occurs in 1 to 2 weeks of abstinence.

Abnormalities of hemostasis result from the diminished production of the vitamin-K-dependent clotting factors (prothrombin, VII, IX, and X), fibrinolysis, and occasionally disseminated intravascular coagulation. Thrombocytopenia may result from decreased production (bone marrow suppression, folate deficiency) or hyperplenism.

Endocrinological Disease

Alcohol interferes with gonadal function even in the absence of cirrhosis by inhibiting normal testicular, pituitary, and hypothalamic function. In males, hypogonadism may cause testicular atrophy, decreased beard growth, diminished sperm count, and a loss of libido. Cirrhosis can lead to feminization, with gynecomastia and changes in the distribution of body hair and fat.

Musculoskeletal Diseases

Acute alcoholic myopathy (rhabdomyolysis) may cause painful tender swelling of one or more large muscle groups. Diagnosis depends on a high index of clinical suspicion, elevation of serum creatine phosphokinase, and myoglobinuria. Chronic alcoholic myopathy may accompany alcoholic polyneuropathy, presenting as painless progressive muscle weakness and wasting.

Alcoholics are at increased risk for metabolic bone disease—both osteoporosis and osteomalacia (Bikle, 1988). Bilateral hip pain may signify osteonecrosis or avascular necrosis of the femoral head.

Dermatology

Dermatological problems that suggest the diagnosis of alcoholism include palmar erythema, spider angiomata, rosacea, rhinophyma and porphyria cutanea tarda, and bronzed cirrhosis (hemochromatosis).

Cancer

It is unclear whether alcoholics have an increased risk of dying from cancer. The American Cancer Society has estimated that 4% of all cancers in men and 1% of all cancers in women can be directly attributed to alcohol abuse. Alcohol abuse probably increases the risk of carcinoma of the pharynx, esophagus, liver, and rectum (Breeden, 1984). The combination of cigarettes and alcohol is clearly synergistic, markedly increasing the incidence of cancer of the mouth and esophagus. In epidemiological and case–control studies, it is difficult to separate the effects of alcohol from those of cigarettes.

Immune System

The effect of alcohol on the immune system includes a direct cell-mediated action that is manifested by depression of the natural killer cell activity and lymphocyte transformation. The effects of heavy alcohol consumption, and the possible increased susceptibility of individuals to human immunodeficiency virus (HIV) and its possible progress to acquired immune deficiency syndrome (AIDS), constitute a current area of study (Petrakis, 1985).

Treatment Priorities

Comorbidity is a common occurrence in alcoholic patients. This potential multiplicity of clinical problems raises questions about treatment priorities, modalities, and settings. An initial guideline is to allow sufficient time in an alcohol- and drug-free state to evaluate potential co-occurring disorders. During this period of evaluation, one of three possible outcomes will present: (1) The acute symptoms, confusion, depression, anxiety, and/or hallucinations will abate as detoxification is completed; in this circumstance an Axis I co-occurring disorder is unlikely, but more time is necessary to rule out a personality disorder. (2) The presenting symptoms remain or become even more pronounced; comorbidity with Axis I and/or Axis II disorders is quite likely. (3) Symptoms not present at initiation of treatment emerge as the alcohol is removed; here also additional Axis I or Axis II diagnosis must be considered. A waiting time of 2 to 4 weeks after use of alcohol or drugs is usually recommended before a diagnosis other than substance use disorder is made. To diagnose a personality disorder, additional time (1 to 2 months) may be necessary. The waiting period is unnecessary if additional psychiatric disorders have been well documented in the past (e.g., a patient with bipolar affective disorder successfully treated with lithium carbonate).

Which disorder should be treated first? A general rule is that the alcoholism is treated first. Little progress in the evaluation and treatment of co-ocurring disorders will take place if drinking continues. As indicated above, the drinking itself usually produces an array of psychiatric symptoms that may be mistaken for evidence of an additional psychiatric disorder. Exceptions to giving the alcoholism treatment priority would be the presence of acute psychiatric states, imminent threat of suicide, profound depression, or any condition that would interfere with the patient's ability to attend to the interpersonal and educational functions of an alcoholism treatment program. It follows that detoxification and treatment of any organic brain syndrome associated with alcoholism should be treated and resolved before attempting rehabilitation.

The question of which disorder to treat first may oversimplify the process being undertaken. The treatment of co-occurring "dual disorders" is more likely to be done in parallel or in synchrony than in a discrete temporal sequence. While the organic symptoms (e.g., withdrawal, hallucinations) are being treated, a therapeutic alliance can be developed with the patient, from which the dependent state can be modified by elimination of denial and restoration of adult ego skills. Specific treatment for anxiety, affective, or other co-occurring disorders may be provided within the treatment setting of psychiatrically based substance abuse programs. For example, antidepressants may be prescribed for depression; biofeedback may be useful in modifying some anxiety disorders; and lithium or neuroleptics can be essential for manic or psychotic patients.

The synchronous treatment of alcoholism and other disorders is well illustrated in the personality-disordered alcoholic patient. The recovery process from alcohol dependence provides a paradigm for strengthening ego and personality growth. Successful treatment of alcoholism involves the patient's development of tolerance for frustration, the ability to delay gratification, the capacity to anticipate consequences of behavior, and a tolerance for affect. These skills are integral to the modification of character pathology as well. Hence, key therapeutic issues in both the treatment of alcoholism and personality disorders are addressed during the recovery process.

Depending on the severity of the patient's alcoholism, the medical status, and the severity of additional psychiatric symptoms, the evaluation for comorbidity may occur in either an inpatient or an outpatient setting.

Pharmacotherapy

The use of psychotropic drugs in alcoholic patients is indicated during the acute stage of withdrawal and in cases when there is a co-occurring psychiatric disorder potentially responsive to medication. Other circumstances indicate use of certain medications with alcoholic patients as well.

Benzodiazepines

Certain specific circumstances may warrant the use of benzodiazepines or sedatives/hypnotics beyond the stage of alcohol withdrawal. For example, periods of severe stress (death of a family member), insomnia, or anxiety may justify a brief period of medication. An additional circumstance is the protracted withdrawal syndrome. Uncomplicated alcohol withdrawal usually lasts 5 days or less, but a protracted withdrawal syndrome may persist for several months (Begleiter & Porjesz, 1979). The risk of cross-dependency limits the use of benzodiazepines in patients with coexisting disorders. Patients with generalized anxiety disorder, social phobia, or agoraphobia without panic disorder may be helped with buspirone. Panic disorder may be responsive to tricyclic antidepressants or monoamine oxidase inhibitors, but may require a benzodiazepine as well. Buspirone is not effective with panic disorders, and alprazolam has been associated with abuse. Clonazepam may be the benzodiazepine of choice for patients with a severe anxiety disorder that is unresponsive to other medications. Its long half-life allows a twice-a-day dosing schedule and minimizes the risk of rebound anxiety, panic, or seizures when it is withdrawn.

The following guidelines should be applied if potentially addicting medications are prescribed (Senay, 1983): Inform the patient of any abuse potential; set a time limit for the use of the medication (e.g., 1 week for a severe grief reaction); explain that the drug is being used until nonpharmacological approaches can be effective; closely evaluate the drug's effect on target symptoms; observe for signs of abuse (e.g., requests for additional prescriptions, obtaining medication from other physicians, or refusal to do anything except take medications).

Lithium

Lithium is indicated in the alcoholic patient with a co-occurring bipolar affective disorder. In a large multicenter, double-blind, placebo-controlled study (Dorus et al., 1989), lithium had no advantage in the treatment of alcoholics. In a more recent double-blind controlled study (Fawcett, 1989), alcoholics treated with lithium achieved a better abstinence rate and were less likely to be rehospitalized. However, lithium therapy did not reduce the amount of drinking if relapse occurred, nor did it have an effect on concomitant affective symptoms.

The use of lithium as a specific treatment for alcohol dependence was not supported in a controlled study (Dorus et al., 1989). Abstinence rates, days of drinking, alcohol-related hospitalizations, and severity of depression did not differ between lithium- and placebo-treated alcoholism in this 52-week trial.

Antidepressants

There is no advantage to using antidepressants in alcoholic patients unless there is an associated depressive disorder, which should be diagnosed only after 2 to 4 weeks of abstinence from alcohol. An exception to these guidelines would be the use of low-dose amitriptyline or other antidepressants with a sedative effect if a sleep disturbance is present.

Major Tranquilizers

Major tranquilizers such as phenothiazines, thiothixene, haloperidol, and other antipsychotics are indicated only if alcoholism is associated with a psychotic disorder. Delirium tremens, alcohol hallucinosis, and agitation associated with alcohol dementia may respond to low doses of a major tranquilizer. Uncomplicated alcohol withdrawal has been treated in the past with phenothiazines, but they lower the seizure threshold, and benzodiazepines are a more suitable choice.

Disulfiram

Disulfiram (Antabuse) is a useful adjunct in the treatment of alcoholism. It is a deterrent drug that has been used in the United States since 1948.

Disulfiram blocks the conversion of acetaldehyde to acetic acid in the liver, leading to a rise in serum acetaldehyde to 5 to 10 times normal levels. The acetaldehyde is toxic and produces the following effects: flushing of the skin, headache, nausea, sweating, hyperventilation and respiratory distress, anxiety, palpitations, and hypotension. The reaction typically occurs within 10 to 20 minutes after ingestion of alcohol and lasts 30 to 60 minutes. The severity of the ethanol–disulfiram reaction is proportional to the dosage of disulfiram and the amount of ethanol ingested. If the reaction is severe, shock and cardiac arrhythmias may occur. A severe reaction may require treatment for shock, administration of oxygen, and use of intravenous antihistamines and vitamin C to abate the symptoms.

Antabuse is available in 250-mg and 500-mg doses. The 250-mg size is adequate in the majority of cases and can be halved if side effects occur.

Disulfiram is taken once a day, can be given 24 hours after the last use of alcohol, and may produce a reaction up to 14 days following the last dose.

Common side effects are fatigue, itching, skin rash, and unpleasant taste in the mouth (garlic or metallic). Other less common effects include impotence, polyneuritis, optic neuritis, and psychosis. Hepatitis may occur in rare, isolated cases. The severe side effects are more likely to occur at higher doses of disulfiram than at the usual 250-mg daily dose.

Contraindications to disulfiram use are few. A history of schizophreniform psychosis or schizophrenia may be a contraindication, because disulfiram inhibits dopamine-β-hydroxylase activity; thus, increased availability of dopamine may potentiate a psychotic reaction. Allergy to the drug and an inability to appreciate the risks associated with drinking are additional contraindications.

The patient should be fully aware of the risks of the ethanol–disulfiram reaction and be instructed to avoid alcohol-containing substances of any type (e.g., cough syrups, mouthwashes). Many patients find Antabuse to be insurance against relapse in the initial 3 to 6 months of recovery as they develop ties with AA and gain support from psychotherapy.

Conclusion

This chapter emphasizes that alcoholism is a condition that becomes manifest through social or medical symptoms. It is a disease, or perhaps a syndrome, amenable to reliable diagnostic criteria. The expressions of alcohol dependence across family, occupational, and social settings often conceal from the naive observer the internal suffering of the alcoholic patient. Subjectively, the alcoholic struggles with prolonged craving for the substance, fear of functioning without alcohol, and doubts about his or her ability to abstain and hence to recover. Concomitant with the ambivalent struggle to change, the alcoholic endures remorse, regret, guilt, and shame.

The physician, if not cognizant of the protean manifestations of this disease, or blinded to the suffering of the patient by the alcoholic's often outrageous behavior, may miss or decline to take the opportunity for a life-changing clinical encounter. On the other hand, the physician prepared for the diagnosis and treatment of addictive disorders will find clinical experiences that contradict the pessimism often instilled during training years.

The psychiatrist's role in the treatment of alcoholism is especially pertinent because of the biopsychosocial orientation of modern psychiatry. Within this chapter, extensive data on the comorbidity of alcoholism with other psychiatric disorders have been presented. With an understanding of the overlapping relationships between substance use and other psychiatric disorders, and an ability to establish treatment priorities, the psychiatrist is in a strong position to provide medical leadership. A leadership role will hinge on an understanding of and respect for both the usefulness and the limitations of pharmacological agents. In addition, effective psychiatric treatment will incorporate the domains of experience formulated by the fellowship of AA.

References

Adams, R. D., & Victor, M. (1981). *Principles of neurology.* New York: McGraw Hill.

Altschuler, H. L., Philips, P. E., & Feinhandler, D. A. (1980). Alteration of ethanol self-administration by naloxone. *Life Sciences, 26:*679–688

American Psychiatric Association (APA). (1980). *Diagnostic and statistical manual of mental disorders* (3rd ed.) Washington, DC: Author.

American Psychiatric Association (APA). (1987). *Diagnostic and statistical manual of mental disorders* (3rd ed., rev.). Washington, DC: Author.

Babor, T. F., & Mendelson, J. H. (1986). Ethnic/religious differences in the manifestation and treatment of alcoholism. *Annals of the New York Academy of Sciences, 472,* 46–59.

Begleiter, H., & Porjesz, B. (1979). Persistence of a "subacute withdrawal syndrome" following chronic ethanol intake. *Drug and Alcohol Dependence, 4,* 353–357.

Bikle, D. (1988). Effects of alcohol abuse on bone. *Comprehensive Therapy, 14*(2), 16–20.

Breeden, J. H. (1984). Alcohol, alcoholism and cancer. *Medical Clinics of North America, 68,* 163–171.

Clark, W., & Midanik, L. (1982). Alcohol use and alcohol problems among U.S. adults. In National Institute on Alcohol Abuse and Alcoholism (Ed.), *Alcohol consumption and related problems* (DHHS Publication No. ADM 82-1190, Alcohol and Health Monograph No. 1, pp. 3–52). Washington, DC: U.S. Government Printing Office.

Davis, L. J., Hunt, R. D., Morse, R. M., & O'Brien, P. C. (1987). Discriminate analysis of the Self-Administered Alcoholism Screening Test. *Alcoholism: Clinical and Experimental Research, 11,* 269–273.

Davis, V. E., & Walsh, M. J. (1970). Alcohol amines and alkaloids: A basis for alcohol addiction. *Science, 167,* 1005–1007.

Donahue, R. P., Abbott, R. D., Reed, D. M., & Yano, K. (1986). Alcohol and hemorrhagic stroke. *Journal of the American Medical Association, 255,* 2311–2314.

Dorus, W., Ostrow, D. G., Anton, R. F., Cushman, P., Collins, J. F., & Shaefer, M. R. (1989, May 10). *Lithium in depressed and nondepressed alcoholics.* Paper presented at the 142nd Annual Meeting of the American Psychiatric Association, San Francisco.

Drake, R. E., & Vaillant, G. E. (1985). A validity study of Axis II of DSM-III. *American Journal of Psychiatry, 142,* 553–558.

Eckardt, M. J., & Martin, P. R. (1986). Clinical assessment of cognition in alcoholism. *Alcoholism: Clinical and Experimental Research, 10*(2), 128–137.

Ewing, J. A. (1984). Detecting alcoholism: The CAGE questionnaire. *Journal of the American Medical Association, 252*(14), 1905–1907.

Fawcett, J. A. (1989, May 10). *Lithium therapy deters relapse drinking.* Paper presented at the 142nd Annual Meeting of the American Psychiatric Association, San Francisco.

Fillmore, K. M. (1974). Drinking and problem drinking in early adulthood and middle age. *Quarterly Journal of Studies on Alcohol, 5,* 819–840.

Galamos, J. T. (1985). Alcoholic liver disease: Fatty liver, hepatitis, and cirrhosis. In J. E. Berk (Ed.), *Gastroenterology* (pp. 2985–3048) Philadelphia: W. B. Saunders.

Grande, T. P., Wolfe, A. W., Schubert, D. S. P., Patterson, M. B., & Brocco, K. (1984). Associations among alcoholics, drug abuse, and anti-social personality: A review of the literature *Psychological Reports, 55,* 455–474.

Haskell, W. L., Camargo, C., Jr, & Williams, P. T. (1984). The effect of cessation and resumption of moderate alcohol intake on serum high density lipoprotein subfractions: A controlled study. *New England Journal of Medicine, 310,* 805–810.

Hebert, V. (Ed.). (1980). Hematologic complications of alcoholism [Special issue]. *Seminars in Hematology, 17,* 83–176.

Helzer, J. E., & Pryzbeck, T. R. (1988). The co-occurrence of alcoholism with other psychiatric disorders in the general population and its impact on treatment. *Journal of Studies on Alcohol, 49*(3), 219–224.

Hesselbrock, M. N., Meyer, R. E., & Keener, J. J. (1985). Psychopathology in hospitalized alcoholics. *Archives of General Psychiatry, 42,* 1050–1055.

Jellinek, E. M. (1960). *The disease concept of alcoholism.* New Haven, CT: Hillhouse.

Koenigsberg, H. W., Kaplan, R. D., Gilmore, M. M., & Cooper, A. M. (1985). The relationship between syndrome and personality disorder in DSM-III: Experience with 2,462 patients. *American Journal of Psychiatry, 142*(2), 207–212.

Kristenson, H., Trell, E., Fex, G., & Hood, B. (1980). Serum Y-glutamyltransferase: Statistical distribution in a middle-aged male population and evaluation of alcohol habits in individuals with elevated levels. *Preventive Medicine, 9,* 108–119.

Lieber, C. S., & Leo, M. A. (1982). Alcohol and the liver. In C. S. Lieber (Ed.), *Medical disorders of alcoholism: Pathogenesis and treatment* (pp. 259–312). Philadelphia: W. B. Saunders.

McEvoy, J. P. (1982). The chronic neuropsychiatric disorders associated with alcoholism. In E. M. Pattison & E. Kaufman (Eds.), *Encyclopedic handbook of alcoholism* (pp. 167–179). New York: Gardner Press.

Morse, R. M., & Hurt, R. D. (1979). Screening for alcoholism. *Journal of the American Medical Association, 242*(24), 2688–2690.

Moser, J.(1980). *Prevention of alcohol-related problems.* Toronto: Alcohol and Drug Addiction Research Foundation.

Moskowitz, H., Burns, M., & Williams, A. (1985). Skills performance at low blood alcohol levels. *Journal of Studies on Alcohol, 46,* 482–485.

Myers, R. D. (1983). Alkaloid metabolites and addiction drinking of alcohol. In N. C. Chang & H. M. Chao (Eds.), *Early identification of alcohol abuse* (pp. 268–284). Rockville, MD: U.S. Public Health Service.

Nace, E. P. (1984). Epidemiology of alcoholism and prospects for treatment. *Annual Review of Medicine, 35,* 293–309.

Nace, E. P., Davis, C., & Gaspari, J. D. (1991). Axis II comorbidity in the substance abuse sample. *American Journal of Psychiatry, 148.*

Nace, E. P., Saxon, J. J., & Shore, N. (1983) A comparison of borderline and non-borderline alcoholic patients. *Archives of General Psychiatry, 40,* 54–56.

National Council on Alcoholism (NCA) Criteria Committee. (1972). Criteria for the diagnosis of alcoholism. *American Journal of Psychiatry, 129,* 127–135.

Orford, J. S., Waller, S., & Peto, J. (1974). Drinking behavior and attitudes and their correlates among university students in England. *Quarterly Journal of Studies on Alcohol, 35,* 1316–1374.

Petrakis, P. L. (1985). *The effects of alcohol on the immune system: Summary of a workshop.* Rockville, MD: National Institute on Alcohol Abuse and Alcoholism.

Porjesz, B., & Begleiter, H. (1985). Human brain electrophysiology and alcoholism. In R. Tarter & D. Van Thiel (Eds.), *Alcohol and the brain* (pp. 139–182). New York: Plenum Press.

Potter, J. F., & Beevers, D. G. (1984). Pressor effect of alcohol in hypertension. *Lancet, ii,* 119–122.

Ranson, J. H. C. (1984). Acute pancreatitis: Pathogenesis, outcome, and treatment. *Clinical Gastroenterology, 13*(3), 343–363.

Regier, D. A., Boyd, J. H., Burke, J. D. Jr., Rae, D. S., Myers, J. K., Kramer, M., Robins, L. N., George, L. K., Karns, M., & Locke, B. Z. (1988). One month prevalence of mental disorders in the United States. *Archives of General Psychiatry, 45,* 977–985.

Ross, H. E., Glaser, F. B., & Germanson, T. (1988). The prevalence of psychiatric disorders in patients with alcohol and other drug problems. *Archives of General Psychiatry, 45,* 1023–1031.

Samson, H. H., Toliver, G. A., & Pfeffer, A. O. (1987). Oral ethanol reinforcement in the rat:

Effect of the partial inverse benzodiazepene agonist RO 15-4513. *Pharmacology, Biochemistry and Behavior, 27,* 517–519.

Schuckit, M. A. (1973). Alcoholism and sociopathy: Diagnostic confusion. *Journal of Studies on Alcohol, 34,* 157–164.

Selzer, M. L. (1971). The Michigan Alcoholism Screening Test: The quest for a new diagnostic instrument. *American Journal of Psychiatry, 127,* 89–94.

Senay, F. C. (1983). *Substance abuse disorders in clinical practice.* Littleton, MA: John Wright/PSG.

Skinner, H. (1981). Early identification of alcohol abuse. *Canadian Medical Journal, 124,* 1279–1295.

Snyder, C. R. (1958). *Alcohol and the Jews: A cultural study of drinking and sobriety.* New Brunswick NJ: Rutgers Center for Alcohol Studies.

Sue, D. (1987). Use and abuse of alcohol by Asian Americans. *Journal of Psychoactive Drugs, 19*(1), 23–26.

Suzdak, P. D., Glowa, J. N., & Crawley, J. N. (1986). A selective imidazobenzodiazepine antagonist of ethanol in the rat. *Science, 234,* 1243–1247.

Suzdak, P. D., Glowa, J. R., & Crawley, J. N. (1987). Is ethanol antagonist RO 15-4513 selective for ethanol? *Science, 239,* 648–650.

Tabakoff, B., Sutker, P. B., & Randall, C. L. (Eds.). (1983). *Medical and social aspects of alcohol abuse.* New York: Plenum Press.

Vaillant, G. E. (1983). *The natural history of alcoholism.* Cambridge, MA: Harvard University Press.

Westermeyer, J. (1986). *A clinical guide to alcohol and drug problems.* New York: Praeger.

Williams, D. H. (1986). The epidemiology of mental illness in Afro-Americans. *Hospital and Community Psychiatry, 37,* 42–49.

World Health Organization. (1952). *Excerpt committee report #48.* Geneva: Author.

4

Sedatives/Hypnotics and Benzodiazepines

ROBERT L. DuPONT

KEITH E. SAYLOR

Introduction

The other drugs dealt with in this book—whether legal, such as alcohol, or illegal, such as cocaine and marijuana, or even the stimulants such as the amphetamines—are not used routinely in medical practice. By contrast, the sedatives and the hypnotics, including the benzodiazepines, are widely used in medical practice in the treatment of anxiety, insomnia, and epilepsy, and for several other indications (Baldessarini, 1985). These medicines are abused by drug addicts and alcoholics, and they can cause physical dependence even when used medically. The combination of abuse by chemically dependent people and the withdrawal symptoms on discontinuation leads to the definition of these as potentially "addictive" drugs.

The rapidly expanding knowledge of the pharmacology and the epidemiology of these drugs is reviewed in this chapter. The chapter focuses primarily on the needs of the clinical practitioner in dealing with the risks and benefits of the benzodiazepines, the safest, most effective, and most widely used members of this class of medicines. There are two distinct, but sometimes overlapping, clinical contexts for these drugs: the treatment of anxiety and the treatment of chemical dependence. Both contexts are dealt with in this chapter.

Although the benzodiazepines have largely replaced the other sedatives and hypnotics in contemporary medical practice, each section of this chapter includes a review of the other members of this class. Before the introduction of the benzodiazepines, the sedatives, especially the barbiturates, were the leading cause of completed suicides in the United States and the rest of the developed world. The barbiturates and other drugs also caused sedation and other impairing effects at effective antianxiety and anti-insomnia doses (Baldessarini, 1985).

Ironically, as the benzodiazepines were introduced as virtually problem-free, and as their popularity reached unprecedented levels in the late 1960s and early 1970s, a growing backlash that we have labeled the "social issues" emerged. This backlash caused a drop in the use of the benzodiazepines during the 1980s, even though there was no drop in the prevalence of the disorders they were used to treat and even though no newer, safer treatments were developed. The recent criticism of the benzodiazepines has focused on the problems of benzodiazepine abuse and dependence.

As the benzodiazepines have become more controversial themselves, and as various regulatory approaches have been employed to limit their use in medical practice, there is a real danger that clinicians will revert to the older and generally more toxic sedatives and hypnotics, which, in the era of the benzodiazepines, have become once more unfamiliar. Thus, there is more than historical interest in looking at these earlier sedatives, because for some younger medical practitioners they seem like "new" drugs. In any event, the pharmacology of these earlier sedating medicines (including the earliest of all, ethyl alcohol) is closely linked with that of the benzodiazepines, so that they fit together, not only in medical practice and drug abuse epidemiology, but in basic biology.

The abuse of benzodiazepines has been recently and comprehensively reviewed in three publications (DuPont, 1988; U.S. Department of Health and Human Services, 1987; Woods, Katz, & Winger, 1988). A fourth major review of the use of the benzodiazepines has been published recently by the American Psychiatric Association (American Psychiatric Association Task Force on Benzodiazepine Dependence, Toxicity and Abuse, 1990). All reached similar conclusions, with one (Woods et al., 1988) concluding with these sentences:

> The vast majority of people actually taking these drugs do manifest the conditions for which benzodiazepine treatment is indicated and efficacious. . . . There is virtually no recreational or other inappropriate use of benzodiazepines among patients for whom these drugs are prescribed. . . . Surveys of patient populations have indicated that patients receiving prescriptions for one of the benzodiazepines or other minor tranquilizers or hypnotics tend to use less than prescribed and to reduce their use over time. (p. 3479)

In contrast, one of the contemporary critics of benzodiazepines calls attention to the possibility that the benzodiazepines are widely prescribed, not because they are efficacious treatments for widespread disorders, but because they cause physical dependence (Tyrer & Murphy, 1987). He argues that if benzodiazepines are to be used at all, "They are best used for periods of no more than 2 weeks in regular dosage, or in intermittent flexible dosage . . . because of the risk of pharmacological dependence" (Tyrer, 1988, p. 183).

Distinguishing Medical and Nonmedical Use

How can medical use be separated from nonmedical use of the same substance? There are five characteristics that distinguish medical from nonmedical use:

1. *Intent.* What is the purpose for the use of the substance? Is it to treat a diagnosed medical problem, such as anxiety or insomnia, or is it to get high (or

to treat the complications of the nonmedical use of other drugs)? Typical medical drug use occurs without use of multiple nonmedical drugs, while nonmedical drug use is usually polydrug abuse. Alcohol is the principal drug abused along with sedatives and benzodiazepines, although other drugs, often cocaine and heroin, are also commonly used simultaneously with sedatives and benzodiazepines. Although chemically dependent people sometimes use the language of medicine to describe their reason for using drugs nonmedically, self-administration of an intoxicating substance outside the boundaries of social control is the hallmark of drug abuse.

2. *Effect.* What is the effect of the drug use on the user's life? The only acceptable standard for medical use is that it helps the user live a better life. Typical nonmedical drug use is associated with deterioration in the user's life, even though continued use and denial of these negative consequences are common.

3. *Control.* Is the substance use controlled only by the user, or does the fully knowledgeable physician share the control of the use? Medical drug use is controlled by the physician as well as the patient, whereas typical nonmedical drug use is solely controlled by the user. When drug abusers use drugs prescribed by physicians, the physician typically does not have all of the facts—including the facts about use of alcohol and other nonmedical drugs, as well as all of the facts about the dose and pattern of the psychotropic drug use.

4. *Legality.* Is the use legal or illegal? Medical drug use is legal; with the exception of alcohol use by adults, nonmedical drug use is illegal.

5. *Pattern.* What is the pattern of the substance use? Typical medical drug use is similar to the use of penicillin or aspirin: It occurs on a regular pattern to treat a health problem. Typical use of nonmedical drugs (e.g., alcohol or marijuana), in contrast, takes place at parties or in other social settings. Medical substance use is stable and at a moderate dose level. Nonmedical drug use is usually polydrug abuse at high and/or unstable doses.

This distinction between medical and nonmedical drug use is central to being able to make a diagnosis of abuse of sedatives, including the benzodiazepines, and to protect the appropriate use of these medicines in medical practice (DuPont, 1989). Warning signs of possible chemical dependence are as follows:

1. Everyday use at levels above "ceiling doses."
2. Use of alcohol or other drugs nonmedically.
3. "Addict behavior," such as "losing" prescriptions or medicine, getting dependence-producing drugs from multiple physicians, or asking for larger doses.
4. Poor therapeutic response.

It should be noted that abuse is more probable for men and for patients under age 40. Protections for the concerned physician include the following:

1. Know the patient.
2. See the patient often enough to monitor medical and nonmedical drug use.
3. Have contact with family members to check for abuse and/or contraindications.
4. Do urine tests for abused drugs.

Definitions

Drug dependence is a mental or a behavioral disorder as defined in the *Diagnostic and Statistical Manual of Mental Disorders*, third edition, revised (DSM-III-R; American Psychiatric Association, 1987). It includes out-of-control drug use, use outside social and medical sanctions, use despite clear evidence of drug-caused problems, and a drug-centered lifestyle. Physical dependence (including withdrawal on discontinuation) is, in contrast, a pharmacological phenomenon in which the user experiences a specific constellation of symptoms for a relatively short period when the substance is no longer used. Here is the way this important distinction is dealt with in DSM-III-R:

> The symptoms of the [psychoactive substance] dependence syndrome include, but are not limited to, the physiologic symptoms of tolerance and withdrawal. . . . Some people with physiologic tolerance and withdrawal may not have the dependence syndrome as defined here. For example, many surgical patients develop a tolerance to prescribed opioids and experience withdrawal symptoms without showing any signs of impaired control of their use of opioids. Conversely, other people may show signs of severely impaired control of psychoactive substance use (e.g., of cannabis) without clear signs of physiologic tolerance or withdrawal. (American Psychiatric Association, 1987, p. 166)

Precisely the same confusion of relatively benign physical dependence with menacing drug dependence occurs in regard to the use of opiates in the treatment of severe pain. Many patients and many physicians undertreat severe pain because they are unable to distinguish benign physical dependence, the simple pharmacological fact, in medical patients from the abuse of opiates by "drug addicts," the serious biobehavioral disorder (Melzack, 1990).

Medical Use and Abuse

Within medical practice, the benzodiazepines, first introduced in the early 1960s, have largely displaced the earlier barbiturates for all the common indications, including antianxiety, anti-insomnia, and anticonvulsant effects, as well as for their muscle-relaxing and anesthetic properties. Before there were barbiturates, which became widely used in medical practice when phenobarbital became available in 1912, the substance most commonly used for these purposes was alcohol (Harvey, 1985). Even today, many non-drug-using patients tend to self-medicate, using alcohol for anxiety and insomnia. However negatively one might view the benzodiazepines, it needs to be clearly understood that they are an enormous improvement for the patient over either alcohol or barbiturates in terms of both safety and efficacy.

The benzodiazepines are among the most widely prescribed psychotropic medicines in the world. The World Health Organization (1988) has labeled them "essential drugs" that should be available in all countries for medical purposes. They are also the least likely to cause any adverse effects, including serious medical complications and death, of all the psychotropic drugs in use today (DuPont, 1988).

The benzodiazepines are primarily used to treat the most widespread mental disorder: clinically significant chronic anxiety. However, the benzodiazepines have become the most controversial psychotropic drugs used in medicine; as noted earlier, there is intense debate about the use and abuse of these medications (DuPont, 1986a). The key to the understanding of this paradox is to understand two potent phenomena: the widespread misunderstanding and minimization of anxiety disorders as clinically important and crippling mental disorders, and the even more complex connection of the benzodiazepines to the problems of chemical dependence, with the magic word "addiction" being at the heart of the contemporary concern.

Several other concerns have been expressed, especially about the long-term use of the benzodiazepines. These concerns include the effects on the brain; the possibility of cerebral atrophy associated with prolonged benzodiazepine use; and other problems, such as memory loss and personality change (Golombok, Moodley, & Lader, 1988; Lader, Ron, & Petursson, 1984; American Psychiatric Association Task Force on Benzodiazepine Dependence, Toxicity and Abuse, 1990; Uhde & Kellner, 1987). The evidence for these problems is both preliminary and controversial, except for the well-studied acute effect of benzodiazepines on memory, which seems to have no clinical significance for most patients.

When a patient using a benzodiazepine experiences a serious adverse effect that may be related to the use of the benzodiazepine, the prudent course is for the prescribing physician to discontinue the medication to see whether that improves the patient's functioning. In our clinical experience, problems do occasionally develop with the long-term use of a benzodiazepine, as described below. However, the large majority of long-term medical benzodiazepine users (especially if prescreened for addiction potential) whose use is within medical guidelines experience no adverse effects, continue to find the medicines effective even after decades of daily use, and do not escalate their dose or add other psychoactive substances, including alcohol.

Pharmacology

The term "sedative" refers to daytime calming, whereas the term "hypnotic" refers to nighttime promotion of sleep. These are two closely related pharmacological functions, so it is hardly surprising that, in general, the same classes of substances are used to produce both daytime and nighttime calming, or what used to be called "tranquilization." In the era before modern psychopharmacology, which can be dated as beginning in the 1950s and 1960s, the drugs used to produce daytime sedation and to induce sleep were limited; the principal substances used were alcohol and narcotics until the early decades of the 20th century, when barbiturates entered medical practice. From that time until the 1960s, the barbiturates dominated medical practice as both daytime and nighttime calming agents.

There were several problems with the barbiturates, however, that limited their usefulness. They were a major cause of overdose death from accidental poisonings and from suicide, and they produced lethargy and drowsiness, even at therapeutic doses. In addition, although this was less noticed at the time than the first two effects, they were frequently abused by what we now call chemically dependent people, including alcoholics (Harvey, 1985).

This class of psychotropics has a wide range of central nervous system (CNS) depressant effects, including antiepileptic and muscle-relaxing effects, as well as amnesia and anesthesia. In this section, the sedatives and hypnotics are divided for convenience into three general groups: the barbiturates; "other sedatives and hypnotics"; and the benzodiazepines. The benzodiazepines, dealt with last, are the principal focus of the chapter.

Barbiturates

Barbital was introduced into medical practice in 1903, and phenobarbital in 1912. Their rapid success led to the development of over 2,000 other derivatives of barbituric acid, with more than 50 being used in medical practice. The only sedatives to precede the barbiturates were bromides and chloral hydrate, both of which were in widespread use before the end of the 19th century.

The most commonly used barbiturates today are amobarbital (Amytal), butabarbital (Butisol), mephobarbital (Mebaral), pentobarbital (Nembutal), secobarbital (Seconal), and phenobarbital (Luminal). The first four are intermediate in their duration of action, while the last, phenobarbital, has a long duration of action. Short-acting barbiturates are used as anesthetics, but not in outpatient medicine.

Barbiturates reversibly suppress the activity of all excitable tissue, with the CNS being particularly sensitive to these effects. Except for the antiepileptic effects of phenobarbital, there is a low therapeutic index for the sedative effects of the barbiturates, with general CNS depression being inescapably linked with the desired therapeutic effects. The dose of barbiturate that causes fatal overdose is relatively close to the therapeutic dose, roughly 10 times the therapeutic dose. Another common problem with the medical use of the barbiturates for both sedation and hypnosis is the rapid development of tolerance, with a common tendency to raise the dose on chronic administration of a barbiturate.

As we describe in more detail in the section on the benzodiazepines, the barbiturates also affect the γ-aminobutyric acid (GABA) system, producing a cross-tolerance to other sedating drugs, including alcohol and the benzodiazepines. In general, the barbiturates are seldom used in medicine today because, compared to the benzodiazepines, they lack specificity in CNS action; they have a lower therapeutic index; tolerance occurs more quickly; and they have a higher abuse potential.

Other Sedatives and Hypnotics

"Other sedatives and hypnotics" constitute a large, heterogeneous class of seldom-used drugs. The most common are chloral hydrate (Noctec), ethchlorvynol (Placidyl), ethinamate (Valmid), glutethimide (Doriden), meprobamate (Miltown, Equanil), methyprylon (Noludar), and paraldehyde (Paral).

Chloral hydrate, the oldest of this class of medicines, produces a decrease in sleep latency and, in therapeutic doses, little effect on respiration or blood pressure. Toxic doses, however, produce severe respiratory depression and hypotension. Chloral hydrate has an unpleasant taste and is irritating to the skin and mucous membranes; therefore, gastric irritation is common, especially if the drug is not well diluted or if it is taken on an empty stomach.

Glutethimide is similar to methyprylon. There is little to recommend the use of these two drugs because of their addictive potential and the severity of withdrawal, and because the treatment of overdoses from these drugs is particularly difficult and hazardous.

Meprobamate was introduced in 1955 and is the first of the postbarbiturate antianxiety medicines. It enjoyed a sudden, wide popularity because of the dissatisfaction with barbiturates at the time, but meprobamate was rapidly and virtually completely displaced by the benzodiazepines in the early 1960s. From today's perspective, meprobamate seems more like a barbiturate than a benzodiazepine, particularly because of the strong likelihood of tolerance to higher doses over time, and because of the potential for lethal overdoses. The largest group of patients using meprobamate today are those who started in the late 1950s and continue taking this medicine because they have been unable or unwilling to stop meprobamate use.

Methaqualone is a hypnotic that possesses anticonvulsant, antispasmodic, local anesthetic, and weak antihistaminic properties. It also has antitussive properties similar to codeine. Within a short time of its introduction, it achieved wide popularity with drug abusers because of its dissociative "high" and reputed aphrodisiac properties. It has been withdrawn from the market because of its popularity as an abused drug and because of its lack of unique therapeutic properties.

Paraldehyde is, like chloral hydrate, an old-fashioned hypnotic that has survived in medical practice for a century, but deserved to be retired decades ago. It produces rapid onset of sleep, but does not possess analgesic properties, so that it may produce excitement in the presence of pain. Although it produces few effects on respiration and blood pressure at therapeutic doses, it produces potentially lethal respiratory depression and hypotension in overdose situations.

Once again, this class of hypnotics is of general pharmacological and historical interest, but it does not contain medicines that have a useful place in contemporary medical practice. In general, these drugs have a narrow therapeutic index (i.e., there is relatively little difference between the therapeutic dose and the dose that causes toxic dose), and they have substantial potential for abuse and overdose death.

Benzodiazepines

The benzodiazepines were recognized in animal experiments in the 1950s for their ability to produce calm without apparent sedation. Cats, which are extremely sensitive to even small electrical shocks, were obviously sedated when given enough alcohol or barbiturates to prevent "anxious" avoidance behavior of impending shocks. But when given benzodiazepines, they appeared normal in all their behavior, except that they did not show the exaggerated anticipatory sensitivity to mild electrical shocks that they had shown prior to treatment with the benzodiazepines.

The identification of the benzodiazepine receptors in 1977 began the modern era of benzodiazepine research, establishing this class as the best understood of all the psychiatric medicines (Paul, 1988). The benzodiazepine receptors are found in approximately 30% of all CNS synapses and in all species above the level of the shark, demonstrating their fundamental biological importance. The benzodiazepine receptors are part of the GABA complex, which is the major quieting, or inhibiting, system in the CNS (see Figure 4.1).

Alcohol and barbiturates, the sedating substances used most widely prior to the introduction of the benzodiazepines, also work through the GABA complex; unlike the benzodiazepines, however, alcohol and barbiturates have a potent, direct effect. This may explain why alcohol and barbiturates, again unlike the benzodiazepines, cause respiratory depression and death in high doses. The benzodiazepines potentiate GABA, which opens the chloride channel, hyperpolarizing these inhibitory neurons. The fact that benzodiazepines potentiate GABA but (unlike alcohol and barbiturates) do not directly activate the system appears to explain the important clinical observation that benzodiazepines potentiate the sedating and the CNS depression effect (and overdose potential) of alcohol and barbiturates, but do not produce unconsciousness or death when taken alone (Paul, 1988).

There are 14 benzodiazepines marketed in the United States today to treat anxiety, insomnia, and epilepsy. They are also used as muscle relaxants and supplemental anesthetic agents. There are pharmacological differences among the individual benzodiazepines that have important clinical significance. The

GABA RECEPTOR COMPLEX

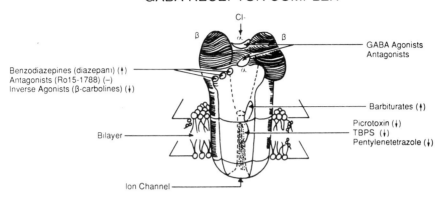

FIGURE 4.1. The benzodiazepine–GABA receptor complex. TBPS, *t*-butylbicyclophosphorothianate. From "Anxiety and Depression: A Common Neurobiological Substrate?" by S. M. Paul, 1988, *Journal of Clinical Psychiatry, 49*(Suppl.), 13–16. Copyright 1988 by Physicians Postgraduate Press. Reprinted by permission.

differences among the benzodiazepines are similar to the differences within the other major classes of psychotropic medicines, the antipsychotics and the antidepressants: While there are many overlapping effects within each class, there are also important differences among the medicines in each class, so that the medicines within a class cannot simply be used interchangeably. These pharmacological differences include the rapidity of onset (distributional half-life), persistence of active drug in the body (elimination half-life), major metabolic breakdown pathways (conjugation vs. oxidation), and specific molecular structure (e.g., alprazolam has a unique triazolo ring that may account for some differences in its clinical effects). Table 4.1 summarizes these differences for the most widely used benzodiazepines. The application of this pharmacological understanding in medical practice is outside the scope of this chapter; however, a few basic facts can be summarized as they relate to the abuse of the benzodiazepines (Scharf, Jennings, & Graham, 1988).

SPEED OF ONSET

The most important distinction among the benzodiazepines in the substance abuse context is the speed of onset, which reflects abuse potential. Those benzodiazepines that have a slow onset (either because they are slowly absorbed or because they must be metabolized to produce an active substance) have a relatively lower abuse potential; those that rapidly reach peak brain levels are relatively more likely to produce euphoria, and therefore abuse, among chemically dependent people (Arendt, Greenblatt, Liebisch, Luu, & Paul, 1987). In this regard, diazepam (Valium) is the most rapidly absorbed and the most effective producer of euphoria. It appears, therefore, to be the

TABLE 4.1. Pharmacological Characteristics of Benzodiazepines

Drug	Trade names[a]	Rate of oral absorption	Rate of metabolism	Metabolized primarily by liver oxidation	Active metabolites	Elimination half-life (hours)	Maximum usual dose (mg/day)
Used primarily to treat anxiety							
Alprazolam	Xanax	Intermediate	Intermediate	Yes	Yes	12–15	4
Chlordiazepoxide hydrochloride	Librium	Intermediate	Long	Yes	Yes	5–30	100
Clonazepam	Klonopin	Fast	Long	Yes	No	18–50	2
Clorazepate dipotassium	Tranxene	Fast	Long	Yes	Yes	36–200	60
Diazepam	Valium	Fast	Long	Yes	Yes	20–50	40
Halazepam	Paxipam	Intermediate	Long	Yes	Yes	50–100	160
Lorazepam	Ativan	Intermediate	Short	No	No	10–14	10
Oxazepam	Serax	Slow	Short	No	No	5–10	120
Prazepam	Centrax	Slow	Long	Yes	Yes	36–200	60
Used primarily to treat insomnia							
Flurazepam hydrochloride	Dalmane	Intermediate	Long	Yes	Yes	40–150	30
Temazepam	Restoril	Intermediate	Short	No	Yes	8–12	30
Triazolam	Halcion	Intermediate	Short	Yes	No	2–5	0.25

Note. From "A Physician's Guide to Discontinuing Benzodiazepine Therapy" by R. L. DuPont, 1990, *Western Journal of Medicine, 152,* 600–603. Copyright 1990 by the *Western Journal of Medicine.* Reprinted by permission.
[a]Some of the drugs are manufactured by more than one company. The names given here are examples only and do not imply endorsement by the author or the editors of the *Western Journal of Medicine.*

most abused of the benzodiazepines. In contrast, the slowly absorbed and activated benzodiazepines, such as oxazepam (Serax) and prazepam (Centrax), appear to have a lower abuse potential. Clorazepate (Tranxene) and prazepam (Centrax), with inactive parent compounds, are also less likely to be abused for their euphoric effects.

The rapidity of onset of diazepam (Valium) does not mean that this benzodiazepine is reinforcing or likely to produce abuse for medical patients who have no chemical dependence history. None of the benzodiazepines, including diazepam (Valium), are reinforcing for patients who do not have a history of chemical dependence. On the other hand, the pharmacology of the benzodiazepines does suggest that, for patients with a history of chemical dependence, diazepam (Valium) is more likely to be abused than oxazepam (Serax) or prazepam (Centrax). In terms of the abuse potential of benzodiaze-pines for chemically dependent people, lorazepam (Ativan) and alprazolam (Xanax) appear to pose an intermediate risk: less than diazepam (Valium), more than oxazepam (Serax).

The issue of the relative abuse potential of the various benzodiazepines in clinical practice is not a settled scientific matter. Some serious students of the pharmacology of benzodiazepines believe that abuse is no more likely for diazepam (Valium) than for oxazepam (Serax) (Woods et al., 1988). The greater liking found for diazepam (Valium), in this view, is the result of dose: Raise the dose of oxazepam (Serax) in the double-blind studies, and the liking scores of oxazepam (Serax) are indistinguishable from those of diazepam (Valium). In contrast, other researchers are convinced that diazepam (Valium) has a greater abuse potential—not solely because of the usual dosage, but presumably because of its more rapid absorption and penetration of the blood–brain barrier, due to its greater lipid solubility (Griffiths & Sannerud, 1987).

METABOLIC PATHWAY

The metabolic pathway of the various benzodiazepines is also important, because those benzodiazepines that are metabolized by oxidation in the liver may alter the effects of other drugs. This is perhaps best illustrated by the "boosting" effect of some benzodiazepines when used by methadone-maintained patients. Although the pharmacology of this effect is not well understood, it appears that simultaneous use of a drug such as diazepam or alprazolam that competes with methadone for oxidative pathways in the liver produces higher levels of methadone in the blood (and brain). Thus, some benzodiazepines may produce a "boosting" of methadone dosages.

Benzodiazepines that have conjugation as the major metabolic pathway are not dependent on liver functioning, so they are less likely to "boost" methadone doses or to build up in patients who have compromised liver functioning, including alcoholics and the elderly. The benzodiazepines metab-olized by conjugation include lorazepam (Ativan), oxazepam (Serax), and temazepam (Restoril). Thus, these are less "liked" by methadone-maintained patients and may be better choices for these patients and for patients with compromised liver functioning if any benzodiazepine is to be used. Oxazepam (Serax) is both a slow-onset and a conjugated benzodiazepine, making it probably the best choice for chemically dependent patients who are treated with a benzodiazepine. On the other hand, oxazepam (Serax) is short-acting, and it is no less likely to produce physical dependence (including difficulties on discontinuation) than any other benzodiazepine.

PERSISTENCE

Persistence of the benzodiazepine (or an active metabolite) in the body is important clinically, because it governs the rapidity of onset of withdrawal symptoms after last dose for people who have used benzodiazepines for prolonged periods of time. The benzodiazepines with shorter elimination half-lives are more likely to produce early and pronounced withdrawal symptoms, whereas those with longer elimination half-lives generally produce more delayed and attenuated withdrawal symptoms. In general, alprazolam (Xanax), lorazepam (Ativan), and oxazepam (Serax) are more rapidly eliminated than are clorazepate (Tranxene), diazepam (Valium), flurazepam (Dalmane), and prazepam (Centrax). Thus, these first three benzodiazepines, with shorter elimination half-lives, are more likely to produce acute withdrawal on abrupt cessation after prolonged use.

REINFORCEMENT

There are three additional aspects of benzodiazepine pharmacology that are relevant to the treatment of chemically dependent patients: reinforcement, withdrawal, and tolerance. Reinforcement is the potential for these drugs to be abused or "liked" by chemically dependent people. There is now controlled research to show that the benzodiazepines are not reinforcing or "liked" by either normal or anxious subjects (de Wit, Johanson, & Uhlenhuth, 1984; de Wit, Uhlenhuth, & Johanson, 1984; Johanson & Uhlenhuth, 1980, 1982). For example, normal and anxious subjects, given a choice between placebos and benzodiazepines, will usually choose the placebo in double-blind acute dose experiments, regardless of the specific benzodiazepine given. In contrast, subjects with a history of chemical dependence, also in double-blind studies, generally prefer benzodiazepines to placebos. These same studies with chemically dependent people have demonstrated that they show a greater preference for short-acting barbiturates and stimulants, as well as narcotics, than for benzodiazepines. Thus, the benzodiazepines are reinforcing for chemically dependent people (though not for normal or anxious people), but they are relatively weak reinforcers.

This research confirms the common clinical observation that benzodiazepines are rarely drugs of choice among the chemically dependent for their euphoric effects. Although it remains unclear why chemically dependent people react differently to the benzodiazepines than do normal or anxious subjects, this phenomenon exists with abused drugs in general and is not limited to the benzodiazepines. Normal subjects do not generally "like" other abused drugs either, including stimulants, narcotics, and even alcohol, in double-blind studies. People who are not chemically dependent do not like the feeling of being intoxicated. Whether chemically dependent people learn to like the intoxicated feeling, or whether they have some innate (perhaps genetically determined) mechanism that explains this characteristic, remains an unanswered question of great importance to the prevention of chemical dependence. Once chemical dependence is established, the reality of the difference in reaction to intoxicating substances needs to be faced by both the physician and the patient.

Clinically, the central point is that chemically dependent people tend to react differently from others not only to the drugs they prefer or have had trouble with in the past, but to all "abused" drugs, whether those drugs are taken medically or nonmedically. In medical practice, this is called "cross-addiction." It means that the abuse or loss of control of the abused substance is generally associated with the abuse or loss of control of all other intoxicating substances these persons use. This makes the point of the unity of the chemical dependence syndrome—it is not "substance-specific." People in treatment for cocaine abuse, for example, can be expected to have problems with (e.g., to "like") not only narcotics, but also alcohol and benzodiazepines if they use these substances, medically or nonmedically.

A related clinically important point is that once a person has been chemically dependent, he or she remains permanently chemically dependent, even after stopping use of all abused drugs. This does not mean that drug abusers will always abuse drugs. Many "recovering" chemically dependent people have stable, lifelong patterns of abstinence. However, the vulnerability and special reactivity to abusable drugs persist for a lifetime.

A physician treating a patient with any controlled substance, including but not limited to the benzodiazepines, needs to know whether that patient has ever been chemically dependent—that is, whether the patient has ever abused or lost control of the use of any drug, including alcohol. The use of any controlled substance in a patient with a history of chemical dependence requires special care on the part of both the patient and the physician. There are many circumstances in which this use can be appropriate and safe, but vigilance needs to be maintained, especially when the controlled substance is used on an outpatient basis and when this use is prolonged.

When it comes to the treatment of anxiety in patients with active chemical dependence (e.g., still or recently abusing), then the use of a controlled substance, including a benzodiazepine, is generally contraindicated. A number of alternative treatments for anxiety are available, including nonpharmacological treatments, some antidepressants, and buspirone (BuSpar), a nonsedating anti-anxiety drug with little abuse potential.

For patients who have been stable in their recovery (including recovering alcoholics) and who need treatment for anxiety, it is generally advisable not to use benzodiazepines unless the physician can be sure that the patient uses the medicine only as prescribed and in the absence of any nonmedical drug use, including alcohol use. We have seen many recovering people who have used benzodiazepines successfully in the treatment of their anxiety disorders and whose sobriety was not threatened by this use of the benzodiazepines. On the other hand, we have seen many chemically dependent people who do not want to use any controlled substance and who have done well with their anxiety problems without using a benzodiazepine. If a benzodiazepine is to be used by a recovering person, it is prudent to use one of the slow-onset medicines (e.g., oxazepam [Serax] or prazepam [Centrax]) and to include a family member in the therapeutic alliance to help ensure that there is no abuse of the benzodiazepine or any other drug, including alcohol.

Some recovering people believe that they are more likely to have withdrawal symptoms when they discontinue a benzodiazepine, even if it has been taken within medical guidelines. What research there is on this topic suggests that this is not the case, but this is best dealt with as an open issue in clinical practice.

WITHDRAWAL

The second general pharmacological aspect of the benzodiazepines that needs to be understood in the context of chemical dependence is that all the drugs that influence the GABA system show cross-tolerance and similar withdrawal problems. Benzodiazepine withdrawal has been recently reviewed (Roy-Byrne & Hommer, 1988). Because of cross-tolerance within this class of sedatives and hypnotics, an alcoholic or barbiturate addict can be withdrawn under medical supervision using a benzodiazepine. The sedatives/hypnotics withdrawal syndrome, including the potential for withdrawal seizures on abrupt discontinuation, is also a general phenomenon of this class of drugs; this factor argues powerfully against abrupt discontinuation of any of these drugs. Cessation of use of the benzodiazepines, along with the other sedatives and hypnotics, can cause withdrawal seizures because they are potent antiepilepsy drugs that raise the seizure threshold. Any medicine that raises the seizure threshold when abruptly withdrawn produces a rebound drop in the seizure threshold that commonly causes seizures, even in people who have not previously had any epileptic seizures (Harvey, 1985).

TOLERANCE

The third pharmacological characteristic of the benzodiazepines of importance in the context of chemical dependence is tolerance. Tolerance is rapid, and all but complete, to the sedative and/or euphoric effects of the benzodiazepines on repeated administration at a steady dose level for even a few days. This rapidly developing tolerance is seen clinically when these medicines are used to treat anxiety. Patients often experience sedation or drowsiness when they take their first few benzodiazepine doses, but within a few days of steady dosing these symptoms of sedation lessen and, for most patients, disappear. In this regard, the benzodiazepines are clinically similar to methadone, which, with continued use at stable doses, does not produce noticeable sedation or euphoria because of tolerance to these effects.

By contrast, tolerance to the antianxiety effect of the benzodiazepines is negligible or nonexistent. Medical patients who are not chemically dependent and who use a benzodiazepine to treat chronic anxiety seem to obtain reproducible effects at standard doses. They rarely escalate their dose beyond common therapeutic levels, even after they have taken the benzodiazepine for many years. A clear example of the lack of tolerance to the antianxiety and antipanic effects of the benzodiazepines was shown in a multisite study we participated in several years ago, in which alprazolam (Xanax) was used to suppress panic attacks. The average dose of alprazolam (Xanax) after 8 weeks of acute treatment was 5.7 mg per day. At follow-up, up to 2 years later, with no attempt by either patients or physicians to limit the dose except to suppress panic with the lowest effective dose, the average dose of alprazolam (Xanax) in this study was 2.7 mg per day. There was no increase in the incidence of panic attacks in this population over the course of the study. If tolerance had occurred, either the dose of alprazolam (Xanax) or the rate of panic attacks (or both) would have increased, but since neither the dose nor the panic increased over time there is reason to believe that tolerance did not occur over this relatively long period of daily benzodiazepine dosing (DuPont et al., unpublished).

This distinction between rapid tolerance to the euphoric effects and the absence of tolerance to the antianxiety effects of benzodiazepines is important for the clinician, since patients who use benzodiazepines to get high typically add other substances and escalate their benzodiazepine dose over time. This commonly observed pattern reflects clinically the existence of tolerance to the euphoric effects of benzodiazepines among chemically dependent people. In contrast, typical medical patients using benzodiazepines for their antianxiety effects use them at low and stable doses, without the addition of other drugs, including alcohol. This also is the commonly observed pattern in clinical practice: Tolerance does not develop to the antianxiety effects of the benzodiazepines among nonabusing patients.

Earlier, we have mentioned that some anxious patients with a personal or family history of chemical dependence believe that they have more severe withdrawal when they stop using a benzodiazepine. Some patients who use benzodiazepines daily, even after a long period of time, escalate their dose beyond the usually prescribed level, add other drugs (especially alcohol), and/or have a poor clinical response to the benzodiazepine use (inadequate suppression of anxiety). Usually, but not always, these patients have a personal or a family history of chemical dependence. These same patients sometimes have unusual difficulty in discontinuing. This syndrome of problems with long-term benzodiazepine use is commonly seen in chemical dependence treatment programs, tending to reinforce the commonly held view in the chemical dependence field that benzodiazepines are ineffective, problem-generating medications, especially on long-term use. Although this pattern certainly exists, it is, in our experience, uncommon in the typical medical or psychiatric practice dealing with anxious patients who do not have a history of chemical dependence. Nevertheless, when it occurs, the best response is discontinuation of benzodiazepine use.

Epidemiology

The epidemiology of the sedatives and hypnotics has largely, in the last two decades, evolved into the epidemiology of the benzodiazepines. However, a review of the most recent drug abuse data from the Drug Abuse Warning Network (DAWN), operated by the National Institute on Drug Abuse (NIDA), shows that some of the nonbenzodiazepines are continuing to cause serious problems. The DAWN covered emergency room (ER) and medical examiner (ME) data from 27 metropolitan areas in the most recent year for which data are available, 1987 (NIDA, 1988b). In that year, DAWN captured the data on 147,778 ER episodes and 4,678 drug-related deaths. Of the top 40 drugs in the ER reports, 12 were sedatives and hypnotics. In order of their occurrence on the list, they were as follows: (6) diazepam, (9) alprazolam, (14) "over-the-counter sleep aids," (18) triazolam, (21) lorazepam, (22) phenobarbital, (24) chlordiazepoxide, (28) flurazepam, (34) butalbital combinations, (35) "benzodiazepine" (unspecified), (39) temazepam, and (40) clorazepate. To put the abuse of benzodiazepines in perspective, the top five spots in the DAWN ER reports were taken, in order, by cocaine, alcohol (in combination with other drugs), heroin, marijuana, and phencyclidine (PCP).

Note that while most of these sedatives and hypnotics on the DAWN top 40 ER list were benzodiazepines (nine), three were not: "over-the-counter sleep aids," phenobarbital, and butalbital combinations.

When it came to the ME data, the sedatives and hypnotics were even more prominent. Fourteen members of this class were in the top 40, as follows: (6) diazepam, (13) phenobarbital, (22) glutethimide, (24) "benzodiazepine" (unspecified), (25) secobarbital, (27) chlordiazepoxide, (30) butalbital, (31) pentobarbital, (32) flurazepam, (33) meprobamate, (35) alprazolam, (36) amobarbital, (36) triazolam, and (39) temazepam. Note that 7 of these 14 sedatives and hypnotics on the top 40 ME list were not benzodiazepines.

The most striking aspect of the DAWN data is the relatively high placement of the nonbenzodiazepine sedatives and hypnotics (despite their low use in medical practice), especially on the ME (death) list. This makes the central point that the nonbenzodiazepine members of this class are generally highly abused and often lethal medicines. It is for this reason that the benzodiazepines have largely replaced them in medical practice over the last two decades.

The DAWN data ranked various medical and nonmedical substances without reference to the relative exposure of the public to these substances. Without the rate at which problems occur relative to use, it is likely that relatively safe substances that are widely used will be ranked higher than relatively dangerous substances less often used. In an attempt to define these rates, Harold Davis, medical epidemiologist for the Food and Drug Administration (FDA), recently wrote a memorandum titled "Reporting Rates of Drug-Abuse Episodes for Prescription Drugs" (Davis, 1989). Using DAWN data from 1976 through 1985, Davis found that DAWN emergency room mentions per 10,000 dispensed prescriptions in the United States showed a striking range. All benzodiazepines averaged 2.4. Phenobarbital was 2.7, while secobarbital was 16.5. Glutethimide was 4.7, and ethchlorvynol was 11.2.

Medical Use

The epidemiology of the benzodiazepines is divided into the medical and the nonmedical use of these substances. A series of national surveys tracking the medical use of the benzodiazepines has shown that their use peaked in 1976, and is now about 25% less than the peak rate (DuPont, 1988). The most recent detailed survey of medical use of the benzodiazepines, taken in 1979 (near the peak of benzodiazepine use in the United States), showed that 89% of Americans aged 18 years and older had not used a benzodiazepine within the previous 12 months. Of those who had used a benzodiazepine, most (9.5% of total adults) had used the medicine either less than every day or for less than 12 months or both, whereas a minority (1.6% of the adult population) had used a benzodiazepine on a daily basis for 12 months or longer. This long-term user group was two-thirds female; 71% were aged 50 or older; and most had chronic medical problems as well as anxiety (DuPont, 1988).

The rates of benzodiazepine use in the society can be compared to the rates of diagnosable anxiety disorders. A recent survey by the National Institute of Mental Health showed that 19% of the adult population suffered from a mental disorder at any time, and that the single most common diagnostic group was the anxiety disorders, which afflicted 8% of the adult population (Robins et al., 1984). Of those with anxiety disorders, three-fourths were receiving no treatment at all, including not using a benzodiazepine. The 1.6% of the population who are chronic benzodiazepine users can be compared to the 8% of the population who are suffering from anxiety disorders. This has led many observers to conclude that the benzodiazepines not only are not overprescribed, but may actually be underprescribed because of the reluctance of both physicians and patients to use these medicines (Mellinger & Balter, 1981).

Nonmedical Use

Nonmedical benzodiazepine use has a somewhat different epidemiology, although the same time course is seen in the general rates in the population: The onset of problems coincided with the introduction of these medicines in the early 1960s and peaked in 1976. The fall in abuse of benzodiazepines has been even sharper than the fall in medical use since 1976, with the most recent rates of ME and ER mentions of benzodiazepines being about 40% lower than in 1976.

These data on abuse have been collected by NIDA since the early 1970s and were most recently summarized for the critical years 1976 to 1985 (NIDA, 1988a). The NIDA study showed that the most comprehensive indicator of benzodiazepine-associated problems—the episodes reported by 564 consistently reporting ERs in 24 metropolitan areas throughout the country—had "decreased sharply, from 24,287 in 1976 to 14,237 in 1985" (p. 7).

NIDA also collects data on the nonmedical use of benzodiazepines in the general population, surveying all Americans over the age of 12 in the National Household Survey on Drug Abuse, as well as separately surveying high school seniors. The Household Survey has been conducted every few years for the last two decades, while high school seniors have been surveyed annually since 1975. Both sets of surveys show a substantial decline of nonmedical use of benzodiazepines since the peak in the mid-1970s. The high school senior data from 1975 through 1987 are reported in Figure 4.2.

The characteristics of benzodiazepine abusers contrast dramatically with the characteristics of the medical users of benzodiazepines. In the 1985 Household Survey (NIDA, 1988c), the benzodiazepine abusers were 61% male, and 74% were under the age of 35. Seventy-two percent had used marijuana, and 49% had used cocaine. This is a typical profile of chemically dependent individuals. Perhaps more striking is the finding that among the 6.5 million people who were estimated to have used a benzodiazepine nonmedically at least once in the last year, 55% had used the benzodiazepine 10 or fewer times in their lifetimes, and only 13% had used a benzodiazepine nonmedically 100 or more times in their lifetimes. This corresponds to an estimate of only 260,000 people in the nation who had used a benzodiazepine nonmedically at least 100 times in their lives. These data from NIDA suggest that a substantial part of the nonmedical use of a benzodiazepine identified in the Household Surveys is occasional use of a benzodiazepine that was prescribed for another person, rather than a consistent pattern of drug abuse.

To put these numbers of people who use benzodiazepines nonmedically into context, the number of people who had used drugs nonmedically in the last month before the 1985 Household Survey (NIDA, 1988c) is shown in Figure 4.3. Note that alcohol had been used by 113 million people within the past month and that 36 million Americans had used an illegal drug within the last month. Only 5 million had used any tranquilizer or sedative, and only 2 million had used a sedative or a tranquilizer without also using some other

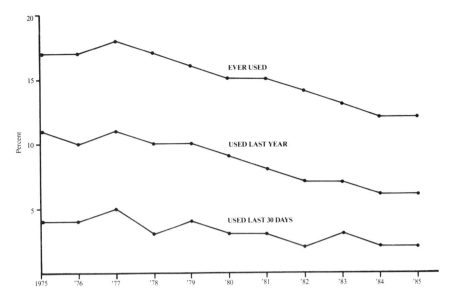

FIGURE 4.2. Nonmedical use of tranquilizers by high school seniors, 1975–1985. From *Drug Use among American High School Students, College Students and Other Young Adults: National Trends through 1985* (DHHS Publication No. ADM 86-1450) by L. D. Johnston, P. M. O'Malley, and J. G. Bachman, 1986, Washington, DC: U.S. Government Printing Office.

illicit drug. Nonmedical benzodiazepine use is different from, and far rarer than, medical use of the benzodiazepines; it is a small part of the overall nonmedical drug problem in the nation.

Diagnosis

There are a number of recent publications on the diagnosis and treatment of chronic anxiety (DuPont, 1986b; McGlynn & Metcalf, 1989; Sheehan, 1986). A simple summary is that anxiety disorders are biologically based, serious, crippling, and often lifelong conditions, which no treatment—pharmacological or nonpharmacological—has been shown to "cure." However, many treatments reduce the symptoms and promote more normal and less troubled living. Neither an automatic use of a benzodiazepine in the treatment of clinically significant anxiety, nor a categorical rejection of the use of these medicines, is in the anxious patient's best interest. The benzodiazepines can be used to treat either acute or chronic anxiety, as well as the panic attacks that are commonly associated with anxiety disorders. The benzodiazepines can be used either as needed or every day, and they can be used either alone or with other medicines, most often in psychiatry with antidepressants.

The connection between anxiety disorders and chemical dependence, with a focus on the role of benzodiazepines in both the anxiety disorders and

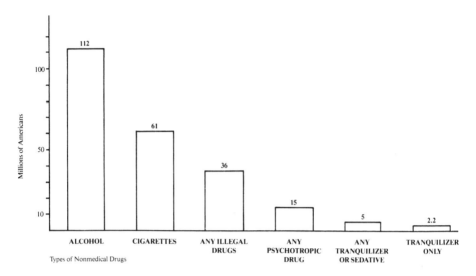

FIGURE 4.3. Nonmedical drug use (in millions) during previous month by Americans 12 years of age and older. From *National Household Survey on Drug Abuse: Main Findings 1985* (DHHS Publication No. ADM 88-1586) by the National Institute on Drug Abuse (NIDA), 1988c, Washington, DC: U.S. Government Printing Office.

chemical dependence, has recently been reviewed (Linnoila, 1989; Roth, 1989). The ongoing epidemiological study of the National Institute of Mental Health (NIMH) found that over their lifetimes 24% of American men and 4.5% of American women will be diagnosable as suffering from alcohol and/or drug abuse, and that 8% of the men and 19.5% of the women will be diagnosable as suffering from an anxiety disorder; these findings establish substance abuse and anxiety disorders as the two most common types of mental disorders (Robins et al., 1984). Bibb and Chambless (1986) reported that 91% of agoraphobics with a history of alcoholism and 43% of those without a history of alcoholism had at some time used alcohol to treat their anxiety. It is clear that both chemical dependence and anxiety disorders are common, often coexistent conditions, which commonly share comorbidity among family members (Noyes, Crowe, & Harris, 1986).

Identification of Problems among Long-Term Benzodiazepine Users

The physician is often confronted by a patient, or the family member of a patient, who is concerned about the possible adverse effects of long-term use of a benzodiazepine in the treatment of anxiety. In helping to structure the decision making for such a patient, we use the Benzodiazepine Checklist (DuPont, 1986a; see Table 4.2). There are four central questions to be answered:

TABLE 4.2. Benzodiazepine Checklist for Long-Term Use

---

1. *Diagnosis.* Does the patient's diagnosis, with accompanying disability and distress, warrant long-term medical treatment?
2. *Drug and alcohol use.* Does the patient's use of the benzodiazepine and of other psychotropic substances demonstrate good therapeutic response to the benzodiazepine with no drug or alcohol abuse?
3. *Toxic behavior.* Is there no evidence of any benzodiazepine-caused problem?
4. *Family monitor.* Does a family member confirm the effectiveness of the benzodiazepine use, and the lack of impairment and chemical dependence?

Standard for continued benzodiazepine use: A "yes" to all four questions.

If problems or possible problems are identified, benzodiazepine discontinuation is probably indicated.

---

1. *Diagnosis.* Is there a current diagnosis that warrants the prolonged use of a prescription medicine? The benzodiazepines are serious medicines that should only be used for serious illnesses.

2. *Medical and nonmedical substance use.* Is the dose of the benzodiazepine the patient is taking reasonable? Is there any use of nonmedical drugs, such as cocaine or marijuana? Is there any excessive use of alcohol (e.g., a total of more than four drinks a week, or more than two drinks a day)? Are there other medicines being used that can depress the functioning of the CNS?

3. *Toxic behavior.* Is there any evidence of slurred speech, staggering, accidents, memory loss, or other mental deficits or evidence of sedation?

4. *Family monitor.* Because people who abuse drugs deny drug-caused problems, or even lie to their doctors, and because many family members are concerned about long-term benzodiazepine use, we generally ask that a family member come to the office with the patient who is taking a benzodiazepine for a prolonged period. This gives us an opportunity to confirm, with the family member, that the benzodiazepine use produces a therapeutic benefit without problems. If there is a problem of toxic behavior or abuse of other drugs, we are more likely to identify it when we speak with the patient's family member; if not, we have an opportunity to educate and reassure both the patient and the family member.

After completion of the Benzodiazepine Checklist, if there is clear evidence that the long-term benzodiazepine use is producing significant benefit and no problems, and if the patient wants to continue using the benzodiazepine (which is, in our experience, a common set of circumstances for chronically anxious patients), then we have no hesitancy in continuing to prescribe a benzodiazepine, virtually for life.

On the other hand, many anxious patients do want to stop using a benzodiazepine. Other patients do not want to stop, but show signs of trouble with the use of a benzodiazepine on this checklist. In either case, discontinuation is in order and is, in our experience, a generally achievable goal. Some critics of benzodiazepines, including Stefan Borg and Curtis Carlson of St. Goran's Hospital in Stockholm, Sweden (Allgulander, Borg, & Vikander, 1984), have expressed concerns about the possibility that benzodiazepine abuse may lead to alcohol problems, especially in women. The simple advice to a long-term benzodiazepine user is not to use alcohol. Most anxious patients who do not have a history of chemical dependence either do not use alcohol at all, or use it only in small amounts. The Benzodiazepine Checklist helps the physician, the patient, and the patient's family identify any problems (including alcohol abuse) at an early stage, and thus facilitates constructive intervention.

Long-Term Dose and Abuse

One clinical observation will help the physician separate anxious benzodiazepine users from people who have chemical dependence problems. Most anxious medical users of benzodiazepines have used them at low and stable doses over time, often for many years. Dose is a critical variable in long-term benzodiazepine use. Chemically dependent people commonly abuse benzodiazepines at high and unstable doses; anxious patients who are not chemically dependent do not. We use a simple standard to assess dose level: If the patient's typical benzodiazepine dose level is stable at or below one-half the ordinary clinical maximum dose of the prescribed benzodiazepine as reported in the *Physicians' Desk Reference* or in the package insert approved by the FDA, we call this the "green light" dose zone. For example, the maximum approved daily doses for the most commonly used benzodiazepines are as follows: alprazolam (Xanax), 4 mg; diazepam (Valium), 40 mg; lorazepam (Ativan), 10 mg; oxazepam (Serax), 120 mg. Thus, patients whose benzodiazepine daily dose is stable at or less than 2 mg of alprazolam (Xanax), 20 mg of diazepam (Valium), 5 mg of lorazepam (Ativan), or 60 mg of oxazepam (Serax) are in the relatively safe or green light zone.

The "red light" or danger zone is above the FDA-approved maximum daily dose (e.g., above 4 mg of alprazolam [Xanax] or 40 mg of diazepam [Valium]). Except in the treatment of panic, when doses up to two or three times the FDA maximum for chronic anxiety are occasionally needed, it is unusual to see an anxious non-drug-abusing patient taking doses this high. Most panic disorder patients, after a few months of treatment, are able to do well (with good panic suppression) in the green light zone without the physician or the patient making any special effort to restrain the dose level.

One common clinical problem is to see a patient, a family member, or sometimes a physician or therapist who is concerned about "tolerance" and "addiction" because the patient feels compelled to raise the dose of the benzodiazepine over time. In our experience, such worries among patients who lack a personal history of chemical dependence are usually the result of underdosing with the benzodiazepine rather than evidence of addiction.

Although some patients with such a presentation are more comfortable taking no medicine at all, most need education about the proper dose of the benzodiazepine. Once the benzodiazepine dose is raised to an ordinary therapeutic level, the patient usually feels much better and has no inner pressure to raise the dose further.

Within the chemically dependent population, several patterns of benzodiazepine abuse can be distinguished. Perhaps the most common pattern is the use of a benzodiazepine to "treat" the adverse effects of the abuse of other, more preferred drugs. Typical is the "treatment" of hangover and other withdrawal phenomena from alcohol use with a benzodiazepine. Patients waking up in the morning after an alcoholic binge may take 10 to 40 mg of diazepam (Valium), for example, just to "face the day."

Other common patterns of self-treatment are to use benzodiazepines (often alprazolam [Xanax] or lorazepam [Ativan]) concomitantly with stimulants (often cocaine) to reduce the unpleasant experience of the stimulant use, and/or to use benzodiazepines (often triazolam [Halcion]) to treat the insomnia that often accompanies and follows stimulant abuse. Benzodiazepines requiring conjugation in the liver can be used to "boost" the effect of methadone among methadone-maintained patients. Benzodiazepines are occasionally used as primary drugs of abuse; in this case, they are typically taken orally at high doses. Chemically dependent patients report using doses of 20 to 100 mg of diazepam (Valium), for example, at one time. Although, in our experience, such benzodiazepine abuse without simultaneous use of other drugs is unusual, it does occur. The hallmarks of benzodiazepine abuse by chemically dependent people are high and unstable dosing and polydrug abuse.

Treatment

There are two general areas of treatment involving the benzodiazepines in the chemical dependence context. The first is the abuse of tnse drugs by chemically dependent people; the second is withdrawal or discontinuation.

Preventing, Detecting, and Treating Benzodiazepine Abuse

With respect to abuse, it is important for the prescribing physician to clearly identify patients who have a current or past chemical dependence problem, including alcohol abuse. Although benzodiazepines have been accepted in the inpatient withdrawal treatment of patients dependent on alcohol and other depressant substances, the use of benzodiazepines in outpatient settings by chemically dependent people, even if they have stable sobriety, is generally discouraged (Castaneda & Cushman, 1989; Ditman, 1964; Kissin & Platz, 1968; Sellers, Naranjo, & Peachey, 1981). Although it is clear that using potentially abusable medicines in the treatment of patients with a history of chemical dependence is hazardous, we believe that it is also unwise to prohibit the medical treatment of serious psychiatric disorders experienced by patients with a history of chemical dependence. A recent review of the evidence of the abuse liability of benzodiazepines among alcoholics concluded,

> Data suggest that the prevalence of benzodiazepine use among alcoholics is greater than in the general population but comparable to the prevalence in psychiatric patients. The liability for abuse may also be greater for alcoholics, but the substantial methodologic deficiencies of existing studies preclude such a conclusion. (Ciraulo, Sands, & Shader, 1988, p. 1505)

Our treatment responses to actively chemically dependent patients with anxiety disorders and/or insomnia are as follows:

1. Do not use benzodiazepines in outpatient treatment.
2. Refer patient to chemical dependence treatment and Alcoholics Anonymous or Narcotics Anonymous.
3. Refer family members to Al-Anon.
4. Work with patient to find nonbenzodiazepine treatments for the anxiety and/or insomnia.

If a medicine is to be used in the treatment of anxiety with a chemically dependent patient, then buspirone (BuSpar) or an antidepressant is desirable as a first choice because these medicines lack abuse potential. Whether, if this approach fails, the patient is better served by the use of an antipsychotic (such as trifluoperazine [Stelazine] or thioridazine [Mellaril]) or a benzodiazepine is a close call, with both having serious drawbacks. Our preference, however, for chemically dependent anxious patients who have not responded to other pharmacological and nonpharmacological treatments, is to use a slow-onset benzodiazepine rather than an antipsychotic. Other treatment alternatives to the benzodiazepines are as follows:

1. Education and support about the problem (help the patient put it into perspective).
2. Nonpharmacological treatments:
   a. Cognitive–behavioral treatments.
   b. Psychotherapy.
   c. Relaxation training.
   d. Assertive training.
   e. Aerobic exercise.

If there is good indication for the use of a benzodiazepine in a chemically dependent patient whose life is stable and who shows no current drug or alcohol abuse, then the choice of a benzodiazepine should be one of slow onset and low abuse potential, such as oxazepam (Serax) or prazepam (Centrax), and most definitely not Valium (diazepam). Alprazolam (Xanax) and lorazepam (Ativan) may be closer to diazepam (Valium) than to oxazepam (Serax) in this regard, and should generally be avoided for such patients.

As a general principle, drug abuse treatment programs should treat benzodiazepine abuse as they treat the abuse of any drug, applying the routine sanctions for this behavior. We recently conducted a study in two methadone maintenance programs, looking for prevalence of abuse of two classes of drugs not often tested for: benzodiazepines and marijuana. We found that the rates of positive urines for marijuana were 27% and 51%, while the rates for benzodiazepines were 4% and 7% (DuPont & Saylor, 1989).

Discontinuation of Benzodiazepine Use

Discontinuation of sedatives and hypnotics, including the benzodiazepines, can be divided into three categories: (1) long-term low-dose benzodiazepine use; (2) high-dose benzodiazepine abuse and multiple-drug abuse; and (3) high-dose abuse of nonbenzodiazepine sedatives and hypnotics (especially intermediate-acting barbiturates). The first group of patients can usually be discontinued on an outpatient basis. Some of the second and even the third group can be treated as outpatients, but most will require inpatient care. Inpatient discontinuation is generally reserved for patients who fail at outpatient discontinuation and for patients who demonstrate potentially life-threatening loss of control over their drug use.

With respect to withdrawal from benzodiazepines in the context of chemical dependence treatment, the biggest problem treatment professionals experience is that some of the patients who take benzodiazepines also suffer chronically from underlying anxiety disorders and panic attacks. Therefore, when the patients stop taking the benzodiazepines, they experience a short-term rebound increase in these distressing symptoms. These rebound symptoms are difficult for the patients or the physicians to separate from withdrawal symptoms because they are often similar and because the time course is also similar, with both types of symptoms occurring at low benzodiazepine doses and peaking during the first or second drug-free week.

There is abundant evidence that most patients who take benzodiazepines at prescribed dose levels can discontinue using them with quite moderate symptoms if the dose reduction is gradual (Busto, Simpkins, & Sellers, 1983; Rickels, Schweizer, Csanalosi, Case, & Chung, 1988). One study found that about half of long-term benzodiazepine users could stop with no withdrawal symptoms (Tyrer, Rutherford, & Huggett, 1981). However, some patients who stop benzodiazepine use, especially after use for many years, do have symptoms that are either prolonged or severe (Noyes, Garvey, Cook, & Perry, 1988). It has been found that about one-third of medical patients with long-term use of a benzodiazepine will have clinically significant symptoms, even after gradual tapering, and that about one in eight patients stopping a benzodiazepine will have prolonged and/or severe symptoms (DuPont, 1988). In any case, discontinuation symptoms (except for abrupt cessation, which can produce seizures and is not indicated) from benzodiazepines are "distressing but not dangerous."

There are two common clinical errors in dealing with benzodiazepine discontinuation symptoms: underestimating the symptoms and overestimating them. Unfortunately, patients taking benzodiazepines today have no trouble finding physicians who do both. Our recommendation is to state the following clearly to the patient: "Withdrawal, especially after many years of daily use of a benzodiazepine, can be hard, but it is not dangerous. It is a solvable problem that is of fairly short duration."

We have found that it is rarely necessary to hospitalize a long-term low-dose benzodiazepine user who is not a drug abuser for benzodiazepine discontinuation. The preferred treatment is gradual reduction of the dose of the usually taken benzodiazepine over a 6- to 12-week period on an outpatient basis, as outlined below.

With respect to a chemically dependent person who typically uses benzodiazepines in high and unstable doses, usually with a variety of other abused drugs, the withdrawal treatment is more complex and sometimes does involve hospitalization. The major clinical problem for this patient population, however, is not so much the acute withdrawal from the benzodiazepine (even though that can be a challenge) as it is the long-term maintenance of a drug-free state. Before admission to a hospital program for detoxification, adequate planning needs to be in place for long-term treatment, to ensure that the patient does not simply leave the hospital and resume the pattern of drug abuse (including the abuse of the benzodiazepine) that produced the chemical dependence in the first place (DuPont, 1984). In this regard, the most potent long-term treatment is usually a Twelve-Step program such as Alcoholics Anonymous (AA) or Narcotics Anonymous (NA).

The use of outpatient treatment that includes drug tests and sanctions against continued drug abuse, combined with regular attendance at AA or NA, will often suffice to get the patient who is abusing a benzodiazepine drug-free without admission to a hospital. Surely, as a general principle, outpatient detoxification should be tried first, if for no other reason than that it is more cost-effective. On the other hand, if outpatient discontinuation—including gradual dose reduction with a long-acting cross-tolerant medication, aggressive counseling, and attendance at Twelve-Step meetings—fails to produce a drug-free outcome, or if the drug-abusing patient fails to comply with the treatment regimen, then inpatient withdrawal treatment is often desirable.

Because of the cross-tolerance of all the substances that affect the GABA receptors, once the patient is admitted to a hospital program a wide variety of medicines can be used for the detoxification, which can generally be accomplished in 1 to 3 weeks of gradually tapering doses. The most widely used cross-tolerant medicines for this purpose are phenobarbital and prazepam (Centrax) (Schuckit, 1984; Smith & Wesson, 1983).

Outpatient treatment is the first response for benzodiazepine discontinuation for medical patients who are taking benzodiazepines at usual therapeutic doses and who are not abusing other drugs, including alcohol. Inpatient treatment is indicated for patients with serious medical or psychiatric complications, as well as for patients who have failed at outpatient discontinuation, for patients who abuse benzodiazepines at high dose, for patients who abuse multiple drugs, and for patients who are unable to manage their own doses as outpatients (usually this means chemically dependent people).

OUTPATIENT DISCONTINUATION

The simplest discontinuation technique is to gradually reduce the patient's dose of the currently used benzodiazepine over a 6- to 12-week period (DuPont, 1987, in press; Sellers, 1988). Patients generally need education and support in this process, since they are likely to feel quite uncomfortable and to worry about their symptoms during discontinuation. We find it helpful to schedule weekly visits and to help each patient carefully structure a discontinuation program in which each dose is planned in advance with the physician. It often helps if the patient has the opportunity to take a small "extra dose" (e.g., 2 mg of diazepam or 0.25 mg of alprazolam) any day during discontinuation, so that the feeling of being trapped is lessened. Patients need to know that their discomfort during dose reduction means that their bodies are getting used to no longer having the benzodiazepine. This discomfort is both healthy and temporary.

The discontinuation symptoms are likely to be most intense at the lowest dose levels and during the first drug-free week. This information helps patients know what to expect, since otherwise they experience the building up of symptoms as they approach zero dose as if the worsening will increase endlessly. The acute benzodiazepine withdrawal symptoms subside by the second drug-free week. Chronic, generally low-level withdrawal distress may continue for several months, or even a year, after becoming drug-free. Along with total duration of benzodiazepine use and maximum dose used, personality factors play a major role in the severity and duration of withdrawal symptoms (DuPont, 1988; Rickels, Schweizer, Case, & Garcia-Espana, 1988). The longer the patient has used the benzodiazepine, the higher the dose used, and the more chronic character pathology the patient has, the more likely a difficult withdrawal is. Nevertheless, in our experience, it is not possible to predict accurately with any particular patient how mild or how severe the withdrawal symptoms will be.

It is of considerable academic interest that three distinct types of symptoms occur on benzodiazepine discontinuation: withdrawal (a response to physical dependence), relapse (of the underlying anxiety disorder), and rebound (a temporary exaggeration of the underlying anxiety disorder, mixed with withdrawal that occurs just at the time of stopping the medication) (DuPont & Pecknold, 1985). All these symptoms overlap both in the quality of the experience and in time course, so it is difficult for either the patient or the physician to distinguish them. The clinically important point is that the up-surge of symptoms during discontinuation is temporary. If the patient sticks with the benzodiazepine discontinuation program, these symptoms can all be overcome.

If gradual benzodiazepine dose reduction does not succeed (though for most anxious patients taking therapeutic doses of a benzodiazepine, it will succeed), then there are two alternatives: using a longer-acting cross-tolerant medication and/or using a medicine to suppress the withdrawal symptoms.

The best choices for cross-tolerant long-acting agents are clonazepam (Klonopin) and phenobarbital. For patients taking the usual therapeutic doses of a benzodiazepine, the standard approach with clonazepam (Klonopin) is to give the patient 0.5 or 1.0 mg at bedtime for 1 week. During that week, the patient may continue to take his or her regular benzodiazepine on an as-needed (p.r.n.) basis, up to the total dose taken prior to the start of discontinuation. After 1 week taking clonazepam, the patient is to stop all use of the original benzodiazepine and to continue taking the clonazepam at the same dose (e.g., usually 0.5 or 1.0 mg at bedtime; however, the dose can be higher or lower and may be divided if the patient has problems with sedation, the most common side effect of clonazepam use). Then the patient reduces the clonazepam dose by 0.25 mg (half a tablet) each week, until reaching a zero dose. This approach, developed by Jerry Rosenbaum, has been labeled the "Klonopin switch" (Herman, Rosenbaum, & Brotman, 1987).

The alternative long-acting cross-tolerant medicine is phenobarbital, which is used in a similar fashion but which is often taken several times a day, with a common starting dose being 30 mg twice a day for patients on usual therapeutic doses of a benzodiazepine. Some patients may require twice that dose, and a few will do well at 30 mg per day to start. As with clonazepam, the primary side effect of phenobarbital is sedation, so that the dose needs to be titrated with the patient to find a dose that suppresses most of the withdrawal symptoms without excess sedation (Ravi, Maany, Burke, Dhopesh, & Woody, 1990). Once that dose has been found, the original benzodiazepine is gradually reduced over 1 week, while the patient's phenobarbital dose is held constant. Then the patient gradually reduces the phenobarbital dose by 30 mg per week to zero. This approach has been developed by Smith and Wesson (1983).

Outpatient discontinuation from long-term benzodiazepine use is usually possible with very gradual dose reduction of the medication the patient was originally taking; when this is not possible, substitution of a longer-acting cross-tolerant agent (usually clonazepam or phenobarbital) is usually success-ful. The outcome is improved if the patient is educated and supported during the benzodiazepine discontinuation process. In our experience, these patients need to have telephone contact with the physician to help them cope with the symptoms they experience. Often simple, direct reassurance that the symptoms are not dangerous and that they will diminish after approximately a week or two of being drug-free is especially helpful. Although we rarely use any adjunctive medicines to treat the symptoms that emerge during benzodiazepine discontinuation, three pharmacological approaches have been tried in recent years, each with some enthusiasm. In our experience, however, these medicines are not generally necessary for outpatient discontinuation.

The three drugs that have shown the most promise in suppressing benzodiazepine withdrawal symptoms are propranolol (Inderol), carbamazepine (Tegretol), and clonidine (Catapres). Smith and Wesson (1983) have used propranolol for many years, usually at doses of 20 mg p.r.n. up to three or four times a day for 2 to 3 weeks just before and just after the patient gets to zero dose of the benzodiazepine (Tyrer et al., 1981).

More recently, Klein (Klein, Uhde, & Post, 1986) and Ries (Ries, Roy-Byrne, Ward, Neppe, & Cullison, 1989) have used carbamazepine (Tegretol) to suppress withdrawal on benzodiazepine discontinuation. Under this approach, carbamazepine is started at 200 mg once a day and gradually raised to 800 mg per day, if this dose is tolerated by the patient. If not, the maximum carbamazepine dose the patient can tolerate is achieved and held steady for a week or two. Then the benzodiazepine dose is gradually reduced over a period of 1 to 3 weeks. The carbamazepine dose is then reduced to zero over a period of 1 week, beginning 1 or 2 weeks after the patient reaches zero dose of benzodiazepine.

A third approach to the suppression of withdrawal symptoms is to use clonidine (Catapres) in p.r.n. doses of 0.1 mg to 0.6 mg/day for a week or two on either side of zero dose (Goodman, Charney, Price, Woods, & Heninger, 1986). Recently, clonidine skin patches have been used in outpatient settings, especially in treating withdrawal symptoms from cigarette smoking (Ornish, Zisook, & McAdams, 1988). The standard approach is to use Catapres-TTS #2, equivalent to 0.2 mg of clonidine per day. If the baseline systolic blood pressure is less than 100 mm Hg, or if the patient is of small build or reports sensitivity to clonidine, a #1 patch can be used. Since it takes 3 or 4 days for adequate blood levels to be reached, it is common to begin tapering only after that interval to accomplish the benzodiazepine discontinuation over about 2 weeks, and to continue the patch for 1 or 2 weeks after reaching zero dose. The rapid development of tolerance to the antiwithdrawal effects of clonidine, along with its hypotensive effects, limits its use.

These three techniques used to suppress benzodiazepine withdrawal symptoms are all new and incompletely studied. They each have their drawbacks, especially in outpatient treatment. All produce sedation and other unpleasant effects for many patients. Propranolol and clonidine can cause distressing, and sometimes dangerous, drops in blood pressure. Carbamazepine can cause a drop in the white blood count, which can occasionally be dangerous and even fatal. Therefore, in using these techniques with outpatients, appropriate care must be taken and the risks must be balanced against the benefits. Since the long-acting cross-tolerant agents used to aid in discontinuation (clonazepam and phenobarbital) also cause sedation, this symptom in particular needs to be watched for with outpatients who are driving or engaged in other possibly dangerous activities during the withdrawal period.

Some patients who use benzodiazepines medically without any nonmedical drug use find it helpful to joing in mutual-aid groups, such as Pills Anonymous or other Twelve-Step programs that focus particularly on the problems of prescription drug dependence, as part of their efforts to stop benzodiazepine use. Such Twelve-Step programs are the foundation of the treatment of all chemically dependent patients who discontinue benzodiazepines.

INPATIENT DISCONTINUATION

As noted earlier, inpatient withdrawal is indicated for patients using sedatives and hypnotics other than the benzodiazepines (especially if that use is at doses higher than usually prescribed), for patients exhibiting polydrug abuse, for patients with severe medical or psychiatric complications, and for patients who have failed in outpatient discontinuation programs. In general, inpatient care permits a more controlled and more rapid discontinuation, because patients will tolerate more distressing symptoms when in a hospital and because they can be observed and managed more carefully. Perhaps the most striking aspect of the care of patients discontinuing benzodiazepines in hospitals, compared to patients stopping other abused drugs, is the severity of their insomnia and the prolonged nature of their subjective distress during and after benzodiazepine discontinuation.

The same pharmacological alternatives described for outpatient discontinuation are available for inpatient care, but the time course is generally much shorter, with most patients being taken from the original dose to zero dose within 2 weeks or less. Inpatient care allows more careful monitoring of sedation and possible side effects of adjunctive treatment (especially leukopenia for carbamazepine and hypotension for propranolol and clonidine). If the patient has concomitant abuse of other drugs, especially alcohol, then that needs to be considered as well in the detoxification process.

For patients using sedatives and hypnotics other than the benzodiazepines, especially at high doses, it may be desirable to use the classic pentobarbital challenge test to set the original dose, and to then withdraw the patient gradually from this intermediate-acting barbiturate (Schuckit, 1984).

In any event, the underlying principle is the same with all patients being withdrawn from any of the sedatives and hypnotics: Either gradually reduce the dose of the original substance or find an equivalent dose of a cross-tolerant substance (of which there are several alternatives, most notably clonazepam and phenobarbital), and then gradually reduce the dose of that substance. For inpatient discontinuation, the period of withdrawal is usually 1 or 2 weeks (followed by a week or two of stabilization off all medicines), whereas on an outpatient basis the duration for dose reduction of a benzodiazepine is usually longer, usually 6 weeks or more.

Summary

The benzodiazepines are useful medicines in the treatment of a wide variety of common disorders. If they are to remain available to doctors and patients, it is essential that clear guidelines be established for when and how they are used and for the recognition of the real problems that can be produced by these generally safe and effective medicines. The two principal problems identified in this chapter are abuse by chemically dependent patients and withdrawal problems after prolonged use. Both problems are serious and require the attention of an educated physician. If these problems are dealt with, the benzodiazepines will remain useful medicines, albeit something less than the "magic bullets" that some of their earlier proponents thought them to be.

References

Allgulander, C., Borg, S., & Vikander, B. (1984). A 4–6 year follow-up of 50 patients with primary dependence on sedative and hypnotic drugs. *American Journal of Psychiatry, 141,* 1580–1582.

American Psychiatric Association. (1987). *Diagnostic and statistical manual of mental disorders* (3rd ed., rev.). Washington, DC: Author.

American Psychiatric Association Task Force on Benzodiazepine Dependence, Toxicity and Abuse. (1990). *Benzodiazepine dependence, toxicity and abuse—A task force report of the American Psychiatric Association.* Washington, DC: American Psychiatric Press.

Arendt, R. M., Greenblatt, D. J., Liebisch, D. C., Luu, M. D., & Paul, S. M. (1987). Determinants of benzodiazepine brain uptake: Lipophilicity versus binding affinity. *Psychopharmacology, 93,* 72–76.

Baldessarini, R. J. (1985). Drugs and the treatment of psychiatric disorders. In A. G. Gilman, L. S. Goodman, T. W. Rall, & F. Murad (Eds.), *The pharmacological basis of therapeutics* (7th ed., pp. 432–439). New York: Macmillan.

Bibb, J. L., & Chambless, D. L. (1986). Alcohol use and abuse among diagnosed agoraphobics. *Behaviour Research and Therapy, 24,* 49–58.

Busto, U., Simpkins, J., & Sellers, E. M. (1983). Objective determination of benzodiazepine use and abuse in alcoholics. *British Journal of Addiction, 48,* 429–435.

Castaneda, R., & Cushman, P. (1989). Alcohol withdrawal: A review of clinical management. *Journal of Clinical Psychiatry, 50,* 278–284.

Ciraulo, D. A., Sands, B. F., & Shader, R. I. (1988). Critical review of liability for benzodiazepine abuse among alcoholics. *American Journal of Psychiatry, 145,* 1501–1506.

Davis, H. (1989, April 25). *Reporting rates of drug-abuse episodes for prescription drugs.* Unpublished memorandum, U.S. Food and Drug Administration.

de Wit, H., Johanson, C. E., & Uhlenhuth, E. H. (1984). Reinforcing properties of lorazepam in normal volunteer subjects. *Drug and Alcohol Dependence, 13,* 31–41.

de Wit, H., Uhlenhuth, E. H., & Johanson, C. E. (1984). Lack of preference for flurazepam in normal volunteers. *Pharmacology, Biochemistry and Behavior, 21,* 865–869.

Ditman, K. S. (1964). Review and evaluation of current drug therapies in alcoholism. *Psychosomatic Medicine, 28,* 667–677.

DuPont, R. L. (1984). *Getting tough on gateway drugs: A guide for the family.* Washington, DC: American Psychiatric Press.

DuPont, R. L. (1986a). *Benzodiazepines: The social issues.* Rockville, MD: Institute for Behavior and Health.

DuPont, R. L. (1986b). *Phobias and panic: A physician's guide to modern treatments.* Rockville, MD: Phobia Society of America.

DuPont, R. L. (1987). Discontinuation of benzodiazepine use: A clinician's guide. *Directions in Psychiatry, 7,* 12.

DuPont, R. L. (Ed.). (1988). Abuse of benzodiazepines: The problems and the solutions. *American Journal of Drug and Alcohol Abuse, 14*(Suppl. 1).

DuPont, R. L. (1989, October). Addiction, withdrawal, and the role of BZs. *The Psychiatric Times,* vi.

DuPont, R. L. (1990). A physician's guide to discontinuing benzodiazepine therapy. *Western Journal of Medicine* [Special issue: *Addiction Medicine*], *152,* 600–603.

DuPont, R. L. (in press). A practical approach to benzodiazepine discontinuation. *Journal of Psychiatric Research.*

DuPont, R. L., & Pecknold, J. C. (1985, May). *Symptoms after alprazolam discontinuation: Withdrawal or relapse?* Paper presented at the annual meeting of the American Psychiatric Association, Dallas, TX.

DuPont, R. L., & Saylor, K. E. (1989). Marijuana and benzodiazepines in patients receiving methadone treatment. *Journal of the American Medical Association, 261,* 3409.

DuPont, R. L., Swinson, R. P., Ballenger, J. C., Burrows, G. D., Noyes, R., Rubin, R. T., Rifkin, A., & Pecknold, J. C. (unpublished). *Discontinuation effects of alprazolam following long-term treatment of panic-related disorders.*

Golombok, S., Moodley, P., & Lader, M. (1988). Cognitive impairment in long-term benzodiazepine users. *Psychological Medicine, 18,* 365–374.

Goodman, W. K., Charney, D. S., Price, L. H., Woods, S. W., & Heninger, G. R. (1986). Ineffectiveness of clonidine in the treatment of the benzodiazepine withdrawal syndrome: Report of three cases. *American Journal of Psychiatry, 143,* 900–903.

Griffiths, R. R., & Sannerud, C. A. (1987). Abuse of and dependence on benzodiazepines and other anxiolytic/sedative drugs. In H. Meltzer, B. S. Bunney, & J. T. Coyle (Eds.), *Psychopharmacology: The third generation of progress* (pp. 1535–1541). New York: Raven Press.

Harvey, S. C. (1985). Hypnotics and sedatives. In A. G. Gilman, L. S. Goodman, T. W. Rall, & F. Murad (Eds.), *The pharmacological basis of therapeutics* (7th ed., pp. 340–351). New York: Macmillan.

Herman, J. B., Rosenbaum, J. F., & Brotman, A. W. (1987). The alprazolam to clonazepam switch for the treatment of panic disorder. *Journal of Clinical Psychopharmacology, 7,* 175–178.

Johanson, C. E., & Uhlenhuth, E. H. (1980). Drug preference and mood in humans: Diazepam. *Psychopharmacology, 71,* 269–273.

Johanson, C. E., & Uhlenhuth, E. H. (1982). Drug preference in humans. *Federation Proceedings, 41,* 228–233.

Johnston, L. D., O'Malley, P. M., & Bachman, J. G. (1986). *Drug use among American high school students, college students and other young adults: National trends through 1985* (DHHS Publication No. ADM 86-1450). Washington, DC: U.S. Government Printing Office.

Kissin, B., & Platz A. (1968). The use of drugs in the long term rehabilitation of alcoholics. In D. H. Efron (Ed.), *Psychopharmacology—A review of progress, 1957–1967* (PHS Publication No. 1836). Washington, DC: U.S. Government Printing Office.

Klein, E., Uhde, T. W., & Post, R. M. (1986). Preliminary evidence for the utility of carbamazepine in alprazolam withdrawal. *American Journal of Psychiatry, 143,* 235–236.

Lader, M. H., Ron, M., & Petursson, H. (1984). Computed axial brain tomography in long-term benzodiazepine users. *Psychological Medicine, 14,* 203–206.

Linnoila, M. I. (1989). Anxiety and alcoholism. *Journal of Clinical Psychiatry, 50,* 26–29.

McGlynn, T. J., & Metcalf, H. L. (Eds.). (1989). *Diagnosis and treatment of anxiety disorders: A physician's handbook.* Washington, DC: American Psychiatric Press.

Mellinger, G. D., & Balter, M. B. (1981). Prevalence and patterns of use of psychotherapeutic drugs: Results from a 1979 national survey of American adults. In G. Tognoni, C.

Bellantuono, & M. Lader (Eds.), *Epidemiological impact of psychotropic drugs* (pp. 117–135). Amsterdam: Elsevier.

Melzack, R. (1990). The tragedy of needless pain. *Scientific American, 262,* 27–33.

National Institute on Drug Abuse (NIDA). (1988a). *A decade of DAWN: Benzodiazepine-related cases, 1976–1985* (DHHS Publication No. ADM 88-1575). Washington, DC: U.S. Government Printing Office.

National Institute on Drug Abuse (NIDA). (1988b). *Annual data 1987: Data from the Drug Abuse Warning Network (DAWN)* (DHHS Publication No. ADM 88-1584). Washington, DC: U.S. Government Printing Office.

National Institute on Drug Abuse (NIDA). (1988c). *National household survey on drug abuse: Main findings 1985* (DHHS Publication No. ADM 88-1586). Washington, DC: U.S. Government Printing Office.

Noyes, R., Crowe, R. R., & Harris, E. L. (1986). Relationship between panic disorder and agoraphobia. *Archives of General Psychiatry, 43,* 227–232.

Noyes, R., Garvey, M. J., Cook, B. L., & Perry, P. J. (1988). Benzodiazepine withdrawal: A review of the evidence. *Journal of Clinical Psychiatry, 49,* 382–389.

Ornish, S. A., Zisook, S., & McAdams, L. A. (1988). Effects of transdermal clonidine treatment on withdrawal symptoms associated with smoking cessation: A randomized, controlled trial. *Archives of Internal Medicine, 148,* 2027–2031.

Paul, S. M. (1988). Anxiety and depression: A common neurobiological substrate? *Journal of Clinical Psychiatry, 49*(Suppl.), 13–16.

Ravi, N. V., Maany, I., Burke, W. M., Dhopesh, V., & Woody, G. E. (1990). Detoxification with phenobarbital of alprazolam-dependent poly-substance abusers. *Journal of Substance Abuse Treatment, 7,* 55–58.

Rickels, K., Schweizer, E., Case, G. W., & Garcia-Espana, F. (1988). Benzodiazepine dependence, withdrawal severity, and clinical outcome: Effects of personality. *Psychopharmacology Bulletin, 24,* 415–420.

Rickels, K., Schweizer, E., Csanalosi, I., Case, G. W., & Chung, H. (1988). Long-term treatment of anxiety and risk of withdrawal. *Archives of General Psychiatry, 45,* 444–450.

Ries, R. K., Roy-Byrne, P. P., Ward, N. G., Neppe, V., & Cullison, S. (1989). Carbamazepine treatment for benzodiazepine withdrawal. *American Journal of Psychiatry, 146,* 536–537.

Robins, L. N., Helzer, J. E., Weissman, M. M., Orvaschel, H., Burke, J. D., & Regier, D. A. (1984). Lifetime prevalence of specific psychiatric disorders in three sites. *Archives of General Psychiatry, 41,* 949–958.

Roth, M. (1989). Anxiety disorders and the use and abuse of drugs. *Journal of Clinical Psychiatry, 50*(Suppl.), 30–35.

Roy-Byrne, P. P., & Hommer, D. (1988). Benzodiazepine withdrawal: Overview and implications for the treatment of anxiety. *American Journal of Medicine, 84,* 1041–1051.

Scharf, M. B., Jennings, S. W., & Graham, J. P. (1988, December). Therapeutic substitution: Clinical differences among benzodiazepine compounds. *U. S. Pharmacist,* pp. H1–H13.

Schuckit, M. A. (1984). *Drug and alcohol abuse: A clinical guide to diagnosis and treatment.* New York: Plenum Press.

Sellers, E. M. (1988). Alcohol, barbiturate and benzodiazepine withdrawal syndromes: Clinical management. *Canadian Medical Association Journal, 139,* 113–120.

Sellers, E. M., Naranjo, C. A., & Peachey, J. E. (1981). Drugs to decrease alcohol consumption. *New England Journal of Medicine, 305,* 1255–1262.

Sheehan, D. V. (1986). *The anxiety disease.* New York: Bantam Books.

Smith, D. E., & Wesson, D. R. (1983). Benzodiazepine dependency syndromes. *Journal of Psychoactive Drugs, 15,* 85–95.

Tyrer, P. (1988). Dependence as a limiting factor in the clinical use of minor tranquilizers. *Pharmacology and Therapeutics, 36,* 173–188.

Tyrer, P., & Murphy, S. (1987). The place of benzodiazepines in psychiatric practice. *British Journal of Psychiatry, 151,* 719–723.

Tyrer, P., Rutherford, D., & Huggett, D. (1981). Benzodiazepine withdrawal symptoms and propranolol. *Lancet, i,* 520–522.

Uhde, T. W., & Kellner, C. H. (1987). Cerebral ventricular size in panic disorder. *Journal of Affective Disorders, 12,* 175–178.

U.S. Department of Health and Human Services. (1987). Sedatives and anti-anxiety agents. In *Drug abuse and drug abuse research: The second triennial report to Congress from the Secretary, Department of Health and Human Services* (DHHS Publication No. ADM 87-1486, pp. 163–181). Washington, DC: U.S. Government Printing Office.

Woods, J. H., Katz, J. L., & Winger, G. (1988). Use and abuse of benzodiazepines: Issues relevant to prescribing. *Journal of the American Medical Association, 260,* 3476–3480.

World Health Organization. (1988). *The use of essential drugs: Third report of the World Health Organization Expert Committee* (WHO Technical Report Series No. 770). Geneva: Author.

5

Opioids

HUBERT H. THOMASON, JR.
STEPHEN L. DILTS

Introduction

Opioids constitute a group of compounds whose pharmacological effects resemble those of morphine. Opioids are commonly used medically for the relief of pain, as an adjunct to anesthesia, for the prevention of an abstinence syndrome, for cough suppression, and occasionally for sedation in the agitated patient. Opioids are also frequently abused for their intoxicating effects.

The history of opioid use goes back thousands of years in human history. The Ebers Papyri from approximately 7000 B.C. refer to the use of opium in children suffering from colic (Deneau & Mule, 1981). In the Victorian era, the use of laudanum was socially acceptable. In the present day, opioids are severely regulated, especially in the United States; however, demand by addicts results in the existence of a "black market" characterized by crime, disease, poverty, and loss of personal and social productivity. An active heroin addict in any major metropolitan city may be responsible for as much as $200,000 in stolen retail goods annually, which are then sold privately to obtain more heroin. Prostitution is closely linked with drug abuse in general and opioid use in particular. The sexually promiscuous intravenous heroin user is a most effective spreader of the deadly acquired immune deficiency syndrome (AIDS) virus, as well as other venereal and infectious diseases. High overall death rates are associated with opioid abuse—approximately 10–15 per 1,000 in the United States (Jaffe, 1989). Opioids have the capacity to commandeer all of an individual's attention, resources, and energy, and to focus these exclusively on obtaining the next dose at any cost. This vicious cycle repeats itself every few hours, 24 hours a day, 365 days a year, for years on end. Comprehending the implications of opioid abuse shocks and staggers the inquiring mind.

Definitions

As a group, the opioids are addicting; that is, they produce a well-defined syndrome characterized by repeated self-administration over time, tolerance to the effects of the drug, and an abstinence syndrome when the drug is no longer available. "Cross-tolerance" refers to the ability of any drug in the opioid class to produce similar effects and block the abstinence syndrome associated with opioids in general as long as equivalent doses are used.

Morphine, codeine, and thebaine are phenanthrane alkaloids naturally occurring in opium, the milky exudate from the unripe capsule of the poppy plant, *Papaver somniferum*. Raw opium contains 4–21% morphine and 0.7–2.5% codeine, and is refined to produce these medically useful products. In practice, most codeine is actually converted directly from morphine, which also can be used to produce hydromorphone (Dilaudid). Thebaine, found in very small concentrations in raw opium, is similar to morphine. It is converted into medically useful compounds such as codeine, hydrocodone (Vicodin), oxycodone (Percodan, Percocet, Tylox), oxymorphone (Numorphan), nalbuphine (Nubain), and diacetylmorphine (heroin). Naloxone (Narcan) is also produced from morphine, but lacks euphoric and analgesic properties; its use in humans is discussed later in this chapter. Etorphine (M99), which is produced from thebaine, is a potent opioid useful mainly in the immobilization of large animals. Raw opium, morphine, codeine, and thebaine are referred to as "naturally occurring" opioids, whereas those compounds mentioned above, which are produced directly from these naturally occurring compounds, are called "semisynthetic" opioids.

Attempts to synthesize opioid-like compounds have produced a variety of agents that are chemically distinct from morphine, yet seem to act via similar mechanisms and also exhibit cross-tolerance. These include meperidine (Demerol), propoxyphene (Darvon), and methadone (Dolophine). Fentanyl (Sublimaze) is a very potent opioid-like compound used mainly as an anesthetic. These compounds are collectively referred to as the "synthetic" opioids.

Most opioids are legitimately used medically for pain relief and therefore are referred to commonly as "analgesics"; yet not all analgesics are opioid-like in their mechanisms of action, nor do they exhibit complete cross-tolerance with the naturally occurring, semisynthetic, and synthetic opioids. Initial hopes were that a nonaddicting analgesic with the same potent pain-relieving properties as the opioids could be produced; unfortunately, this has not come to pass, and the following examples are known to produce dependence along with analgesia. Pentazocine (Talwin) and butorphanol (Stadol) will produce analgesia in the opioid-free individual, but when given to someone who is opioid-dependent, they will produce an abstinence syndrome. The semisynthetic compound nalbuphine (Nubain), mentioned above, has similar properties. This mixed agonist-antagonist phenomenon highlights an important aspect of opioid pharmacology, the "opioid receptor."

Discovery of the opioid receptor in relation to both endogenous and exogenous compounds that may bind to it has broadened the definition of "opioid" to include any substance that binds specifically to the opioid receptor site and produces an agonistic action. Further investigations have described opioid receptor subtypes. For example, the μ receptor is occupied preferentially by the classic morphine-like opioids, but butorphanol (Stadol) and nalbuphaine (Nubain) prefer the κ receptor. Both receptors are highly specific, and an abstinence syndrome mediated by the κ receptor will not be relieved if a μ receptor compound is administered. There are also compounds that bind selectively to the receptor site yet produce no agonistic action. These compounds are antagonistic in nature, since they occupy the receptor site and exclude agonist opioids; examples include naloxone (Narcan) and naltrexone (Trexan). These opioid antagonists are useful as treatment agents, and are discussed later in the chapter in connection with pharmacotherapy. Also of interest is the discovery and description of endogenous opioid substances in humans, which operate at the κ receptor site along the spectrum from agonistic to antagonistic function. To date, no endogenous μ receptor opioid has been discovered (Jaffe, 1989).

Diagnosis

In the framework provided by the revised third edition of the *Diagnostic and Statistical Manual of Mental Disorders* (DSM-III-R; American Psychiatric Association, 1987), the problem of opioid abuse is divided into four categories among which there may be some overlap. Opioid-induced organic mental disorders of two types are defined: intoxication and withdrawal. Opioid intoxication is defined in Table 5.1, and opioid withdrawal is defined in Table 5.2. Facility in making these diagnoses requires a clear understanding of the clinical features associated with opioids, as discussed later in this chapter. In addition to intoxication or withdrawal, it is important to characterize the individual's relationship to the use of opioids over time. Tables 3.1 and 3.2 in Chapter 3 of this volume give the DSM-III-R criteria for psychoactive substance dependence and abuse, respectively.

Initial assessment always includes a thorough history of the individual's

TABLE 5.1. DSM-III-R Diagnostic Criteria for Opioid Intoxication

A. Recent use of an opioid.

B. Maladaptive behavioral changes, e.g., initial euphoria followed by apathy, dysphoria, psychomotor retardation, impaired judgment, impaired social or occupational functioning.

C. Pupillary constriction (or pupillary dilation due to anoxia from severe overdose) and at least one of the following signs:

   (1) drowsiness
   (2) slurred speech
   (3) impairment in attention or memory

D. Not due to any physical or other mental disorder.

Note: When the differential diagnosis must be made without a clear-cut history, testing with an opioid antagonist, or toxicologic analysis of body fluids, it may be qualified as "Provisional."

Note. From the *Diagnostic and Statistical Manual of Mental Disorders* (3rd ed., rev., p. 152) by the American Psychiatric Association, 1987, Washington, DC: Author. Copyright 1987 by the American Psychiatric Association. Reprinted by permission.

TABLE 5.2. DSM-III-R Diagnostic Criteria for Opioid Withdrawal

A. Cessation of prolonged (several weeks or more) moderate or heavy use of an opioid, or reduction in the amount of opioid used (or administration of an opioid antagonist after a brief period of use), followed by at least three of the following:

   (1) craving for an opioid
   (2) nausea or vomiting
   (3) muscle aches
   (4) lacrimation or rhinorrhea
   (5) pupillary dilation, piloerection, or sweating
   (6) diarrhea
   (7) yawning
   (8) fever
   (9) insomnia

B. Not due to any physical or other mental disorder.

Note: When the differential diagnosis must be made without a clear-cut history or toxicologic analysis for body fluids, it may be qualified as "Provisional."

substance use over time, with corroboration from outside sources if possible. This corroboration of the individual's history is essential because of the universal presence of denial in the nonrecovered substance abuser. Minimization of the frequency and amounts of opioid use is common, as is the illusion of control characterized by the often-heard phrase, "I can stop any time I want to." Progression in the pattern of usage is the rule, as the reinforcing qualities of the opioid and tolerance exert their powerful influence. Critical to the initial assessment is an accurate answer to this question: "When did you last use and how much did you use?" With this information, one can begin to assess the impact of intoxication or withdrawal upon the immediate clinical presentation. It is also necessary to understand the crises or events precipitating contact with the health care system, in order to assess whether the patient has truly "hit bottom" or merely experienced a temporary loss of ability to obtain opioids. This information may be useful in predicting readiness to accept treatment interventions.

    A family history of substance abuse provides data reflective of the genetic influences in opioid dependence, as well as the contribution of learned behavior and sanction of substance abuse within the family structure. This information is particularly useful in planning a strategy for recovery and relapse prevention. Returning an individual to contact with family members and/or friends who are still using opioids and other drugs will virtually guarantee a quick relapse.

    Also important are inquiries into the individual's functioning in the workplace, at home, and in the social arena. Trouble may occur in each area because of the competition between dependence-driven drug-seeking behavior and the demands of everyday living. It is important to ask specifically about legal difficulties, arrests, convictions, or restrictions of freedom (e.g., loss of professional licensure).

A medical review of systems in tandem with a thorough physical examination, including a neurological examination and a mental status examination, will almost always reveal actual signs of intoxication or withdrawal as outlined below. Stigmata of opioid use, such as fresh or old needle marks around superficial veins in the extremities and neck, are readily observed. These often appear as increased lines of pigmentation. There may be evidence of old and new skin abscesses; clotted or thrombosed veins; an enlarged and tender liver; swollen lymph nodes; a heart murmur caused by endocarditis; hypo- or hyperactive bowel sounds; and pupillary abnormalities, which depend on the stage of intoxication or withdrawal. Significant weight loss is common, though weight gain is occasionally reported.

Useful laboratory studies include serum liver function studies, which may show inflammation in the form of elevated serum glutamic-oxaloacetic transferase (SGOT), serum glutamic-pyruvic transferase (SGPT), bilirubin, or alkaline phosphatase, and reduction in total protein and immunoglobulins. Blood urea nitrogen (BUN) may also be elevated, though the meaning of this finding is unclear. Further testing may include hepatitis A and B screening; human immunodeficiency virus (HIV) testing; complete blood count; and urine and/or serum analyses for the presence of opioids, cocaine metabolites, marijuana, alcohol, benzodiazepines, barbiturates, other stimulants, and hallucinogens. If possible, the collection of urine samples should be actively observed to assure that the samples are not falsified in some manner by the individual. "Scams" for avoiding detection of illicit drugs in urine are diverse and imaginative: Some men have provided "clean" urine from a small tube alongside the penis, and some women have concealed a balloon of "clean" urine in the vagina to be lacerated with a fingernail, while apparently positioning the specimen cup near the urethral meatus as the sample is collected.

As evidence of opioid abuse or dependence grows, the clinician can mount a firm but respectful confrontation of the individual, who will frequently admit the problem because he or she now recognizes that there may exist an opportunity for treatment. Use of the "addiction as an illness" concept can be useful at this critical juncture in the physician's interactions with an opioid-dependent person. If the patient's denial prevents engagement in treatment, leverage on his or her behavior may be gained by involving significant others, employers, or the legal system.

Clinical Features and Pharmacology

Clinical features of opioid abuse are logically divided into three categories: features associated with intoxication, withdrawal, and overdose. These are outlined in Tables 5.3, 5.4, and 5.5, respectively. The features listed in these

TABLE 5.3. Signs of Opioid Intoxication

1. Euphoria immediately following ingestion; profound relief from anxiety and tension.
2. Apathy following euphoria.
3. An initial mild to moderate burst of energy in the minutes following ingestion, ultimately replaced with psychomotor retardation.
4. "Nodding," a "twilight state" in between alertness and sleep during which the individual is quiescent but arousable.
5. Pupillary constriction (myosis).
6. Hypoactive bowel sounds.
7. Slow regular respiration.
8. Slurred speech.
9. Impaired judgment, attention, concentration, and memory.
10. Physical evidence of recent use, including needle marks, hyperemic nasal mucosa if insufflation was the route of administration, and positive opioid blood or urine screen.

tables are directly related to the pharmacological actions of the opiates and are uniform in humans, with the occasional exception of the individual who experiences an idiosyncratic reaction.

Analgesia is the principal useful effect of the opioids. It seems not to matter whether the pain is physical or emotional; relief is significant. The addiction potential of a given opioid appears to be at least partly related to the

TABLE 5.4. Opioid Withdrawal

Stage I—begins within hours of last dose and peaks at 36–72 hours:

1. Craving for the drug.
2. Tearing (lacrimation).
3. "Runny nose" (rhinorrhea).
4. Yawning.
5. Sweating (diaphoresis).

Stage II—begins at 12 hours and peaks at 72 hours:

6. Mild to moderate sleep disturbance.
7. Dilated pupils (mydriasis).
8. Loss of appetite (anorexia).
9. "Goose flesh" or "cold turkey" (piloerection).
10. Irritability.
11. Tremor.

Stage III—begins at 24–36 hours and peaks at 72 hours:

12. Severe insomnia.
13. Violent yawning.
14. Weakness.
15. Nausea, vomiting, diarrhea.
16. Chills, fever.
17. Muscle spasms or "kicking the habit" (especially in the lower extremities).
18. Flushing.
19. Spontaneous ejaculation.
20. Abdominal pain.

TABLE 5.5. Opioid Overdose

1. Signs of recent ingestion.
2. Profoundly decreased respirations or apnea.
3. Pale skin and blue mucous membranes.
4. Pinpoint pupils unless prolonged cerebral apnea has caused some brain damage, in which case pupillary dilatation may occur.
5. Pulmonary edema resulting in characteristic gasping and audible rhonchi; occasional froth in the upper airway.
6. Cardiovascular collapse.
7. Cardiac dysrhythmias.
8. Convulsions, especially with meperidine (Demerol), propoxyphene (Darvon), or codeine.
9. Semicoma or coma.

analgesic affect. Analgesia is increased in a dose-related manner, to a point beyond which larger doses cause greater side effects but no greater analgesia (Deneau & Mule, 1981). Contravening side effects include respiratory depression, sedation, seizures, and loss of motor control. Heroin, morphine, and hydromorphone (Dilaudid) are among the best analgesics because of rapid absorption into the central nervous system and a relatively higher threshold for side effects. Meperidine (Demerol) and codeine are less effective in this regard. Route of administration significantly affects analgesic effectiveness. Parenteral use is the most efficient, since oral administration subjects the opioid to erratic absorption in the gastrointestinal tract as well as passage through the portal system before reaching the central nervous system. Codeine and methadone (Dolophine) are reliably absorbed orally; morphine and meperidine (Demerol) are not.

Opioids are potent suppressors of the cough reflex, and this antitussive action is most often accomplished with codeine or hydrocodone. A related phenomenon is that of respiratory depression. Opioids cause the central respiratory center to become less sensitive to carbon dioxide, which in rising concentrations ordinarily stimulates breathing. The mechanism of death in acute opioid overdose is respiratory arrest.

Opioids have pronounced gastrointestinal effects. Initially the user may experience nausea and emesis due to central stimulation; however, this is followed by depression of the central structures controlling emesis, and even emetic agents will frequently fail to produce vomiting. The intestinal smooth muscle is stimulated to contract by opioids, thus reducing peristalsis. Although this action may be desirable in preventing loss of water through diarrhea, the related undesirable effect of constipation routinely appears.

Smooth muscle in the urinary bladder is also stimulated by opioids, sometimes resulting in an unpleasant sensation of nearly constant urinary urgency. Although uterine muscle is not seriously affected by opioids, labor is frequently prolonged. Since opioids do cross the placental barrier, newborn infants can show all the adult signs of intoxication, withdrawal, and overdose.

Blood vessels in the periphery are generally dilated as a result of opioid-induced histamine release; this sometimes causes a blush of the skin with itching, especially in the face. By a separate mechanism, reflex vasoconstriction is inhibited, resulting in significant orthostasis. This opioid effect usually disappears as tolerance develops.

Some endocrine effects have also been noted. Thyroid activity, output of gonadotropins, and adrenal steroid output are all reduced. These effects are caused by opioid actions on the pituitary gland.

The concept of tolerance has been previously mentioned. Repeated administration of opioids results in decreasing levels of euphoria and analgesia over time. The user also becomes less affected by respiratory depression, nausea and emesis, and impairment of consciousness. Less tolerance develops to orthostasis and very little to myosis, constipation, and urinary urgency; however, these side effects may be counteracted by the euphoric and analgesic properties of opioids, in which individuals remain aware of unpleasant physical sensations but insist that they are no longer bothered by these. Tolerance is reversed during periods of abstinence.

Tolerance is the direct result of neuroadaptive change at the opioid receptor site during a period of continuous occupation by an exogenous opioid. A state of physical dependence is reached when removal of the opioid from its receptor site produces an abstinence syndrome. A more sudden removal of the opioid from its receptor site produces a more intense abstinence syndrome. The most rapid removal of opioid from its receptor site is accomplished by the opioid antagonists, which selectively compete for the site but have no agonist properties. Shorter-acting opioids exit the receptor site system more quickly than opioids with longer half-lives. Thus heroin and morphine produce intense abstinence syndromes with relatively rapid onset and progression, whereas methadone produces an abstinence syndrome of less overall intensity but with slower progression through the stages of acute abstinence to resolution, which, for a short-acting drug such as heroin, arrives at 5–10 days. Abrupt methadone withdrawal produces an abstinence syndrome that is largely resolved at 14–21 days. Following resolution of the acute abstinence syndrome, a longer-lasting and more subtle abstinence syndrome may occur and last for many months. Symptoms include hyposensitivity to the respiratory stimulant effect of carbon dioxide, disturbed sleep, preoccupation with physical discomfort, poor self-esteem, and diminished ability to tolerate stress. Risk of relapse is higher during this period (Martin & Jasinski, 1969).

Course

The natural history of opioid addiction is influenced by many complex factors. Overall, the course is one of relapse and remission. Attempts to define the opioid abusers as a group are difficult, since long-term contact with these frequently itinerant persons is difficult and because only a minority of opioid abusers can be studied effectively (namely, those who elect to enter treatment).

Given these obstacles to accurate understanding, some generalizations can still be made. The vast majority of active opioid abusers are between the ages of 20 and 50 years. Age at first use is usually in the teens or 20s. Race, ethnicity, and socioeconomic status variables are important. Though opioid addiction affects persons from all groups in the United States, black or Hispanic persons who are poor are overrepresented. The reasons for this finding are enormously complex, and much literature is available addressing the question of who gets addicted to opioids and why (Lowinson & Ruiz, 1981; Meyer, 1986). True iatrogenic opioid dependence rarely persists to become chronic, although the risk exists for those with chronic, painful medical or surgical problems. Although men and women seek treatment in roughly equal numbers, women who are mothers of dependent children may benefit from a more favorable prognosis.

Opioid addiction follows a relapsing and remitting course until middle age, when its relentless grip on the individual seems to abate slowly and spontaneously. Some experts have estimated 9 years as the average duration of active opioid addiction (Jaffe, 1989). Criminal activity, usually in support of addiction, is very common during periods of active use. In periods of remission, criminal activity drops off significantly. The overall death rate in opioid abusers is estimated to be as much as 20 times that of the general population. The proximate cause of death is usually overdose, use-related infections, suicide, homicide, or accidental death.

Significant psychiatric comorbidity has been observed; depression and personality disorder are diagnoses most frequently made. Polysubstance abuse is common in opioid addicts. Almost all are nicotine-addicted, and many have serious alcohol-related problems as well. Benzodiazepine use is common and probably underestimated, since it may not be specifically assayed in urine specimens. Sporadic use of cocaine and other stimulants is common, as is the use of marijuana. A few opioid addicts also use hallucinogens or toxic vapors.

The medical complications of opioid abuse are many and diverse. They stem most commonly from the following:

1. The failure to use aseptic techniques during injection.
2. The presence of particulate contaminants in the injected solution.
3. The direct pharmacological actions of the drug.

The consequences of infection are the most frequently encountered medical complications of opioid abuse. Skin abscesses, lymphadenopathy, osteomyelitis, septic emboli in the lungs, endocarditis, septicemia, glomerulonephritis, meningitis, and brain abscesses are encountered with regularity when "dirty needles" are used. A low-level immunodeficiency exists in chronic opioid addicts, causing them to be more susceptible to infectious processes such as tuberculosis, syphilis, malaria, tetanus, and hepatitis (Senay, 1983). HIV infection may result from sharing needles with an infected individual. Risk of this complication is highest in the northeastern United States, where a survey of opioid addicts in methadone treatment programs showed seropositivity in 60% of those who reported sharing needles (Jaffe, 1989). Fortunately, the percentage drops dramatically in most other parts of the country, and aggressive efforts at education of both addicts and those who treat them in clinics and elsewhere have helped slow the spread of this deadly virus.

Addicts frequently inject opioid solutions contaminated with adulterants such as talc and starch; these substances are used to increase the bulk of the illicit powder and thus to increase profits for the drug dealer. Addicts will mix the powder with water, heat it, and use cotton or a cigarette filter to block the entry of undissolved particles as the solution is drawn into the syringe. As a result, fibers enter the venous blood stream and lodge in the lungs, where conditions become favorable for the development over time of pulmonary emboli, pulmonary hypertension, and right-side heart failure. Opioid abusers are at further risk of compromised pulmonary function if they use cigarettes and marijuana, as they usually do. The antitussive effect of opioids also compromises pulmonary function, contributing to frequent pneumonia and other respiratory tract infections.

A number of lesions may occur in the central nervous system of those persons who have survived overdoses in which anoxia and coma were featured. The residual effects of such trauma include partial paralysis, parkinsonism, intellectual impairment, personality changes, peripheral neuropathy, acute transverse myelitis, and blindness.

Psychiatric complications caused by opioid dependence frequently occur most commonly in the form of depression. When this is observed during the recovery period, treatment with antidepressants and psychotherapy is indicated and frequently helpful if the individual is abstinent from illicit drug use. Some experienced clinicians have felt that doses of methadone greater than 30–40 mg per day interfere with the individual's motivational state and undermine efforts at psychotherapy.

Psychiatric comorbidity is also common. Though not necessarily caused by drug abuse, the following disorders are seen in association with opioid dependence:

1. Depression.
2. Antisocial personality disorder.
3. Anxiety disorders.
4. Other personality disorders, including paranoid, schizoid, schizotypal, histrionic, narcissistic, borderline, dependent, compulsive, passive–aggressive, and mixed.
5. Organic brain syndrome (rare).
6. Schizophrenia (very rare).

Depression may be diagnosable in as many as 60% of opioid addicts (Dackis & Gold, 1984; Khantzian & Treece, 1985; Mirin, Weiss, Michael, & Griffin, 1989; Rounsaville, Weissman, Kleber, & Wilber, 1982). It may have preceded the onset of drug abuse as chronic, episodic low-grade depression or dysthymia, and a full-blown major depressive episode may develop in the stressful and traumatic context of opioid addiction. Depression occurs more frequently in women than in men. Depression coexisting with opioid dependence is more strongly associated with a history of concomitant polydrug abuse.

Of the personality disorders, antisocial personality is the most commonly diagnosed and can be seen in as many as 55% of opioid addicts enrolled in treatment programs; the vast majority of these are men (Khantzian & Treece, 1985). It is inaccurate to assume that drug-seeking behavior learned during years of addiction is responsible for the high percentage of antisocial personalities among opioid addicts. Antisocial personality disorder can be reliably diagnosed historically in most individuals at a young age prior to the onset of opioid dependence. The relationship between opioid abuse and antisocial personality is complicated and appears to be influenced by a non-sex-linked genetic factor. When antisocial personality and opioid dependence are found together, the treatment course is frequently stormy, and the overall outcome is poor with regard to adequate length of time in treatment, relapse, criminal behavior during treatment, and ability to establish rapport with a therapist or counselor. The one exception appears to be the antisocial addict who also has a diagnosable depression. This group responds much better to treatment, on a par with the average opioid addict without significant psychiatric comorbidity (Woody, McLellan, Luborsky, & O'Brien, 1985).

Anxiety disorders, such as panic disorder, obsessive–compulsive disorder, generalized anxiety disorder, and phobia, are seen in approximately 10% of opioid addicts. This group is typically somewhat younger in age and higher in socioeconomic status, and their drug use histories are not as extensive.

Other personality disorders from DSM-III-R Axis II are regularly found coexisting with opioid abuse, but are not as significant a factor in treatment as is antisocial personality. Organic brain syndrome, and psychotic disorders such as schizophrenia, mania, and psychotic depression, are not usually seen in opioid clinic populations. The presence of both a DSM-III-R Axis I diagnosis (depression or an anxiety disorder) and an Axis II diagnosis (a personality disorder) in the same opioid-dependent individual is frequently observed; the proportion of such patients may approach 50% in clinic populations (Khantzian & Treece, 1985).

Treatment

The various nonpharmacological treatment modalities used to treat other types of substance abusers are also useful in treating opioid addicts and are discussed elsewhere in this text. The focus of this chapter is on pharmacotherapy of situations commonly found in the context of opioid abuse, including overdose, withdrawal, detoxification, and maintenance. In addition, we discuss the usefulness of blocking agents and some experimental agents currently on the horizon.

The management of opioid overdose is best accomplished in a medical facility with the availability of sophisticated expertise and technology. These can be brought to bear on the potential "worst-case scenario"—for example, opioid overdose in a pregnant female with septicemia, pulmonary edema, and coma. In addition to intensive physiological support needed in opioid overdose, the use of an opioid antagonist can be life-saving. Naloxone (Narcan) is the drug of choice because it does not further depress respiratory drive (Berger & Dunn, 1986). A regimen of 0.4 to 0.8 mg, administered intravenously several times over the course of 20 to 30 minutes, is conservative but avoids the pitfall of precipitating full-blown opioid withdrawal, which can be a greater threat than respiratory depression because of the possible occurrence of emesis, seizure, or combative delirium. If after 10 mg of naloxone there is no improvement in the patient's condition, one must question the diagnosis of opioid overdose. Other drugs may be involved, or other central nervous system processes may exist. One also must remember that the action of naloxone almost always will be shorter than the action of the opioid, necessitating close attention to the re-emergence of the opioid's physiological effects (Wilford, 1981).

The opioid withdrawal syndrome can easily be suppressed by administering any opioid with significant same-receptor activity as the drug that originally produced the addiction. However it is more useful to prevent opioid withdrawal symptoms pharmacologically with a nonaddicting drug. This approach will further the goals of detoxification and abstinence. When circumstances force addicts to treat their withdrawal symptoms without opioids, they most commonly use alcohol and/or benzodiazepines. The main disadvantage to this approach is that because of the lack of cross-tolerance between opioids and alcohol/benzodiazepines, blockade of withdrawal symptoms requires the ingestion of large amounts of these sedatives to achieve suppression, thus rendering the individual almost totally nonfunctional during the course of acute withdrawal.

Clonidine, an α-2 agonist originally marketed as an antihypertensive, represents an effective and safer alternative for the treatment of opiate withdrawal symptoms (Koob & Bloom, 1988). It can partially suppress many (but not all) elements of opioid withdrawal, so that the risk of immediate relapse is reduced (Jasinski, Johnson, & Kocher, 1985). Withdrawal symptoms less relieved by clonidine include insomnia, muscle aches, craving, lethargy, and restlessness (Charney, Sternberg, Kleber, Heninger, & Redmond, 1981). Clonidine is most effective for those motivated persons who are involved in their overall treatment program and are using small amounts of opioid (Kleber et al., 1985). Outpatients who are on less than 20 mg methadone per day and detoxifying at rates approaching 1 mg per day make ideal candidates for the adjunctive use of clonidine. These individuals can be given 0.1 to 0.3 mg up to three or four times a day throughout the withdrawal period with good effect.

Sometimes only small amounts of clonidine (on the order of 0.1 mg per day) may be useful, to be administered at the time of day that is most problematic for the patient. Clonidine is not generally useful beyond 2 weeks after the last dose of methadone (Gold, Pottash, Sweeney, & Kleber, 1980). A newly available transdermal delivery system (Catapres-TTS), which is active over a 7-day period, is useful in the outpatient setting because the indiscriminate use of large amounts of clonidine by the individual can be avoided, thus limiting the risk of adverse reactions (Spencer & Gregory, 1989). A major side effect of clonidine is hypotension, which can be profound. Lethargy is also a common side effect.

In a hospital setting, clonidine has been used in concert with abstinence and an opioid antagonist to produce tolerable withdrawal and detoxification in a short period of time (5–6 days) for persons on methadone doses of 50 mg or less; various protocols exist (Charney, Heninger, & Kleber, 1986). This treatment can be complicated by delirium and/or psychosis (Brewer, Rezae, & Bailey, 1988). The treatment involves sudden cessation of opioid ingestion, precipitation of an acute abstinence syndrome with an opioid blocker, and aggressive treatment of the withdrawal symptoms with large doses of clonidine throughout the day and benzodiazepines at night. Over the 5- to 6-day course, the clonidine and opioid blocker are tapered. Benzodiazepines are not routinely used after the second or third night. Bed rest is often necessary in the early phases of treatment. A less aggressive, but more time-consuming, approach would involve abstinence (not precipitated suddenly by an opioid blocker) and more aggressively used clonidine than could practically be used on an outpatient basis. These approaches are appropriate for those individuals who are highly motivated to become drug-free quickly in a controlled manner, for reasons related to employment or to impending incarceration.

Clonidine is of no use in maintaining abstinence after withdrawal is complete. Other agents, including lofexidine and guanabenz, may have properties that would be useful in managing opioid withdrawal, but the use of these drugs is only being investigated at the present time (Jaffe, 1989).

It is generally recognized that abrupt withdrawal from opioids is almost always followed by relapse. The risk of relapse can be lessened by following a rational plan for detoxification, using decreasing amounts of an opioid over time. In this way the withdrawal syndrome is minimized, rendering the individual more responsive to other, nonpharmacological therapies during this high-risk phase of treatment. In the United States, the usual first step toward detoxification is to switch the addicted individual to a longer-acting opioid. Methadone is the obvious choice, with a half-life of 15–25 hours in comparison to 2–3 hours for morphine, heroin, and many other commonly available opioids. In addition to methadone's pharmacological advantage, it is the only narcotic drug approved by the federal government for detoxification and maintenance treatment of opioid addiction. It is strictly controlled, and clinicians should refer to federal, state, and local regulations regarding its use. Generally speaking, for every 2.0 mg of heroin, 1.0 mg of methadone may be substituted. The same is true for 4 mg of morphine, 20 mg of meperidine, 50 mg of codeine, and 12 mg of oxycodone. Other equivalencies are available in standard pharmacology texts.

Usually, it is not possible to know how much heroin a user is actually administering in a 24-hour period, because of the impure nature of the product available on the street. Experience shows that an initial dose of 20–30 mg of methadone will block most withdrawal symptoms in moderate to heavy users who may inject from 4 to 12 or more times in 24 hours. For those who inject 2 to 3 times per day, a starting dose of 10–20 mg of methadone is usually sufficient. Methadone may be given every 24 hours, and the dose may be adjusted daily up or down by 5- to 10-mg increments, based on observable symptoms of withdrawal or intoxication. The peak plasma levels from methadone occur between 2 and 6 hours after ingestion. Over time, methadone becomes tissue-bound throughout the body, creating a buffer against significant withdrawal in those persons who occasionally miss a daily dose. This phenomena also facilitates a smooth detoxification over time as daily dosage is reduced. Stabilization on methadone can usually be accomplished with 20–50 mg daily. Detoxification may then begin.

Regulations at the various levels of government have historically mandated that detoxification be accomplished within 21 days. Unfortunately, this period of time has been too short for all but the most minimally addicted individuals, and has frequently resulted in relapse. Fortunately, the regulations are now being liberalized, largely because of recognition that HIV/AIDS is spread very rapidly among intravenous drug abusers who share needles. Changes in the regulations are intended to allow more addicts to enter and stay in treatment. As a practical matter, 30 days is the minimum amount of time required for successful detoxification, and 45 days or more may often be needed. For those individuals with long abuse histories and high doses of opioids, 6 months or more may be required. Veteran opioid users are extremely sensitive to even small reductions in their daily dose of methadone. The critical stage of detoxification occurs below 20 mg of methadone daily, and the use of clonidine is helpful in blocking withdrawal symptoms. In some individuals detoxification will be successful, but symptoms of insomnia, malaise, irritability, fatigue, gastrointestinal hypermotility, and even premature ejaculation may persist for months. Clonidine is less effective in this situation.

After detoxification, relapse prevention must be actively addressed with whatever treatment interventions are available. A pharmacological agent in the form of an opioid antagonist can be a useful adjunct in relapse prevention. A long-acting agent such as naltrexone (Trexan) is effective in blocking the euphoric effects of opioids and ultimately leads to the extinction of operantly conditioned drug-seeking behaviors. Naltrexone is given orally in the opioid-free individual three times a week in doses of 50–150 mg, and will block the effects of relatively large doses of opioids. This adjunctive therapy works best in the context of ongoing treatment and support. Its administration should be monitored over time because compliance with voluntary, unsupervised self-administration of naltrexone is notoriously poor. Length of treatment with this agent is a therapeutic issue, having mainly to do with the individual's ability to embrace a drug-free lifestyle consistently over time.

Some addicts seem unable to tolerate acute withdrawal, to succeed at controlled detoxification, or to remain drug-free. Methadone maintenance may then become the treatment of choice. Administered on a once-a-day schedule, methadone in appropriate doses will block opioid withdrawal, thus reducing compulsive drug-seeking behavior and use. The individual may then focus energy and attention on more productive behaviors. Indications for the use of methadone maintenance include the following:

1. A history of chronic high-dose opioid abuse.
2. Repeated failures at abstinence.
3. History of prior successful methadone maintenance.
4. History of drug-related criminal convictions or incarcerations.
5. Pregnancy, especially first and third trimesters.
6. HIV seropositivity.

Relative contraindications to methadone maintenance are as follows:

1. Being less than 16 years of age.
2. The expectation of incarceration within 30–45 days.
3. History of abuse of methadone maintenance, including diversion of methadone to "the street" and failure to cease illicit use despite adequate doses.

The administration of methadone, as noted earlier, is heavily regulated by federal and state governments. Very specific requirements must be met by individuals and clinics offering this service. Generally, after the individual's history and physical condition are assessed, methadone dosing is begun according to the protocol previously described in this chapter. A period of 4–10 days may be required to stabilize the patient at an appropriate dose. When stabilization has occurred, the individual's illicit drug use should cease, as evidenced by regular monitored urinalysis showing only methadone. A pitfall here is that individuals may supplement their maintenance dose with "black market" methadone. Urinalyses will not be helpful in detecting this behavior, since quantification techniques are not generally employed. Dosage requirements should not change after stabilization unless something has occurred to change the body's absorption, metabolism, distribution, or excretion of methadone. Emesis following within 20–30 minutes after the oral ingestion of methadone is an obvious example of disruption to absorption. Metabolism of methadone may be affected by the use of phenytoin and rifampin, both of which can precipitate withdrawal symptoms by reducing methadone plasma levels. Concealed or denied regular use of other opiates in addition to methadone will result in the user's asking for more methadone because the development of tolerance has outpaced current stable dosing. Abusive use of alcohol and/or benzodiazepines with methadone maintenance will also cause individuals to request more methadone, possibly because of enhanced hepatic metabolization and/or significant withdrawal symptoms from these agents that do not share cross-tolerance with methadone. Administering Antabuse with methadone is a common and highly useful therapeutic approach.

Certain individuals will report that heavy labor with much perspiration will reduce the effectiveness of methadone in a 24-hour period. This phenomenon is usually easily addressed with a small increase in dose unless the individual is not being truthful. After months or years of methadone maintenance, most individuals will be able to tolerate a slow taper of a few milligrams per week or month. For those persons who become suspicious or psychologically unstable as their dose is lowered, a "blind" detoxification schedule may be used in which the individual never knows the exact amount of methadone he or she is receiving.

Pregnancy is a special situation for which continued methadone maintenance is recommended, since any withdrawal symptoms place the fetus at risk (Finnegan, 1979). In addition, the risk of relapse to street drugs after detoxification also places the fetus at risk. Therefore, maintenance at a level of 20 mg is the safest plan. Slow detoxification down to this level can be achieved safely during the second trimester.

Other agents have been studied that may be useful in maintenance of opioid users. An experimental drug, levo-alpha acetyl methadol (LAAM), is similar to methadone but longer-acting and may be given three times per week instead of daily. It has more side effects than methadone, including some that are stimulant-like; in addition, its pharmacology is complicated, requiring the attention of a more sophisticated clinician. For these and possibly other reasons, dropout rates for LAAM exceed those for methadone in maintenance settings (Blaine, Thomas, Barnett, Whysner, & Renoult, 1981). Another agent, buprenorphine, is a mixed agonist–antagonist agent that has been shown to be acceptable to addicts, is long-acting (daily administration is sufficient), and blocks the effects of other opiates. An additional benefit is that it can be discontinued more easily than methadone because it produces less physical dependence. Unfortunately, it appears that buprenorphine cannot be substituted completely for methadone without some withdrawal symptoms appearing during the transition period (Bickel et al., 1988). Neither of these agents has compelling advantages over methadone as an agent for maintenance in opioid addiction.

Although this section has presented only pharmacotherapies for opioid addiction, it is crucial that psychosocial interventions be used to help these patients change their lifestyles. It is generally accepted that escape from drug seeking and the accompanying antisocial impulses requires a change in deeply rooted behavioral patterns. Individual and group psychotherapy may be useful in approaching this goal. The various Twelve-Step programs such as Narcotics Anonymous are also useful adjuncts to treatment and facilitate significant degrees of change. For those persons who continue to relapse in less restrictive treatment settings, a "therapeutic community" may be the appropriate next step (O'Brien & Biase, 1981). These nonhospital, community-based, 24-hour live-in programs are geared to subject the addict to continuous treatment pressure for as long as 1 or 2 years. Personal freedom is severely curtailed and community rules are rigorously enforced. Ex-addicts usually play a prominent role in the treatment process, sometimes to the exclusion of mental health professionals (Deitch & Zweben, 1981). The goal is to use nonviolent but highly confrontational tactics in the context of peer pressure, for the purpose of breaking down denial and exposing destructive attitudes and behaviors that formerly led to drug use (Rosenthal, 1989). A growth process may then occur, allowing the individual to achieve a degree of personal integrity that is un-related to the former identity of drug abuser. When successful, this type of personal transformation can lead to permanent recovery. However, this form of treatment requires a total commitment, which many opioid abusers are unable to make; thus the dropout rate is high. As with any treatment modality, selection of appropriate candidates leads to greater success.

References

American Psychiatric Association. (1987). *Diagnostic and statistical manual of mental disorders* (3rd ed., rev.). Washington, DC: Author.

Berger, P. A., & Dunn, M. J. (1986). The biology and treatment of drug abuse. In S. Arieti (Ed.-in-Chief), *American handbook of psychiatry* (Vol. 8, pp. 811–822). New York: Basic Books.

Bickel, W. K., Stitzer, M. L., Bigelow, G. E., Liebson, I. A., Jasinski, D. R., & Johnson, R. E. (1988). A clinical trial of buprenorphine: Comparison with methadone in the detoxification of heroin addicts. *Clinical Pharmacology and Therapeutics, 43,* 72–78.

Blaine, G. D., Thomas, D. B., Barnett, G., Whysner, J. A., & Renoult, P. F. (1981). Levo-alpha acetylmethadol (LAAM): Clinical utility and pharmaceutical development. In J. H. Lowinson & P. Ruiz (Eds.), *Substance abuse: Clinical problems and perspectives* (pp. 356–370). Baltimore: Williams & Wilkins.

Brewer, C., Rezae, H., & Bailey, C. (1988). Opioid withdrawal and naltrexone induction in 48–72 hours with minimal drop-out, using a modification of the naltrexone–clonidine technique. *British Journal of Psychiatry, 153,* 340–343.

Charney, D. S., Sternberg, D. E., Kleber, H. D., Heninger, G. R., & Redmond, D. E., Jr. (1981). The clinical use of clonidine in abrupt withdrawal from methadone: Effects on blood pressure and specific signs and symptoms. *Archives of General Psychiatry, 38,* 1273–1277.

Charney, D. S., Heninger, G. R., & Kleber, H. D. (1986). The combined use of clonidine and naltrexone as a rapid, safe, and effective treatment of abrupt withdrawal from methadone. *American Journal of Psychiatry, 143,* 831–837.

Dackis, C. A., & Gold, M. S. (1984). Depression in opiate addicts. In S. M. Mirin (Ed.), *Substance abuse and psychopathy* (pp. 20–40). Washington, DC: American Psychiatric Press.

Deitch, D. A., & Zweben, J. E. (1981). Synanon: a pioneering response in drug abuse treatment and a signal for caution. In J. H. Lowinson & P. Ruiz (Eds.), *Substance abuse: Clinical problems and perspectives* (pp. 289–302). Baltimore: Williams & Wilkins.

Deneau, G. A., & Mule, S. J. (1981). Pharmacology of the opiates. In J. H. Lowinson & P. Ruiz (Eds.), *Substance abuse: Clinical problems and perspectives* (pp. 129–139). Baltimore: Williams & Wilkins.

Finnegan, L. P. (Ed.). (1979). *Drug dependency in pregnancy: Clinical management of mother and child*. Rockville, MD: National Institute on Drug Abuse.

Gold, M. S., Pottash, A. C., Sweeney, D. R., & Kleber, H. D. (1980). Opiate withdrawal using clonidine. *Journal of the American Medical Association, 243*(4), 343–346.

Jaffe, J. H. (1989). Psychoactive substance use disorders. In H. I. Kaplan & B. J. Sadock (Eds.), *Comprehensive textbook of psychiatry* (5th ed., pp. 642–698). Baltimore: Williams & Wilkins.

Jasinski, D. R., Johnson, R. E., & Kocher, T. R. (1985). Clonidine in morphine withdrawal: Differential effects on signs and symptoms. *Archives of General Psychiatry, 42*, 1063–1066.

Khantzian, E. J., & Treece, C. (1985). DSM-III psychiatric diagnosis of narcotic addicts: Recent findings. *Archives of General Psychiatry, 42*, 1067–1071.

Kleber, H. D., Riordan, C. E., Rounsaville, B., Kosten, T., Charney, D., Gaspari, J., Hogan, I., & O'Connor, C. (1985). Clonidine in outpatient detoxification from methadone maintenance. *Archives of General Psychiatry, 42*, 391–394.

Koob, G. F., & Bloom, F. E. (1988). Cellular and molecular mechanisms of drug dependence. *Science, 242*, 715–723.

Lowinson, J. H., & Ruiz, P. (Eds.). (1981). *Substance abuse: Clinical problems and perspectives*. Baltimore: Williams & Wilkins.

Martin, W. R., & Jasinski, D. R. (1969). Physiological parameters of morphine dependence in men: Tolerance, early abstinence, protracted abstinence. *Journal of Psychiatric Research, 7*, 9–17.

Meyer, R. E. (Ed.). (1986). *Psychopathology and addictive disorders*. New York: Guilford Press.

Mirin, S. M., Weiss, R. D., Michael, J., & Griffin, M. L. (1989). Psychopathology in substance abusers: Diagnosis and treatment. *American Journal of Drug and Alcohol Abuse, 14*, 139–157.

O'Brein, W. B., & Biase, D. V. (1981). The therapeutic community: The family-milieu approach to recovery. In J. H. Lowinson & P. Ruiz (Eds.), *Substance abuse: Clinical problems and perspectives* (pp. 303–316). Baltimore: Williams & Wilkins.

Rosenthal, M. S. (1989). The therapeutic community: Exploring the boundaries. *British Journal of Addiction, 84*(2), 141–150.

Rounsaville, B. J., Weissman, M. M., Kleber, H., & Wilber, C. (1982). Heterogeneity of psychiatric diagnosis in treated opiate addicts. *Archives of General Psychiatry, 39*, 161–166.

Senay, E. C. (1983). *Substance abuse disorders in clinical practice*. Littleton, MA: John Wright/PSG.

Spencer, L., & Gregory, M., (1989). Clonidine transdermal patches for use in outpatient opiate withdrawal. *Journal of Substance Abuse, 6*, 113–117.

Wilford, B. B. (1981). *Drug abuse for the primary care physician*. Chicago: American Medical Association.

Wood, G. E., McLellan, A. T., Luborsky, L., & O'Brien, C. P. (1985). Sociopathy and psychotherapy outcome. *Archives of General Psychiatry, 42*, 1081–1086.

6

Cocaine

LORI D. KARAN
DEBORAH L. HALLER
SIDNEY H. SCHNOLL

History

With all of the current publicity about cocaine use, many believe that it is a modern phenomenon. However, the use of cocaine dates back to the beginnings of recorded history in the Andean region of South America. Although the Incas had no written history, there are depictions of coca use in drawings on pottery and on buildings. Cocaine was initially used by the priests of the Incan civilization and gradually became used by the general population. The leaves of the coca plant were chewed, and coca is still used in this form by the Indians in the Andes Mountains. The use of coca is so prevalent in that region that the distance a person can travel in the time it takes to chew a wad of coca leaves is called a *cocada*.

When the Spanish arrived in South America, they recognized the widespread use of coca and tried to control the native populations by controlling the coca leaves. They brought the leaves back to Europe, and in the mid-1800s, cocaine was extracted from coca leaves by Gaedecki. The use of coca leaves and cocaine in patent medicines, wines, and other beverages was soon widespread; several such preparations, particularly Coca-Cola, became extremely popular.

Sigmund Freud performed some of the earliest experiments with cocaine and postulated a large number of potential uses for the drug. Kohler and Halstead experimented with the drug as a local anesthetic. Because of the epidemic use of cocaine and coca-containing beverages during this period, large numbers of users became dependent on cocaine. Knowledge of the problems associated with cocaine use is clearly demonstrated in Sir Arthur Conan Doyle's stories about Sherlock Holmes. In the stories, Holmes uses cocaine and develops paranoia secondary to its use.

A reduction in cocaine use occurred in the United States following the passage of the Pure Food and Drug Act. Under the regulations of the Act, cocaine became available only by prescription and was characterized as a narcotic drug. Despite this, there was a resurgence of cocaine use during the 1920s, with several popular novels and songs written about the effects of cocaine and the problems associated with its use. The advent of Prohibition and the Depression resulted in a decrease in cocaine use,

The latest resurgence of cocaine use occurred in the late 1970s. Early in this recent epidemic, cocaine's availability was limited and the price was high, with a gram of cocaine costing between $100 and $120 on the street and the purity of that cocaine running approximately 25–30%. Because of the high price, cocaine was considered to be a drug of the wealthy and was called the "champagne" of drugs. There was increasing use among young, upwardly mobile middle-class people, who looked at cocaine as an enhancement of their lifestyle. As more information became available regarding the negative consequences of cocaine use, and middle-class users began to see friends develop problems associated with their cocaine use, we have seen a gradual reduction in the recreational use of cocaine by the middle class. However, because of cocaine's easy availability, its rapidly decreasing cost, and the well-developed distribution networks in the inner city, the problem of cocaine use among lower socioeconomic groups has continued to climb at an alarming rate. Unfortunately, this has been associated with addicted persons' having an earlier onset of use, decreased maturation, and increased psychiatric comorbidity. Cocaine is associated with getting rich quickly and having status, power, and control within the community. The current cocaine epidemic has had a substantial impact on the economic framework of the inner city, and is inexorably linked to the increasing rates of violence there.

Ethnography

Data from the National Household Survey on Drug Abuse (Adams, Blanken, Ferguson, & Kopstein, 1989) show that past-year users of cocaine decreased from 12 million in 1985 to 8 million in 1988 and that past-month users of cocaine decreased from 5.8 million people in 1985 to 2.9 million people in 1988. In 1988, among youths 12 to 17 years of age, the past-year prevalence of cocaine use was highest for Hispanics (4%), as compared with that of whites (3%) and blacks (1%). The rates among young adults aged 18 to 25 were 13% for Hispanics, 13% for whites, and 8% for blacks; the rates among young adults aged 26 to 34 were 9% for blacks, 8% for Hispanics, and 8% for whites. Although lifetime prevalence of cocaine remained stable for blacks and whites between 1985 and 1988, an increase from 7% to 11% occurred among Hispanics.

Despite the decreasing numbers of cocaine users, information collected from the Drug Abuse Warning Network (DAWN; National Institute on Drug Abuse [NIDA], 1989) shows that the number of hospital emergencies associated with the use of cocaine increased from 8,831 in 1984 to 46,020 in 1988, and that the number of cocaine-related deaths increased from 628 in 1984 to 1,589 (provisional data) in 1988. Crack (freebase cocaine that can be smoked) may be responsible for this trend, since its strength and nearly immediate onset of action cause increased toxicity.

In 1987, more than one out of every five homicide victims in the United States were found to have evidence of recent cocaine use in their blood or body tissues. In Los Angeles County, persons dying with evidence of recent cocaine use were 736, 818, and 1,160 in 1986, 1987, and 1988, respectively. Robert Budd (1989) analyzed the causes of death in the first 114 Los Angeles County coroner's cases with positive drug toxicology for cocaine in the period from January 1, 1988, to February 24, 1988. He found that 70 (61.4%) of these persons died a violent death, with over 68% of these deaths resulting from shootings and stabbings. Nonviolent deaths included overdose (73%), illness (20.5%), and stillbirth (6.8%). Although blacks compose only 15% of the Los Angeles County population, they were overrepresented in both violent (36%) and nonviolent (18%) deaths. Interestingly, over 50% of the violent-death victims had used both alcohol and cocaine just prior to their death, while over 50% of the nonviolent-death victims used cocaine in combination with at least one drug other than alcohol. Traffic accident victims had the lowest average levels of cocaine (0.62 ± 0.59 μg/ml) and the least amount of alcohol and other drugs in their systems prior to death, while the victims of three falls, two drownings, and one fire had the highest cocaine levels (2.29 ± 2.55 μg/ml).

Preparation and Routes of Administration

Cocaine is a benzoylmethylecgonine. It is an ester of benzoic acid and a nitrogen-containing base. Cocaine occurs naturally in the leaves of *Erythroxylon coca* and other species of *Erythroxylon* indigenous to Peru, Bolivia, Java, and Colombia. Andean natives who chew coca leaves experience diminished hunger and fatigue and an improved sense of well-being without evidence of chronic toxicity and dependence. However, other preparations and routes of administration of cocaine have a more rapid onset of action and are more problematic.

Cocaine hydrochloride is frequently snorted (insufflation) or "tooted" in "lines" or "rails" about $1\frac{1}{2}$ to 2 inches long and an eighth of an inch thick. Users pour the powdered cocaine onto a hard surface such as a mirror, glass, or slab of marble, and arrange it into lines with a razor blade, knife, or credit card. One line is snorted into each nostril via a rolled bill, straw, or miniature coke spoon, or a specially grown fingernail. From a street purchase of a single gram of cocaine about 30 lines can be made, each averaging 10 to 35 mg of powder. The actual amount of cocaine hydrochloride present in each line depends upon the purity of the drug. The bioavailability of intranasal cocaine is about 60%. Peak plasma levels occur over a range of 30 to 120 minutes (Barnett, Hawks, & Resnick, 1981). Intranasal cocaine limits its own absorption by causing vasoconstriction of the nasal mucous membranes. Cocaine is a topical anesthetic and will cause numbness of the nose during snorting. Nasal congestion with stuffiness and sneezing may occur after snorting cocaine, because of its vasoconstrictive properties as well as the contaminants in the preparation. Users may flush out the inside of the nose with a salt–water mixture after a round of snorting. Decongestants and antihistamines are also commonly employed to relieve these symptoms.

Cocaine can be injected intravenously. This is called "shooting" or "mainlining." The cocaine is mixed in a spoon or bottle cap with water to form a solution. Unlike heroin, cocaine hydrochloride may not need to be heated over a candle to enter solution. "Kicking" or "booting" refers to drawing blood from the vein back into the syringe and reinjecting it with each cocaine mixture. This process is felt by users to produce a heightened drug sensation or "rush," despite the lack of a pharmokinetic basis for this. Following intravenous administration, peak plasma levels are achieved almost instantaneously.

The smoking of coca paste, popularly called "pasta" or "bazooka," is prevalent in South America and also occurs in the United States. The paste is an intermediate product in the processing of cocaine hydrochloride. This results in a grey-white or dull brown powder with a slightly sweet smell, which is 40–85% cocaine sulfate.

Freebase cocaine is obtained by extracting cocaine hydrochloride with an alkali such as buffered ammonia, and then mixing it with a solvent, which is usually ether. The solvent fraction is separated and volatilized, leaving very small amounts of residual freebase material. Cocaine freebase is most often smoked in a water pipe with a fine stainless steel screen upon which the cocaine is vaporized. Cigarettes are rarely used because only a small amount of cigarette smoke actually enters the lungs, wasting valuable cocaine. Cocaine hydrochloride is soluble in water and has a melting point of 195°C. In contrast, cocaine freebase is lipid-soluble and has a melting point of 98°C. Thus, cocaine freebase vaporizes and readily crosses the blood–lung barrier (DePetrillo, 1985). This results in nearly immediate peak plasma levels, which are achieved at a rate similar to that of injecting cocaine hydrochloride.

"Crack" or "rock" is a prepackaged, ready-to-use form of freebase cocaine that is inexpensive and has been widely available on the streets in many American cities since 1985. The processing does not necessarily remove the impurities and adulterants in the cocaine, nor the baking soda that is now presently used in the preparation. "Crack" is named for the crackling sound heard when the mixture is heated, and "rock" describes its crystalline appearance. The drug is sold in vials or foil packets, which are then smoked in a pipe. Its rapid onset of action and rapid dissipation are problematic, because the user wants to repeat the effects of the intense but short-lived high. The cost of a 300-mg dose on the street has been reported to be as low as $5 to $10.

In America, popular street names for cocaine include "blow," "flake," "girl," "white lady," "nose candy," "paradise," and "snow." Adulterants commonly found in illicitly purchased cocaine include inert substances such as talc, flour, cornstarch, and various sugars (lactose, inositol, sucrose, maltose, and mannitol). Local anesthetics such as procaine, lidocaine, tetracaine, and benzocaine may be added to replace or enhance the local anesthetic effect of cocaine. Cheaper stimulants, including amphetamines, caffeine, methylphenidate, ergotamine, aminophylline, and strychnine ("death hit"), may be added to the preparation. Quinine may be added for taste, and other compounds such as thiamine, tyramine, sodium carbonate, magnesium silicate, magnesium sulfate, salicylamide, and arsenic (Lombard, Levin, & Weiner, 1989) may be found. Contaminants may also include bacteria, fungi, and viruses (Goldfrank, Lewin, & Weisman, 1981).

As the efforts to control the importation and sale of cocaine have increased, there has been a rise in the availability of domestically produced methamphetamine, or "ice." This is made in clandestine laboratories and is full of impurities. Users like the fact that methamphetamine can be taken orally, injected, or smoked. It has a duration of action of 12 hours, in contrast to the 20- to 120-minute duration of action of cocaine.

Users frequently take cocaine in combination with other drugs, citing the need to take the edge off the abrupt effects and "crash" from cocaine. Intravenous injection of heroin and cocaine mixed together is called "speedballing," and ingesting alcohol in conjunction with taking cocaine may be referred to as having "liquid lady." Any drug combination is possible; other opioids, depressants, hallucinogens, phencyclidine (PCP), and marijuana are frequently used in conjunction with cocaine.

Pharmacokinetics and Assays

Cocaine is metabolized by both microsomal enzymes in the liver and serum cholinesterase. It is hydrolyzed to form ecgonine methyl ester, and cleavage of the methyl ester group yields benzoylecgonine. These two inactive metabolites compose about 75–90% of cocaine's elimination products in the urine (Jatlow, 1988). Liver disease or a decrease in cholinesterase activity (e.g., as a result of genetic inheritance, some carcinomas, or exposure to anticholinesterase drugs) is postulated to result in increased toxicity at lower doses. About 1–5% of cocaine is eliminated in the urine unchanged. N-Demethylation of cocaine in hepatic microsomes produces norcocaine, the only pharmacologically known active metabolite of cocaine. This may be important in the fetal metabolism of cocaine. Because of its immature esterase system, the human fetus may form decreased benzoylecgonine and increased norcocaine. Norcocaine is water-soluble and less able to cross back through the placenta. Thus, the fetus, who continuously swallows amniotic fluid, is hypothesized to experience prolonged effects of cocaine (Chasnoff, 1988).

The enzyme multiplied immunoassay test (EMIT) uses antibodies to detect benzoylecgonine in the urine. This metabolite can be detected in urine specimens as early as 4 hours and as long as 48 hours after cocaine inhalation (Quandt, Sommi, Pipkin, & McCallum, 1988), and for longer periods of time in pregnant women. Infants born to mothers who had used intranasal cocaine just prior to delivery excreted unchanged cocaine for 12 to 24 hours and benzoylecgonine for over 5 days after delivery (Chasnoff & Schnoll, 1987).

There are relatively few compounds that cross-react with the EMIT's benzoyl-ecgonine-specific antibodies, and therefore few false-positive urine tests occur. Blood toxicology can be performed, but its utility in screening for prior cocaine use is limited by its high cost and the rapid disappearance of active cocaine from the bloodstream. In the future, it may be possible to develop a saliva test for cocaine. Analysis of saliva extracts by gas chromatography and mass spectrometry shows that saliva levels parallel plasma cocaine levels (Thompson, Yousefnejod, Kumor, Sherer, & Cone, 1987).

Hair analysis for benzoylecgonine may have specific forensic and therapeutic uses, such as in determining gestational cocaine exposure in infants less than 2 months of age (Graham, Gideon, Klein, Schneiderman, & Greenwald, 1989). Hair analysis detects long-term rather than recent exposure to cocaine. However, relatively complex laboratory methods, in addition to false-positive and false-negative results due to the assay itself, confounding hair preparations, and environmental hazards, may limit the use of this biotechnology (Bailey, 1989).

Neurotransmitters and Behavioral Pharmacology

Cocaine is both a stimulant of the central nervous system and a local anesthetic. Cocaine facilitates the effects of dopamine, norepinephrine, and serotonin on autoinhibitory receptors to inhibit the spontaneous firing of neurons in the ventral tegmental area, the locus coeruleus, and the dorsal raphe, respectively (Lakoski & Cunningham, 1988). Cocaine inhibits neuronal uptake of dopamine, norepinephrine, and serotonin. Its potent reinforcing qualities are felt to be closely linked to dopamine, the neural substrate for reward. In animal experiments, the binding of a drug to the dopamine uptake site correlated with continued drug self-administration, whereas there was little correlation with the ability of a drug to inhibit the uptake of serotonin or norepinephrine (Kuhar, Ritz, & Sharkey, 1988). Both the nucleus accumbens and the medial prefrontal cortex receive dopamine projections from the ventral tegmental area and may be important areas in drug reinforcement and reward. Animals, when allowed to freely self-administer cocaine, rapidly escalate their doses and prefer taking cocaine to meeting their biological and psychological needs. Dose escalation with cocaine occurs more rapidly, resulting in death of the animal, than does dose escalation with amphetamines or heroin (Johanson, Balster, & Bonese, 1976). It is not yet known how each biochemical action of cocaine corresponds to the components of behavioral processes such as drug reinforcement and reward. Cocaine's actions may also involve a variety of peptides and transmitter systems in ways that remain undetermined.

Local anesthetics induce unique patterns of spindling in olfactory and limbic brain regions. One hypothesis is that this may initially contribute to the euphoric effects of cocaine, but that it may later (following pharmacologically induced kindling) lead to adverse effects, including decreased seizure threshold and panic attacks (Post & Weiss, 1988). Although the local anesthetic properties of cocaine would be expected to make it an antiarrhythmic drug, both its effects upon the central nervous system (increased sympathetic tone) and the ability of cocaine to potentiate the effects of norepinephrine released at synapses are arrhythmogenic (Wilkerson, 1988). Further research is needed to understand cocaine's local anesthetic actions upon the central nervous system and upon the heart.

Clinical Features

Intoxication/Overdose

With intoxication, cocaine blocks monamine neuronal reuptake, initially leading to increased dopamine and norepinephrine availability at receptor sites. Acute dopaminergic stimulation of the endogenous pleasure center results in euphoria, increased energy and libido, decreased appetite, hyperalertness, and increased self-confidence when small initial doses of cocaine are taken. Exaggerated responses such as grandiosity, impulsivity, hyperawareness of the environment, and hypersexuality may also occur. The acute noradrenergic effects of small doses of cocaine include a mild elevation of pulse and blood pressure. Insomnia results both from increased dopamine and norepinephrine concentrations and from decreased serotonin synthesis and turnover.

Higher doses of cocaine are accompanied by increasing toxicity. Not only is there intensification of the "high," but anxiety, agitation, irritability, confusion, paranoia, and hallucinations may also occur. Sympathomimetic effects include dizziness, tremor, hyperreflexia, hyperpyrexia, mydriasis, diaphoresis, tachypnea, tachycardia, and hypertension. These symptoms can be accompanied by a sense of impending doom, and they may have important ramifications in overdose situations. Overdose complications may become manifest as muscle twitching, rhabdomyolysis, convulsions, cerebral infarction and hemorrhage, cardiac ischemia and arrhythmias, and respiratory failure. Acute intoxication with cocaine is more frequently characterized by convulsions and cardiac arrhythmias than intoxication with other amphetamines, possibly because of cocaine's lack of tolerance to these effects and its local anesthetic qualities. Death may be caused by peripheral autonomic toxicity and/or paralysis of the medullary cardiorespiratory centers (Gay, 1982).

Chronic Use

In contrast to acute cocaine intoxication, chronic cocaine administration is believed to result in neurotransmitter depletion. This is evidenced by a compensatory increase in postsynaptic receptor sensitivity for dopamine and norepinephrine, increased tyrosine hydroxylase activity (a major enzyme in norepinephrine and dopamine synthesis), and hyperprolactinemia. These are expected results for a negative feedback system. Clinical features of chronic cocaine use include depression, fatigue, poor concentration, loss of self-esteem, decreased libido, mild parkinsonian features (myoclonus, tremor, brady-kinesis), paranoia, and insomnia. Tolerance to the stimulant effects of cocaine, particularly the anorexic effects, develops rapidly. However, repeated phasic use of low-dose cocaine can lead to enhanced sensitivity and potentiation of motor activity, including exaggerated "startle" reactions, dyskinesias, and postural abnormalities. Increased stereotypical behavior and a toxic psychosis can occur after repeated cocaine use (Jaffe, 1985).

The elimination half-life of cocaine is under 1 hour by the intravenous route and just over 1 hour by the intranasal route. The physiological and subjective effects of cocaine correlate well with plasma levels (Javaid, Fisch-man, Schuster, Dekirmenjian, & Davis, 1978), although with repeated use pharmacodynamic tachyphylaxis does occur. The cocaine euphoria is only of short duration, with a 10- to 20-second "rush" followed by 15 to 20 minutes of a lower level of euphoria and the subsequent onset of irritability and craving. Cocaine users who try to maintain the euphoric state readminister the drug frequently until their supply disappears. Cocaine binges average 12 hours, but can last as long as 7 consecutive days (Gawin & Kleber, 1985).

Withdrawal

A withdrawal syndrome, often referred to as the "crash," has been demon-strated; it consists of strong craving, electroencephalographic (EEG) abnor-malities, depression, alterations in sleep patterns, hypersomnolence, and hy-perphagia (Jones, 1984). However, because abrupt discontinuation of cocaine does not cause any major physiological sequelae, cocaine is stopped and not tapered off or replaced by a cross-tolerant drug during medically supervised withdrawal.

Following the resolution of intoxication and acute withdrawal symptoms, there is a 1- to 10-week period of chronic dysphoria, anergia, and anhedonia. Relapses frequently occur because the memory of cocaine euphoria is quite compelling in contrast to a bleak background of intense boredom. If patients can remain abstinent from illicit mood-altering drugs during this period of time, the dysphoria gradually improves. Thereafter, intense cocaine craving is replaced by episodic craving, which is frequently triggered by environmentally conditioned cues during an indefinite extinction phase.

Abuse and Addiction

The NIDA has estimated that of 30 million Americans who have tried cocaine intranasally, 80% have not become regular users and 95% do not develop compulsive use or addiction (Gawin & Ellinwood, 1988). No one has yet identified a set of characteristics that will predict whether or not a given recreational cocaine user will become chemically dependent. Abusers commonly report that their controlled use shifted to compulsive use either when they attained increased access to cocaine and escalated their dosage, or when they switched to a more rapid route of administration, such as from intranasal administration to intravenous injection or smoking freebase or crack (Gawin & Kleber, 1985).

With recreational use, the cocaine user's initial experience of elation and heightened energy, with increased sexuality and self-esteem, appears to be free of negative consequences. Abusers may experience occasional problems associated with their drug use. Because cocaine use in the United States is illegal, recreational users can be considered abusers. Persons addicted to cocaine, however, have a compulsion to use this drug despite disastrous consequences. In search of the illusive "high," increased doses are taken with more rapid routes of administration and increased frequency. In comparison to daily use, which is common with alcohol and opiate dependence, binge use is more frequent with cocaine dependence. With chronic and increased use there is increased drug toxicity, dysphoria, and depression. The addict has irresistible cravings for cocaine and focuses on pharmacologically based cocaine euphoria, despite progressive inability to attain this state and adverse physical, psychological, and social sequelae. Loved ones are neglected; responsibility becomes immaterial; financial hardships occur; and nourishment, sleep, and health care are ignored. It is lucky that most addicts, unlike most animal models, deplete their cocaine supplies or are confronted by the harsh reality of their losses before death ensues.

Psychiatric Comorbidity and Sequelae

Patients with concomitant psychiatric and substance abuse diagnoses constitute up to 50% of psychiatric populations and up to 80% of addict populations (Crowley, Chesluk, Dilts, & Hart, 1974; Hall, Popkin, DeVaul, & Stickney, 1977; Khantzian & Treece, 1985; Rounsaville, Weissman, Crits-Christoph, Wilber, & Kleber, 1982). Mood and anxiety disorders are the most common concurrent Axis I disorders found in substance abusers (Rounsaville et al., 1982), and Khantzian and Treece (1985) have documented a 65% rate of Axis II personality disorders in three independent samples of narcotic addicts.

It has previously been reported that as few as 10% of cocaine abusers have diagnosable psychiatric disorders (U.S. Department of Health and Human Services, 1987; Smith, 1984). However, as the demographics of cocaine continue to shift, it is likely that the clinical picture of those persons who abuse cocaine is also being altered. Weiss, Mirin, Michael, and Sollogub (1986), studying inpatients, and Gawin and Kleber (1986), studying outpatients, both found that 50% met criteria for the diagnosis of mood disorder. It is known that the subgroup of cocaine users with attention deficit disorder (ADD) is overrepresented in the treatment population (Gawin & Kleber, 1985, 1986; Weiss et al., 1986). Weiss et al. (1986) also noted in their sample of 30 chronic cocaine abusers that 27%, 23%, 17%, and 3% met *Diagnostic and Statistical Manual of Mental Disorders,* third edition (DSM-III) criteria for borderline, narcissistic, histrionic, and antisocial personality disorders, respectively. There is a need for further research on the prevalence of other psychiatric diagnoses, including compulsive disorders, among cocaine-dependent persons.

Distinguishing primary from secondary diagnoses is important, both in determining the proper pharmacological and psychotherapeutic interventions for a given patient and in determining the patient's long-term prognosis. Although most of the work in this area to date has involved opiate- and alcohol-dependent subjects, these concepts would intuitively appear to apply to cocaine abusers as well. Schuckit (1985), in his work with alcoholics, argues that the antisocial behavior predating the onset of heavy drinking differs from the antisocial behavior occurring within the context of addiction. Similarly, symptoms of ADD in cocaine-dependent individuals, which in fact date from early childhood, are indicative of an independent disorder. The temporal relationships between onset of drug use, period(s) of drug abstinence, and psychiatric symptoms are key in determining whether or not a psychiatric disorder is independent of drug use. Since cocaine intoxication and withdrawal can cause various psychiatric disturbances, a careful history and psychiatric assessment need to be completed after the period of acute withdrawal.

Although an Axis I substance abuse disorder and additional Axis I or Axis II diagnoses may be "independent" of one another, this does not mean that they are unrelated. It is frequently the case that the drug use represents an attempt at management of pre-existing psychiatric symptoms. This idea that the patient has serendipitously learned that a certain drug (or class of drugs) will alleviate psychiatric symptoms and therefore uses it to this end is termed the "self-medication hypothesis." Khantzian (1985) argues that addicts do not select their drug of choice on a random basis. Rather, they demonstrate preference for various substances based on their pharmacological action. More specifically, he believes that the appeal of cocaine lies in its ability to relieve feelings of depression, hypomania, and hyperactivity. This theoretical concept coincides with the previously noted finding that as many as half of all cocaine abusers meet criteria for a diagnosis of depressive disorder. With ADD, patients often report the paradoxical reaction of being calmed by stimulants. Interestingly, there are multiple reports of stimulant-abusing patients who have discontinued use of illicit drugs when properly medicated (Khantzian, Gawin, Kleber, & Riordan, 1984; Weiss & Mirin, 1986). It would thus appear that some psychiatric disorders may indirectly contribute to, or predispose an individual to, chronic cocaine use and dependence.

The self-medication view emerged from the work of a number of modern-day psychoanalytic theorists. Early on, Milkman and Frosch (1973) suggested that drug of choice is related to "defensive style." Their findings supported the hypothesis that opiate users prefer the calming effects of narcotics and use them to bolster weak defenses, whereas amphetamine users utiltize the stimulation provided by the drug to increase their sense of self-worth and to support a confrontive, interactive style with the environment. Similarly, Wieder and Kaplan (1969) noted that stimulants increase feelings of self-esteem, assertiveness, and frustration tolerance. Wurmser (1974) suggested that stimulants allow the addict to cope better with feelings of boredom and emptiness. In sum, this school of thought views stimulants as a "chemical defense" for individuals with inherently weak ego defenses. The drugs help them to alleviate overwhelming and negative affective states.

It also needs to be recognized that addicts' lifestyle and social setting are important in determining their drug of choice, the dosage they use, and even the route by which they administer that drug. Substance abusers have switched their primary drug of preference and pattern of drug use over time, according to changes in the popularity, economics, availability, and perceptions of given drugs, as well as alterations in the drug paraphernalia industry (Siegel, 1985). Finally, some addicted persons have emotional and behavioral difficulties that result from drug taking and resolve with abstinence and a program of recovery. Clearly, there are multiple subgroups of cocaine addicts: some who use stimulants to experience euphoria; others who wish to escape dysphoria; some who are influenced by their peers and social setting; and still others who are compensating for ego deficits (Haller, Karan, & Schnoll, 1990).

When comorbidity is a factor, primary versus secondary diagnostic distinctions must be made. The differential diagnosis of primary or secondary depression, and whether or not there is coexisting residual ADD, are particularly important when evaluating stimulant abusers. Depression that predates drug use or persists beyond the 1 to 2 weeks characteristic of cocaine withdrawal may indicate a primary depressive disorder. Also, if a cocaine abuser becomes acutely depressed or suicidal after ingesting only very small amounts of the drug, a primary depressive disorder (Kosten, Rounsaville, & Kleber, 1987) may be indicated. In order for ADD (or attention-deficit hyperactivity disorder, as it is now called) to be formally diagnosed, there must be evidence of symptomatology prior to age 7 (American Psychiatric Association, 1987). Thus, while cocaine users may present with many of the symptoms of ADD, the date of onset is again critical in making this differential diagnosis. Collateral reports from relatives, along with school reports, frequently aid in making this distinction. Kosten and Kleber (1988) note that, in general, there is an inverse relationship between the actual amount of drug being used and the presence of underlying psychopathology for those seeking treatment. They emphasize that, in addition to the route and amount of drug use, psychiatric status should also be taken into consideration in determining the intensity of treatment needed for a given individual.

It is interesting to note that recent studies are beginning to identify male–female differences in relation to the issue of comorbidity in cocaine users

(Griffin, Weiss, Mirin, & Lange, 1989). The data suggest that men who are hospitalized for cocaine abuse use drugs as part of a larger pattern of social behavior and that they tend to have higher rates of antisocial personality disorder. Their female counterparts, by contrast, are much more likely to have diagnoses of major depression. These results parallel those previously reported for alcoholic men and women by Hesselbrock, Meyer, and Keener (1985).

Cocaine may also exacerbate known psychiatric disorders. Schizophrenics are more susceptible to relapse if they abuse cocaine, and persons with panic disorder may have attacks of increased frequency and intensity as a result of their cocaine use (Estroff & Gold, 1986).

In addition, cocaine may cause isolated psychiatric symptoms. Bruxism, picking at the face and body, and other stereotypical or repetitious behaviors may occur. Cocaine hallucinosis may include visual, tactile, auditory, and olfactory hallucinations, along with delusions. Cocaine users commonly perceive "cocaine bugs" in their skin and visual "snow lights" (Jaffe, 1985). In less severe cases, the users are aware that the hallucinations and delusions are not real. In more severe cases, individuals may show a full-blown toxic psychosis with extreme paranoia, hypervigilance, and ideas of persecution. This can potentially lead to unusual aggressiveness, damaged property, and homicidal or suicidal behavior. Luckily, these effects are often limited to the time of cocaine intoxication.

Another important differential diagnosis is the distinction between cocaine addiction and human immunodeficiency virus (HIV) infection, because these diseases may present with similar psychiatric symptoms. Depression, impaired memory, agitation, panic attacks, anorexia, seizures, impaired concentration, delusional thinking, and hallucinations may occur with either illness (Shaffer & Costikyan, 1988); other historical, physical, and laboratory data are required for distinction.

Medical Complications

Direct Results of Cocaine Use

Medical consequences of acute and chronic cocaine abuse may be categorized as those caused directly by cocaine, those caused by adulterants, and those related to the route of administration. An increasing number of cases relating cardiovascular toxicity to cocaine use and withdrawal are being reported. Cocaine may decrease coronary flow during a period of increased oxygen demand. There have been reports of cocaine-induced coronary artery vasoconstriction during both cocaine intoxication and withdrawal. In one study (Lange et al., 1989), persons undergoing cardiac catheterization for the evaluation of chest pain were given intranasal cocaine (2 mg/kg body weight). Although no patient had chest pain or electrocardiographic (EKG) evidence of myocardial ischemia, the heart rate and arterial pressure rose, the coronary sinus blood flow fell, and the diameter of the left coronary artery decreased by 8–12% after the application of cocaine. These values returned to baseline after administration of phentolamine, an α-adrenergic blocking agent. Another study (Nademanee et al., 1989) related S-T elevation upon Holter monitoring to cocaine withdrawal. Eight of 21 consecutive male patients admitted to a 28-day inpatient treatment program for cocaine addicton had a total of 45 episodes of ST elevation during the first several weeks of their withdrawal. Eighty-seven percent of these episodes of ST elevation were not accompanied by chest pain, and the mean duration of each episode was 57 ± 77 minutes. It is possible that a deficiency of dopamine may cause coronary vasoconstriction and release norepinephrine at the presynaptic junction. Alternatively, cocaine may affect vascular smooth muscle tone by affecting calcium channels. In addition, procoagulant effects of combined protein C and antithrombin III depletion have been found in a person with cocaine-related arterial thromboses (Chokshi, Miller, Rongione, & Isner, 1989). Singly or in combination, these factors may lead to vasospasm and myocardial ischemia.

Cocaine is also arrhythmogenic. Sinus tachycardia, ventricular premature contractions, ventricular tachycardia, and fibrillation and asystole may occur as results of the direct effect of cocaine, its effects on catecholamines, or myocardial ischemia. Propranolol, amitriptyline, lidocaine, and some calcium channel blockers have all been recommended for treatment of ventricular arrhythmias associated with cocaine use (Cregler & Mark, 1986; Kunkel, 1986). A recent study of massive cocaine overdosage in mice showed decreased mortality after β-adrenergic blockade with propranolol. The mechanism is not yet explained; propranolol, unlike its effect on other neurogenic edemas, did not alter the increased amount of lung water and transudative ascites present (Robin, Wong, & Ptashne, 1989).

Central nervous system manifestations of cocaine abuse include seizures, status epilepticus, cerebral hemorrhage, cerebral vascular accidents, and transient ischemic attacks. Cocaine may produce hyperpyrexia through its direct effect on thermoregulatory centers. Depression of the medullary centers may result in respiratory paralysis, and sudden death may be caused by respiratory arrest, myocardial infarction or arrhythmia, or status epilepticus (Cregler & Mark, 1986). Migraine-like headaches have been associated with cocaine withdrawal and may be linked to serotonin disregulation (Satel & Gawin, 1989).

Rhabdomyolysis is a complication of cocaine use. When it is accompanied by acute renal failure, severe liver dysfunction, and disseminated intravascular coagulation, the fatality rate is high (Rogh, Alarcon, Fernandez, Preston, & Bourgoignie, 1988).

Given cocaine's widespread use, the relatively low frequency of cocaine-induced morbidity is surprising. Predictors of these medical sequelae have not yet been ascertained. It is possible that low cholinesterase activity and/or liver disease can impede the metabolism of cocaine and result in increased toxicity at lower cocaine doses. Pre-existing conditions such as coronary artery disease, seizures, and hypertension will also place a person at higher risk of medical complications.

Difficulties associated with chronic cocaine use include weight loss, dehydration, nutritional deficiencies (particularly of vitamin B_6, vitamin C, and thiamine), and endocrine abnormalities. Neglect of self-care may be evident, including multiple dental caries and periodontitis exacerbated by bruxism. Addicts may medicate their pain with cocaine or other mood-altering drugs and seek medical attention only after prolonged existence of their problem(s).

Results of Adulterants and Routes of Administration

Adulterants may play a role in the development of medical complications. Local anesthetics and stimulants may increase cocaine's inherent toxicity by increasing the risk of hypertension and cardiovascular complications. Sugars, though relatively benign, may encourage development of bacteria that becomes problematic when injected intravenously.

Other complications of cocaine may result from the route of administration of this drug. Intestinal ischemia caused by vasoconstriction and reduced blood flow in the mesenteric vasculature from catecholamine stimulation of α receptors has been reported after oral cocaine ingestion (Texter, Chou, Merrill, Laureton, & Frohlich, 1964). A 58% mortality rate has occurred in smugglers or "body packers" of cocaine whose packets have ruptured (McCarron & Wood, 1983). This problem is also seen in persons who swallow their cocaine stores to escape police, either because an actual "bust" is occurring or because they are paranoid about this potential. Depending upon the packaging material, partially radiopaque material or gas halos can be seen on abdominal roentgenography. In recent years, professional smugglers have been using more durable packages with multiple layers, instead of condoms and plastic food wrap. Treatment consists of activated charcoal and sorbitol to absorb released cocaine and to facilitate expulsion (Buchanan, 1988). Nonstimulant laxatives are used to avoid compromising the integrity of the packets. Endoscopic removal can sometimes be performed in those whose packets have been recently swallowed. Surgical removal of packets lower in the intestine should be reserved for cases of gastrointestinal obstruction or serious intoxication. The patient needs to be monitored until all packets are expelled.

Complications of intranasal administration include loss of sense of smell, atrophy and inflammation of the nasal mucosa, necrosis, and perforation of the nasal septum. Snorting cocaine may anesthetize and paralyze the pharynx and larynx, not only causing hoarseness but predisposing the person to aspiration pneumonia (Estroff & Gold, 1986). There is a recent report of osteolytic sinusitis with optic disc swelling, optic atrophy, and visual field defects (Newman, Diloreto, Ho, Klein, & Birnbaum, 1988).

Pneumomediastinum and cervical emphysema have been reported after the smoking of freebase cocaine, due to alveolar rupture with prolonged deep inspiration and Valsalva's maneuver (Aroesty, Stanley, & Crockett, 1986). Other respiratory complications of inhaling or smoking freebase cocaine include abnormal reductions in carbon-monoxide-diffusing capacity (Itkonen, Schnoll, & Glassroth, 1984), granulomatous pneumonitis (Cooper, Bai, Heyderman, & Lorrin, 1983), and pulmonary edema (Alfred & Ewer, 1981). Inhalation of hot cocaine vapors may also result in bilateral loss of eyebrows and eyelashes (Tames & Goldenring, 1986), and preparation of freebase cocaine with solvents such as ether may result in accidental burns and explosions.

Complications of intravenous drug use are multiple. Intravenous drug abusers are particularly at risk for contracting acquired immune deficiency syndrome (AIDS). Although direct inoculation of this virus into the bloodstream is the most efficient way of obtaining this disease, unsafe sexual practices are also a major concern with this population. The Centers for Disease Control have documented increases in several sexually transmitted diseases among heterosexuals and noted a correlation with regions of heavy crack use (Goldsmith, 1988). Ethnographic "street" researchers of HIV-infected intravenous drug abusers in Chicago showed hyposexuality in one group of chronic drug users and hypersexuality in another group of heavy drug users, some of whom exchanged sex for drugs (Raymond, 1988). Finally, the effects of the drugs themselves on the immune system and malnutrition may be cofactors promoting opportunistic infection.

In a recent study of cocaine use and HIV infection among heterosexual intravenous drug users in public methadone treatment programs in San Francisco during 1986 and 1987, multivariate analysis demonstrated independent predictors of HIV infection to include black race; daily cocaine injection by blacks and Hispanics; all other cocaine injection; heavy use prior to entry into methadone treatment by blacks; and use of drugs in "shooting galleries" (Chaisson et al., 1989). It is plausible that more frequent daily injections of cocaine, caused by its short half-life and highly addictive nature, increase the risk of HIV infection. Shooting galleries were more often used by regular cocaine users who were black. Also, other socioeconomic, behavioral, and biological variables may explain the higher HIV-1 seroprevalence in black and Hispanic intravenous drug users. Interestingly, methadone therapy was associated with substantial reductions in heroin use and some reduction in cocaine use, but 24% of cocaine users receiving methadone began or increased cocaine injection after entry into treatment.

Additional complications of intravenous cocaine use include skin abscesses; phlebitis and cellulitis; and septic emboli resulting in pneumonia, pulmonary abscesses, subacute bacterial endocarditis, ophthalmological infections, and fungal cerebritis (Wetti, Weiss, Cleary, & Gyori, 1984). Injected talc and silicate may cause granulomatous pneumonitis with pulmonary hypertension, as well as granulomata of the liver, brain, or eyes (Estroff & Gold, 1986). Hepatitis B, hepatitis C (hepatitis non-A–non-B), and δ-agent are all too frequent by-products of intravenous drug abuse. In the past several years, concomitant with the increase in HIV infection, there has been an increase in pneumonia, endocarditis, tuberculosis, hepatitis D, and other sexually transmitted diseases in drug users.

Obstetric Complications

Cocaine exposure *in utero* can lead to serious complications for the fetus. Maternal cocaine use may result in complications of labor and delivery and may influence the outcome of pregnancy. Increases in spontaneous abortion, preterm labor, and abruptio placentae among cocaine-using mothers have all been reported. Recent findings indicate that maternal cocaine use is associated with alterations in fetal birth weight, length, and head circumference (Zuckerman et al., 1989). There are reports of these infants' having genitourinary abnormalities, including ambiguous genitalia, hypospadias, "prune belly," and hydronephrosis. There are also reports of ileal atresia, seizures, and cerebral infarction in neonates whose mothers abused cocaine during their pregnancy (Chasnoff, 1988; Chasnoff & Schnoll, 1987). Fetal hypoxia induced by placental vasoconstriction and altered circulating levels of dopamine and norepinephrine may explain both intrauterine growth retardation and the increased rate of congenital malformations. Even women who stop using cocaine during their first trimester are at increased risk for preterm labor (Chasnoff, Griffith, MacGregor, Dirkes, & Burns, 1989) and have babies with neurobehavioral abnormalities. Measurements of these children on the Brazelton Neonatal Assessment Scale show significant depression of interactive behavior and a poor organizational response to environmental stimulus (Chasnoff, Burns, Schnoll, & Burns, 1985; Chasnoff et al., 1989). These infants are also at high risk for sudden infant death syndrome (SIDS).

Assessment

Initial evaluation of the cocaine abuser begins with a medical, psychiatric, and psychosocial history, as well as a physical examination. Confirming and augmenting the patient's history through collateral reports of family members and significant others are often helpful. On an emergency basis, the following laboratory tests need to be considered based upon the patient's clinical presentation: complete blood count, chemical profile (SMA 12), urinalysis, urine and/or blood toxicology, EKG, and chest X-ray.

Indications for acute hospitalization include (1) serious medical or psychiatric problems, either caused by the stimulant drugs or independently coexisting; and (2) concurrent dependency on other drugs such as alcohol or sedatives/hypnotics, necessitating a more closely supervised withdrawal. As yet, there is no validated, widely accepted tool to assess the severity of addiction specifically to cocaine. There are DSM-III-R diagnostic criteria for cocaine intoxication, withdrawal, delirium, delusional disorder, dependence, and abuse (American Psychiatric Association, 1987), which are based on the symptoms described in this chapter. Evaluation for direct addiction treatment needs to address a variety of issues, including the dosage, patterns, chronicity, and method of cocaine use; other drug use; antedating and drug-related medical, social, and psychological problems; the patient's cognitive ability and social skills; and the patient's knowledge, motivation, attitude, and expectations of treatment (Washton, Stone, & Hendrickson, 1988). Additional factors indicating increased severity of addiction, which may necessitate inpatient treatment, include chronic freebase smoking or intravenous cocaine use, demonstrated inability to abstain from use while in outpatient treatment, and lack of family and social supports.

Once the patient is stabilized and assigned to an appropriate level of care, a more detailed medical, psychiatric, and psychosocial history and physical examination should be performed. The search for evidence of medical and psychiatric sequelae should be stressed, as well as consequences of self-neglect. The following laboratory tests should be considered as supplements to those obtained previously on an acute care basis: pulmonary function testing with diffusing capacity of carbon monoxide (DLCO, DCO) in smokers of freebase and crack cocaine; purified protein derivative (PPD) tubercular skin testing with controls; rapid plasma reagin agglutination test (RPR; syphilis serology); hepatitis B surface antigen; and HIV serology in intravenous users. Since these patients generally have poor follow-up rates, immunizations should be given and general preventive health maintenance should be performed at this time as well.

Treatment

In the case of a massive cocaine overdose, the patient is likely to present with advanced cardiorespiratory distress and seizures. Treatment is life support. The principles of resuscitation, along with the administration of thiamine, glucose, and naloxone (Narcan), are necessary. Naloxone is important because narcotics and cocaine are often taken concomitantly. Oxygen is helpful in light of increased anaerobic metabolism with muscle hyperactivity, seizures, and hyperthermia. Treatment of metabolic and lactic acidosis, often accompanied by respiratory alkalosis due to hyperventilation, is critical.

Suggestions for symptom-specific therapies to counteract the effects of cocaine overdose follow. Nitrates and calcium channel blockers can be used for coronary artery spasm, and arrhythmias can be treated with propranolol, lidocaine, and calcium channel blockers as appropriate. Sodium nitroprusside, phentolamine, and calcium channel blockers are effective therapies for hypertension. The use of propranolol is controversial here because of resultant unopposed α receptor stimulation. Dantrolene is advocated for severe hyperthermia, in addition to physical cooling techniques and possibly muscle paralysis. Paralysis with pancuronium (Pavulon) may be helpful to allow intubation of the patient or to control persistent seizure activity. Succinylcholine has rapid paralytic effects, but it can worsen muscle fasiculations and aggravate hyperthermia (Kunkel, 1986). Benzodiazepines, such as diazepam or lorazepam, or barbiturates are helpful to control severe agitation or seizure activity. Whenever seizures occur, their etiology should be carefully assessed, as these may not be stimulant-related. Hypotension may necessitate norepinephrine tartrate (Levophed) and/or dopamine (Intropin). A pneumomediastinum or pneumothorax may require a chest tube but can often be treated supportively.

Intoxicated persons who seek assistance with less severe cocaine complications are more likely to present with panic, irritability, hyperreflexia, paranoia, hallucinations, and stereotyped repetitive movements. Assurance in a calm, nonthreatening environment is a prerequisite for successful patient management. Psychosis can be treated with haloperidol, although caution is necessary, since this medication can lower the seizure threshold. Monoamine oxidase inhibitors are contraindicated, since they block neurotransmitter degradation. Infectious diseases and other complications need to be treated appropriately.

Benzodiazepines may be considered to ameliorate the "crash" or early phase of withdrawal from cocaine. However, the high abuse potential of benzodiazepines limits their therapeutic value (Kosten, 1988). The most serious complication of early withdrawal is depression with the potential for suicide. Patients must be watched closely when manifesting depression and agitation. If symptoms of depression do not remit within 10 days to 2 weeks and with relative normalization of sleep patterns, then this is suggestive of underlying major depression requiring psychiatric intervention.

The protracted withdrawal phase is characterized by anhedonia, anergia, and dysphoria, and can persist for up to 18 weeks following the cessation of cocaine. Potential pharmacological treatments include (1) monoamine oxidase inhibitors, which block neurotransmitter metabolism both intraneuronally and at the synaptic cleft; (2) amantadine, which by an unknown mechanism increases brain dopamine levels; (3) bromocriptine, a dopamine receptor agonist; and (4) L-dopa. Large-scale controlled double-blind studies demonstrating the efficacy of these drugs are lacking. Tricyclic antidepressants—including desipramine, a norepinephrine reuptake blocker, and trazodone, a triazolopyridine derivative that blunts the response to exogenous catecholamines—are being tested for their efficacy in relieving craving. Although desipramine reduces cocaine abuse in some patients, Weiss (1988) reported three cases of a "jitteriness syndrome" in abstinent individuals caused by desipramine, which precipitated cocaine craving and relapse. These drugs may be most helpful in treating persons who are both depressed and cocaine dependent. Neurotransmitter precursors, including L-tyrosine, L-tryptophan, and multivitamins with B complex, have been postulated but not demonstrated in double-blind controlled studies to help the cocaine-dependent patient (Dackis & Gold, 1985).

Preclinical studies with buprenorphine may offer a promising future direction for the pharmacological therapy of both cocaine and opiate addiction. Buprenorphine, an opioid mixed agonist–antagonist, not only suppressed heroin use by heroin addicts (Mello & Mendelson, 1985), but also significantly suppressed cocaine self-administration by rhesus monkeys for 30 consecutive days (Mello, Mendelson, Bree, & Lukas, 1989). To date, a low potential for abuse and minimal adverse side effects have been noted. The mechanism by which buprenorphine suppresses cocaine self-administration is not yet clear. Since opioid antagonists by themselves do not suppress cocaine self-administration in primates, either the opioid agonist portion or the opioid agonist–antagonist combination may cause this action. This is consistent with new evidence of comodulatory relationships between opioid and dopaminergic systems in the brain.

Pharmacological treatments of concurrent psychiatric conditions are diagnosis-specific. As previously mentioned, desipramine and other antidepressants are helpful with depressed patients. Lithium can be used with individuals who have bipolar illness. Pemoline, with its longer onset and duration of action, is less likely to be abused and therefore is preferred over methylphenidate (Ritalin) for the treatment of those with ADD. Full psychiatric evaluation and treatment of coexisting disorders are necessary, in addition to the traditional therapeutic interventions of drug programs. Unfortunately, too often coexisting disorders are overlooked and the patient who fails to improve is mistakenly blamed for continuing "denial" or lacking motivation; this in turn leads to frustration and a negative outcome for therapist and patient alike.

Nonpharmacological treatments emphasize abstinence from cocaine and other nonprescribed mood-altering drugs, including alcohol and marijuana. Persons who are addicted have tendencies toward compulsive and uncontrolled use of these substances. Relapse is frequently caused when the nonprescribed use of mood-altering substances is associated with reinitiation of craving and reduction of inhibitions in a social situation that is not supportive of recovery. Unfortunately, many persons will need to learn this by experience before they will agree to abstinence from these drugs.

Therapies specific to cocaine may be educational, psychodynamic, supportive, and behavioral in nature. The first goal of treatment is to interrupt the recurrent binges or daily use of cocaine and to overcome drug craving, despite a patient's initial agitation and/or depression and later anhedonia. A highly structured outpatient program can be tried in patients without unstable medical or other psychiatric disorders to accomplish this goal before physically removing them from their drug-using environment via hospitalization. Treatment during the initiation of abstinence should include daily or multiple weekly contacts and urine monitoring with as many external controls as possible. Explicit practical measures to limit exposure to stimulants and high-risk situations should be individualized, but might include having drug-free significant others provide monitoring and support; discarding drug supplies and paraphernalia; breaking off relationships with dealers and drug-using comrades; limiting finances; changing one's telephone number and/or geographic location; and structuring one's time during all waking hours.

It is important to educate the patient and his or her family about cocaine addiction and its biological, psychological, and social ramifications. Cocaine differs from alcohol in that it is not known to have prolonged adverse effects on cognitive function. Education along with psychotherapeutic techniques may help the patient better understand the role cocaine has played in his or her life, overcome acute cocaine urges and cravings, and gain awareness of early signs of relapse. An early goal of therapy is to motivate the client toward abstinence; memories of cocaine euphoria, glamour, and a sense of identity need to be set against the reality of long-term injury and destruction. Later therapeutic goals include enhancing affect management and improving interpersonal skills.

Supportive therapies, including self-help groups, may provide positive role models, a group spirituality, and the backing needed to assist in change. Special Cocaine Anonymous groups may be beneficial in addressing issues especially pertinent to cocaine's strong reinforcing properties and associated lifestyle. On the other hand, these separate meetings may have detrimental effects by continuing to foster a sense of cocaine elitism.

Although the actual treatment modalities for cocaine-addicted persons may well be the same as for other drug abusers (education, individual therapy, and group therapy), the intensity of the treatment must be greater. Also, an acute emphasis must be placed on the acquisition of skills that will give the cocaine abuser more internal control and the ability to return to the outside environment without quickly relapsing. This means that treatment must have multiple "practical" components. These may include desensitization training, in which patients are repeatedly exposed to drug stimuli and given the opportunity to deal *in vivo* with them. Behavioral rehearsal is the key to being prepared to deal with the real-life, drug-laden situations that exist outside the protection of the treatment center. Patients also need to develop concrete relapse prevention plans. They must know, *a priori*, what situations are likely to be dangerous for them and precisely how to avoid them. Finally, they must be afforded the opportunity to try out new coping strategies under controlled conditions.

With a chronic disease such as addiction, relapses and remissions are expected. When a person does relapse, more intense treatment and cognitive restructuring are necessary to help prevent a "slip" from escalating (Marlatt & Gordon, 1985). Reminding the patient of prior progress, focusing on making the "slip" an isolated event, and maximizing the learning value of this experience are constructive ways of handling the situation.

Instead of simply taking away cocaine's central role in the patient's existence, emphasizing lifestyle changes (including stress reduction, wellness, exercise, and leisure activities) is important. This may be more difficult for persons of lower socioeconomic classes and/or those with an earlier onset of addiction. These persons lack the knowledge, experience, and resources with which to make these changes. Such patients may need linkage to other social services and habilitation, in addition to the rehabilitation just discussed.

Conclusion

The American public has become increasingly concerned about drug abuse. Cocaine use has spread through all segments of society and has implications for adults, adolescents, and our unborn. In Illinois, the number of "cocaine babies" born during July to December 1988 increased by 78.8% (to 978) over the same period in 1987, according to that state's Department of Children and Family Services (Silverman, 1989). It is feared that between 5% and 10% of children in our next generation will be handicapped at birth because of their mothers' addiction. Research efforts are now underway to determine optimal interventions for this problem.

Cocaine abuse is a complex and multidetermined disorder. As we continue to gain knowledge about the relationships between cocaine abuse and other medical, psychiatric, and obstetric disorders, we can become more sophisticated in our approach to diagnosis and treatment. As health care professionals, we need a full array of interdisciplinary assessment tools and threapeutic modalities to target the individual needs of our patients.

The cocaine epidemic has allowed us to learn a great deal about the successful marketing of illicit drugs; the interactions between neurotransmitters on the one hand and drug reinforcement and reward on the other; and strategies for behavioral relapse prevention to overcome environmental conditioning and cues. Let us hope that this knowledge will enable us to prevent and treat drug addiction more effectively in the future.

References

Adams, E. H., Blanken, A. J., Ferguson, L. D., & Kopstein, A. (1989). *Overview of selected drug trends* (NIDA Publication No. RP0731). Rockville, MD: National Institute on Drug Abuse.

Alfred, R. J., & Ewer, S. (1981). Fatal pulmonary edema following intravenous "freebase" cocaine use. *Annals of Emergency Medicine, 10,* 441–442.

American Psychiatric Association. (1987). *Diagnostic and statistical manual of mental disorders* (3rd ed., rev.). Washington, DC: Author.

Aroesty, D. J., Stanley, R. B., Jr., & Crockett, D. M. (1986). Pneumomediastinum and cervical emphysema from inhalation of "free-based" cocaine: Report of three cases. *Otolaryngology—Head and Neck Surgery, 94,* 372–374.

Bailey, D. N. (1989). Drug screening in an unconventional matrix: Hair analysis. *Journal of the American Medical Association, 262,* 3331.

Barnett, G., Hawks, R., & Resnick, R. (1981). Cocaine pharmacokinetics in humans. *Journal of Ethnopharmacology, 3,* 353–366.

Buchanan, J. F. (1988, March). Cocaine intoxication: A review of the presentation and treatment of medical complications. *Hospital Physician,* 24–29.

Budd, R. D. (1989). Cocaine abuse and violent death. *American Journal of Drug and Alcohol Abuse, 15*(4), 375–382.

Chaisson, R. E., Bacchetti, R., Osmond, D., Brodie, B., Sande, M., & Moss, A. (1989). Cocaine use and HIV infection in intravenous drug users in San Francisco. *Journal of the American Medical Association, 261,* 561–565.

Chasnoff, I. J. (1988). *Cocaine use in pregnancy: Pre- and postnatal effects.* Paper presented at a technical review meeting, Clinical Applications of Cocaine Research: From Bench to Bedside, National Institute on Drug Abuse, Rockville, MD.

Chasnoff, I. J., Burns, W. J., Schnoll, S. H., & Burns, K. A. (1985). Cocaine use in pregnancy. *New England Journal of Medicine, 313,* 666–669.

Chasnoff, I. J., Griffith, D. R., MacGregor, S., Dirkes, K., & Burns, K. A. (1989). Temporal patterns of cocaine use in pregnancy. *Journal of the American Medical Association, 261,* 1688–1689.

Chasnoff, I. J., & Schnoll, S. H. (1987). Consequences of cocaine and other drug use in pregnancy. In A. Washton & M. S. Gold (Eds.), *Cocaine: A clinician's handbook* (pp. 241–251). New York: Guilford Press.

Chokshi, S. K., Miller, G., Rongione, A., & Isner, J. M. (1989). Cocaine and cardiovascular diseases: The leading edge. *Cardiology, 111,* 1–6.

Cooper, C. B., Bai, T. R., Heyderman, C., & Lorrin, B. (1983). Cellulose granulomas in the lungs of a cocaine sniffer. *British Medical Journal, 286,* 2121–2022.

Crowley, T. J., Chesluk, D., Dilts, S., & Hart, R. (1974). Drug and alcohol abuse among psychiatric admissions. *Archives of General Psychiatry, 30,* 13–20.

Cregler, L. L., & Mark, H. (1986). Special report: Medical complications of cocaine abuse. *New England Journal of Medicine, 315,* 1495–1500.

Dackis, C. A., & Gold, M. S. (1985). Pharmacological approaches to cocaine addiction. *Journal of Substance Abuse Treatment, 2,* 139–145.

DePetrillo, P. (1985). Getting to the base of cocaine. *Emergency Medicine, 8,* 8.

Estroff, T. W., & Gold, M. S. (1986). Medical and psychiatric complications of cocaine abuse with possible points of pharmacological treatment. In B. Stimmel (Ed.), *Controversies in alcoholism and substance abuse* (pp. 61–75). New York: Haworth Press.

Gawin, F. H., & Ellinwood, E. H., Jr. (1988). Cocaine and other stimulants: Actions, abuse, and treatment. *New England Journal of Medicine, 318,* 1173–1182.

Gawin, F. H., & Kleber, H. D. (1985). Cocaine use in a treatment population: Patterns and diagnostic distinctions. In N. J. Kozel & E. H. Adams (Eds.), *Cocaine use in America: Epidemiologic and clinical perspectives* (NIDA Research Monograph No. 61, DHHS Publication No. 85-1414, pp. 182–192). Washington, DC: U.S. Government Printing Office.

Gawin, F. H., & Kleber, H. D. (1986). Abstinence symptomatology and psychiatric diagnosis in cocaine abusers. *Archives of General Psychiatry, 43,* 107–113.

Gay, G. R. (1982). Clinical management of acute and chronic cocaine poisoning. *Annals of Emergency Medicine, 11,* 562–572.

Goldfrank, L., Lewin, N., & Weisman, R. (1981). Cocaine. *Hospital Physician,* 17–26.

Goldsmith, M. F. (1988). Sex tied to drugs: STD spread. *Journal of the American Medical Association, 260,* 2009.

Graham, K., Gideon, K., Klein, J., Schneiderman, J., & Greenwald, M. (1989). Determination of gestational cocaine exposure by hair analysis. *Journal of the American Medical Association, 262,* 3328–3330.

Griffin, M. L., Weiss, R. D., Mirin, S. M., & Lange, U. (1989). A comparison of male and female cocaine abusers. *Archives of General Psychiatry, 46,* 122–126.

Hall, R. C. W., Popkin, N. K., DeVaul, R., & Stickney, S. K. (1977). The effect of unrecognized drug abuse on diagnosis and therapeutic outcome. *American Journal of Drug and Alcohol Abuse, 4,* 455–465.

Haller, D., Karan, L., & Schnoll, S. (1990). Treatment of stimulant dependence. In W. Lerner & M. Barr (Eds.), *Handbook of hospital based substance abuse treatment* (pp. 118–131). New York: Pergamon Press.

Hesselbrock, M. N., Meyer, R. E., & Keener, J. J. (1985). Psychopathology in hospitalized alcoholics. *Archives of General Psychiatry, 42,* 1050–1055.

Itkonen, J., Schnoll, S., & Glassroth, J. (1984). Pulmonary dysfunction in freebase cocaine users. *Archives of Internal Medicine, 144,* 2195–2197.

Jaffe, J. H. (1985). Drug addiction and drug abuse. In A. F. Gilman, L. S. Goodman, T. W. Rall, & F. Murad (Eds.), *The pharmacological basis of therapeutics* (7th ed., pp. 550–554). New York: Macmillan.

Jatlow, P. (1988). Cocaine: Analysis, pharmacokinetics, and metabolic dispostion. *Yale Journal of Biology and Medicine, 61,* 105–113.

Javaid, J. I., Fischman, M. W., Schuster, C. R., Dekirmenjian, H., & Davis, J. M. (1978). Cocaine plasma concentration: Relation to physiological and subjective effects in humans. *Science, 202,* 227–228.

Johanson, C. E., Balster, R. L., & Bonese, K. (1976). Self-administration of psychomotor stimulant drugs: The effects of unlimited access. *Pharmacology, Biochemistry and Behavior, 4,* 45–51.

Jones, R. T. (1984). The pharmacology of cocaine. In J. G. Grabowski (Ed.), *Cocaine: Pharmacology, effects and treatment of abuse* (DHHS Publication No. ADM AD4-1325, pp. 34–53). Washington, DC: U.S. Government Printing Office.

Khantzian, E. J. (1985). The self-medication hypothesis of addictive disorders: Focus on heroin and cocaine dependence. *American Journal of Psychiatry, 142,*(11), 1259–1264.

Khantzian, E. J., Gawin, F., Kleber, H. D., & Riordan, C. E. (1984). Methylphenidate treatment of cocaine dependence: A preliminary report. *Journal of Substance Abuse Treatment, 1,* 107–112.

Khantzian, E. J., & Treece, C. (1985). DSM-III psychiatric diagnosis of narcotic addicts: Recent findings. *Archives of Genral Psychiatry, 42,* 1067–1071.

Kosten, T. R. (1988). *Cocaine treatment: Pharmacotherapies.* Paper presented at a technical review meeting, Clinical Applications of Cocaine Research: From Bench to Bedside, National Institute on Drug Abuse, Rockville, MD.

Kosten, T. R., & Kleber, H. D. (1988). Differentiated diagnosis of psychiatric comorbidity in substance abusers. *Journal of Substance Abuse Treatment, 5,* 201–206.

Kosten, T. R., Rounsaville, B. J., & Kleber, H. D. (1987). A 2.5 year follow-up of cocaine use among treated opioid addicts: Have our treatments helped? *Archives of General Psychiatry, 44,* 281–284.

Kuhar, M. J., Ritz, M. D., & Sharkey, J. (1988). Cocaine receptors on dopamine transporters medicate cocaine-reinforced behavior. In D. Clouet, A. Khursheed, & R. Brown (Eds.), *Mechanisms of cocaine abuse and toxicity* (NIDA Research Monograph No. 88, DHHS Publication No. ADM 88-1585, pp. 14–22). Washington, DC: U.S. Government Printing Office.

Kunkel, D. B. (1986, July 15). Cocaine then and now: Part II. Of pharmacology and overdose. *Emergency Medicine,* 168–173.

Lakoski, J. M., & Cunningham, K. A. (1988). The interaction of cocaine with central serotonergic neuronal systems: Cellular electrophysiologic approaches. In D. Clouet, A. Khursheed, & R. Brown (Eds.), *Mechanisms of cocaine abuse and toxicity* (NIDA Research Monograph No. 88, DHHS Publication No. 88-1585, pp. 78–91). Washington, DC: U.S. Government Printing Office.

Lange, R. A., Cigarroa, R. G., Yancy, C. W., Jr., Willard, J. E., Popma, J. J., Sills, M. N., McBride, W., Kim, A. S., & Hillis, L. D. (1989). Cocaine-induced coronary-artery vasoconstriction. *New England Journal of Medicine, 321,* 1557–1562.

Lombard, J., Levin, J. H., & Weiner, W. J. (1989). Arsenic intoxication in a cocaine abuser. *New England Journal of Medicine, 320,*(13), 869.

Marlatt, G. A., & Gordon, J. R. (Eds.). (1985). *Relapse prevention: Maintenance strategies in the treatment of addictive behaviors.* New York: Guilford Press.

McCarron, M. M., & Wood, J. D. (1983). The cocaine "body packer" syndrome: Diagnosis and treatment. *Journal of the American Medical Association, 250,* 1417–1420.

Mello, N. K., & Mendelson, J. H. (1985). Behavioral pharmacology of buprenorphine. *Drug and Alcohol Dependence, 14,* 283–303.

Mellow, N. K., Mendelson, J. H., Bree, M. P., & Lukas, S. E. (1989). Buprenorphine suppresses cocaine self-administration by rhesus monkeys. *Science, 245,* 859–861.

Milkman, H., & Frosch, W. A. (1973). On the preferential abuse of heroin and amphetamine. *Journal of Nervous and Mental Disease, 156,* 242–248.

Nademanee, K., Gorelick, D., Josephson, M., Ryan, M., Wildins, J., Robertson, H., Mody, F. V., & Intarachot, V. (1989). Myocardial ischemia during cocaine withdrawal. *Annals of Internal Medicine, 111,* 876–880.

Newman, N. M., Diloreto, P. A., Ho, J. T., Klein, J. C., & Birnbaum, N. S. (1988). Bilateral optic neuropathy and osteolytic sinusitis. *Journal of the American Medical Association, 259,* 72–74.

National Institute on Drug Abuse (NIDA). (1989, March). *Drug abuse warning network (DAWN)* [Data file]. Rockville, MD: Author.

Post, R. M., & Weiss, S. R. B. (1988). Psychomotor stimulant vs. local anesthetic effects of cocaine: Role of behavioral sensitization and kindling. In D. Clouet, A. Khursheed, & R. Brown (Eds.), *Mechanisms of cocaine abuse and toxicity* (NIDA Research Monograph No. 88, DHHS Publication No. ADM 88-1585, pp. 217–238). Washington, DC: U.S. Government Printing Office.

Quandt, C. M., Sommi, R. W., Jr., Pipkin, T., & McCallum, M. H. (1988). Differentiation of cocaine toxicity: Role of the toxicology drug screen. *Drug Intelligence and Clinical Pharmacy, 22,* 582–587.

Raymond, C. A. (1988). Study of IV drug users and AIDS finds differing infection rate, risk behaviors. *Journal of the American Medical Association, 260,* 3105.

Robin, E. D., Wong, R. J., & Ptashne, K. A. (1989). Increased lung water and ascites after massive cocaine overdosage in mice and improved survival related to beta-adrenergic blockage. *Annals of Internal Medicine, 110,* 202–207.

Roth, D., Alarcon, F. J., Fernandez, J. A., Preston, R. A., & Bourgoignie, J. J. (1988). Acute rhabdomyolysis associated with cocaine intoxication. *New England Journal of Medicine, 319,* 673–677.

Rounsaville, B. J., Weissman, M. M., Crits-Christoph, K., Wilber, C. H., & Kleber, H. D. (1982). Diagnosis and symptoms of depression in opiate addicts: Course and relationship to treatment outcome. *Archives of General Psychiatry, 39,* 151–156.

Satel, S. L., & Gawin, F. H. (1989). Migrainelike headache and cocaine use. *Journal of the American Medical Association, 261,* 2995–2996.

Schuckit, M. A. (1985). The clinical implications of primary diagnostic groups among alcoholics. *Archives of General Psychiatry, 42,* 1043–1049.

Shaffer, H. J., & Costikyan, N. S. (1988). Cocaine psychosis and AIDS: A contemporary diagnostic dilemma. *Journal of Substance Abuse Treatment, 5,* 9–12.

Siegel, R. K. (1985). New patterns of cocaine use: Changing doses and routes. In N. J. Kozel & E. H. Adams (Eds.), *Cocaine use in America: Epidemiologic and clinical perspectives* (NIDA Research Monograph No. 61, DHHS Publication No. ADM 85–1414, pp. 204–226). Washington, DC: U.S. Government Printing Office.

Silverman, S. (1989). Scope, specifics of maternal drug use, effects on fetus are beginning to emerge from studies. *Journal of the American Medical Association, 261,* 1688–1689.

Smith, D. E. (1984). Diagnostic, treatment and aftercare approaches to cocaine abuse. *Journal of Substance Abuse Treatment, 1,* 5–9.

Tames, S. M., & Goldenring, J. M. (1986). Madarosis from cocaine use. *New England Journal of Medicine, 314,* 1324.

Texter, E. C., Chou, C. C., Merrill, S. L., Laureton, H. C., & Frohlich, E. D. (1964). Direct effects of vasoactive agents on segmental resistance of the mesenteric and portal circulation: Studies with l-epinephrine, levarterenol, angiotensin, vasopressin, acetylcholine, methacholine, histamine, and serotonin. *Journal of Laboratory and Clinical Medicine, 64,* 624–633.

Thompson, L. K., Yousefnejod, D., Kumor, K., Sherer, M., & Cone, E. J. (1987). Confirmation of cocaine in human saliva after intravenous use. *Journal of Analytical Toxicology, 11,* 36–38.

U.S. Department of Health and Human Services. (1987). *Drug abuse and drug abuse research: The second triennial report to Congress from the Secretary, Department of Health and Human Services* (NIDA Publication No. 152, DHHS Publication No. ADM 87-1486). Washington, DC: U.S. Government Printing Office.

Washton, A. M., Stone, N. S., & Hendrickson, E. C. (1988). Cocaine abuse. In D. M. Donovan & G. A. Marlatt (Eds.), *Assessment of addictive behaviors* (pp. 364–389). New York: Guilford Press.

Weiss, R. D. (1988). Relapse to cocaine abuse after initiating desipramine treatment. *Journal of the American Medical Association, 260,* 2545–2546.

Weiss, R. D., & Mirin, S. M. (1986). Subtypes of cocaine abusers. *Psychiatric Clinics of North America, 9,* 491–501.

Weiss, R. D., Mirin, S. M., Michael, J. L., & Sollogub, A. C. (1986). Psychopathology in chronic cocaine abusers. *American Journal of Drug and Alcohol Abuse, 12,*(1–2), 17–29.

Wetti, C. V., Weiss, S. D., Cleary, T. J., & Gyori, E. (1984). Fungal cerebritis from intravenous drug use. *Journal of Forensic Science, 29,* 260–268.

Wieder, H., & Kaplan, E. H. (1969). Drug use in adolescents: Psychodynamic meaning and pharmacogenic effect. *Psychoanalytic Study of the Child, 24,* 399–431.

Wilkerson, R. D. (1988). Cardiovascular toxicity of cocaine. In D. Clouet, A. Khursheed, & R. Brown (Eds.), *Mechanisms of cocaine abuse and toxicity* (NIDA Research Monograph No. 88, DHHS Publication No. ADM 88–1585, pp. 304–324). Washington, DC: U.S. Government Printing Office.

Wurmser, L. (1974). Psychoanalytic considerations of the etiology of compulsive drug use. *Journal of the American Psychoanalytic Association, 22,* 820–843.

Zuckerman, B., Frank, D., Hingson, R., Amaro, H., Levenson, S., Kayne, H., Parker, S., Vinci, R., Aboagye, K., Fried, L. E., Cabral, H., Timperi, R., & Bauchner, H. (1989). Effects of maternal marijuana and cocaine use on fetal growth. *New England Journal of Medicine, 320,* 762–768.

7

Hallucinogens, Phencyclidine, Marijuana, Inhalants

CAROL J. WEISS
ROBERT B. MILLMAN

Hallucinogens

The term "hallucinogens" is used to describe a group of naturally occurring and synthetic drugs that alter consciousness or produce changes in thought, mood, and perception. "Hallucinogens" is not an accurate term, however, as the drugs in this group rarely produce true hallucinations. Rather, pseudohallucinations or perceptual distortions are more common.

The major effects of hallucinogens—their mind-altering and perceived mystical/transcendent effects—inspired the term "psychedelic" (mind-manifesting, mind-revealing) for this class of drugs, as well as other less popular names, including "psychodysleptic" (mind-disrupting), "psycholytic" (mind-loosening), and "mysticomimetic" (Grinspoon & Bakalar, 1986; Hollister, 1984). "Psychotomimetic" is also a term sometimes applied to this drug class, though it too is not adequate: It describes an inconsistent effect that may also occur with use of many licit and illicit drugs other than hallucinogens, such as stimulants and steroids.

Classification

The hallucinogens are primarily derivatives of indoles or phenylalkylamines, though other drugs may also be classified as part of this group, such as phencyclidine (PCP) and ketamine (see the section of PCP, below). There are about a dozen natural hallucinogens and over 100 synthetic ones (Grinspoon & Bakalar, 1986). The drugs in this class that are most abused in Western society are as follows (this summary draws on the reviews of Climko, Roehrich, Sweeney, & Al-Razi, 1986–1987; Cohen, 1989; and Ungerleider & DeAngelis, 1981):

Indolealkylamine Derivatives
1. D-Lysergic acid diethylamide (LSD; "acid"). Synthesized from ergot (*Claviceps purpurea*), a fungus, and chemically related to certain alkaloids found in morning glory seeds. First synthesized in 1938.

2. Psilocybin (dimethyl-4-phosphoryltryptamine; "magic mushrooms"). Found in *Psilocybe mexicana* and over 100 related species of mushrooms.
3. Dimethyltryptamine (DMT). Found in cohaba snuff from the seeds of *Piptadenia peregrina*, but made synthetically for street sale. Named the "businessman's LSD" for its rapid onset and short duration of action.
4. Harmine, harmaline, and ibogaine. Naturally occurring, rarely used in Western societies.

Phenylalkylamine Derivatives
1. Mescaline (3,4,5-trimethoxyphenylethylamine). Found in the buttons of the peyote cactus *(Lophophora williamsii)*. Available legally in the United States as part of Native American religious ceremonies.
2. Ring-substituted amphetamines.
   a. 3,4-Methylenedioxyamphetamine (MDA). Known as Ecstasy before MDMA became popular; differs from it by one methyl group. First synthesized in 1910. Widely used in the United States between 1960 and 1973. Classified as a Schedule I drug in 1973.
   b. 3,4-Methylenedioxymethamphetamine (MDMA), also known as Ecstasy, XTC, DOM, MDM, Adam, and STP. First synthesized in 1914. Classified as a Schedule I drug in 1985.
   c. 3,4-Methylenedioxyethamphetamine (MDEA), also called Eve. A new, weaker version of MDMA, which has not yet been classified as a Schedule I drug.

MDA, MDMA, and MDEA are considered "designer drugs" (i.e., new chemical analogues or variations of existing controlled substances that have psychedelic, stimulant, or depressive effects and high potential for abuse). Other designer drugs include fentanyl and meperidine analogues.

History

Ritual and recreational use of naturally occurring hallucinogens goes back to antiquity (Siegel, 1984). Mescaline is still used in certain Native American rituals. The modern age of synthetic hallucinogens began with the first "trip" taken in 1943 by Albert Hoffman, when he accidentally ingested the LSD he had created 5 years earlier (Ungerleider & De Angelis, 1981).

Fascination with hallucinogens was a prominent feature of the social, cultural, and sexual revolution of the 1960s. "Psychedelic" art, language, music, and clothing suffused the culture; all were referential to the hallucinogen experience. Though this experience could be hedonic and sensory, it was also perceived by many to be meaningful and enlightening.

Hallucinogens, particularly LSD, psilocybin, and mescaline, were investigated as a possible adjunct to psychotherapy. By the time LSD became illegal in the mid-1960s, over 1,000 articles on its use had appeared in the medical literature (Ungerleider & De Angelis, 1981). By virtue of the drug's unpredictability and the poorly controlled studies done, it was not shown to be helpful for the many conditions for which it was tried. In the early 1970s, MDMA began to replace LSD as the psychotherapy adjunct that might promote insight and therapeutic communication (Greer & Strassman, 1985). Though many psychotherapists were dismayed by the Drug Enforcement Agency's emergency classification of MDMA as a Schedule I drug in 1985, there is little in the medical literature to support its actual therapeutic value. At the same time, some workers believe that if better research could be done, appropriate indications for the use of these substances might be found.

Epidemiology

Use of hallucinogens peaked during the era of a media-popularized counterculture in the late 1960s and early 1970s, in association with remarkable increases in the use of marijuana and other drugs. It has been estimated that at least one-third of college students experimented with hallucinogens in the 1969–1972 period; currently those numbers are considerably lower (Millman, 1982). It should be noted, however, that most epidemiological studies of drug abuse are limited. Many surveys are conducted in treatment or academic facilities; the significant numbers of drug users in disenfranchised, illiterate, and homeless populations are not represented. There may be many people who use them rarely on special occasions and do not develop adverse sequelae. Also, responses to self-report surveys are often colored by what the respondent believes is an acceptable response. Moreover, given the prevalence of polysubstance abuse, the variable quality of drugs, the uncertain composition of street drugs, and the confusion resulting from intoxication, many drug users themselves do not truly know what they use, how much, and how often. Interestingly, many hallucinogen users of the 1960s were "purists" and did not use other classes of drugs, whereas contemporary users tend to use a variety of drugs.

According to the National Annual High School Senior and Young Adult Survey, in 1988, 7.7% of 16,000 high school students had ever tried LSD, down from 11.3 in 1975; 4.8% had used LSD within the past year, down from 7.2% in 1975; and 1.8% has used LSD within the past month, down from a peak of 2.5% in 1981. Also in 1988, 3.6% of 1300 college students had used LSD in the past year, down from 6.0% in 1980. Among 7,300 follow-up respondents who were from 1 to 11 years beyond high school, 2.8% had used LSD in 1988 (Johnston, O'Malley, & Bachman, 1989). It would seem that psychedelic use has moved from an epidemic situation, where large numbers of people tried the drug, to an endemic situation, where only those at risk or those who continue to subscribe to the cultural mores and music of the earlier era continue to use.

Pharmacology

LSD is the most potent of the hallucinogens, with effects recorded after 20–30 μg; most of the agonist effects of the other hallucinogens are similar to those of LSD. The usual street dose of LSD is 200 μg. It is 4,000 to 6,000 times more potent than mescaline and 100 to 200 times more potent than psilocybin (Halikas, Weller, & Morse, 1982). LSD is usually ingested in the form of impregnated paper or sugar cubes, capsules, and tablets. Intravenous use is rare (Millman, 1982).

The physiological effects of LSD and mescaline are seen within 20 minutes after ingestion; the psychoactive effects appear within 2 to 4 hours. Effects may last from 6 to 24 hours. DMT's and psilocybin's effects last 2 to 6 hours.

The usual dose of MDMA is 75–150 mg. It is commonly available on the street in 100-mg gelatin capsules or loose powder. It is occasionally insufflated (sniffed) and rarely injected by intramuscular or subcutaneous route. It has a rapid onset, usually within 30 minutes, and its duration of action is 4 to 8 hours.

Most hallucinogens produce central sympathomimetic stimulation: mydriasis, hyperthermia, tachycardia, and slightly elevated blood pressure. Piloerection, flushed face, quickened reflexes, and increased alertness may also be present. Delirium and sedation are rare. Peyote characteristically causes dramatic nausea and emesis.

Tolerance to repeated doses develops and is lost rapidly. LSD, mescaline, and psilocybin are cross-tolerant. True craving and physiological dependence do not occur. There is no hallucinogen withdrawal syndrome or need for detoxification. There is no known pharmacologically lethal dose of LSD (Ungerleider & De Angelis, 1981). Cases have been reported of people surviving 10,000 mg of LSD (Cohen, 1982). Deaths have been attributed to PCP and to the ring-substituted amphetamines; these are probably due to the known toxicity of stimulants (Dowling, McDonough, & Bost, 1987).

Patterns of Use and Abuse

Hallucinogens are generally used intermittently by youthful people to punctuate an occasion such as a concert or party. Some adolescents take the drug more regularly, sometimes every day, though this pattern usually lasts only for short periods. When used in this way, the hallucinogen's effects are decreased because of the advent of tolerance.

Effects

Varied and often quite poetic descriptions have been used to convey the psychological aspects of the hallucinogenic experience. The experience varies remarkably from person to person, and in the same person under different conditions (Zinberg, 1984). Usually perceptions are heightened and may become overwhelming. Afterimages are prolonged and overlap with ongoing perceptions. Objects may seem to move in a wave-like fashion or to melt. Overflow of one sense modality to another is common. There may be a sense of unusual clarity, and one's thoughts may assume unusual importance. Time may seem to pass slowly. Illusions and body distortions are commonly perceived. True hallucinations with loss of insight may occur in susceptible individuals. Mood is highly variable and labile, and may range from euphoria and self-confidence to depression and panic (Millman, 1982).

The ring-substituted amphetamines have different and varying properties. MDA is mildly hallucinogenic, and has been described as producing "a warm glow," increased aesthetic sense, increased spirituality and sense of "oneness," and heightened tactile sensation. It has also been described as producing increased desire for interpersonal contact, increased sense of well-being, increased insight, heightened self-awareness, and diminished anxiety and defensiveness (Climko et al., 1986–1987). MDMA has minimal hallucinogenic properties. Its popularity is attributed mostly to effects such as positive mood changes, enhanced communication and intimacy, improved interpersonal relationships, and increased self-esteem. Though MDMA has been called a "sex drug," a survey of 76 users in San Francisco did not confirm any actual aphrodisiacal properties; in fact, decreased ability to reach orgasm or ejaculation was reported by 70% of males surveyed (Buffum & Moser, 1986).

ADVERSE PSYCHOLOGICAL EFFECTS

Adverse psychological effects of hallucinogens are classified as acute or chronic. The main acute adverse reaction is the "bad trip." This is a general term used to describe an acute anxiety/panic reaction, dysphoric reaction, or paranoid state. These are a result of a combination of factors, including the user's psychological state before using, the environment in which the drug is being used, the quality of the drug, and the nature of the user's drug-induced distorted perceptions. The reactions vary in intensity and on rare occasions have led to suicide attempts and accidents.

Chronic adverse effects include a prolonged psychotic state resembling schizophrenia or mania (Bowers, 1977; Lake, Stirba, Kinneman, Carlson, & Holloway, 1981); depression; chronic anxiety state; and chronic personality changes, sometimes with persistent evidence of magical thinking. Some users continue to experience, for months to years, mild perceptual changes such as intensified colors and sounds or trails of images from moving objects. These symptoms are often experienced within a context of otherwise normal functioning.

Sequelae that last more than 4 to 6 weeks often suggest the likelihood of a premorbid vulnerability to psychiatric illness uncovered or exposed by the drug experience. One wonders whether the person would have developed the chronic state if he or she had never used the drug. Did the drug open the gate, or kindle certain neurotransmitters, that led to psychosis or schizoid personality? And once the gate was opened, could it not be closed? In one 2- to 6-year follow-up study of hallucinogen-induced prolonged psychotic reactions, half of the 15 patients had poor outcome, including two who had committed suicide (Bowers, 1977).

"Flashbacks" are recurrences of the drug-induced state that may appear days to years after the drug exposure. They can be pleasurable or distressing, depending on their content and the context in which they occur. They are usually brief and spontaneous, though stress, fatigue, and certain drugs such as marijuana may precipitate them (Cohen, 1989). Flashbacks have been divided into three categories: perceptual, somatic, and emotional. Perceptual flashbacks are the most common; they are most often visual, although any sensory modality may be affected. Somatic flashbacks can consist of feelings of depersonalization, and emotional flashbacks often consist of distressing emotions originally associated with the acute LSD reaction (Shick & Smith, 1970).

Shared paranoid disorder, such as that seen with Charles Manson and his "family," has been described in connection with the use of hallucinogens (Cohen, 1989). However, this phenomenon is usually complicated by factors other than drugs, including the presence of psychiatric illness in the group, isolation, or the power of a charismatic leader and group forces.

MEDICAL CONSEQUENCES

Despite numerous articles and great concern in the late 1960s that LSD might cause chromosomal damage, there are no convincing data showing that LSD is a mutagen. Any mutagenic effects shown were more likely to be due to the lifestyle of the user or to impurities (Cohen, 1989).

Currently, a number of investigations are being undertaken to study the possible neurotoxic effects of MDMA. (Battaglia & DeSouza, 1987; Kolata, 1989; Peroutka, 1989). Neurotoxic effects have been demonstrated in rats and monkeys, but not yet in humans.

Treatment

Treatment of the acute reaction should be directed toward relieving the patient's overwhelming anxiety and protecting him or her from harm. The person should be placed in a calm environment with someone present to provide reassurance by "talking down." He or she should be told that the present state is due to the drug and will soon pass. The patient should be frequently oriented and discouraged from closing his or her eyes, as this may worsen the symptoms. Restraints should be avoided, though they may be necessary if agitation becomes too severe. The preferred medication is a benzodiazepine, such as lorazepam or diazepam. Chlorpromazine or haloperidol may be necessary if there is no response to the benzodiazepine, though adverse reactions have been seen in response to the neuroleptics.

Treatment is often complicated by use of other psychoactive drugs or a toxic reaction to an adulterant. In these instances, too, benzodiazepines are preferred over neuroleptics as the first treatment choice. The presence of a clear sensorium can help differentiate an acute hallucinogen reaction from a toxic reaction; a clouded sensorium or delirium is more common in the latter condition.

Chronic states should be treated with the modality appropriate for that disorder. Neuroleptics, antidepressants, benzodiazepines, psychotherapy, and/ or behavioral interventions should be used when indicated. Serotonergic agents have been suggested for persistent perceptual disorders, though this data is based on anecdotal reports.

Few patients use hallucinogens compulsively or require traditional chemical dependency rehabilitation for their hallucinogen use. This may be indicated, however, if other drugs are also being abused. Some young people use these drugs as self-medication of severe premorbid psychopathology; they are attempting to distance themselves from their functional psychopathology with the hallucinogen.

Cultural biases in diagnosing mental illness may arise when one is evaluating a hallucinogen user. Today, one might diagnose a hallucinogen user who extols the magical and mystical states induced by frequent hallucinogen use as a schizotypal personality or worse. Twenty years ago, the same patient might have been perceived as a normal college student or professor seeking deeper meaning.

Phencyclidine

PCP is an inexpensive, easily available, widely abused drug that alters perception and affect. It has been associated with violence, psychosis, and delirium. Although it shares some properties with LSD and other hallucinogens, it is sufficiently different to be considered as a separate entity.

Classification

PCP (1-[1-phenylcyclohexyl] piperidine monohydrochloride) and related aryl-cyclohexylamines are classified as dissociative or cataleptoid anesthetics. PCP is classified as a Schedule II drug along with morphine and amphetamines. It has approximately 30 chemical analogues, several of which have appeared on the illicit market (Grinspoon & Bakalar, 1986). These include PCE (N-ethyl-1-phencyclohexalamine), TCP (1-[1-2-thienyl-cyclohexyl] piperidine), PHP (1-[1-phencyclohexyl] pyrrolidine), PCC (1-piperidinocyclohexane carbonitrile), and ketamine (2-2-[chlorophenyl]-2-[methylamino]-cyclohexanone).

On the street, PCP has many names, including "angel dust," "mist," "THC," "PeaCePill," "Shermans," "tranq," and "whack" (Schuckit, 1985). A general rule of thumb is that a new drug with a strange name that profoundly alters perception in a bizarre way is likely to be PCP unless proven otherwise (Luisada, 1981). Since it is so inexpensive, PCP has been used to adulterate or enhance other drugs, such as LSD, cannabis, and cocaine.

History

PCP was developed in the late 1950s as an anesthetic agent. It was found to have a calming and sedating effect on nonhuman primates. When used in humans, it had the advantage of inducing anesthesia through a dissociative state without significant depression of vital signs. However, as patients emerged from anesthesia, some became agitated, bizarre, psychotic, or delirious. PCP was quickly removed from the market as a human anesthetic, but became valuable as a research drug that could induce psychosis. Numerous studies of the drug's psychotomimetic effects in humans were published prior to 1965, when PCP was withdrawn from human experimentation. PCP is now used legally only as a veterinary tranquilizer under the trade name Sernylan. Most of the drug that is available for street use has been produced in illicit laboratories.

Ketamine was synthesized in 1962 and has been available by prescription since 1969 as a surgical anesthetic. It has anesthetic effects similar to PCP and has been subject to abuse, though it has not been manufactured illicitly and was never as widely used as PCP.

PCP first appeared as a drug of abuse in the mid-1960s in San Francisco and New York City. It was ingested in the form of a pill called the "PeaCePill," but it did not become a widely abused drug because of a high incidence of adverse reactions.

A few years later, PCP emerged as a white powder or solution that could be insufflated or ingested or combined with parsley, tobacco, or marijuana leaves that would be suitable for smoking. The smokeable form became particularly popular, since if offered a rapid onset and short duration of psychoactive effects. It was also easily synthesized in illicit laboratories, so that it was inexpensive and widely available. The current popularity of "crack" use owes much to similar factors.

Epidemiology

PCP is used primarily by young adults, adolescents, and even young children, most of whom also abuse other substances, particularly marijuana and alcohol. PCP abuse has tended to be a regional phenomenon; it has been a much greater problem in Washington, D.C., than in New York City, and in inner-city minority groups rather than the middle class. Studies from a Los Angeles hospital published in 1980 and 1981 reported that 43% of 145 consecutive emergency room patients and 79% of 135 consecutive psychiatric admissions tested positive for PCP (Aniline, Allen, Pitts, Yago, & Pitts, 1980; Yago et al., 1981)

According to the National Annual High School Senior and Young Adult Survey, PCP use has decreased significantly in recent years (Johnston et al., 1989). In 1988, 2.9% of high school seniors had ever used PCP, down from 12.8 in 1979; 1.2% has used it in the past year, down from 7.0% in 1979; 0.3% had used it in the past month, down from 2.4% in 1979; and 0.1% had used it daily, which was essentially unchanged from 1979. A reported 0.3% had used PCP daily in 1985 and 1987.

Pharmacology

PCP is usually smoked, though it can also be insufflated in powder form or ingested in pill or liquid form. Intravenous or intramuscular use is rare. There is great variation in the amount of PCP per cigarette or capsule, ranging from 2 to 25 mg (Grinspoon & Bakalar, 1986; Schuckit, 1985). Experienced users report that the effects of 2–3 mg of smoked PCP begin within 5 minutes and plateau within 30 minutes. The effects usually last 4 to 6 hours, though it may take 1 to 2 days to recover completely. Toxic effects may persist for significantly longer periods. PCP is metabolized by the liver, is stored in adipose tissue, and has a long half-life (up to 3 days). Tolerance and craving have been reported by chronic users, though there is no withdrawal syndrome (Luisada, 1981).

Effects

INTOXICATION

The PCP user is seeking an altered state of consciousness marked by bizarre perceptions. Incoordination, a euphoric floating feeling, and heightened emotionality can be experienced with 1–5 mg of PCP and usually lasts hours; 5–10 mg can produce an intoxicated state marked by numbness of extremities and perceptual illusions (Schuckit, 1985).

Confusion and disorientation often accompany these sensations. The user may appear agitated and hyperactive or catatonic and withdrawn, or may vacillate between these two states. The agitated state is notable for its high incidence of violence. The catatonic state is marked by a blank stare, facial grimacing, stereotyped movements, little spontaneous speech, and at times waxy flexibility. Speech, when present, is often slurred or perseverative.

Characteristic physiological hallmarks of PCP intoxication include both sympathomimetic and cholinergic effects. Sympathomimetic properties account for increased muscle tone; increased deep tendon reflexes; and moderately increased temperature, pulse, blood pressure, and respiration. Cholinergic effects are increased lacrimation, salivation, diaphoresis, and pupillary constriction. Cerebellar disturbances such as dizziness, ataxia, uncoordination, and nystagmus are common. Horizontal nystagmus should be present; vertical nystagmus may be absent at lower doses. Nystagmus may persist for 48 hours after cessation of drug use (Luisada, 1981).

OVERDOSE, POISONING, TOXIC REACTION

The primary distinction between intoxication and overdose is level of consciousness and autonomic hyperactivity. Doses greater than 10 mg can produce delirium, catalepsy, mutism, severe sedation, and stupor; greater than 20 mg may produce convulsions and/or coma.

The overdose state is marked by dramatic and persistent hypertension. Hypertensive crisis has been reported to persist for up to 3 days after PCP ingestion. Muscular rigidity and horizontal and vertical nystagmus are invariably present. Increased oral and bronchial secretions and profuse sweating are common. Repetitive, purposeless movements may be present. Cardiac, respiratory, and renal failure are life-threatening complications.

The PCP coma can last up to 10 days, leaving a residual organic brain syndrome that can last over a month. The electroencephalogram (EEG) may show rhythmic theta activity, sometimes interrupted by periodic slow- or sharp-wave complexes (Luisada, 1981).

ORGANIC BRAIN SYNDROME, DELIRIUM

A waxing and waning confusional state, disorientation, and clouded sensorium are characteristic of PCP-induced intoxication, overdose, and psychosis. The organic brain syndrome may occur as an element of the acute effects, though it may last for more than a month after the acute effects have resolved. The presence of an organic brain syndrome often helps to differentiate PCP-related disturbances from hallucinogen effects or functional psychoses.

PSYCHOSIS

PCP can precipitate a psychotic reaction in normals, though this disorder is more likely in predisposed individuals. The drug may markedly exacerbate a psychotic disorder in schizophrenic patients. PCP psychosis is defined as a schizophreniform psychosis that occurs after PCP use and persists for days or weeks with no additional PCP use. The features that differentiate this disorder from functional schizophrenia, other than a history of recent PCP use, are a higher incidence of violent behavior and clouded sensorium, though these distinctions may not be present. Patients with functional psychosis tend to have poorer premorbid functioning than those admitted with PCP psychosis.

Schizophrenic patients admitted with exacerbations due to PCP tend to exhibit more violent and unpredicatable behavior during their PCP-related admissions than during admissions not related to PCP (Luisada, 1981). It should be understood that a PCP-precipitated psychotic disorder, if it persists, may be indistinguishable from a functional psychotic reaction.

The psychosis has been characterized as having three phases, each lasting from 1 day to more than 1 week, though these have not been well documented (Luisada, 1981). The initial (agitated) phase is characterized by violent, psychotic behavior. During the second (mixed) phase, behavior is more controlled, but patients remain restless and unpredictable. Resolution of psychotic processes occurs in the final (resolution) phase. A clouded sensorium may be present or may remit during any of these phases.

According to one study, one-fourth of the patients treated for PCP psychosis returned to the hospital within a year with a schizophrenic psychosis in the absence of drug use (Luisada, 1981). These patients tended to be the ones with the longest initial PCP-related psychosis.

Treatment

Treatment is aimed at four functions: protecting the patient and others from harm, maintaining necessary life support, enhancing excretion of the toxic agent, and ameliorating symptoms with medication.

Violent or medically ill patients require hospitalization, often against their will. Restraints may exacerbate muscle damage and agitation and should be avoided, but at times they may be necessary.

A toxic reaction to PCP should be considered a medical emergency. Vital functions may need to be supported. Body cooling and antihypertensive agents may be required, as well as intravenous benzodiazepines to treat convulsions. When PCP has been taken orally, gastric lavage with activated charcoal may prevent further absorption of the drug (Schuckit, 1985). To enhance excretion of the drug, the urine should be acidified to a pH of less than 5.0 with 500 mg of intravenous ammonium chloride every 4 hours or 500 mg of oral ascorbic acid every 4 hours, though this should only be attempted in an appropriately equipped and staffed medical setting. Repeated monitoring of blood pH, blood gases, blood urea nitrogen (BUN), blood ammonia, and electrolytes is necessary.

Mild psychiatric symptomatology, including anxiety and paranoia, should be treated with reassurance in a warm, supportive, low-stimulation atmosphere ("talking down"), as with hallucinogen and marijuana reactions. Sensory deprivation should be avoided. More severe acute psychiatric complications usually do not respond to this intervention and may necessitate pharmacotherapy early on. Benzodiazepines are preferable to neuroleptics, as the latter may exacerbate cholinergic imbalance, muscle damage, or vulnerability to seizures. There is no evidence to support earlier concerns that benzodiazepines might delay excretion of PCP. Low-potency neuroleptics, such as chlorpromazine and thioridazine, have undesirable anticholinergic effects that may worsen the delirium and psychosis (Miller, Gold, & Millman, 1988). High-potency neuroleptic medication is recommended for patients who do not respond to benzodiazepines or who develop protracted psychoses. PCP precipitates psychotic disorders that persist for weeks after the drug ingestion and should be treated as a functional psychosis.

One recent study suggests that ascorbic acid may enhance the therapeutic effects of haloperidol in the treatment of PCP psychosis (Giannini, Loiselle, DiMarzio, & Giannini, 1987). Electroconvulsive therapy (ECT) has also been recommended as an effective treatment for patients with PCP psychosis who are refractory to antipsychotic medication (Rosen, Mukherjee, & Shinbach, 1984).

Chronic PCP users often abuse other substances and/or have concomitant psychiatric illnesses. After the resolution of acute symptoms, conventional chemical dependency treatment should be provided to promote abstinence and prevent relapse. Severe psychopathology must be treated with the drug dependence. Psychiatric evaluation should continue throughout the early treatment stages, since symptomatology may change with continued abstinence.

Marijuana

Marijuana is the most widely used illicit substance in Western society. The term "marijuana" refers to various preparations obtained from the upper leaves and flowering tops of the Indian hemp plant, *Cannabis sativa*. The resin obtained from the plant contains over 60 cannabinoids and 400 different chemicals, of which δ-9-tetrahydrocannabinol (THC) is the major chemical with psychoactive properties. The THC content can vary from 0.1% in the type of plant grown for fiber to 60% in hashish oil, a concentrated resin distillate (Cohen, 1986; Grinspoon & Bakalar, 1981). Marijuana as used in the United States may contain from 1% to 10% THC. In recent years, the cultivated plant has yielded preparations with increasingly high THC content. The least potent grade of cannabis, called "bhang," is derived from uncultivated flowers and tops with a low resin content comprising 1–2% THC. Most of the marijuana used in the United States is of this grade. "Ganja" refers to the product of the carefully cultivated flowers with a high resin content. "Hashish" is an extremely potent form of cannabis derived mostly from the resin itself. "Sinsemilla" is a potent cannabis preparation that can contain THC concentrations of greater than 10%.

Although marijuana alters perceptions and heightens sensory awareness as do the hallucinogens, the drug differs from this class of substances in a number of ways and should therefore be classified separately. In distinction to the hallucinogens, it is generally smoked; its consciousness-altering properties at the doses generally used are less profound; and it is sedating, whereas LSD and most of the other hallucinogens are activating.

History and Epidemiology

Like the other naturally occurring drugs of abuse, cannabis has been used since ancient times, having first been described in an ancient Chinese medical text. It has been used all over the world in a variety of ways by diverse people, including religious mystics, Persian and Jamaican laborers, and European literati.

In the mid-19th century, marijuana was introduced to England and the United States as both a medicinal agent and a euphoriant. Prior to World War II in this country, use of marijuana was confined to the very wealthy, the underworld classes, and the entertainment profession (Millman & Sbriglio, 1986). Following the war, use increased significantly in urban ghetto populations in association with other drugs of abuse such as heroin and cocaine. During the 1960s and 1970s, marijuana use assumed epidemic proportions, spreading to the middle class as well as to youthful, female, and rural populations.

According to the National Annual High School Senior and Young Adult Survey, the use of marijuana peaked in 1979 and has declined since then (Johnston et al., 1989). According to the survey, 51% of all high school seniors reported some use in the year 1979; that figure fell to 33% by 1988. Similarly, 51% of college students reported marijuana use in 1981; in 1988, that figure dropped to 35%. In 1978, 10.7% of high school seniors were daily marijuana users; in 1988, only 2.7% used the drug daily. In 1988, 47% of seniors had ever used marijuana, down from 60% in 1979. 18% of seniors had used marijuana in the 30 days preceding the study, down from 37% in 1978. Among follow-up respondents who were 1 to 11 years beyond high school, 31.3% had used marijuana in 1988, down from 34.3% in 1987. Interestingly, alcohol use has remained constant in all these categories of respondents.

This decline has been attributed to a changed perception of marijuana. In 1978, 35% of seniors thought there was a "great risk" associated with regular marijuana use. By 1988, that number rose to 77%. It is likely that changing cultural styles in this country, with a move toward a more conservative, self-protective stance, have contributed to the decline as well. There is also evidence to suggest a natural history of marijuana use, such that as people grow older in Western society, the psychoactive effects of the drug are perceived to be less attractive, and use declines (Millman & Sbriglio, 1986). It should also be understood that surveys of marijuana use (or any other drug use, for that matter) are unable to characterize the many young people who do not go to school or those people who do not live in stable situations.

Marijuana has been called a "gateway" drug, leading to the abuse of other classes of drugs. This has also been called the "stepping-stone" theory (Clayton & Voss, 1981; O'Donnell & Clayton, 1979; O'Donnell, Voss, Clayton, et al., 1976). Alcohol and tobacco have a similar correlation with other drug use. It is likely that positive experiences with one illicit psychoactive drug may encourage use of other drugs; the extent of marijuana use correlates positively with the use of other drugs (Halikas et al., 1982). Also, the acquisition and use of marijuana usually encourage association with people who use or have access to other drugs (Cohen, 1986; Millman, 1989).

Patterns of Use and Abuse

The patterns of marijuana use are quite varied and depend upon social and cultural factors as well as individual personality factors. Many young people experiment with the drug for periods of time, and then relegate it to a peripheral status in their lives or stop using it completely; others continue to use it intermittently to punctuate particular occasions. Regular smokers include those who use the drug three to five times a week; chronic users are those who smoke every day, often throughout the day so that they remain intoxicated.

Dependence on marijuana and compulsive use are often associated with psychopathology, though the relationship is often complex. In some cases, the drug may be a cause of the psychopathology noted, though in others it may be seen as self-medication of a pre-existing psychological disorder. For example, some people use the drug for its sedative properties, to decrease symptoms of anxiety or depression. It is striking that a subset of chronic psychiatric patients, including those with psychotic disorders, will use a drug that may increase their feelings of paranoia or unreality and that often results in their readmission to hospitals. It is as if they are seeking distance from their symptoms, or some control over their thoughts and feelings. Perhaps they are able to derive some comfort from the idea that their symptoms are drug-induced, under their control, and not due to their own psychopathology. It is also somewhat more socially acceptable to be a "drug abuser" or a "pothead" than it is to be a "mental patient."

Pharmacology

Marijuana is generally smoked, though it can be ingested. When it is smoked, much of the THC content is lost by pyrolysis. After smoking, effects begin within minutes and last 2 to 4 hours; after ingestion, effects begin within 30 to 60 minutes and last 5 to 12 hours (Jaffe, 1985). The delay in effects after ingestion is not satisfying to most drug users who are seeking rapid change in affect or perceptual state. Moreover, this delay makes it difficult to titrate dosage against effects; often larger quantities of the drug are consumed because no immediate effects are experienced. This in part contributes to the greater incidence of adverse sequelae experienced with oral ingestion.

THC is highly lipid-soluble, and quickly passes from the blood to the brain and other lipid-rich tissues (Cohen, 1986). It is extensively metabolized in the liver. The metabolites are excreted in the bile, urine, and feces. After high-dose or chronic use, traces of THC and its metabolites persist in blood for several days or weeks and even longer in urine.

Significant tolerance develops to the physiological effects of the drug; tolerance to its psychoactive subjective effects is markedly variable. After cessation of high-dose chronic use, a mild withdrawal syndrome occurs. This is characterized by 4 to 5 days of irritability, restlessness, nervousness, decreased appetite, weight loss, and insomnia (with rebound increase in rapid eye movement [REM] sleep) (Jaffe, 1985). This syndrome is quite variable and much influenced by set and setting. Fatal overdoses due to marijuana alone have not been reported.

Effects

The physiological effects of marijuana include a rise in systolic blood pressure while supine and a decrease while standing (though these changes are inconsistent), tachycardia, conjunctival vascular injection, and dry mouth. There is no significant change in pupil size (Jaffe, 1985). REM sleep decreases. Appetite is increased, though it seems to be quite dependent upon expectation and setting.

The psychoactive effects of cannabis are remarkably varied and are profoundly dependent upon the personality of the user, his or her expectation, and the setting, though relaxation, a sense of well-being, and enhanced somatosensory perceptions are quite common.

Marijuana intoxication is often associated with labile affect, impaired short-term memory, and altered time perception (such that time seems to pass more slowly). Enhanced sociability and giddy laughter occur, but so may social withdrawal and extreme self-consciousness. Information processing is altered, such that boring and repetitive tasks may be performed with enhanced interest and concentration, while the ability to carry out complex goal-oriented tasks is impaired. Ideas may seem to change in importance and relevance.

ADVERSE PSYCHOLOGICAL EFFECTS

The most common acute adverse psychological reactions to marijuana are anxiety reactions and frank panic attacks. These reactions are usually brief and do not persist beyond the period of intoxication. The anxiety can range from mild to severe, depending on the amount used, the degree of experience of the user, the setting in which the drug is used, and the psychological predisposition of the user.

Cannabis-induced panic attacks may occur in patients with no psychiatric history, though they occur more often in those with a history of a panic disorder, a generalized anxiety disorder, or other related psychopathology. Most users who develop panic attacks while intoxicated do not continue to experience these reactions; others find that these reactions occur frequently with the drug, and so discontinue its use. There are a few reported cases of patients who developed panic attacks and/or agoraphobia that continued to recur despite the cessation of marijuana use. It may be postulated that in these instances, the drug and its psychoactive sequelae represented a sensitization or kindling phenomena that led to the persistence of psychiatric symptomatology.

Frank hallucinations and/or delusions occur infrequently with acute marijuana reactions. They are usually associated with high doses, oral ingestion, or psychiatric vulnerability. Rarely, these symptoms may be manifestations of a hallucinogen flashback precipitated by marijuana, the most common precipitant. Delirium is rare but can occur in the setting of high-dose use, particularly after oral ingestion. Adulterants such as PCP may be associated with delirium or other adverse effects.

Psychotic disorders precipitated by cannabis use are usually short-lived, but may last days to weeks or longer. Prolonged and severe psychotic disorders indistinguishable from schizophrenia have been attributed to high-dose and chronic cannabis use, though it is likely that these reactions occurred in predisposed individuals whose drug use triggered expression of premorbid psychopathology.

An "amotivational" or "chronic" cannabis syndrome, marked by apathy, dullness, diminished goal-directed activities, impaired concentration, and deterioration in personal appearance, has been described in some chronic marijuana users (Stefanis, Boulougouris, & Liakos, 1976). It is likely that the psychoactive effects of the drug in the setting of premorbid psychopathology may present as this syndrome. In the absence of severe psychopathology, cessation of drug use leads to improvement in symptoms and performance; for others, abstinence may reveal the complex and disturbing symptoms that were previously being medicated with the drug.

A subgroup of chronic users who have been described as having an amotivational syndrome actually manifest remarkable energy and enthusiasm in the pursuit of other goals, such as involvement with particular kinds of music or identification with drug-using cults. Hence the term "aberrant motivational syndrome" has been suggested as a more precise description of the phenomenon (Millman & Sbriglio, 1986).

MEDICAL CONSEQUENCES

The most notable adverse physiological effects of marijuana smoking are its effects on lung and pulmonary function. These effects are proportionally greater than the effects of smoking tobacco and may be additive with tobacco. Habitual smoking of three to four marijuana cigarettes a day is associated with the same frequency of bronchitis and the same epithelial damage in the central airways as regular smoking of more than 20 tobacco cigarettes a day (Wu, Tashkin, Djahed, & Rose, 1988). These differences are due to the irritants in marijuana as well as to the smoking behavior of marijuana users, who take larger and longer inhalations than cigarette smokers.

Aphrodisiac properties have been attributed to marijuana, as well as to many of the other drugs of abuse. Self-report surveys support claims of both enhanced and impaired sexual function secondary to marijuana use (Cohen, 1982; Halikas et al., 1982). Cannabis may lower testosterone levels after chronic and acute use, and may affect all phases of reproductive physiology in both sexes (Kolodny, Masters, Kolodner, & Toro, 1974; Kolodny, Lessin, Toro, Masters, & Cohen, 1976; Powell & Fuller, 1983). Gynecomastia may occur in male chronic users. Chromosomal damage, teratological effects, and increased fetal loss have been suggested but not documented.

Treatment

Treatment of the acute adverse effects of cannabis, including anxiety reactions, panic attacks, and flashbacks, consists of calm and gentle reassurance in a warm and supportive atmosphere ("talking down"). When these people are brought to an emergency room, an attempt should be made to find a quiet place for them out of the mainstream of traffic (Millman, 1989). It is useful to remind a patient that the symptoms are drug-induced and will pass quickly. When necessary, a benzodiazepine anxiolytic should be administered. As with adverse reactions from hallucinogens, neuroleptics are usually not necessary and should be avoided except when severe agitation has not been adequately managed with benzodiazepines. Protracted psychotic symptoms, when severe, usually require neuroleptics. The presence of delirium necessitates the consideration of etiologies other than cannabis. Management is similar to that of any delirium: close monitoring of vital functions and metabolic status, and supportive care. Benzodiazepines are indicated if withdrawal from depressants is also suspected.

It is necessary to define the meaning of the drug for individual patients in order to develop the most appropriate treatment for chronic users. The therapist or counselor needs to be mindful of the interrelationship of character, psychopathology, and addictive behavior when evaluating any substance abuse patient. Moreover, this evaluation should be an ongoing process, with new information being uncovered as the patient faces the challenges of the treatment process.

Chronic marijuana users and other chemically dependent patients who also abuse marijuana should be afforded treatment based on the disease model of chemical dependence, including Twelve-Step programs as well as relapse prevention techniques. Although most marijuana-dependent people can be managed as outpatients, institutionalization in a therapeutic community, rehabilitation program, or psychiatric hospital with a coordinated drug treatment program may be indicated. Surprisingly, given the widespread use and abuse of this substance, there are few Twelve-Step groups aimed specifically at marijuana users.

Treatment programs for marijuana-dependent people, many of whom are adolescents, are often indistinguishable from those aimed at adults who are dependent on alcohol and other drugs. These programs may not be sensitive to the particular needs and cultural mores of this youthful population. Many young people are unable or unwilling to accept the tenets of adult programs, such as the admission that they have the disease of chemical dependence and that they may never again use another psychoactive drug, including alcohol. Programs aimed specifically at this younger population, which emphasize identification with a non-drug-using group and the development of alternatives to drug use, have shown promise.

Treatment of patients with premorbid psychopathology depends on the characterization of symptomatology and behavioral patterns after cessation of marijuana use. This may take days or weeks. It may be necessary to institute treatment presumptively before abstinence is obtained or drug effects have disappeared. Patients should be carefully educated with respect to relapse prevention techniques and their attempts at self-medication or rationalization of their psychopathology (Millman, 1989).

Inhalants

The term "inhalants" refers to a category of diverse substances that produce psychoactive but generally short-lived effects after inhalation. They are relatively inexpensive, easily available, and subject to a wide variety of abuse patterns.

Classification

Many substances that are classified as inhalants are quite disparate; they may contain multiple ingredients, with differing desired and toxic effects. The inhalants that are commonly subject to abuse are listed below, with their general composition (Fornazzari, 1988; Sharp & Korman, 1981).

Commonly Abused Inhalants
Alkyl nitrites—amyl nitrite ("amies," "poppers," "snappers"), butyl nitrite ("rush," "locker room"). Amyl nitrite is available by prescription; butyl nitrites are available over the counter.
Glues, adhesives, cements.
Paints and paint thinners.
Gasoline, lighter fluid.
Aerosols, including nitrous oxide ("whippets").
Nail polish remover.
Dry cleaning fluid, cleaning solutions.
Typewriter correction fluid.
Antifreeze.

Common Contents of Inhalants

Amyl nitrite, butyl nitrite.

Toluene and toluene mixtures—glues, adhesives, cements, paint and cement cleaners and thinners.

Benzene and substances containing benzene—gasoline, glues, paints.

Hexane—gasoline, some glues, spray adhesives, rubber cement.

Ketones—rubber cement, printing ink, paint, nail polish remover (acetone).

Halogenated hydrocarbons (halocarbons): Methylene chloride—spray paints, paint thinner. Trichloroethylene—typewriter correction fluid, dry cleaning solvent. Halothane—surgical anesthetic. Chloroform, methylchloroform—typewriter correction fluid, household cleaning fluids.

Fluorocarbons—aerosols, freon.

Nitrous oxide—aerosols.

Ethylene glycol—antifreeze.

Epidemiology and Patterns of Use and Abuse

The fact that certain smells and vapors alter consciousness has been known since antiquity, though the first characterization of glue and gasoline sniffing as substance abuse and dependence did not occur in the United States until the 1950s (Brecher, 1972). Abuse of these substances increased significantly in the late 1960s and early 1970s, in association with the increased use of other psychoactive substances.

According to the National Annual High School Senior and Young Adult Survey, inhalant use has fluctuated within a narrow, relatively stable range since 1979 (Johnston et al., 1989). In 1988, 17.5% of high school seniors had ever used inhalants, down from 18.2% in 1979 and a high of 20.1% in 1986. In 1988, 7.1% had used inhalants in the past year, which was a decrease from the reported 8.9% in 1979 and 1986. In 1988, 3.0% had used the drugs in the past 30 days, down from 3.2% in 1979 and a high of 3.5% in 1987. Daily use was 0.3%, up from 0.1% in 1979 and down from a high of 0.4% in 1985–1987. Use among college students ranged from a low of 2.4% in 1984 to a high of 4.1% in 1988. Among follow-up respondents who were 1 to 11 years beyond high school, 1.7% has used inhalants in 1988, 2.0% in 1987.

Inhalants come in a variety of forms, from tanks of nitrous oxide to ampules of butyl nitrite or bottles of occupational fluids. Nitrous oxide is also available as cartridges that are used in whipped cream dispensers (hence the name "whippets"). These cartridges can be purchased in large quantities in hardware, gourmet, restaurant supply, and drug paraphernalia stores. The cartridge is placed in an empty whipped cream canister or a special "charger" that can be purchased at a drug paraphernalia store. The user places his or her mouth over the dispensing spout and pushes down on the dispensing lever, which punctures the opening to the ampule, releasing its contents. Some adolescents have learned to extract the gas from whipped cream dispensers on supermarket shelves, leaving behind a contaminated can of flat whipped cream to be sold to unwitting customers.

Amyl nitrite ampules are available by prescription, whereas the butyl nitrites may be purchased in drug paraphernalia stores as "aromas." The ampule is broken and inhaled, or placed in a metal container to prolong its effects. During the peak of nitrite popularity in the mid-1970s, the wearing of the metal container around one's neck conferred a status akin to wearing a cocaine spoon.

Organic solvents can be inhaled from a hand, rag, or jar. Gasoline is commonly inhaled from portable plastic gas cans. An opening is created as a vent, and the user places his or her mouth over the spout. Solvents such as glue or cement are often deposited in a plastic bag, which is secured around the face or head so as to create a closed system.

Most surveys report a marked male preponderance of users. Initial and experimental use is generally by young people in a group setting; chronic or compulsive use is generally a solitary practice. Solitary use is also more common with older users. Most users state that inhalants are not their drugs of choice; abuse of other substances is common.

Though solvent abuse is frequently perceived as a problem of adolescence, abuse among adults, including the educated middle class, is not uncommon. During the past two decades, alkyl nitrites became popular with young adults (most visibly, homosexual men) to enhance social and sexual encounters. Reports of nitrous oxide abuse by dentists, who have access to large quantities of it, are not uncommon. Intermittent and compulsive use of nitrous oxide cartridges continues to be common. High-functioning individuals, the affluent, and the educated middle class often use nitrous oxide or the nitrites because of their legality and easy availability.

Pharmacology

Inhalants are quickly absorbed over the large surface of the lungs, accounting for their almost instantaneous psychoactive effects. It has been estimated that solvent abusers inhale a concentration of about 1,000–5,000 parts per million, as compared to factory workers, who may be exposed to solvent concentrations not greater than 100–500 parts per million (Fornazzari, 1988; Ron, 1986). The solvents are deposited in organs and tissues with high lipid contents, including the central nervous system. Inhalant effects generally persist for minutes, though some of the preparations may exert effects for up to an hour. Inhalation can be repeated an indefinite number of times; some users do it over a hundred times a day. It is likely that the rapid onset and waning of effects account for the liability to develop compulsive use. Abusers seek rapid, predictable change, often in any direction, and continue to seek this change. The drugs are reinforcing rather than classically addicting. The recent epidemic of compulsive cocaine use by inhalation ("freebase" cocaine and "crack") probably relates in part to similar mechanisms.

Tolerance has been reported with toluene and nitrous oxide; some degree of subjective tolerance probably occurs with all of the inhalants. Whereas profound dependence marked by craving and compulsive use is common, a physiological withdrawal syndrome does not occur with these drugs, though one case of a phenomenon similar to delirium tremens has been reported (Ron, 1986).

Contrary to popular belief, many of the inhalants or their metabolites can be detected in blood and urine, albeit very transiently. For toluene, the blood concentration reaches its peak 15 to 30 minutes after use and cannot be detected after 4 to 6 hours. Urine levels peak after 1 hour and rapidly wane after 4 hours (Ron, 1986). According to one report, toluene is detectable by portable mass spectrometry 4 days after the last inhalation (Fornazzari, 1988).

It is believed that the mechanism of action of most inhalants is to reduce excitatory impulses on neuronal membranes, possibly after an initial enhanced excitation. The nitrites differ from the other inhalants in that they are smooth muscle relaxants and dilate blood vessels; this may relate to their use as a sexual aid.

Psychoactive Effects and Toxicity

Initial psychoactive effects of the various inhalants have some features similar to alcohol intoxication. Users seek the "rush," the rapid onset of a euphoric feeling that may be associated with a sensation of floating and decreased inhibitions. The initial excitation is generally followed by sedation. Irritability may occur with continued use. Nitrous oxide use is characteristically accompanied by giddy laughter. Though use of all inhalants is associated with the rapid onset of effects, the nitrite "rush" is most often associated with the attempt to enhance sexuality, particularly the experience of orgasm.

Tinnitus, blurry or double vision, eye irritation, light sensitivity, and a characteristic taste in the mouth are common concomitants of nitrite use. Sneezing, rhinorrhea, and coryza often occur after chronic use. Illusions, hallucinations, other perceptual distortions, and clouding of consciousness may also occur after chronic use. Chronic users often appear to be intoxicated, though the characteristic inhalant breath smell and perioral rash are useful diagnostic clues.

Aftereffects of the inhalants almost invariably include headache; gastrointestinal symptoms such as abdominal cramps, nausea, vomiting, and diarrhea may be present. Transient central nervous system toxicity is manifested by cerebellar dysfunction, paresthesias, and (rarely) seizures.

Arrhythmias secondary to cardiac toxicity have been reported with use of the solvents. Other associated medical complications include restrictive ventilatory defects, bronchitis, and pneumonias. Acidosis and hyperchloremia may be present in plasma or cerebrospinal fluid (Fornazzari, 1988). Asphyxiation and death have occurred when the plastic bag that was used to increase the concentration of organic solvents collapsed around the user's head. Anoxia and death have also occurred when users inhaled nitrous oxide with a fixed face mask that did not allow sufficient oxygen to enter the closed system.

Multiple organ systems are adversely affected by the various inhalants. Benzene can produces hematotoxic changes such as anemia, leukopenia, pancytopenia, and leukemia. The halogenated hydrocarbons are associated with significant hepatorenal toxicity, including renal tubular acidosis. The hydrocarbons are also associated with carcinogenesis, abortions, and developmental defects. Halothane has been associated with delayed-onset behavioral changes after perinatal exposure. The fluorocarbons are significantly cardiotoxic and are the primary etiological agents in deaths due to cardiac sensitization (Sharp & Korman, 1981). Methemoglobin is formed after nitrite inhalation. Though hemoglobin is re-formed from the methemoglobin, patients with an enzyme deficiency or cardiac sensitivities are at risk for serious complications.

Many of the inhalants are associated with the development of both transient and persistent neuropathies. The production of ketones has been implicated as the cause of the most rapidly developing neuropathies. Hexane is especially associated with sensorimotor neuropathies due to myelin degeneration, characterized by symmetrical numbness, weakness, and ataxia. Benzene's motor and sensory neurotoxic effects are characterized by dysmetria and dysarthria. Toluene actually presents a low risk for the development of neuropathies, though rare optic neuropathy and sensorineural hearing loss have been reported with its use. The distal paresis and numbness reported with nitrous oxide use are also likely to be due to a neuropathic process.

A persistent cerebellar syndrome characterized by nystagmus, titubating gait, ataxia, and limb tremor has been convincingly attributed to toluene. ("Titubating gait" is a characteristic staggering gait seen in cerebellar diseases.) These findings were correlated with cerebellar atrophy on computed tomography (Fornazzari, 1988). The same author has also demonstrated cerebral atrophy associated with toluene use, though complicating factors (such as other drug use) and lack of controls were not adequately addressed (Ron, 1986).

Many studies have attempted to demonstrate a causal relationship between persistent neuropsychological deficits and inhalant use. To date, studies addressing cognitive, reading, and memory impairments and defective visual scanning have all been inconclusive (Ron, 1986).

Severe psychiatric morbidity (including an organic mental syndrome, psychiatric reactions, and personality disorders) is frequent in chronic inhalant abusers, though it has been difficult to determine whether the inhalant use is causal, what the contribution of other drug use is, or whether the psychopathology preceded the inhalant use and may have determined the drug abuse pattern. As with all substance abusers who present with psychiatric illness, a careful and ongoing evaluation is critical to determine the relationship of the drug and the psychiatric symptomatology.

Treatment

Intermittent or experimental inhalant users do not generally come to medical attention. Inhalant abuse is often considered unimportant and frivolous both by the users themselves and by health professionals, possibly because the substances are legal and are integral parts of everyday life. However, due to their short duration of action, easy availability, cheapness, and licitness, inhalants lend themselves to compulsive use patterns that may be associated with severe behavioral and psychiatric impairment. Other drug use is generally present as well.

Inhalant abusers should be treated in well-coordinated chemical dependency treatment programs; adolescents should optimally be treated in programs focused particularly on this age group. Although outpatient treatment should be attempted initially, institutionalization is indicated when the use cannot be controlled or severe psychiatric sequelae are present. A number of studies have indicated that adolescent inhalant abusers tend to respond poorly to traditional treatment programs (Mason, 1979). This has been attributed to a number of factors, including a high incidence of antisocial personality disorders and other severe psychopathology.

Hospitalization is required for such severe medical sequelae as arrhythmia, seizure, coma, or unmanageable agitation. Most neurological symptoms, such as cerebellar disturbance or paresthesias, are quickly reversible. Psychiatric disturbances are also usually transient and will remit with no medication or, on occasion, benzodiazepines. In more severe or protracted disturbances, neuroleptics may be necessary.

Methylene blue has been suggested as a treatment for high methemoglobin levels due to nitrous oxide abuse. Renal tubular acidosis, associated with fluorocarbon use, responds to intravenous bicarbonate and potassium chloride (Sharp & Korman, 1981).

Prevention programs aimed at making inhalants and related paraphernalia less accessible or adding noxious additives to the substances of abuse have been suggested, but not instituted.

References

Aniline, O., Allen, R. E., Pitts, F. N., Yago, L. S., & Pitts, A. F. (1980). The urban epidemic of phencyclidine use. *Biological Psychiatry, 15*, 813–817.
Battaglia, G., & DeSouza, E. B. (1987). Long term effects of Ecstasy. *NIDA Notes, 2*(3), 7.
Bowers, M. B. (1977). Psychoses precipitated by psychomimetic drugs. *Archives of General Psychiatry, 34*, 832–835.

Brecher, E. M. (1972). *Licit and illicit drugs.* Boston: Little, Brown.

Buffum, J., & Moser, C. (1986). MDMA and human sexual function. *Journal of Psychoactive Drugs, 18*(4), 355–359.

Clayton, R. R., & Voss, H. L. (1981). *Young men and drugs in Manhattan: A causal analysis* (NIDA Research Monograph No. 39). Washington, DC: U.S. Government Printing Office.

Climko, R. P., Roehrich, H., Sweeney, D. R., & Al-Razi, J. (1986–1987). Ecstasy: A review of MDMA and MDA. *International Journal of Psychiatry in Medicine, 16*(4), 359–371.

Cohen, S. (1982). Cannabis and sex. *Journal of Psychoactive Drugs, 14*(1–2), 55–58.

Cohen, S. (1986). Marijuana. In A. J. Frances & R. Hales (Eds.), *Annual review of psychiatry* (Vol. 5). Washington, DC: American Psychiatric Press.

Cohen, S. (1989). The hallucinogens. In T. B. Karasu (Ed.), *Treatment of psychiatric disorders.* Washington, DC: American Psychiatric Press.

Daghestani, A. N., & Schnoll, S. H. (1989). Phencyclidine abuse and dependence. In T. B. Karasu (Ed.), *Treatment of psychiatric disorders.* Washington, DC: American Psychiatric Press.

Dowling, G. P., McDonough, E. T., & Bost, R. O. (1987). A report of five deaths associated with the use of MDEA and MDMA. *Journal of the American Medical Association, 257*(12), 1615–1617.

Fornazzari, L. (1988). Clinical recognition and management of solvent abusers. *Internal Medicine, 9*(6), 99–109.

Giannini, A. J., Loiselle, R. H., DiMarzio, L. R., & Giannini, M. C. (1987). Augmentation of haloperidol by ascorbic acid in phencyclidine intoxication. *American Journal of Psychiatry, 144*(9), 1207–1209.

Greer, G., & Strassman, R. J. (1985). Information of "Ecstasy." *American Journal of Psychiatry, 142*(11), 1391.

Grinspoon, L., & Bakalar, J. B. (1981). Marihuana. In J. H. Lowinson & P. Ruiz (Eds.), *Substance abuse: Clinical problems and perspectives.* Baltimore: Williams & Wilkins.

Grinspoon, L., & Bakalar, J. B. (1986). Psychedelics and arylcyclohexylamines. In A. J. Frances & R. Hales (Ed.), *Annual review of psychiatry* (Vol. 5). Washington, DC: American Psychiatric Press.

Halikas, J., Weller, R., & Morse, C. (1982). Effects of regular marijuana use on sexual performance. *Journal of Psychoactive Drugs, 14*(1–2), 59–70.

Hollister, L. E. (1984). Effects of hallucinogens in humans. In B. L. Jacobs (Ed.), *Hallucinogens: Neurochemical, behavioral, and clinical perspectives.* New York: Raven Press.

Jaffe, J. (1985). Drug addiction and drug abuse. In A. G. Gilman, L. S. Goodman, T. W. Rall, & F. Murad (Eds.), *The pharmacological basis of therapeutics* (7th ed.). New York: Macmillan.

Johnston, L. D., O'Malley, P. M., & Bachman, J. G. (1989). *National trends in drug use and related factors among American high school students and young adults, 1975–1988* (DHHS Publication No. ADM 87–1535). Washington, DC: U.S. Government Printing Office.

Kolata, G. (1989, February 7). Worried doctors seek new clues to the drug Ecstasy's effect on brain. *New York Times,* p. C1.

Kolodny, R. C., Lessin, P., Toro, G., Masters, W. H., & Cohen, S. (1976). Depression of plasma testosterone with acute marijuana administration. In M. C. Braude & S. Szara (Eds.), *The pharmacology of marijuana.* New York: Raven Press.

Kolodny, R. C., Masters, W. H., Kolodner, R. M. & Toro, G. (1974). Depression of plasma testosterone levels after chronic intensive marijuana use. *New England Journal of Medicine, 290*(16), 872–874.

Lake, C. R., Stirba, A. L., Kinneman, R. E., Carlson, B., & Holloway, H. C. (1981). Mania associated with LSD ingestion. *American Journal of Psychiatry, 138*(11), 1508–1509.

Luisada, P. V. (1981). Phencyclidine. In J. H. Lowinson & P. Ruiz (Eds.), *Substance abuse: Clinical problems and perspectives.* Baltimore: Williams & Wilkins.

Mason, T. (1979). *Inhalant use and treatment* (NIDA Research Monograph). Washington, DC: U.S. Government Printing Office.

Miller, N. A., Gold, M. S., & Millman, R. B. (1988). PCP: A dangerous drug. *American Family Physician, 38*(3), 215–218.

Millman, R. B. (1982). Psychedelics. In J. B. Wyngaarden & L. H. Smith (Eds.), *Cecil textbook of medicine* (16th ed.) Philadelphia: W. B. Saunders.

Millman, R. B. (1989). Cannabis use and dependence. In T. B. Karasu (Ed.), *Treatment of psychiatric disorders.* Washington, DC: American Psychiatric Press.

Millman, R. B., & Sbriglio, R. (1986). Patterns of use and psychopathology in chronic marijuana users. *Psychiatric Clinics of North America, 9*(3), 533–545.

O'Donnell, J. A., & Clayton, P. R. (1979). Determinants of early marijuana use. In G. M. Bechner & A. S. Friedman (Eds.), *Youth drug abuse: Problems, issues and treatment.* Lexington, MA: Lexington Books.

O'Donnell, J. A., Voss, H. L., Clayton, R. R., et al. (1976). *Young men and drugs: A nationwide survey* (NIDA Research Monograph No. 42, DHEW Publication No. ADM 76–311). Washington, DC: U.S. Government Printing Office.

Peroutka, S. J. (1989). Ecstasy: A human neurotoxin? *Archives of General Psychiatry, 46,* 191.

Powell, D. J., & Fuller, R. W. (1983). Marijuana and sex. *Journal of Psychoactive Drugs, 15*(4), 269–280

Ron, M. A. (1986). Volatile substance abuse: A review of possible long-term neurological, intellectual, and psychiatric sequelae. *British Journal of Psychiatry, 148,* 235–246.

Rosen, A. M., Mukherjee, S., & Shinbach, K. (1984). The efficacy of ECT in phencyclidine-induced psychosis. *Journal of Clinical Psychiatry, 45*(5), 220–222.

Schuckit, M. A. (1985). *Drug and alcohol abuse.* New York: Plenum Press.

Sharp, C. W., & Korman, M. (1981). Volatile substances. In J. H. Lowinson & P. Ruiz (Eds.), *Substance abuse: Clinical problems and perspectives.* Baltimore: Williams & Wilkins.

Shick, J. F., & Smith, D. E. (1970). Analysis of the LSD flashback. *Journal of Psychedelic Drugs, 3,* 13–19.

Siegel, R. K. (1984). The natural history of hallucinogens. In B. L. Jacobs (Ed.), *Hallucinogens: Neurochemical, behavioral, and clinical perspectives.* New York: Raven Press.

Smith, D. E., Wesson, D. R., Buxton, M. E., et al. (1978). The diagnosis and treatment of the PCP abuse syndrome. In *PCP abuse: An appraisal* (NIDA Research Monograph No. 21). Washington, DC: U.S. Government Printing Office.

Stefanis, C., Boulougouris, I., & Liakos, A. (1976). Clinical and psychophysiological effects of cannabis in long term users. In M. C. Braude & S. Szara (Eds.), *Pharmacology of marijuana.* New York: Raven Press.

Ungerleider, J. T., & De Angelis, G. G. (1981). Hallucinogens. In J. H. Lowinson & P. Ruiz (Eds.), *Substance abuse: Clinical problems and perspectives.* Baltimore: Williams & Wilkins.

Wu, T. C., Tashkin, D. P., Djahed, B., & Rose, J. E. (1988). Pulmonary hazards of smoking marijuana as compared with tobacco. *New England Journal of Medicine, 318,* 347–351.

Yago, K. B., Pitts, F. N., Burgoyne, R. W., Aniline, O., Yago, L. S., & Pitts, A. F. (1981). The urban epidemic of phencyclidine use. *Journal of Clinical Psychiatry, 42,* 193–196.

Zinberg, N. (1984). *Drug, set, and setting.* New Haven, CT: Yale University Press.

8

Tobacco

NORMAN HYMOWITZ

Introduction

The use of tobacco *(Nicotine tobaccum)* has been traced to early American civilizations, where it played a prominent role in religious rites and ceremonies. Among the ancient Maya, tobacco smoke was used as "solar incense" to bring rain during the dry season. Shooting stars were believed to be burning butts cast off by the rain god (Schultes, 1978). The Aztecs employed tobacco *(Nicotine rustica)* as a powder, which was used in ceremonial rites as well as chewed as a euphoric agent with lime (Schultes, 1978).

In 1492, Columbus and his crew observed natives lighting rolls of dried leaves, which they called *tobacos* (cigars), and "swallowing" the smoke (Schultes, 1978). Twenty years later, Juan Ponce de Leon brought tobacco back to Portugal, where it soon was grown on Portuguese soil. Sir Walter Raleigh introduced smoking to England in 1565, and the English, too, successfully grew their own tobacco (Vogt, 1982). The growth of world trade led to the spread of tobacco to every corner of the globe.

The popular "weed" was not without its detractors. James I of England published a "counterblaste to tobacco" in 1604, and he arranged a public debate on the effects of tobacco in 1605. Pope Urban III condemned tobacco use in 1642, threatening excommunication of offenders. In Russia, a decree in 1634 punished tobacco users by nose slitting, castration, flogging, and banishment. These harsh measures were abolished by Peter the Great, who took to smoking a pipe in an effort to open a window to the West (Van Lancker, 1977).

It is believed that smoking of cigarettes first occurred in Mexico, where chopped tobacco was wrapped in corn husks (Van Lancker, 1977). The most popular forms of tobacco use in the United States in the past were chewing and dipping snuff, as evidenced by spittoons in homes and public places. In the late 1800s, cigarette smoking grew in popularity. James Buchanan Duke brought Polish and Russian Jews to the United States to manufacture cigarettes in 1867, and he used advertising to enlighten Americans about the pleasures of smoking. Cigarettes were first mass-produced in Durham, North Carolina, in 1884, when Washington Duke used a newly invented cigarette machine to produce some 120,000 cigarettes per day, thus ushering in the era of cheap, abundant tobacco products for smoking and setting the stage for 20th-century epidemics of lung cancer, emphysema, and coronary heart disease (Vogt, 1982).

In 1900, the total consumption of cigarettes in the United States was 2.5 billion (U.S. Department of Health and Human Services [DHHS], 1989a), and cigarette smoking was largely restricted to males. Major advances in agriculture, manufacturing, and marketing; two world wars; and changing cultural norms led to a marked increase in smoking rates. In the United States, total consumption of cigarettes increased from 2.5 billion in 1900 to 631.5 billion in 1980 (U.S. DHHS, 1989a). Cigarette consumption peaked in 1981 (640 billion), but has since declined to an estimated 574 billion in 1987 (U.S. DHHS, 1989a), the equivalent of more than 6 trillion doses of nicotine (Jones, 1987). By 1935, 52.5% of adult American males smoked cigarettes, and at the age of peak smoking prevalence (roughly from the age of 20 through the early 30s), more than 70% of all American males were smokers in 1947 (Warner, 1986).

Cigarettes are the nation's most heavily advertised consumer product (Warner, 1986). Advertising expenditures were estimated at more than $2 billion for 1985—twice the annual expenditures of the National Cancer Institute (American Cancer Society, 1986). Tobacco advertisers have expanded existing markets and opened new ones, contributing to significant changes in the demography of smoking. Tobacco advertisements in magazines targeted to women (Albright, Altman, Slater, & Maccoby, 1988) and minorities (Cummings, Giovino, & Mendicino, 1987) have increased markedly, as have smoking rates in both population groups. American women are now almost as likely to smoke as men, and teenage girls are more likely to begin smoking than teenage boys (U.S. DHHS, 1989a). The prevalence of smoking among blacks is higher than among whites (U.S. DHHS, 1989a), as are rates of lung cancer (Devesa & Diamond, 1983) and coronary heart disease (Sempos, Cooper, Kovar, & McMillan, 1988).

The occurrence of cigarette smoking as a mass phenomenon in the 20th century gave rise to new information about the adverse health consequences of smoking. Dr. Luther Terry, who served as Surgeon General of the U.S. Public Health Service from 1961 to 1965, noted that the landmark 1964 Surgeon General's Advisory Committee Report, *Smoking and Health,* was the culmination of growing scientific concern over a period of more than 25 years (Terry, 1983). This report documented the etiological link between cigarette smoking and cancer, coronary artery disease, and chronic obstructive pulmonary disease. The report also recognized the "habitual" nature of tobacco use, but stopped short of recoginizing tobacco use as an addiction.

Data on the health effects of cigarette smoking and other forms of tobacco continue to accumulate, documenting adverse effects of maternal smoking on the developing fetus (Asmussen, 1980) and of "secondhand" smoke on nonsmokers (Kauffmann, Tessier, & Oriol, 1983). The 1979 Report of the Surgeon General presented the most comprehensive review of health effects of smoking ever published (U.S. Department of Health, Education and Welfare [DHEW], 1979). Subsequent reports focused on women, the "changing cigarette," cancer, cardiovascular disease, chronic obstructive lung disease, the workplace, and involuntary smoking (U.S. DHHS, 1989a).

The 1988 Surgeon General's Report was entitled *The Health Consequences of Smoking: Nicotine Addiction* (U.S. DHHS, 1988). Major conclusions from this report were as follows: (1) Cigarettes and other forms of tobacco are addicting; (2) nicotine is the drug in tobacco that causes addiction; and (3) the pharmacological and behavioral processes that determine tobacco addiction are similar to those that determine addiction to drugs such as heroin and cocaine.

These conclusions were based on years of observation and study. Nicotine was isolated from tobacco leaves in 1828 by Posselt and Reimen; pharmacological studies of the physiological actions of nicotine were well underway by the end of the 19th century; and the central nervous system effects of nicotine were clearly documented in the 1950s (Henningfield & Jasinski, 1988). Attempts to market nicotine-free cigarettes have been commercial failures. Relapse rates among ex-smokers are remarkably similar to relapse rates among ex-heroin and alcohol users (cf. Hunt & Bespalec, 1974), and persons trying to quit smoking or other forms of tobacco use often experience intense withdrawal symptoms that can be relieved by ingestion of nicotine (Russell, 1986).

Studies of the conditioned, discriminative, and reinforcing functions of nicotine, in animals as well as humans (Henningfield & Goldberg, 1988), have underscored nicotine's dependence potential. Experiments in behavioral pharmacology showed that pretreatment of smokers with nicotine led to a reduction in smoking (Lucchesi, Schuster, & Emley, 1967); that smokers compensated for lower-nicotine cigarettes by smoking more (Ashton, Watson, Marsh, & Sadler, 1970); and that central nicotine antagonists, such as mecamylamine, led to an increase in cigarette smoking (Stolerman, Goldfarb, Fink, & Jarvik, 1973). These findings suggest that nicotine regulation plays an important role in smoking behavior, and that the effects of nicotine on the brain may be an important factor in understanding tobacco use. Studies of nicotine receptors in the brain (e.g., Sloan, Todd, & Martin, 1984), and a greater understanding of the role of cigarettes and other forms of tobacco as "nicotine delivery systems" (see Henningfield & Goldberg, 1988), served as additional bases for the 1988 report.

Definitions

Henningfield (1986) compared tobacco dependence to other forms of drug dependence and concluded that there are more similarities than differences. He noted that (1) tobacco dependence, like other forms of drug dependence, is a complex process, involving interactions between drug and nondrug factors; (2) tobacco dependence is an orderly and lawful process governed by the same factors that control other forms of drug self-administration; (3) tobacco use, like other forms of drug use, is sensitive to dose manipulation; (4) development of tolerance (diminished response to repeated doses of a drug or the requirement for increasing doses to have the same effect) and physiological dependence (termination of nicotine followed by a syndrome of withdrawal phenomena) when nicotine is repeatedly administered is similar to the development of tolerance and dependence of other drugs of abuse; and (5) tobacco, like many other substances of abuse, produces effects often considered of utility or benefit to the user (e.g., relief of anxiety or stress, avoidance of weight gain, alteration in mood).

Although the similarities between tobacco or nicotine dependence and other forms of drug dependence are noteworthy, there are features of tobacco use that make it unique. In contrast to many other drugs of abuse, tobacco products are legal and readily available. When used as intended, tobacco products lead to disease and death. Unlike alcohol, a legal drug that can be consumed socially and in moderation without ill effects, all levels of tobacco use are harmful (U.S. DHHS, 1988).

Large sums of money are spent each year to advertise and market tobacco products, particularly cigarettes. This adds an important dimension to tobacco dependence that is not present to the same degree with other substances, with the possible exception of alcohol. Few children in our society grow up free of the tobacco advertisers' reach; this provides unique opportunities for the tobacco companies to teach them about the virtues of tobacco, the manner in which it should be used, and the role it should play in their daily lives. So pervasive is the positive imagery associated with cigarette smoking that it is almost impossible to distinguish the reinforcing qualities of cigarettes that derive from past conditioning and learning from those that derive from nicotine per se.

Subtle behavioral factors may also assume a relatively greater role in controlling smoking than other forms of substance dependence. Daily, repetitive smoking patterns make cigarette smoking an overpracticed, unconscious behavior that is associated via conditioning mechanisms with almost every other behavior in the smoker's repertoire. So insidious is the moment-to-moment role of smoking in daily life that smokers often do not even know what to do with their hands when they stop smoking.

Diagnosis

According to the *Diagnostic and Statistical Manual of Mental Disorders*, third edition, revised (DSM-III-R), nicotine dependence is considered to be a psychoactive substance use disorder (American Psychiatric Association [APA], 1987). This diagnostic class covers symptoms and maladaptive behaviors associated with regular use of psychoactive substances that affect the central nervous system. The main features of psychoactive substance dependence are cognitive, behavioral, and physiological symptoms suggesting that the individual has impaired control of psychoactive substance use and continues to use the substance despite adverse consequences (APA, 1987).

The symptoms of dependence are the same across all categories of psychoactive substances (see Table 3.1 in Chapter 3 for the complete list), but for some classes some of the symptoms are less salient. At least three of the nine characteristic symptoms of dependence are necessary to make the diagnosis. In addition, the diagnosis of the dependence syndrome requires some symptoms of the disturbance to have persisted for at least 1 month, or to have occurred repeatedly over a longer period of time, as in binge drinking (APA, 1987).

The diagnosis of nicotine dependence in DSM-III-R is fairly straightforward. Information needed to make the diagnosis can be obtained through interview and questionnaire and can readily be collected along with other medical history data. Two National Institutes of Health publications, *Clinical Opportunities for Smoking Intervention* (U.S. DHHS, 1986) and *How to Help Your Patients Stop Smoking* (U.S. DHHS, 1989b), provide guidelines to help physicians inquire about smoking, assess their patient's needs, and encourage patients to quit smoking. The American Heart Association and the American Academy of Family Physicians also have prepared "quit-smoking kits" to enable physicians to intervene on smoking in their offices.

It is important to be aware that verbal report data can be misleading. Patients may underreport the number of cigarettes smoked per day, and, depending on the "demand" characteristics of the situation, may report that they have stopped smoking when they have not. Objective measures of smoking, such as expired air carbon monoxide, serum or saliva thiocyanate, and cotinine (U.S. DHEW, 1979), are available and readily applicable to clinical and research settings. Self-monitoring of smoking behavior and verification of smoking status by checking with an informant are additional ways of improving or monitoring the accuracy of verbal reports.

Most of the criteria for psychoactive substance dependence are characteristic of cigarette smoking and other forms of tobacco use. Cigarette smokers often smoke more than they intend to; have difficulty quitting or simply cutting down; spend a great deal of time procuring cigarettes and smoking them; persist in smoking despite known risk and/or current illness; and readily develop tolerance, enabling them to smoke a larger number of cigarettes per day than they did when they first started smoking. The fact that most smokers who quit smoking in the past did so on their own, without formal treatment, seems to be somewhat at odds with the popular notion of addiction. However, it is important to note that most former heroin users also gave up heroin without formal treatment (Johnson, 1977).

When smokers stop smoking, they may experience nicotine withdrawal as defined by DSM-III-R (APA, 1987). Diagnostic criteria for nicotine withdrawal are presented in Table 8.1. Associated features include increased slow rhythms on an electroencephalogram (EEG), decreased catecholamine, decreased metabolic rate, tremor, increased coughing, rapid eye movement (REM) change, gastrointestinal disturbance, headaches, insomnia, and impairment of performance on tasks requiring vigilance (APA, 1987). When smokers return to smoking after a period of prolonged abstinence, they often react

TABLE 8.1. DSM-III-R Criteria for Nicotine Withdrawal

A. Daily use of nicotine for at least several weeks.

B. Abrupt cessation of nicotine use, or reduction in the amount of nicotine used, followed within
    24 hours by at least four of the following signs:
    (1) craving for nicotine
    (2) irritability, frustration, or anger
    (3) anxiety
    (4) difficulty concentrating
    (5) restlessness
    (6) decreased heart rate
    (7) increased appetite or weight gain

Note. From the *Diagnostic and Statistical Manual of Mental Disorders* (3rd ed., rev., p. 151) by the American
Psychiatric Association, 1987, Washington, DC: Author. Copyright 1987 by the American Psychiatric Association. Reprinted by permission.

adversely to the first few cigarettes. However, tolerance develops quickly, and
they are able to resume earlier rates of smoking within a short time.

   Withdrawal symptoms begin within 24 hours of cessation or reduction of
nicotine use and usually decrease in intensity over a period of a few days to
several weeks. While the occurrence of withdrawal symptoms is evidence for
the physiological effects of nicotine, conditioning factors, particularly as they
interact with nicotine, also play a significant role. Stimuli in the environment
may trigger or inhibit the "urge" to smoke. School teachers, for example, go
several hours between cigarettes without discomfort, despite the fact that they
may "chain-smoke" in other environments.

   The fourth diagnostic criterion for psychoactive substance dependence
(i.e., frequent intoxication and withdrawal symptoms interfering with obligations at work, home, or school; APA, 1987) probably is less applicable to
nicotine dependence than to other forms of dependence, since nicotine rarely
causes any clinically significant state of intoxication. Even the "pleasure"
obtained from cigarette smoking is likely to be of a qualitatively different ilk
than the euphoric pleasure derived from other drugs (Kozlowski et al., 1989).
Tobacco withdrawal symptoms may produce considerable discomfort for
some smokers, and they could conceivably interfere with activities at work or
home. Smokers miss more days from work than nonsmokers because of illness
(U.S. DHEW, 1979), and when smokers develop frank disease, the disruption
of daily activities is greater. The fifth criterion (important social, occupational,
or recreational activities given up or reduced because of substance abuse; APA,
1987) will become more applicable in the future as more public places and
worksites post no-smoking signs and implement smoke-free policies.

   Psychoactive substance dependence is also conceptualized as occurring in
different degrees, including mild, moderate, and severe dependence; moreover,
dependence may be in partial or full remission (APA, 1987). "In partial
remission" means that during the past 6 months, some use of the substance
and some symptoms of dependence occurred. "In full remission" refers to the

fact that during the past 6 months, either there was no use of the substance or there was use of the substance but no symptoms of dependence (APA, 1987). For research purposes, 1 year of abstinence serves as the "gold standard" for successful treatment (Schwartz, 1987).

The concept of relative severity is an important one, as it is associated with the likelihood of developing adverse health consequences of tobacco dependence and the ease with which complete abstinence can be obtained. Heavy smokers (25 or more cigarettes per day) are at higher risk of disease than light smokers (fewer than 25 cigarettes per day), and they are less successful in quitting smoking than light smokers are (U.S. DHHS, 1988). The idea of remission also plays a significant role in understanding tobacco dependence. Adult smokers quit and start smoking many times before finally achieving long-term abstinence. The term "lapse" is used to describe a return to smoking that is short-lived and does not lead to a pattern of regular smoking. "Relapse" signifies a return to regular cigarette use.

Clinical Features

Under normal circumstances, cigarette smoking and other forms of tobacco use do not cause obvious states of intoxication, nor does their chronic use lead to organic brain damage, although acute effects of nicotine may affect vigilance and memory (U.S. DHHS, 1988). Overdose typically is not a problem, and acute effects of nicotine on health have received less attention in the medical literature than have chronic effects.

A number of poisonings and deaths from ingestion of nicotine, primarily involving nicotine-containing pesticides, have been reported, and acute intoxication has been observed in children after swallowing tobacco materials (U.S. DHHS, 1988). The lethal oral dose of nicotine in adults has been estimated as 40–60 mg (U.S. DHHS, 1988). Nicotine intoxication produces nausea, vomiting, abdominal pain, diarrhea, headaches, sweating, and pallor. More severe intoxication results in dizziness, weakness, and confusion, progressing to convulsions, hypotension, and coma. Death is usually due to paralysis of respiratory muscles and/or central respiratory control (U.S. DHHS, 1988).

Chronic effects of cigarette smoking take a massive toll, and the role of cigarette smoking and other forms of tobacco use in the pathogenesis of coronary heart disease, lung cancer, and chronic obstructive lung disease, as well as in many other forms of illness, have been widely documented and described (U.S. DHEW, 1979). The U.S. Surgeon General has estimated the annual U.S. mortality toll due to cigarette smoking to be 350,000 (Warner, 1986). Among these 350,000 are 130,000 cancer deaths, 170,000 coronary heart disease deaths, and 50,000 chronic obstructive lung disease deaths (80–90% of fatalities from emphysema and chronic bronchitis) (Warner, 1986). To put these numbers into perspective, Warner (1986) noted that the death toll associated with smoking is the equivalent of three fully loaded jumbo jets crashing and leaving no survivors, every single day of the year!

Several acute effects of nicotine also are important. Acute effects of nicotine have been implicated in sudden heart attack death (U.S. DHEW, 1979). Cigarette smoking and other forms of tobacco use are contraindicated in patients with frank heart disease, hypertension, diabetes, chronic obstructive lung disease, and diseases of the gastrointestinal tract for fear that nicotine and other components of tobacco will exacerbate existing illness, as well as contribute to progressive pathogenesis (U.S. DHEW, 1979).

Evidence of the harmful effects of cigarette smoking also may be observed in smokers in whom frank disease has not yet developed. Shortness of breath, cough, excessive phlegm, and nasal catarrh are common symptoms, which readily subside when smokers stop smoking (Hymowitz, Lasser, & Safirstein, 1982). Smokers often report a dulling of the senses of taste and smell, and smokers, as well as their family members, generally experience more colds and illness than nonsmokers (U.S. DHEW, 1979). Tobacco smoke and products may interact with other drugs that patients are taking (American Pharmacy, 1986). Drugs that show the most significant interactions with tobacco smoke include oral contraceptives, theophylline, propranolol, and other antianginal drugs. Drugs with moderately significant clinical interactions with smoking include propxyphene, pentazocene, phenylbutazone, phenothiazine, tricyclic antidepressants, benzodiazepines, amobarbital, heparin, furosemide, and vitamins (American Pharmacy, 1986).

A recent study (Bansil, Hymowitz, & Keller, 1989) showed that schizophrenic outpatients who smoked cigarettes required significantly more neuroleptic medication to control psychiatric symptoms than comparable nonsmokers, despite the fact that the patients were identical with respect to initial severity of illness. Multivariate analyses showed that the difference between the groups was not due to age, weight, sex, alcohol consumption, or tea/coffee intake. In view of the side effects profile of many drugs used in psychiatry, and the fact that the prevalence of tardive dyskinesia may be higher in mentally ill patients who smoke than in patients who do not smoke (Yassa, Lal, Korpassy, & Ally, 1987), it is important to achieve clinical effectiveness with as low a dose as possible. Cigarette smoking compromises this important goal.

Despite apparent discomfort, the evidence clearly indicates that smokers benefit in many ways when they stop smoking. Carbon monoxide is eliminated from their systems within 24 hours, and within a few months ex-smokers report a lessening of pulmonary symptoms, such as shortness of breath, cough, phlegm, and nasal catarrh (Hymowitz et al., 1982). Their senses of taste and smell return; peripheral vascular circulation improves; and ex-smokers report feeling healthier. Within a year's time, ex-smokers may experience an improvement in small-airway disease and a slowing in the rate of decline of pulmonary function (U.S. DHEW, 1979). Most important, risk of serious disease and premature death declines markedly over the course of several years following smoking cessation, and in people already disabled by frank disease, prospects for recovery improve greatly (U.S. DHEW, 1979).

Course

Cigarette smoking starts at an early age, usually in response to peer pressure and/or curiosity (Sachs, 1986). Personal characteristics, family, and cigarette marketing (U.S. DHHS, 1989a) also exert important influences. A sizeable proportion (one-third or more) of children as young as 9 years old have engaged in experimental "puffing," and there is a steady rise with age in the proportion of children who report becoming involved with smoking (Oei & Fea, 1987). Among American children 13 years old and older, only about one-third of those surveyed had not at least puffed a cigarette (Chassin et al., 1981). By age 14 or 15, smoking or nonsmoking behavior is an established pattern, and little experimentation takes place thereafter (Aitken, 1980).

While experimentation by young children is quite prevalent, few children 12 years old or under smoke on a regular basis, and very few have smoked more than one cigarette (Oei & Fea, 1987). As with experimentation, more regular use of cigarettes increases steadily with age. Approximately 6–8% of seventh- and eighth-graders report smoking "occasionally" (twice a month or more) (see Hurd et al., 1980). At the high school level, "regular" smoking is much more prevalent, with about one-fifth smoking on a daily basis, and no significant differences between the sexes (Oei & Fea, 1987).

As in the general population, the prevalence of smoking among young people has declined during the past decade. Reported daily smoking of cigarettes has decreased among high school seniors from a peak prevalence of 29% in 1976 to 19% in 1987, although the decrease has not been linear. Teenage smoking prevalence has remained fairly stable since 1980.

Although psychosocial factors play a major role in the initiation of smoking in adolescence, pharmacological and conditioning factors are also important. Like adults, young people often have difficulty stopping smoking (Green, 1980). The reasons they give for this difficulty—social pressure, urges, and withdrawal symptoms—implicate behavioral and physiological dependence on tobacco (Biglan & Liechtenstein, 1984). Hansen (1983) studied abstinence and relapse in high-school-age smokers (16–18 years old) who smoked an average of 15–20 cigarettes per day. As with adults, most relapse occurred within 3 months of stopping smoking. Variables that predicted relapse were the number of cigarettes smoked per day and the regularity of a teenager's smoking pattern—findings that are also indicative of tobacco dependence.

The early initiation of smoking is of considerable concern to the public health community. The pathogenesis of diseases such as chronic obstructive lung disease and atherosclerotic heart disease begins early in life, and duration of exposure to tobacco contributes to the likelihood of suffering adverse consequences as an adult (U.S. DHEW, 1979). However, it is not necessary to wait until adulthood to see signs of impaired health. Seely, Zuskin, and Bouhuys (1971) reported that cough, phlegm, and shortness of breath were more common among high school students who smoked than among non-smokers, with no significant differences between sexes. Pulmonary function testing showed that V_{max} at both 50% and 25% vital capacity (midmaximal flow rates) were significantly below expected levels in boys who smoked more than 15 cigarettes per day and in girls who smoked more than 10 cigarettes per day (Seely et al., 1971). The authors concluded that regular smoking for 1–5 years is sufficient to cause demonstrable decreases of lung function.

After high school, there is a gradual transition to regular adult smoking levels, and the relative influence of dependence on nicotine increases (Sachs, 1986). For most, smoking rates will hover around one pack per day and remain quite stable for most of their adult lives. Others will progress to higher smoking rates, again revealing marked day-to-day stability in nicotine ingestion. Recent surveys have shown that the percentage of adult smokers who smoke 25 or more cigarettes per day (heavy smokers) has increased since the 1960s, primarily because heavy smokers are least likely to stop smoking on their own or in formal smoking cessation programs (U.S. DHHS, 1988).

Inevitably, adverse consequences of cigarette smoking and other forms of tobacco use take their toll. Smokers experience excess illness and absence from work; diseases of the small and large airways of the lungs; and adverse complications of diseases that are exacerbated but not caused by smoking, such as diabetes and hypertension (U.S. DHEW, 1979). Most importantly, risk of life-threatening illness, such as chronic obstructive lung disease, lung cancer, and coronary heart disease, is significantly higher in smokers than in nonsmokers (U.S. DHEW, 1979). Most smokers are aware of these facts, and a majority admit that they would like to stop smoking (U.S. DHHS, 1989a). Approximately 2% per year succeed (U.S. DHHS, 1989a), most making a number of attempts before succeeding. Nearly half of all living adults who ever smoked have quit (U.S. DHHS, 1989a), and most did so "on their own" (Schachter, 1982). In 1965, 29.6% of those who had ever smoked had quit. By 1987, this proportion had increased to 44.8%. Whites have quit at a higher rate than blacks (46.4% vs. 31.5% in 1987), with black females being least likely to quit. College graduates have quit at a much higher rate than smokers with less education (U.S. DHHS, 1989a), although smoking cessation has become prevalent at all educational levels (Van Reek & Adriaanse, 1988). Today, approximately 29% of the adult population smokes cigarettes (U.S. DHHS, 1989a).

Many smokers do not quit smoking until they suffer serious illness, such as a heart attack. Others still do not stop, or they return to smoking as soon as they recover (U.S. DHHS, 1989a). Some smokers will continue smoking until the day they die. Unfortunately, statistics show that they die at younger ages than nonsmokers or former smokers; even for those who survive to a ripe old age, the quality of their health suffers in comparison to that of age-matched peers who do not smoke (U.S. DHEW, 1979).

Differential Diagnosis

The diagnosis of nicotine dependence is relatively simple, and, under normal circumstances, it is not difficult to distinguish nicotine dependence and withdrawal from other clinical syndromes. The clinician may wish to determine the severity of tobacco dependence, since such information may guide decisions to recommend behavioral or pharmacological approaches to smoking intervention (see Fagerstrom, 1988). Fagerstrom (1978) has developed a brief "physical dependence" questionnaire, which is helpful in identifying smokers for whom the physiological effects of nicotine are most likely to play a significant role. Among the most discriminating questions are "How soon after you wake up do you smoke your first cigarette?", "How many cigarettes a day do you smoke?", and "Have you stopped smoking or tried to stop smoking in the past?" (Kozlowski et al., 1989). According to Fagerstrom (1988), smokers who score high on the questionnaire are most likely to benefit from nicotine replacement thereapy.

My colleagues and I (Hymowitz, Sexton, Shekelle, Ockene, & Grandits, in press) studied the relationship between baseline variables and smoking cessation and relapse in the Multiple Risk Factor Intervention Trial (MRFIT). Variables that, upon multivariate analysis, were significantly associated with smoking cessation at Year 1 for Special Intervention (SI) participants were age, education, quit smoking in the past, alcoholic drinks per week, and baseline cigarettes per day. Older participants and those with the most education were most likely to quit smoking by Year 1 of the 6-year trial. Those who smoked the most, never quit smoking in the past (approximately 20% of smokers at baseline), and consumed the most alcohol per week were least likely to quit. Among Usual Care (UC) participants, who were referred to their own physicians for treatment of smoking and other risk factors, the presence of a wife who smoked and the number of life events endorsed on the Social Readjustment Rating Scale (Holmes & Rahe, 1967) also were significantly and negatively associated with quitting smoking.

Variables that influenced relapse differed from those that influenced cessation. For SI participants, only the number of alcoholic drinks per week emerged as a significant predictor of relapse upon multivariate analysis. For UC participants, education, past success in quitting, alcohol, and life events predicted relapse. It is likely that the formal group cessation program and follow-up support provided to SI men accounted for the differences between the SI and UC groups (Hymowitz et al., in press).

Ethnicity

Nationally, smoking rates for blacks exceed those for whites (U.S. DHHS, 1989a), and survey data reveal a lower percentage of blacks in the "former smoker" column. Although blacks are less likely to be classified as heavy smokers than whites (U.S. DHHS, 1988), they are more likely to smoke high-tar, high-nicotine, and mentholated brands (Cummings et al., 1987). At the same time, blacks suffer from the ravages of cigarette smoking at a level that may exceed the burden among whites. Recent analyses of data from the

American Cancer Society's prospective study of 1 million Americans (Garfinkel, 1984) shows that cigarette smoking may be particularly lethal to blacks by virtue of its synergistic effects with hypertension. Blacks also suffer from lung and other smoking-related cancers at rates that exceed those for whites (Devesa & Diamond, 1983).

Surveys of Hispanic smoking rates in the United States (Marcus & Crane, 1985) show that Hispanic males smoke as much as or more than white males, while Hispanic females smoke less than white females. In the 1979–1980 Health Interview Survey (Marcus & Crane, 1985), males of Puerto Rican origin averaged 40.2 cigarettes per day, while females smoked 24.6 cigarettes per day. Marked increases in tobacco-related morbidity and mortality in the Hispanic community can be expected. The Colorado Tumor Registry showed a 132% increase in lung cancer for Hispanic males between 1970 and 1980, compared to a 12% increase for white males during the same time period (Berg, 1983).

Although emerging epidemiological data underscore the need for intervention on smoking in minority populations, behavioral data on which to base the interventions are weak. Virtually no studies have specifically compared the efficacy of different interventions in different ethnic groups, and few studies have included sufficient numbers of minorities in their sample size to permit unambiguous generalization of results. Data from the MRFIT are an important exception (Hymowitz et al., in press). Blacks were as likely to stop smoking as whites, and they were as likely to remain abstinent (Hymowitz et al., in press). These findings held both for UC participants, who stopped smoking on their own, and for SI participants, who were offered group intervention and follow-up. For both blacks and whites, low socioeconomic status (SES), as measured by income and years of education, was negatively associated with success in stopping smoking. More effective intervention among low-SES populations is important for both whites and minorities.

Pharmacology

Nicotine is a tertiary amine composed of a pyridine and a pyrrolidine ring (U.S. DHHS, 1988). Absorption of nicotine across biological membranes depends on pH. Modern cigarettes produce smoke that is suitably flavored and sufficiently nonirritating to be inhaled deeply into lung alveoli (see Jones, 1987). When tobacco smoke reaches the small airways and alveoli of the lung, the nicotine is readily absorbed. The rapid absorption of nicotine from cigarette smoke through the lung occurs because of the huge surface area of the alveoli and small airways and because of the dissolution of nicotine at physiological pH, which facilitates transfer across cell membranes. Concentrations of nicotine in blood rise quickly during cigarette smoking and peak at its completion (U.S. DHHS, 1988).

Chewing tobacco, snuff, and nicotine polacrilex gum are of alkaline pH as a result of tobacco selection and/or buffering with additives by the manufacturer. The alkaline pH facilitates absorption of nicotine through mucous membranes. The rate of nicotine absorption from smokeless tobacco depends on the product and the route of administration. With fine-ground nasal snuff, blood levels of nicotine rise almost as fast as after cigarette smoking. The rate of nicotine absorption with the use of oral snuff, chewing tobacco, and nicotine polacrilex gum is more gradual (U.S. DHHS, 1988). Swallowed nicotine is poorly absorbed because of the high acidity of the gut.

Nicotine inhaled in tobacco smoke enters the blood very rapidly, with uptake into the brain occurring withing 1–2 minutes. After smoking, the action of nicotine on the brain occurs very quickly. Rapid onset of effects after a puff is believed to provide optimal reinforcement for the development of drug dependence (U.S. DHHS, 1988). The effects of nicotine decline after it is distributed to other tissues. The distribution half-life, which describes the movement of nicotine from the blood and other rapidly perfused tissues (such as the brain) to other body tissues, is approximately 9 minutes (U.S. DHHS, 1988).

After absorption into the blood, which is at pH 7.4, about 69% of the nicotine is ionized and 31% nonionized. Binding to plasma protein is less than 5%. The drug is distributed to body tissues with a steady-state volume of distribution averaging 180 liters. Spleen, liver, lungs, and brain have a high affinity for nicotine, whereas the affinity of adipose tissue is very low (U.S. DHHS, 1988). Nicotine binding sites or receptors in the brain have been identified and differentiated as very-high-affinity, high-affinity, and low-affinity types (U.S. DHHS, 1988). The most intense localization of labeled nicotine has been found in the interpeduncular nucleus and medial habenula.

Nicotine is extensively metabolized, primarily in the liver, but also to a small extent in the lung. Renal excretion of unchanged nicotine depends on urinary pH and urine flow, and may range from 2% to 35%, but typically accounts for 5–10% of elimination (U.S. DHHS, 1988).

The relationship between the dose of nicotine and the resulting response (dose–response relationship) is complex and varies with the specific response that is measured. Nicotine is commonly thought of as an example of a drug that in low doses causes ganglionic stimulation and in high doses causes ganglionic blockade following brief stimulation (U.S. DHHS, 1988). At very low doses, similar to those seen during cigarette smoking, cardiovascular effects appear to be mediated by the central nervous system, either through activation of chemoreceptor afferent pathways or by direct effects on the brain stem. The net result is sympathetic neural discharge with an increase in blood pressure and heart rate. At higher doses, nicotine may act directly on the peripheral nervous system, producing ganglionic stimulation and the release of adrenal catecholamine. With high doses or rapid administration, nicotine produces hypotension and slowing of heart rate, mediated either by peripheral vagal activation or by direct central depressor effects (U.S. DHHS, 1988).

Humans and other species readily develop tolerance to the effects of nicotine. Studies of tolerance to nicotine on *in vitro* tissue preparations may be summarized as follows: (1) With repeated dosing, responses diminished to nearly negligible levels; (2) after tolerance occurred, responsiveness could be restored by increasing the size of the dose; and (3) after a few hours without nicotine, responsiveness was partially or fully restored (U.S. DHHS, 1988). It is apparent that cigarette smokers reveal evidence for both acute tolerance (tachyphylaxis) and chronic tolerance to nicotine. This is consistent with the fact that smokers increase their tobacco consumption and intake of nicotine with experience (chronic tolerance). When they abstain for a while, the first few cigarettes they smoke produce a variety of bodily symptoms. Thereafter, they quickly become less sensitive (acute tolerance). Tolerance may be related to an increase in central nicotine-binding sites, or to a decrease in their sensitivity (U.S. DHHS, 1988).

Psychopharmacotherapy

Successful intervention on smoking and other forms of tobacco use must address many contributing factors. These include acquired associations between smoking and environmental events, the use of tobacco to regulate mood and cope with stress, subtle relationships between smoking and other features of the smoker's behavioral repertoire, many idiosyncratic ways in which tobacco dependence interweaves itself within the psychosocial fabric of each smoker's life, and pharmacological properties of tobacco. Withdrawal symptoms, the tendency for environmental stimuli to elicit the urge to smoke, and the need to cope actively with potential obstacles to abstinence represent important issues once smokers stop smoking.

There are numerous approaches to smoking cessation in adults, and many comprehensive reviews and critiques of the literature have been published (e.g., Leventhal & Cleary, 1980; Schwartz, 1987). Although many approaches to smoking cessation have been successful in the short run, few if any have proved satisfactory in terms of long-term abstinence. Relapse seems to be the rule rather than the exception (Hunt & Bespelac, 1974), with most smokers relapsing within 3 months after the end of treatment. Of the many nonpharmacological approaches to smoking cessation, behavioral approaches are most germane to the present chapter: They have undergone the most extensive experimental study, they are suitable for office- and clinic-based physician interventions, and they may be used in combination with pharmacological approaches to smoking cessation (Fagerstrom, 1988).

Behavioral programs, whether in group, individual, or "self-help" formats, typically include a number of strategies (self-monitoring, stimulus control procedures, behavioral contracting, relaxation training, advice on diet and exercise, "quit dates," self-management skill training for relapse prevention, etc.) to motivate smokers and to help them gain control over smoking and systematically eliminate smoking from their behavioral repertoire. Once smokers stop smoking, many of the very same behavioral skills that helped them quit smoking are used to help them cope with stress and problematic situations to prevent relapse. Aversive conditioning procedures may also be used, either alone or in combination with other behavioral techniques, and they are among the most successful approaches to initial smoking cessation (Leventhal & Cleary, 1980). However, the initial success is usually compromised by high relapse rates (Raw & Russell, 1980).

"Multicomponent" behavioral programs include diverse behavioral strategies to help smokers modify their behavior. Success rates vary, depending on selection factors, cost, and whether aversive conditioning procedures are used. Schwartz (1987) reported that 1-year quit rates for multicomponent programs averaged 40%. This figure seems somewhat inflated. When objective measures of smoking and completeness of follow-up are taken into account, 1-year quit rates of 20–30% are more common. End-of-treatment quit rates may be higher, but relapse again compromises the long-term success of the intervention.

The MRFIT employed diversified behavioral strategies for initial smoking cessation and long-term smoking abstinence (Hughes, Hymowitz, Ockene, Simon, & Vogt, 1981). The reported quit rates for SI men were 43.1% at Year 1 and 50% at Year 6 (Hymowitz, 1987). These quit rates were significantly superior to those for UC participants (13% and 29% at Years 1 and 6, respectively). When serum thiocyanate, a breakdown product of hydrogen cyanide, was used as an objective measure of smoking, the Year 6 quit rate for SI participants was reduced to 46% (Hymowitz, 1987).

Most of the SI men quit smoking during the first year of the program, whereas quitting for UC men was more evenly distributed over the 6 years of the program (Ockene, Hymowitz, Sexton, & Broste, 1982). This is consistent with the overall trend toward quitting smoking in the United States during the same time period (U.S. DHHS, 1989a). Of the SI smokers who reported not smoking at Year 1, 65% continued to report abstinence at each follow-up visit through Year 6 (U.S. DHHS, 1987). These findings compare quite favorably with those of most studies in the literature, and they show that large numbers of adult smokers can quit smoking and remain abstinent (Hymowitz, 1987).

Heavy smokers in the MRFIT were less likely to stop smoking than light smokers. Ockene (1988) reported that the Year 6 quit rate for SI light smokers (fewer than 25 cigarettes per day) was 61.6%. The quit rate for SI heavy smokers (more than 25 cigarettes per day) was 37.6%. A similar differential was observed for UC smokers. These findings, which are consistent with other reports in the literature (U.S. DHHS, 1988), suggest that the medical, educational, and behavioral strategies used in the MRFIT were more effective for the lighter smokers. Those at greater risk of heart disease, the heavy smokers, were less likely to achieve abstinence.

In view of the fact that the percentage of smokers in our society who smoke heavily has increased dramatically over the past decade (U.S. DHHS, 1988), there is a need to develop interventions that are more helpful to heavy smokers. Pharmacological therapies may help fill this void. Lighter smokers generally report fewer or less intense withdrawal symptoms than heavier smokers (Stitzer & Gross, 1988), and it is likely that heavy smokers are relatively more dependent on nicotine than light smokers. Pharmacological agents that counteract withdrawal symptoms may be of particular value to heavy smokers, either when used alone or as a component of a multicomponent behavioral program.

At present, there are two pharmacological approaches to minimize withdrawal symptoms. One approach is to use a pharmacological agent to block or minimize withdrawal symptoms. Another is to use a nicotine replacement strategy, providing an alternative, less harmful form of nicotine within a therapeutic context, so that smokers can abstain from smoking without experiencing excessive withdrawal symptoms (Jasinski & Henningfield, 1988).

Clonidine, a noradrenergic agonist used in the treatment of hypertension, diminishes symptoms of both opiate withdrawal (Gold, Redmond, & Kleber, 1978) and alcohol withdrawal (Bjorkqvist, 1975). Glassman, Stetner, and Raizman (1986) showed that clonidine significantly diminished withdrawal symptoms of cigarette smokers who were abstinent for 24 hours. Compared to placebo treatment and to a benzodiazepine-like substance, alprazolam, clonidine was significantly more effective in reducing complaints of craving. For anxiety, irritability, concentration, and tension, clonidine and alprazolam were clearly better than placebo and essentially identical to each other (Glassman et al., 1986).

A more recent study (Glassman et al., 1988) showed that clonidine may have efficacy for smoking cessation. Following brief behavioral counseling, smokers who were able to reduce smoking levels by 50% were randomly assigned to clonidine or placebo therapy. Four-week and 6-month follow-up of smokers revealed significantly more abstinence for clonidine-treated subjects than for those who received placebo. At the end of 4 weeks, during which time subjects received clonidine (210–246 μg per day) or placebo, 61% of clonidine-treated subjects were abstinent, compared to 26% of placebo-treated subjects (verified by serum cotinine measurement). Six months after discontinuing medication, 27% of clonidine-treated patients and 5% of controls were abstinent (according to verbal report). This difference is highly significant, and further research on the efficacy of clonidine therapy for smoking cessation is warranted.

Other examples of drugs used to minimize withdrawal symptoms are meprobamate, intended to counter anxiety, and amphetamine, used to overcome sleepiness (Schwartz, 1987). Neither has proved more successful than placebo in helping people quit smoking, although systematic study of their efficacy (or that of other anxiolytic, stimulant, or antidepressant agents) within the context of a comprehensive intervention program has not been undertaken. In view of the fact that stress and the regulation of affect are important determinants of adult smoking behavior, it is somewhat surprising that more systematic study of the utility of antidepressants and anxiolytic agents for smoking cessation and relapse prevention has not been undertaken (see Jarvik & Henningfield, 1988). Research has shown, however, that alcohol intake is associated with increased smoking (see Jarvik & Henningfield, 1988), as is heroin self-administration (Mello, Mendelson, Sellers, & Kuenle, 1980). In view of the lack of a necessary data base, the side effects profile of many antidepressants, and the addictive potential of the benzodiazepines, their use for smoking cessation at this time is probably best restricted to carefully selected and monitored clinical encounters.

Nicotine polacrilex gum, a nicotine-containing chewing gum marketed by Lakeside Pharmaceutical, a division of Merrell Dow, may play an important role in replacement therapy for smoking cessation. Interest in nicotine gum derives from several quarters. The concept of nicotine replacement is consistent with renewed interest in the addictive properties of nicotine, and use of nicotine gum for treatment of tobacco dependence is viewed in the same light as methadone maintenance therapy for heroin addicts (Jasinski & Henningfield, 1988). From the public health point of view, nicotine gum offers the potential of providing effective therapy to large numbers of smokers at minimal cost. It has been estimated that 70% of smokers visit a physician each year (U.S. DHHS, 1989a). Brief physician counseling and prescription of nicotine gum have the potential for a significant impact on nationwide smoking rates, even if quit rates are not as great as those obtained in labor-intensive treatment programs. Finally, heavy smokers have been relatively unresponsive to behavioral interventions in the past. Nicotine replacement therapy may represent a new opportunity for successful intervention with this important subgroup of smokers.

Fagerstrom (1988) reviewed findings from four placebo-controlled studies of the effects of nicotine polacrilex gum on tobacco withdrawal symptoms. Although 2-mg gum had little if any effect on "craving," it did reduce the symptom of irritablility/impatience in each of the studies. Other symptoms that were reduced in at least one of the four studies (but not in all of them) were depression, somatic complaints, sleepiness/trouble sleeping, sociability, hunger, difficulty in concentrating, restlessness, feeling annoyed, hostility, mood fluctuations, and total withdrawal discomfort. Fagerstrom (1988) suggested that 4-mg nicotine gum, which has not received Food and Drug Administration approval for clinical use in the United States, yields higher blood nicotine levels and may be more effective in relieving withdrawal symptoms than 2-mg gum (but see Tønnesen et al., 1988).

Schwartz (1987) summarized data from 28 trials of nicotine gum by 20 different investigative groups. He noted that follow-up "quit rates" have been treated differently for nicotine polacrilex gum than for other quit-smoking therapies. In most studies, the quit rate at 1 year means that a year has passed since the termination of therapy. This is not the case for nicotine gum, as follow-up starts with initiation of gum use, not termination. Very often, gum use is encouraged through the first 6 months of follow-up, and approximately 10% of participants continue using the gum for 1 year, accounting for a sizeable percent of "abstinent" smokers at follow-up.

Schwartz (1987) evaluated the results of nine trials of nicotine gum alone from 1979–1986. Average 1-year quit rates were 11%, with many of the studies failing to document superiority over placebo treatment. Improper use of the gum, poor compliance, and failure to maintain proper blood nicotine levels suggest that proper supervision and follow-up are critical to successful treatment.

Even when appropriate care is taken, the efficacy of nicotine gum alone for smoking cessation is modest at best. Recent studies of gum use within physician practices underscore this point. Wilson et al. (1988) assessed the impact of three conditions on 1-year smoking cessation rates. Physicians in 70 community general practices were randomly allocated by practice to one of three groups: Usual-care, gum-only, and gum-plus groups. In the third group, physicians received training in how to advise patients to stop smoking, set a quit date, offer nicotine gum, and conduct at least four follow-up visits. According to a criterion of at least 3 months of abstinence (validated by saliva cotinine), 8.8% of the patients of the trained physicians had "quit" smoking at 1 year, compared to 4.4% and 6.1% of the patients in the usual-care and gum-only groups, respectively (Wilson et al., 1988). These differences were not statistically significant, although the "quit rate" was doubled in the gum-plus compared to the usual-care group.

Hughes, Gust, Keenan, Fenwick, and Healey (1989) similarly failed to obtain greater quit rates at 1 year for smokers in a family practice clinic given nicotine gum than for comparable smokers given placebo. Ten percent of those who received nicotine gum and 7% of those who received placebo reported continuous abstinence for 11 months. The initial results from the Stanford Stop Smoking Project were positive, with abstinence rates at 6 months of 31% for nicotine gum and 22% for placebo (Fortmann, Killen, Telch, & Newman, 1988). It is hoped that the difference between groups will be sustained at 1 year, by which time a majority of participants will stop using the gum.

The efficacy of nicotine polacrilex gum is greater when it is incorporated into a comprehensive behavioral treatment program (Schwartz, 1987). From 1973 to 1986, 11 studies combined nicotine gum and behavioral treatment/therapy and reported 1-year follow-up data (Schwartz, 1987). The average quit rate at 1 year was 29%; rates ranged from 12% to 49%. Many of the studies reported that the gum conferred significant advantage over behavioral treatment alone, and some (e.g., Jarvis, Raw, Russell, & Feyerabend, 1982) reported more than a 2 : 1 advantage (47% vs. 21% at 12-month follow-up for nicotine gum and placebo, respectively).

A recent study by Hall, Tunstall, Rugg, Jones, and Benowitz (1985) compared the effects on smoking cessation of a behavioral treatment program (B), which included aversive smoking, relapse prevention training, and relaxation, to the effects of nicotine gum alone (N) and nicotine gum plus behavioral treatment (NB). Nicotine gum was dispensed to appropriate subjects for the first 6 months of the study.

Each treatment yielded high initial cessation rates (78%, 81%, and 95%

for B, N, and NB, respectively). At Week 26, quit rates were 31%, 47%, and 59% for B, N, and NB, respectively. These differences achieved statistical significance, despite the fact that considerable relapse had occurred in each group. At Year 1, the quit rates were 28%, 37%, and 44% for B, N, and NB, respectively. These differences were not statistically significant, although the differences were in the expected direction.

Two other aspects of the data are noteworthy. First, between 6 months and 1 year, relatively more relapse took place for the two nicotine-gum-treated groups (N and NB) than for the B group. This may have been due to the fact that nicotine gum was no longer dispensed after 6 months. Although nicotine polacrilex is not a benign substance, it is less harmful than cigarette smoking; it may be of value to encourage longer use of the gum, perhaps at a low-maintenance dose, rather than run the risk of relapse.

Second, subjects with the highest cotinine levels at the start of the study (heavy or dependent smokers) responded better to nicotine gum therapy than subjects with lower cotinine levels (light smokers) (Hall, et al., 1985). For the behavioral treatment, subjects with lower levels did better. At this time, nicotine polacrilex therapy is the only intervention on smoking that has achieved better quit rates for heavy smokers than for light smokers. Although not all studies have replicated this finding (e.g., DeWitt & Camic, 1986; Tønnesen et al., 1988), a number of others have (cf. Fagerstrom, 1988). Additional research on the utility of nicotine gum for heavy smokers is needed. The answer, no doubt, will have a great impact on the course of nicotine replacement therapy in the future.

Another approach to the pharmacological management of smoking may be classified as "deterrant therapy." In a manner analogous to disulfiram therapy with alcoholics (Jarvik & Henningfield, 1988), a pharmacological agent is used to pair smoking or other forms of tobacco use with an aversive sensation, thereby counteracting the urge and tendency to smoke. Silver acetate products, such as Tabmint and Respaton (Rosenberg, 1974), have been available as over-the-counter stop-smoking aids in Europe for more than a decade. Smokers are instructed to chew the gum or lozenge approximately four to six times per day. If they light up a cigarette within several hours of chewing, they experience an aversive metallic taste and possibly nausea. Excessive use of the gum may lead to argyrism, a permanent discoloring of the skin due to accumulation of silver.

Malcolm, Currey, Mitchell, and Kiel (1986) reported that, in a double-blind controlled study that employed objective measures of smoking, subjects using Tabmint for 3 weeks of treatment had a smoking cessation rate of 11%. Placebo subjects had a smoking cessation rate of 4%. At 4 months, the quit rate for Tabmint subjects was 7%; for controls, it was 0%. Long-term follow-up data for silver acetate products are currently lacking, nor have the effects of silver acetate on smoking cessation and relapse prevention been studied within the context of a comprehensive multicomponent behavioral program.

Nicotine blockade therapy (see Jarvik & Henningfield, 1988) represents another approach to smoking cessation. Antagonists that act both centrally and peripherally (e.g., mecamylamine), but not those that only act peripherally (e.g., pentolinium), are known to influence smoking under experimental conditions—causing, for example, an increase in smoking (Stolerman et al., 1973). Although nicotine antagonists would not be expected to be of benefit for initial cessation (i.e., antagonists would lead to an increase in smoking), they may be of therapeutic value in programs aimed at preventing relapse. Daily treatment with an antagonist, for example, would decrease the tendency to lapse in the same manner that naltrexone treatment may be advantageous to ex-opioid users (Jarvik & Henningfield, 1988). At this time, the efficacy of this mode of therapy for modification of tobacco use has not been systematically studied.

References

Aitken, P. P. (1980). Peer group pressures, perental controls and cigarette smoking among ten-to-fourteen year olds. *British Journal of Social and Clinical Psychology, 19,* 141–146.

Albright, C. L., Altman, D. G., Slater, M. D., & Maccoby, N. (1988). Cigarette advertisements in magazines: Evidence for a differential focus on women's and youth magazines. *Health Education Quarterly, 15,* 225–233.

American Cancer Society. (1986). *Facts and figures on smoking, 1976–1986* (Publication No. 5650-LE). New York: Author.

American Pharmacy. (1986). Pharmacists' "helping smokers quit" program. *American Pharmacy,* NS26(7), 25–33.

American Psychiatric Association (APA). (1987). *Diagnostic and statistical manual of mental disorders* (3rd ed., rev.). Washington, DC: Author.

Ashton, H., Watson, D. W., Marsh, R., & Sadler, J. (1970). Puffing frequency and nicotine intake in cigarette smokers. *British Medical Journal, iii,* 679–681.

Asmussen, I. (1980). Effects of maternal smoking on the fetal cardiovascular system. In R. M. Lauer & R. B. Shekelle (Eds.), *Childhood prevention of atherosclerosis and hypertension* (pp. 235–250). New York: Raven Press.

Bansil, R. K., Hymowitz, N. & Keller, S. (1989, May). *Cigarette smoking and neuroleptics.* Paper presented at the annual meeting of the American Psychiatric Association, San Francisco.

Berg, J. (1983). *Cancer in Colorado: A new high.* Denver: AMC Cancer Research Center.

Biglan, O., & Lichtenstein, E. (1984). A behavior-analytic approach to smoking acquistion: Some recent findings. *Journal of Applied Social Psychology, 14,* 207–223.

Bjorkqvist, S. E. (1975). Clonidine in alcohol withdrawal. *Acta Psychiatric Scandinavica, 52,* 256–263.

Chassin, L., Corty, E., Presson, C. C., Olshovsky, R. W., Bensenberg, M., & Sherman, S. J. (1981). Predicting adolescents' intentions to smoke cigarettes. *Journal of Health and Social Behavior, 22,* 445–455.

Cummings, K. M., Giovino, G., & Mendicino, A. J. (1987). Cigarette advertising and black–white differences in brand preference. *Public Health Reports, 102,* 698–701.

Devesa, S. S., & Diamond, E. L. (1983). Socioeconomic and racial differences in lung cancer incidence. *American Journal of Epidemiology, 118,* 818–831.

DeWitt, H., & Camic, P. M. (1986). Behavioral and pharmacologic treatment of cigarette smoking: End of treatment comparisons. *Addictive Behaviors, 11,* 331–335.

Fagerstrom, K. O. (1978). Measuring degree of physician dependence to tobacco smoking with reference to individualization of treatment. *Addictive Behaviors, 3,* 235–241.

Fagerstrom, K. O. (1988). Efficacy of nicotine chewing gum: A review. In O. F. Pomerleau & C. S. Pomerleau (Eds.), *Nicotine replacement* (pp. 109–128). New York: Alan R. Liss.

Fortmann, S. P., Killen, J. D., Telch, M. J., & Newman, B. (1988). Minimal contact treatment for smoking cessation. *Journal of the American Medical Association, 260,* 1575–1580.

Garfinkel, L. (1984). Cigarette smoking and coronary heart disease in blacks: Comparisons to whites in a prospective study. *American Heart Journal, 108,* 802–807.

Glassman, A. H., Stetner, F., & Raizman, P. (1986). Clonidine and cigarette smoking withdrawal. In J. K. Ockene (Ed.), *The pharmacologic treatment of tobacco dependence: Proceedings of the World Congress* (pp. 174–180). Cambridge, MA: Institute for the Study of Smoking Behavior and Policy.

Glassman, A. H., Stetner, F., Walsh, T., Raizman, P. S., Fleiss, J. L., Cooper, T. B., & Covey, L. S. (1988). Heavy smokers, smoking cessation, and clonidine. *Journal of the American Medical Association, 259,* 2863–2866.

Gold, M. S., Redmond, D. E., Jr., and Kleber, H. D. (1978). Clonidine blocks acute opiate-withdrawal symptoms. *Lancet, ii,* 599–601.

Green, D. E. (1980). Beliefs of teenagers about smoking and health. In R. M. Leauer & R. B. Shekelle (Eds.), *Childhood prevention of atherosclerosis and hypertension* (pp. 223–228). New York: Raven Press.

Hall, S. M., Tunstall, C., Rugg, D., Jones, R. T., & Benowitz, N. L. (1985). Nicotine gum and behavioral treatment in smoking cessation. *Journal of Consulting and Clinical Psychology, 53,* 256–258.

Hansen, W. B. (1983). Behavioral predictors of abstinence: Early indicators of a dependence on tobacco in adolescents. *International Journal of the Addictions, 18,* 913–920.

Henningfield, J. E. (1986). How tobacco produces drug dependence. In J. K. Ockene (Ed.), *The pharmacologic treatment of tobacco dependence: Proceedings of the World Congress* (pp. 19–31). Cambridge, MA: Institute for the Study of Smoking Behavior and Policy.

Henningfield, J. E., & Goldberg, S. R. (1988). Pharmacologic determinants of tobacco self-administration by humans. *Pharacology, Biochemistry and Behavior, 30,* 221–226.

Henningfield, J. E., & Jasinski, D. R. (1988). Pharmacologic basis for nicotine replacement. In O.F. Pomerleau & C. S. Pomerleau (Eds.), *Nicotine replacement* (pp. 35–61). New York: Alan R. Liss.

Holmes, T. H., & Rahe, R. H. (1967). The Social Readjustment Rating Scale. *Journal of Psychosomatic Research, 11,* 213–218.

Hughes, J. R., Gust, S. W., Keenan, R. M., Fenwick, J. W., & Healey, M. L. (1989). Nicotine vs. placebo gum in general medical practice. *Journal of the American Medical Association, 261,* 1300–1305.

Hughes, G. H., Hymowitz, N., Ockene, J. K., Simon, N., & Vogt, T. M. (1981). The Multiple Risk Factor Intervention Trial (MRFIT): V. Intervention on smoking. *Preventive Medicine, 10,* 476–500.

Hunt, W. A., & Bespalec, D. A. (1974). An evaluation of current methods of modifying smoking behavior. *Journal of Clinical Psychology, 30,* 431–438.

Hurd, P. D., Johnson, C. A., Pechacek, T., Bast, L. P., Jacobs, D. R., and Luepker, R. V. (1980). Prevention of cigarette smoking in seventh grade students. *Journal of Behavioral Medicine, 3,* 15-27.

Hymowitz, N. (1987). Community and clinical trials of disease prevention: Effects on cigarette smoking. *Public Health Reviews, 15,* 45–81.

Hymowitz, N., Lasser, N. L., & Safirstein, B. H. (1982). Effects of graduated external filters on smoking cessation. *Preventive Medicine, 11,* 85–95.

Hymowitz, N., Sexton, M., Shekelle, R., Ockene, J., & Grandits, G. (in press). Relationship between baseline variables and smoking cessation and relapse in MRFIT smokers. *Preventive Medicine.*

Jarvik, M. E., & Henningfield, J. E. (1988). Pharmacological treatment of tobacco dependence. *Pharmacology, Biochemistry and Behavior, 30,* 279–294.

Jarvis, M. D., Raw, M., Russell, M. A. H., & Feyerabend, C. (1982). Randomised controlled trial of nicotine chewing-gum. *British Medical Journal, 285,* 537–540.

Jasinski, D. R., & Henningfield, J. E. (1988). Conceptual basis of replacement therapies for chemical dependence. In O. F. Pomerleau & C. S. Pomerleau (Eds.), *Nicotine replacement* (pp. 13–34). New York: Alan R. Liss.

Johnson, B. D. (1977). The race, class, and irreversibility hypotheses: Myths and research about heroin. In J. D. Rittenhouse (Ed.), *The epidemiology of heroin and other narcotics* (NIDA Research Monograph No. 16, pp. 51–60). Washington, DC: U.S. Government Printing Office.

Jones, R. T. (1987). Tobacco dependence. In H. Y. Meltzer (Ed.), *Psychopharmacology: The third generation of progress* (pp. 1589–1995). New York: Raven Press.

Kauffmann, F., Tessier, J. F., & Oriol, P. (1983). Adult passive smoking in the home environment: A risk factor for chronic airflow limitation. *American Journal of Epidemiology, 117,* 269.

Kozlowski, L. T., Wilkinson, A., Skinner, W., Kent, C., Franklin, T., & Pope, M. (1989). Comparing tobacco cigarette dependence with other drug dependencies. *Journal of the American Medical Association, 261,* 898–901.

Leventhal, H., & Cleary, P. P. (1980). The smoking problem: A review of the research and theory in behavioral risk modifiction. *Psychological Bulletin, 88,* 370–405.

Lucchesi, B. R., Schuster, C. R., & Emley, A. B. (1967). The role of nicotine as a determinant of cigarette smoking frequency in man with observations of certain cardiovascular effects associated with the tobacco aklaloid. *Clinical Pharmacology and Therapeutics, 8,* 789–796.

Malcolm, R., Currey, H. S., Mitchell, M. O., & Kiel, J. E. (1986). Silver acetate gum as a deterrent to smoking. *Chest, 90,* 107–111.

Marcus, A. C., & Crane, L. A. (1985). Smoking behavior among U.S. Latinos: An emerging challenge for public health. *American Journal of Public Health, 75,* 169–172.

Mello, N. K., Mendelson, J. H., Sellers, M. L., & Kuenle, J. C. (1980). Effects of heroin self-administration on cigarette smoking. *Psychopharmacology, 67,* 45–52.

Ockene, J. K. (1988, March). *Why are there differences in reduction of lung cancer versus heart disease risk after quitting smoking?* Paper presented at the American Heart Association 28th Annual Conference on Cardiovascular Disease Epidemiology, Santa Fe, NM.

Ockene, J. K., Hymowitz, N., Sexton, M., & Broste, S. K. (1982). Initial and long-term cessation of smoking after four years of the Multiple Risk Factor Intervention Trial (MRFIT). *Preventive Medicine, 11,* 621–638.

Oei, T. S., & Fea, A. (1987). Smoking prevention program for children: A review. *Journal of Drug Education, 17,* 11–42.

Raw, M., & Russell, M. A. H. (1980). Rapid smoking, cue exposure, and support in the modification of smoking. *Behaviour Research and Therapy, 18,* 363–372.

Rosenberg, A. (1974). An investigation into the effect on cigarette smoking of new anti-smoking preparation. *Journal of International Medicine Research, 4,* 310–313.

Russell, M. A. H. (1986). Conceptual framework for nicotine substitution. In J. K. Ockene (Ed.), *The pharmacologic treatment of tobacco dependence: Proceedings of the World Congress* (pp. 90–107). Cambridge, MA: Institute for the Study of Smoking Behavior and Policy.

Sachs, D. P. L. (1986). Nicotine polacrilex: Clinical promises delivered and yet to come. In J. K. Ockene (Ed.), *The pharmacologic treatment of tobacco dependence: Proceedings of the World Congress* (pp. 120–140). Cambridge, MA: Institute for the Study of Smoking Behavior and Policy.

Schachter, S. (1982). Recidivism and self-cure of smoking and obesity. *American Psychologist, 37,* 436–444.

Schultes, R. E. (1978). Ethnopharmacological significance of psychotropic drugs of vegetal origin. In W. G. Clark & J. del Giudice (Eds.), *Principles of psychopharmacology* (pp. 41–70). New York: Academic Press.

Schwartz, J. L. (1987). *Smoking cessation methods: The United States and Canada, 1978–1985* (DHHS Publication No. NIH 87-2940). Washington, DC: U.S. Government Printing Office.

Seely, J. E., Zuskin, E., & Bouhuys, A. (1971). Cigarette smoking: Objective evidence for lung damage in teen-agers. *Science, 172,* 741–743.

Sempos, C., Cooper, R., Kovar, M. G., & McMillen, M. (1988). Divergence of the recent trends in coronary mortality for the four major race–sex groups in the United States. *American Journal of Public Health, 78,* 1422–1427.

Sloan, J. W., Todd, G. D., & Martin, W. R. (1984). Nature of nicotine binding to rat brain P_2 fraction. *Pharmacology, Biochemistry and Behavior, 20,* 899–909.

Stitzer, M. L., & Gross, J. (1988). Smoking relapse: The role of pharmacological and behavioral factors. In O. F. Pomerleau & C. S. Pomerleau (Eds.), *Nicotine replacement* (pp. 163–184). New York: Alan R. Liss.

Stolerman, I. P., Goldfarb, T., Fink, R., & Jarvik, M. E. (1973). Influencing cigarette smoking with nicotine antagonists. *Psychopharmacologia, 28,* 237–259.

Terry, L. L. (1983). The Surgeon General's first report on smoking and health. *New York State Journal of Medicine, 83,* 1254–1255.

Tønnesen, P., Fryd, V., Hansen, M., Helsted, J., Gunersen, A. B., Forchammer, H., & Stockner, M. (1988). Two and four mg nicotine chewing gum and group counseling in smoking cessation: An open, randomized, controlled trail with a 22 month follow-up. *Addictive Behaviors, 13,* 17–27.

U.S. Department of Health, Education and Welfare (DHEW). (1979). *Smoking and health: A report of the Surgeon General* (DHEW Publication No. PHS 79-50066). Washington, DC: U. S. Government Printing Office.

U.S. Department of Health and Human Services (DHHS). (1986). *Clinical opportunities for smoking intervention: A guide for the busy physician* (NIH Publication No. 86-2178). Washington, DC: U.S. Government Printing Office.

U.S. Department of Health and Human Services (DHHS). (1987). *Smoking and health: A national status report. A report to Congress* (DHHS Publication No. CDC 87-8396). Washington, DC: U.S. Government Printing Office.

U.S. Department of Health and Human Services (DHHS). (1988). *The health consequences of smoking: Nicotine addiction. A report of the Surgeon General* (DHHS Publication No. CDC 88-8406). Washington, DC: U.S. Government Printing Office.

U.S. Department of Health and Human Services (DHHS). (1989a). *Reducing the health consequences of smoking: 25 years of progress* (DHHS Publication No. CDC 89-8411). Washinton, DC: U.S. Government Printing Office.

U.S. Department of Health and Human Services (DHHS). (1989b). *How to help your patients stop smoking: A National Cancer Institute manual for physicians* (NIH Publication No. 89-3064). Washington, DC: U.S. Government Printing Office.

Van Lancker, J. (1977). Smoking and disease. In M. E. Jarvik, J. W. Cullen, E. R. Gritz, T. M. Vogt, & L. J. West (Eds.), *Research on smoking behavior* (NIDA Research Monograph No. 17, DHEW Publication No. ADM 78-581, pp. 230–283). Washington, DC: U.S. Government Printing Office.

Van Reek, J., & Adriaanse, H. (1988). Cigarette smoking cessation rates by level of education in five Western countries. *International Journal of Epidemiology, 17,* 474–475.

Vogt, T. M. (1982). Cigarette smoking: History, risks, and behavior change. *International Journal of Mental Health, 11,* 6–43.

Warner, K. E. (1986). *Selling smoke: Cigarette advertising and public health.* Washington, DC: American Public Health Association.

Wilson, D. M., Taylor, W., Gilbert, J. R., Best, J. A., Lindsay, E. A., Wilms, D. G., & Singer, J. (1988). A randomized trial of a family physician intervention for smoking cessation. *Journal of the American Medical Association, 260*(11), 1570–1574.

Yassa, R., Lal, S., Korpassy, A., & Ally, J. (1987). Nicotine exposure and tardive dyskinisia. *Biological Psychiatry, 22,* 67–72.

9

Special Problems of the Alcohol and Multiple-Drug Dependent: Clinical Interactions and Detoxification

NORMAN S. MILLER

Introduction

Dependence on drugs other than alcohol by alcoholics, and dependence on alcohol by drug dependents, have been noted by clinicians and researchers over recent decades. However, because there has been a recent explosion of such multiple dependences, a more uniform terminology is required to describe contemporary alcoholics and drug dependents. The two major classes are no longer sufficiently mutually exclusive to enable us to apply the traditional nosology.

There is a growing acknowledgment in clinical practice of the frequent inability to make clear clinical distinctions between the alcoholic and the drug dependent. The simultaneous and concurrent use of multiple drugs and alcohol has become extraordinarily common (e.g., alcohol and cocaine, heroin and cocaine, marijuana with alcohol or cocaine). This large overlap between the use of drugs and of alcohol has significant ramifications for diagnosis and treatment as they are traditionally practiced (Kreek, 1987; Sokolow, Welte, Hynes, & Lyons, 1981).

Importantly, the formulation of research models for dependence on alcohol and drugs is also affected by multiple use and dependence. In actual practice, one drug is frequently substituted for another, and the majority of the individuals develop alcohol and multiple-drug dependence. The concurrent and simultaneous occurrence of multiple-drug and alcohol dependence suggest an overlapping susceptibility to the various types of dependence (Kreek, 1987; Miller, Gold, Belkin, & Klahr, 1990; Miller & Mirin, 1989).

Definitions

In this chapter, "multiple dependence" is defined as dependence on more than one psychoactive substance (drugs, alcohol) simultaneously or concurrently, including the predominant practice in which the user has a hierarchy of

194

substance use. Simultaneous use of drugs and alcohol is within the same week, and concurrent use is within the last year. "Multiple dependence" as used here is more broadly defined than the diagnosis of "polysubstance dependence" according to *Diagnostic and Statistical Manual of Mental Disorders,* third edition, revised (DSM-III-R) criteria; DSM-III-R requires a period of at least 6 months in which the person has repeatedly used at least three categories of psychoactive substances (not including nicotine and caffeine), but no single psychoactive substance has predominated. During this period the criteria should have been met for dependence on psychoactive substances as a group, but not for any specific substance (American Psychiatric Association, 1987). Because most multiply dependent individuals use some drug or other predominantly, the term "polysubstance dependence" has limited application in actual clinical practice (Miller & Gold, 1989).

The drugs sought by multiply dependent individuals have become increasingly extensive and exotic. The traditional boundaries of dependent use of illicit and therapeutic use of prescribed medications are considerably less distinct. The nonmedical use of medical drugs by drug dependents is widespread. The drug dependent who is dependent on only one drug is becoming a rare species. Many heroin dependents are also dependent on marijuana and/or alcohol, and more recently cocaine. The common practice of adulteration (mixing in the preparation before selling) of one illicit drug with another drug makes it difficult and at times impossible for the dependent to maintain a self-determined monodrug addiction, particularly, when the drugs are obtained on the street (Redda, Walker, & Barnett, 1989).

Natural History and Epidemiology

The natural history of alcoholism and drug addiction is being altered by the emergence of multiple dependence. The course of one substance dependence in duration and severity is significantly affected by the addition of another such dependence. It is clinically acknowledged that the course of alcoholism is often drastically telescoped and the need for treatment is apparent earlier because of the dependence on another drug, although this has not been documented and is not easily demonstrated, except by retrospective analysis. Correspondingly, the course of a drug addiction is altered by repeated alcohol use, which may precipitate a relapse to drugs (Miller et al., 1990).

The widespread practice of multiple-drug and alcohol use began in adolescent cohorts as a cultural phenomenon in the 1960s with the "hippie" generation. Epidemiological evidence confirms that large numbers of individuals with extensive drug experiences entered the age of risk for alcoholsim during their adolescent period. The risk for alcoholics to develop a drug dependence is also high in early adolescence. On the other hand, on a cross-sectional analysis, a gradual transition from common to uncommon dependence on other drugs by alcoholics is evident as age increases, perhaps in roughly a linear progression (Miller & Mirin, 1989; Hoffman, 1983).

The most complete and most often cited reference for alcohol and drug use in adolescence is a monitoring survey conducted annually since 1975 by the National Institute on Drug Abuse (NIDA). A nationally representative sample of enrolled high school seniors is interviewed, usually by telephone. Although these surveys may underestimate prevalence of drug use, because the 20% of the high-school-age seniors who have dropped out of school or are chronically absent are not polled and are often afflicted with drug and alcohol problems, the results may nonetheless be taken to be indicative. The NIDA survey in 1985 showed the following lifetime use rates by high school seniors: alcohol, 93%; marijuana, 59%; cocaine, 16%; other stimulants, 16%; and tranquilizers, 14%. The use rates in the last month for the same drugs were 70%, 29%, 5%, 14%, and 2%, respectively (Johnston, O'Malley, & Bachman, 1986).

The Drug Abuse Warning Network (DAWN), which records drug-related visits to emergency rooms in the United States, in 1985 found that alcohol used in combination with other drugs was most frequently cited and accounted for 24% of all drug-related episodes. Data were not collected for episodes related to alcohol alone (NIDA, 1985).

The National Youth Polydrug Study revealed that the mean number of drugs regularly used by alcoholic youths was 4.4. Marijuana and alcohol were the drugs most frequently used on a regular basis (by 86% and 80% of the sample of 2,750 youths, respectively). Amphetamines had the third highest prevalence at 45%, followed by hashish, barbituates, hallucinogens, and phencyclidine (PCP) at 42%, 40%, 40%, and 32%, respectively (Watkins & McCoy, 1980).

As far back as 1930 and throughout each decade into the 1980s, alcoholics have used other drugs in alarming frequency. Freed (1973) reviewed 15,447 cases in 46 studies carried out between the 1930s and 1970s and found 3,046 alcoholics who were also dependent on another drug—in other words, a 20% rate of drug dependence among alcoholics. Some of the same drugs prevalent today were used then (i.e., barbiturates, opiates, benzodiazepines and marijuana).

Few of the available studies have established the actual prevalence of multiple dependence in the general population. Until recently, the prevalence of alcoholism and drug addiction was based on "estimates" of consumption rates of alcohol and drugs or medical consequences of alcohol and drug use. The high prevalence of the actual diagnosis of alcoholism was only recently verified in the Epidemiologic Catchment Area (ECA) study. The ECA study is the first national account of the prevalence of alcoholism and drug dependence in the general population, collected according to diagnostic criteria contained in DSM-III (Robins, Helzer, Pryzbeck, & Regier, 1988). This standarized five-city study administered structured diagnostic questions to subjects in personally conducted interviews. The lifetime prevalence of alcoholism in the total population in the ECA sample was 13.8% (23.8% for men and 4.6% for women). Almost 7% of the total population had had active alcohol dependence in the past year. The 1-year: lifetime prevalence ratio for the total sample was .49; that is, half of those who had been alcoholic had active alcoholism in the past year. Another important finding was that the prevalence of alcoholism was significantly higher in men and women under the age of 45 years. For men, the lifetime prevalence of alcohol dependence in the age group 18–29 years was 27%, and for the age groups 30–44 years and 45–65 years it was 28% and 21%, respectively. For women, lifetime prevalences for the corresponding age groups were 7%, 6%, 3%, and 1.5%, respectively (Robins et al., 1988).

The ECA study also established alcohol dependence as a youthful disorder; almost 40% of the cases began between the ages of 15 and 19 years, and 80% of the cases began by the age of 30 years. Men had an earlier onset of alcoholism then women: The average age of onset of alcoholism was 22 years old in men and 25 years old in women. The age of risk for alcoholism was clearly established as beginning in adolescence in this study. Over half (54%) had a duration of alcohol dependence of 5 years of less (Robins et al., 1988; see Table 9.1).

The prevalence of drug dependence among alcoholics was reasonably high in the ECA study, with as many as 30% of the alcoholics qualifying for a drug dependence. Marijuana dependence was the highest. The reverse, the prevalence of alcohol dependence among drug dependents, was also illuminating: Alcoholism among marijuana dependents was 36%, among barbiturate dependents was 71%, among amphetamine dependents was 62%, among hallucinogen dependents was 64%, among opiate dependents was 67%, and among cocaine dependents was 84%. Less than 1% of the total sample admitted to cocaine dependence at some time in their lives. Clearly, in this survey that examined the general population, alcohol dependence was a common com-

TABLE 9.1.   Rates of Lifetime Alcohol Disorder by Age, Sex, and Race (All Sites)

Age	Men			Women		
	White	Black	Other	White	Black	Other[a]
18–29	29	13[b]	27	7	4[b]	5
30–59	24	32	29	4	7	5
60 +	13	24	22	2	3	1
All ages	23	24	28	4	6	5

Note. From "Alcohol Disorders in the Community: A Report from the Epidemiologic Catchment Area" by L. N. Robins, J. E. Helzer, T. R. Pryzbeck, and D. A. Regier, 1988, in R. M. Rose and J. Barrett (Eds.), *Alcoholism: Origins and Outcomes* (p. 19), New York: Raven Press. Copyright 1988 by Raven Press, Ltd. Reprinted by permission.
[a]This category is dominated by Los Angeles Hispanics, whose male rates exceed whites, and whose female rates are below whites.
[b]The low rate in young blacks is found in all four sites with substantial black populations.

plicating dependence in the majority of those dependent on drugs. Furthermore, these estimates were conservative, because they were based on self-report; drug dependents often do not admit readily to type, amount, and duration of drug use (Robins et al., 1988).

Many studies of both alcoholics and drug dependents of any age in general and patient populations indicate that alcohol is the first drug used and often is used dependently. The natural history of alcohol dependence in conjunction with drug dependence is highly variable and age-dependent. Older alcoholics (over the age of 30) typically began drinking in adolescence and progressed to diagnosable alcohol dependence in their 20s. A certain proportion (perhaps 10–20%) began using cannabis in their 20s. Another 10% began using stimulants (including cocaine and amphetamines), while 20% began using sedatives/hypnotics (predominantly benzodiazepines, barbiturates, and meprobamate). About 50% may continue their alcohol dependence without significant use of any additional drugs (Smith, 1986; Sokolow et al., 1981; Miller, Millman, & Keskinen, in press; Miller et al., 1990; see Table 9.2).

When a select population, such as those entering a treatment program, is examined, the overlap of alcohol and drug dependence is intensified and the occurrence of multiple dependence increases significantly. This is probably because it takes greater clinical severity to be admitted to inpatient units, and multiple dependence adds to the severity.

The prevalence of multiple use or dependence that includes alcohol is very high for contemporary drug dependents being admitted for both inpatient and outpatient treatment. In large-scale studies of inpatient populations of adult and adolescent alcoholics and drug dependents in various treatment facilities, the number of cocaine dependents with the additional diagnosis of alcohol dependence was in the 70%–90% range. Similar studies of methadone and heroin dependents show rates of alcohol dependence between 50% and 75%. Approximately 80–90% of admitted cannabis dependents are also dependent on alcohol (Sokolow et al., 1981; Miller et al., 1990, in press).

Over 80% of alcoholics in treatment populations are dependent on at

TABLE 9.2. Estimate of Drug Use and Dependence among the Multiply Dependent Population

Index drug	Additional drug					
	Alcohol	Cocaine	Cannabis	Benzodiazepines	PCP	Opiates
Alcohol	—	20–30%	20–30%	20–30%	20–30%	15%
Cocaine	80–90%	—	70–80%	20–30%	30–40%	5–10%
Cannabis	80–90%	20–30%	—	10–20%	80–80%	10–20%
Benzodiazepines	50–60%	5–10%	5–10%	—	5–10%	15%
PCP	80–90%	50–60%	80–90%	10–20%	—	5–10%
Opiates	50–60%	30–40%	80–90%	30–40%	30–40%	—

Note. These are estimates based on multiple studies of use and dependence, both simultaneous and concurrent. See text for references.

least one other drug, and usually more than one. A triad of alcohol, marijuana, and cocaine dependence is a regular occurrence among the alcoholics currently being admitted to inpatient and outpatient facilities. According to many studies, the younger alcoholic begins using alcohol in early teenage years (i.e., at about 13 to 15 years of age) and progresses to dependent use of alcohol by 15 to 16 years of age. A year or two after the onset of alcohol and tobacco use, other drugs are tried and some used dependently; these include marijuana, tobacco, and then cocaine, followed by hallucinogens (PCP), benzodiazepines, and barbiturates in frequency. Cigarette smoking is particularly troublesome; unlike some other drug use, which may wax and wane, the use of tobacco often remains persistent well into adulthood, with its particular well-known medical complications. The pattern of cocaine use has changed dramatically and continues to do so to the present day, most remarkably in the progressively earlier age of onset of use. The skillful marketing techniques for the initially cheaper form of cocaine, "crack," have lured younger individuals to addictive use (NIDA, 1988).

The predictors of cessation of marijuana and cocaine use were examined in a longitudinal cohort of young adult men and women ($n = 1,222$). Six domains of predictors were examined: socioeconomic background variables, participation in the social roles of adulthood, degree of drug involvement, social context of drug use, health status, and deviant activities and conventionality of life experiences. Factors that predicted cessation of use in adulthood paralleled those that predicted lack of initiation in adolescence: conventionality in social role performance, social context unfavorable to the use of drugs, and good health. A most important predictor was prior degree of involvement in licit and illicit drugs (Kandel & Raveis, 1989; Kandel, Murphy, & Karus, 1985).

Pharmacology

Alcohol is a sedative/hypnotic drug by pharmacological classification. Alcohol intoxication is characterized by the effects of sedation, which include slowness of mental and physical function. Thinking, speech, and actions are sluggish and uncoordinated, punctuated by errors and miscalculations. Memory and cognitive abilities are impaired, so that functional intelligence may be reduced in chronic drinkers. Insight and judgment are distorted and produce decisions and actions that are counterproductive and destructive in both acute and chronic use (Ritchie, 1985).

Anxiety and depression commonly arise as a result of chronic alcohol use. The anxiety may take the form of generalized anxiety, panic attacks, and phobias, such as agoraphobia. The depression may be minor or particularly severe; the latter may produce a disturbed mood, vegetative symptoms, and suicidal thoughts and actions that are similar to the symptoms of major depression (American Psychiatric Association, 1987).

In many respects, chronic withdrawal is an exaggeration of the acute withdrawal from alcohol. Studies have demonstrated that acute alcohol withdrawal typically includes anxiety, depression, irritability, elevated blood pressure and pulse, mild tremors, and insomnia. Blood pressure and pulse are nearly always elevated over baseline during withdrawal for an individual, although not necessarily in the abnormal range. Mild positional tremors of the hands, sweating, facial flushing, fatigue, malaise, anorexia, irritability, diarrhea, myalgias, and arthralgias are well known to those who have withdrawn from a particularly heavy bout of drinking.

Marijuana is the second most commonly used drug by the multiply dependent alcoholic, next to alcohol. Marijuana is classified as a hallucinogen as much for historical reasons as for pharmacological rationale. Marijuana also produces a wide array of psychiatric symptoms that are indistinguishable from those of other psychiatric disorders, including paranoid delusions, panic attacks, phobias, and severe depression. The hallmark of a hallucinogen is that it alters and distorts perceptions and may produce hallucinations. These distortions may involve vision, hearing, touch, time, and space, as well as other subjective sensations (Redda et al., 1989).

The withdrawal syndrome from marijuana is subtle and protracted, but definite. There may be tachycardia and blood pressure elevation (usually mild), restlessness, malaise, anxiety, panic, depression, emotional lability, acute intermittent euphoria and depression, apathy, anhedonia, and suspiciousness. The withdrawal syndrome may persist with gradual diminution over weeks and months. Tetrahydrocannabinol (THC) is the chief psychoactive ingredient among several hundred chemical compounds in marijuana. THC is taken up and stored in muscle and fat, where it can be detected for months after a single low-dose administration in animals. The THC is gradually released in low amounts over time in humans. THC metabolites can be detected in urine for months after the cessation of chronic use (Hoffman, 1983; see Verebey & Turner, Chapter 10, this volume).

Acute and chronic cocaine intoxication includes euphoria, hyperactivity, arousal, hypertension, tachycardia, tremors, palpitations, anxiety, panic, irritability, aggressiveness, violence, and poor judgment and insight. The chronic use of cocaine, particularly higher doses, frequently results in a delusional syndrome similar to that described for other sympathomimetic drugs, such as amphetamines. Paranoid ideation with delusions of persecution in a clear sensorium, visual and auditory hallucinations with distortion of faces, and disturbances of body image occur with chronic use (Hoffman, 1983; Post, 1975; Gold & Verebey, 1984).

The withdrawal from cocaine commences within hours of cessation of use and reaches a peak intensity within 1 to 3 days. The prominent signs and symptoms are depression, hypersomnolence, fatigue, disturbed sleep, anxiety, panic, agitation, suicidal thinking, irritability, apathy, and hyperphagia. Depression and irritability may persist for months in varying and fluctuating degrees. The risk of suicide is particularly high within the acute withdrawal period in the first week (Gold & Verebey, 1984; Gawin & Kleber, 1986).

PCP is classified as hallucinogen; it is similar to the classical hallucinogens as well as the stimulants. The characteristics of intoxication are euphoria, anxiety, depression, hostility, grandiosity, disorientation, marked visual and auditory hallucinations, and suicidal thinking. The patient may be labile and impulsive, exhibiting feats of great strength without clear or specific triggers, alternating with a placid and cooperative demeanor. The PCP user (particularly the chronic user) may be violent toward self or others while intoxicated (Hoffman, 1983).

The withdrawal from PCP is similar to withdrawal from marijuana and cocaine, with a more protracted and more pronounced subjective component. The patient is anxious, depressed, suicidal, restless, agitated, suspicious, guarded, and at times combative. The vital signs usually return to normal within a few hours or days following intoxication. The patient may remain intermittently confused, with periods of disorientation, anxiety, and depression that may take days to weeks to clear. Occasionally, a toxic delirium persists for months or indefinitely in some heavy users. Cases of a permanent psychosis have been reported in which the users failed to emerge from a toxic delirium. These individuals may have had large overdoses of PCP (Hoffman, 1983).

Opiate intoxication is characterized by signs of sedation, a clouded sensorium, hypotension, bradycardia, depressed respirations, hyporeflexia, pupillary constriction, and slowed motor movements. In high enough doses, even in tolerant individuals, respiratory arrest and coma may result. The symptoms of intoxication include an intense euphoria, sedation, depression, profound analgesia, ennui, and fatigue. Chronic use leads to less euphoria and increasing anxiety and depression, largely because of the development of tolerance and pharmacological dependence.

The withdrawal from opiates is similar for all compounds. The various opiate compounds include morphine, methadone, meperidine (Demerol), oxycodone (Percodan), propoxyphene (Darvon), heroin, hydromorphone (Dilaudid), fentanyl, codeine, pentazocine (Talwin), nalbuphine, buprenorphine, and butorphanol. The withdrawal syndrome varies in duration and intensity, according to the duration of action of the particular opiate. The short-acting heroin has an onset of signs and symptons of withdrawal within a few hours and peaks at 3 days, whereas methadone withdrawal may take a day or two to begin and peaks at 7 to 10 days. Also, the more potent the narcotic, the more severe the withdrawal state; for example, the withdrawal from morphine is more severe than that from codeine.

Benzodiazepines and other sedatives/hypnotics such as barbiturates produce intoxications that are similar to alcohol, with which they have cross-tolerance and dependence. They affect mood initially with a calming euphoria, followed after chronic use with anxiety and depression. Acute effects include impairment of concentration and memory, slow thinking, and even amnestic states of "blackouts" as with alcohol. Chronic use leads to irritability, emotional lability, slurred speech, and decreased self-control (Harvey, 1985).

The short-acting benzodiazepines, such as alprazolam, are particularly likely to produce an intense, severe, and medically significant withdrawal syndrome. The long-acting benzodiazepines produce a less intense but nonetheless remarkable withdrawal syndrome. The signs of long-acting benzodiazepine withdrawal are anxiety, agitation, depression, seizures, muscular weakness, tremulousness, hyperpyrexia, sweating, convulsions, delirium, elevated pulse and blood pressure, and tremors of extremities and tongue. The symptoms of short-acting benzodiazepine withdrawal are intense anxiety, insomnia, nausea, vomiting, malaise, irritability, illusions, depression, visual hallucinations, paranoid ideation, confusion, and delirium (Harvey, 1985).

Other less commonly used, but nonetheless addicting and dependence-producing, drugs are hallucinogens such as lysergic acid diethylamide (LSD); "ice" and Ecstasy, which are derivatives of methamphetamines; and others. Other sedatives/hypnotics include methaqualone, chloral hydrate, and others. Nicotine in tobacco, and caffeine in coffee, are drugs on which alcoholics and drug addicts become commonly dependent.

Table 9.3 presents, in chart form, the intoxication and withdrawal symptoms for the major substances described here.

Biological Mechanisms in Multiple Dependence

The interactions between multiple drugs and the frequency of their concurrent and simultaneous use suggest a common biological determinant. Several neurotransmitters may be involved in the various systems that underlie addictive behaviors. The major neurotransmittors that have been implicated are the opioid peptides, dopamine, serotonin, and norepinephrine. These neurotransmittors have individual functions and interactive relationships in the reward center, as well as in drive states and other behaviors that appear to involve common neurochemical mechanisms associated with addiction (Blum, 1989; Blum, Briggs, & Trachtenberg, 1989).

Opiates have been shown to connect with the reward center through opiate receptors that are located on dopamine neurons in the ventral tegmentum in the midbrain. These dopamine neurons project to the mesolimbic system and, when stimulated, support heroin, cocaine, and ethanol self-administration. Self-administration paradigms confirm the participation of the reward center in addictive use of drugs. Blockade of dopamine receptors prevents the self-administration of opiates and cocaine, and blockade of norepinephrine sites reduces alcohol intake. Moreover, antagonism with narcotic blocking agents attenuates reward behavior from cocaine, heroin, and ethanol. These findings suggest that the common denominator of a wide range of addictive drugs is their ability to activate the dopaminergic fibers in the mesolimbic system (Blum & Briggs, 1989; Trachtenberg & Blum, 1987).

Other more direct theories are based on the findings that alcohol, through

TABLE 9.3. Symptoms of Intoxication and Withdrawal for Major Substances of Abuse

Symptom	Intoxication						Withdrawal					
	Alcohol	Cocaine	Cannabis	Benz.	PCP	Opiates	Alcohol	Cocaine	Cannabis	Benz.	PCP	Opiates
Euphoria	XX	XXX	XX	XX	XX	XXX	XXX	XXX	XX	XX	XX	XX
Depression	XX	X	X	XX	XX	X	XXX	XXX	XX	XXX	XX	XX
Anxiety	X	X	X	X	XX	X	XX	XX		XX	X	
Delusions	X	XXX	XXX		XX		XX	XX		XX	X	
Hallucinations	X	XXX	X		XXX		XXX		X	XXX	X	XX
Hyperactivity	X	XXX	X		XXX		XXX		X	XX	X	X
Tremulousness	X	XXX	X		XX		XX	X				X
Pupil dilation	X	XXX			XX		XXX			X		X
Hypertension	X	XXX	X		XX		XXX			X		X
Tachycardia	XX	XXX	X		XX		XXX			X		X
Hyperthermia		XXX	X		XX		XXX			X		X
Suicidal activity	XXX	XXX	XX	XX	XX	XX	XXX	XXX	XXX	XXX	XXX	XX
Reduced insight and judgment	XXX	XXX	XXX	XXX	XXX	XXX	XXX	XXX	XXX	XXX	XXX	XXX
Memory	XX	X	XX	XX	X	X	X	X	X	X	X	X

Note. Relative weighting: ×, mild; ××, moderate; ×××, marked. See text for references.

the formation of condensation products termed *tetrahydroisoquinolines* (TIQs), may interact with opioid receptors to stimulate the mesolimbic catecholaminergic systems. TIQs that form following ethanol ingestion and metabolism can function as opiates, and provide a link between the two-carbon ethanol molecule and the more complex phenanthrene alkaloids. The metabolic product from ethanol, acetaldehyde, condenses noncovalently with dopamine to form TIQs. The TIQs act as agonists at enkephalin and endorphin binding sites to further substantiate the link between alcohol and opiates through a common mechanism. A TIQ, salsolinol, has been found in the urine and in postmortem brains of alcoholics (Blum, 1989; Blum et al., 1989).

Cerebrospinal fluid endorphin levels and plasma enkephalin levels are reduced in human alcoholics. Inbred mice (C57BL/6J) that show a preference for ethanol over water exhibit lower than normal levels of the opiate peptides, endorphins, and enkephalins than do mice (DBA2/J) that avoid alcohol. Long-term ethanol ingestion significantly reduces brain endorphins and enkephalins in animals. Both acute and chronic treatment with the carboxypeptidase A (enkephalinase) inhibitors D-phenylalanine and hydrocinnamic acid, which raise brain enkephalin levels, significantly attenuates both forced and volitional ethanol intake in mice with a genetic preference for alcohol (Blum & Briggs, 1988; Blum, Briggs, & Trachtenberg, 1987).

In humans, administration of serotonin (5-HT) reuptake inhibitors (zimelidine, fluoxitine, citalopram) to nondepressed, heavy drinkers is associated with a decrease in the number of drinks consumed. Serotonin neurons in the hypothalamus project to the met-enkephalin neurons that inhibit mesencephalic projections of γ-aminobutyric acid (GABA) neurons. GABA interacts to inhibit dopamine neurons in the ventral tegmentum.

Clinical Features

Multiple-substance use will determine the clinical presentation of the acute and chronic intoxication syndromes in the multiply dependent individual. The clinical features are understandably a result of the combined effects of multiple substances during intoxication, withdrawal, and prolonged abstinence syndromes, as well as toxic and psychosocial consequences. The challenge to the physician to diagnose multiple dependence and to determine detoxification schedules has been increasing dramatically in recent years. The resultant mixture of signs and symptoms may complicate the clinical picture sufficiently to make the diagnosis of any one drug intoxication impossible. Furthermore, other psychiatric syndromes that may be induced by alcohol and particularly by drugs make diagnosis and treatment more complex.

Considerable overlap occurs among drug effects. The intoxicated state of one drug may mimic the withdrawal state of another. A stimulant picture is produced during intoxication and a depressant state during withdrawal by stimulants, whereas a depressant picture is produced during intoxication and a stimulant state during withdrawal by depressants. Psychotic symptoms are produced during intoxication by some drugs and during withdrawal by others (e.g., cocaine produces hallucinations and delusions during intoxication, and alcohol produces them during withdrawal). Moreover, because all the drugs involved in a multiple dependence produce psychiatric symptoms and syndromes, the clinical state of the multiply dependent individual frequently includes more severe psychopathological consequences (Gold & Verebey, 1984; Jaffe, 1983).

Addicts use combinations of drugs for a variety of reasons. The high (euphoria) from a stimulant is better maintained with a depressant (e.g., alcohol is often used with cocaine for this reason). A drug may be used to "treat" unwanted side effects of another drug (e.g., the undesirable effects of a cocaine high can be counteracted by opioids, alcohol, or sedatives/hypnotics). Moreover, depressants such as alcohol or benzodiazepines are used to "come down" or to "sedate" a cocaine-induced anxiety. As discussed earlier, one drug may be used as a substitute for another drug (e.g., over-the-counter stimulants, anticholinergics, and antihistamines may be used in lieu of cocaine or opiates when the latter are not available). A withdrawal effect of one drug may be alleviated by the intoxicating effect of another drug (e.g., a cocaine-induced depression may be temporarily relieved by alcohol, benzodiazepines, or marijuana).

Medical syndromes as sequelae of chronic alcoholism are not particularly common in the overall population of alcoholics, but still are present in a substantial minority. These include alcoholic liver disease, cardiomyopathy, oropharyngeal cancers, gastrointestinal ulcerations, and others. Accidents and trauma are also leading causes of morbidity and mortality in alcoholics, particularly among adolescents. Alcoholics represent from 25% to 50% of the total suicides in the United States and Europe. Although acute overdose from alcohol is rare, associated drug overdoses with alcohol use are common. The leading drugs that alcoholics tend to use in overdoses are benzodiazepines, tricyclic antidepressants, barbiturates, and other psychotropic medications. However, use of other drugs of dependence in overdoses may be higher than investigators have recorded, because of the difficulty in obtaining evidence for other drug use in clinical situations (Ritchie, 1985).

The medical complications of multiple-drug dependence are numerous but not nearly as common as the psychiatric complications, with the exception of intravenous drug use, which is associated with substantial morbidity and mortality. Accidental, suicidal, and homicidal deaths remain common, especially among the young, for whom multiple-drug use is significantly more predominant.

Persons dependent on intravenous drugs are at high risk of developing acquired immune deficiency syndrome (AIDS). Approximately 30% of AIDS cases in the United States are among intravenous drug addicts or are attributable to intravenous drug use. The intravenous drug addicts who themselves have AIDS readily transmit the virus to other drug dependents by sharing syringes and needles, having sexual contact, and engaging in other activities that involve an exchange of blood between donor and recipient. As many as 55–60% of intravenous drug dependents are seropositive for human immunodeficiency virus (HIV) in some cities such as New York. Intravenous drug dependents represent about 1% of the population, or 2.5 million individuals (Des Jarlais, & Friedman, 1988).

Other relatively common sequelae from intravenous drug use are viral and toxic hepatitis, endocarditis, lethal overdoses, pulmonary infections and allergic reactions, meningoencephalitis, brain abscesses, accidents, and trauma (Hoffman, 1983).

Because of the use of denial and rationalization, alcoholics and drug dependents tend to minimize the nature and amount of their drug use. The sources of denial are diverse; they include organicity, the psychopathology of addiction, and the psychodynamics of conflict. The major mechanism by which the illogical state of dependence is allowed to continue, inspite of sometimes overwhelming adverse consequences from alcohol and drug use, is denial. The denial is both unconscious and conscious, so the dependence is generated by forces often unrecognized by the dependent. Multiple dependence appears to reinforce this denial more strongly and makes it more difficult for the dependent to abstain from drug use because of the substitution of one substance for another. Importantly, the loss of control over one drug extends to another drug: The use of one psychoactive drug will disinhibit the individual and tend to lead to use of another (Miller & Mirin, 1989; Milam & Ketchum, 1981).

Diagnosis

The findings of an important study have supported a common dependence syndrome for alcohol and drugs, particularly alcohol, opiates, and cocaine (Kosten, Rounsaville, Babor, Spitzer, & Williams, 1987). The practice of multiple-substance use by today's dependent has many practical implications for diagnosis. The identification of only alcohol dependence in a patient is often tenuous and misleading. Because denial is a part of the dependence process, and because drugs are illegal and socially unacceptable, underreporting and underestimation of multiple use are to be expected in a clinical interview, especially if only the dependent person is interviewed. Corroborative sources increase the likelihood of obtaining a more accurate history; however, because of similar denial, these sources still may not reveal the total pattern and amount of alcohol and drug use. These corroborative sources may include family members, employer, and legal agencies, and may be supported by urine and blood testing for alcohol and drugs.

Although the contemporary alcoholic usually becomes dependent on alcohol first, most alcoholics under the age of 30 are dependent on at least one other drug and more often multiple drugs. Studies also show that a majority of drug dependents who become dependent on a drug first develop alcohol dependence later. Moreover, for many drug dependents, alcohol is the first drug used dependently. Finally, even in cases where alcohol is not the drug of choice for the drug dependent, it continues to be used dependently as an adjunct with a drug or in substitution of a drug (Galizio & Maish, 1985; Freed, 1973; Miller et al., 1990; Miller & Mirin, 1989).

It is a frequent clinical observation that the multiply dependent individual has greater behavioral and mental disturbances than the person who is dependent on only one substance. Frequently, the multiple dependence begins in adolescence, when the personality is developing and the individual has not yet achieved a stable, integrated identity of self. However, the effects of alcohol and drug dependence on an immature personality and personality development have not been well studied. The salient clinical observation is that the personality is adversely affected by acute and chronic use of alcohol and drugs; the questions of how long these changes last and to what degree they change with recovery have not been addressed in studies.

Specifically, the pharmacological interactions with the brain critically affect the mind and behavior. Alcohol, marijuana, cocaine, opiates, sedatives/ hypnotics, and other drugs produce signs and symptoms of intoxication and withdrawal that include disturbances in mood, thinking, and vegetative states. These psychoactive effects on the brain and behavior are often chronic and cumulative in multiply dependent individuals. The degree of mental and cognitive disorganization is sometimes especially marked in this population because of the chronic dependence on multiple substances (Hoffman, 1983; Schuckit, 1983; Miller, Dackis, & Gold, 1987).

Obtaining answers to questions regarding the essentials of diagnosis is difficult with these reticent and impaired patients, even in obvious cases. The criteria for dependence, which include a preoccupation with, compulsive use of, and relapse to alcohol and drugs, are denied by many alcoholics and drug dependents who are actively using these substances. Obtaining answers to questions regarding the development of tolerance and dependence on alcohol and drugs is equally difficult. Persistent pursuit of such a patient in subsequent interviews, and a knowledge of the diagnostic characteristics of alcohol and drug use and dependence (particularly in the multiply dependent individual), will often yield rewarding results (Miller & Gold, 1989).

Differential Diagnosis

Both acute and chronic alcohol and drug intoxication and withdrawal produce syndromes that must be differentiated from bipolar, depressive, anxiety, psychotic, personality, and other psychiatric disorders (Schuckit, 1983; Post, 1975; Gold & Verebey, 1984). Alcohol-induced depression must be differentiated from major depression due to other causes, as defined in DSM-III-R.

Alcohol hallucinosis with auditory and sometimes visual hallucinations needs to be differentiated from schizophrenia. The anxiety produced by repeated stimulation of the sympathetic nervous system in alcohol intoxication and withdrawal must be distinguished from the anxiety disorders of generalized anxiety, panic attacks, and phobias. Phobias such as agoraphobia, which are quite common in alcoholics, often resolve with abstinence from alcohol (Schuckit, 1983).

Cocaine and other stimulant intoxication produce effects that must be distinguished from mania; euphoria, hyperactivity, and distorted self-image (the triad in mania) are principal pharmacological effects of cocaine intoxication. The withdrawal from cocaine, particularly in chronic use, is characterized by severe depression, with attendant signs and symptoms that resemble major depression. The chronic effects of cocaine are to induce paranoid delusions and hallucinations, both visual and auditory, which must be distinguished from schizophrenia. Furthermore, the anxiety generated by the pharmacological effects of chronic cocaine use is in the form of generalized anxiety, panic attacks, and intense agoraphobia (Gold & Verebey, 1984; Gawin & Kleber, 1986).

Marijuana, PCP, and other hallucinogens are drugs that produce intense distortions of mood, affect, thinking, and perceptions. The resulting development of depression, manic behavior, delusions, and hallucinations must be differentiated from affective and psychiatric disorders. Other hallucinogens, such as LSD, methamphetamine, and psilocybin, share properties with marijuana (Redda et al., 1989).

All these drugs have adverse effects on personality when used chronically in a dependent mode. Deterioration in personality and interference with development of the personality are produced by all the drugs when taken individually, including alcohol. The multiply dependent individual is more severely affected and experiences a more pronounced effect on the personality, which is manifested by a disturbance in interpersonal relationships (Poldrugo & Forti, 1988; Miller & Gold, 1989; Miller & Mirin, 1989).

Of foremost importance is maintaining a differential diagnosis with continuous review; the clinician should not be compelled to make a single, final, and irreversible diagnosis. Furthermore, it is essential to keep in mind that alcohol and drug dependence are primary disorders that produce these symptoms and syndromes. The treatment of multiple dependence with detoxification and abstinence will frequently be sufficient to establish the definitive diagnosis within days to weeks. However, occasionally the effects of alcohol and drugs will persist for protracted periods, so that a prolonged period of observation may be necessary before these effects can be ruled out. The mood disturbances and anxiety produced by alcohol, cocaine, and marijuana may endure for weeks and months, although they may lessen with the passing of time. The delusions and hallucinations will sometimes continue in all the drug states for prolonged periods. Finally, the deterioration in personality may take years to reverse, although a substantial start is initiated with abstinence and a commitment to a treatment program (Schuckit, 1983; Hoffman, 1983).

Laboratory testing for drugs of dependence can be useful in differentiating psychiatric from drug-induced syndromes and identifying use of specific drugs. The accuracy depends on the sensitivity and specificity of the test employed, the recency of onset, the dose of the drug, and the method of specimen collection and cutoff value. A positive test is almost certain evidence of use of a particular drug, wherein a negative result is not confirmatory, although it suggests lack of recent use. The rate of false positives is low, and the rate of false negatives is high (see Verebey & Turner, Chapter 10). As with any laboratory test in medicine, the results should be interpreted in the context of the clinical setting. It is imperative not to treat a particular result without a coresponding clinical syndrome that is relevant.

Psychiatric Disorders

The findings of the ECA study for prevalence rates for comorbid psychiatric diagnoses (Helzer & Pryzbeck, 1988) indicate that psychiatric disorders are common in alcohol and drug dependence. One-third of the total population in the ECA sample met lifetime criteria for one of the DSM-III psychiatric diagnoses, and one-third of those with one diagnosis had a second diagnosis. The lifetime prevalence rates for psychiatric disorders were higher among those with alcoholism than those without alcoholism in the general population.

Among those with the diagnosis of alcoholism, almost half (47%) had a second psychiatric diagnosis. The co-occurrence of psychiatric disorders with alcoholism was more common in women than in men: 64% of female alcoholics had a second diagnosis, compared to 44% of men. In men, antisocial personality disorder was second to drug dependence as the most common psychiatric disorder among alcoholics, with a substantial relative risk for the presence of antisocial personality if alcoholism was diagnosed. Phobias were particularly common among male alcoholics, followed by depression, schizophrenia, panic, and mania.

In alcoholic women, phobias and depression, followed by antisocial personality, panic, schizophrenia, and mania, were the psychiatric disorders cited in descending prevalence. Interestingly, the *relative risk* of a psychiatric diagnosis for women with alcoholism in relation to the general population was greatest for antisocial personality and least for depression and phobias, owing to the high rates of these latter disorders among nonalcoholic women in the general population. Furthermore, the prevalence of *relative risk* for psychiatric disorders was the same for women alcoholics as for men alcoholics, suggesting a common contribution from the alcoholism (Helzer & Pryzbeck, 1988).

Other studies indicate further that those patients with multiple-substance dependence and psychiatric disorders have an overall poorer prognosis. These "dual-diagnosis" patients tend to be younger, are more often male, and have poorer medication compliance. In addition, they are nearly twice as likely to be rehospitalized at a 1-year follow-up. Multiple dependence appears to add to the problems of disruptive, disinhibited, and noncompliant behaviors in chronic mental illness (Drake & Wallach, 1989).

Hereditary Factors

Recent studies have demonstrated genetic factors in the development of alcoholism. Twin, adoption, familial, and high-risk studies have revealed a significant genetic predisposition to alcoholism (Frances, Timm, & Bucky, 1980; Goodwin, 1985). Identical twins are more concordant for alcoholism than fraternal twins. The biological parent of an adoptee is a more important determinant of alcoholism than the foster parent who reared the adoptee (Goodwin, 1985). Over 50% of alcoholics have a family history positive for alcoholism (Goodwin, 1985). A child of an alcoholic is more likely to have certain neurophysiological and behavioral manifestations in common with other offspring of alcoholics than with matched controls without an alcoholic parent (Tarter, 1981; Begleiter, Porjesz, & Kissin, 1982).

Corresponding studies for the prevalence of the family history of alcohol dependence in cocaine and opiate addicts and other drug dependents have been performed. In one study, the rate of the diagnosis of alcohol dependence in first- or second-degree relatives in the families of 263 cocaine dependents was greater than 50%; in other words, 132 cocaine dependents had at least one relative with alcohol dependence by DSM-III-R criteria (Miller et al., 1990).

Opiate dependents with a parental history of alcoholism were more frequently diagnosed with concurrent alcoholism. In one study, 21.3% of opiate dependents with a diagnosis of alcohol dependence ($n = 638$) had at least one parent with alcohol dependence. Opiate dependents without the diagnosis of alcohol dependence ($n = 422$) had a 12.5% rate of parental alcohol dependence. Among the opiate dependents with alcohol dependence, those with parental alcoholism had more severe problems with alcohol (Kosten, Rounsaville, & Kleber, 1987).

A study of young alcohol users in their 20s revealed a higher rate of alcohol-related problems and drug use if a family history of alcoholism was present in the first- and second-degree relatives. Young alcohol users without alcoholic relatives, or with fewer relatives with alcoholism, had a lower rate of alcohol-related problems and drug use (Schuckit, 1986). These genetic and familial studies of alcoholics and familial studies of drug dependents, in addition to the concept of the multiple-drug and alcohol dependent, support a possible common genetic transmission of alcohol and drug dependence.

The existence of a single personality disorder that predisposes individuals to alcoholism and drug dependence or to the addictive process has not been confirmed. No one type of personality determines the biological development of alcoholism and drug dependence. However, some personality disorders, including antisocial, narcissistic, and borderline personality, may especially affect the development of multiple dependence. Antisocial personality in adults and conduct disorder in children enhance the potential for exposure to alcohol and drugs, particularly at a young age. Because early and significant exposure to multiple drugs is more common in these personality types, the addictive process is perhaps more likely to develop (Vaillant, 1983; Poldrugo & Forti, 1988).

Pharmacotherapy

The knowledge of the drugs used by the multiply dependent individual has important implications for treatment in the acute detoxification period, as well as for the sustaining of recovery in relapse prevention (Kern, Hassett, Cohen, Lennon, & Schmelter, 1983; Crane, Sereny, & Gordis, 1988). Different substances may require individualized detoxification schemes that do not always overlap. The physiological withdrawal from alcohol is treated with benzodiazepines, whereas the delusional and hallucinatory symptoms of PCP are treated with a neuroleptic and opiate withdrawal is treated with clonidine or methadone. Furthermore, the protracted withdrawal from hallucinogens, cannabis, and stimulants may require pharmacological intervention with neuroleptics and antidepressants if psychotic, anxiety, and depressive symptoms persist.

Caution is urged in using combinations of medications for detoxification. In general, the use of sedatives in combination for detoxification from a sedative should be avoided. An example might be detoxifying a methadone addict who is also alcoholic with methadone, plus a barbiturate (phenobarbital) or a benzodiazepine (chlordiazepoxide) for the alcohol withdrawal. The synergistic effect of the two sedatives might produce a compromise of sensorium, respirations, and cardiovascular function. An alternative would be to use clonidine instead of methadone and an as-needed (p.r.n.) schedule of chlordiazepoxide instead of a fixed dose for the alcohol withdrawal.

Detoxification from stimulants, cannabis, and hallucinogens usually does not require a medication for medical sequelae. The use of neuroleptics and antidepressants in a fixed schedule might be needed for the symptoms of psychosis, depression, or anxiety.

Detoxification from sedatives/hypnotics and benzodiazepines is often done with benzodiazepines, although barbiturates are also effectively used. Chlordiazepoxide is the drug my colleagues and I prefer, because of its intermediate half-life, its potential dual use in a simultaneous alcohol withdrawal, and its lower drug-seeking properties. The duration of the half-life provides a smoother, more gradual withdrawal than does a short-acting drug, and less accumulation than does a long-acting benzodiazepine. Chlordiazepoxide is given on a tapered schedule for 7–10 days for detoxification from short-acting, and for 10–14 days for detoxification from long-acting, benzodiazepines.

General principles that may serve as clinical guidelines for detoxification of the multiply dependent individual are the following:

1. The clinician should treat objective signs of withdrawal, such as disturbed vital signs (blood pressure, pulse, temperature), tremors, pupillary changes, diaphoresis, and agitation. Subjective signs as a rule are unreliable, because the basic defect of the multiply dependent individual is a loss of control over drugs; thus self-report is likely to be directed toward obtaining drugs, not withdrawing from them.

2. The clinician should re-evaluate a fixed regimen daily, or more frequently, in regard to the need to continue. That is, there may be a need to decrease dose or shorten duration, or (in exceptional circumstances) to increase dose and duration. A p.r.n. regimen should be used whenever possible. Generally, withdrawal from alcohol and sedatives carries some medical risk, whereas withdrawal from opiates and cocaine carries little or no medical risk. Frequent monitoring of vital signs and clinical presentation will adequately cover these risks.

3. The clinician should be skeptical about a patient's self-report or even corroborative accounts of drug types and doses, frequency, and duration. Because of the denial of the dependence syndrome and the adverse effects of intoxication on judgment, alcohol/drug dependents often omit and underestimate alcohol and drug use. Again, objective monitoring of behavior and vital signs will reveal other drug withdrawals. The clinician should keep an open mind. The alcoholic frequently denies the use of other drugs such as marijuana and sedatives/hypnotics; the cocaine dependent frequently denies the use of alcohol and marijuana; the opiate dependent denies the use of alcohol, marijuana, and benzodiazepines. The need to obtain drug screens is especially significant in multiply dependent populations, in order to diagnose and treat the various withdrawal syndromes.

4. Finally, detoxification is almost a subspecialty in itself. Experience is required to assess and treat drug withdrawal adequately. Outside consultation is suggested until familiarity with the complex issues of drug detoxification is achieved. A "cookbook" approach, as in other areas of medicine, has limited application.

The management of overdose or intoxification should include a thorough history and physical examination, as well as drug screens for blood and urine. In the case of overdoses, when patients are conscious, the stomach should be emptied by inducing vomiting or using activated charcoal. If the clinical condition does not improve, other medical and surgical states should be considered. Emergency rooms give naloxone to attempt to reverse opiate drugs in all overdoses. The respiratory and cardiovascular systems may need support in cases of multiple-substance overdoses on alcohol, opiates, sedative/hypnotic drugs, and antidepressants. These substances have a consistent synergistic depressant effect on respirations and generate arrhythmias in the cardiovascular system. Constant monitoring of the vital signs in intensive care units may be required in cases of overdose.

Because of the multiply dependent individual's apparent generalized vulnerability to alcohol and drugs, the use of any psychoactive drugs or medications creates a risk of developing a new dependence or of reactivating the old alcohol and drug dependence. The use of anticholinergic and antihistaminic drugs, including antidepressants and antipsychotics, may have addictive potential and produce pharmacological dependence in multiply dependent patients (Dilsaver, Greden, & Snider, 1987; Dilsaver & Alessi, 1988). Even aspirin or Tylenol may be used dependently, particularly by this population.

Bromocriptine and desipramine have been used in treating the craving for cocaine during the acute and subacute withdrawal period. Limited experimental success has been achieved with these drugs in treating the cocaine dependent (Gawin et al., 1989). Moreover, studies have been performed on "pure" cocaine-dependent populations, and therefore the generalizability of this treatment to the multiply dependent population needs further study. The use of blocking agents for opiates, such as naltrexone, has met with some clinical success. Naltrexone is an antagonist that interacts at the opiate receptor to block the effects of opiate agonists. Naltrexone is given orally and may neutralize intravenous injections of heroin or morphine. Naltrexone by itself has no opiate agonist properties.

Antabuse (disulfiram) is a drug that has been used with limited efficacy over the years. Antabuse is a competitive inhibitor of aldehyde dehydrogenase, an enzyme that is responsible for degrading acetaldehyde, the breakdown product of the action of the enzyme alcohol dehydrogenase on alcohol. Acetaldehyde is a noxious intermediary that produces an unpleasant syndrome of nausea, vomiting, lightheadedness, and cardiovascular collapse in severe reactions. The more alcohol consumed and the higher the dose of Antabuse, the more severe the adverse reaction. A major limiting stipulation is that the alcoholic must continue to take Antabuse daily in order for the reaction to take place when alcohol is imbibed. It may only take a day or two for the Antabuse to be sufficiently washed out before alcohol can be consumed without significant interactive effect. At times, the alcoholic is able to drink "through" or in spite of the Antabuse reaction. However, it should be cautioned that other alcoholics may need as long as a week or two before it is safe for them to drink alcohol.

Methadone maintenance for opiate dependence in the multiply dependent individual is covered in another chapter of this book (see Dilts & Thomason, Chapter 5).

Treatment of Multiple Dependence

It may be desirable, because of the special issues regarding the multiply dependent patient, to employ more than a single modality of treatment simultaneously and/or sequentially. Many approaches may be employed in treatment of such a patient.

Contemporary inpatient and outpatient programs are designed to treat multiple dependence, because it now represents the most common presentation of alcohol and drug dependence. The decision to select either inpatient or outpatient treatment can be determined by several clinical factors. Inpatient hospitalization is indicated for heavy and prolonged alcohol/drug use, complicating medical and/or psychiatric comorbidity, poor premorbid personality, lack of family support or organization, significant others who are manifesting drug/alcohol dependence, unemployment, and previous failures at outpatient forms of treatment (Washton, & Gold, 1987; Pattison & Kaufman, 1982). Correspondingly, the decision to select outpatient treatment is determined by less severe substance use and fewer complicating factors.

Individual psychotherapy and group therapy directed at the addiction component can be utilized during both inpatient and outpatient treatment, as well as the long-term recovery period called "aftercare." These important therapies may be based on approaches oriented to the "here-and-now" intrapsychic and interpersonal processes of the multiply dependent individual. Generally, supportive, confrontational, and cognitive approaches are the most effective in directing such a patient to minimize conflict and to remain abstinent from drugs and alcohol during the acute and subacute period of the recovery. Insight- and dynamic-oriented therapy can be very valuable in the more advanced stages of recovery, after a year or two of the other therapies and abstinence (Pattison & Kaufman, 1982; Kaufman, 1989).

Traditional alcohol and drug treatment programs that utilize a Twelve-Step approach are effective for multiply dependent patients (Miller et al., in press). Because of the common dependence syndrome in this patient population, a uniform treatment approach involving group and individual therapies directed at the addiction component can be effectively employed.

Some studies show favorable responses to treatment administered for concurrent, multiple dependence. A recent study (Miller et al., in press) determined outcome rates for inpatient treatment based on a Twelve-Step approach for alcohol, cocaine, and other drug dependence. Demographic information and abstinence rates at 6 and 12 months postdischarge were compiled for 1,627 patients admitted to an inpatient treatment unit for the rehabilitation of cocaine, alcohol, and other drug dependence. Of these patients, 42% were diagnosed as alcohol dependent; 25% as cocaine, alcohol, and other drug dependent; and 28% as alcohol and other drug dependent. The abstinence rate at 6 months for patients with alcohol dependence only was 75%, for alcohol and other drug dependence 82%, and for cocaine dependence 76%; at 12 months, the abstinence rates were 71%, 66%, and 62%, respectively.

For the total sample, 77% of the respondents were attending Alcoholics Anonymous at the 12-month follow-up. Forty-six percent had used other group and individual therapy modalities and 35% were attending other support groups to assist their recovery. The rate for Alcoholics Anonymous attendance by respondents decreased from the 6th to the 12th month posttreatment. Attendance at Alcoholics Anonymous of one or more times per week decreased from 64% to 55% for the cocaine-dependent group, from

80% to 71% for the alcohol- and drug-dependent group, and from 73% to 60% for the alcohol-dependent group.

The treatment modalities for the dependence (addiction component) may be affected by type of substance use. Individualized education and support groups may be indicated for specific drugs such as cocaine and opiates (i.e., Cocaine and Narcotics Anonymous). However, the principles of an abstinence-based treatment program that includes Alcoholics Anonymous will work for the alcoholic who has additional drug dependence or the multiple-drug dependent with an alcohol dependence diagnosis. The similarities in the addictive disorders are greater than the differences, so that recovery by multiply dependent individuals self-help groups such as Alcoholics Anonymous and Narcotics Anonymous is common.

Psychiatric evaluations and interventions may be necessary as discussed earlier (see "Psychiatric Disorders," above). For those patients with psychiatric disorders and concurrent alcohol and drug dependence, specific pharmcotherapy may be indicated for the psychiatric disorder. In general, the same pharmacological agents used in psychiatric disorders in the absence of a "dual diagnosis" may be used with some notable exceptions. As discussed, antidepressants and antipsychotic medications with low anticholinergic and low sedative properties are preferred, because of the abuse/addiction potential of drugs with stronger anticholinergic and sedative effects (Dilsaver & Alessi, 1988; Dilsaver et al., 1987). Importantly, the use of sedatives/hypnotics, including benzodiazepines, is to be avoided because of their addictive potential, particularly in the high-risk population of alcoholics and drug dependents (DuPont, 1988). The abuse/addiction potential of newer agents such as buspirone is yet unknown.

Individual and group therapies aimed at the comorbid psychiatric disorders are often indicated in the dual-diagnosis populations. These therapies may be employed on a short- or long-term basis, depending on the type and severity of the psychiatric disorders. Comorbid personality disorders in particular have been shown to respond to behavioral, cognitive, and psychodynamic therapies. Rewarding results may be obtained when these therapies are used alone or in conjunction with specific treatments of addiction such as Twelve-Step programs (see Chapters 17–20, this volume).

References

American Psychiatric Association. (1987). *Diagnostic and statistical manual of mental disorders* (3rd ed., rev.). Washington, DC: Author.

Begleiter, H., Porjesz, B., & Kissin, B. (1982). Brain dysfunction in alcoholics with and without a family history of alcoholism. *Alcoholism: Clinical and Experimental Research, 6*, 36.

Blum, K. (1989). A commentary on neurotransmitter restoration as a common mode of treatment for alcohol, cocaine and opiate abuse. *Integrative Psychiatry, 6*, 199–204.

Blum, K., & Briggs, A. H. (1988). Opioid peptides and genotypic responses to ethanol. *Biogenic Amines, 5*(6), 527–533.

Blum, K., Briggs, A. H., & Trachtenberg, M. C. (1987). Enkephalinase inhibition: Regulation of ethanol intake in genetically predisposed mice. *Alcohol, 4,* 449–456.

Blum, K. Briggs, A. H., & Trachtenberg, M. C. (1989). Ethanol ingestive behavior as a function of central neurotransmission. *Experientia, 45,* 445–451.

Crane, M., Sereny, G., & Gordis, E. (1988). Drug use among alcoholism detoxification patients: Prevalence and impact on alcoholism treatment. *Drug and Alcohol Dependence, 22,* 33–36.

Des Jarlais, D. C., & Friedman, S. R. (1988). HIV and intravenous drug use. *AIDS, 2*(Suppl. 1), S65–S69.

Dilsaver, S. C., & Alessi, N. E. (1988). Antipsychotic withdrawal symptoms: Phenomenology and pathophysiology. *Acta Psychiatrica Scandinavica, 77*(3), 241–246.

Dilsaver, S. C., Greden, J. F., & Snider, R. M. (1987). Antidepressant withdrawal syndromes: Phenomenology and pathophysiology. *International Clinical Psychopharmacology, 2*(1), 1–19.

Drake, R. E., & Wallach, M. A. (1989). Substance abuse among the chronic mentally ill. *Hospital and Community Psychiatry, 40*(10), 1041–1045.

DuPont, R. L. (Ed.). (1988). Abuse of benzodiazepines: The problems and the solutions. A report of a committee of the Institute for Behavior and Health, Inc. *American Journal of Drug and Alcohol Abuse, 14*(Suppl. 1), 1–69.

Frances, R., Timm, S., & Bucky, S. (1980). Studies of familial and nonfamilial alcoholism: I. Demographic studies. *Archives of General Psychiatry, 37,* 564–566.

Freed, E. X. (1973). Drug abuse by alcoholics: A review. *International Journal of the Addictions, 8,* 451–473.

Galizio, M., & Maish, S. A. (1985). *Determinants of substance abuse* New York: Plenum.

Gawin, F. H., & Kleber, H. D. (1986). Abstinence symptomatology and psychiatric diagnosis in cocaine abusers: Clinical observations. *Archives of General Psychiatry, 43,* 107–113.

Gawin, F. H., Kleber, H. D., Byck, R., Rounsaville, B. J., Kosten, T. R., Jatlow, P. I., & Morgan, C. (1989). Desipramine facilitation of initial cocaine abstinence. *Archives of General Psychiatry, 46,* 117–121.

Gold, M. S., & Verebey, K. (1984). The psychopharmacology of cocaine. *Psychiatric Annals, 14*(10), 714–723.

Goodwin, D. G. (1985). Alcoholism and genetics: The sins of the fathers. *Archives of General Psychiatry, 42,* 171–174.

Harvey, S. C. (1985). Hypnotics and sedatives. In A. G. Gilman, L. S. Goodman, T. W. Rall, & F. Murad (Eds.), *The pharmacological basis of therapeutics* (7th ed., pp. 339–371). New York: Macmillan.

Helzer, J. E., & Pryzbeck, T. R. (1988). The co-occurrence of alcoholism with other psychiatric disorders in the general population and its impact on treatment. *Journal of Studies on Alcohol, 49*(3), 219–224.

Hoffman, F. G. (1983). *A handbook of drug and alcohol abuse* (2nd ed.). New York: Oxford University Press.

Jaffe, J. H. (1985). Drug addiction and drug abuse. In L. S. Goodman & A. G. Gilman (Eds.), *The pharmacological basis of therapeutics* (6th ed, pp. 532–581). New York: Macmillan.

Johnston, L. D., O'Malley, P. M., & Bachman, J. G. (1986). *Drug use among American high school students, college students and other young adults: National trends through 1985* (DHHS Publication No. 86-1450). Washington, DC: U.S. Government Printing Office.

Kandel, D. B., Murphy, D., & Karus, D. (1985). Cocaine use in young adulthood: Patterns of use and psychosocial correlates. In N. J. Kozel & E. H. Adams (Eds.), *Cocaine use in America: Epidemiologic and clinical perspectives* (NIDA Research Monograph No. 61, DHHS Publication No. 85-1414, pp. 76–110). Washington, DC: U.S. Government Printing Office.

Kandel, D. B. & Raveis, V. H. (1989). Cessation of illicit drug use in young adulthood. *Archives of General Psychiatry, 46,* 109–116.

Kaufman, E. (1989). The psychotherapy of dually diagnosed patients. *Journal of Substance Abuse Treatment, 6,* 9–18.

Kern, J. C., Hassett, C. A., Cohen, M., Lennon, F., & Schmelter, W. (1983). Comparison of pure and polydrug alcoholics: Its implication for alcohol detoxification in the 1980s. *Journal of Psychiatric Treatment and Evaluation, 5,* 263–267.

Kosten, T. R., Rounsaville, B. J., Babor, T. F., Spitzer, R. L., & Williams, J. B. W. (1987). Substance use disorders in DSM-III-R: Evidence for the dependence syndrome across different psychoactive substance. *British Journal of Psychiatry, 151,* 834–843.

Kosten, T. R., Rounsaville, B. J., & Kleber, H. D. (1987). Parental alcoholism in opioid addicts. *Journal of Nervous and Mental Disease, 173*(8), 461–468.

Kreek, M. J. (1987). Multiple drug abuse patterns and medical consequence. In H. Y. Meltzer (Ed.), *Psychoparmacology: The third generation of progress* (pp. 1597–1604). New York: Raven Press.

Milam, J. R., & Ketchum, K. (1981). *Under the influence.* Seattle: Madrona.

Miller, N. S., Dackis, C. A., & Gold, M. S. (1987). The relationship of addiction, tolerance and dependence: A neurochemical approach. *Journal of Substance Abuse Treatment, 4,* 197–207.

Miller, N. S., & Gold, M. S. (1989). Suggestions for changes in DSM-III-R criteria for substance use disorders. *American Journal of Drug and Alcohol Abuse, 15*(2), 223–230.

Miller, N. S., Gold, M. S., Belkin, B., & Klahr, A. L. (1990). The diagnosis of alcohol and cannabis dependence in cocaine dependents and alcohol dependence in their families. *British Journal of Addiction, 84,* 1491–1498.

Miller, N. S., Millman, R. B., & Keskinen, S. (in press). The treatment outcome at six and twelve months for alcohol dependence among cocaine addicts in an inpatient population. *Advances in Alcohol and Substance Abuse.*

Miller, N. S., & Mirin, S. M. (1989). Multiple drug use in alcoholics in practical and theoretical implications. *Psychiatric Annals, 19*(5), 248–255.

National Institute on Drug Abuse (NIDA). (1985). *Demographic trends and drug abuse, 1980–1985* (NIDA Research Monograph No. 335). Washington, DC: U.S. Government Printing Office.

National Institute on Drug Abuse (NIDA). (1988). *National household survey on drug abuse* (DHHS Publication No. ADM 89-1636). Washington, DC: U.S. Government Printing Office.

Pattison, E. M., & Kaufman, E. (1982). *The encyclopedic handbook of alcoholism.* New York: Gardner Press.

Poldrugo, F., & Forti, B. (1988). Personality disorders and alcoholism treatment outcome. *Drug and Alcohol Dependence, 21,* 171–176.

Post, R. M. (1975). Cocaine psychosis: A continuum model. *American Journal of Psychiatry, 132,* 225–231.

Redda, K. K., Walker, C. A., & Barnett, G. (1989). *Cocaine, marijuana, designer drugs: Chemistry, pharmacology, and behavior.* Boca Raton, FL: CRC Press.

Ritchie, J. M. (1985). The alipathic alcohols. In A. G. Gilman, L. S. Goodman, T. W. Rall, & F. Murad (Eds.), *The pharmacological basis of therapeutics* (7th ed., pp. 372–386). New York: Macmillan.

Robins, L. N., Helzer, J. E., Pryzbeck, T. R., & Regier, D. A. (1988). Alcohol disorders in the community: A report from the Epidemiologic Catchment Area. In R. M. Rose & J. Barrett (Eds.), *Alcoholism: Origins and outcome* (pp. 15–29). New York: Raven Press.

Schuckit, M. A. (1983). Alcoholism and other psychiatric disorders. *Hospital and Community Psychiatry, 34*(11), 1022–1027.

Schuckit, M. A. (1986). Genetic and clinical implications of alcoholism and affective disorders. *American Journal of Psychiatry, 143*(2), 140–147.

Smith, D. E. (1986). Cocaine–alcohol abuse: Epidemiological, diagnostic and treatment considerations. *Journal of Psychoactive Drugs, 18*(2), 117–129.

Sokolow, L., Welte, J., Hynes, G., & Lyons, J. (1981). Multiple substance abuse by alcoholics. *British Journal of Addiction, 76,* 147–158.

Tarter, R. (1981). Minimal brain dysfunction as an etiological predisposition to alcoholism. In R.

E. Meyer, B. C. Glueck, J. E. O'Brien, T. F. Babor, & J. H. Jaffe (Eds.), *Evaluation of the alcoholic: Implications for research, theory and treatment* (NIAAA Publication No. ADM 81-1033, pp. 167–191). Rockville, MD: U.S. Department of Health and Human Services.

Trachtenberg, M. C. & Blum, K. (1987). Alcohol and opioid peptides: Neuropharmacological rationale for physical craving of alcohol. 1987, *American Journal of Drug and Alcohol Abuse, 13*(3), 365–372.

Vaillant, G. E. (1983). *The natural history of alcoholism*. Cambridge: Harvard University Press.

Washton, A. M., & Gold, M. S. (Eds.). (1987). *Cocaine: A clinician's handbook*. New York: Guilford Press.

Watkins, V. M., & McCoy, C. B. (1980). Drug use among urban Appalachian youths. In V. M. Watkins & C. B. McCoy (Eds.), *Drug abuse patterns among young polydrug abusers and urban Appalachian youths* (NIDA Services Research Report, DHHS Publication No. 80-1002, pp. 17–34). Washington, DC: U.S. Government Printing Office.

PART THREE

DIAGNOSTIC INSTRUMENTS

10

Laboratory Testing

KARL VEREBEY

CARLTON E. TURNER

Introduction

Although drug abuse testing by qualified laboratories is extremely reliable, frequent criticism of inaccurate results appears in the popular press. The adverse publicity has resulted in distrust of drug testing by the general public. The authors of such anti-drug-testing articles either show no scientific data or provide out-of-context quotes from scientific articles attempting to discredit drug testing. On the other hand, many carefully controlled scientific studies support the reliability of testing when performed properly by locally and nationally accredited laboratories (Frings, Battaglio, & White, 1989).

The confusion surrounding drug abuse testing is a result of large numbers of variables. Each individual drug is unique, and detectability depends on the type of drug, size of the dose, frequency of use, the route of administration, differences in individual drug metabolism, the sample collection time, and the sensitivity of the analytical method used to test the sample. All these variables make each test request an individual case, and general rules for all drugs and all situations are extremely difficult to set.

Modern analytical toxicology deals with the detection and identification of minute amounts of drugs or alcohol in body fluids. This branch of science has grown and expanded tremendously in the last few decades, with the recognition of widespread drug abuse in the United States. Qualified drug-testing laboratories, providing objective qualitative and quantitative urinalysis results, are now easily accessible to physicians. Laboratory accreditations must be checked by the physicians before ordering tests, however, because poor-quality laboratories still exist. This chapter examines detailed drug-testing issues and the clinical and forensic utility of drug abuse testing.

Rationale for Testing

Drug abuse is characterized by impulsive drug-seeking behavior, with paroxysmal breaks in use and almost certain relapses. A common feature of all drug abusers is denial. The patients lie to themselves, as well as to the forbidding outside world, to protect the continuity of their obsessive addiction to drugs and/or alcohol. For this reason, physicians dealing with drug abusers are seldom given voluntarily the diagnostically important information about the patients' addictive habits.

The drug abuse pattern is an important part of the medical history. The attending physician cannot properly design treatment when kept in the dark about a patient's addiction. Depending on the drug or drugs used, symptoms of physical and/or psychiatric illness may be simulated by the presence or the absence of the particular drug(s). The dichotomy of symptoms associated with drug presence or absence is best illustrated with the opioid class of drugs (Jaffe & Martin, 1985). While under the influence of an opioid, the addict experiences euphoria, anxiolytic sedation, mental clouding, sweating, and constipation. In the absence of opioid, the common withdrawal signs and symptoms appear: pupillary mydriasis, agitation, anxiety, panic, muscle aches, gooseflesh, rhinorrhea, salivation, and diarrhea. Thus, the two different sets of diagnostic symptoms belong to the abuse of the same drug, observed at different times in the presence and absence of an opioid.

Behavior similar or identical to textbook descriptions of psychosis can be triggered in predisposed individuals by drugs. For example, phencyclidine (PCP), D-lysergic acid diethylamide (LSD), amphetamines, or cocaine can cause toxic psychosis that is indistinguishable from paranoid schizophrenia; drug-induced model psychosis can be produced in anyone given the adequate dose of one of these drugs. Drug-induced psychosis has a different prognosis and must be treated differently from psychosis related to endogenous organic, anatomical, or neurochemical disorders (Gold, Verebey, & Dackis, 1985).

Treatment of identified drug abusers would be extremely handicapped if drug abuse testing were not utilized. Therefore, comprehensive drug testing is important for psychiatrists in making precise follow-up evaluations and selecting appropriate treaments for their patients. The first good reason for laboratory drug testing is to provide objective identification of drug abusers and the substances they are abusing (Pottash, Gold, & Extein, 1982).

Testing is also of great value after drug abusers are identified. Current treatment strategies are intimately tied to frequently scheduled urinalyses to monitor recovering addicts. Negative results support the success of treatment, while positive test results alert the treating physician to relapses. This is the reason why objective testing is a necessary component of modern treatment of ex-drug abusers.

Drug abuse testing, in some cases, is forensic in nature. Ex-drug abusers, after release from incarceration, are monitored by parole officers. A positive drug test may invalidate the parole and signal to law enforcement the involvement of the parolee with criminal elements.

Health professionals, such as doctors, dentists, and nurses, are afflicted with drug abuse problems more often than the general population. Once their involvement with drug abuse is exposed, their professional licenses are in danger of suspension. The rehabilitation of addicted health professionals is tied to urine testing as a condition of probation.

Professional athletes often abuse drugs. Teams and national or international sport associations may prohibit the use of performance-enhancing drugs, and staying drug-free is often the condition athletes must fulfill in order to be allowed to compete. Laboratory testing of body fluids for drugs of abuse is the objective technique used to enforce these rules (Wadler & Heinline, 1989).

Finally, the conduct of business and the public safety may be endangered by intoxicated employees. Bankers and stockbrokers handle investors' money; such business professionals should not be influenced by psychoactive drugs, especially drugs that cause delusions and impulsive risk-taking behavior. Similarly, drug abuse by other professionals may endanger the public. Drug abuse has been identified among airline pilots, bus drivers, railroad engineers, and police officers. In all these examples, drug abuse testing is advantageous to both the drug abuser and his or her environment (his relatives and the general public). The abuser gets early treatment and a chance for early rehabilitation, and the public is saved from potential wrongdoing under the influence of drugs. Success of drug abuse testing by decreasing drug abuse has been clearly demonstrated in the military. Prior to the institution of testing in 1981, 48% of armed services personnel used illegal drugs. After 3 years of testing, fewer than 5% were found to be using drugs (Willette, 1986). Although critics often attack testing as ineffective, drug use clearly decreases in situations where serious drug testing is in place.

Tests Available

A number of different laboratory methods are available for comprehensive drug screening. When the drug abuse habit of the patient is unknown, physicians request a "comprehensive drug screen" (Verebey, Martin, & Gold, 1986). Some laboratories usually perform the most inexpensive procedure, the relatively insensitive thin-layer chromatography (TLC) test. Many results are negative because of the low sensitivity of this screening procedure, not because a drug or its metabolite is not present in the sample. By "comprehensive drug testing," different laboratories mean different things. Unless the physician is familiar with the laboratory procedures and technical language, he or she will be less effective in diagnosing drug-induced psychiatric symptoms when the use of drugs is the true cause of a patient's problems.

Urine samples are most commonly sent for "routine drug screen" analysis. The psychiatrists or other physicians may assume that this test will detect all abused drugs. The problem is that the TLC drug screen will detect only high-level drug use of a select group of drugs. TLC is not sensitive enough to detect marijuana, PCP, LSD, 3,4-methylenedioxyamphetamine (MDA), 3,4-methylenedioxymethamphetamine (MDMA), mescaline, and fentanyl, among others (see Table 10.1). Thus, a negative TLC drug screen does not mean that the patient has not used drugs. What it means is that there is no evidence of high-dose abuse of morphine, quinine (a diluent of heroin), methadone, codeine, dextromethorphan, propoxyphene, barbiturates, diphenylhydantoin, phenothiazines, cocaine, amphetamine, or phenylpropanolamine. Again, low-dose abuse of these drugs is not likely to be detected. Thus, false negatives are very high for the "routine drug screen" performed by TLC (Manno, 1986). Table 10.1 presents the time frames within which TLC can detect various drug groups; it also lists drugs not detected by routine TLC.

If, for example, a physician suspects marijuana abuse, he or she must specifically request that a marijuana screen be performed, usually by enzyme immunoassay (EIA; Verebey et al., 1986). Currently, screening for prescription drugs and drugs of abuse is performd by EIA, such as the enzyme multiplied immunoassay test (EMIT); radioimmunoassay (RIA); fluorescent polarization immunoassay (FPIA); and a modern version of the TLC, called "ToxiLab," which has improved sensitivity over conventional TLC systems. In exceptional laboratories, drug screening is performed by capillary gas–liquid chromatography (GLC) equipped with nitrogen–phosphorous detector (NPD). In a single analysis, 25 compounds or more can be identified. This system is advantageous when there is no clue to the identity of the abused or toxic substance in the sample; however, GLC-NPD is time-consuming, labor-intensive, and usually expensive. High-performance liquid chromatography (HPLC) is similar to GLC in principle. It is usually less sensitive than GLC but sample preparation is easier. The EMIT and RIA tests are significantly cheaper and more practical than the more specific gas chromatography (GC) and gas chromatography–mass spectrometry (GC/MS) methods. The EIA and FPIA have technical advantages over other screening techniques, in that no extrac-

TABLE 10.1. Drugs That Can and Cannot Be Detected by Thin-Layer Chromatography (TLC)

Detected by TLC for 24 hours or longer after use
1. Amphetamine, methamphetamine, ephedrine, pseudoephedrine, phenylpropanolamine, etc.
2. Benzodiazepines: Librium, Valium, Dalmane, etc.
3. Barbiturates: phenobarbital, secobarbital, pentobarbital, etc.
4. Methadone, propoxyphene.
5. Tricyclic antidepressants: imipramine, desipramine.

Detected by TLC for 3 to 12 hours
1. Opiates.
2. Cocaine (benzoylecgonine).
3. Talwin.

Not detected by TLC
1. Cannabinoids. [a]
2. PCP.
3. LSD, psilocybin, MDA, MDMA.
4. Designer drugs: fentanyl derivatives.

Note. Adapted from Manno (1986).
[a]Routine TLC does not detect tetrahydrocannabinol (THC); however, special TLC procedures do.

tion of drugs or metabolites is required. Thus, these procedures are easily adaptable for high-volume automated screening analysis of drugs. In fact, most good laboratories offer a 5- or 10-drug panel with or without alcohol (Hawks, 1986). These tests are usually performed by EIA. An example of EIA selection of a 10-drug panel plus alcohol is presented in Table 10.2. Comparative "sensitivity ranges" and "cost per sample" for the various analyses are shown in Table 10.3.

Analytical Methodology

The choice of methods for the identification of drugs or their metabolites in body fluids depends on the patient's history, physical examination, past history, and available biological samples. Sometimes there is some hint or knowledge about the type of substances used by the subject, which needs to be confirmed. These are the simplest situations because the analyst can compare the suspected drug in the sample with a known standard by GC or a specific and sensitive EIA procedure. Also, the method of choice is determined by knowledge of the drug's identity, biotransformation pathway, and pharmacokinetic pattern (Chiang & Hawks, 1986).

Most often, however, there is no clue about the substance(s) used. Such samples are tested to rule out the drug-related symptoms. In this case, a broad drug screen is required. There are various types of drug screens available, with markedly different panels of drugs, sensitivity, specificity, and cost. Analytical methods are described below, with specific examples for specific needs.

Extraction

With the exception of some immunoassays, such as EIA, FPIA, and RIA, most methods require isolation of drugs from body fluids before instrumental analy-

---

TABLE 10.2 Ten Drugs and Alcohol Screened by Enzyme Immunoassay (EIA)

Alcohol (ethanol)
Amphetamine
Barbiturate
Benzodiazepines (including Librium, Valium, and Dalmane)
Cocaine and metabolite (benzoylecgonine)
Methaqualone (Quaalude)
Opiates, morphine, codeine, monoacetyl morphine (heroin metabolite),
    and hydrocodone (Dilaudid)
Methadone
PCP
Propoxyphene (Darvon)
Cannabinoids (THC metabolites)

TABLE 10.3. Sensitivity and Cost Ranges for Various
Analytic Methods

Method	Sensitivity ranges (ng/ml)	Cost per sample range ($)
Chromatography		
TLC	1,000–2,000	5–10
GLC	10–300	40–50
HPLC	20–300	40–60
GC/MS	5–100	50–100
Immunoassays		
EMIT	200–1,000	4–6
RIA	2–20	5–15

sis. This is accomplished by extraction, using appropriate organic solvents at the specific hydrogen ion concentration (or pH) at which the drug molecules favor movement from aqueous biofluids into organic solvents. Basic drugs (such as morphine, methadone, and amphetamine) are favorably extracted at alkaline pH, whereas acid drugs (such as the barbiturates and phenytoin) are more soluble in organic solvents at near-neutral or acid pH. There is an advantage to the analytical chemist when the abused substance is known; thus, the proper conditions can be selected for isolation. Samples containing unknown substances are extracted at acidic, basic, and neutral conditions, hoping to create the most favorable condition to isolate the abused substance (Verebey et al., 1986).

Preparing the cleanest extract possible, so that interference by unrelated molecules is minimized, is of great importance. Biofluids are rank-ordered as follows from clean to dirty: saliva, cerebrospinal fluid (CSF), serum, urine, and whole blood (hemolyzed). In other words, the least interference is in saliva and CSF, whereas urine and hemolyzed whole blood have the most background materials. Depending on the distribution of the drug in the body, which in turn is dependent on the drug's physicochemical properties, one or another biofluid may be best suited for analysis. As a rule, urine has from 100 to a 1,000 times more drug or metabolite in it than serum. Following extraction and "cleanup" of samples, the extracts are analyzed by various methods differing in sensitivity and specificity.

Thin-Layer Chromatography

TLC is a technique that is utilized to separate different molecules in a mixture, based on their polarity and their chemical interaction with developing solvents and the thin-layer coating. A specific substance, given the same physical and chemical conditions, will always migrate the same distance from the origin. Thus, if cocaine is in a mixture, a spot characterized by the cocaine standard will travel to the same location on the TLC plate as the cocaine standard. Unfortunately, similar molecules, interfering substances in an extract, and various drugs may also travel to approximately the same location. This makes TLC a crude, nonspecific method. The spot location is identified by an Rf number, which is the ratio calculated from the distance traveled by the drug divided by the distance traveled by the solvent front from the origin, where the mixture was originally spotted. TLC is a qualitative method, and, as emphasized earlier, it is the least sensitive among the methods for most drugs. Visualization of the spots on TLC is achieved in different ways. The plate can be illuminated by ultraviolet or fluorescent lights. Migration of molecules to speccific Rf zones can be further identified by color reactions of the spots after spraying with chemical dyes. Identical molecules are expected to migrate to the same Rf zone and give identical color reactions (Gold et al., 1985).

Traditional "toxicology screen" by TLC was primarily designed to detect high-dose recent drug abuse or toxic levels of drugs. It is the ideal test for emergency room use in cases where the drugs taken are unknown, the concentrations are expected to be high, and quick determination of the toxic substance is the primary task. Psychiatrically and forensically relevant low-level substance abuse, or drug use long before the sample is collected, is not readily identified by traditional TLC. Thus, TLC toxicology screen is often not sufficiently sensitive for the differential diagnosis of drug-induced toxic psychosis that mimicks depression, mania, or schizophrenia. Nor is it very well suited for diagnosis of chronic low-dose use of illicit drugs. Such TLC screens are generally no longer admissible as forensic evidence in most court proceedings. In addition to emergency rooms, TLC is also used in methadone progams as a "routine drug screen" or a "tox screen." When TLC is used, false negatives are the rule rather than the exception, thereby confusing the meaning of negative and positive drug screens. It must be understood that very often whether a sample is called "positive" instead of "negative" depends on the concentration of the drug in the sample or the sensitivity of the assay. With TLC for most drugs, sensitivity is in the low-microgram range (about 2 μg/ml); thus a "negative" urine smple by TLC may be positive by other methods, such as RIA, EIA, FPIA, and/or GC/MS. Exceptions to the rule of insufficient sensitivity are new TLC methods, such as high-performance TLC, ToxiLab, and bounded phase adsorption–thin-layer chromatography (BPA/TLC). Some of these methods use a larger-volume urine sample, and are therefore sensitive to lower drug concentrations than the traditional TLC.

It should be emphasized that when a TLC is ordered, a positive result should be confirmed by a scientifically different method. The color specificity and differential migration make the TLC assay reliable in the hands of experienced toxicologists; however, the boredom and labor-intensive nature of TLC make experienced TLC toxicologists hard to find (Verebey et al., 1986). And, again, negative results by TLC screen are not always negative by other, more sensitive analytical methods. Table 10.3 shows some of the sensitivity ranges for commonly abused drugs detected by TLC as opposed to the more sensitive EIA, RIA, and GC/MS.

Most substances are detected by conventional TLC only when the level of drug in the urine is above 2 μg/ml. This makes cocaine, for example, very difficult to detect by routine TLC since the half-life of cocaine is only 1 hour in humans and the levels in body fluids quickly diminish (Baselt & Cravey, 1989). Marijuana, PCP, LSD, an other important drugs of abuse are not identified at all in most conventional TLC systems (Manno, 1986).

Enzyme Immunoassay and Radioimmunoassay

The various immunoassays operate on the principle of antigen–antibody interactions. These techniques are commonly used to measure hormones, neurochemicals, and drugs. Antibodies are produced against the drug or metabolite of interest by coupling them to large immunoactive molecules and injecting the haptene-bound drug into rabbits or sheep. The animals produce antibodies against the drug that is used in the immunoassay. Immunological methods used for drug detection utilize these antibodies to seek out the drug in biofluids. In the sample containing one or more unknown drugs, competition exists for available antibody-binding sites between the tagged drug in the test and drug or drugs in the unknown sample. The binding ratio determines the presence or absence of specific drugs.

The specificity and sensitivity of the antibodies to a given drug compound differ, depending on the particular assay and the manufacturer. Immunoassay can be very specific; however, compounds structurally similar to the drug of interest (their metabolites) often do cross-react. Thus, in general, the specificity of the immunoassays is considered far less than that of GLC and GC/MS (Hawks, 1986). Lack of specificity may be an advantage in some cases, because interaction of the antibody with drugs plus metabolites in a sample increases sensitivity in "total" detection of a drug class. In chromatography, single specific molecules are determined. Thus, quantitatively less drug is detected by GLC and GC/MS than by immunoassays. For EIA, FPIA, and RIA, the ranges of sensitivity are between micrograms and picograms.

EIA systems are very popular and commonly used for drug abuse screening because no extraction or centrifugation is required, and the system lends itself to easy automation. Although an EIA screen is more costly than TLC, toxicological screens using EIA are much more sensitive for most drugs and are more likely to detect lower drug concentrations. The user of EIA screening should know what drugs are on the panel offered by the laboratory and what the sensitivity cutoffs for these drugs are.

Gas–Liquid Chromatography and Gas Chromatography–Mass Spectrometry

GLC is an analytical technique that separates molecules by principles similar to those of TLC, except that the TLC plate is replaced by glass or metal tubing (1 to 2 meters long) packed with materials of particular polarity or capillary columns 15 to 30 meters long. The sample is vaporized by heat at the injection port and carried through the column by a steady flow of gas. The column terminates at the detector, which registers a response to the drugs, and the response can be graphically recorded and quantitated. The response is proportional to the amount of substance present in the sample. Identical compounds travel through the column at the same speed, since their interaction with the column packing is the same. The time from injection until a response at the recorder is observed is referred to as the "retention time." Identical retention times of substances run on two different polarity columns constitute strong evidence that the substances are identical (Verebey et al., 1986).

Even stronger evidence can be obtained by the use of GC/MS, which analyzes the substance by its fragmentation pattern. Since in various molecules not all bonds are of equal strength, the weak ones are more likely to break under stress. Bombardment of the molecules by an electron beam in the mass detector fragments molecules at the weak bonds. The exact mass of the fragments or breakage products is measured by the mass spectrometer. GC/MS is considered as the most reliable, most definitive forensically accepted procedure. The breakage of molecules results in unique fragments that are in specific ratios to one another; thus the GC/MS method is often called "molecular fingerprinting" (Gold et al., 1985).

Information on the fragmentation pattern is checked with a computer library that lists the mass of the parent compound, as well as its most likely fragments and their relative ratios. A perfect match with a control is considered absolute confirmation of a particular compound. The use of GC/MS has been out of the reach of most laboratories in the past because of high cost of equipment, high level of technical expertise needed for operation, and complex sample preparation. However, recent advances in computerization, automated sample preparation, and less expensive analytical technology are now placing GC/MS capabilities within the reach of forensic analytical laboratories and clinicians. The sensitivity of GLC for most drugs is in the nanogram range, but with special detectors some compounds can be measured at picogram levels. GC/MS can also be used quantitatively, which sometimes provides additional information that may help to interpret a clinical syndrome or to explain corroborating evidence in forensic cases. Although identification of compounds by GC/MS is considered absolute, this is only true when the instrument is operating in the scanning mode looking at full framentation spectra. When the GC/MS is in the selected-ion-monitoring (SIM) mode, some of the specificity of the MS technique is lost, yet sensitivity for quantitation is increased. The probability of interfering substances' having the same molecular ion fragments as the drug of interest is very low. Therefore, the chances for error by GC/MS are much reduced when the instrument is in the "full-scan" mode, and ion ratios of the most characteristic fragments are calculated and compared to known controls.

GLC for most drugs is about 100 to 1,000 times more sensitive than TLC;

it is also more specific, especially when the unknown substance is analyzed on two different polarity columns and the commonly abused drugs are readily identified by both GLC and GC/MS (e.g., marijuana, cocaine, amphetamines, and opiates). GC/MS is also 100 to 1,000 times more sensitive than conventional TLC systems, and when it is operated in the "full-scan" mode, identification of drugs is considered absolute.

When a routine toxicological screen is ordered, it may be performed by the cheapest technique (TLC). The physician is often not aware that he or she has options for more sensitive toxicological analyses by either GLC, GC/MS, or the more recently introduced and practical EIA, FPIA, and RIA techniques. Table 10.4 shows a comparative sensitivity of the three major methods for a selected group of abused drugs.

The Choice of Body Fluids and Time of Sample Collection

Some drugs are metabolized extensively and are very quickly excreted, whereas others stay in the body for an extended period of time. Thus, success of detection depends not only on the time of sample collection after the last drug use, but also on the particular drug used and whether the analysis is performed for the drug itself or for its metabolites. In Table 10.5, expected time scales of detectability are shown for some commonly abused drugs (Wadler & Heinline, 1989).

When drug abuse detection is the goal, the following questions should be asked: (1) How long does the particular drug stay in the body, or what is its half-life? (2) How extensively is the drug biotransformed? Thus, should one look for the drug itself or its metabolite(s)? (3) Which body fluid should be analyzed, or what is the major route of excretion (Chiang & Hawks, 1986)? The importance of asking these questions is illustrated by cocaine and methaqualone (Quaalude), which are biotransformed significantly differently.

TABLE 10.4. Sensitivity of Methods (Employing Urine Samples) for Testing Specific Drugs

	Sensitivity (ng/ml)		
Drug	TLC	EIA, RIA, TDX, EMIT	GC/MS
Amphetamines	2,000	300	25
Barbiturates	2,000	300	50
Benzodiazepines	—	300	50
Cocaine (benzoylecgonine)	2,000	75–300	20
Marijuana (THC)	20[a]	20–100	10
Opiates (morphine)	2,000	300	20
PCP	—	25–75	10

[a]Special procedure; not detected by routine TLC.

TABLE 10.5. Detectability of Drug Use

Drug	Half-life (hours)	EIA cutoff (ng/ml)	GC/MS cutoff (ng/ml)	Detection after last use (days)
Amphetamines	10–15	300	100	1–2
Barbiturates				
Short-acting	20–30	300	100	3–5
Long-acting	48–96	—	—	10–14
Benzodiazepines				
Diazepam	20–35	300	—	2–4
Nordiazepam	50–90	300	100	7–9
Cocaine				
Cocaine proper	0.8–1.5	—	—	0.2–0.5
Benzoylecgonine	—	300	50	2–4
Methaqualone	20–60	300	50	7–14
Opiates (morphine, codeine)	2–4	300	100	1–2
PCP	7–16	75	10	2–8
Cannabinoids (THC)	10–40	20–100	10	14–42 (chronic) 2–8 (acute)

Cocaine has a half-life of about 1 hour in humans. It is rapidly biotrans-formed into inactive metabolites of benzoylecgonine and ecgoninemethyl ester. Less than 10% of unchanged cocaine and more than 45% of benzoylecgonine is excreted into the urine. Unchanged cocaine is detectable only from 0 to 12 hours after use. What does all this suggest to the clinician who wants to know whether or not a patient is taking cocaine? The short half-life indicates that unless use is suspected within hours, or the patient is suspected of being currently under the influence of cocaine, the parent compound is not likely to be found in detectable concentration in either the blood or the urine. However, a blood test that includes cocaine and the cocaine metabolite may be reliable for many hours after use to document or exclude recent exposure to cocaine. Plasma enzymes continue to metabolize cocaine even after the blood is taken from the subject. *Therefore, blood samples should be collected into sodium fluoride, which inactivates these enzymes.* Benzoylecgonine is the major metabolite of cocaine; its half-life is about 6 hours, and, as noted above, it is excreted in urine at levels totaling approximately 45% of the dose. Clearly, detection is best accomplished by collecting urine and analyzing it for ben-zoylecgonine. In one study, it was observed that of those subjects who had enough benzoylecgonine in their urine to be detected, only 2% had enough cocaine present for detection. Thus, 98% of the subjects, if tested for cocaine specifically, would have been found negative (Verebey, 1987).

A contrasting example is methaqualone. This substance is, like cocaine, extremely lipid-soluble, but it has a half-life of 20 to 60 hours. Because it is not biotransformed rapidly, either blood or urine tests are effective for detection of the parent compound itself. In our studies, we were able to detect methaqualone for 21 days in the urine after a single 300-mg oral dose, and in blood for 7 days (Kogan, Jukofsky, Verebey, & Mulé, 1978). Thus information about pharmacokinetics and excretion is important in deciding which chemical to look for and in which body fluid.

Urine is the most suitable biofluid for drug detection analysis. *As a rule, urine has about 1,000 times more drug present in it than blood or plasma.* On the other hand, it is often much easier to prepare cleaner extracts from plasma than from urine. A cleaner extract greatly reduces background interference, and makes it easier for the chromatographer to interpret and confirm results. Background interference is less important in the immunoassays, where no extraction is needed.

Many physicians prefer blood to urine for drug screening because they believe that blood levels constitute stronger evidence of recent use and that they are more closely related to brain levels and drug-related behavior changes than urine levels. For example, amphetamine blood levels are directly related to the emergence and persistence of amphetamine-induced psychoses. Since urine is an ulatrafiltrate of plasma, it is also sufficiently accurate for drug and metabolite determination as proof of drug use. However, the collection of urine specimens must be supervised in order to insure that the person in question is the source of the sample and to guarantee the integrity of the specimen. It is not unusual to receive someone else's or a highly diluted sample when collection of samples is not supervised or screened by the laboratory for pH, specific gravity, or creatinine. First morning urine samples are preferred, because they are more concentrated and drugs are more readily detected (Verebey et al., 1986). The decision to use blood or urine should be based on the specific drug's pharacokinetic and excretion data. As a rule, urine drug levels are higher and should be the biofluid of choice for drug and metabolite detection.

The Meaning of Positive and Negative Reports

Psychoactivity of most drugs lasts only a few hours after drug ingestion, while urinalysis can detect many drugs and/or metabolites for days or even weeks. Thus, the qualitative presence of drugs (or metabolites) in urine is only an indication of prior exposure, not proof of intoxication or impairment at the time of sample collection. In some cases, quantitative data in blood or urine can corroborate observed behavior or action of a subject, especially when the levels are so high that it is impossible for the subject to be free of drug effects. Thus, drug-induced behavior and laboratory data should be interpreted by experts in pharmacology, toxicology, and pharmacokinetics (Verebey et al., 1986).

When one receives drug analysis reports, whether positive or negative, there are certain questions about the absolute truth of the results. The following should be asked to clarify questions about the testing procedure: (1) What method was used? (If the lab does not make this clear on the report, the clinician should call and ask.) (2) Did the assay analyze for the drug alone, metabolite only, or both? What is the "cutoff" value for the assay? (Again, the clinician should call and ask if anything seems unclear.) (3) Was the sample time close enough to the suspected drug exposure? (This information is usually unavailable, since denial is one of the most typical features of drug abusers. Their use pattern is usually hidden.)

First, let us examine positive results. Some scrutiny of the method is needed to determine whether or not a false-positive result is a possibility. Knowledge of the method of determination is helpful. TLC, although not very sensitive, is reasonably specific for drugs that have both the parent drug and its metabolite identified on the TLC plate. Also, specific color reactions help to eliminate false positives for certain drugs. However, if GLC or GC/MS is the analytical technique, positive results are usually acceptable. Either RIA or EMIT is considered rather sensitive, but chemically similar compounds may cross-react with the antibody, registering positive results. Cross-reactivity depends on the specificity of the antibody used for a particular drug and drug metabolite. Some antibodies are more specific than others; therefore, each test should be individually evaluated for specificity. Positive test results for amphetamines and opiates must be further defined for specific substances if the results are to be legally and medically acceptable. Usually, an immunoassay can be confirmed by a chromatographic procedure, and vice versa.

False-negative results can occur more easily than false positives, mainly once a test is screened negative it is not tested further. Also, negative reports based on TLC alone are not conclusive. Additionally if the screening method is RIA or EIA, the cutoff that separates positives and negatives may have been set too high. Another possibility for false negatives is that the sample was taken too long after the last drug exposure. Whatever the case may be, if the suspicion of drug use is strong, the clinician should have the testing repeated and inquire at the laboratory for more sensitive drug-screening procedures.

In general, analytical toxicology methods have significantly improved in the past decades, and the trend is toward further improvement. As technology continues to improve, more drugs and chemicals will be analyzed in biofluids at the nanogram and picogram level. Advancement, however, does not mean that modern methodologies are infallible, nor do they replace the clinician. Theoretically and practically, technical or human error can influence testing results. A solid laboratory, locally and nationally certified, with a full spectrum of drug abuse tests, enables the well-trained clinician to make drug abuse diagnoses that were not possible in the past. With knowledge of the available analytical methods, one can scrutinize the laboratory test results and be more confident about their validity.

Ethical Considerations

The legitimate utilization of drug abuse testing in the clinical setting is indisputable. Denial makes identification of drug abuse difficult; therefore, testing is necessary both in identification and in monitoring treatment outcome. However, drug testing at the workplace and in sports is more controversial. For example, positive test results may be used (or abused) in termination of long-time employees or refusal to hire new ones.

Private companies feel that it is their right to establish drug- and alcohol-free workplaces and sport arenas. The opposition feels that it is ill advised to terminate individuals for a single positive test result even when it is confirmed by forensically acceptable procedures. A testing program is more reasonable when a chance for rehabilitation is offered. Probationary periods would provide individuals with an opportunity to stop using drugs through treatment or self-help programs (Verebey et al., 1986). Employee assistance programs, which refer employees to drug counseling, are available in larger companies and governmental organizations.

It is important that this new powerful tool, drug testing, be used not as a weapon but judiciously as a means of early detection and prevention of disability. Test results must be interpreted only by individuals who understand drugs of abuse medically and/or pharmacologically. The federal government requires that in its drug-testing program the results go directly to medical review officers, who are trained to interpret such reports. Improper testing in the laboratory or improper interpretation of drug-testing data, which may destroy innocent lives, must be prevented.

Federal employees may be tested for drugs of abuse only by locally and nationally certified laboratories. The two most respected regulatory agencies for forensic toxicology laboratories are the National Institute on Drug Abuse (NIDA) and the College of American Pathologists (CAP). Only the most proficient and competent laboratories in the nation are certified by these organizations. The laboratories must pass a stringent 2-day "on-site" inspection and frequent proficiency testing throughout the year. Because of the serious consequences of positive test results, employee and pre-employment testing by private companies should also be conducted in certified laboratories.

Is society placed in jeopardy by the drug-related actions of certain drug abusers? How should the test results be used? Who should know the results and under what circumstances? These are just some of the questions asked by private citizens. The verdict on random testing is not yet decided, but in a case of "for-cause testing," the U.S. Supreme Court was on the side of testing. The Court determined that public safety supersedes individual rights to privacy, especially when the job in question has a significant impact on society. It is predictable that the controversy regarding the civil rights issues and legality of drug abuse testing will continue for some time.

Conclusions

As long as illegal drug use is prevalent in our society, drug abuse testing will have an important clinical and forensic role. Testing in the clinical setting will aid the physician in treating subjects with psychiatric signs and symptoms secondary to drug abuse, in monitoring treatment outcome, and in handling serious overdose cases. Drug testing in the forensic setting will be used in the workplace and in monitoring parolees convicted of drug-related charges.

Several civil rights concerns must be enforced to protect the innocent. Names of subjects should be known only to the medical office where the sample is collected. Testing must follow strict chain-of-custody procedures to insure anonymity and prevent sample mixup during testing. Some progressive laboratories (e.g., Princeton Diagnostic Laboratories of America) have instituted bar-code labeling of samples and related documents to insure confidentiality. Bar-coding also improves the accuracy of reporting, tracking of samples, and records. This system ultimately prevents sample mixup due to human error during accessioning.

The reliability of testing procedures is also of foremost importance. Good laboratories institute internal (both open and blind) and external quality control systems to assure high quality of testing (Blanke, 1986).

Before issuing licenses, governmental agencies require laboratories to adhere to strict standards in personnel qualifications, experience, quality control, quality assurance programs, chain-of-custody procedures and multiple data review prior to the reporting of results.

Two nationally recognized agencies are protecting the rights of individual citizens who might be tested by assuring proper procedures in forensic drug testing: NIDA (through its National Laboratory Certification Program) and CAP (through its Forensic Toxicology Proficiency Program). In addition, numerous city and state regulatory agencies inspect and license drug-testing laboratories. Good laboratories are easily identified by having current certificates of qualification and licenses issued by national and local regulatory agencies.

In conclusion, drug abuse testing has come a long way in accuracy and reliability. Testing started in traditional "wet chemistry" laboratories, using huge sample volumes and crude methodologies of low sensitivity. Now autoanalyzers perform hundreds of test on minute sample volumes, measuring accurately low-nanogram amounts of substances. Thus, the insecurity expressed in the popular press about drug abuse testing should not be a concern to anyone using properly certified, licensed laboratories.

References

Baselt, R. C., & Cravey, R. H. (Eds.). (1989). *Disposition of toxic drugs and chemicals in man* (3rd ed.). Chicago: Year Book Medical.

Blanke, R. V. (1986). Accuracy in urinalysis. In R. L. Hawks & N. C. Chiang (Eds.), *Urine testing for drugs of abuse* (NIDA Research Monograph No. 73, pp. 43–53). Washington, DC; U.S. Government Printing Office.

Chiang, N. C., & Hawks, R. L. (1986). Implications of drug levels in body fluids: Basic concepts. In R. L. Hawks & N. C. Chiang (Eds.), *Urine testing for drugs of abuse* (NIDA Reseach Monograph No. 73, pp. 62–83). Washington, DC: U.S. Government Printing Office.

Frings, C. S., Battaglio, D. J., & White, R. M. (1989). Status of drugs of abuse testing in urine under blind conditions: An AACC study. *Clinical Chemistry, 35*(5), 891–844.

Gold, M. S., Verebey, K., & Dackis, C. A. (1985). Diagnosis of drug abuse, drug intoxication and withdrawal states. *Fair Oaks Hospital Psychiatry Letter, 3*(5), 23–34.

Hawks, R. L. (1986). Analytical methodology. In R. L. Hawks & N. C. Chiang (Eds.), *Urine testing for drugs of abuse* (NIDA Research Monograph No. 73, pp. 30–42). Washington, DC: U.S. Government Printing Office.

Jaffe J. H., & Martin, W. R. (1985). Opioid analgesics and antagonists. In A. G. Gilman, L. S. Goodman, T. W. Rall, & F. Murad (Eds.), *The pharmacological basis of therapeutics* (7th ed., pp. 491–531). New York: Macmillan.

Kogan, M. J., Jukofsky, D., Verebey, K., & Mulé, S. J. (1978). Detection of methaqualone in human urine by radioimmunoassay and gas–liquid chromatography after a therapeutic dose. *Clinical Chemistry, 24,* 1425–1427.

Manno, J. E. (1986). Interpretation of urinalysis results. In R. L. Hawks & N. C. Chiang (Eds.), *Urine testing for drugs of abuse* (NIDA Research Monograph No. 73, pp. 54–61). Washington, DC: U.S. Government Printing Office.

Pottash, A. L. C., Gold, M. S., & Extein, I. (1982). The use of the clinical laboratory. In L. Sederer (Ed.), *Inpatient psychiatry: Diagnosis and treatment* (pp. 205–221). Baltimore: Williams & Wilkins.

Verebey, K. (1987). Cocaine abuse detection by laboratory methods. In A. M. Washton & M. S. Gold (Eds.), *Cocaine: A clinician's handbook* (pp. 214–228). New York: Guilford Press.

Verebey, K., Martin, D., & Gold, M. S. (1986). Drug abuse: Interpretation of laboratory tests. *Psychiatric Medicine, 3*(3), 155–166.

Wadler, G. I., & Heinline, B. (1989). *Drugs and athletes: Contemporary exercise and sports medicine.* Philadelphia: F. A. Davis.

Willette, R. E. (1986). Drug testing programs. In R. L. Hawks & N. C. Chiang (Eds.), *Urine testing for drugs of abuse* (NIDA Research Monograph No. 73, pp. 5–12). Washington, DC: U.S. Government Printing Office.

11

Psychometric Assessment

RALPH E. TARTER
PEGGY J. OTT
ADA C. MEZZICH

Introduction

All psychometric procedures have one characteristic in common—they selectively evaluate cognitive, emotional, or behavioral processes. Because it is not technically feasible or practical to attempt to learn everything about an individual, the psychometric evaluation necessarily focuses on the accrual of information in selected areas of psychological functioning from among the total repertoire of the individual. Information obtained from a psychometric examination should ideally reveal treatment needs so as to maximize prognosis, as well as to elucidate the etiological factors underlying a known or suspected disorder. The psychometric assessment can be especially arduous because of the multifactorial causes underlying these disorders and because there are usually numerous psychological disturbances that either presage, or are concomitant to, or are consequences of alcohol abuse and other types of substance abuse.

This chapter is divided into three main sections. First, the scope of a comprehensive psychometric assessment is discussed. In order to familiarize the clinician with the purpose and context of a psychometric assessment, the first section of the chapter describes the attributes of such an assessment and briefly reviews the issues that, from a psychological perspective, are particularly pertinent to understanding alcohol and drug abuse. Second, the methods for conducting a psychometric assessment are described. The areas of required coverage for a comprehensive evaluation are identified, and specific instruments for clinical assessment are discussed. Finally, the third and concluding section presents a decision tree format for conducting a psychometric evaluation so that the results can be linked to specific modes of treatment.

Scope and Attributes of a Comprehensive Psychometric Assessment

Figure 11.1 depicts the three broad categories of psychological processes requiring psychometric evaluation in cases of known or suspected substance

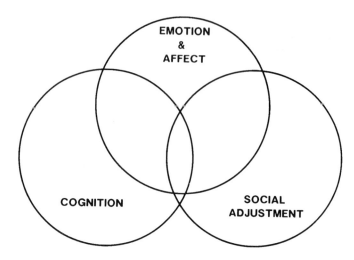

FIGURE 11.1. Interrelationships among cognition, emotion, and social adjustment that influence the unique clinical presentation revealed by psychometric assessment.

abuse. A disturbance in one category may or may not involve also a disturbance in another. That is to say, these three categories of psychological functioning are not necessarily causally related to one another. For instance, some drug addicts may be more disturbed emotionally, whereas others are more affected socially. Hence, within a given diagnostic category (e.g., substance abuse disorder), there is substantial heterogeneity in the population with respect to the component disturbances contributing to the overall psychological presentation. A major task, therefore, in the psychometric assessment is to ascertain what processes are disturbed. Once these are assessed, the task then becomes analyzing the causal interrelationships among the disturbances.

Moreover, the psychological characteristics observed, encompassing the cognitive, emotional, and psychosocial spheres of functioning, depend to a great extent on the type of facility in which the alcoholic or substance abuser is seeking treatment. For example, alcoholics who present for treatment at a liver unit or gastroenterology service typically manifest less severe emotional disorder and present with better social adjustment than alcoholics who are admitted to psychiatric facilities (Ewusi-Mensah, Saunders, & Williams, 1984). In contrast, they may be more likely to manifest either an acute or low-grade hepatic encephalopathy than persons who are admitted to psychiatric facilities, for whom adjustment problems rather than disease effects from chronic alcoholism precipitated treatment. Thus, clinicians must be cognizant of the general characteristics of the population from which their clients are drawn, so as to focus and structure the psychometric examination accordingly. A point to be emphasized in this regard is that a diagnostic label alone conveys very little useful information. Rather, by contributing to an understanding of cognitive, emotional, and social processes within the individual, the comprehensive psychometric evaluation can substantially assist in clarifying the factors that are etiologically related to the abuse of alcohol and other drugs.

In summary, the goals of a comprehensive psychometric evaluation are fourfold: (1) to acquire objective and quantitative information about current cognitive, emotional, and social functioning; (2) to facilitate an understanding of the idiosyncratic and causal interrelationships among these three spheres of functioning; (3) to elucidate the etiology of the substance use disorder with respect to the origin and relative contribution of cognitive, emotional, or social disturbances; and (4) to accrue information that identifies the treatment needs of the client.

Requirements of a Comprehensive Psychometric Evaluation

The information acquired from the psychometric assessment must satisfy two basic requirements: validity and reliability.

Validity

The tests administered must have proven validity. This insures that the findings are factual so that the clinician can have confidence in the information obtained. "Construct validity" means that the psychological processes claimed to be measured are, in fact, what are being assessed. For instance, for a given patient or client, it is essential to know that poor performance on a neuropsychological test of memory capacity is due to a central nervous system (CNS) injury and is not the consequence of emotional problems or any other factor unrelated to neurological status. Numerous other examples can be provided. However, the point to be made is that the ultimate utility of any psychometric instrument (and therefore the safeguard against misinterpretation) depends on its capacity to evaluate accurately the processes intended to be measured.

In addition, psychometric instruments should be selected that have "predictive validity." That is, the psychological processes sampled and measured by the test should yield scores that facilitate prediction of some aspect of the individual's behavior in the natural environment. For example, low scores on tests of educational aptitude should be associated with academic underachievement. High scores on tests of anxiety should be found in conjunction with avoidant social behavior. Thus, predictive validity enables the clinician to make inferences about how the individual is ordinarily functioning beyond the circumscribed context of the assessment. These predictions should be oriented to meaningful and specific domains of functioning, such as the person's potential to respond to a particular type of treatment, hold a certain type of job, or attend college. Although psychometric tests must be recognized as not being the absolute or even the only method for making predictions, they should nevertheless be administered to gather the type of information that can maximize the client's prognosis in multiple spheres of everyday functioning. Clearly, predictive validity is an essential ingredient in a comprehensive assessment, because it yields information that can help guide the particular type of rehabilitation, which can then promote the best prognosis.

Finally, it should be noted that psychometric testing is warranted only where the obtained data have "incremental validity." That is, the test should yield information beyond what can be acquired from informal interviewing or casual observation. It is pointless to measure depression if the self-report of symptoms and observed pathognomonic signs are readily obtained. Psychometric procedures are most prudently utilized in cases where the objectivity of measurement and quantification of the process, against either population norms or criterion cutoff scores, yield information that is either too complex or too subtle to be obtained from casual observation. In this fashion, information accrued from psychometric tests increases the level of understanding to sophisticated intelligibility. Because it is both expensive and labor-intensive, the psychometric evaluation should not be requested merely to confirm clinical impressions.

Reliability

Of the various types of psychometric reliability, two need to be considered here: test–retest and interrater reliability. "Test–retest reliability" refers to the stability of the individual on the measured characteristic. The clinical meaningfulness of any set of test results is contingent on their repeatability. Changes monitored in the individual using a particular instrument, therefore, should truly reflect a change in the person's status. Thus, for example, if the psychometric instrument has established test–retest reliability, the test can be used repeatedly to monitor any changes in status occurring between any two points in time during the course of treatment or aftercare.

The second type of reliability is "interrater reliability." A test score obtained by one psychometrician should nearly equal the score obtained if the test is administered by another person. Confidence can then be placed in the results accrued as being an accurate description of the client, and not the product of idiosyncratic interaction between the psychometrician and the client.

In summary, the data accrued from the psychometric evaluation must satisfy several fundamental requirements pertaining to validity and reliability. In essence, the scores obtained must consistently and accurately reflect the psychological process claimed to be measured, must have predictive value, must be stable over time, and should not be an artifact of the particular assessment context. These requirements apply regardless of the psychological process evaluated.

Before we proceed with a discussion of specific instruments and domains of psychometric assessment, the following section examines the three broad categories of processes that are integrally related to both the etiology and consequences of a substance use disorder. From this discussion, it should become apparent that a substance use disorder typically has a multifactorial etiology. Hence, a comprehensive multivariate psychometric assessment protocol is necessary in order to characterize the individual fully.

Psychological Processes Integral to Substance Abuse

Cognition

Cognitive processes encompass both cognitive style and cognitive capacity. Both aspects are relevant to understanding alcoholism and drug abuse. "Cognitive style" refers to the general strategy the individual uses to process information. For example, there is substantial evidence indicating that substance abusers and alcoholics are more inclined than the general population to analyze perceptual stimuli in a global, inarticulate manner (Sugerman & Schneider, 1976). This rather stable trait is referred to as "perceptual field dependency." Significantly, this cognitive style appears to be related to treatment prognosis (Karp, Kissin, & Hustmeyer, 1970). Another type of cognitive style commonly found among substance abusers is "stimulus augmentation" (Buchsbaum & Ludwig, 1980). Stimulus augmentation (the propensity to magnify sensory input) is related to a motivational disposition characterized by impulsivity, behavioral disinhibition, and sensation or novelty seeking. Interestingly, this cognitive style is found primarily among persons with low platelet monoamine oxidase (MAO) activity (Schooler, Zahn, Murphy, & Buchsbaum, 1978). Low platelet MAO activity is particularly associated with alcoholism in cases where there is a conjoint antisocial disorder (Von Knorring, Bohman, Von Knorring, & Oreland, 1985).

Understanding the person's cognitive style may thus assist in treatment planning and in formulating a differential diagnosis. Unfortunately, the techniques for assessing this aspect of cognition have not been inculcated into general psychometric assessment practice, although it is possible to make inferences about perceptual field dependency by using a simple test measuring flexibility of perceptual closure (Jacobson, Pisani, & Berenbaum, 1970), and about stimulus augmenting by measuring sensation-seeking behavior (Zuckerman, Bone, Neary, Mangelsdorff, & Brastman, 1972).

Cognitive capacities are commonly impaired in alcoholics because of CNS injury that is either directly caused by alcohol neurotoxicity or indirectly mediated by organ/system damage (e.g., hepatic encephalopathy, obstructive pulmonary disease, hypertension). CNS functioning is typically compromised by multiple sources where cognitive deficits are found. In other words, besides the specific effects of drugs or alcohol on the brain, neglectful lifestyle, trauma from accidents and fights, and poor overall health status may contribute to the CNS disturbances. The psychometric evaluation must therefore not only be aimed at detecting and describing the pattern of disturbances in CNS functioning by means of validated neuropsychological tests, but should additionally attempt to determine from other psychometric instruments (as well as from biomedical or laboratory tests) the possible etiological bases for the manifest disturbances.

Approximately 75% of alcoholics demonstrate some form of CNS disturbance as measured by neuropsychological tests (Tarter & Edwards, 1985). Emerging findings also suggest that other forms of substance abuse are frequently associated with deficits on neuropsychological tests (Grant, Mohns, Miller, & Reitan, 1976); however, the research literature is far less conclusive than the findings obtained on alcoholics. Impairments are most frequently observed on tasks measuring abstract thinking and memory capacity, as well as on tests measuring visuospatial processes (Tarter & Ryan, 1983). These deficits appear to be most pronounced in individuals who are in less than optimal health or who have experienced the cumulative effects of multiple CNS insults (Grant, Adams, & Reed, 1979). With respect to biomedical factors, a low-grade chronic hepatic encephalopathy may contribute substantially to the cognitive deficits found in cirrhotic alcoholics; this neuropsychiatric disturbance itself has a complex etiology. For example, the encephalopathy, revealed as poor performance on cognitive tests, may be produced by the liver's failure to catabolize circulating neurotoxins (Tarter, Edwards, & Van Thiel, 1986), in addition to the liver's failure to absorb and store vitamin E. Hence, neuronal membranes are injured because of the absence of vitamin E to protect them from oxidation by free radicals. Furthermore, it should be noted that a hepatic encephalopathy may have a variety of other etiological determinants (Tarter et al., 1986). The point to be made is that the manifest cognitive deficits found in alcoholics have a multifactorial etiology.

Neuropsychological deficits associated with alcoholism are well documented. Indeed, two syndromes of cognitive disorder have been described. A dementia has been observed in alcoholics that is distinguishable according to both neuroanatomical and cognitive manifestations from the more florid amnestic or Korsakoff's syndrome (Wilkinson & Carlen, 1980). A number of other neurological conditions have also been described in alcoholics, although their neuropsychological manifestations have not yet been studied.

Less is known regarding the neuropsychological sequelae of other drugs having abuse liability. Evidence has been presented indicating that the chronic use of such drugs as phencyclidine (PCP), inhalants, benzodiazepines, heroin, cocaine, and amphetamines may be associated with neuropsychological impairments in some individuals (Grant & Judd, 1976; Parsons & Farr, 1981); however, the results regarding the neurotoxic effects of specific drugs are still inconclusive. One major methodological problem in this area of study is that it is not possible to ascertain the specific effects of a certain drug on CNS functioning, since polydrug abuse is the typical pattern of consumption. Also, the frequency and quantity of drug use are extremely variable among consumers. Hence, determining dose–effect relationships vis-à-vis cognitive functioning is difficult if not impossible. These qualifications notwithstanding, the available evidence does indicate that as a group, substance abusers perform deficiently on certain neuropsychological tests indexing CNS integrity. As is the case among alcoholics, poor neuropsychological test performance probably has a multifactorial etiology. For instance, the poor performance may be reflective of multiple minor brain injuries, poor overall health, and premorbid neurodevelopmental disorder.

Neuropsychological tests are very sensitive indicators of cerebral integrity (Lezak, 1983). Their sensitivity surpasses that of either the clinical neurological examination or the electroencephalogram (EEG) (Goldstein, Deysach, & Kleinknecht, 1973). Moreover, in the early stages of a dementing disease, psychometric procedures probably also exceed the diagnostic sensitivity of neuroradiological procedures, where gross morphological injury may not be present or detectable upon visual inspection. More importantly, perhaps, neuropsychological tests are especially informative for rehabilitation purposes because the data obtained describe functional cerebral integrity; as such, they characterize the person according to commonly recognized psychlogoical processes (e.g., attention, memory, language, learning, concentration) that are generally understood to be important for educational, vocational, and social adjustment. Indeed, it is the relationship between neurological status and these latter processes, rather than the test scores per se, that underscores the importance of the neuropsychological assessment.

Documenting cognitive capacity and efficiency via neuropsychological assessment is important for several reasons. During the drug withdrawal phase at the onset of rehabilitation, cognitive capacity may be too impaired for the person to achieve meaningful gains from didactic therapy or counseling. A brief cognitive screening used on repeated occasions can thus determine the client's readiness for rehabilitation. Cognitive limited individuals may not be able to solve daily problems, develop broad strategic plans to restructure their lives, acquire insight into their problems, or benefit from vocational rehabilitation. Neuropsychological assessment can assist in the formulation of a treatment plan and aftercare program for individuals with these types of difficulties. For instance, among alcoholics whose thinking is concrete, structured interventions not requiring insight are most beneficial (Kissin, Platz, & Su, 1970). Furthermore, it is important to note that everyday activities such as driving a car, using power machinery, or performing tasks where there are safety risks may be impaired because of CNS damage from chronic substance abuse. Neuropsychological testing, particularly in the area of psychomotor capacities, may therefore assist in a determination of injury risk to self and/or others.

Neuropsychological assessment has also been increasingly utilized as part of forensic evaluation. In criminal cases, the objective, quantitative assessment of cognitive capacities can contribute to a better understanding of behavior that may be due to CNS injury. In this regard, the expertise of the neuropsychologist who understands the neurobehavioral mechanisms associated with alcohol or substance abuse disturbances (e.g., blackouts, anterograde amnesia) can provide important information about the severity of the addiction, its consequences for the functional capacities of the particular individual, and the impact of cognitive deficits on emotional and psychosocial processes.

The systematic delineation of cognitive strengths and weaknesses, particularly as they relate to the onset and pattern of substance use behavior, is important for several additional reasons. This type of evaluation may yield important information about etiology. For example, an attentional disorder or learning disability often precedes the onset of substance abuse (Tarter, Alterman, & Edwards, 1985). This has treatment implications because it may be possible to prevent or treat the substance use behavior for some individuals by ameliorating the problem that initially motivated drug use. In addition, the assessment of cognitive deficits has importance for understanding the person's everyday abilities, such as remembering appointments, following simple as well as complex directions, and learning new material. Demonstrating the presence of a deficit lends itself to implementing a treatment program that also encompasses cognitive rehabilitation. For example, cognitive retraining—either teaching the person compensatory strategies where there is an irreversible deficit, or re-establishing a capacity that was not permanently impaired—affords the opportunity to maximize social and vocational adjustment as part of multidisciplinary rehabilitation. It is noteworthy that cognitive rehabilitation as a subspeciality of clinical neuropsychology has been shown to be a useful adjunct to treatment of neurologically impaired individuals, although these procedures have yet to be applied to alcoholics and other drug abusers.

Emotion

The intensity of emotional experience and appropriate expression of emotion are strongly associated with overall quality of psychological well-being. Conflicts over anger and guilt, or the display of intense emotional reactions such as rage or panic, have long been known to accompany substance use behavior in many individuals. These disruptive emotions may either presage substance abuse or emerge following drug use onset. Not uncommonly, the consumption of psychoactive substances is motivated by a need to ameliorate negative affective states. The inability to express emotions effectively in the social context, particularly negative feelings, is also frequently associated with drug abuse.

Emotional disturbance is often encompassed within psychopathology. Although not all drug or alcohol users demonstrate psychopathology, the range of manifest psychopathology includes the spectrum of neurotic, characterological, and psychotic disturbances. From the psychometric perspective, clinically significant psychopathology is present in cases where the severity exceeds two standard deviations above the population mean. That is to say, individuals who rank in excess of the 95th percentile in the population on a trait qualify for a diagnosis. Commonly, psychopathology is present in substance abusers, although often not to diagnostic threshold. Whether such psychopathological disturbances requires treatment can only be determined by integrating the findings obtained from the psychiatric and psychometric assessments. For example, a chronic state of tension or depression may be integral to substance abuse for an individual, even if it is not of sufficient severity to qualify for a diagnosis. Under these circumstances, the negative affective states may contribute directly to drug-seeking motivation. At the other extreme, it is important to be cognizant of the possiblity that a psychopathological disorder, even if qualifying for a psychiatric diagnosis, may spontaneously remit following effective treatment for substance use. Indeed, it is not uncommon for psychopathology symptoms to dissipate in conjunction with sobriety or abstinence from drugs. Furthermore, it is essential to recognize that emotional distress (e.g., anger, helplessness, guilt) can both precipitate and sustain a psychopathological disorder. Hence, characterizing the client's emotional status should enable the clinician to determine whether an emotional disturbance underlies the emergence of psychopathology or, alternatively, is a symptomatic correlate of the psychopathology. For example, intense unresolved anger can either provoke or be concomitant to a psychopathological disorder such as depression.

Psychometric tests measure traits or dimension, in comparison to a psychiatric assessment, which is concerned with assigning the person to a diagnostic category. Traits are usually measured on a continuum that ranges from low to high. Structured psychiatric interviews (e.g., the Schedule for Affective Disorders and Schizophrenia, the Diagnostic Interview Schedule, the Structured Clinical Interview for DSM-III-R) characterize the person dichotomously according to the presence or absence of symptoms. The aggregate of symptoms determines the severity of the syndrome. Whether a categorical or dimensional approach is utilized, the most frequently observed psychopathological disturbances comorbid to alcohol or drug abuse are anxiety and depression. However, virtually every Axis I and Axis II disturbance has been observed concomitant to substance abuse (Helzer & Pryzbeck, 1988; Weissman, 1988; Daley, Moss, & Campbell, 1987; Peace & Mellsop, 1987; Dackis, Gold, Pottash, & Sweeney, 1985).

In addition to recognizing the importance of objectively evaluating emotion and affect in the context of both psychopathology and substance abuse, the clinician must be aware of the complexity of this task. Emotional disturbance as well as psychopathology can emerge at any time during the natural history of the substance use disorder, and often has a complicated etiological basis. Disturbances, for example, may be manifested as the result of genetic predisposition or life stress, or may appear as neuropsychiatric sequelae emanating from the drug's actions on the CNS. With respect to genetic predisposition, a careful and systematic evaluation of the first- and second-degree relatives of the client can help the clinician to ascertain whether the psychopathology or the substance abuse is the primary disorder. One objective of the psychometric assessment should be directed to determining the likely etiological basis for the observed disturbances through an examination of family psychiatric history, so that the most effective interventions can be applied.

Social Adjustment

The third component of a comprehensive psychometric assessment pertains to the degree to which substance use relates to social role performance and interpersonal adjustment. Role performance can be considered at two levels—functioning within the microenviroment (e.g., the family) and the macroenvironment (e.g., work, community). There is abundant evidence indicating, for example, that family disruption may be the most salient problem contributing to alcohol or drug use for one person, whereas occupational maladjustment may be most problematic for another. Also, for some individuals, chronic substance abuse is associated with generalized psychosocial maladjustment or an antisocial disposition. For others, the psychosocial disturbance may be circumscribed and confined to only one or a few particular areas of functioning. The point to be emphasized is that psychosocial adjustment is not a unitary dimension, but rather consists of numerous processes. Disturbances in one or more of these processes may either presage or emerge as a result of prolonged alcohol or drug abuse. Moreover, the particular areas of disturbance vary widely in the population. If the matter is considered in the context of heterogeneous presentation in the previously discussed areas of cognitive and emotional functioning, it is apparent that the overall clinical presentation for any given individual is unique. In other words, alcoholism or substance abuse dichotomies such as primary–secondary (Tarter, McBride, Buonpane, & Schneider, 1977), essential–reactive (Rudie & McGaughran, 1974), or Type 1–Type 2 (Cloninger, Bohman, & Sigvardsson, 1981) are, at best, general categorizations. Subtyping alcoholics or substance abusers into more categories is similarly beset with the problem of obscuring the marked individuality of antecedent characteristics and potential range of consequences. Thus, from a clinical perspective, the evaluation must be idiographic to the extent that it identifies the unique characteristics and their interrelationships within the client, so as to help the clinician arrive at an understanding of the current predicament. In this way, a comprehensive psychometric evaluation surpasses merely assigning the person to a diagnostic category.

Evaluating psychosocial adjustment is thus an integral component of the overall clinical examination. Commonly, social stress precipitates the initiation of substance use, which can subsequently evolve into a substance use disorder.

Under these circumstances, substance use may reflect an attempt by the individual to cope with a discrete stressor (e.g., death of parent, loss of employment, accidental injury, chronic illness), or cumulative conflicts in meeting the challenges of everyday living. Furthermore, a change in lifestyle may trigger drug use. In this regard, it is noteworthy that the risk for substance abuse is augmented among newly retired individuals, who may for the first time in their lives have extensive free time and an accompanying lack of daily challenges revolving around their job or parenting responsibilities. The point to be made is that disturbed psychosocial process can be either etiologically related to a substance use disorder or consequential to such a condition. This disturbance can involve any of a number of social roles (e.g., parent, spouse, employee) or center around interpersonal matters (e.g., conflicts, social skill deficits). In conducting the psychometric evaluation, it is essential, therefore, that information be obtained about the specific areas of maladjustment, as well as the time of their emergence in the context of the natural history of the substance use disorder.

Summary

The three broadly defined categories of psychological functioning—cognition, emotion, and social adjustment—form an interrelated unity. A disruption in one area may affect other areas of functioning. Hence, severe emotional disorder, for example, can produce disturbances in cognitive efficiency and capacity as well as in psychosocial adjustment. Many different patterns of disturbance may be manifested. In substance abusers, disturbance may be confined to one area of functioning, may pervade all psychological domains, or (theoretically, at least) may not be present at all in any of the three areas. The major objective of the psychometric assessment is to analyze the relationships among these three categories of psychological functioning with respect to the etiology and consequences of alcoholism and other types of substance abuse. The discussion to follow describes the procedures for accomplishing this objective.

Methods of Psychometric Assessment

Evaluation in the three broad areas described above—namely, cognition, emotion, and social adjustment—is useful only to the extent that the information obtained contributes to a better understanding of the onset and course of substance abuse, so that affected individuals may be effectively treated. The evaluation must entail identifying the individual's specific problems that are amenable to intervention. The psychometric techniques employed need to focus on characterizing the client–environment interrelationship, in order to elucidate how each reciprocally affects the other to culminate in alcohol or drug abuse. Hence, interventions can be directed to changing either the individual's psychological makeup or the environment that may have triggered or helped maintain the substance abuse disorder.

In addition to promoting an intervention strategy, psychometric assessment offers the opportunity to quantitatively monitor changes occurring during the course of treatment. The use of brief standardized self-report checklists or rating scales, for example, facilitates the objective and systematic charting of therapeutic progress. This information not only provides feedback to the clinician, but also serves the purpose of goal setting for the client. Furthermore, demonstrating to the client via objective and quantitative indices that he or she is benefiting from treatment serves the important purpose of sustaining motivation for continued involvement in rehabilitation.

Alcohol or drug abuse is almost invariably embedded in a variety of other psychological, social, or psychiatric disturbances. Within the three categories of processes illustrated in Figure 11.1, 12 specific domains of processes comprise the comprehensive psychometric evaluation. From such an evaluation, a description of the client's status is obtained in each domain, and an overall understanding of the person is acquired by learning how the domains are interrelated to culminate in the individualized pattern of maladjustment. In conducting this type of examination, it is essential to be cognizant of the reciprocal relationships that exist among the 12 domains; that is, a disturbance in one domain may directly or indirectly affect adjustment in another. Similarly, resources in one domain may offset the deleterious effects caused by disturbances in other domains. For example, strong social support may compensate for the effect of a psychiatric disorder on overall adjustment. The ensuing discussion describes the most clinically relevant and standardized psychometric instruments presently utilized in the evaluation of known or suspected substance abusers. It is necessary to reiterate, however, that although this discussion organizes the assessment procedures according to 12 discrete domains, the information acquired must be interpreted with respect to their interrelationships.

Alcohol and Drug Use

The first requirements in the assessment is to characterize the substance use behavior. The onset of each type of substance used needs to be documented, so that drug use progression may be explicitly described. As each type of substance use emerges in the person's history, it is essential to ascertain whether it reached problematic severity so as to warrant a diagnosis of abuse or dependence. In addition, the occurrence of remission and number of lifetime episodes should be described. Also, the quantity and frequency of consumption within a typical 30-day period should be recorded for each episode, so that a picture of the person's total involvement with alcohol and drugs can be obtained. Table 11.1 lists the most common types of drugs that require assessment and the dosage units that are familiar to the consumer.

TABLE 11.1. Drugs Having Abuse Potential

Wine	Phencyclidine (PCP, angel dust, sherms)
Beer	Ecstasy (MDMA, MDA)
Liquor	Downers (Xanax, Ativan, Librium,
Cocaine (powder, crack, snow, rock,	Quaaludes, ludes, Seconal, reds, Valium,
freebase, etc.)	Halcion, Dalmane, Serax)
Amphetamines (uppers, crystal, meth, speed,	Amyl nitrates (poppers, rush, locker room)
speedball, ice, crank, dexedrine, Ritalin,	Nitrous oxide (laughing gas, whippets,
black beauties)	chargers)
Morphine	Marijuana (hashish, pot, reefer, shish)
Opium	Anabolic steroids (roids, juice)
Methadone	Sominex
Heroin (smack, horse)	No-Doze
Synthetic heroin (China white, T's, blues)	Diet pills (prescription: Preludin, Tenuate,
Codeine products (codeine, Percodan)	Tepanil, Sanorex, etc.)
Prescription painkillers (Darvon, Dilaudid,	Diet pills (over-the-counter: Dexetrim,
Demerol)	Acutrim, Apadrine, caffeine, etc.)
Tobacco for smoking (cigarettes, pipe, cigar)	Wite-Out (Correct-O-Type)
Tobacco for chewing (snuff)	Cough syrup
LSD (acid)	Nyquil
Psilocybin (magic mushrooms)	Other drugs
Peyote (buttons, mescaline)	

In addition, polydrug use should be investigated because of the substantial lethal risk posed by the synergistic effects of the combined use of psychoactive drugs. For example, conjointly using alcohol and benzodiazepines is especially dangerous because of the risk of respiratory arrest.

For adults, a number of unidimensional rating scales quantifying severity of alcohol problems are routinely used. The Michigan Alcoholism Screening Test (Selzer, 1971) is best known for this purpose. Alcohol problems can also be evaluated from a multivariate perspective, employing the Alcohol Use Inventory (AUI; Wanberg & Horn, 1985). The specific scales of the AUI are listed in Table 11.2; it can be seen that this instrument attempts to capture both the motivational and consequential aspects of alcohol use.

Drug problem severity can be quantified using the Addiction Severity Index (ASI; McClellan, Luborsky, Woody, & O'Brien, 1980). This semistructured interview yields an evaluation of the impact of drug use on various aspects of daily living. The scales comprising the ASI are listed in Table 11.3. To date, no standardized self-report measure of drug use behavior for adults has been published.

Psychometric tests for known or suspected adolescent drug users have been recently validated. The Personal Experience Inventory (PEI; Henly & Winters, 1988) and the Chemical Dependency Assessment Survey (Oetting, Beauvais, Edwards, & Waters, 1984) are the two best-developed instruments, with the PEI being more suitable for a clinical population. A teen version of the ASI is presently undergoing psychometric validation (Kaminer, Bukstein, &

TABLE 11.2. Scales of the Alcohol Use Inventory (AUI)

Primary scales	Secondary scales	General factor
Drinking to Improve Sociability	Drinking to Enhance Functioning	General Alcohol Involvement
Drinking to Improve Mental Functioning	Obsessive Sustained Drinking	
Gregarious vs. Solo Drinking	Anxious Concern about Drinking	
Sustained Drinking	Uncontrolled, Life Functioning Disruption (1)	
Obsessive–Compulsive Drinking	Uncontrolled, Life Functioning Disruption (2)	
Guilt and Worry Associated with Drinking		
Drinking Helps Manage Mood		
Prior Attempts to Stop Drinking		
Lose Control over Behavior When Drinking		
Social Role Maladaptation		
Psychoperceptual Withdrawal		
Psychophysical Withdrawal		
Quantity of Daily Alcohol Use		
Drinking Used to Cope with Marital Stress		
Marital Problems Associated with Drinking		

Tarter, 1991). Finally, the Drug Use Screening Inventory (DUSI; Tarter, 1990) is also presently undergoing validation studies; this self-report measure profiles substance use involvement in conjunction with severity of disturbance in nine spheres of everyday functioning. The DUSI measures the absolute and relative severity of problems in 10 problem domains.

It is readily apparent that psychometric techniques have not been developed to encompass the measurement of alcohol and drug abuse in all of their multifaceted aspects. The above-described procedures serve only to clarify present or current use pattern and problem severity. Other types of information are also important to obtain; these can most easily be gathered during the course of an interview or from self-report. Questioning should therefore be directed to determine the following:

1. Pattern of substance use (e.g., episodic vs. continuous).
2. Context of substance use (solitary vs. social consumption).
3. Availability of drugs in the social environment.
4. Perceived importance of drugs in the person's life.
5. Expected and experienced effects of drugs on mood and behavior.
6. Family history of drug and alcohol abuse.
7. Access to drugs (dealer vs. consumer).

TABLE 11.3. Scales of the Addiction Severity Index

General Information	Legal Status
Medical Status	Family/Social Relationships
Employment/Support Status	Psychiatric Status
Drug/Alcohol Use	

Psychiatric Disorder

Substance abuse can occur conjointly with virtually any Axis I or Axis II psychiatric disorder. This has important treatment implications, of which the most obvious is that for some individuals, alcohol or drug consumption may constitute an attempt at self-medication. Hence, treatment of the primary disorder may in some circumstances be sufficient to ameliorate the substance use disorder. Alternatively, prolonged drug abuse many precipitate a psychiatric disturbance, either directly by inducing neurochemical changes or indirectly through the stress or maladjustment concomitant to a substance-abusing lifestyle. A major task, therefore, is to delineate the type and severity of psychiatric morbidity that may be present and to determine whether it preceded or developed after the substance use disorder.

Structured interviews have been increasingly utilized in the objective formulation of substance use disorder diagnoses as well as other psychiatric diagnosis. Several instruments, all with good reliability, are currently available. The Structured Clinical Interview for DSM-III-R (SCID; Spitzer, Williams, & Gibbon, 1987) is the most recent interview schedule to be introduced. Other structured interviews are the Diagnostic Interview Schedule (Robins, Helzer, Croughan, & Ratcliff, 1981) and the Schedule for Affective Disorders and Schizophrenia (Spitzer, Endicott, & Robins, 1975); both of these latter instruments are based on the older DSM-III criteria. Employing a structured interview makes it possible, at the diagnostic threshold level of psychiatric disorder, to relate substance use behavior to psychiatric status. The ramification for treatment is that the information gleaned may suggest a particular type of intervention. For example, if an affective disorder preceded the substance use disorder and is still present at the time of the assessment, it would suggest the need to treat this disorder as the primary condition.

Three diagnostic interviews are available for adolescents. These include the Diagnostic Interview Schedule for Children—Revised (Costello, Edelbrock, & Costello, 1984), the Kiddie Schedule for Affective Disorders and Schizophrenia (Orvaschel, Puig-Antich, Chambers, Tabrizi, & Johnson, 1982), and the Diagnostic Interview for Children and Adolescents (Wellner, Reich, Herjanic, Jung, & Amado, 1987). Each of these interviews also has a version to be administered to a parent in order to obtain convergent validity of the findings accrued from the youngster. These latter instruments are, however, limited because they permit a psychiatric diagnosis according to only

DSM-III criteria. Because alcohol and drug use commonly begins in adolescence and often rapidly progresses to a level of severity qualifying for a psychiatric diagnosis, it is informative to obtain accurate and clinically relevant information. Hence, the use of a structured interview for evaluating adolescents in treatment is strongly recommended for the same reasons as for adults.

Self-report questionnaires can also reveal important information by quantifying the presence and severity of psychiatric disorder that may not be severe enough to warrant a diagnosis (e.g., an affective disturbance that, although not qualifying for a diagnosis, may nonetheless be a contributor to or a consequence of substance abuse). Thus, self-rating scales may provide a more valid picture of the severity of psychopathology than that afforded by only an interview. For example, the Minnesota Multiphasic Personality Inventory (MMPI; Hathaway & McKinley, 1951) contains three validity scales that also measure some test-taking attitudes, Hence, truthfulness or a response bias toward either over- or underreporting symptoms is documented. A disadvantage is that the profile obtained from the MMPI does not translate to diagnosis in any taxonomic system, but rather quantifies severity across multiple dimensions. However, the configuration of scores among the scales, in conjunction with the many specialized scales that have been derived from the MMPI, makes it possible to comprehensively identify personality disorder, family problems, health disturbances, and social maladjustment. Another valuable feature of the MMPI is that it can be scored and interpreted by computer, thereby minimizing the time-consuming effort and expense of a clinician.

Other self-report dimensional rating scales can be employed where either the time or expertise is not available to conduct a structured interview or to obtain an MMPI profile. The most commonly used test in this regard is the Symptom Checklist 90—Revised (SCL-90-R; Derogatis, 1983). This self-rating scale is brief, is easily scored, and yields indices of severity of psychopathology across nine specific dimensions of psychopathology in addition to three summary global scales.

Under certain circumstances, it may be desirable to quantify only one specific psychopathological condition. Self-rating scales for assessing anxiety (Spielberger, Gorsuch, & Lushene, 1970) and depression (Beck & Beck, 1972) have been standardized and provide a simple method for monitoring changes during the course of treatment.

Table 11.4 presents the primary scales for the MMPI and the SCL-90-R. However, with respect to the MMPI, it should be noted that the richness of clinical information lies in the configuration comprising the overall profile of the primary scales, combined with the numerous other specialized scales.

The importance of evaluating psychopathology in the substance abuse disorders cannot be overemphasized. In many cases, treatment of the underlying psychiatric disorder may itself be sufficient to ameliorate a substance abuse disorder. For this reason, it is essential to document the type, onset, and presentation of psychopathology as it relates to alcohol or drug use behavior.

TABLE 11.4. Major Scales of the Minnesota Multiphasic Personality Inventory (MMPI) and Symptom Checklist 90—Revised (SCL-90-R)

MMPI	SCL-90-R
Hypochondriasis	Somatization
Depression	Depression
Hysteria	Phobic Anxiety
Psychopathic Deviate	Obsessive–Compulsive
Masculinity–	Anxiety
Feminity	Paranoid Ideation
Paranoia	Interpersonal Sensitivity
Psychasthenia	Hostility
Schizoprhrenia	Psychoticism
Hypomania	
Social Introversion	

In addition, documentation of psychiatric illness in other family members, using such instruments as the Family History Chart (Mann, Sobell, Sobell, & Pavan, 1985) or the Family Informant Schedule and Criteria (Manuzza, Fryer, Endicott, & Klein, 1985), can assist in obtaining a clear picture of the primary psychiatric disorder when it is unclear whether the substance abuse or another psychiatric disturbance constitutes the fundamental problem.

Cognition

A neuropsychological evaluation is important for a variety of reasons. It provides information regarding the patient's ability to respond to treatment. For example, individuals who are retarded, have suffered severe neurological injury, or are demented as a result of their alcoholism or drug use are unlikely to profit from insight-oriented forms of therapy. In the early stages of withdrawal, cognitive assessment can help determine whether mental confusion is present to a degree that would militate against a patient's accruing any benefits from individual or group therapy. The presence of acute neurological injury from trauma, fights, falls, or automobile accidents is also important to document, insofar as such injury affects cognitive capacity. This information can also help characterize the person's lifestyle and overall association with psychoactive drugs. In addition, the behavioral changes associated with these types of injuries, such as behavioral disinhibition, social inappropriateness, and emotional lability, may impede rehabilitation. Hence, clarifying cognitive impairment due to CNS injury and dysfunction facilitates the comprehensive characterization of neuropsychiatric disorder, which in turn has treatment and posttreatment ramifications.

Although neuropsychological testing to evaluate CNS integrity is labor-intensive, the unique contribution of such testing is that it enables determination of the presence and location of cerebral lesions while quantifying severity in the context of readily understood psychological processes (e.g., language, memory, abstracting, attention, learning). In the early stages of dementia, neuropsychological tests may be more sensitive than neuroradiological procedures for detecting CNS pathology. Moreover, by delineating the person's cognitive strengths and weaknesses, these specialized psychometric tests afford the important advantage of yielding information pertinent to vocational rehabilitation, educational planning, and treatment.

The desire for a comprehensive neuropsychological evaluation of the client's abilities must be balanced against the time and resources available for such an evaluation. In order to be efficient, the neuropsychological evaluation should be conducted in three stages. As described by Tarter and Edwards (1987), the first stage is an initial screening to determine whether there is evidence of a CNS disturbance. This stage of testing requires sensitive but nonspecific tests. Various brief instruments such as the Mini Mental Status Exam (Folstein, Folstein, & McHugh, 1975), the Trail Making Test (Armitige, 1946), and the Symbol Digit Modalities Test (Smith, 1973) adequately serve this purpose. The second stage of the evaluation is the delineation of cognitive abilities and limitations. At this stage, standardized batteries, complemented where necessary by specialized tests should be used to quantify the severity of cognitive impairment. The processes evaluated typically include speech and language, attention, psychomotor skill, learning and memory, and abstract reasoning ability. At this stage of the evaluation, hypotheses can be formulated about lesion localization and lateralization. Several standardized neuropsychological batteries are currently in wide use. The Halstead–Reitan Neuropsychological Test Battery (Reitan, 1955), the Luria–Nebraska Neuropsychological Test Battery (Golden, 1981), and the Pittsburgh Initial Neuropsychological Testing System (Goldstein, Tarter, Shelly, & Hegedus, 1983) provide perhaps the most comprehensive suveys of the major cognitive domains.

Finally, if significant impairment is noted in a specific cognitive domain, specialized comprehensive testing should be conducted to elucidate its severity and breadth. This is the third stage of the assessment. It is not only important for purposes of lesion localization, but is perhaps even more critical for posttreatment planning. For example, it is important to describe psychomotor impairments fully if the client works with power machinery or if there are other safety risks. Visuoperceptual disturbances must be comprehensively documented if the person drives a car, and especially when driving at night might pose a significant risk. Similarly, if a learning or memory deficit is identified in the second stage of testing, it should be further evaluated if the posttreatment plan includes educational or vocational rehabilitation. For example, memory testing at the third stage can be most easily accomplished using the California Verbal Learning Test (Fridlund & Dellis, 1987). This test can provide detailed information about learning and memory when it is found in the second stage of assessment that there is evidence of a memory disorder.

Such comprehensive evaluation of memory capacities, can be used to implement targeted cognitive rehabilitation. Specialized tests for other aspects of cognitive and psychomotor abilities can yield further data essential for making decisions about the client's treatment needs.

In interpreting the results of a neuropsychological evaluation, it is important to be cognizant of the multifactorial etiology of any identified impairment. Not only do alcohol and other drugs act directly on the brain, but their use may induce injury to other organs or systems, which in turn can disrupt CNS integrity. For example, cirrhosis, independently of alcoholism, is associated with hepatic encephalopathy. Thus, the neuropsychological deficits seen in alcoholics may be in large part due to liver disese (Tarter, Van Thiel, & Moss, 1988). This fact is not inconsequential, because treatment of low-grade hepatic encephalopathy caused by alcoholic liver disease has been tentatively shown to improve cognitive capacities (McClain, Potter, Krombout, & Zieve, 1984). Thus medically significant problems should be recorded, particularly hypertension, malnutrition, and pulmonary insufficiency, insofar as these latter disturbances are correlated with impaired cognitive capacity. Other neurological problems frequently found in alcoholics and drug abusers are developmental disability and head trauma. The extent to which these factors contribute to neuropsychological test performance should be studied, particularly if they preceded the substance use disorder. Our point here is that it is not sufficient merely to describe the presence of a neuropsychological disorder. It is essential also to attempt to identify the causes underlying the manifest impairments. This latter objective can be accomplished where the neuropsychological assessment is conducted in tandem with documentation of the medical and psychiatric history.

Family Adjustment

Family organization and interactional patterns have been demonstrated to contribute to the etiology and maintenance of substance abuse. Indeed, the transmission of alcoholism across generations is to some degree influenced by familial attitudes and rituals surrounding alcohol consumption and the meanings attached to alcohol ingestion (Steinglass, Bennett, Wolin, & Reiss, 1987). Two self-report instruments quantifying the severity of family problems are presently available. The Family Environment Scale (Moos & Moos, 1981) assesses family values and behaviors across 10 dimensions. The more recently developed Family Assessment Measure emphasizes interactional patterns among family members (Skinner, Steinhauer, & Santa Barbara, 1983). Table 11.5 lists the scales comprising these two instruments.

The family is the organizational unit in society. It is the primary influence shaping the values and behavior patterns of children. Without doubt, parenting style and family environment exercise the most profound influence on the child's development up until at least the time of adolescence, when psychoactive substance use may first become problematic. From the standpoint of

TABLE 11.5. Scales of Family Assessment Instruments

Family Environment Scale	Family Assessment Measure
Cohesion	Task Accomplishment
Expressiveness	Role Performance
Conflict	Communication
Independence	Affective Expression
Achievement Orientation	Affective Involvement
Intellectual–Cultural Orientation	Control
Active–Recreational Orientation	Values and Norms
Moral–Religious Emphasis	
Organization	
Control	

clinical diagnosis, a number of issues need to be addressed. First, it is essential to characterize the contribution of psychiatric disorder, including substance abuse, in the family. The greater the density of psychiatric disorder in family members of the client undergoing evaluation, the more problematic both the family and the client are likely to be. Among young substance-abusing clients, it may be especially important to record past or present physical or sexual abuse of the clients as one critical index of family dysfunction. Second, the causal relationship between family dysfunction and drug use behavior needs to be ascertained. How drug use precipitated the family problems, or, conversely, how family problems triggered drug use, needs to be investigated in the course of the diagnostic evaluation. Third, the reinforcement contingencies, if any, exercised by the family on the member having the drug use problem needs to be analyzed. That is, is drug use ignored, punished, or positively reinforced? And fourth, the roles and status of each family member must be understood, to the extent that maladjustment, conflict, or instability contributes to the family dysfunction that propels one member to seek alcohol or drugs as a means of coping with the ensuing stress.

Besides identifying the liabilities, the evaluation should also clarify the family's resources or strengths. This is particularly important for engaging the family in a therapeutic alliance. Whereas most evaluations of the family are typically limited to a description of its structure, the point to be emphasized herein is that it is more important to understand the family as an organizational system involving complex interactional patterns. These dynamic relationships occurring within the family, as well as values and rituals transmitted across generations, have the most influence on the onset and persistence of substance abuse.

Social Skills

Social skill deficits are common among alcoholics and drug abusers (Van Hasselt, Hersen, & Milliones, 1978). Deficiencies in assertiveness skills, refusal skills, and compliment-giving skills have all been well documented. Poor ability to manage conflict in interpersonal situations may also be linked to alcohol or drug abuse. Moreover, the exacerbation of poor social skills by the stress or anxiety they induce may lead to substance use as a learned coping response. Consequently, coping style needs to be determined as one component of social skills assessment.

There are currently no psychometrically standardized instruments for evaluating social skills. Various self-rating scales, although lacking in normative scores, have been employed for identifying the presence and severity of social skill deficits and for targeting behaviorally focused interventions. The same limitations exist with respect to coping style; however, two measures that have been found to be informative are the Ways of Coping Scale (Folkman & Lazarus, 1980) and the Constructive Thinking Inventory (Epstein, 1987). The scales compromising these two instruments are listed in Table 11.6.

In addition to social skills, the comprehensive evaluation should document the individual's capacity to exercise the skills required for everyday living. As society becomes more and more technologically complex, it is desirable to learn whether the individual is capable of performing everyday tasks required for adaptive social adjustment. For example, can the individual manage a bank account, use bank card machines, access directories, obtain appropriate service information, utilize public transportation, satisfy personal needs with respect to food and clothing, or apply for a job? Deficiencies in any of these areas may exacerbate the level of experienced stress and thus serve to promote further alcohol or drug abuse.

Vocational Adjustment

The rapid expansion of employee assistance programs illustrates the extent to which alcohol or drug abuse impacts on the workplace and the extent to which the workplace may influence alcohol or drug use. Stress in the workplace can have a multifactorial basis: It may occur as a consequence of inability to meet performance standards, conflicts with other employees or supervisors, disruptive work schedules, and low job satisfaction. In the most extreme cases,

TABLE 11.6. Scales of Instruments for Assessment of Coping Skills

Ways of Coping Scale	Constructive Thinking Inventory
Conformative Coping	Constructive Thinking
Distancing	Emotional Coping
Self-Controlling	Behavioral Coping
Seeking Social Support	Categorical Thinking
Accepting Responsibility	Superstitious Thinking
Escape–Avoidance	Naive Optimism
Planful Problem Solving	Negative Thinking
Positive Reappraisal	

unemployment as well as underemployment needs to be evaluated as one factor underlying substance abuse. In addition, for some individuals, extensive travel and associated social obligations place the individual in social situations where alcohol consumption is expected. It is apparent that no single factor in the workplace predisposes a person to substance abuse. Hence, for the individual presenting for drug abuse or alcoholism treatment, it is necessary to analyze, in detail, performance and adjustment in the workplace as an etiological determinant.

Besides evaluating the job demands and workplace environment, it is necessary to evaluate the client's behavioral disposition. For example, premorbid personality disorders (particularly antisocial personality disorder or social phobias) may contribute to job failure, which in turn may predispose the individual to a substance use disorder. Furthermore, it is important to evaluate the particular job in the context of normative behaviors with respect to alcohol and drug use. For instance, individuals who work in the entertainment industry, in the military, or in bars and lounges are more inclined to use alcohol and drugs than other individuals in the population. Access to addictive substances places the person at heightened risk simply by virtue of their availability among professionals. Not surprisingly, physicians have a very high prevalence of opiate abuse. The vocational evaluation must therefore not only identify specific job-related characteristics that predispose a client to alcohol or drug abuse, but must also elucidate the personality and behavioral characteristics of the person. In particular, it should clarify how the vocational maladjustment results from an interaction between the person and the job environment.

Recreation and Leisure Activities

Alcohol and drug use is commonly associated with recreational and leisure time activities. An individual who does not have socially satisfying recreational activities, hobbies, or other leisure time opportunities may resort to the use of alcohol or drugs as a means of passing time or otherwise coping with the stress of boredom. This may be particularly problematic among members of the elderly population who are no longer gainfully employed and productive and have not developed adequate or satisfying substitute behaviors. A somewhat similar problem may confront members of the adolescent population who have substantial free or unstructured time.

Assessment and counseling related to recreational and leisure time activities constitute a newly developing specialty. Presently, there are no standardized evaluation procedures. It therefore remains for the clinician to gather this information informally. Once it is determined that the absence of positively reinforcing pastimes may be associated with substance abuse, or that the recreational activities the client engages in involve peers who use psychoactive substances, it is possible to help the person to restructure this important aspect of his or her life.

Personality

Certain dispositional behaviors or personality traits of the individual are commonly associated with the etiology and maintenance of alcohol or drug abuse. The extent to which certain personality traits presage the onset of substance use, or are shaped by the long-term consequence of drug abuse, needs to be ascertained on a case-by-case basis. Features such as low self-esteem, impulsivity, aggressiveness, behavioral disinhibition, and sex-role conflict are more prevalent in the drug-abusing than in the normal population.

No single instrument currently assesses all dimensions of personality that may be relevant to understanding drug use behavior. The MMPI, described previously, is very useful for profiling psychopathology and facilitating the formulation and testing of heuristic hypotheses about specific personality characteristics. However, more specialized personality assessment focusing on discrete traits is required to determine which dispositional behaviors are linked to drug use motivation. The Multidimensional Personality Questionnaire (MPQ) provides information about personality traits that have frequently been found to be deviant in alcoholics or drug abusers. Significantly, the scales comprising the MPQ are quite independent of one another and measure traits having a strong heritable basis (Tellegen, 1982, 1985; Tellegen et al., 1988). Table 11.7 summarizes the MPQ scales. Numerous other personality questionnaires have been developed; however, none measure traits that are so integrally linked to substance abuse as those assessed by the MPQ.

Self-esteem disturbances may be also related in some individuals to drug use. Low self-esteem can occur in a number of areas of daily living and may be secondary to psychopathology. Its important role in drug abuse is well known. The Self-Esteem Inventory (Epstein, 1976) is a multidimensional scale having good breadth of coverage and superior psychometric properties. Table 11.8 lists the scales comprising this inventory. As can be seen, the test taps aspects of psychological well-being that are not ordinarily covered by personality tests and that may contribute to a better understanding of the causes and consequences of substance use disorder in the individual.

TABLE 11.7. Scales of the Multidimensional
Personality Questionnaire

Well-Being	Control (vs. Impulsiveness)
Social Potency	Harm Avoidance
Achievement	Traditionalism
Social Closeness	Absorption
Stress Reaction	Positive Affectivity
Alienation	Negative Affectivity
Aggression	Constraint

TABLE 11.8. Scales of the Self-Esteem Inventory

Global Self-Esteem	Competence
Lovability	Likability
Self-Control	Personal Power
Moral Self-Approval	Body Appearance
Body Functioning	Identity Integration
	Defensive Self-Enhancement

School Adjustment

For young alcohol or drug abusers, it is important to document school adjustment and performance. The school is the primary social environment during adolescence. Drug accessibility in school, and particularly the peer affiliation network of the adolescent, are especially influential as determinants of drug use initiation. Conduct problems and deviance from normative behavior are commonly associated with current substance abuse and future psychopathology. The teacher version of the Child Behavior Checklist (CBCL; Achenbach & Edelbrock, 1983) affords the opportunity to identify and quantify severity of behavior problems in the school environment. Also, comparing the findings to the parallel parent version enables the clinician to ascertain whether adjustment problems are confined to school or are also present in the home. The scales comprising the CBCL are presented in Table 11.9.

Assessing the teacher's perceptions of a child's behavior in the classroom is an essential component of a comprehensive evaluation. The Disruptive Behavior Rating Scale (Pelham & Murphy, 1987) is a measure based on DSM-III-R criteria for diagnosing conduct disorder, attention-deficit hyperactivity disorder, and oppositional defiant disorder. Another brief rating scale that can be completed by the teacher is the Iowa Conners Teachers Rating Scale (Loney & Milich, 1982).

One important aspect of social adjustment is the extent to which a youngster participates in athletics and other extracurricular activities. These types of activities indicate how well the person is socially integrated and accepted by peers. In addition, it is essential to evaluate academic achievement and learning aptitude in the basic skills areas. For example, learning disability, compounded by low self-esteem, may be a major factor propelling the youngster toward drug use as well as other non-normative behaviors. Standardized learning and achievement tests may need to be administered to the adolescent alcohol- or drug-abusing client to document the extent to which cognitive impairments and low achievement are involved in the motivation to use alcohol or drugs. A quick indication of whether such testing is needed is whether the client has been held back at least two grades or cannot master specific subjects. The Peabody Individual Achievement Test (Dunn & Markwardt, 1970) and the Wide Range Achievement Test (Jastak & Wilkinson,

TABLE 11.9. Child Behavior Checklist: Social Competence Scales

Externalizing Factors	Internalizing Factors
Hyperactivity	Schizoid Withdrawal
Aggression	Depression
Delinquency	Uncommunicativeness
Sexual Activity	Obsessive–Compulsive Phenomena
Cruelty	Sanitization
	Immaturity

1965) are the tests most commonly used by psychologists to evaluate a learning disability, in conjunction with the Wechsler Intelligence Scale for Children—Revised (Wechsler, 1974). However, testing by a learning disabilities specialist may be required to reveal the array of cognitive processes that are developmentally delayed. In the context of such an evaluation, emphasis should be placed on the youngster's ability to use language. Communication skills are integral to social adjustment, because language mediates or regulates overt behavior. The Test of Language Competence (Wiig, 1985) is one test specifically developed to assess everyday or practical language capacity.

Peer Affiliation

A social network where drug use is commonplace will increase the likelihood that the individual will also engage in this behavior. Drug and alcohol accessibility and availability are thus important to evaluate, because ameliorating the substance use disorder may require abandoning long-standing peer affiliations. Hence, changing peer involvement may be necessary for preventing relapse. The extent to which peer relationships are embedded in a pattern of non-normative or antisocial behavior also needs to be evaluated, since such maladjustment interacts with other aspects of role performance maladjustment at work, at school, and in family life. Standardized psychometric instruments for evaluating peer affiliation patterns have not been developed. Consequently, this information must be accrued during the course of the diagnostic interview. One newly developed self-report measure, the DUSI (Tarter, 1990), enables assessment of peer problems in adolescents. Normative data have yet to be published for this instrument; however, the DUSI permits the clinician to quantify the severity of social relationship problems relative to the severity of problems in nine other areas

Because the social environment is a major source of reinforcement, it is essential to learn about the reward contingencies, role models, and social contextual characteristics associated with alcohol or drug use for the individual. It should be recognized that the individual not only responds to the particular social environment, but also seeks out an environment that has reinforcing value. Hence, during the course of the psychometric assessment, attempts should be made to learn why the drug- or alcohol-abusing client seeks out social interactions that have maladaptive consequences. From such an evaluation, social needs and motivational patterns that bear directly on the etiology and persistence of substance abuse for the individual may be elucidated.

Legal Status

As part of the diagnostic formulation, it is essential to obtain a lifetime history of criminal activity and prosecutions, including incarcerations. This information is important for diagnosing antisocial personality disorder and for assessing the type and severity of substance use involvement as well as drug preference. Criminal behavior can begin at a very young age; it is not uncommon, for example, for preadolescents to engage in drug selling. Other criminal behaviors that support the drug use lifestyle (e.g., theft, prostitution) also require documentation in the course of diagnostic assessment.

In addition, the evaluation should address the possibility of victimization by other drug-using individuals. Physical and sexual abuse by alcoholics of their children and spouses is not uncommon. Crimes associated with a peer culture of violence is common and requires evaluation. Furthermore, debts from gambling may predispose an individual to criminal behavior.

Standardized instruments have not been developed to evaluate legal status. Thus, information must be acquired from informal interview, as well as gleaned from the other diagnostic instruments described herein.

Health

Health can be compromised both by the direct effects of chronic drug use and by the associated effects of a personally neglectful or irresponsible lifestyle. Physical examination supported by appropriate laboratory assessment is mandatory as part of a comprehensive diagnostic workup. Self-report measures of health status can provide additional useful information that may be otherwise overlooked (Schinka, 1984). The Millon Behavioral Health Inventory (Millon, Green, & Meagher, 1982) evaluates somatic status insofar as it bears on psychological well-being, health habits, and attitudes.

Summary

An evaluation of the alcoholic or substance abuser involves a mixture of art and science. The 12 domains of assessment described above are important for understanding the etiology and development of these disorders. How the various processes interact to sustain a substance abuse disorder needs to be ascertained, so that a program of intervention can be conceptualized and implemented. Ultimately, this requires clinical judgment based on experience and knowledge. The schema described below does, however, have the advantage of providing a systematic framework for relating psychometric assessment information to the treatment process.

Diagnostic Procedure

Comprehensive diagnostic assessment of alcohol or drug abuse requires an interdisciplinary effort. Once tasks are defined for the primary care physician, psychologist, social worker, psychiatrist, and other members of the rehabilitation team, it is necessary to devise procedures for efficient and coordinated evaluation. Figure 11.2 summarizes a decision tree format for assessing adolescents. Based on a three-stage evaluation procedure, this approach to assessment not only enables an integrated synthesis of diagnostic findings, but also yields findings that identify specific treatment needs (Tarter, 1990). Following a quick initial assessment using the self-report DUSI, comprehensive evaluations are then conducted in selected areas. The information obtained in both phases of assessment points to areas of disturbance requiring targeted interven-

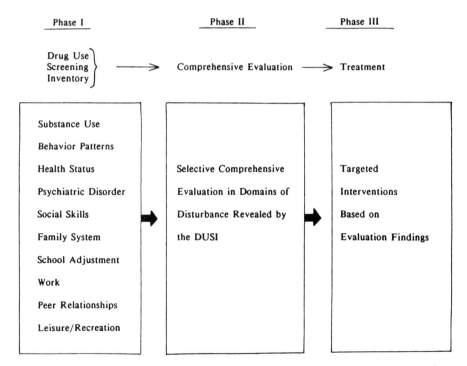

FIGURE 11.2. Decision tree format for conducting a psychometric assessment of suspected or known substance abusers.

tion. The strength of this approach is that it explicitly defines the disturbances and treatment needs and links them together in the diagnostic workup. An analogous evaluation system has also been prepared for adults.

There are several advantages to using a multistage decision tree evaluation procedure. First, the areas of disturbance can be identified quickly and at minimal cost. Second, labor-intensive comprehensive diagnostic evaluation only needs to be targeted to specific areas suggested by initial screening. Third, the aggregate findings from initial screening and the comprehensive diagnostic evaluation delineate the client's rehabilitation needs. And fourth, once the required treatment interventions are specified, a coordinated intervention program can be developed. In this fashion, evaluation and treatment are integrally linked in an ongoing and interactive manner.

Acknowledgment

The writing of this chapter was supported by Grant No. DA05605 from the National Institute on Drug Abuse.

References

Achenbach, T., & Edelbrock, C. (1983). *Manual for the Child Behavior Checklist and Revised Child Behavior Profile.* Burlington: University of Vermont, Department of Psychiatry.

Armitage, S. (1946). An analysis of certain psychological tests used for the evaluation of brain surgery. *Psychological Monographs, 60* (Whole No. 277).

Beck, A., & Beck, R. (1972). Screening depressed patients in family practice: A rapid technique. *Postgraduate Medicine, 52,* 81–85.

Buchsbaum, M., & Ludwig, A. (1980). Effects of sensory input and alcohol administration on visual evoked potentials in normal subjects and alcoholics. In H. Begleiter (Ed), *Biological effects of alcohol.* New York: Plenum.

Cloninger, C., Bohman, M., & Sigvardsson, S. (1981). Inheritance of alcohol abuse: Cross fostering analysis of adopted men. *Archives of General Psychiatry, 38,* 361–868.

Costello, J., Edelbrock, C., & Costello, A. (1984). *The reliability of the NIMH Diagnostic Interview Schedule for Children: A comparison between pediatric and psychiatric referrals.* Pittsburgh: Western Psychiatric Institute and Clinic.

Dackis, C. A., Gold, M. S., Pottash, A. L. C., & Sweeney, D. R. (1985). Evaluating depression in alcoholics. *Psychiatry Research, 17,* 105–109.

Daley, D., Moss, H. B., & Campbell, F. (1987). *Dual disorders: Counseling clients with chemical dependency and mental illness.* Center City, MN: Hazelden.

Derogatis, L. R. (1983). *SCL-90-R: Administration, scoring and procedures manual II (revised).* Towson, MD: Clinical Psychometric Research.

Dunn, L. M., & Markwardt, F. C., Jr. (1970). *Peabody Individual Achievement Test.* Circle Pines, MN: American Guidance Service.

Epstein, S. (1976). Anxiety, arousal and the self-concept. In I. G. Sarason & C. D. Spielberger (Eds.), *Stress and anxiety.* Washington, DC: Hemisphere.

Epstein, S. (1987). *The Constructive Thinking Inventory.* Amherst: University of Massachusetts, Department of Psychology.

Ewusi-Mensah, I., Saunders, J., & Williams, R. (1984). The clinical nature and detection of psychiatric disorders in patients with alcoholic liver disease. *Alcohol and Alcoholism, 39,* 297–302.

Folkman, S., & Lazarus, R. (1980). An analysis of coping in middle aged community sample. *Journal of Health and Social Behavior, 21,* 219–239.

Folstein, M. F., Folstein, S. E., & McHugh, P. R. (1975). Mini Mental State. *Journal of Psychiatric Research, 12,* 189–198.

Fridlund, A. J., & Dellis, D. C. (1987). *California Verbal Learning Test (research edition).* New York: Psychological Corporation.

Golden, C. J. (1981). A standardized version of Luria's neuropsychological tests. In S. Filskov & T. J. Boll (Eds.), *Handbook of clinical neuropsychology.* New York: Wiley-Interscience.

Goldstein, G., Tarter, R., Shelly, C., & Hegedus, A. (1983). The Pittsburgh Initial Neuropsychological Testing System (PINTS): A neuropsychological screening battery for psychiatric patients. *Journal of Behavioral Assessment, 5,* 227–238.

Goldstein, S., Deysach, R., & Kleinknecht, R. (1973). Effect of experience and amount of information on identification of cerebral impairment. *Journal of Consulting and Clinical Psychology, 41,* 30–34.

Grant, I., & Judd, L. (1976). Neuropsychological and EEG disturbances in polydrug users. *American Journal of Psychiatry, 133,* 1039–1042.

Grant, I., Mohns, L., Miller, M., & Reitan, R. (1976). A neuropsychological study of polydrug users. *Archives of General Psychiatry, 33*(8),973–978.

Grant, I., Adams, K., & Reed, R. (1979). Normal neuropsychological abilities of alcoholic men in their late thirties. *American Journal of Psychiatry, 136,* 1263–1269.

Hathaway, S. R., & McKinley, J. C. (1951). *The Minnesota Multiphasic Personality Inventory manual (revised).* New York: Psychological Corporation.

Helzer, J. E., & Pryzbeck, T. R. (1988). The co-occurrence of alcoholism with other psychiatric disorders in the general population and its impact on treatment. *Journal of Studies on Alcohol, 49,* 219–224.

Henly, G., & Winters, K. (1988). Development of problem severity scales for the assessment of adolescent alcohol and drug abuse. *International Journal of the Addictions, 23,* 65–85.

Jacobson, G., Pisani, V., & Berenbaum, H. (1970). Temporal stability of field dependence among hospitalized alcoholics. *Journal of Abnormal Psychology, 76,* 10–12.

Jastak, S. F., & Wilkinson, G. S. (1984). *Wide Range Achievement Test—Level I and II* (rev. ed.). Wilmington, DE: Jastak Associates.

Kaminer, Y., Bukstein, O. G., & Tarter, R. E. (1991). The Teen Addiction Severity Index: Rationale and reliability. *International Journal of the Addictions, 26.*

Karp, S., Kissin, B., & Hustmeyer, F. (1970). Field-dependence as a predictor of alcoholic therapy dropouts. *Journal of Nervous and Mental Disease, 15,* 77–83.

Kissin, B., Platz, A., & Su, W. (1970). Social and psychological factors in the treatment of chronic alcoholism. *Journal of Psychiatric Research, 8,* 13–27.

Lezak, M. (1983). *Neuropsychological assessment.* New York: Oxford University Press.

Loney, J., & Milich, R. (1982). Hyperactivity, inattention, and aggression in clinical practice. In M. Wolraich & D. Routh (Eds.), *Advances in developmental and behavioral pediatrics.* Greenwich, CT: JAI Press.

Mann, R. E., Sobell, L. C., Sobell, M. B., & Pavan, D. (1985). Reliability of family tree questionnaire for assessing family history of alcohol problems. *Drug and Alcohol Dependence, 15,* 61–67.

Manuzza, S., Fyer, A. J., Endicott, J., & Klein, D. F. (1985). *Family Informant Schedule and Criteria (FISC).* New York: New York State Psychiatric Institute.

McClain, C., Potter, L., Krombout, J., & Zieve, L. (1984). The effect of lactulose on psychomotor performance test of alcoholic cirrhotics without hepataic encephalopathy. *Journal of Clinical Gastroenterology, 6,* 325–329.

McLellan, A., Luborsky, L., Woody, G., & O'Brien, C. (1980). An improved diagnostic evaluation instrument for substance abuse patients: The Addiction Severity Scale Index. *Journal of Nervous and Mental Disease, 168,* 26–33.

Millon, T., Green, C., & Meagher, R. (1982). *Millon Behavioral Health Inventory manual.* Minneapolis: National Computer Systems.

Moos, R., & Moss, B. S. (1981). *Family Environment Scale manual.* Palo Alto, CA: Consulting Psychologists Press.

Oetting, E., Beauvais, F., Edwards, R., & Waters, M. (1984). *The Drug and Alcohol Assessment System.* Fort Collins, CO: Rocky Mountain Behavioral Sciences Institute.

Orvaschel, H., Puig-Antich, J., Chambers, W., Tabrizi, M. A., & Johnson, R. (1982). Retrospective assessment of prepubertal major depression with the Kiddie-SADS-E. *Journal of the American Academy of Child Psychiatry, 21,* 392–397.

Parsons, A., & Farr, S. (1981). The neuropsychology of alcohol and drug abuse. In S. Filskov & T. Boll (Eds), *Handbook of clinical neuropsychology* (pp. 320–365). New York: Wiley.

Peace, K., & Mellsop, G. (1987). Alcoholism and psychiatric disorder. *Australian and New Zealand Journal of Psychiatry, 21,* 94–101.

Pelham, W. E., & Murphy, D. A. (1987). *The DBD rating scale: A parent and teacher rating scale for the disruptive behavior disorders of childhood in DSM-III-R.* Unpublished manuscript, University of Pittsburgh.

Reitan, R. (1955). An investigation of the validity of Halstead's measures of biological intelligence. *Achives of Neurology and Psychiatry, 73,* 28–35.

Robins, L., Helzer, J., Croughan, J., & Ratcliff, K. (1981). National Institute of Mental Health Diagnostic Schedule: Its history, characteristics and validity. *Archives of General Psychiatry, 38,* 381–389.

Rudie, R., & McGaughran, L. (1974). Differences in developmental experience, defensiveness and personality organization between two classes of problem drinkers. *Journal of Abnormal and Social Psychology, 83,* 655–666.

Schinka, J. A. (1984). *Health Problems Checklist.* Odessa, FL: Psychological Assessment Resources.

Schooler, C., Zahn, T., Murphy, D., & Buchsbaum, M. (1978). Psychological correlates of monoamine oxidase activity in normals. *Journal of Nervous and Mental Disease, 166,* 177–186.

Selzer, M. (1971). The Michigan Alcoholism Screening Test: The quest for a new diagnostic instrument. *American Journal of Psychiatry, 127,* 1653–1658.

Skinner, H. A., Steinhauer, P. D., & Santa Barbara, J. (1983). The Family Assessment Measure. *Canadian Journal of Community Mental Health, 2,* 91–105.

Smith, A. (1973). *Symbol Digit Modalities Test.* Los Angeles: Western Psychological Services.

Spielberger, C., Gorsuch, R., & Lushene, R. (1970). *Manual for the State–Trait Anxiety Inventory.* Palo Alto, CA: Consulting Psychologists Press.

Spitzer, R. L., Endicott, J., & Robins, E. (1975). Clinical criteria for psychiatric diagnosis and DSMIII. *American Journal of Psychiatry, 132,* 1187–1192.

Spitzer, R. L., Williams, J. B. W., & Gibbon, M. (1987). *Instruction Manual for the Structured Clinical Interview for DSM-III-R (SCID, 4/1/87 revision).* New York: New York State Psychiatric Institute.

Steinglass, P., Bennett, L., Wolin, S., & Reiss, D. (1987). *The alcoholic family.* New York: Basic Books.

Sugerman, A., & Schneider, D. (1976). Cognitive styles in alcoholism. In R. Tarter & A. Sugerman (Eds), *Alcoholism: Interdisciplinary approaches to an enduring problem.* Reading, MA: Addison-Wesley.

Tarter, R. 1990. Evaluation and treatment of adolescent substance abuse: A decision tree method. *American Journal of Drug and Alcohol Abuse, 16,* 1–46.

Tarter, R., Alterman, A., & Edwards, K. (1985). Vulnerability to alcoholism in men: A behavior-genetic perspective. *Journal of Studies on Alcohol, 46,* 329–356.

Tarter, R., & Edwards, K. (1985). Neuropsychology of alcoholism. In R. Tarter & D. Van Thiel (Eds.), *Alcohol and brain: Chronic effects.* New York: Plenum.

Tarter, R., & Edwards, K. (1987). Brief and comprehensive neuropsychological assessment of alcoholism and drug abuse. In L. Hartlage, M. Ashen, & L. Hornsby (Eds.), *Essentials of neuropsychological assessment* (pp. 138–162). New York: Springer.

Tarter, R., Edwards, K., & Van Thiel, D. (1986). Hepatic encephalopathy. In G. Goldstein & R. Tarter (Eds.), *Advances in clinical neuropsychology* (vol. 3, pp. 243–263). New York: Plenum.

Tarter, R., McBride, H., Buonpane, N., & Schneider, D. (1977). Differentiation of alcoholics: Childhood history of minimal brain dysfunction, family history and drinking pattern. *Archives of General Psychiatry, 34,* 761– 768.

Tarter, R., & Ryan, C. (1983). Neuropsychology of alcoholism: Etiology, phenomenology, process and outcome. In M. Galanter (Ed.), *Recent developments in alcoholism* (pp. 449–469). New York: Plenum.

Tarter, R., Van Thiel, D., & Moss, H. (1988). Impact of cirrhosis on the neuropsychological test performance of alcoholics. *Alcoholism: Clinical and Experimental Research, 12,* 619–621.

Tellegen, A. (1982). *A manual for the Differential Personality Questionnaire.* Unpublished manuscript.

Tellegen, A. (1985). Structures of mood and personality and their relevance to assessing anxiety, with an emphasis on self-report. In A. H. Tuma & J. D. Maser (Eds.), *Anxiety and the anxiety disorders.* Hillsdale, NJ: Erlbaum.

Tellegen, A., Lykken,. D., Bourchard, T., Wilcox, K., Segal, N., & Rich, S. (1988). Personality similarity in twins reared apart and together. *Journal of Personality and Social Psychology, 54*(6), 1031–1039.

Van Hasselt, V. B., Hersen, M., & Milliones, J. (1978). Social skills for alcoholics and drug addicts: A review. *Addictive Behaviors, 3,* 221–233.

Von Knorring, A., Bohman, M., Von Knorring, L., & Oreland, L. (1985). Platelet MAO activity as a biological marker in subgroups of alcoholism. *Acta Psychiatrica Scandinavica, 72,* 51–58.

Wanberg, K., & Horn, J. (1985). *The Alcohol Use Inventory: A guide to the use of the paper and pencil version.* Fort Logan, CO: Multivariate Measurement Consultants.

Wechsler, D. (1974). *Wechsler Intelligence Scale for Children—Revised.* New York: Psychological Corporation.

Weissman, M. (1988). Anxiety and alcoholism. *Journal of Clinical Psychiatry, 49*(10), 17–19.

Wellner, Z., Reich, W., Herjanic, B., Jung, D., & Amado, K. (1987). Reliability, validity and parent–child agreement studies of the Diagnostic Interview for Children and Adolescents (DICA). *Journal of the American Academy of Child Psychiatry, 26,* 649–653.

Wiig, E. H. (1985). *Test of Language Competence.* San Antonio, TX: Psychological Corporation.

Wilkinson, D., & Carlen, P. (1980). Relationship of neuropsychological test performance to brain morphology in amnesic and non-amnesic chronic alcoholics. *Acta Psychiatrica Scandinavica, 62,* 89–102.

Zuckerman, M., Bone, R., Neary, R., Mangelsdorff, D., & Brastman, B. (1972). What is the sensation seeker? Personality and trait experience correlates of the Sensation Seeking Scales. *Journal of Consulting and Clinical Psychology, 39,* 308–321.

PART FOUR

EMERGING TREATMENT ISSUES FOR SPECIAL POPULATIONS

12

Substance Abuse and Mental Illness

STEVEN M. MIRIN
ROGER D. WEISS

Clinical Considerations in the Evaluation of Dual-Diagnosis Patients

Relationship of Substance Abuse to Onset, Course, and Severity of Other Psychiatric Disorders

Clinical and research experience, particularly in the last decade, has demonstrated that a substantial minority of substance abusers are concurrently suffering from other psychiatric disorders. Among these are patients with affective disorders (e.g., depression or bipolar disease), anxiety disorders, organic conditions, and a wide range of personality disorders (Rounsaville, Weissman, Crits-Christoph, Wilber, & Kleber, 1982; Rounsaville, Weissman, Kleber, & Wilber, 1982; Mirin, Weiss, Sollogub, & Michael, 1984b).

Although there has been considerable emphasis on the concept of dual diagnosis in patients initially identified as substance abusers, there has been relatively less attention paid to the problem of substance abuse in patients seeking treatment for acute or chronic psychiatric problems (other than substance abuse). However, studies of the prevalence of substance abuse among inpatients being treated for other psychiatric disorders are remarkably similar in finding that approximately one-third of such patients have an active drug or alcohol problem at the time of admission (Eisen, Grob, & Dill, 1987, 1988; Crowley, Chesluk, Dilts, & Hart, 1974; Davis, 1984; Fischer, Halikas, Baker, & Smith, 1975). The detrimental effects of substance abuse on the clinical course and treatment response of these patients have also been well documented (McLellan, Druley, & Carson, 1978; Schwartz & Goldfinger, 1981, Helzer & Pryzbeck, 1988). Compared to patients of similar age, gender, and socioeconomic status, psychiatric patients with concurrent substance use disorders experience more social disability (e.g., divorce, unemployment), display more problems with impulsivity, are less compliant with treatment recommendations, and in general have a poorer prognosis. Yet, despite the high prevalence and profound impact of substance abuse among psychiatric patients, these disorders are frequently missed (i.e., not diagnosed); even when they are diagnosed, treatment is often nonspecific and inadequate.

By the time they first present for treatment, most dual-diagnosis patients have experienced many of the psychosocial sequelae of chronic drug use, including loss of relationships, occupational failure, incarceration, and repetitive relapse to drug use. In addition, they have experienced the impact of whatever psychiatric disorder developed prior to, or in conjunction with, their substance abuse problem. Often, the interplay of the various disorders is quite evident. For example, in patients with high genetic loading for alcoholism, one may discern a pattern of early heavy drinking with rapid progression to alcohol dependence. In such patients, the concurrent presence of antisocial personality traits appears to increase the risk that this type of progression will take place. Similarly, in drug abusers with concurrent affective disorder, episodes of depression (or mania) can be observed to trigger relapse to drug or alcohol use. Conversely, drug or alcohol use may exacerbate signs and symptoms of a concurrent affective illness.

Problems in the Evaluation of Dual-Diagnosis Patients

The evaluation of substance abusers who may also be suffering from additional psychiatric disorder(s) can be quite complex. In the evaluation of such patients, clinicians are often faced with the task of distinguishing whether the patients' presenting signs and symptoms are manifestations of an underlying psychiatric disorder or consequences of drug intoxication or withdrawal. For example, in the chronic opiate user with concurrent depression, it is often difficult to discern whether the depression is the result of an organic affective disorder induced by chronic drug use; an expectable response to the psychosocial sequelae of life as an opiate addict; or a primary depressive disorder that preceded, and played an etiological role in the development of, the patient's drug dependence. The fact that many of these patients abuse multiple substances complicates the evaluative process further. Finally, it is also important to distinguish whether one of the disorders is primary, in the sense of being a causal or precipitating factor in the development of the other, or whether each has developed independently. As we discuss in detail later in this chapter, these distinctions are important not only from the standpoint of diagnosis, but also for treatment planning, since each disorder requires an array of treatment approaches specifically tailored to what the clinician believes are the important psychological, biological, and psychosocial factors at work.

Typically, dual-diagnosis patients present with long drug use histories, and in this respect they are indistinguishable from the rest of their drug-using peers. Their initial drug experience most frequently involves alcohol use in the early teenage years, followed by use of other drugs including marijuana, hallucinogens, phencyclidine (PCP), and central nervous system (CNS) stimulants, including cocaine. Opioid use, where it occurs, frequently begins with prescription drugs (e.g., Dilaudid) taken orally and often progresses to street drugs (e.g., heroin) taken intravenously.

Characteristically, casual experience with multiple drugs gives way to more regular use of fewer drugs, with the eventual emergence of a drug of choice. The progression is accompanied by experimentation with more efficient methods of drug self-administration (e.g., intravenous use, freebasing); in some patients, these methods become the preferred routes of administration.

As drug abusers work their way through the menu of available drugs, drug preference is shaped by a host of factors, including current fashion, drug availability, peer influences, and of course the subjective response of the user to the pharmacological effects of the drugs themselves. To some extent, sociocultural characteristics of the user appear to be correlated with drug preference. For example, among upper-middle-class whites, stimulant abuse is relatively common, while among lower-class blacks and Hispanics, marijuana and alcohol use is more popular (Fernandez-Pol, Bluestone, & Mizruchi, 1988). Gender-related differences also play a role in the epidemiology of drug use (e.g., abuse of sedative hypnotics by women; Quitkin, Rifkin, Klein, & Kaplan, 1972), as do genetic factors (e.g., alcoholism in males; Goodwin, 1971).

The Self-Medication Hypothesis

A Psychodynamic Perspective

Viewing substance abuse from a psychodynamic perspective, some have hypothesized that specific drug effects may help shape drug preference by ameliorating specific deficiencies in ego development or interpersonal relatedness (Milkman & Frosch, 1973; Khantzian, 1985). For example, introverts with poor interpersonal skills may find that CNS stimulants, in addition to their euphorigenic effects, allow them to feel less inhibited, more confident, more outgoing, and more aggressive. By the same token, individuals burdened by feelings of tension and anger may prefer drugs with predominantly sedative effects (e.g., opioids). Thus, in addition to pharmacological reinforcement, the user also experiences social reinforcement as a consequence of the short-term effects of these drugs on affect and behavior.

Though the self-medication hypothesis has clinical face validity in selected patients, there is also evidence that some drugs of abuse are perceived as highly aversive by specific diagnostic subgroups. For example, some have reported that schizophrenics find the effects of hallucinogens highly unpleasant and therefore tend to avoid them (Vardy & Kay, 1983).

It is also important to note that the acute effects of various drugs of abuse on behavior and mood may be quite different from the effects one observes when the same drugs are taken chronically. Observations of heroin users in varying stages of intoxication and withdrawal illustrate this point. In the mid-1970s, our group (Meyer & Mirin, 1979) carried out a study in which previously detoxified heroin addicts were allowed to self-administer increasing doses of heroin over a 10-day period in a controlled research environment.

This attenuated cycle of addiction took place in the context of a larger study designed to assess the efficacy of naltrexone, a narcotic antagonist, in the treatment of opiate addiction.

In the above-mentioned study, acute administration of heroin was quickly followed by euphoria and tension relief. With continued use, however, subjects developed increasing dysphoria, motor retardation, and social withdrawal. Although acute administration of heroin briefly reversed these chronic effects, tolerance eventually developed to the acute euphorigenic effects of the drug. A similar dichotomy between acute and chronic effects may be observed in cocaine users: Whereas initial low-dose use usually produced euphoria in most users, chronic high-dose use is often accompanied by an agitated dysphoric state (Post, 1975; Post, Kotin, & Goodwin, 1974).

Neurochemical Considerations

Psychodynamic theories that attempt to explain drug preference are not necessarily incompatible with what we understand about the effects of these drugs on brain neurotransmitters, neuromodulators, and neurohormones. For example, acute administration of cocaine, in both animals and humans, has been found to facilitate release of catecholamines (i.e., norepinephrine and dopamine) from presynaptic neurons (Wise, 1984; Gawin & Ellinwood, 1988). The drug also blocks norepinephrine reuptake in a manner similar to some of the tricyclic antidepressants and is a weak inhibitor of monoamine oxidase (MAO), an enzyme responsible for the intracellular degradation of various monoamines, including norepinephrine and serotonin (Gudeman et al., 1982). These, and perhaps other actions of cocaine on central neurotransmitter systems, are postulated to be responsible for the drug's reinforcing properties (Wise, 1984). Chronic cocaine administration has been shown to result in both depletion of brain catecholamines and alterations in the sensitivity of their respective postsynaptic neuronal receptors. These changes are thought to provide the neurophysiological substrate for the depression that often accompanies cocaine withdrawal (Gawin & Ellinwood, 1988).

In the case of the opioids, the direct effect of these agents on central neurotransmitter systems is less well understood. However, the discovery of endogenous opioid compounds in the brain (i.e., endorphins), and their demonstrated role as neuromodulators in the CNS, suggests at least a preliminary model as to how these drugs exert their acute reinforcing effects, as well as their intermediate and chronic effects on mood and behavior. In addition, both opioid agonists and antagonists appear to have profound effects on neuroendocrine systems, mediated through their effects on the hypothalamic pituitary axis (Mirin, Meyer, Mendelson, & Ellingboe, 1980). These perturbations in the endocrine system may also play a role in changes in mood and various drive states (e.g., aggression, sexuality) observed during acute and chronic opioid use.

In summary, although the precise mechanisms and pathways have yet to be identified, various drugs of abuse, particularly the CNS stimulants and opioids, exert their subjective reinforcing effects through acute alterations in CNS neurophysiology. For the individual user, these effects may be reinforcing and subsequently desirable, or they may be aversive, depending upon the psychological and biological substrate upon which these changes are imposed. In substance abusers with concurrent psychiatric disorder, the interplay between psychodynamic factors and neurochemical changes resulting from acute and/or chronic drug use, as well as drug withdrawal, are obviously more complex. These issues are explored in more detail in the sections that follow.

Substance Abuse and Affective Illness

Surveys carried out in both inpatient and outpatient settings reveal that during periods of either chronic intoxication or withdrawal, many substance abusers manifest a substantial degree of depressive symptomatology (Rounsaville, Weissman, Crits-Christoph, et al., 1982; Mirin et al., 1984b; Weiss, Mirin, Michael, & Sollogub, 1986). In addition to low mood, such patients often report sleep and appetite disturbances and diminished libido. Pessimism, low self-esteem, guilt, and suicidal preoccupation are also common in these patients. Moreover, in some individuals, these signs and symptoms persist long after drug detoxification is completed, raising the possibility that the patients, in addition to their substance use disorder, are also suffering from a concurrent affective illness (e.g., major or atypical depression or dysthymic disorder).

Opiate Abusers

In exploring this issue, Rounsaville, Weissman, Crits-Christoph, et al. (1982) evaluated a group of opiate addicts entering a multimodality treatment program, and found that 17% met Research Diagnostic Criteria for major depression. The same group of investigators (Rounsaville, Weissman, Kleber, et al., 1982), using the Schedule for Affective Disorders and Schizophrenia (SADS), found that approximately 30% of opiate addicts in outpatient treatment met SADS criteria for *current* major depression and almost 75% had met SADS criteria for this disorder at some point during their lifetimes. Other investigators (Kleber & Gold, 1978; Mirin et al., 1984b) have reported similar findings in both active and recently detoxified opiate addicts.

As previously noted, it is often difficult to distinguish between the signs and symptoms of an endogenous depression and the manifestations of chronic opiate intoxication or withdrawal in these patients. In exploring this issue, Dackis and Gold (1983, 1984) found a significantly higher prevalence of what they called "organic affective disorder" (i.e., depression) in patients withdrawn from methadone compared to those withdrawn from heroin (60% vs. 25%).

They postulated that the longer-acting drug methadone had induced changes in brain neurophysiology, which contributed to the depression seen in these patients, and that these took longer to reverse themselves once patients were detoxified.

Stimulant Abusers

The prevalence of affective disorder among users of cocaine, amphetamines, and other CNS stimulants has also been a subject of recent study (Weiss et al., 1986; Weiss & Mirin, 1986; Griffin, Weiss, Mirin, & Lange, 1989). Users frequently cite the euphorigenic effects of these drugs as their primary reason for using them; clearly, they are powerfully reinforcing in both animals and humans (Javaid, Fischman, & Schuster, 1978). As noted previously, their acute euphorigenic effects are attributable to their effects on brain catecholamines, specifically norepinephrine and dopamine, as well as serotonin (Wise, 1984). Each of these neurotransmitters has also been implicated in the pathophysiology of depressive disorder (DeLeon-Jones, Maas, Dekirmanjian, & Sanchez, 1975; Schildkraut et al., 1978).

Given the ability of stimulant drugs to induce euphoria and behavioral activation, it is not surprising that some individuals with endogenous depressive disorders should find them attractive. It should be noted, however, that the efficacy of drugs such as cocaine in relieving endogenous depression is quite variable. For example, in a study of depressed patients, Post et al. (1974) found that while low doses of cocaine induced euphoria in some depressed patients, most experienced either no change in mood or a mild dysphoria. Moreover, at higher doses, cocaine seemed to intensify the depressive symptomatology in these patients. Thus, despite its reinforcing properties, cocaine's variable effect on mood, coupled with its short duration of action, makes the drug a poor antidepressant.

Chronic stimulant use leads to depletion of catecholamines from central presynaptic neurons, with a corresponding increase in the sensitivity of both noradrenergic and dopaminergic postsynaptic receptors (Carr & Moore, 1969; Schildkraut, Watson, Draskoczy, & Hartman, 1971). Chronic use has also been demonstrated to deplete intracellular stores of 5-hydroxytryptamine (serotonin) from presynaptic neurons and to block the neuronal uptake of tryptophan, an amino acid precursor important in serotonin synthesis (Ross & Renyi, 1969; Taylor & Ho, 1977). Collectively, these changes in neurotransmitter homeostasis are thought to play a role in the pathogenesis of the depression that accompanies stimulant withdrawal, and in the accompanying craving for cocaine (which, in some individuals, may be prolonged beyond the acute withdrawal period) (Gawin & Kleber, 1986; Gawin et al., 1989).

Clinically, patients in acute stimulant withdrawal manifest persistent anhedonia, with accompanying reversal of many of the vegetative changes that characterize stimulant intoxification. Thus, agitation gives way to fatigue, insomnia is replaced by hypersomnolence, and anorexia is followed by a rebound hyperphagia. Since cocaine and other CNS stimulants suppress rapid eye movement (REM) sleep, individuals in stimulant withdrawal also experience REM rebound and increased dreaming (Watson, Hartmann, & Schildkraut, 1972). During what Gawin and Kleber (1986) have described as the intermediate phase of cocaine withdrawal (i.e., between 1 and 10 weeks after the last dose), depression gradually abates, sleep becomes normalized, anxiety is diminished, and craving for the drug is relatively low in most patients. However, in some, depression, anergia, anxiety, and a high degree of drug craving may persist. In these individuals, evaluation for concurrent underlying affective illness is clearly warranted.

Evaluating Substance Abusers for Affective Disorder: The McLean Hospital Study

CLINICAL INTERVIEW AND RATING SCALE DATA

The diagnostic issues posed by detoxified substance abusers with persistent depressive symptomatology have led a number of investigators to attempt to develop a systematic approach to evaluating such patients at varying phases of the addiction cycle. In one such study, our group (Mirin, Weiss, & Michael, 1988) used structured and unstructured clinical interviews, psychiatric rating scales, and family pedigree data to assess 160 substance abusers for other forms of psychopathology. The patient group consisted of individuals dependent on opioids (53.3%), cocaine (33.7%), or CNS depressants (13.1%). The mean age of the group was approximately 30 years; three-quarters were men; 92% were Caucasians; and about 30% were professionals or executives. At the time of admission, these patients had been using illicit drugs for an average of about 10 years and had been involved in heavy drug use for about 6 years. About two-thirds could be classified as polydrug users, defined as individuals who frequently used two or more drugs in addition to their stated drug of choice. Finally, in addition to their drug dependence, slightly over 50% met *Diagnostic and Statistical Manual of Mental Disorders,* third edition (DSM-III; American Psychiatric Association, 1980) criteria for a diagnosis of alcohol abuse or dependence.

On admission, most of these patients manifested significant depressive symptomatology, as measured by their scores on the Hamilton Depression Rating Scale (HDRS; Hamilton, 1960), the Beck Depression Inventory (BDI; Beck, Ward, Mendelson, Mock, & Erbaugh, 1961), and the Depression subscale of the Symptom Checklist 90 (SCL-90; Derogatis, Rickels, & Rock, 1976). Over a 4-week period of inpatient treatment, however, the vast majority demonstrated substantial improvement, with more than a 60% reduction on the various rating scale measures of depression. There was, however, a subgroup (approximately 14%) who met DSM-III criteria for a diagnosis of major or atypical depression, both currently and during a prior period in their lives in which they had been drug-free. More than half had experienced their first affective episode (i.e., depression, mania of hypomania) prior to the initiation of frequent (i.e., daily) drug use. An additional 10% were found to meet DSM-III criteria for bipolar or cyclothymic disorder.

Among the opiate abusers, 14.2% met DSM-III criteria for major or atypical depression, while another 4.9% were suffering from concurrent bipolar or cyclothymic disorder. Depressed opiate abusers could be distinguished from those who did not meet criteria for this diagnosis by their significantly higher scores on the HDRS, the BDI, and the SCL-90 Depression subscale, on admission and at 2 and 4 weeks into their hospital stay. In many instances, depression was accompanied by a high degree of agitation in these patients, which persisted even after the acute withdrawal phase.

Among the cocaine abusers, rating scale data also revealed moderate to high levels of depressive symptomatology on admission, with substantial improvement over time. Although much of this improvement can probably be attributed to recovery from acute cocaine withdrawal, it is noteworthy that cocaine abusers who eventually received a DSM-III diagnosis of major or atypical depression (11.6%) scored significantly higher on the HDRS, BDI, and SCL-90 on admission, at 2 weeks, and at 4 weeks, compared to those who were not so diagnosed.

Another subgroup of cocaine abusers consisted of individuals with cyclothymic or bipolar disorder (18.5%). It should be noted that although such patients expectably used cocaine in an attempt to self-medicate dysphoric mood, or to switch themselves out of depression and into hypomania or mania, we observed that they also used cocaine while hypomanic or manic, in an attempt to accelerate and accentuate their endogenously produced high. The grandiosity, impulsivity, and poor judgment characteristic of these patients during their hypomanic or manic periods also seemed to play a role in their decision to use cocaine. In our experience, treatment of such patients with lithium carbonate and/or anticonvulsants such as carbamazepine or sodium valproate may have salutary effects, not only on the patients' affective disorder, but on their propensity to abuse cocaine as well.

FAMILY PEDIGREE DATA

Family pedigree data, obtained by interviewing all available first-degree relatives (approximately 46%), tended to independently confirm our clinical and rating scale data in these patients. Drug abusers with concurrent affective disorder had significantly more first-degree relatives with affective illness than did drug abusers without affective disorder. This finding, which was consistent across all drug-using subgroups, suggests that in substance abusers the development of affective disorder is in part influenced by familial, and perhaps genetic, factors. Moreover, in these patients, pre-existing affective illness may play an etiological role in the subsequent development of their substance use disorder. Supporting this hypothesis is our finding that among the cocaine abusers, those with concurrent affective illness began drug use at an early age and had a longer history of drug use prior to coming to treatment, compared to cocaine abusers without affective disorder. Thus, the presence of affective illness may have functioned as a risk factor in this population, predisposing them to earlier onset of cocaine abuse.

The Problem of Suicidal Behavior in Substance Abusers

Numerous studies (Schuckit, 1986; Hawton, 1987; Murphy, 1988; Norstrom, 1988) have found that the frequency of both suicide attempts and completed suicides is substantially higher among substance abusers than in the general population. Indeed, most surveys report that between 20% and 30% of substance abusers entering treatment programs have made a suicide attempt at some point in the past, and the incidence of completed suicide is probably three to four times that found in the general population (Murphy, 1988). The lifetime mortality from suicide among substance abusers may be as high as 15% (Hawton, 1987). Finally even among individuals who do not regard themselves as substance abusers, approximately half of all completed suicides are associated with excessive intake of drugs and/or alcohol just prior to the event.

Though most studies have not controlled for the presence or absence of concurrent affective illness in this group of patients, it is evident to clinicians that the presence of major or atypical depression in an individual who also abuses drugs and/or alcohol substantially increases the risk of suicide, compared to having either disease alone (Dorpat, 1974). In addition to the effects of the illicit drugs themselves, there is also a degree of risk imposed by the psychosocial sequelae of life as a chronic drug abuser. School and vocational failure, disrupted interpersonal relationships, alienation of friends and family members, and being branded as deviant by both the legal and health care systems—all these factors contribute to the sense of helplessness and hopelessness experienced by most chronic substance abusers. Thus, even individuals currently engaged in treatment and/or the recovery process may mourn the years of lost opportunities, irretrievably damaged relationships, and limited hopes for the future that may result from even a brief period of substance abuse, and these factors contribute to the increased risk of eventual suicide.

Finally, it should be noted that the vast majority of substance abusers, regardless of whether they have a concurrent psychiatric illness, tend to be individuals who have difficulty tolerating frustration and display impulsivity and poor judgment, particularly in stressful situations. As a consequence of their lifestyle, they are frequently exposed to other individuals with similar personality traits, some of whom have died as a result, either from drug overdose, drug-related violence, or suicide. In addition, some of the character disorders frequently found among substance abusers (e.g., antisocial personality disorder and borderline personality disorder) by themselves carry an increased risk of impulsivity and self-destructive behavior.

The Substance Abuser with Anxiety

Clinical Issues

A number of studies have documented the relatively high prevalence of anxiety disorders (i.e., generalized anxiety and/or panic disorder) in patients being treated for substance abuse problems (Quitkin et al., 1972; Mirin et al., 1988). Conversely, abuse of a variety of psychoactive drugs, including hypnotics/sedatives, benzodiazepines (BZDs), and alcohol, is a frequent complication in patients presenting for treatment of anxiety disorders in traditional psychiatric settings (Eisen et al., 1987, 1988).

As in the case of the affective disorders, it is often difficult to discern the precise causal relationship between substance abuse and anxiety disorders of various types. Clearly, there are many patients with anxiety or panic disorder who discover that they can obtain short-term relief of anxiety symptoms through the use of prescribed or nonprescribed drugs with anxiolytic properties. Sleep disturbance, particularly difficulty falling asleep, may also prompt the prescription of antianxiety and/or sedative drugs.

With frequent use, tolerance develops rapidly to the antianxiety and sedative effects of these agents. In addition to both dispositional (i.e., metabolic) and pharmacodynamic tolerance, cross-tolerance also develops to the effects of other CNS depressants, including alcohol (Braestrup & Squires, 1978; Smith, Wesson, & Seymour, 1979). The rapidity of tolerance development depends on a variety of factors, including the drug used, the frequency of its use, and individual physiological variables. In some cases, tolerance may be evident within several days.

Unfortunately, an all-too-common medical response to the development of tolerance is to raise the dose of the original drug, or to add yet another drug in the same general class (e.g., adding a long-acting BZD such as flurazepam to induce sleep in a patient already taking a short-acting BZD such as lorazepam during the day for relief of anxiety). Since cross-tolerance develops to all BZDs (as well as to hypnotics/sedatives and alcohol) in such patients, these therapeutic maneuvers simply accelerate the development of tolerance, and eventually of physical dependence.

Once physical dependence is present, abrupt or even gradual withdrawal of one or more of these drugs may be accompanied by abstinence symptoms, including anxiety, restlessness, tachycardia, postural hypotension, hyperreflexia, tremor, sleep disturbance, and seizures and/or delirium in more severe cases (Pevnik, Jasinski, & Haertzen, 1978; Noyes, Clancy, & Coryell, 1985). Onset of withdrawal symptoms is more rapid following the use of shorter-acting agents (including alcohol), and users may experience some degree of withdrawal symptomatology 6–12 hours after their last dose, prompting a pattern of repetitive drug self-administration. In such patients, it soon becomes impossible to discern whether drug use constitutes an attempt to self-treat anxiety stemming from underlying anxiety or panic disorder, or to treat the symptoms that arise as the result of acute or chronic withdrawal of the drugs used to treat these disorders.

Epidemiological Data

Data from the National Institute of Mental Health (NIMH) Epidemiologic Catchment Area survey suggest that, compared to other major psychiatric disorders, anxiety disorders and alcohol and drug abuse have a relatively early onset. Indeed, in one study, Christie et al. (1988) found that the mean age of onset for anxiety disorders in this population was 15 years; for drug abuse it was 19 years, and for alcohol abuse it was 21 years. Among respondents aged 18 to 30, 22.3% had a substance use disorder, and 6.2% had experienced both a substance use disorder and either a major depressive episode or an anxiety disorder.

These investigators also examined the relationship between age of onset of mental disorder and the subsequent risk of drug abuse in young adults. In so doing, they found that the presence of an anxiety disorder or a major depressive episode substantially increased the risk for the subsequent development of drug abuse or dependence. Among substance abusers with anxiety or depressive disorder, the vast majority (approximately 75%) had developed their illness prior to the onset of their drug abuse problem. This suggests that anxiety disorders may increase the risk of experimentation and repetitive use, particularly of those drugs that relieve anxiety and tension (e.g., alcohol, marijuana, BZDs); in some cases, this pattern of use evolves into drug dependence.

In yet another study, Kashani and Orvaschel (1988) reported that the 6-month prevalence of anxiety disorders in a community sample of 150 adolescents aged 14–16 was 17%, with 8.7% having symptoms severe enough, in the opinion of the authors, to require some form of treatment intervention. Within the latter group, the coexistence of an anxiety disorder and depression was quite common. Anxiety disorders were the most common psychiatric diagnoses in this group of adolescents, as they are in surveys of adults. Anxiety disorders were also more common among females (23%) than among males (12%).

In the previously mentioned McLean study (Mirin et al., 1988), our group found that approximately 10% of patients presenting for treatment of a substance use disorder met DSM-III criteria for generalized anxiety disorder or panic disorder. These disorders were far more common among abusers of CNS depressants than among those who abused opioids or cocaine. These patients (most of them women) characteristically abused BZDs (primarily diazepam), often in combination with alcohol; almost half met DSM-III criteria for alcohol abuse or dependence. The relatively high prevalence of anxiety disorders in women appears to serve as a risk factor for the subsequent development of depressant abuse in this population. In addition, depressant abuse may be relatively more common among women for other reasons, including easier access to depressant drugs through legitimate sources (i.e., prescriptions), and a preference for drugs that can be administered orally as opposed to intravenously.

The presence of anxiety or panic disorder in patients with an abuse problem poses not only diagnostic problems, but also a number of issues related to the treatment of such patients. Most prominent among these is the acknowledged hazard of prescribing BZDs to patients who have already demonstrated a propensity to abuse these drugs and/or alcohol. Some patients with panic disorder clearly benefit from treatment with tricyclic antidepressants or MAO inhibitors, but there are few data to support the efficacy of antidepressants in the treatment of generalized anxiety disorder (Sheehan, Ballenger, Jacobson, 1980). In addition, although psychotherapy may facilitate the development of insight in such patients, its usefulness in reducing their overall levels of anxiety appears limited. Behaviorally oriented techniques, including relaxation training and systematic desensitization to situations that are particularly anxiety-provoking, appear to hold more promise (Sheehan, 1982). The use of β blockers in the treatment of chronic (as opposed to situational) anxiety is controversial, with most studies demonstrating less than impressive results (Jefferson, 1974).

Organic Conditions Associated with Substance Abuse

Psychoactive drug use may give rise to a wide range of organic conditions ranging from mild intoxication to drug-induced psychosis. After chronic use, withdrawal from some of these agents may also be accompanied by changes in mental state; at times, such changes may be indistinguishable from naturally occurring (i.e., non-drug-induced) psychiatric disorders. It is beyond the scope of this chapter to describe all of the various drug-induced organic conditions, so we focus here on those conditions most frequently seen in clinical practice.

Psychosis, Mania, and Confusional States

FOLLOWING USE OF CNS STIMULANTS

Acute intoxication with a number of psychoactive drugs may produce states closely resembling naturally occurring psychiatric disorders, including hypomania, mania, and acute psychosis. For example, in low doses, CNS stimulants such as dextroamphetamine (Dexedrine), methaphetamine (Desoxin), methylphenidate (Ritalin), and cocaine usually produce acute excitation, enhanced mental acuity, and mood elevation. Hyperactivity, appetite suppression, and insomnia are also part of the intoxication syndrome, particularly in nontolerant individuals (Ellinwood, 1972, 1979; Kramer, Fischman, & Littlefield,

1967). At higher doses, stimulant drugs (particularly cocaine and methamphet-amine) may result in restlessness, irritability, hyperactivity, and emotional lability, along with more prominent signs of autonomic nervous system hyper-arousal, including increased heart rate, hypertension, tremulousness, and agitation. Hyperthermia is also a frequent finding (Ellinwood, 1979; Cregler & Mark, 1986).

Severe intoxication with CNS stimulants may closely mimic hypomania, mania, or acute psychosis. Indeed, emotional lability, hyperactivity, irritabil-ity, and signs of autonomic arousal are seen both in acute stimulant intoxica-tion and during hypomania or manic states. Moreover, the propensity of bipolar patients to abuse these drugs may cloud the clinical picture further (Weiss et al., 1986). It should be noted, however, that stimulant overdose is more frequently accompanied by headache, chills, vomiting, and hyperther-mia. Parasitosis (i.e., picking at imaginary bugs under the skin) and curious forms of repetitive stereotyped behavior (e.g., taking television sets apart and putting them back together) are also characteristic of chronic stimulant abus-ers.

The suspiciousness, agitation, delusions, emotional lability, and hallucina-tions that may accompany acute stimulant intoxication may also be confused with a non-drug-related psychotic episode. However, visual auditory hallu-cinations are more common in the former, whereas visual hallucinations are more common among the latter. Thus, in acutely psychotic patients, the presence of tactile hallucinations and/or parasitosis, coupled with signs of autonomic nervous system hyperactivity and a known history of drug abuse, should cause the clinician to suspect an acute toxic state secondary to stimu-lant overdose.

Treatment of acute stimulant toxicity is primarily directed toward reduc-ing both CNS irritability and central and peripheral autonomic arousal. In acutely agitated and/or psychotic patients, steps must be taken to prevent the individuals from harming themselves or others. Treatment measures may include the use of long-acting BZDs (e.g., diazepam) to reduce CNS irritabil-ity and prevent seizures, and steps to counteract tachycardia, hypertension, and hyperthermia (Pollock, Brotman, & Rosenbaum, 1989). In psychotic pa-tients, neuroleptic drugs are useful, but should be confined to those agents with minimal anticholinergic effects, since some illicitly obtained CNS stim-ulants may be adulterated with other drugs that have anticholinergic prop-erties.

Fortunately, in most individuals, acute intoxication with CNS stimulants is of relatively short duration (i.e., 20 minutes to 4 hours), and most patients recover without medical intervention. Even the psychosis associated with acute stimulant toxicity clears within 2–3 days, if drug use has also stopped. In chronic users, however, psychotic symptomatology may persist for long per-iods of time and often requires aggressive neuroleptic treatment (Ellinwood, 1972).

FOLLOWING HALLUCINOGEN USE

Another class of drugs that may produce a condition resembling acute psychosis are the hallucinogens, such as lysergic acid diethylamide (LSD) and mescaline. Acute intoxication with these agents is characterized by alterations in body boundaries, perceptual distortions, illusions, hallucinations, and emotional lability. Patients are often agitated and confused, and their judgment is impaired, but reality testing usually remains intact and overt thought disorder is uncommon (Bowers, 1972a, 1972b). Characteristically, the affective, cognitive, and behavioral sequelae of hallucinogen intoxication are time-limited, with gradual recovery 8–24 hours after drug ingestion, depending on the duration of action of the drug used. A somewhat longer period of apathy and exhaustion may follow.

In rare instances, hallucinogen use may precipitate an acute toxic delirium, characterized by agitation, disorientation, and paranoid delusions (Bowers, 1972b). Unprovoked violence, directed toward oneself or others, may occur under such conditions. Unlike schizophrenia or bipolar disorder, there is usually no prior history of mental illness, and the patient is often at least partially aware that his or her symptomatology is the result of drug intoxication. In some patients, the psychotic symptomatology may persist. In these individuals, one often finds a prior history of schizophrenia or affective illness that has been exacerbated by hallucinogen use (Freedman, 1968; Tucker, Quinlan, & Harrow, 1972; Naditch, 1974).

Recurrent perceptual disturbances (i.e., flashbacks) may occur up to a year after hallucinogen use. These are usually brief events (i.e., lasting seconds to hours), often precipitated by stress, use of other drugs (e.g., marijuana) or environmental stimuli that are reminiscent of the earlier hallucinogenic experience (Cohen, 1977; Abraham, 1983). In individuals with no other mental disorder, the periods between flashbacks are usually devoid of psychiatric symptomatology. However, the experience of flashbacks in an otherwise normal individual may precipitate profound anxiety, a fear of "going crazy," and a reactive depression. In those individuals who report flashbacks, but whose last experience with hallucinogens was more than a year ago, one should strongly suspect the presence of a "functional" (i.e., non-drug-related) psychiatric disorder.

FOLLOWING ALCOHOL USE

Acute alcohol intoxication, with its accompanying disinhibition, impaired judgment, diminished attention span, and emotional lability, can also be confused with a number of other psychiatric conditions. For example, the disinhibition, sense of increased confidence, talkativeness, and interpersonal aggressivity that accompany alcohol intoxication may be confused with hypomania or mania. At higher blood alcohol levels (i.e., > 150 mg/dl) with more severe intoxication, the euphoria evident at lower blood alcohol levels may be replaced by dysphoria, confusion, disorientation, and loosening of associations, which may resemble acute manic excitement or the acute psychosis associated with schizophrenia or schizoaffective disorder (Liskow & Goodwin, 1987). In some users who are acutely sensitive to the effects of alcohol, profound intoxication may develop even after a single drink (idiosyncratic intoxication; Cohen, 1981b). Delusions, hallucinations, impulsivity, and rage reactions may occur in such individuals.

The diagnostic dilemmas posed by the interaction of acute alcohol intoxication with pre-existing personality traits and/or concurrent psychiatric disorder are exacerbated by the high prevalence of alcohol abuse and dependence among patients with other psychiatric disorders—in particular, affective disorder and schizophrenia (Liskow, Mayfield, & Thiele, 1982; Mendelson, Babor, Mello, & Pratt, 1986). Fortunately, alcohol intoxication is relatively easy to diagnose, and in the absence of further drinking most episodes clear within 12 hours, as the blood and brain alcohol concentration drops. Persistent signs of intoxication should lead the clinician to suspect concurrent use of other drugs. In the absence of signs of alcohol withdrawal, persistent signs and symptoms of hyperactivity, aggressivity, hallucinations, and delusions suggest the presence of an underlying psychiatric disorder complicated by alcohol abuse.

Following chronic high-dose use, abrupt withdrawal from alcohol is accompanied by a characteristic abstinence syndrome, which has been well described in the literature (Brown, 1982; Liskow & Goodwin, 1987). In addition to anxiety and restlessness, there are numerous signs of CNS irritability, including hyperreflexia, tremor, and agitation. Both auditory and visual hallucinations, as well as delusions, may accompany the withdrawal state; these may lead to initial diagnostic confusion with other conditions, including mania and acute psychosis. In its advanced stages, severe alcohol withdrawal is accompanied by disorientation, confusion, and an agitated delirium (delirium tremens). In addition to manifestations of CNS irritability (e.g., seizures), there is profound hyperarousal of the autonomic nervous system, as well as fluid and electrolyte imbalance (Mendelson & Mello, 1979). In their initial presentation, such patients may be misdiagnosed as suffering from an acute manic or psychotic episode or catatonic excitement. In patients who are also being treated with neuroleptic drugs, the autonomic nervous system hyperarousal and hyperthermia seen in delirium tremens may be confused with neuroleptic malignant syndrome. A history of chronic heavy drinking and recent withdrawal, coupled with the presence of elevated liver function tests and other neurological and metabolic sequelae of chronic alcohol abuse, usually clarifies the diagnosis (Mendelson & Mello, 1979; Brown, 1982).

Finally, some chronic alcohol patients experience the onset of visual and auditory hallucinations within 48 to 72 hours after their last drink. This alcoholic hallucinosis may last for several weeks or even months and may be exacerbated by subsequent alcohol use. Unlike patients with delirium tremens, however, these patients are oriented and not confused. They are frequently misdiagnosed as schizophrenic (Saravay & Pardes, 1967).

The veterinary tranquilizer phencyclidine (PCP) was a popular drug of abuse in the late 1970s; although its popularity has declined, it is still a problem in some urban areas.

In low doses, PCP functions primarily as a depressant, producing a mild intoxication with accompanying analgesia. Acute intoxication takes many forms, however, and in some ways resembles intoxication with alcohol or sedative/hypnotics (Domino, 1980; Clouet, 1986). At lower doses, the user characteristically experiences changes in body image, perceptual distortions, elevated mood, and hypersensitivity to stimulation. High-dose use (i.e., > 20 mg) is associated with a number of medical sequelae, including muscular rigidity, catalepsy, hypertension, seizures, and respiratory depression. Agitation may alternate with periods of stupor and, in some patients, coma. Psychiatric sequelae may include hallucinations, delusions, stereotypic behavior, and paranoia, all of which may easily be mistaken for an acute schizophrenic episode or acute manic state (Luisada, 1978). However, the presence of motor disturbances, including dystonia, tremor, athetosis, and seizures, along with signs of autonomic nervous system hyperactivity (e.g., sweating, salivation, hypertension, tachycardia, and hyperthermia), in a patient who intermittently becomes stuporous or comatose suggests acute PCP intoxication.

The acute psychosis produced by PCP intoxication may last several weeks, with early, intermediate, and late phases. Initially, agitation, hyperactivity, and paranoia predominate; during the intermediate phase, some control over behavior is obtained, though patients may still harbor paranoid delusions. In the late phase, psychotic symptoms gradually resolve and are often replaced by depression (Gelenberg, 1977).

Chronic PCP use is sometimes accompanied by a chronic psychosis, which persists even when patients are drug-free (Luisada, 1978). Since most PCP users also tend to abuse other drugs, it is difficult to attribute this state to PCP alone. It is also difficult to discern whether these individuals were already schizophrenic and have simply been made worse by chronic use of PCP (Fauman & Fauman, 1978). Given the distinctive syndrome that develops following chronic use, however, it appears that the drug is capable of producing both acute and chronic psychosis in otherwise normal individuals—a state that unfortunately may persist, despite treatment with neuroleptic drugs (Graeven, 1978).

Acute Anxiety and Panic Reactions

Use of a number of drugs, particularly cocaine, hallucinogens, and marijuana, may precipitate acute panic reactions that may be difficult to distinguish from generalized anxiety or panic disorder (Gawin & Ellinwood, 1988; Freedman, 1968; Melges, Tinklenberg, Hollister, & Gillespie, 1970). In the case of marijuana, these episodes usually occur in individuals with pre-existing anxiety over drug use (i.e., novice users), or in experienced users who have taken more than their usual dose and as a result are experiencing more profound drug effects than they are accustomed to. There is usually an awareness that the panic is directly related to drug use. Fear of loss of control, confusion, and disorientation are common during such episodes, as is some degree of paranoia. On the other hand, most patients are oriented to time, place, and person; hallucinations are rare; and reality testing remains intact. Some users may benefit from being given low doses of BZDs (Weil, 1970; Tennant & Groesbeck, 1972; Meyer, 1975).

In cocaine or hallucinogen users, anxiety or panic is usually short-lived, but marijuana-induced panic may persist for several days because of the long half-life of its active ingredient, δ-9-tetrahydrocannabinol (THC), and its metabolites. In contrast to patients with panic disorder, patients with drug-induced anxiety/panic usually have no prior history of panic episodes (other than those precipitated by drug use) and no history of agoraphobia. It should be noted, however, that some patients with panic disorder may experience panic attacks precipitated by cocaine use.

DURING AND AFTER ALCOHOL WITHDRAWAL

During and after acute alcohol withdrawal, patients often experience anxiety, restlessness, and difficulty in sleeping. They also may complain of fatigue and a host of other somatic symptoms (Brown, 1982). This syndrome may be mistaken for generalized anxiety disorder or atypical affective disorder, and failure to accurately diagnose alcohol abuse and withdrawal as its cause may lead to the ill-advised prescribing of anxiolytic or antidepressant medication in such patients. Conversely, in patients with underlying anxiety disorders or affective illness who also abuse alcohol, the prescription of psychotropic medication without recognition of or attention to the alcohol problem is a serious pitfall in treatment.

Chronic Apathy and Dysphoria

ACCOMPANYING HALLUCINOGEN OR MARIJUANA USE

Chronic use of hallucinogens and/or marijuana may be accompanied by the development of chronic apathy, anhedonia, inability to concentrate, and social withdrawal—what some have called an "amotivational syndrome" (Blacker, Jones, Stone, & Pfefferbaum, 1968; Cohen, 1980, 1981a). Controversy exists as to the relative importance of pre-existing psychopathology in these patients, since some investigators have noted that chronic high-dose marijuana use in otherwise functional individuals may not result in any demonstrable psychopathology (Kupfer, Detre, & Koral, 1973; Meyer, 1975; Millman & Sbriglio, 1986). Thus, amotivational syndrome may be more common in chronic drug users with pre-existing passive/dependent or avoidant personality disorders, schizoaffective disorder, or dysthymic disorder. Although individuals with amotivational syndrome may superficially resemble patients with schizoaffective disorder or chronic undifferentiated schizophrenia, there is usually no evidence of thought disorder. Depression, where present, is not as severe as in patients with chronic affective illness.

IN CHRONIC ALCOHOLISM

Chronic alcohol abuse may induce a range of CNS pathology (Adams & Victor, 1985), with chronic apathy and dysphoria as prominent features. For example, in Wernicke's disease, patients are usually apathetic, drowsy, and disoriented, and may be misdiagnosed as depressed. However, the concurrent presence of ataxia, nystagmus, palsy of the sixth cranial nerve, and a paralysis of conjugate gaze helps clarify the diagnosis. In Korsakoff's psychosis (alcohol-induced amnestic disorder), patients may be alert, but respond to questioning with confabulation. Careful memory testing reveals both anterograde and retrograde amnesia. In many such patients, there are also coexisting signs of Wernicke's disease, suggesting that the condition is related to chronic alcohol use and should not be confused with the dementia seen in Alzheimer's disease, or with the pseudodementia that frequently accompanies depression in elderly patients (Weissman & Myers, 1980).

Personality Disorder in Substance Abusers

Although the clinical literature is rich in descriptions of the various personality disorders manifested by substance abusers, well-controlled studies on this subject are relatively rare. In general, the early psychoanalytic writers (Glover, 1932; Rado, 1933) tended to emphasize similarities in personality traits among substance abusers (the so-called "addictive personality"). Frequently cited were the passive/dependent, manipulative characteristics of these patients. Their inability to tolerate frustration, their tendency to regress in the face of external stress, and their need to be taken care of by others in a hostile/dependent relationship were also emphasized. More recent psychodynamic formulations (Zinberg, 1974; Khantzian, 1974, 1985) have focused on the role of particular drugs of abuse in ameliorating intrapsychic conflicts and compensating for pre-existing ego deficits. In this paradigm, depressed and angry individuals who decide to use illicit drugs in an attempt at self-treatment may prefer substances with acute euphorigenic and tension relieving effects (e.g., opioids). In contrast, passive and inhibited individuals, who have difficulty asserting themselves, may prefer substances that have a disinhibiting effect on behavior and enhance aggressivity in social situations (e.g., alcohol, cocaine).

A major obstacle to understanding the role of character pathology in the development and maintenance of substance use disorders is the difficulty in separating those personality traits that predate the onset of drug abuse from those that develop in the context of such abuse. Thus, for some individuals, being hostile and manipulative may be a useful adaptation to life as an addict. For others, passivity, dependency, and the ability to elicit caring from others may insure that substance abuse can continue unabated, with the conscious or unconscious support of spouses, physicians, or other unwitting accomplices, who either supply the drugs themselves or fail to intervene effectively in the drug-using behavior. Finally, it should be noted that some drugs of abuse provide a powerful, albeit temporary, relief from feelings of sadness, helplessness, anger, and a host of other uncomfortable feelings; by taking these drugs, individuals obviate the need to develop more effective coping strategies to deal with such feelings. As a result, most chronic drug users experience a gradual atrophy in their coping skills as they come to depend more and more on drug effects to solve their intrapsychic and interpersonal problems.

Among the personality disorders classified under Axis II of the multiaxial system of DSM-III, only antisocial personality disorder (APD) and borderline personality disorder (BPD) have been well studied with respect to their interaction with drug abuse. The diagnostic criteria for these two groups of patients have been relatively well defined and tend to emphasize enduring patterns of behavior, which are present even during drug-free periods. For these reasons, this section focuses primarily on these two diagnostic entities as they occur in substance abusers.

Antisocial Personality Disorder

IN ALCOHOLICS

There is a great deal of evidence that APD tends to co-occur with certain forms of substance use disorder, particularly alcoholism (Stabenau, 1984; Hesselbrock, Meyer, & Kenner, 1985) and opioid dependence (Khantzian & Treece, 1985; Rounsaville et al., 1986). Some surveys suggest that APD occurs in about 15–20% of alcoholic men and approximately 10% of alcoholic women (Helzer & Pryzbeck, 1988). Other studies (Koenigsberg, Kaplan, Gilmore, & Cooper, 1985; Mirin, Weiss, Griffin, & Michael, in press) have found an even higher rate of APD among alcoholics and drug abusers, ranging from 20% to 45%, depending on the sample. Higher prevalence rates are found in persons screened through the criminal justice system, and lower rates are found in substance abusers seeking outpatient treatment. All of these rates are substantially higher than those found in the general population (about 4% for men and 1% for women; Helzer & Pryzbeck, 1988). Though APD is more common among the first-degree relatives of alcoholics (Cloninger, Bohman, & Sigvardsson, 1981; Stabenau & Hesselbrock, 1984), the two disorders appear to be transmitted through separate modes of inheritance. On the other hand, the presence of APD in an alcoholic male appears to increase the risk of alcoholism in his offspring (Bohman, 1978).

In the diagnostic evaluation of substance abusers with possible APD one is faced with the dilemma of distinguishing between antisocial behavior that occurs in the context of substance abuse (or other psychiatric disorders that may be present) and behavior that is due to APD per se. Nevertheless, when the two disorders do co-occur, there are important clinical implications. Thus, alcoholics with concurrent APD appear to have an earlier onset of alcoholism, are more likely to be polydrug users, and have a generally poorer prognosis (Hesselbrock et al., 1985; Schuckit, 1985). Social adjustment in these individuals is generally poor, and they also have more alcohol-related medical and social problems than do alcoholics without APD (Stabenau, 1984; Cadoret, Troughton, & Widmer, 1984). Alcoholics with APD have also been found to have a more prominent family history of APD and more family disruption during their childhoods, which is not surprising, considering their early onset of heavy drinking and relatively poor response to treatment (Stabenau & Hesselbrock, 1984). It should be noted, however, that such individuals also have poor adjustment during periods in which they are alcohol-free. In essence, their alcoholism is superimposed on an already chronic and severe illness (i.e., APD), which is made worse by a career of chronic drinking.

IN OTHER TYPES OF DRUG ABUSERS

Among abusers of drugs other than alcohol, APD is also quite common. For example, our group (Mirin et al., in press) looked at the prevalence of various Axis II disorders in a group of 382 patients admitted for treatment of drug dependence, half of whom were also alcoholic. Approximately 95% of all patients met DSM-III criteria for an Axis II disorder, and 23% were diagnosed as suffering from APD. When patients were grouped by drug of choice, APD was significantly more prevalent among opioid abusers (about 32%) than among those who abused cocaine or CNS depressants (16% and 8%, respectively). Not surprisingly, patients with APD were almost exclusively male (92%).

With respect to clinical and demographic differences, patients with APD were, in general, less likely to have graduated from high school and more likely to be unemployed. Compared to patients without APD, they exhibited earlier onset of heavy drug use and were more likely to be alcoholic. In addition, substance abusers with APD more frequently cited the recreational aspects of drug use as their reason for initiating and maintaining their drug dependence. In comparison, substance abusers with concurrent BPD frequently cited the wish for self-treatment of anxiety or depression as their primary reason for initiating substance use.

In summary, it appears that APD, a disorder frequently found in substance abusers, has a profound effect on the risk for and subsequent course of substance use disorder, including alcoholism. Characteristically, these patients present for treatment with more severe illness and are more difficult to engage, particularly in treatments that require interpersonal relatedness, sincerity, and motivation. Once they have left a treatment setting, they tend to relapse more quickly. Many also have repetitive contact with the criminal justice system. Incarceration, though not a substitute for treatment, may actually prolong life in some of these individuals, allowing them to "mature out" of their APD and render them more amenable to treatment for their substance use disorder. This hypothesis, however, requires more rigorous longitudinal study.

Borderline Personality Disorder

Among other Axis II disorders found among substance abusers, BPD has been the most extensively studied. The work of Gunderson (1984) and others (Drake & Vaillant, 1985) in establishing the validity of and criteria for the BPD diagnosis has been an important factor in this regard.

As in the case of APD, the prevalence of BPD among substance abusers varies with the population studied. Gender, drug of choice, age of the sample, and the setting in which data are gathered all play a role. In general, the prevalence of BPD appears to range from 10% to 20% in most samples (Nace, Saxon, & Shore, 1983, 1986; Koenigsberg et al., 1985). Our group (Mirin et al., in press) found that substance abusers with concurrent BPD were predominantly female (80%) and preferred CNS depressants to cocaine or opioids. Borderlines were also more likely to be suffering from a concurrent Axis I disorder, primarily major depression, than individuals with other personality disorder diagnoses. Conversely, among substance abusers with concurrent affective disorder, borderline pathology was diagnosed in approximately 25%—two and a half times the rate found in substance abusers without affective illness. Among the possible explanations for this finding include overlap in the diagnostic criteria for major depression and BPD, or alternatively, the hypothesis that affective illness, particularly when coupled with substance abuse, places an individual at increased risk for the development of those personality traits and behaviors that satisfy the DSM-III diagnostic criteria for BPD. Included among these are impulsivity, unpredictability, a tendency to develop intense and often unstable interpersonal relationships, marked shifts of attitude, devaluation and manipulation of others, and affective instability with frequent bouts of anxiety and depression. Feelings of emptiness or boredom and periods of intense anger (particularly in the face of perceived or actual rejection), as well as self-destructive acts, are also more prevalent among substance abusers with BPD and/or affective disorder.

From a clinical perspective, the diagnosis of BPD in a substance-abusing patient has practical implications. Drug treatment staff are frequently bewildered when drug-free borderlines continue to manifest a great deal of impulsivity, affective instability, manipulativeness, and difficulties in their interpersonal relationships. All too often, the interpersonal and behavioral characteristics of these patients are attributed to acute or chronic drug intoxication or withdrawal, rather than to their personality disorder; failure to recognize and treat the latter clearly precludes therapeutic progess.

In a study of inpatient substance abusers, Inman, Bascue, and Skoloda (1985) used a structured interview to identify a sample of patients with BPD. Psychological testing revealed that borderlines manifested more depression, more difficulty with impulse control, poorer reality testing, and more antisocial behavior than did substance abusers without borderline pathology. These data are consistent with the findings of Zanarini, Gunderson, and Frankenburg (1989), who found that borderlines were more likely to meet DSM-III criteria for affective illness (particularly dysthymic disorder) than were antisocial controls. In our studies (Mirin et al., in press), borderlines frequently cited the anxiety-relieving and antidepressant properties of illicit drugs as their primary reason for initiating and maintaining drug use, particularly in the face of perceived or actual rejection.

Other Personality Disorders

In addition to APD and BPD, substance abusers as a group display a wide range of personality disorders, including schizoid, schizotypal, compulsive, dependent, avoidant, and passive/aggressive personality types (Khantzian & Treece, 1985; Rounsaville et al., 1986). Preliminary data from our studies (Mirin et al., in press) suggest that these diagnoses are unevenly distributed across different drug-using subtypes. Specifically, histrionic and narcissistic personality disorders appear to be more common among cocaine abusers than among those who abuse opioids or CNS depressants, while APD appears to be more common among opioid abusers, and BPD more prevalent among depressant abusers.

The elucidation of specific personality disorders among substance abusers has important implications for both diagnosis and treatment planning. Unfortunately, the validity and reliability of the diagnostic criteria for these disorders have not been subject to the same degree of scrutiny as those for Axis I disorders. The development of more rigorous methods for arriving at Axis II diagnoses, such as the Structured Clinical Interview for DSM-III (SCID), is a step in the right direction. Once the validity and reliability of these diagnoses are established for well-defined populations of substance abusers, the role of specific personality disorders in the development, course, and outcome of drug or alcohol dependence in these patients can be more accurately assessed.

Summary

Among substance abusers presenting for treatment, a substantial minority are also found to be suffering from one or more concurrent psychiatric disorders.

In such patients, the presence of affective illness, generalized anxiety disorder, panic disorder, and a host of other clinical entities may influence the decision to experiment with illicit drugs or alcohol, as well as the risk of progressing from casual to regular use. The presence or absence of "nondrug" psychopathology also colors the perceived subjective effects of these drugs, and affects an individual's ability to enter into and benefit from treatment.

The development of more reliable techniques for the diagnostic assessment of substance abusers has lent credence to the dual-diagnosis concept and made clinicians increasingly aware of the complexity of these patients. At the same time, we have made considerable progress in the development of treatment modalities designed to address the specific needs of individual patients. As the interplay among substance use disorders and other forms of psychopathology becomes better understood, we may hope that dogmatic and monolithic approaches to etiology and treatment will fade into obscurity.

Acknowledgment

We gratefully aknowledge the assistance of Susanne Daley and Claire Ryan in the preparation of the manuscript. All studies reported by the authors were supported by a grant from the Engelhard Foundation.

References

Abraham, H. D. (1983). Visual phenomenology of the LSD flashback. *Archives of General Psychiatry, 40,* 884–889.

Adams, R. D., & Victor, M. (1985). *Principles of neurology.* New York: McGraw-Hill.

American Psychiatric Association. (1980). *Diagnostic and statistical manual of mental disorders* (3rd ed.). Washington, DC: Author.

Beck, A. T., Ward, C. H., Mendelson, M., Mock, J., & Erbaugh, J. (1961). An inventory for measuring depression. *Archives of General Psychiatry, 4,* 561–571.

Blacker, K. H., Jones, R. T., Stone, G. C., & Pfefferbaum, D. (1968). Chronic users of LSD: The "acidheads." *American Journal of Psychiatry, 125,* 341–351.

Bohman, M. (1978). Some genetic aspects of alcoholism and criminality: A population of adoptees. *Archives of General Psychiatry, 35,* 269–276.

Bowers, M. B., Jr. (1972a). Acute psychosis induced by psychotomimetric drug abuse: 1. Clinical findings. *Archives of General Psychiatry, 27,* 437–439.

Bowers, M. B., Jr. (1972b). Acute psychosis induced by psychotomimetric drug abuse: 2. Neurochemical findings. *Archives of General Psychiatry, 27,* 440–442.

Brown, C. G. (1982). The alcohol withdrawal syndrome. *Annals of Emergency Medicine, 11*(5), 276–280.

Braestrup, C., & Squires, R. F. (1978). Brain specific benzodiazepine receptors. *British Journal of Psychiatry, 133,* 249–260.

Cadoret, R. J., Troughton, E., & Widmer, R. B. (1984). Clinical differences between antisocial and primary alcoholics. *Comprehensive Psychiatry, 25,* 1–8.

Carr, L. A., & Moore, K. E. (1969). Norepinephrine: Release from brain by d-amphetamine in vivo. *Science, 164,* 322–323.

Christie, K. A., Burke, J. D., Regier, D. A., Rae, D. S., Boyd, J. H., & Locke, B. Z. (1988). Epidemiologic evidence for early onset of mental disorders and higher risk of drug abuse in young adults. *American Journal of Psychiatry, 145*(8), 971–975.

Cloninger, C. R., Bohman, M., & Sigvardsson, S. (1981). Inheritance of alcohol abuse. *Archives of General Psychiatry, 38,* 861–868.

Clouet, D. H. (Ed.). (1986). *Phencyclidine: An update* (DHHS Publication No. ADM 86-1443, NIDA Research Monograph No. 64). Washington, DC: U.S. Government Printing Office.

Cohen, S. (1977). Flashbacks. *Drug Abuse and Alcoholism Newsletter, 6,* 1–3.

Cohen, S. (1980). Cannabis: Impact on motivation. Part I. *Drug Abuse and Alcoholism Newsletter, 9,* 1–3,

Cohen, S. (1981a). Cannabis: Impact on motivation. Part II. *Drug Abuse and Alcoholism Newsletter, 10,* 1–3.

Cohen, S. (1981b). Pathological intoxication. *Drug Abuse Alcoholism and Newsletter, 10*(5), 1–5.

Cregler, L. L., & Mark, H. (1986). Medical complications of cocaine abuse. *New England Journal of Medicine, 315,* 1495–1500.

Crowley, T., Chesluk, D., Dilts, S., & Hart, R. (1974). Drug and alcohol abuse among psychiatric admissions. *Archives of General Psychiatry, 30,* 13–20.

Dackis, C. A., & Gold, M. S. (1983). Opiate addiction and depression: Cause or effect? *Drug and Alcohol Dependence, 2,* 105–109.

Dackis, C. A., & Gold, M. S. (1984). Depression in opiate addicts. In S. M. Mirin (Ed.), *Substance abuse and psychopathology* (pp. 20–40). Washington, DC: American Psychiatric Press.

Davis, D. I. (1984). Differences in the use of substances of abuse by psychiatric patients compared with medical and surgical patients. *Journal of Nervous and Mental Disease, 172,* 654–657.

DeLeon-Jones, F., Maas, J. W., Dekirmenjian, H., & Sanchez, J. (1975). Diagnostic subgrougs of affective disorders and their urinary excretion of catecholamine metabolites. *American Journal of Psychiatry, 132,* 1141–1148.

Derogatis, L., Rickels, K., & Rock, A. (1976). The SCL-90 and the MMPI: A step in the validation of a new self-report scale. *British Journal of Psychiatry, 128,* 280–289.

Domino, E. F. (1980). Treatment of phencyclidine intoxication. *Psychopharmacology Bulletin, 16,* 83–85.

Dorpat, T. L. (1974). Drug automatism, barbiturate poisoning and suicide behavior. *Archives of General Psychiatry, 31,* 216–220.

Drake, R. E., & Vaillant, G. E. (1985). A validity study of Axis II of DSM-III. *American Journal of Psychiatry, 142,* 555–558.

Eisen, S. V., Grob, M. C., & Dill, D. L. (1987). *Substance abuse in a generic inpatient population* (McLean Hospital Evaluative Service Unit, Report No. 71). Belmont, MA: McLean Hospital.

Eisen, S. V., Grob, M. C., & Dill, D. L. (1988). *Substance abuse in an inpatient population: A comparison of patients on Appleton and generic units* (McLean Hospital Evaluative Service Unit, Report No. 75). Belmont, MA: McLean Hospital.

Ellinwood, E. H., Jr. (1972). Amphetamine psychosis: Individuals, settings and sequences. In E. H. Ellinwood, Jr. & S. Cohen (Eds.), *Current concepts on amphetamine abuse* (pp. 143–158). Washington, DC: U.S. Government Printing Office.

Ellinwood, E. H., Jr. (1979). Amphetamines/anorectics. In R. L. DuPont, A. Goldstein, & J. O'Donnell (Eds.), *Handbook on drug abuse* (pp. 221–231). Washington, DC: U.S. Government Printing Office.

Fauman, M. A., & Fauman, B. J. (1978). The psychiatric aspects of chronic phencyclidine use: A study of chronic PCP users. In R. C. Peterson & R. C. Stillman (Eds.), *PCP: Phencyclidine abuse: An appraisal* (DHEW Publication No. 78–728, NIDA Research Monograph No. 21, pp. 183–200). Washington, DC: U.S. Government Printing Office.

Fernandez-Pol, B., Bluestone, H., & Mizruchi, M. S. (1988). Inner-city substance abuse patterns: A study of psychiatric inpatients. *American Journal of Drug and Alcohol Abuse, 14*(1), 41–50.

Fischer, D., Halikas, J., Baker, J., & Smith, J. (1975). Frequency and patterns of drug abuse in psychiatric patients. *Diseases of the Nervous System, 36,* 550–553.

Freedman, D. X. (1968). The use and abuse of LSD. *Archives of General Psychiatry, 18,* 330–347.

Gawin, F. H., & Ellinwood, E. H., Jr. (1988). Cocaine and other stimulants: Actions, abuse, and treatment. *New England Journal of Medicine, 318,* 1173–1182.

Gawin, F. H., & Kleber, H. D. (1986). Abstinence symptomatology and psychiatric diagnosis in cocaine abusers: Clinical observations. *Archives of General Psychiatry, 43,* 107–113.

Gawin, F. H., Kleber, H. D., Byck, R., Rounsaville, B. J., Kosten, T. R., Jatlow, P. I., & Morgan, C. (1989). Desipramine facilitation of initial cocaine abstinence. *Archives of General Psychiatry, 46,* 117–121.

Gelenberg, A. J. (1977). Psychopharmacology update: Phencyclidine, *McLean Hospital Journal, 2,* 89–96.

Glover, E. G. (1932). On the etiology of drug addiction. *International Journal of Psycho-analysis, 13*(3), 298–328.

Goodwin, D. W. (1971). Is alcoholism hereditary? A review and critique. *Archives of General Psychiatry, 25,* 545.

Graeven, D. B. (1978). Patterns of phencyclidine use. In R. C. Peterson & R. C. Stillman (Eds.), *PCP: Phencyclidine abuse: An appraisal* (DHEW Publication No. 78–728, NIDA Research Monograph No. 21, pp. 176–182). Washington, DC: U.S. Government Printing Office.

Griffin, M. L., Weiss, R. D., Mirin, S. M., & Lange, U. (1989). A comparison of male and female cocaine abusers. *Archives of General Psychiatry, 46,* 122–126.

Gudeman, J. E., Schatzberg, A. F., Samson, J. A., Orsulak, P. J., Cole, J. O., & Schildkraut, J. J. (1982). Toward a biochemical classification of depressive disorders: VI. Platelet MAO activity and clinical symptoms in depressed patients. *American Journal of Psychiatry, 139,* 630–633.

Gunderson, J. G. (1984). *Borderline personality disorder.* Washington, DC: American Psychiatric Press.

Hamilton, M. (1960). A rating scale for depression. *Journal of Neurology, Neurosurgery and Psychiatry, 23,* 56–62.

Hawton, K. (1987). Assessment of suicide risk. *British Journal of Psychiatry, 150,* 145–153.

Helzer, J. E., & Pryzbeck, T. R. (1988). The co-occurrence of alcoholism with other psychiatric disorders in the general population and its impact on treatment. *Journal of Studies on Alcohol, 49*(3), 219–224.

Hesselbrock, M. N., Meyer, R. E., & Kenner, J. J. (1985). Psychopathology in hospitalized alcoholics. *Archives of General Psychiatry, 42,* 1050–1055.

Inman, D. J., Bascue, L. O., & Skoloda, T. (1985). Identification of borderline personality disorders among substance abuse inpatients. *Journal of Substance Abuse and Treatment, 2*(4), 229–232.

Javaid, J. I., Fischman, M. W., & Schuster, C. R. (1978). Cocaine plasma concentration: Relation to psychological and subjective effects in humans. *Science, 202,* 227–228.

Jefferson, J. W. (1974). Beta-adrenergic receptor blocking drugs in psychiatry. *Archives of General Psychiatry, 31,* 681–691.

Kashani, J. H., & Orvaschel, H. (1988). Anxiety disorders in mid-adolescence: A community sample. *American Journal of Psychiatry, 145*(8), 960–964.

Khantzian, E. (1974). Opiate addiction: A critique of theory and some implications of treatment. *American Journal of Psychotherapy, 28,* 59–70.

Khantzian, E. J. (1985). The self-medication hypothesis of addictive disorders: Focus on heroin and cocaine dependence. *American Journal of Psychiatry, 142,* 1259–1264.

Khantzian, E. J., & Treece, C. (1985). DSM-III psychiatric diagnosis of narcotic addicts. *Archives of General Psychiatry, 42,* 1067–1071.

Kleber, H. D., & Gold, M. S. (1978). Use of psychotropic drugs in the treatment of methadone maintained narcotic addicts. *Annals of the New York Academy of Sciences, 331,* 81–98.

Koenigsberg, H. W., Kaplan, R. D., Gilmore, M. M., & Cooper, A. M. (1985). The relationship between syndrome and personality disorder in DSM-III: Experience with 2,462 patients. *American Journal of Psychiatry, 142,* 207–212.

Kramer, J. C., Fischman, V. S., & Littlefield, D. C. (1967). Amphetamine abuse: Pattern and effects of high doses taken intravenously. *Journal of the American Medical Association,* 201, 89–93.

Kupfer, D. J., Detre, T., & Koral, J. (1973). A comment on the "amotivational syndrome" in marijuana smokers. *American Journal of Psychiatry, 130,* 1319–1322.

Liskow, B. I., & Goodwin, D. W. (1987). Pharmacological treatment of alcohol intoxification, withdrawal and dependence: A critical review. *Journal of Studies on Alcohol, 48*(4), 356–370.

Liskow, B., Mayfield, D., & Thiele, J. (1982). Alcohol and affective disorder: Assessment and treatment. *Journal of Clinical Psychiatry, 43*(4), 144–147.

Luisada, P. V. (1978). The phencyclidine psychosis: Phenomenology and treatment. In R. C. Peterson & R. C. Stillman (Eds.), *PCP: Phencyclidine abuse: An appriasal* (DHEW Publication No. 78–728, NIDA Research Monograph, No. 21, pp. 241–253). Washington, DC: U.S. Government Printing Office.

McLellan, A., Druley, K., & Carson, J. (1978). Evaluation of substance abuse problems in a psychiatric hospital. *Journal of Clinical Psychiatry, 39,* 425–430.

Melges, F. T., Tinklenberg, J. R. Hollister, L. E., & Gillespie, H. K. (1970). Temporal disintegration and depersonalization during marijuana intoxication. *Archives of General Psychiatry, 23,* 204–210.

Mendelson, J. H., Babor, T. F., Mello, N. K., & Pratt, H. (1986). Alcoholism and prevalence of medical and psychiatric disorders. *Journal of Studies on Alcohol, 47*(5), 361–366.

Mendelson, J. H., & Mello, N. K. (1979). Biologic concomitants of alcoholism. *New England Journal of Medicine, 301,* 912–921.

Meyer, R. E. (1975). Psychiatric consequences of marijuana use: The state of the evidence. In J. R. Tinklenberg (Ed.), *Marijuana and health hazards: Methodological issues in current research* (pp. 133–152). New York: Academic Press.

Meyer, R. E., & Mirin, S. M. (1979). *The heroin stimulus: Implications for a theory of addiction.* New York: Plenum Press.

Milkman, H., & Frosch, W. A. (1973). On the preferential abuse of heroin and amphetamine. *Journal of Nervous and Mental Disease, 156,* 242–248.

Millman, R. B., & Sbriglio, R. (1986). Patterns of use and psychopathology in chronic marijuana users. *Psychiatric Clinics of North America, 9,* 533–545.

Mirin, S. M., Meyer, R. E., Mendelson, J. H., & Ellingboe, J. (1980). Opiate use and sexual function. *American Journal of Psychiatry, 137,* 909–915.

Mirin, S. M., Weiss, R. D., & Michael, J. (1988). Psychopathology in substance abusers: Diagnosis and treatment. *American Journal of Drug and Alcohol Abuse, 14*(2), 139–157.

Mirin, S. M., Weiss, R. D., Sollogub, A., & Michael, J. (1984a). Psychopathology in the families of drug abusers. In S. M. Mirin (Ed.), *Substance abuse and psychopathology* (pp. 80–106). Washington, DC: American Psychiatric Press.

Mirin, S. M., Weiss, R. D., Sollogub, A., & Michael, J. (1984b). Affective illness in substance abusers. In S. M. Mirin (Ed.), *Substance abuse and psychopathology* (pp. 58–77). Washington, DC: American Psychiatric Press.

Mirin, S. M., Weiss, R. D., Griffin, M. L., & Michael, J. L. (in press). Psychopathology in drug abusers and their families. *Comprehensive Psychiatry.*

Murphy, G. E. (1988). Suicide and substance abuse. *Archives of General Psychiatry, 45,* 593–594.

Nace, E. P., Saxon, J. J., Jr., & Shore, N. (1983). A comparison of borderline and non-borderline alcoholic patients. *Archives of General Psychiatry, 40,* 54–56.

Nace, E. P., Saxon, J. J., Jr., & Shore, N. (1986). Borderline personality disorder and alcoholism treatment: A one-year follow up study. *Journal of Studies on Alcohol, 47,* 196–200.

Naditch, M. P. (1974). Acute adverse reactions to psychoactive drugs, drug usage and psychopathology. *Journal of Abnormal Psychology, 83*(4), 394–403.

Norstrom, T. (1988). Alcohol and suicide in Scandinavia. *British Journal of Addiction, 83,* 553–559.

Noyes, R., Jr., Clancy, J., & Coryell, W. H. (1985). A withdrawal syndrome after abrupt discontinuation of alprazolam. *American Journal of Psychiatry, 142*(1), 114–116.

Pevnick, J. S., Jasinski, D. R., & Haertzen, C. A. (1978). Abrupt withdrawal from therapeutically administered diazepam. *Archives of General Psychiatry, 35,* 995–998.

Pollack, M. H., Brotman, A. W., & Rosenbaum, J. F. (1989). Cocaine abuse and treatment. *Comprehensive Psychiatry, 30,* 31–44.

Post, R. M. (1975). Cocaine psychosis: A continuum model. *American Journal of Psychiatry, 132,* 225–231.

Post, R. M., Kotin, J., & Goodwin, F. K. (1974). The effects of cocaine on depressed patients. *American Journal of Psychiatry, 131,* 511–517.

Quitkin, F. M., Rifkin, A., Klein, D. F., & Kaplan, J. (1972). Phobic anxiety syndrome complicated by drug dependence and addiction. *Archives of General Psychiatry, 27,* 159–162.

Rado, S. (1933). Psychoanalysis of pharmacothymia. *Psychoanalytic Quarterly, 2,* 1–23.

Ross, S. B., & Renyi, A. L. (1969). Inhibition of the uptake of 5-hydroxytryptamine in brain tissue. *European Journal of Pharmacology, 7,* 270–277.

Rounsaville, B. J., Kosten, T. R., & Kleber, H. D. (1986). Long-term changes in current psychiatric diagnosis of treated opiate addicts. *Comprehensive Psychiatry, 27,* 480–498.

Rounsaville, B. J., Weissman, M. M., Kleber, H., & Wilber, C. (1982). Heterogeneity of psychiatric diagnosis in treated opiate addicts. *Archives of General Psychiatry, 39,* 161–166.

Rounsaville, B. J., Weissman, M. M., Crits-Christoph, C., Wilber, C., & Kleber, H. (1982). Diagnosis and symptoms of depression in opiate addicts: Course and relationship to treatment outcome. *Archives of General Psychiatry, 39,* 151–156.

Saravay, S. M., & Pardes, H. (1967). Auditory elementary hallucinations in alcohol withdrawal psychosis. *Archives of General Psychiatry, 16,* 652–658.

Schildkraut, J. J., Orsulak, P. J., Schatzberg, A. F., Gudeman, J. E. Cole, J. O., Rohde, W. A., & La Brie, R. A. (1978). Toward a biochemical classification of depressive disorders: I. Differences in urinary excretion of MHPG and other catecholamine metabolites in clinically defined subtypes of depression. *Archives of General Psychiatry, 35,* 1427–1433.

Schildkraut, J. J., Watson, R., Draskoczy, P. R., & Hartman, E. (1971). Amphetamine withdrawal depression and MHPG excretion. *Lancet, i,* 485–486.

Schuckit, M. A. (1985). The clinical implications of primary diagnostic groups among alcoholics. *Archives of General Psychiatry, 42,* 1043–1049.

Schuckit, M. A. (1986). Primary male alcoholics with histories of suicide attempts. *Journal of Studies on Alcohol, 47,* 78–81.

Schwartz, S., & Goldfinger, S. (1981). The new chronic patient: Clinical characteristics of an emerging subgroup. *Hospital and Community Psychiatry, 32*(7), 470–474.

Sheehan, D. V. (1982). Current views of the treatment of panic and phobic disorders. *Drug Therapy. Hospital Edition,* 74–93.

Sheehan, D. V., Ballenger, J., & Jacobson, G., (1980). The treatment of endogenous anxiety with phobic, hysterical and hypochondriacal symptoms. *Archives of General Psychiatry, 37,* 51–59.

Smith, D. E., Wesson, D. R., & Seymour, R. B. (1979). The abuse of barbituates and other sedative-hypnotics. In R. L. DuPont, A. Goldstein, & J. O'Donnell (Eds.), *Handbook on drug abuse* (pp. 233–240). Washington, DC: U.S. Government Printing Office.

Stabenau, J. R. (1984). Implications of family history of alcoholism, antisocial personality, and sex differences in alcohol dependence. *American Journal of Psychiatry, 141,* 1178–1182.

Stabenau, J. R., & Hesselbrock, V. M. (1984). Psychopathology in alcoholics and their families and vulnerability to alcoholism: A review and new findings. In S. M. Mirin (Ed.), *Substance abuse and psychopathology* (pp. 108–132). Washington, DC: American Psychiatric Press.

Taylor, D., & Ho, B. T. (1977). Neurochemical effects of cocaine following acute and repeated injection. *Journal of Neuroscience Research, 3,* 95–101.

Tennant, F. S., Jr., & Groesbeck, C. J. (1972). Psychiatric effects of hashish. *Archives of General Psychiatry, 27,* 133–136.

Tucker, G. J., Quinlan, D., & Harrow, M. (1972). Chronic hallucinogenic drug use and through disturbance. *Archives of General Psychiatry, 27,* 443–447.

Vardy, M. M., & Kay, S. R. (1983). LSD psychosis or LSD-induced schizophrenia? A multimethod inquiry. *Archives of General Psychiatry, 40*(8), 877–883.

Watson, R., Hartmann, E., & Schildkraut, J. J. (1972). Amphetamine withdrawal: Affective state, sleep patterns, and MHPG excretion. *American Journal of Psychiatry, 129*(3), 39–45.

Weil, A. T. (1970). Adverse reactions to marijuana: Classification and suggested treatment. *New England Journal of Medicine, 282*, 997–1000.

Weiss, R. D., & Mirin, S. M. (1986). Subtypes of cocaine abusers. *Psychiatric Clinics of North America, 9*, 491–501.

Weiss, R. D., Mirin, S. M., Michael, J. L., & Sollogub, A. (1986). Psychopathology in chronic cocaine abusers. *American Journal of Drug and Alcohol Abuse, 12*, 17–29.

Weissman, M. M., & Myers, J. K. (1980). Clinical depression in alcoholism. *American Journal of Psychiatry, 137*, 372–374.

Wise, R. A. (1984). Neural mechanisms of the reinforcing action of cocaine. In J. Grabowski (Ed.), *Cocaine: Pharmacology, effects, and treatment of abuse* (DHHS Publication No. ADM 84-1326, NIDA Research Monograph No. 50, pp. 15–34). Washington, DC: U.S. Government Printing Office.

Zanarini, M. C., Gunderson, J. G., & Frankenburg, F. R. (1989). Axis I phenomenology of borderline personality disorder. *Comprehensive Psychiatry, 30*(2), 149–156.

Zinberg, N. E. (1974). Addiction and ego function. *Psychoanalytic Study of the Child, 30*, 507–588.

13

AIDS and Addictions

STEVEN J. SCHLEIFER
BEVERLY R. DELANEY
SUSAN TROSS
STEVEN E. KELLER

Introduction

Since its appearance in 1981, the acquired immune deficiency syndrome (AIDS) epidemic has become the focus of worldwide attention. In 1988, health departments in the United States and U.S. territories reported over 10,000 cases of AIDS in intravenous drug users (IVDUs), in their sex partners, and in children born to mothers who were IVDUs or sex partners of IVDUs (Centers for Disease Control, 1989). These IVDU-associated AIDS cases accounted for one-third of AIDS in the United States reported in 1988. Male homosexual/ bisexual male IVDUs made up approximately one-fifth of all IVDU-associated cases; however, proportions varied widely from region to region. In the Northeast, this group accounted for 7.7% of IVDU-associated cases, whereas in the West they accounted for 56.8% of IVDU-associated cases (Centers for Disease Control, 1989).

Transmission of human immunodeficiency virus (HIV), the putative causative agent, occurs through direct entry of the virus into the bloodstream. This can occur by direct transfer of blood or blood products, by sexual contact, or by perinatal transfer from mother to infant. High-risk behaviors for exposure to the virus include unprotected vaginal or anal intercourse and use of shared intravenous needles with HIV-positive partners (Miles, 1988).

In some cities, a large majority of IVDUs have become seropositive for HIV, representing substantial morbidity and a serious potential for spread into the general population. There is considerable geographic variation within the United States. Seroprevalence rates among IVDUs in U.S. cities range from 2% in southern New Jersey and New Orleans to 50–60% in New York City and Northern New Jersey (Des Jarlais & Friedman, 1987). Studies show that once the virus has been introduced into a local community of IVDUs, spread is rapid. Two years after the first seropositive sample in Manhattan was identified, the seroprevalence rose to over 40% (Des Jarlais et al., 1987). IVDUs are becoming the primary source of heterosexual and perinatal transmission. An analysis of the first 1,000 AIDS cases in the United States found that 73% of heterosexuals with AIDS have had sexual contact with an IVDU; 7% of homosexual/bisexual men with AIDS reported a history of intravenous drug use; and 51% of children with AIDS had at least one parent who used intravenous drugs (Jaffe, Bregman, & Selik, 1983). IVDUs have been the probable source of infection in 93% of heterosexual cases in New York City and 80% of infected *in utero* children (Des Jarlais & Friedman, 1987). In view of the increasing incidence of HIV infection among IVDUs and the increasing contribution of IVDU-related transmission to the epidemiology of AIDS, it is essential that health and mental health professionals working with addictive disorder patients be cognizant of the clinical parameters of this problem.

Although IVDUs represent the major heterosexual at-risk and vector population for AIDS, abuse of substances such as alcohol may play an increasing, albeit less direct, role in AIDS risk and disease progression. Intoxicated states caused by the use of alcohol, opiates, or other drugs can influence an individual's sexual behavior, resulting in unsafe sexual practices that may increase risk of exposure to HIV. Behavioral strategies to minimize such behaviors are required. There is also evidence that psychoactive substances such as alcohol and opiates have suppressive effects on immune function, possibly placing individuals at greater risk for infection or further compromising the immune systems of those already infected. This chapter reviews basic aspects of HIV and AIDS in relation to current and potential consequences for substance abusers and their health care providers.

Etiology and Pathogenesis

AIDS is caused by infection with HIV (Fauci, 1985), an agent that had not been identified before the current epidemic. This retrovirus, originally named human T-cell lymphotropic virus type III (HTLV-III) and lymphadenopathy-associated virus (LAV), has been termed HIV since 1986 by agreement of viral taxonomists and AIDS investigators. HIV is considered to be the primary cause of a progressive and fatal disease related to impairment of the immune system. HIV is more complex than other known animal retroviruses, containing at least eight functional genes (Carpenter & Mayer, 1988; Fauci, 1988).

Immune responses are mediated primarily by T- and B-lymphocytes. These cell types are responsible for cell-mediated and humoral (antibody-mediated) responses to antigenic challenge. In addition, specific subclasses of T-cells are involved in the regulation of both cell-mediated and humoral responses. Among these, T-helper cells are required for effective augmentation of responses to antigenic challenge, and T-suppressor cells are involved in dampening and terminating immune responses. T-helper cells can be detected by their expression of the phenotypic surface marker CD4 and are therefore often referred to as "T4-cells." HIV has a particular predilection for T4-cells, and the infection and destruction of such cells are believed to constitute the primary source of morbidity in AIDS. HIV is believed to bind to the CD4 surface molecule, allowing it to enter the T4-cell. Once in the cell, viral ribonucleic acid (RNA) is transcribed to deoxyribonucleic acid (DNA) and integrated into the host cell's chromosomal DNA. HIV infection may then enter a latent phase. Subsequent cell activation, which may be triggered by host factors, results in transcription of viral RNA, protein synthesis, virus assembly, budding of the mature virus from the cell surface, cell death, and dissemination of viral particles (Fauci, 1988). Destruction or impaired functioning of T-helper lymphocytes will result in diminished capacity to respond to antigenic challenge, with consequent susceptibility to neoplasia and infection, often by organisms that would pose little threat in the presence of an intact immune system.

Diagnosis and Staging

Since 1984, serum tests to detect HIV antibody have become available for screening and diagnosis of both symptomatic and asymptomatic cases. There are presently three serological tests for determining the presence of HIV infection. Table 13.1 presents possible test results and interpretations for two of these, the enzyme-linked immunosorbent assay (ELISA) and the Western blot. ELISA is widely available and is the most frequently used test. Available since 1985, ELISA determines the presence of HIV infection by detecting and measuring antibodies in the blood through a colorimetric reaction (Stimmel, 1988). Positive results on ELISA should be confirmed by the Western blot, a more complicated and expensive assay with higher predictive value. False-positive results on ELISA are especially common in multiparous women, drug

TABLE 13.1. Possible Test Results and Interpretations for the Enzyme-Linked Immunosorbent Assay (ELISA) and the Western Blot

Test results	Interpretation
ELISA negative Western blot negative	Because of "window" period, negative testing should be repeated at 6-month intervals for at least 1 year when index of suspicion is high.
ELISA negative Western blot positive	HIV antibodies are present.
ELISA negative Western blot indeterminate	Test should be repeated. In high-risk patients, repeat testing is often confirmed as positive. In difficult cases, PCR technique may be helpful.
ELISA positive Western blot negative	False-positive ELISA is common in drug users and individuals with collagen vascular disease. Should be repeated in 3–6 months.
ELISA positive Western blot positive	HIV antibodies are present.

users, and individuals with collagen vascular diseases (Carpenter & Mayer, 1988).

In the Western blot or immunoblot, viral antigens are separated on a gel, transferred to a blotting strip, and exposed to a patient's serum. HIV antibodies attach themselves to the denatured HIV antigens; after processing, bands corresponding to the major and minor HIV antigens can be visualized. At times, some but not all bands are visualized, making results indeterminate—an indication for repeat testing. A negative Western blot following a positive ELISA should be repeated within 3 to 6 months. Finally, it should be noted that both tests detect the presence of antibodies to HIV rather than the HIV antigen itself. Seroconversion requires several weeks or more following exposure, with 90% of seropositives showing an antibody response within 42 days (J. Jacobs, personal communication, 1988). Infected individuals who have yet to develop an antibody response due to recent exposure (<2 months), or who cannot mount an antibody response due to impaired immunity (including impaired immunity as a result of advanced HIV infection), may test negative but be wholly capable of transmitting HIV infection. HIV results cannot therefore be used to assure safety to unprotected sex partners, particularly among high-risk subjects such as needle-sharing IVDUs.

Recent studies utilizing the polymerase chain reaction (PCR) technique show that HIV can be detected before antibodies develop (Laure et al., 1988; Schindzielorz, 1989). The PCR technique uses enzymes and highly specific primers to generate multiple copies of the original viral nucleic acid, increasing its numbers to levels that can be detected. This currently experimental and high-cost technique may eventually lead to more efficient screening methodologies. At present, it is used primarily to provide alternative confirmation or to screen selected very-high-risk groups (e.g., newborns of HIV-infected mothers) (Schindzielorz, 1989).

Initial approaches to classification of HIV infection distinguished symptomatic patients without opportunistic infection or neoplasia (AIDS-related complex, or ARC) from those with clinical AIDS. Patients with ARC could exhibit generalized lymphadenopathy, frequent fevers, anorexia, weight loss, and malaise. The diagnosis of AIDS was made in the presence of opportunistic infections such as pneumocystis pneumonia (PCP) or Kaposi's sarcoma (Carpenter & Mayer, 1988). With further clinical experience and identification of HIV as the etiological agent of AIDS, a more refined classification system has been developed (Centers for Disease Control, 1986). Four categories are defined. Group I consists of individuals with acute symptomatic HIV infection; Group II consists of individuals with asymptomatic HIV infection; Group III includes individuals with asymptomatic generalized lymphadenopathy, previously classified as having ARC; Group IV includes patients with active disease, and is further subdivided into five subgroups. Individuals with constitutional symptoms such as progressive fevers, sweats, chills, and weight loss (formerly classified in ARC) are included in Group IV,A. Patients with HIV infections and neurological disease are now classified in Group IV,B. Groups

IV,C and IV,D include individuals with opportunistic infection (IV,C) or secondary cancers such as lymphoma and Kaposi's sarcoma (IV,D). The latter three subgroups were previously defined as having clinical AIDS.

After initial exposure to HIV, an acute viral syndrome, the clinical significance of which is unknown, may occur (Carpenter & Mayer, 1988). Symptoms of the acute syndrome may include fever, malaise, and generalized lymphadenopathy; these last for about 1 week and then subside. Antibodies to HIV are generally detectable within 4–12 weeks following exposure (Curran et al., 1985). Once seroconversion occurs, the rate of development of AIDS and other clinical symptoms is variable, and the infected individual may remain asymptomatic for an extended and unpredictable period of time. Current evidence suggests, however, that given sufficient time all infected persons will eventually experience disease progression. Signs or symptoms of progressive HIV disease often precede the occurrence of opportunistic infection or malignancy. These include generalized extrainguinal lymphadenopathy, persistent fevers, diarrhea, anorexia, weight loss, and malaise.

Once full-blown AIDS has developed, the patient's deterioration may be quite rapid. IVDUs with AIDS have been observed to have an even more severe and rapidly progressive clinical course than other AIDS patients, and recent studies show a broad spectrum of severe HIV-associated diseases in IVDUs. HIV infection is believed to result in an exacerbation of illnesses common in IVDUs, often through reactivation of latent disorders. Studies by Selwyn and others (Selwyn et al., 1988, 1989; Stoneburner et al., 1988) found that deaths due to infections, endocarditis, and pulmonary tuberculosis occurred more frequently among IVDUs with HIV infection than among IVDUs without HIV infection.

Neuropsychiatric Complications of AIDS

The extent to which neuropsychiatric complications occur in patients with HIV infection was not initially appreciated. It is becoming increasingly apparent, however, that the cognitive, affective, and behavioral manifestations in AIDS patients may often be manifestations of organic mental disorders rather than psychological reactions to life-threatening illness. Central nervous system (CNS) effects may constitute the initial presentation of HIV infection and should be considered in the differential diagnosis of IVDUs exhibiting cognitive, affective, or personality changes. Navia, Jordan, and Price (1986) found that 25% of 121 AIDS cases exhibited CNS manifestations that accompained or preceded other AIDS symptoms; 10% exhibited CNS manifestations as the presenting sign of AIDS. Awareness of such disorders by health professionals working with IVDUs and other high-risk groups may be critical to diagnosis and management.

HIV may affect the CNS in several ways: (1) direct effects on the CNS; (2) opportunistic infections and HIV-related tumors of the CNS; (3) CNS effects of systemic illness; and (4) CNS effects of medications used to treat the disorder and its complications.

Mass lesions and infectious processes in the CNS, including cryptococcus neoformans, toxoplasmosis, cytomegalovirus, and lymphoma, are not uncommon and often treatable; however, they account for only 30% of CNS complications of AIDS (Navia et al., 1986). More frequently, AIDS patients develop a progressive dementia with diffuse cerebral atrophy demonstrable on computed tomography (CT) scan. The terms "AIDS dementia complex," "subacute encephalitis," or "subacute encephalopathy" may be used. Patients often present with psychological symptoms as their first manifestation of AIDS dementia complex. Frequently the presentation involves a mild degree of cognitive impairment and disturbance of affect. Navia et al. (1986) described a triad of cognitive, motor, and behavioral symptoms. Their patients tended to appear depressed initially, with complaints of apathy and social withdrawal, difficulty in concentration, forgetfulness, and psychomotor slowing. Behavioral changes were noted in one-third of the patients. Irritability, emotional lability, confusion, agitated psychosis with visual hallucinations, bilateral chronic headaches, and generalized seizures were also seen, but less commonly. In the full-blown syndrome, which tended to develop over several months, patients exhibited global cognitive impairment. Motor symptoms were present in half of the patients studied. Patients most frequently complained of progressive loss of balance or leg weakness. Deterioration of handwriting, reflecting a loss of motor coordination, or tremor was elicited in some patients (Navia et al., 1986).

Physicians treating alcohol-addicted and other substance abusing patients have additional diagnostic concerns in evaluating cognitive impairment. The CNS effects of alcohol by themselves commonly pose diagnostic problems. Alcohol use, in addition to its more focal syndromes, causes diffuse brain dysfunction that may persist for months, years, or indefinitely even after withdrawal of the drug (Pohl, 1988). Cognitive impairment has been shown in 70–90% of alcoholics after detoxification (Pohl, 1988). Symptoms of alcoholic organic brain syndrome, such as loss of intellectual abilities, memory deficits, and personality change, may be difficult to differentiate from early HIV-associated cognitive impairment. In alcoholics, however, the impairment is usually mild and often can be stabilized or reversed by abstinence. In the AIDS patient, the impairment is progressive and, by the terminal phase of the disease, severe. Alcoholics who develop AIDS may suffer from both drug- and infection-related cognitive impairment. The diagnosis of HIV infection should therefore be considered actively in the assessment of alcoholics and other substance abusers with cognitive impairment in areas of endemic HIV, especially when the symptoms do not improve with abstinence.

Zidovudine, originally known as azidothymidine (AZT), is now commonly used in the treatment of AIDS and HIV infection. Zidovudine, a thymidine analogue, blocks viral replication by inhibiting reverse transcriptase. The drug is virustatic but not virucidal; that is, it blocks the replication of the virus but does not kill it. Studies have shown that zidovudine decreases mortality and morbidity, thus increasing survival time (Schmitt et al., 1988). Incidence and severity of opportunistic infections are reduced after approximately 6 weeks of therapy. Symptoms such as night sweats, fever, and neuropsychological manifestations may resolve or diminish. A recent study examining the neuropsychological outcome of zidovudine treatment of patients with AIDS and ARC found that patients receiving zidovudine, particularly those with AIDS, showed improved cognition when compared to those receiving placebo (Schmitt et al., 1988). This finding suggests that the neurological dysfunction caused by HIV infection may to some extent be reversible by zidovudine treatment. In general, symptoms improve for 6 to 8 months but then often recur. The mechanisms involved in this process are currently unknown. Most patients tolerate zidovudine well, but adverse side effects can occur. Major adverse effects are hematological and include anemia and granulocytopenia; others include headache, nausea, vomiting, insomnia, and restlessness. Those patients who are more debilitated are more susceptible to adverse side effects.

Substance Abuse and Risk of HIV Infection

A variety of exposure and host factors may influence seroconversion and progression of disease. Although these factors are not well understood, they may include altered baseline immune capacity and the presence of concurrent infections, most notably viral (herpes simplex, cytomegalovirus) and sexually transmitted diseases, all of which may have increased prevalence in substance-abusing populations. The classes of abused substances where both behavioral and biological risk factors for AIDS are of a major concern are considered here in brief.

Opiates

The exceptionally high risk of HIV transmission in opiate abusers has already been described. In addition, compromised immune function as a result of exposure to opiates may add to the risk of infection and disease progression. Brown, Stimmel, Taub, Kochwa, and Rosenfeld (1974) found reduced lymphocyte stimulation in response to various mitogens in heroin addicts, suggesting a possible impairment in cell-mediated immunity. Other studies found that, in addition to decreased lymphocyte functional responses, addicts had a significant reduction in numbers of T-cells when compared with normals (McDonough et al., 1980). Incubation of the addicts' cells with naloxone (an opiate antagonist) reversed some of the immune effects. It has been postulated that opiates bind reversibly to lymphocytes, blocking T-cell receptors and diminishing the ability to proliferate when stimulated (MacGregor, 1988).

Other reported immune abnormalities in opiate addicts include hyperactive B-cell activity, hyperglobulinemia, and increased opsonic capacity (MacGregor, 1988). The role of these factors in the development and progression of HIV-related disease requires investigation.

Alcohol

Alcoholics, who may also be polysubstance abusers, may be at increased risk of exposure to HIV by virtue of high-risk behaviors while under the disinhibiting influence of the drug. Stall, McKusick, Wiley, Coates, and Ostrow (1986) examined sexual behaviors of homosexual men under the influence of alcohol and other drugs such as marijuana and amyl nitrate. Men with high-risk sexual behaviors were 2 to 3.5 times more likely to use drugs during their sexual encounters than men who were considered at no risk for HIV exposure. In follow-up studies, Stall et al. (1986) found that men who remained at high risk were more than twice as likely to use alcohol during sexual activity, and 8 times more likely to use other drugs. Men who were originally at no risk but who showed increased risk at follow-up were more likely to use drugs during sexual activity than those remaining at low risk, and decreasing risk was associated with less frequent use of alcohol and drugs during sexual activity.

Once exposed to HIV, alcoholics may also be at increased risk of infection as a result of alcohol-related alterations in the immune system. Acute alcohol consumption has been implicated experimentally in the impairment of both cellular and humoral immunity (Smith & Palmer, 1976; Adams & Jordan, 1984; National Institute on Alcohol Abuse and Alcoholism, 1986; MacGregor, 1988). Lymphocyte function, antibody response to novel antigens, serum bactericidal activity, phagocyte function, and neutrophil migration and granulopoiesis are reported to be altered by alcohol. It is difficult, however, to extrapolate these experimental results to naturalistic settings in human users and abusers of alcohol. Moreover, the extent to which clinically relevant immunosuppression occurs in alcohol abusers without clinical liver disease is unclear. Patients with a history of excessive prolonged consumption of alcohol (Lieber, Seitz, Garro, & Worner, 1979; U.S. Department of Health and Human Services, 1987; Jerrels, Marietta, Bone, Weight, & Eckardt, 1988) and alcoholic liver disease (Kanagasundaram & Leevy, 1979) appear to have alterations in host defense mechanisms. In one study, alcoholics showed decreased delayed cutaneous hypersensitivity, compared with normal controls; the degree of inhibition was associated with the extent of liver damage (MacGregor, 1988). Alcoholics may also have decreased circulating lymphocytes, which return to normal levels after several days of abstinence. The decrease may be related to hepatocellular injury (MacGregor, 1988). Natural killer cell activity, which plays a role in resistance to viral infection and neoplasia and may be involved in progression of HIV infection (Fauci, 1988), is also inhibited by alcohol use (Ristow, Starkey, & Hass, 1982). Alterations in immune function are thought to play a role in the increased susceptibiltiy to infection found in alcoholics (Smith & Palmer, 1976; Adams & Jordan, 1984).

Other Drugs

Animal studies reveal that tetrahydrocannabinol (THC) in marijuana has an effect on cell-mediated immunity (Holsapple & Munson, 1985). *In vivo* studies in rodents show decreased delayed hypersensitivity reactions, depressed lymphocyte transformation, and decreased natural killer cell activity (MacGregor, 1988). Studies in humans, however, have been inconsistent. Some studies show reduced numbers of T-lymphocytes and impaired lymphocyte transformation, whereas others find normal functioning (MacGregor, 1988).

Several studies have examined the effects of cocaine on the immune system. Studies done in rodents show suppressed antibody response (Holsapple & Munson, 1985; Faith & Valentine, 1983), whereas reports on cocaine's effects on cell-mediated immunity have been conflicting (MacGregor, 1988).

The abuse of drugs in combination may have consequences for the immune system. There may be important interactions in relation to the immune system among opiates, alcohol, and cocaine (Donahoe & Falek, 1988). These interactions may either exaggerate or mitigate the immune effects of any single drug. Studies by Donahoe and Falek (1988), for example, suggest that opiates depress immune function and that cocaine reverses this depression when used in combination. However, when alcohol is used simultaneously with opiates and cocaine, the ability of cocaine to reverse the effects of opiates is attenuated. Since many alcoholics and other substance abusers do not restrict their substance use to a single drug, counseling concerning such drug use patterns in relation to AIDS risk may be of importance.

Behavior–Immune System Interactions

Other factors that are prevalent in alcoholics, opiate addicts, and other substance abusers may further compromise the immune system and increase the risk of HIV infection and disease. Malnutrition is an important factor suppressing various components of the immune system (MacGregor, 1988). Immune system effects associated with life stress, poor coping, and depression, which are highly prevalent in alcoholics and other substance abusers (Jaffe & Ciraulo, 1986; Schuckit & Bogard, 1986), may further exacerbate AIDS risk and disease progression in these populations. Research on life stress and immunity in humans has identified conditions in which altered (primarily suppressed) immunity, as well as increased medical morbidity, occurs. These conditions include losses such as the death of a spouse (Helsing, Szklo, & Comstock, 1981; Schleifer, Keller, Camerino, Thornton, & Stein, 1983; Bartrop, Lazarus, Luckherst, & Kiloh, 1977; Irwin, Daniels, Bloom, Smith, &

Weiner, 1987) and acute short-term stressors (Glaser & Kiecolt-Glaser, 1988). Depressive disorders and depressive reactions to life stress are also associated with altered immunity (Cappel, Gregoire, Thiry, & Sprecher, 1978; Kronfol et al., 1983; Schleifer et al., 1984; Schleifer, Keller, Siris, Davis, & Stein, 1985; Schleifer, Keller, Bond, Cohen, & Stein, 1989; Irwin et al., 1987; Avery & Winokur, 1976). Interventions to treat affective disorders in substance abusers may therefore have both medical and psychosocial benefits.

AIDS in Addiction Treatment

Introduction

Treatment of alcohol and drug abuse in persons infected with HIV or at risk for HIV infection raises special issues and concerns. First, those treating alcohol- and drug-addicted individuals must introduce prevention strategies into treatment plans, since these individuals are known to be at great risk of HIV infection. There is also a need for special interventions aimed at those individuals suffering from chemical dependency who already have AIDS or HIV infection.

Assessment of HIV risk behavior should be undertaken in the initial phases of drug treatment with frequent reassessments, and AIDS education should be a regular component of the treatment. IVDU patients should be instructed on the hazards of needle sharing and methods of needle sterilization, and all patients should be educated concerning safe sex. This includes explicit discussion of proper techniques of condom usage, as well as the importance of using condoms from the initiation of intercourse and other sex practices in which body fluids are transmitted. It is apparent, however, that altering risk behaviors in this population has many impediments. In general, substance abusers have been found to be relatively resistant to changing drug use behaviors. Reducing injection risk in IVDUs is hampered by conditions in which individuals may not invest time in finding clean needles or in needle cleaning because of their intense drug craving and the resulting urgency to inject. Engaging in sex to obtain drugs is common and may involve circumstances where safe sex practices are unlikely to be maintained. Intravenous cocaine users deserve special attention, since they are more likely to be exposed to multiple injections during drug use episodes. Counseling for non-IVDU substance abusers is no less important, especially when sex partners may be IVDUs (see "Prevention and Public Health," below). Crack users should be specifically targeted for counseling on sexual practices during intoxicated states. When intoxicated, individuals may exhibit hypersexuality or engage in sex in order to obtain more of the drug. It is also important to inquire and educate about occasional intravenous drug usage, especially in polydrug users who do not consider themselves to be IVDUs.

HIV testing in patients enrolling in substance abuse programs entails special clinical considerations, which are considered further below. At intake, a thorough assessment of HIV risk behavior and physical examination, including stigmata of HIV disease, should be undertaken. HIV testing at intake, however, may undermine participation in the program for some patients and may best be deferred until such patients have been engaged in treatment. At that time, they should receive counseling on HIV testing and be given an opportunity to take the test. For some individuals, either a positive or a negative HIV test can be a powerful motivating factor for continued treatment. Therapists can help facilitate this by stressing the connection between continued drug use and AIDS.

HIV Testing: Clinical Considerations

Screening for HIV infection within substance abuse programs is extremely controversial. It has been suggested by the Centers for Disease Control that all patients admitted to substance abuse programs be screened for the presence of HIV antibodies (Hawthorne & Siegel, 1988). Proponents of routine screening reason that knowledge of positive HIV status would encourage safe sex practices and discourage needle sharing. Another consideration in favor of routine screening is that early identification of seropositive individuals would allow prophylactic treatment with zidovudine (see the discussion of zidovudine treatment, above). Literature on the behavioral impact of HIV testing is mixed. Recent studies report that, at least for seropositive subjects, HIV testing and notification constitute a catalyst for needle use risk reduction among IVDUs in treatment (Casadonte, Des Jarlais, Smith, Novatt, & Hemdal, 1986; Cox, Selwyn, Schoenbaum, O'Dowd, & Drucker, 1986). From a study of 324 gay men, with a 3-month follow-up after testing, Farthing, Jesson, Taylor, Laurence, and Gazzard (1987) concluded that the majority of men wanted to know their antibody status and that having the test did encourage safer sex practices. By contrast, one study showed that 18 of 27 IVDU subjects dropped out of a methadone maintenance program over the short term, going back to intravenous drug use after learning that they were seropositive; at follow-up, however, the majority had returned to treatment (Marlink et al., 1987).

Knowledge of positive antibody status may have important implications for an individual's health care. Information on HIV status will aid physicians in evaluating patients with nonspecific medical, neurological, and psychiatric symptoms and will assist in the prompt recognition and treatment of infection (Stimmel, 1988). Women with positive HIV status may wish to avoid pregnancy, since there is a substantial risk (50%) of transmission to the fetus *in utero* (Abrams, 1987; Scott, Mastrucci, Hutto, & Parks, 1987). The impact HIV testing has had on pregnancy decisions is unclear. A study done in Paris reported that 38% of women studied terminated their pregnancies after learning they were seropositive (Ciraru-Vigneron et al., 1988). A study done in New York reported that 67% of a group of women found to be seropositive opted

to terminate their pregnancies, but this percentage was not significantly different from that of seronegative women (E. Schoenbaum, personal communication to Polly Thomas, M.D., Director of AIDS Surveillance, New York City
Department of Health, 1988).

Opponents of routine screening point to the lack of proven treatments for
asymptomatic HIV-positive persons, as well as the psychological and social
risks to those found to be positive. Studies of homosexual and bisexual men by
Ostrow (1987) suggested that knowledge of HIV viral status does not alter
sexual behaviors. Opponents argue that routine screening may stigmatize
those in high-risk groups, leading to discrimination and denial of health
insurance benefits. There are also reports of knowledge of positive HIV status
having adverse psychological effects, including suicidal behavior (Glass, 1988).

With respect to IVDUs and other substance-abusing persons, the impact
of HIV testing on behaviors is even less clear. Such individuals may have
underlying personality and behavioral problems that may make them especially likely to act out in a self-destructive manner, including relapse into
substance abuse, when confronted with HIV testing results (whether positive
or negative). Substance abusers may also be less likely to respond emotionally
and behaviorally to what may be perceived as just one more health risk
identified by health care providers.

Although no general consensus among physicans treating drug-addicted
individuals regarding routine HIV testing has been reached, the need for
effective counseling regarding disease prevention and HIV testing is apparent.
Substance-abusing patients should be educated about the significance of positive and negative results. Pre- and posttest counseling is indicated and should
also address the issue of modifying risk behaviors such as needle sharing and
unsafe sex. Patients should be counseled on the symptoms associated with
altered immunity and the possible effects of alcohol and drugs on the immune
system (Stimmel, 1988). The fact that substance abuse may influence both
susceptibility to and progression of HIV disease (see below) should be included
in therapeutic work with IVDUs and other substance abusers.

HIV testing raises ethical issues that are not readily resolved. For example,
if an individual is found to be HIV-antibody-positive, is there a duty to warn
the spouse or partner of such an individual? How will this affect the therapeutic relationship? The ethical and legal aspects of such questions are being
actively considered; these may vary from state to state in relation to social as
well as psychological considerations.

HIV Testing: Guidelines for Counseling

Before HIV testing is done, an individual should receive pretest counseling
(Smith, 1988). The therapist should first assess the patient's current knowledge
about AIDS and AIDS testing. He or she should then explain what the test
means in clear, easy-to-understand language. It is important to assess the
individual's risk factors: What substances are used? In what social context?

Does this patient share needles or engage in risky sexual behaviors (especially when intoxicated)? Does the individual live in or frequent areas of endemic HIV? Answers to these questions may be difficult to obtain, because some patients may not be truthful and others may not remember their behaviors. Once the patient's risk status is defined, he or she should be informed of this status and counseled on effective means of reducing risk behavior.

The therapist should also assess the individual's anticipated emotional and behavioral response to a positive test result. The patient's social support system and coping strategies should be evaluated, and it may be helpful for the patient to participate in a cognitive rehearsal of adaptive coping skills. Before testing is done, the patient's informed consent must be obtained and adequate follow-up arrangements made.

Posttest counseling and follow-up involve additional considerations. When the clinician is informing an individual of a positive test result, it is important to explain the several possible meanings of a positive test. That is, in most cases, the virus should be considered to be present and potentially active, although the individual should not assume that he or she has AIDS. At present, between 10% and 40% of HIV-positive individuals are expected to develop AIDS over the next 10 years.

Once the patient has been informed of a positive test result, he or she should be monitored closely for delayed emotional reactions. Special attention should be given to those individuals with concurrent depression and other mental disorders. Suicide risk cannot be ignored. The patient should be given an opportunity to ask questions about the test and to respond to the results. The therapist should also provide the patient with appropriate referrals for medical and psychological follow-up, and should educate the patient on methods for preventing transmission of the virus to others. It should also be emphasized that the majority of people becoming seropositive do not develop AIDS over the short term but can still transmit the infection.

Counseling for persons testing negative should emphasize the limitations of the test (see above), including the possibility that they have in fact been infected; the need for continued HIV precautions should be reiterated. IVDUs who test negative may conclude they they are resistant to HIV infection and therefore free to undertake or continue high-risk behavior. Such erroneous conclusions should be pre-emptively addressed. The counselor should be aware that receiving a negative HIV report may pose psychological risks for some individuals who have been expecting positivity and for whom the test has substantial or idiosyncratic affective loading. Factors such as survival guilt may be relevant.

Clinical Assessment and Management

AIDS has many physical and emotional effects that complicate the treatment of patients with both AIDS and chemical dependency. Substance abuse treatment units may expect an increased need for medical involvement in the treatment of chemically dependent patients, because of the increased incidence of HIV seropositivity among this population. The presence of AIDS patients in drug treatment units elicits complex feelings in the staff and in other patients. Issues of death and dying are prevalent; patients may express feeling of hopelessness and question the value or practicality of abstinence from drug and alcohol use. Arrangements for aftercare and placement of patients with AIDS following inpatient treatment may be difficult. Issues of confidentiality and required HIV testing are of special concern (see the discussion of legal issues, below).

The dual diagnoses of AIDS and substance abuse make treatment of chemical dependency difficult. A patient's family members and significant others, who are often instrumental in motivating a drug-addicted individual for treatment, may, in the the face of AIDS, overlook or be reluctant to confront the substance abuse problem. Physicians and other health workers may also tend to overlook an individual's addiction in light of his or her overwhelming physical illness. The medical, psychosocial, and social morbidity of substance abuse, however, is no less catastrophic in the AIDS patient and may actually be exacerbated. For example, continued drug use in HIV-infected individuals may accelerate the course of AIDS (Rothenberg et al., 1987). Dismissal of a patient's addiction problem may also convey the dehumanizing message that the patient's problems of life are no longer relevant since he or she is "terminal" and "hopeless."

It is also important not to focus on substance abuse issues alone, to the point of excluding AIDS-related psychological needs. Anxiety and depression, complicated at times by cognitive impairment, may accompany the progression of the disease, and suicidal ideation is common. These symptoms should be evaluated frequently throughout the course of treatment. The therapist should also be aware that the patient may at times become overwhelmed by his or her illness, with grief and a sense of loss.

The family members of HIV-infected substance abusers require special consideration. Family difficulties may arise or be heightened as a result of the diagnosis of AIDS and its protean clinical manifestations. The HIV-positive individual may have difficulty in confiding in family members about his or her seropositivity. He or she may fear rejection or reprisal from others. The family may feel overwhelmed by the immense caretaking needs that the patient may have or develop. Feelings of helplessness and hopelessness in the family may result in passive or active undermining of substance abuse treatment. The therapist must take a flexible approach and be willing to discuss openly the feelings and problems that will arise as the result of AIDS diagnosis. It is important for the therapist to realize that the family may go through a bereavement process when a loved one is diagnosed with AIDS. A lover or spouse may experience survivor guilt, wondering why the patient was diagnosed with AIDS and he or she was not (Faltz & Madover, 1988). The family members may benefit from referral to AIDS support groups in their community during this time. Finally, a person with AIDS may receive care from a variety of health professionals and social service agencies; it is important that the therapist make some contact with these agencies, in order to coordinate and promote cooperation among the various caregivers.

It is not only the patient and family members who will have difficulty coping with the diagnosis of AIDS and its course. In therapists and other staff members, countertransference issues linked to fear of contagion, addictophobia, fear of homosexuality, denial of helplessness, and need for professional omnipotence often arise when treating AIDS patients (Faltz & Madover, 1988). The fear of contagion can be exaggerated and may stem from an unconscious need to avoid the illicit impulses these patients represent. Mechanisms such as displacement and reaction formation may be involved (Perry & Markowitz, 1986) and can result in failure to maintain appropriate empathic distance from the patients. The therapist must be careful to avoid becoming overwhelmed by what he or she feels the patient is experiencing. Taking a moralistic attitude toward the patient's drug use and sexual behaviors must be assiduously avoided, and the therapist must confront his or her own feelings and attitudes toward drug addiction, homosexuality and AIDS. Fears and countertransference of the staff and caregivers can be partly assuaged by providing specific information about transmission precautions and by support from supervisors and coworkers.

Legal Issues Involving the Treatment of Patients Infected with HIV

Substance abuse professionals must be aware of the legal concerns involved in caring for persons infected with HIV. AIDS-related legal issues are a developing area of the law; as such, it is impossible to give definitive guidelines.

Issues of confidentiality arise when treating individuals with drug addiction and HIV infection. Pascal (1987) points out that federal law protects the confidentiality of the patient records for persons under treatment for drug abuse. This includes drug-abusing patients who have AIDS. (There is, however, no general federal confidentiality protection for medical records of AIDS patients who are not being treated for drug abuse.) These federal regulations protect oral as well as written communications.

Treatment programs may identify patients with HIV infection to staff members, so that appropriate precautions and guidelines for clinical care can be followed. Laboratory personnel may also be advised of an individual's HIV status, since they are handling infected body fluids; however, a written agreement to protect patient confidentiality must be obtained from lab personnel (Pascal, 1987). Disclosure to those outside the clinical setting is permitted only with the patient's written consent. Reporting of HIV status to public health authorities may be required in some states, and such status may be disclosed without the patient's consent to the extent required by law. In all other situations, disclosure without the patient's consent must be obtained through a court order based on a finding of good cause (Pascal, 1987).

Once a caregiver has knowledge of a positive HIV status, he or she is obligated to inform that individual. Failure to do so may make the caregiver liable for any harm that results to the individual or his or her partners (Pascal, 1987).

Since AIDS is a fatal communicable disease, situations may arise in which the physician or therapist is aware of a danger posed to a third party, such as a spouse, cohabitant, or sexual partner. HIV-positive patients should be counseled on their responsibilities and encouraged to voluntarily report their status to third parties who may be at risk for infection (Pascal, 1987). If a substance abuse program considers it indicated to warn a third party concerning a patient's HIV status, either the patient's consent or a court order must be obtained, in order to comply with federal confidentiality regulations. An alternative to warning specific individuals may be to institute a policy of universal education for all patients, their spouses, significant others, and caregivers. Whether such a policy would be an acceptable legal defense is not known. The policy is consistent, however, with the consensus public health viewpoint that education, prevention, and voluntary measures are the best approaches to stemming the AIDS epidemic, and that punitive approaches are counterproductive (Pascal, 1987).

During the final stages of illness, AIDS patients may experience cognitive deficits, and issues of competency should be addressed in an appropriate manner.

Prevention and Public Health

As already noted, no effective cure for AIDS has yet been identified; therefore, prevention is the strongest defense against further spread of this fatal disease. Studies examining behavioral changes in response to the AIDS epidemic indicate that some IVDUs are attempting risk reduction, especially in needle sharing (Des Jarlais & Friedman, 1987; Selwyn, Cox, Feiner, Lipshutz, & Cohen, 1985). Prevention strategies to reduce the risk of exposure to contaminated needles include (1) cessation of intravenous drug use; (2) cessation of needle sharing; (3) methadone maintenance and drug-free treatment programs; and (4) needle sterilization.

Although needle sharing is quite common, it is not a universal pattern among IVDUs. Sharing practices are influenced by many factors, including economics, regional drug norms, needle availability, length of habit, drug of choice (e.g., heroin, cocaine, multiple substances, etc.), and others. Abusers who frequent "shooting galleries," where needles and syringes are anonymously shared by multiple IVDUs, may be at particular risk. However, in some places, these have also become sites for bleach distribution. Intravenous cocaine users may use multiple injections in a drug use episode, which further increases their risk of infection. In addition, the practice of needle sharing is associated with socialization processes (Howard & Borges, 1970). Individuals may share needles not only because of a shortage of clean needles, but also because they wish to foster feelings of camaraderie and brotherhood. Those who refuse to share needles may be distrusted by others and suspected of having disease.

There is some indication that IVDUs are attempting to reduce their risk by altering needle-sharing behaviors. In a study of 59 patients attending a methadone maintenance program, 59% reported some form of risk reduction; 31% increased their use of clean needles and/or the cleaning of needles; 29% reduced needle sharing; and 14% reported reduced drug injection (Des Jarlais & Friedman, 1987). IVDUs with appropriate AIDS knowledge reported that their consistent use of sterile, new needles was dependent on availability (Des Jarlais, Friedman, & Hopkins, 1985). If clean needles were unavailable, whatever needles that were handy were used. Individuals were most likely to obtain needles at the time of the drug purchase, and desire to use the drug immediately influenced the decision to use whatever needles were available.

Outreach programs have been developed to teach needle sterilization techniques as a form of AIDS prevention. Newmeyer and colleagues (see Smith, 1988) have developed an outreach program in which IVDUs are instructed in the sterilization technique and then provided with bottles of bleach and condoms for their own use. The IVDUs are given firsthand instruction and education in prevention, and immediately provided with the necessary tools to begin utilizing this technique. This program also serves to trigger discussion about AIDS and risk behaviors and encourages IVDUs to actively protect themselves from the AIDS virus (Smith, 1988).

An area of much debate is whether or not sterile needles and syringes should be made available to drug-addicted individuals. This practice has been undertaken in Europe, but its proposed introduction in New York City and other U.S. locations has been highly controversial. Proponents note the importance of clean-needle availability in this population and advocate a needle exchange program in addition to education. Those opposing the needle exchange programs feel that providing free needles to drug-addicted individuals will encourage increased intravenous drug use. Studies of needle exchange programs in Amsterdam do not show decreased enrollment in drug treatment programs, nor has there been an increase in intravenous drug use (Des Jarlais & Friedman, 1987).

Increasing the numbers of IVDUs enrolled in methadone maintenance and drug-free programs has been considered as a means of reducing intravenous drug use. One concern about such a strategy relates to the effects of opiates on the immune system and the possibility that methadone may have an immunosuppressant effect (Smith, 1988).

The potential for the spread of AIDS through heterosexual transmission among IVDUs, as well as transmission from IVDUs to non-IVDU heterosexual partners, is a challenging public health problem. At present, sexual contact with IVDUs is the most common mode of transmission for heterosexual cases of AIDS (Murphy, 1988). Male IVDUs are an especially important vector for the spread of HIV into the general population. Murphy (1988) found that male IVDUs reported a greater percentage of non-IVDU heterosexual contacts than did female IVDUs. Similar findings were reported by Des Jarlais et al. (1987). In contrast, female IVDUs may be at particular risk for being exposed to HIV as a result of heterosexual behaviors and needle sharing. Des Jarlais et al. (1987) reported that female IVDUs were more likely than male IVDUs to have sexual contacts who were also IVDUs and who also tended to be needle sharers. Women who shared needles had twice as many IVDU sexual partners as did females who did not share needles, while the majority of sexual partners of male needle sharers were not themselves needle sharers. These findings are consistent with other observations of social, psychological, and sexual affiliations among IVDUs (Howard & Borges, 1970).

Summary

IVDUs are becoming a primary vector in the transmission of HIV to other adults and to children in the general population. Health care providers have a major responsibility to provide education and promote prevention in this group. HIV testing and counseling should be made readily available to those who desire it. Those IVDUs who are unable to abstain from intravenous drug use may benefit from therapeutic educational strategies concerned with reducing needle sharing and using needle sterilization techniques. Counselors involved in the treatment of drug-addicted individuals should be prepared to discuss issues of safe sex and condom usage openly, as well as to discuss the effects of intoxication on sexual behavior and AIDS risk. Those involved in the care of drug-addicted individuals should be aware of the wide range of presenting signs and symptoms of HIV infection.

The extraordinary rates of HIV infection among substance abusers suggest that these individuals will occupy an increasing proportion of inpatient beds. Places for those with HIV infection or AIDS will be increasingly required on alcohol and drug treatment units. Education concerning substance abuse for medical staff and about AIDS for drug treatment staff is required to minimize difficulties in managing these patients. As the incidence of HIV infection increases among the drug-addicted population, the potential for spread into other populations is also increasing. Additional resources for drug education treatment, prevention, rehabilitation, and research are urgently needed.

References

Abrams, E. (1987). *New York City Collaborative Study Group of Maternal Transmission of Human Immunodeficiency Virus: Longitudinal study on infants born to women at risk for AIDS. One year report.* Paper presented at the 27th Interscience Conference on Antimicrobial Agents and Chemotherapy, New York.

Adams, H., & Jordan, C. (1984). Infections in the alcoholic. *Medical Clinics of North America, 68,* 179–200.

Avery, D., & Winokur, G. (1976). Mortality in depressed patients treated with electroconvulsive therapy and antidepressants. *Archives of General Psychiatry, 33,* 1029–1037.

Bartrop, R. W., Lazarus, L., Luckherst, E., & Kiloh, L. H. (1977). Depressed lymphocyte function after bereavement. *Lancet, i,* 834–836.

Brown, S., Stimmel, B., Taub, R., Kochwa, S., & Rosenfeld, R. (1974). Immunological dysfunction in heroin addicts. *Archives of Internal Medicine, 134,* 1001–1006.

Cappel, R., Gregoire, L., Thiry, L., & Sprecher, S. (1978). Antibody and cell mediated immunity to herpes simplex virus in psychotic depression. *Journal of Clinical Psychiatry, 39,* 266.

Carpenter, C. J., & Mayer, K. (1988). Advances in AIDS and HIV infection. *Advances in Internal Medicine, 33,* 45–80.

Casadonte, P., Des Jarlais, D., Smith, T., Novatt, A., & Hemdal, P. (1986). *Psychological and behavioral impact of learning HTLV III/LAV antibody test results.* Paper presented at the Second International Conference on AIDS, Paris.

Centers for Disease Control. (1986). CDC classification system for HIV infection. *Morbidity and Mortality Weekly Reports, 35,* 334–339.

Centers for Disease Control. (1989). CDC update: Acquired immunodeficiency syndrome associated with intravenous drug use—United States, 1988. *Morbidity and Mortality Weekly Reports, 38,* 165–170.

Ciraru-Vigneron, N., Nguyen, Tan Lung, R., Bereau, G., Sauvanet, E., Bitton, C., Brunner, C., Boizard, B., Wautier, J. L., & Ravina, J. H. (1988). *Prospective study for HIV infection among high risk pregnant women: Follow-up of 60 women, 37 children and 30 families.* Paper presented at the Fourth International Conference on AIDS, Stockholm.

Cox, C., Selwyn, P., Schoenbaum, E., O'Dowd, M., & Drucker, E. (1986). *Psychological and behavioral consequences of HTLV-III/LAV antibody testing among intravenous drug users in a methadone maintenance program in New York.* Paper presented at the Second International Conference on AIDS, Paris.

Curran, J. W., Morgan, W., Hardy, A. M., Jaffe, H. W., Darrow, W. W. & Dowdle, W. R. (1985). The epidemiology of AIDS: Current status and future prospects. *Science, 229,* 1352–1357.

Des Jarlais, D. C., Friedman, S. R., & Hopkins, W. (1985). Risk reduction for AIDS among intravenous drug users. *Annals of Internal Medicine, 103,* 755–759.

Des Jarlais, D. C., & Friedman, S. (1987). HIV infection among intravenous drug users: Epidemiology and risk reduction. *AIDS, 1,* 67–76.

Des Jarlais, D. C., Wish, E., Friedman, S. R., Stoneburner, R., Yancovitz, S. R., Mildvan, D., el Sadr, W., Brady, E., & Cuadrado, M. (1987). Intravenous drug use and the heterosexual transmission of the human immunodeficiency virus: Current trends in New York City. *New York State Journal of Medicine,* 283–286.

Donahoe, R. M., & Falek, A. (1988). Neuroimmunomodulation by opiates and other drugs of abuse: Relationship to HIV infection and AIDS. *Advances in Biochemical Psychopharmacology, 44,* 145–158.

Faith, R. E., & Valentine, J. L. (1983). Effects of cocaine exposure on immune function. *Toxicology, 3,* 56.

Faltz, B., & Madover, S. (1988). Treatment of substance abuse in patients with HIV infection. *Advances in Alcohol and Substance Abuse, 7*(2), 143–157.

Farthing, C. F., Jesson, W., Taylor, H. C., Laurence, A. G., & Gazzard, B. G. (1987, June). *The HIV antibody test: Influence on sexual behavior of homosexual men.* Paper presented at the National Institutes of Health AIDS Conference, Bethesda, MD.

Fauci, A. S. (1985). The acquired immunodeficiency syndrome: An update. *Annals of Internal Medicine, 102,* 800–813.

Fauci, A. S. (1988). The human immunodeficiency virus: Infectivity and mechanisms of pathogenesis. *Science, 239,* 617–622.

Glaser, R., & Kiecolt-Glaser, J. (1988). Stress-associated immune suppression and acquired immune deficiency syndrome (AIDS). *Advances in Biochemical Psychopharmacology, 44,* 203–205.

Glass, R. M. (1988). AIDS and suicide [Editorial]. *Journal of the American Medical Association, 259*(9), 1369–1370.

Hawthorne, W., & Siegel, L. (1988). Should there be HIV testing in chemical dependency treatment programs? *Advances in Alcohol and Substance Abuse, 7*(2), 15–19.

Helsing, K. J., Szklo, M., Comstock, G. W. (1981). Factors associated with mortality after widowhood. *American Journal of Public Health, 71,* 802–809.

Holsapple, M. P., & Munson, A. F. (1985). Immunotoxicology of abused drugs. In J. Dean, M. I. Luster, A. E. Munson, & H. Amos (Eds.), *Immunotoxicology and immunopharmacology* (pp. 381–392). New York: Raven Press.

Howard, J., & Borges, P. (1970). Needle sharing in the Haight: Some social and psychological functions. *Journal of Health and Social Behavior, 11*(3), 220–230.

Irwin, M. R., Daniels, M., Bloom, E. T., Smith, T. L., & Weiner, H. (1987). Life events, depressive symptoms and immune function. *American Journal of Psychiatry, 144,* 437–441.

Jaffe, H. W., Bregman, D. J., & Selik, R. M. (1983). AIDS in the U.S.: The first 1,000 cases. *Journal of Infectious Diseases, 148,* 339–345.

Jaffe, J. H., & Ciraulo, D. A. (1986). Alcoholism and depression. In R. E. Meyer (Ed.), *Psychopathology and addictive disorders* (pp. 293–320). New York: Guilford Press.

Jerrels, T. R., Marietta, C. A., Bone, G., Weight, F. F., & Eckardt, M. J. (1988). Ethanol-associated immunosuppression. *Advances in Biochemical Psychopharmacology, 44,* 173–186.

Kanagasundaram, N., & Leevy, C. (1979). Immunologic aspects of liver disease. *Medical Clinics of North America, 63,* 631–642.

Kronfol, Z., Silva, J., Greden, J., Dembinski, S., Gardner, R., & Carroll, B. (1983). Impaired lymphocyte function in depressive illness. *Life Sciences, 33,* 241–247.

Laure, F., Rouzioux, C., Veber, F., Jacomet, C., Courgnaud, V., Blanche, S., Burgard, M., Griscelli, C., & Brechot, C. (1988). Detection of HIV1 DNA in infants and children by means of the polymerase chain reaction. *Lancet, ii,* 538–541.

Lieber, C. S., Seitz, H. K., Garro, A. J., & Worner, T. M. (1979). Alcohol-related diseases and carcinogenesis. *Cancer Research, 39,* 2863–2886.

MacGregor, R. (1988). Alcohol and drugs as co-factors for AIDS. *Advances in Alcohol and Substance Abuse, 7*(2), 47–71.

Marlink, R., Foss, B., Swift, R., Davis, W., Essex, M., & Groopman, J. (1987). *High rate of HTLVIII/HIV exposure in IVDA's from a small sized city and the failure of specialized methadone maintenance to prevent further drug use.* Paper presented at the Third International Conference on AIDS, Washington, DC.

McDonough, R. J., Madden, J. J., Falek, A., Shafer, D. A., Pline, M., Gordon, D., Bokos, P., Kuehnle, J. C., & Mendelson, J. (1980). Alteration of T- and null lymphocyte frequencies in the peripheral blood of human opiate addicts: In vivo evidence for opiate receptor sites on T-lymphocytes. *Journal of Immunology, 125,* 2539–2543.

Miles, S. A. (1988). Diagnosis and staging of HIV infection. *American Family Physician, 38*(4), 248–256.

Murphy, D. L. (1988). Heterosexual contacts of intravenous drug abusers: Implications for the next spread of the AIDS epidemic. *Advances in Alcohol and Substance Abuse, 7*(2), 89–97.

National Institute on Alcohol Abuse and Alcoholism. (1986). *The effects of alcohol on the immune system: Summary of a workshop to provide policy and research recommendations to the NIAAA* (Alcohol Research Utilization System Working Document No. 85-02). Rockville, MD: Author.

Navia, B. A., Jordan, B. D., & Price, R. W. (1986). The AIDS dementia complex: I. Clinical features. *Annals of Neurology, 19*(6), 517–524.

Ostrow, D. (1987). Antibody testing won't cut risky behavior. *AMA News,* June 5.

Pascal, C. B. (1987). Selected legal issues about AIDS for drug abuse treatment programs. *Journal of Psychoactive Drugs, 19*(1), 1–12.

Perry, S. W., & Markowitz, J. (1986). Psychiatric interventions for AIDS spectrum disorders. *Hospital and Community Psychiatry, 37,* 1001–1006.

Pohl, M. (1988). Neurocognitive impairment in alcoholics: Review and comparison with cognitive impairment due to AIDS. *Advances in Alcohol and Substance Abuse, 7*(2), 107–116.

Ristow, S. S., Starkey, J. R., & Hass, G. M. (1987). Inhibition of natural killer cell activity *in vitro* by alcohols. *Biochemistry and Biophysics Research Communications, 105,* 1315–1321.

Rothenberg, R., Woefel, M., Stoneburner, R., Milberg, J., Parker, R., & Truman, B. (1987). Survival with the acquired immunodeficiency syndrome. *New England Journal of Medicine, 317,* 1297–1302.

Schindzielorz, A. (1989). HIV-1 serology and AIDS testing: A practical approach to understanding. *Southern Medical Journal, 82,* 1529–1533.

Schleifer, S. J., Keller, S. E., Bond, R., Cohen, J., & Stein, M. (1989). Major depressive disorder and immunity. *Archives of General Psychiatry, 46,* 81–87.

Schleifer, S. J., Keller, S. E., Camerino, M., Thornton, J. C., & Stein, M. (1983). Suppression of lymphocyte stimulation following bereavement. *Journal of the American Medical Association, 250,* 374.

Schleifer, S. J., Keller, S. E., Meyerson, A. T. Raskin, M. J., Davis, K. L., & Stein, M. (1984). Lymphocyte function in major depressive disorder. *Archives of General Psychiatry, 41,* 484–486.

Schleifer, S. J., Keller, S. E., Siris, S. G., Davis, K. L., & Stein, M. (1985). Depression and immunity. *Archives of General Psychiatry, 42,* 129–133.

Schmitt, F. A., Bigley, J. W., McKinnis, R., Logue, P., Evans, R., & Drucker, J. (1988). Neuropsychological outcome of zidovudine (AZT) treatment of patients with AIDS and AIDS-related complex. *New England Journal of Medicine, 319,* 24.

Schucket, M., & Bogard, B. (1986). Intravenous drug use in alcoholics. *Journal of Clinical Psychiatry, 47,* 11.

Scott, G. G., Mastrucci, M. T., Hutto, S. C., & Parks, W. P. (1987). *Mothers of infants with HIV infection: Outcome of subsequent pregnancies.* Paper presented at the Third International Conference on AIDS, Washington, DC.

Selwyn, P. A., Cox, C. P., Feiner, C., Lipshutz, C., & Cohen, R. L. (1985, September). *Knowledge about AIDS and high risk behavior among intravenous drug abusers in New York City.* Paper presented at the annual meeting of the American Public Health Association, Washington, DC.

Selwyn, P. A., Feingold, A. R., Hartel, D., Schoenbaum, E. E., Alderman, M. H., Klein, R. S., & Friedland, G. H. (1988). Increased risk of bacterial pneumonia in HIV-infected intravenous drug users without AIDS. *AIDS, 2,* 267–272.

Selwyn, P. A., Hartel, D., Lewis, V., Schoenbaum, E., Vermund, S., Klein, R., Walker, A., & Friedland, G. (1989). A prospective study of the risk of tuberculosis among intravenous drug users with human immunodeficiency virus infection. *New England Journal of Medicine, 320,* 545–550.

Smith, D. (1988). The role of substance abuse professionals in the AIDS epidemic. *Advances in Alcohol and Substance Abuse, 7*(2), 175–195.

Smith, F. E., & Palmer, D. L. (1976). Alcoholism, infection and altered host defenses: A review of clinical and experimental observations. *Journal of Chronic Diseases, 29,* 35–49.

Stall, R., McKusick, L., Wiley, J., Coates, T. J., & Ostrow, D. G. (1986). Alcohol and drug use during sexual activity and compliance with safe sex guidelines for AIDS: The AIDS Behavior Research Project. *Health Education Quarterly, 13*(4), 359–371.

Stimmel, B. (1988). To test or not to test: The value of routine testing for antibodies to the human immunodeficiency virus (HIV). *Advances in Alcohol and Substance Abuse, 7*(2), 21–28.

Stoneburner, R. L., Des Jarlais, D. C., Benzra, D., Gorelkin, L., Sotheran, J., Friedman, S., Schultz, S., Marmor, M., Mildvan, D., & Malansky, R. (1988). A larger spectrum of severe HIV-1 related disease in intravenous drug users in New York City. *Science, 242,* 916–919.

U.S. Department of Health and Human Services. (1987). *Alcohol and health: Sixth special report to the U.S. Congress.* Washington, DC: U.S. Government Printing Office.

14

Adolescent Substance Abuse

YIFRAH KAMINER

Research on substance abuse in adolescents started to gain momentum in the 1970s, when epidemiological and etiological issues became the foci of investigation. Treatment-related issues in this age group were not really explored until the 1980s. Unfortunately, the published research examining substance abuse in adolescents is still meager, compared to the adult substance abuse literature.

The relative scarcity of results derived from methodologically sound investigations among adolescent substance abusers creates difficulties with the interpretation, practical implications, and generalization of the findings. Because the rates of substance use and abuse among American high school seniors and college students are still the highest in the industrialized world (Johnston, Bachman, & O'Malley, 1988), not to mention the rates among high school dropouts, the concern among health professionals who are looking for reliable solutions to substance abuse and problems related to substance abuse is clear and justified.

For example, the following are important questions that need to be researched further: What, if any, differences exist between adolescent and adult substance abuse? What is the natural history of substance abuse in adolescents? Are the present nosology, treatment, and prevention strategies relevant and satisfactory to the needs of this age group? The situation of adolescent substance abuse at present is similar to that of other domains of child and adolescent psychiatry, such as affective disorders, during the course of their conceptual and historical development: It is trying to achieve "separation–individuation" from the corresponding domain in general psychiatry.

Nosology

The ideal diagnostic label indicates the cause of a disorder, the most likely prognosis, and the best available treatment, (Schuckit, Zisook, & Mortola, 1985). The various substance abuse diagnostic systems proposed for adults through the years have been changed frequently. The National Council on Alcoholism's criteria, the Feighner criteria, and the Research Diagnostic Criteria (Spitzer, Endicott, & Robins, 1978) were criticized for various impediments; one of the most prominent of them was overemphasis on the physical consequences of alcohol use and on the later stages of the illness.

In the third edition of the *Diagnostic and Statistical Manual of Mental Disorders* (DSM-III; American Psychiatric Association, 1980), a separate category of substance use disorders was created, and a separate diagnosis of substance abuse was added as distinct from the diagnosis of substance dependence. However, the DSM-III diagnosis of substance dependence, because it relied on physical evidence of dependence, could rarely apply to adolescents due to the infrequent occurrence of physical sequelae in this young age group (Filstead, 1982).

The category of psychoactive substance use disorders in the revised third edition of DSM (DSM-III-R; American Psychiatric Association, 1987) represents a substantial change from the DSM-III criteria. Despite a field trial finding high levels of agreement between DSM-III and DSM-III-R in an adult clinical population (Rounsaville, Spitzer, & Williams, 1986), the value of the DSM-III-R psychoactive substance use diagnoses in terms of relevance to adolescents has not been established. The distinction between adult and adolescent substance abusers is important because of the many differences between the two populations. For example, chronicity and pervasiveness of drinking are more frequent among adult alcoholics than in drinking adolescents (Blane, 1979). Also, adolescents are less commonly diagnosed with immediate, severe physical effects of substance abuse, such as craving and withdrawal symptoms (Filstead, 1982). In view of these basic differences between substance abuse patterns and consequences, one cannot predict that even a valid diagnostic system for adult substance use would be as valid for adolescents.

It appears that the following criteria serve at present as a basis for operational definitions and diagnosis of adolescent substance abuse:

1. Objective use characteristics, such as quantity and frequency. For example, problem drinking by adolescents, as defined by the National Institute on Alcohol Abuse and Alcoholism (NIAAA, 1981–1982), is drinking to the point of being drunk six or more times a year.

2. "Symptomatic" use behaviors, such as intoxication, blackout, and the like.

3. Areas of functional impairment presumed to be due to substance abuse (Pandina, 1986). Such negative consequences, according to the NIAAA (1981–1982), must occur at least twice per year in order to be considered part of the problem drinking syndrome. They include impaired relationships with family, peers, or teachers; problems with school, police, or dates; and/or driving after drinking (Pandina, 1986).

The diagnosis of adolescent substance abusers may be made more difficult than necessary by the patient's and peers' withholding of information. The possible legal and disciplinary consequences followng under-age drinking or illicit substance abuse are some of the main reasons why diagnosis based solely on adolescent self-report may be incomplete and distorted. Unfortunately, parents are in many cases a poor source for information, especially regarding the type and patterns of substances used, because adolescents will withhold the truth from them as well.

It appears that the present DSM-III-R criteria for the diagnosis of adolescent substance abuse compensate to a substantial degree for the relative lack of relevance to this age group of some of the criteria for the separate diagnosis of psychoactive substance dependence, and enable us to lower the threshold for this diagnosis. The advantage in lowering the threshold for the diagnosis of substance abuse among adolescents lies in the increased potential of identifying adolescents at the onset of their substance abuse or when the symptomatology is mild. However, there are at least two disadvantages to be considered; (1) Lowering the threshold may increase the difficulty in differentiating between use (in its various forms) and abuse, and consequently raises the question of when the identified adolescent needs treatment; (2) the drug and alcohol treatment community, which is strongly loyal to the "disease" concept of addiction, is reluctant to accept operational criteria that do not overlap with the "disease" model. Such a conflict may hamper the integration of the adolescent substance abuser into self-help groups, which play an important role in the community. So although the ideal diagnosis should indicate the cause of the disorder, the most likely prognosis, and the best available treatment, caution is warranted when the scientific merits of a psychiatric diagnosis of substance abuse are being contrasted with the practical implications of such a diagnosis to the young patient.

Several present and future directions appear to be promising in the quest for an appropriate classification of substance abuse among adolescents. There is growing evidence that alcoholism may not be a unitary concept and that a subdivision of population of alcohol abusers into homogeneous subgroups may have impact on further development of the nosology (Meyer, 1986). For instance, subgroups can be classified on the basis of similar etiology, family history, age of onset, course, prognosis, and treatment response (Bukstein, Brent, & Kaminer, 1989).

The reports that Type 2 alcohol abusers (see "Genetic and Biological Factors," below) have been found to begin using alcohol at an early age (usually under age 20), and to have different associated psychopathology, may indicate that this type may have a different clinical course, prognosis, and treatment implications than other types (Buydens-Branchey, Branchey, & Noumair, 1989).

Future classification may also rely on biological markers or on biochemical parameters, such as relationship of susceptibility to serotonin precursor availability (Buydens-Branchey, Branchey, Noumair, & Lieber, 1989).

Consideration of the natural history of various subgroups of adolescent substance abusers may establish an interesting direction. Adolescent alcohol abusers who recover without treatment, or who may be able to achieve nonabusive drinking, may create a nosological challenge to be explored that may be comparable, for example, to "good-prognosis schizophrenia." Further empirical study that considers the constant changes and developments in the typologies of substance abuse will certainly emerge to explore the nosology of adolescent substance abuse.

In this chapter, the terms "substance abuse" and "drug and alcohol abuse" are used interchangeably as generic terms, unless one of these or other terms are specifically used as part of a formal classification system. Also, most of the examples pertain to the alcohol research, because much more research to date has been conducted on adolescent alcohol abuse than on abuse of illegal substances.

The Extent of the Problem

The measurement of the substance abuse problem is complicated by the fact that drug abuse is an illicit behavior and that populations of interest may not volunteer the essential information (Kozel & Adams, 1986). Repeated cross-sectional surveys are used to monitor trends, changes in the attitudes of the adult and adolescent population, and the prevalence of drug use. The National Institute on Drug Abuse (NIDA) sponsors two continuing nationwide monitoring programs that contribute most of the knowledge currently available on substance use and abuse among adolescents. First, a survey called Monitoring the Future has been conducted annually since 1975 among nationally representative samples of about 16,000 high school seniors from 130 schools (Johnston, Bachman, & O'Malley, 1987). It should be noted that the study contains data from only those seniors present on the day each year that the survey is administered; therefore, school dropouts and those who are chronically absent are not adequately represented. Although these coverage limitations may somewhat affect the results obtained regarding use of various drugs, they do not appear so far to have had much impact on the trend lines from year to year. Second, the National Household Survey on Drug Abuse is a general population survey of household members aged 12 and above that has been conducted every 2 to 3 years since 1971.

Other information is derived from two NIDA data systems that have been used to monitor drug abuse trends and health consequences: (1) the Drug Abuse Warning Network (DAWN), which reports consequences of drug abuse as reflected by emergency room episodes for drug-related problems and medical examiner cases for drug-related fatalities; and (2) the Client Oriented Data Acquisition Process (CODAP), which reports treatment data.

Johnston, O'Malley, and Bachman (1989) reported that the general downward trend in drug use by high school seniors that started in 1979 has continued through 1988 (except for the year 1985), but has tapered off more recently. A salient exception to the general pattern was the rapid increase in the use of cocaine, which reached a record high in 1985 before significantly declining in 1986, 1987, and 1988.

Cigarette smoking bears a strong positive relationship to the use of alcohol and illicit drugs (marijuana in particular), and is usually initiated in seventh through ninth grades, with rather little further initiation after high school. Of the pack-a-day smokers in high school, 95% had used an illicit drug, 81% had used an illicit drug other than marijuana, and 26% were currently daily users of some illicit drug (mostly marijuana) (Johnston et al., 1987, 1988).

The present trend toward polydrug abuse and the early onset of alcohol and marijuana use may have significant impact on the probability of use of additional illicit substances. A recent survey of high school seniors regarding the grade in which they first used substances revealed that 8.4% reported first use of alcohol, 2.8% first use of marijuana, and 0.2% first use of cocaine in the sixth grade (Johnston et al., 1987). These data are depicted in Table 14.1.

Over half (57%) of high school seniors in the class of 1986 reported ever trying an illicit drug—a decline from 61% in 1984 and 58% in 1985, respectively (Johnston et al., 1987). Thirty-six percent had tried an illicit drug other than marijuana (polydrug abusers). The prevalence and recency of use of 11 drugs are depicted in Figure 14.1.

Although the use of marijuana, sedatives, and stimulants has declined, the Monitoring the Future survey has found little change in the use of LSD, heroin, or other opiates, and some evidence of a continuing gradual increase in the use

TABLE 14.1. Grade of First Use for 16 Types of Drugs, Class of 1986

Substance	Grade in which drug was first used		
	Sixth	Seventh–eighth	Ninth
Marijuana	$2.8	11.2	11.5
Inhalants	1.9	$3.7	2.8
Amyl/butyl nitrites	0.4	1.3	0.9
Hallucinogens	0.2	0.6	2.1
LSD	0.1	0.4	1.3
PCP	0.6	0.8	0.6
Cocaine	0.2	0.6	2.0
Heroin	0.1	0.1	0.1
Other opiates	0.2	1.0	1.9
Stimulants	0.3	3.8	6.9
Sedatives	0.5	2.4	2.9
Barbiturates	0.4	1.7	2.5
Methaqualone	0.3	1.2	1.4
Tranquilizers	0.4	1.5	2.5
Alcohol	8.4	21.9	24.6
Cigarettes	22.7	20.3	10.0

Note. Entries are percentages. Adapted from National Trends in Drug Use and Related Factors among American High School Students and Young Adults, 1975–1986 (DHHS Publication No. ADM 87-1535) by L. Johnston, J. G. Bachman, and P. M. O'Malley, 1987, Washington, DC: U.S. Government Printing Office.

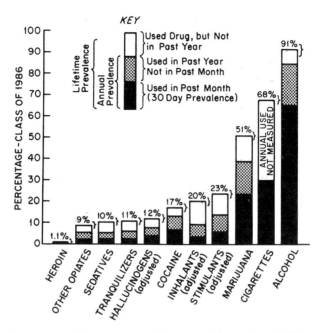

FIGURE 14.1. Prevalence and recency of use of 11 types of drugs, class of 1986. From *National Trends in Drug Use and Related Factors among American High School Students and Young Adults, 1975–1986* (DHHS Publication No. ADM 87-1535) by L. Johnston, J. G. Bachman, and P. M. O'Malley, 1987, Washington, DC: U.S. Government Printing Office.

of inhalants. The use of alcohol and cigarette smoking has not dropped among high school seniors since 1984 (Johnston et al., 1988). Perceived availability of drugs and alcohol has likewise not changed among adolescents. Regarding sex differences, males are more likely to use most illict drugs; the only exception is the use of stimulants (especially "diet pills"), which is more frequent among females in high school. The sexes attain near-parity on tranquilizer use.

Alcohol, marijuana, and cocaine are the three drugs most frequently used by high school seniors. The most recent information available about their patterns of use is as follows:

1. *Alcohol.* In 1987, 92% of high school seniors reported having used alcohol; 66% were current users, 5% were daily drinkers, and 37.5% reported at least one occasion of heavy drinking (five or more drinks in a row). None of these figures had shown any improvement in the past 3 years (Johnston et al., 1988). A biracial comparison of adolescent alcohol use revealed that white males demonstrated a higher amount of alcohol use, while white females reported drinking rates comparable to those of black males. Also, white respondents tended to have their initial drinking experiences almost a year earlier than their black counterparts (Johnston et al., 1988).

2. *Marijuana.* Marijuana is the most widely abused illegal drug in the country, yet the decline from 1978 to 1987 figures is impressive. In 1978

monthly prevalence among high school seniors was at 37% and daily use at
10.7%, while 35% of seniors perceived great risk with regular use. By 1987,
regular use was perceived as risky by 74% of seniors, and daily use fell to
3.3%, less than one-third or the 1978 figure (Johnston et al., 1988).

Marijuana has been called a "gateway" drug (Kandel, 1982), and indeed
the single best predictor of cocaine use is frequent use of marijuana during
adolescence. Only 1% of those not regularly using any drug and 4% of legal
drug users had experimented with opiates, cocaine, and hallucinogens, as
compared to 26% of marijuana users (Kandel, 1982).

3. *Cocaine.* Cocaine is the second most frequently used illicit substance
after marijuana. Lifetime, annual, and 30-day prevalence of cocaine use
reached their highest levels ever in 1985. The data from 1975 to 1987 (Johnston et al., 1988) are depicted in Figure 14.2 and Table 14.2. Among 1985
high school seniors, 6.7% had used cocaine in the 30 days previous to the
survey. Lifetime prevalence (ever used) was 17.3% among 1985 seniors as
compared to 9.7% among 1976 seniors. (At the 11-year follow-up of 1976
seniors, 40% reported using cocaine at least once; therefore, many individuals
were initiating cocaine use after they graduated from high school.) In 1987,
however, lifetime prevalence declined to 15.2%, and only 4.3% of high school
seniors had used cocaine during the 30 days previous to the survey (the lowest
rate since 1979). The number of seniors who disapproved of cocaine use, even
at experimental levels, increased dramatically to 87%.

The rate of cocaine use suggests a revolutionary change in personal
attitudes and peer norms in response to cocaine use. One might actually have
expected a rise in the rates of use with the introduction of different modes of
administration, such as intravenous use and the "freebase" use of crack; the

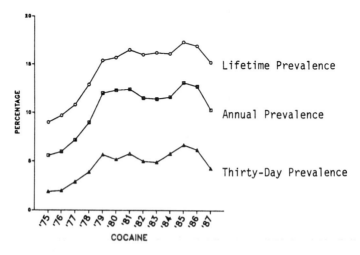

FIGURE 14.2. Trends in lifetime, annual, and 30-day prevalence of cocaine use: All seniors,
1975–1987. From "Details of Annual Survey" by L. Johnston, J. G. Bachman, and P. M. O'Malley,
1988, *University of Michigan News and Information Services, 1,* 1–5.

TABLE 14.2. Trends in Lifetime, Annual, and 30-Day Prevalence of Cocaine Use: All Seniors, 1975–1987

Year	Prevalence		
	Lifetime	Annual	30-day
1975	9.0	5.6	1.9
1976	9.7	6.0	2.0
1977	10.8	7.2	2.9
1978	12.9	9.0	3.9
1979	15.4	12.0	5.7
1980	15.7	12.3	5.2
1981	16.5	12.4	5.8
1982	16.0	11.5	5.0
1983	16.2	11.4	4.9
1984	16.1	11.6	5.8
1985	17.3	13.1	6.7
1986	16.9	12.7	6.2
1987	15.2	10.3	4.3

Note. Entries are percentages. Adapted from "Details of Annual Survey" by L. Johnston, J. G. Bachman, and P. M. O'Malley, 1988, University of Michigan News and Information Services, 1, 1–5.

latter was included for the first time in the 1986 survey, when 4.1% of seniors reported its use. It is noteworthy that crack was reported to have spread from 50% of schools in the survey of 1986 to 75% of schools in 1987 (Johnston et al., 1988). The most important developments in 1988, however, were the drop in crack use and the continued decline of cocaine use in any form (Johnston et al., 1989). Perceived availability of cocaine did not change and was still high, and the price was still relatively low and stable (Siegel, 1987). Therefore, the most likely explanation for the decline in cocaine use may be a change of attitude toward cocaine.

Johnston et al. (1988) summarized the findings of 1987 as follows: "The overall picture has improved considerably in the past years but the amount of illicit as well as licit drug use among America's younger age groups is still striking" (p. 5).

The Development of Substance Use and Abuse in Adolescence

There is evidence that substance abuse has origins in the family. Parental substance use is associated with use by adolescents; children of alcoholic parents are four to five times more likely to become alcoholics than are children of nonalcoholic parents (Goodwin, 1985).

The link between parental substance abuse and the initiation of substance use and abuse in their children is an intriguing issue, but it appears that whether or not an individual actually develops alcohol abuse depends on social and environmental circumstances. Hence, the typological and dimensional perspectives are both appropriate, but at different levels of observation about the pathway from genotype to phenotype (Cloninger, Reich, Sigvardsson, Von Knorring, & Bohman, 1987). The dilemma of substance abuse inheritance is being complicated even further by the question of whether alcoholism or other substance abuse is inherited as a syndrome that stands by itself, or perhaps as a part of a broader syndrome, such as the three family types of alcohol abuse: the milieu-limited (Type 1), the male-limited (Type 2), and the antisocial personality (Meyer, 1986).

Genetic and Biological Factors

Most of the data regarding the genetic and biological contribution to the development of substance abuse are being derived from alcoholism research. It has been suggested that individuals may enter life with a certain level of a genetically influenced biological predisposition toward alcoholism or other substance abuse. Convergent evidence from twin, adoption, and biological response studies suggests that genetic factors may indeed play a role in the etiology of alcoholism (Bohman, Sigvardsson, & Cloninger, 1981; Cloninger, Bohman, & Sigvardsson, 1981). Investigations of neuropsychological and physiological precursors or markers of alcoholism, conducted with sons of alcoholics and nonalcoholics, suggest some possible biological differences that may increase vulnerability to alcoholism. Goodwin (1985) has suggested that children of alcoholics may be deficient in serotonin or may have an increased level of serotonin in the presence of alcohol. The "addictive cycle"—a pattern in which a person initially drinks to feel good, and then later has to resume drinking after an abstinence period in order to stop feeling bad—may result from such a problem with serotonin. Children of alcoholics are also suspected to have increased tolerance to alcohol. Ten more differences are reviewed by Kumpfer and Demarsh (1986).

There are indications that adolescent substance abuse may be part of a broader genetic constellation. Some theorists have suggested that polydrug abuse (abuse of a wide variety of substances) constitutes evidence against a genetic interpretation of addiction. Cadoret, Troughton, O'Gorman, and Heywood (1986) suggest instead that some underlying biochemical route may be involved both in substance abuse and in problem or deviant behavior, especially delinquency. They have summarized their findings of an adoption study as follows: "There appear to be two genetic pathways to drug abuse: one through antisocial personality (and indirectly from biologic parents with anti-social behavior) and the second from biologic parents with alcohol problems to individuals who themselves are not antisocial" (p. 1136).

Adoption studies support this approach by introducing the male-limited alcoholism (Type 2) model versus the milieu-limited alcoholism (Type 1) model (Cloninger et al., 1981). Type 2 alcoholism is found exclusively in young males (teenage/early adulthood onset), and is strongly correlated with severe alcoholism and criminality in the biological father. Type 1 alcoholism is found in mild and severe forms in both sexes, is influenced by alcoholism in both biological parents, and is characterized by adult onset and no criminality. The investigation of Type 2 alcoholism among adults demonstrates that the natural history of these male adolescent alcohol abusers is characterized by continuity to adult alcohol abuse (Buydens-Branchey, Branchey, & Noumair, 1989). So it appears that unless the theory of the three family types of alcohol abuse is challenged, only two of the three types (Type 1 excluded) are relevant to adolescence.

Environmental Theories

The evidence supporting a genetic factor in alcoholism and substance abuse is paralleled by evidence supporting the role of psychosocial, familial, peer, and other environmental and interactional variables. Lettieri (1985) listed over 40 articles covering a wide range of mainly psychosocial hypotheses about initiation and continuation of substance use, and eventual transition from use to abuse. Two of the most influential theories have been postulated by the Jessors and by Kandel.

The Jessors have formulated the problem behavior theory, which explains substance use as a component of a "deviance" syndrome or "proneness" to problem behavior (Jessor, 1987). This model extends beyond genetic and biological considerations. The primary focus of the theory is on three systems of psychosocial influence: the personality system, the perceived environment system, and the behavior system. Together, these three systems generate a dynamic state called "proneness," which specifies the likelihood of occurrence of normative development or problem behavior that departs from the social and legal norms.

Also, longitudinal studies have documented that personality characteristics such as aggressiveness and rebelliousness are predictive factors that precede the use of substances and can be identified in preschoolers. Kandel (1982) has formulated four broad classes of predictors: (1) parental influences, (2) peer influences, (3) adolescent beliefs and values, and (4) adolescent involvement in various shared activities. "Each of these clusters as well as single variables within each cluster assume[s] differential importance for predicting each stage of drug behavior" (p. 338).

PARENTAL INFLUENCES

Three different types of parental characteristics predict initiation of substance use: parental substance use/abuse behaviors; parental attitudes toward substances, and parental–child interactions. Studies suggest that exposing a child (particularly a young child) to substance abuse behavior by the caretaker and to the nonfulfillment of parental responsibilities that follows affects the child by providing models and by reinforcement of related behaviors. Ahmed, Bush, Davidson, and Iannotti (1984) have reported on a measure of "salience," defined as the number of household users of a substance and the degree of children's involvement in parental substance-taking behavior; this measure was found to be the best predictor of both expectations of use and actual abuse of alcohol. Salience was also a strong predictor of children's cigarette and marijuana use. Among the environmental characteristics of these families, the following factors were noted: high stress, poor and inconsistent family management skills, increased separation, divorce, death, and prison terms, and decreased family activities.

Chemically dependent families are often socially isolated from the community, partly because of their need for secrecy and partly because of community rejection. Parents in substance-abusing families have fewer friends and are less involved in recreational, social, religious, and cultural activities (Kumpfer & Demarsh, 1986). Because of such families' social isolation, the children have fewer opportunities to interact with other children, have fewer friends, and express desire to have more friends but doubt their abilities to make friends. Emotional neglect has been reported frequently; substance-abusing parents have only a limited ability to involve themselves meaningfully and emotionally with their children, and also have been found to spend less time in planned and structured activities with their children (Kumpfer & Demarsh, 1986). In addition, more psychopathology and significantly more depression have been detected in substance-abusing parents. The emotional impact on children from these families results in the children's having difficulty with identifying and expressing positive feelings. Parents who are substance abusers are also characterized by difficulty in coping with everyday realities and responsibilities. Lack of energy for better parenting, because of the drain on the family's time, finances, and emotional/social resources created by the substance abuse, has been noted (Kumpfer & Demarsh, 1986).

Feelings that are often identified or reported among these children are resentment, embarrassment, anger, fear, loneliness, depression, and insecurity. Intense fear of separation and abandonment is very common. Since psychopathology and emotional disturbances often precede substance abuse, these children are at high risk for the development of substance abuse and dependence. Kumpfer and Demarsh (1986) also found that children of alcoholic parents scored lower than children of nonalcoholics on measures of intelligence and cognitive performance and on two measures of self-concept.

PEER INFLUENCES; BELIEFS AND VALUES; SHARED ACTIVITIES

Peer influences play a crucial role in the process of involvement in the use and abuse of all substances—tobacco, alcohol, and illicit substances (especially marijuana). Parental influences are probably more important in the socialization process during preadolescence, whereas peer influences become more important during adolescence. Peer relationships have a significant effect on the initiation, development, and maintenance of substance abuse. The most consistent and reproducible finding in substance abuse research is the strong relationship between an individual's substance behavior and the concurrent substance use of his or her friends (Jessor & Jessor, 1977). Such an association may result from socialization, but also from a process of interpersonal selection (assortative pairing), in which adolescents with similar values and behaviors seek each other out as friends (Kandel, 1982). Susceptibility to peer influence is related to involvement in peer-related activities and to a degree of attachment and reliance on peers rather than parents (Kandel, 1978).

Regarding values and attitudes in adolescent substance abusers, substance abuse is correlated negatively with conventional behaviors and beliefs, such as church attendance, good scholastic performance, value of academic achievement, and beliefs in the generalized expectations, norms, and values of society (Jessor, 1987). Substance abuse is correlated positively with risk-taking behavior, sensation-seeking behavior, early sexual activity, higher value of independence, and greater involvement in delinquent behavior (Jessor, 1987).

Delinquency may reach a point at which adolescent gangs, groups, and cults engage in one or more of the following shared activities: using the same drugs of choice, Satanism and related rituals, drug trafficking, and violence. Such activities are deeply rooted in the identity-creating process of these groups and are inseparable components of their code of values. Although a relatively small number of adolescents are reporting or are reported to be engaged in such activities, they constitute a growing reason for concern, because they comprise a new trend that we see increasing among our patients.

The "Gateway" Theory

Early initiation of substance use predicts subsequent abuse of that substance, as well as greater extensive and persistent involvement in other drug use (Kandel, 1982).

Kandel initiated the use of the term "gateway drug" in regard to marijuana, which is considered to lead to the use/abuse of other illicit drugs. Kandel's (1975) simplistic but practical model of adolescent involvement with legal and illegal substances includes at least four distinct developmental stages: (1) beer or wine, (2) cigarettes or hard liquor, (3) marijuana, and (4) other illicit drugs. Kandel also suggested that a fifth stage, problem drinking, takes place between the use of marijuana and other illicit drugs. She qualified her presentation of the model, however, by indicating that position on a particular point in the sequence is a necessary but not sufficient condition for participation in a later stage. It appears that users in a peer group who become abusers progress on the chain of the stages of substance involvement almost simultaneously.

Comorbidity and Adolescent Substance Abuse

A comorbid disorder is defined as "any distinct additional clinical entity that has existed or may have occurred during the clinical course of a patient who has the index disease under study" (Feinstein, 1970, p. 455). Comorbid disorders may affect the severity and expression of the index disorder, thereby affecting the diagnosis and the choice of therapeutic strategies.

Many adolescents who come to treatment for substance abuse also manifest psychiatric symptomatology. Affective disorders, conduct disorders, and anxiety disorders appear to be the most common ones. In the National Youth Polydrug Study, 28% of the adolescents reported that they sought help for emotional and psychiatric problems (Friedman & Glickman, 1986). In adolescents with a dual psychiatric and substance abuse diagnosis, it is not always easy to determine which disorder came first. Most of the existing studies that have examined the occurrence of comorbidity in hospitalized or clinic samples might lead one to conclude that the above-noted comorbid symptoms or disorders may be intrinsic to the illness, rather than secondary to the sampling frame.

What are the possible relationships between coexisting substance abuse and psychopathology?

1. Kandel (1982) pointed out that "one of the most intriguing findings to emerge from longitudinal drug studies is that the antecedents of adolescent drug use appear to be similar in certain respects to those linked in other studies to various forms of psychopathology" (p. 343); in other words, substance abuse and psychopathology may originate from a common vulnerability.
2. Psychiatric symptoms or disorders may develop or be exacerbated as a consequence of use or abuse of mood-altering substances.
3. Substance abuse may develop as a consequence of psychiatric disorders (self-medication).
4. Psychiatric disorders may alter the course of substance abuse.
5. Substance abuse may alter the course of psychiatric disorders.
6. Psychiatric disorder and substance abuse may be mutually exclusive but coincidentally manifested.

Research on this topic in adolescent psychiatry is scarce; however, affective disorders, conduct disorder/antisocial personality, attention-deficit disorder/hyperactivity (ADDH), and eating disorders have been explored in regard to their comorbidity with substance abuse in adolescents and young adults. It appears that the coexistence of psychopathology and substance abuse in adolescents is highly prevalent and cannot be underestimated if treatment is to be effective. However, Swaim, Oetting, Edwards, and Beauvais (1989) could not confirm the validity of the self-medication theory and its applicability to adolescent substance abuse. A path model analysis carried out concluded that emotional distress variables accounted for less than 5% of the variance of drug use. Moreover, it was found that anger was the only variable that was linked to drug use. Finally, except for family studies that probed into the clustering in families of the comorbidity of anxiety disorders, mood disorders, and substance abuse (as reviewed by Bukstein et al., 1989), the comorbidity of anxiety disorders and substance abuse in adolescents has not yet been carefully studied.

Affective Disorders

Affective symptomatology and affective disorders are perhaps the most frequently studied psychiatric problems coexisting with substance abuse. Clinical experience suggests that 60–80% of adolescent substance abusers are diagnosed as depressed on admission to inpatient treatment programs; however, many of them experience a gradual lifting of the depression without drug therapy between 10 and 21 days after admission. This phenomenon may be attributed to various factors other than primary depression, such as substance abuse or withdrawal; loss of the substance of abuse or related lifestyle; or a reaction to loss of freedom due to the admission. Also, the diagnosis of depression may be difficult to make, because adolescents may deny or hide their depressive mood in order to avoid hospitalization.

In a study of adolescents seen for psychiatric evaluation in a general hospital emergency room, Reichler, Clement, and Dunner (1983) found that almost half of those with elevated blood alcohol levels (17% of the total sample) had at least one additional psychiatric diagnosis; the most common such diagnosis was depression. Kashani, Keller, Solomon, Reid, and Mazzola (1985) interviewed 100 adolescent substance abusers in a youth drop-in counseling center and found that 16% showed evidence of double depression (i.e., a major depression superimposed on a dysthymic disorder). Deykin, Levy, and Weller (1986) found in a cross-sectional study of 424 college students that alcohol abuse was associated with major depression, but not with other diagnoses. The onset of the major depression almost always preceded the alcohol or substance abuse, thus supporting the view of depression and anxiety disorders as risk factors for subsequent substance abuse in adolescence and young adults (Christie et al., 1988; Helzer & Pryzbeck, 1988). Mania was reported to have an odds ratio of 6.2 to comorbidity with alcoholism, second only to the ratio for antisocial personality (Helzer & Pryzbeck, 1988).

Conduct Disorder and Antisocial Personality

Conduct disorder and antisocial personality have long been strongly associated with substance abuse. According to the Epidemiologic Catchment Area (ECA) research, it has an odds ratio of 21 to comorbidity with alcoholism (Helzer &

Pryzbeck, 1988). However, this association may be in part due to the fact that substance abuse is one of the diagnostic criteria for antisocial personality. In addition, intoxication with various substances leads to behavioral disinhibition, thus decreasing the threshold for antisocial behavior. Several investigators have noted that childhood behavior problems appear to predispose individuals to the later development of alcoholism.

Attention-Deficit Disorder/Hyperactivity

It is common to associate ADDH with substance abuse, and a number of retrospective studies have reported increased frequencies of childhood histories of hyperactivity or minimal brain dysfunction among adult substance abusers. However, Weiss and Hechtman (1986) reported in a follow-up review of subjects diagnosed with childhood ADDH that these subjects did not engage in significant drug or alcohol use in adolescence, compared with controls; nor did these subjects show significant evidence of greater alcohol use or abuse as young adults. Although Gittelman, Mannuzza, Shenker, and Bonagura (1985) reported that substance abuse was more prevalent in adolescents formerly diagnosed as hyperactive, in all cases those hyperactives who later used drugs showed conduct disorder either before or coincident with the onset of substance abuse. Alterman and Tarter (1986) reviewed the literature on hyperactivity as a risk factor for alcoholism and confirmed Gittelman et al.'s (1985) findings. A later study by Gittelman and her colleagues found that the presence of antisocial personality or conduct disorder in young adulthood almost completely accounted for the increased risk of criminal activities in subjects diagnosed as hyperactive in childhood, whether or not it was accompanied by a substance use disorder (Mannuzza et al., 1989).

Eating Disorders

Many patients with eating disorders, especially bulimia nervosa, manifest substance abuse. A substance abuse diagnosis is also frequently made in the first-degree relatives of such patients (Kaminer, Feingold, & Lyons, 1988). Bulimia, according to one theory, is more prevalent among women than among men because it may represent an alternative expression of addiction among females (Bulik, 1987).

Suicide

Suicide is frequently associated with substance abuse among adolescents. Suicide rates for adolescents have almost tripled in the last three decades, and suicide is now the second leading cause of death for this group (Committee on

Adolescent Suicide, 1988). Also, the age group of 15 to 24 years displays the highest involvement with alcohol and illicit substances. Rich, Young, and Fowler (1986) reported in the San Diego Suicide Study that substance abuse diagnosis was strongly associated with 70% of suicides among victims under 30 years of age. They concluded that their findings would appear to support Miles's (1977) conclusion that drug usage may be the most important single factor in the suicide rate increase among youth in the United States.

Intoxication often precedes suicide attempts and suicide. Detectable blood alcohol levels were found in adolescent suicide attempters and completers, and a positive correlation between intoxication and choice of firearm as means for suicide was reported by Brent, Perper, and Allman (1987) in their research on adolescent suicides.

The typical adolescent at risk for suicide appears to be a white male who is likely to be intoxicated and prefers to commit suicide by firearm without seeking help from mental health professionals. It appears that the association between adolescent substance abuse and suicide may be an exclusive one and may in fact cut cross a shared association with other disorders (e.g., mood disorders, anxiety disorders, conduct disorders), impulsivity, genetic variables, or neurobiological factors. Or perhaps the association is only causal (substances serve as a trigger that is dose-related). The subject has been recently reviewed elsewhere (Crumley, 1990).

The Assessment of the Adolescent Substance Abuser

At least 10 problem domains need to be evaluated in order to assess the severity of an adolescent's substance abuse and substance-abuse-related problems: (1) the substance abuse itself; (2) psychiatric disorders; (3) family functioning; (4) school performance; (5) peer relationships; (6) social skills; (7) vocational status; (8) legal status; (9) medical status; and (10) recreational activities.

Two types of rating scales are commonly used for the assessment of adolescent substance abuse: self-reports and interviews. It is widely asserted that "You cannot believe an addict." However, there is a growing body of evidence suggesting that information obtained from adult substance abusers is reliable and valid, regardless of the sensitivity of the information sought, the specificity of the validation criteria, or the type of information-gathering procedure used (Sobell & Sobell, 1978). Campanelli, Dielman, and Shope (1987) concluded that self-report data on adolescent alcohol use and abuse were valid when confidentiality was maintained.

Only a handful of instruments for the clinical assessment of adolescent substance abuse have been described, and none of them is widely tested and accepted as yet. Tarter (1990) has reviewed the following instruments.

An instrument developed by Cohen, Karras, and Hughes (1977) specifically measures drug use severity in adolescents. The component areas assessed include history, effects, usage pattern, utility, and social basis for consumption. Several other questionnaires, also unstandardized, have been devised to measure particular features of drug use. Jessor's (1976) self-report questionnaire emphasizes the quantity–frequency characteristics of drug use, the context of drug use, and stated reasons for use within the framework of problem or non-normative behavior. A brief questionnaire of six items was created by Smart and Jones (1970) to measure frequency of drug use, availability (source), and history of professional contacts for drug use problems. A similar scale, consisting of 72 items, has been developed by Gossett, Lewis, and Phillips (1972).

Substantial advances in the field of adolescent substance abuse assessment were made with the Personal Experience Inventory (PEI; Henly & Winters, 1988). Although standardization data are not yet available, the PEI attempts to (1) measure the adolescent's behavioral involvement with drugs and alcohol; (2) assess the frequency, style, duration, and sequelae of drug use; (3) evaluate personality characteristics and environmental circumstance of the user, (4) assist in the formulation of DSM-III-R diagnoses; (5) identify pyschosocial stressors; and (6) examine for the presence of other disorders besides drug abuse. In addition, there are three validity scales that evaluate response style to the test items; these may suggest an inclination to be defensive or reflect attempts to present an overly negative picture of oneself. The PEI consists of two general parts. The first part consists of 15 clinical scales that measure the severity of drug use. The second part contains 17 scales to evaluate psychosocial functioning; these latter scales consist of items pertaining to self-esteem, peer relationships, family functioning, behavioral disturbance, achievement motivation, and social adjustment.

Several other instruments, each in various stages of development and standardization, are also noteworthy. The Client Substance Abuse Index, developed by Moore (1980), focuses on drug use severity within the DSM-III diagnostic scheme. As such, the items pertain specifically to pathological use, social impairment, symptom aggregation, and physical dependence. Another instrument, also in the development stages, is the Adolescent Drug Abuse Diagnosis (Friedman, 1987). This is an interview-based evaluation of an adolescent, to be used for treatment planning. It evaluates drug and alcohol use patterns, medical and legal status, family problems and background, school or employment record, psychological well-being, and social as well as peer relationships. This instrument does not as yet have normative data or proven validity. The Teen Addiction Severity Index (T-ASI) is an interview utilizing a dimensional approach and is based on the Addiction Severity Index (McLellan, Luborsky, Woody, & O'Brien, 1980). The T-ASI (Kaminer, Bukstein, & Tarter, 1991) includes seven domains: substance use, school, employment, family, peer/social, legal, and psychiatric. The T-ASI's psychometric properties are still being investigated; however, partial results indicate that its reliability is good (average correlation of .78).

Treatment

Not much has been documented about the treatment of adolescent substance abuse. Paucity of reports from treatment services, scarce treatment quality assessments, and, above all, much disagreement about major treatment approaches account for the difficulty in suggesting optimal treatment strategies for substance-abusing adolescents. I describe the current state of this field by answering five questions.

What Is a Successful Treatment Outcome?

Regardless of the expressed goals and underlying philosophy of substance abuse treatment programs, the usual measure of effectiveness is abstinence after treatment completion. There are two other common measures of successful treatment outcome. The first of these is treatment retention; Rush (1979) argues that retention in the treatment program is the primary goal and is also positively correlated to productivity among adolescents (an index score combining education, training, and employment; Friedman & Glickman, 1986). The second measure is a goal of combined abstinence and productivity, intended to help an adolescent achieve a drug-free lifestyle.

Are the Various Treatment Facilities/Modalities Differentially Effective?

Frequently, adolescents are incorporated into mixed patient populations or provided with adult services that are not adapted to their specific needs. Many times, a referral to a certain facility is based on availability of space and not necessarily on patient's needs. The most common treatment facilities are outpatient clinics (which serve 80% of adolescents who receive treatment), drop-in centers, therapeutic communities, residential programs, halfway houses, and inpatient units.

An inpatient setting provides an immediate interruption of the negative, self-destructive lifestyle by removing the adolescent from the "infectious" environment and by providing a substitute—usually a drug-free, highly structured therapeutic community. Inpatient treatment is indicated for the following adolescents:

1. Patients who are severely physically dependent; such patients need to be detoxified under medical supervision, in order to prevent potentially life-threatening withdrawal symptoms.
2. Patients who have failed in or do not qualify for outpatient treatment.
3. Intravenous drug abusers and freebasers

4. Dual-diagnosis patients with moderate to severe psychiatric disorders requiring treatment simultaneously with the substance abuse.

5. Patients who need to be isolated from influential relapse-promoting environmental factors in order to provide them with proper treatment without interruption.

The prevailing therapeutic approach in many substance abuse treatment centers is the "shotgun" approach, in which all modalities are targeted to each patient diagnoses as chemically dependent. The philosophy behind this approach is that in a drug-free therapeutic environment, one or several modalities will provide the "corrective emotional experience" that will facilitate change and help the patient overcome the physical dependency. It is commonly believed that most adolescents at the admission stage are reluctant to make a commitment to treatment; many of them arrive involuntarily, usually under the pressure of a family member or some representative of a social or legal agency. Commitment to change as a result of a resolution to stop drug consumption is crucial. The typical adolescent substance abuser who starts treatment exhibits a sense of ambivalence about his or her drug use, with the perceived adverse consequences, costs, and problems being counterbalanced by the immediate benefits of use.

The focus in treatment is shifting at present from relying only on type of treatment facility and length of stay to matching the "dosage" of treatment, including content, quality, quantity, frequency, and intensity of treatment, to the individual (an analogy to dosage in pharmacotherapy). This movement toward a differential treatment approach makes excellent sense because of the differences between patients. Examples of some of the commonly used treatment modalities for adolescents are individual therapy, cognitive and behavioral therapy, individual- and multiple-family therapy, various group therapies, social skills training, and support groups for both the adolescents and their families. Vocational counseling is important for school dropouts, and recreational counseling is crucial in order to fight boredom, a frequent emotional state among adolescent substance abusers.

However, it is also important to find out what the adolescent patient, the referral source, and the caretakers expect from the treatment program (i.e., hidden and covert agendas) at the outset of treatment; otherwise, dropout rates shortly after admission to the program will surge (Zweben & Li, 1981). There is no single strategy that appears to be superior in dealing with the problem of attrition. This may be due to the complexity of the issue; to lack of knowledge about the meaning of attrition in various stages of the treatment; and to a similar lack of knowledge about the relative weight and interaction among patient, staff, and treatment variables. The study of the relationship between the treatment process and context of treatment on the one hand, and outcome on the other, is difficult. Cronkite and Moos (1978) found that the combined explanatory power of the program-related variables was considerably more than would be expected from previous research, and that both the treatment experience and the patient's perception of the treatment environment were strong predictors of outcome.

What Relationships Exist between Patient Variables and Treatment Modalities?

The adolescent patient variables usually receive more attention than the variables of the program. Patient characteristics such as being white, not using opiates, being enrolled in an educational program, and being older when the drug abuse was first tried were found to be positively related to completion of treatment among adolescents (Rush, 1979). Polydrug abuse was negatively related to completion of treatment in the same study.

Perhaps the most important patient variable for predicting treatment outcome among adult substance abusers is patient psychopathology. Indeed, psychiatric diagnosis frequently accompanies substance abuse in adolescents, and dual-diagnosis rates range between 16% and 71% in various reports (Deykin et al., 1986; Kashani et al., 1985; Reichler et al., 1983).

In one study, adult alcoholics with severe psychiatric disorders showed low levels of improvement and significantly less improvement than those with mild and moderate psychiatric problems (Rounsaville, Kosten, Weissman, & Kleber, 1986). Those with additional concurrent family problems showed even poorer outcome. The patients with middle-severity psychiatric pathology achieved significant benefit from patient–program matching (Rounsaville, Kosten, et al., 1986). The fewer problems a patient had upon admission, the more likely he or she was to benefit from a program. Personality disorders, especially antisocial personality, were correlated with poor treatment outcome in any treatment modality (Rounsaville, Kosten, et al., 1986; Woody, McLellan, Luborsky, & O'Brien, 1985). No such research on adolescent substance abusers has been reported yet.

Is There a Need to Treat Adolescent Substance Abusers Differently from Adults?

Adolescent substance abusers appear to differ from adult substance abusers in aspects such as these: Their history of substance abuse is much shorter, they infrequently manifest physical long-term side effects, and they are more vulnerable to peer pressure to use alcohol or drugs. Furthermore, the cognitive development of youths in their early and even middle adolescent years is not complete; they face difficulties in internalizing values, ideas, and concepts that are based partially or completely on formal operational (abstract) thinking. Consequently, they face difficulty in internalizing and implementing treatment concepts. Most adolescents are still in school, live at home and have achieved partial or no economic independence, and need a great deal of family involvement in their treatment. Adolescents who are substance abusers are not attracted by long-term treatment goals, such as preventing liver cirrhosis from alcohol, or lung cancer from cigarette smoking (Botvin, Baker, Remick, Filazzola, & Botvin, 1984). Immediate and short-term goals thus need to be designed in order to increase adolescent substance abusers' motivation to treatment.

My colleagues' and my experience is that information about acquired immune deficiency syndrome (AIDS) and sex education should be components of the treatment curriculum. Adolescent females who abuse alcohol and other substances are increasng their risk of pregnancy, and therefore their risk of giving birth to infants with fetal alcohol syndrome or other drug-related morbidity. Adolescent parents should also be guided and taught parenthood skills, in order to prevent and reduce child abuse behavior to their offspring—a phenomenon commonly found among alcoholic and substance-abusing parents.

How Can We Improve the Quality of Treatment Provided to the Adolescent Substance Abuser?

Recommendations on how to improve treatment programs for adolescent substance abusers are clearly needed, and clinical exploration into the high rates of attrition from treatment (which average 50%) is imperative. However, the suggestions found in the literature are not data-based.

To conclude, it appears that Longabaugh's (1987) summary may serve as a framework. Longabaugh suggests, based on his experience and on a literature review, three areas that need to be further explored in order to improve treatment outcome:

1. The strength of the active ingredients of the treatment program.
2. Treatment integrity—the operationalization of the treatment plan as designed.
3. Measurement of the treatment as it is delivered.

Prevention

Controlled research findings regarding substance abuse prevention among children and adolescents are scarce. It is noteworthy to focus on the primary prevention efforts based on the behavioral domain, which offers at present the most promise for school-based prevention programs. Based upon the theoretical and experimental research into social learning theory (Bandura, 1977), four major components are being employed in the process: (1) role modeling, (2) reinforcement, (3) establishment of normative expectations, and (4) coping with social pressure. Sometimes a fifth component, training for generalization, is employed. The premise of substance abuse prevention programs based upon these principles is that cigarette smoking, alcohol consumption, and other drug use are acquired behaviors, derived from social pressures and reinforced by peers, family, the media, and community norms (Tucker, 1985).

Rather than focusing primarily on resistance training, Botvin et al. (1984) have developed and tested a more generalized but comparable behavioral approach. This program, entitled Life Skills Training (LST), includes resistance training only as one of several social skills taught to sixth- and seventh-graders. A peer-led LST program for the use of alcohol and marijuana indicated significant improvement.

The problem of drug and alcohol use should be addressed by the media as well as by the schools. Curiosity and boredom are ranked by adolescents as the two most common reasons for initiating the use of drugs. (Jalali, Jalali, Crocetti, & Turner, 1980). The media indirectly stimulate adolescents' curiosity to seek out alcohol and other drugs and to experience their effects. A study of television's role in alcohol use among adolescents indicated that heavy viewers consumed alcohol significantly more often than did light and moderate viewers (Tucker, 1985). The data indicated that the association was linear; this implies that television may have a greater influence on the attitude and lifestyles of youths than initially believed. Adolescents watch characters who rarely refuse a drink or express disapproval of drinking. Moreover, intoxication is often portrayed as humorous and is commonly justified as a reaction to acute stress. Evidently the media do not convey health-promoting messages, and it is time to extend prevention efforts to this dimension as well.

It is argued that alcohol abuse is sensitive to price and that the government's policy of maintaining excise taxes at a relatively low level may actually exacerbate the problem of alcohol use and abuse among adolescents because of increased availability. Cook and Tauchen (1982) have reported that use of alcohol by youths declines when either the price of alcoholic beverages or the legal drinking age increases. It is hoped in states taking these measures that alcohol-related motor vehicle accident mortality and other drug-related morbidity and mortality will decrease among adolescents.

Many unanswered questions still remain to be assessed by future research into prevention programs. Kumpfer and Demarsh (1986) have listed several major research issues that need further investigation:

1. The etiology of substance abuse, including prospective longitudinal studies in which low- and high-risk children are followed, in order to improve our understanding of why children do or do not become substance abusers.
2. The efficacy of prevention programs on various levels (school, national policies, etc.), in order to understand why they succeed or fail.
3. Side effects of prevention policies.
4. Cost-effectiveness of prevention programs, in order to find which

approaches are likely to produce the best ratio of benefit to cost and under what circumstances.

5. Clearer definitions of the goals of preventive programs (e.g., controlled drinking, drinking and not driving).

AIDS and the Adolescent Substance Abuser

Toward the end of 1987, 195 cases of AIDS in the age range of 13 to 19 years were diagnosed (Centers for Disease Control, 1987). Adolescents may contract AIDS through sharing dirty needles while abusing drugs intravenously, as well as through sexual contact. The adolescent substance abuser tends to initiate precocious drug and sexual activity, thus putting himself or herself at increased risk of contracting AIDS. Remafedi (1987) reported that gay and bisexual male adolescents had problems related to substance abuse as well. Adolescents may also contract AIDS through prostitution and sexual assaults. An increasing number of adolescent girls exchange sexual favors for drugs ("crack house girls") and may thus contract the fatal disease. High-risk populations such as adolescent substance abusers should be educated about the AIDS danger. Sex and AIDS education should be part of every curriculum in substance abuse treatment programs.

Testing for AIDS among substance abusers in general and among adolescents in particular is a sensitive issue. Conflicting opinions regarding whether, when, and to whom the test for the detection of human immunodeficiency virus (HIV) should be given divide the medical community. However, physicians and other mental health professionals should be aware that state laws may restrict actions recommended by the various available guidelines. It also appears that consensus regarding confidentiality, notification of third parties, and informed consent by the adolescent and his or her family is still far from being reached in the pediatric and psychiatric community. The need to solve this problem in communication, policy setting, and legislation is urgent.

Conclusion

This chapter has attempted to shed light on various aspects of adolescent substance abuse. It is impossible at this stage to answer many of the burning questions in the field, especially when the data generated by research are so scanty.

Future research should be based on rigorously controlled studies with random assignments if possible. Clinicians should exchange information on recent findings in this dynamic and constantly changing field, in order to identify new trends, prevent problems early where possible, and treat the afflicted adolescents. Last but not least, the medical education of students, residents, child fellows, and other health professionals in substance abuse is limited and needs to be more widespread and intensified. Only conjoint effort of all segments of health and education agencies will contribute to reduction of the magnitude of substance use, abuse, and dependence in adolescents, who are already or will shortly become the parents of the next generation of children of alcoholics and substance abusers.

Acknowledgment

The editors and I wish to acknowledge the late Joaquim Puig-Antich, M.D., for his valuable suggestions in preparing this chapter.

References

Ahmed, S. W., Bush, P. J., Davidson, F. R., & Iannotti, R. J. (1984). *Predicting children's use and intentions to use abusable substances.* Paper presented at the annual meeting of the American Public Health Association, Anaheim, CA.

Alterman, A. I., & Tarter, R. E. (1986). An examination of selected typologies: Hyperactivity, familial and antisocial alcoholism. In M. Galanter (Ed.), *Recent developments in alcoholism* (Vol. 4). New York: Plenum Press.

American Psychiatric Association. (1980). *Diagnostic and statistical manual of mental disorders* (3rd ed.). Washington, DC: Author.

American Psychiatric Association. (1987). *Diagnostic and statistical manual of mental disorders* (3rd ed., rev.). Washington, DC: Author.

Bandura, A. (1977). *Social learning theory.* Englewood Cliffs, NJ: Prentice-Hall.

Blane, H. (1979). Middle-aged alcoholics and young drinkers. In H. Blane & M. Chafetz (Eds.), *Youth, alcohol and social policy.* New York: Plenum Press.

Bohman, M., Sigvardsson, S., & Cloninger, C. R. (1981). Maternal inheritance of alcohol abuse. *Archives of General Psychiatry, 38,* 965–969.

Botvin, G., Baker, E., Remick, N., Filazzola, N., & Botvin, A. (1984). A cognitive behavioral approach to substance abuse prevention. *Journal of Addictive Behavior, 9,* 137–147.

Brent, D. A., Perper, J. A., & Allman, C. J. (1987). Alcohol, firearms, and suicide among youth. *Journal of the American Medical Association, 257,* 3369–3372.

Bulik, C. M. (1987). Drug and alcohol abuse by bulimic women and their families. *American Journal of Psychiatry, 144,* 1604–1606.

Bukstein, O. G., Brent, D. A., & Kaminer, Y. (1989). Comorbidity of substance abuse and other psychiatric disorders in adolescents. *American Journal of Psychiatry, 146,* 1131–1141.

Buydens-Branchey, L., Branchey, M. H., & Noumair, D. (1989). Age of alcoholism onset: I. Relationship to psychopathology. *Archives of General Psychiatry, 46,* 225–230.

Buydens-Branchey, L., Branchey, M. H., Noumair, D., & Lieber, C. S. (1989). Age of alcoholism onset: II. Relationship to susceptibility to serotonin precursor availability. *Archives of General Psychiatry, 46,* 231–236.

Cadoret, R. J., Troughton, E., O'Gorman, T. W., & Heywood, E. (1986). An adoption study of genetic and environmental factor in drug abuse. *Archives of General Psychiatry, 43,* 1131–1136.

Campanelli, P. C., Dielman, T. E., & Shope, J. T. (1987). Validity of adolescents' self-reports of alcoholic use and misuse using a bogus pipeline procedure. *Adolescence, 85,* 7–22.

Centers for Disease Control. (1987). Update: Acquired immunodeficiency syndrome—United States. *Morbidity and Mortality Weekly Report.*

Christie, K. A., Burke, J. D., Regier, D. A., Rae, D. S., Boyd, J. H., & Locke, B. Z. (1988).

Epidemiologic evidence for early onset of mental disorders and higher risk of drug abuse in young adults. *American Journal of Psychiatry, 145,* 971–975.

Cloninger, C. R., Bohman, M., & Sigvardsson, S. (1981). Inheritance of alcohol abuse. *Archives of General Psychiatry, 38,* 861–871.

Cloninger, C. R., Reich, T., Sigvardsson, S., Von Knorring, A. L., & Bohman, M. (1987). Effects of changes in alcohol use between generations on inheritance of alcohol abuse. In R. M. Rose & J. Barrett (Eds.), *Alcoholism: Origins and outcome.* New York: Raven Press.

Cohen, M., Karras, A., & Hughes, R. (1977). The usefulness and reliability of a drug severity scale. *International Journal of the Addictions, 12,* 417–422.

Committee on Adolescent Suicide. (1988). Suicide and suicide attempts in adolescents and young adults. *Pediatrics, 81,* 322:324.

Cook, P. J., & Tauchen, G. (1982). The effect of liquor taxes on heavy drinking. *Bell Journal of Economics, 13,* 379–390.

Cronkite, R. C., & Moos, R. H. (1978). Evaluating alcoholism treatment programs. *Journal of Consulting and Clinical Psychology, 45,* 1105–1119.

Crumley, F. E. (1990). Substance abuse and adolescent suicidal behavior. *Journal of the American Medical Association, 263,* 3051–3056.

Deykin, E. Y., Levy, J. C., & Weller, V. (1986). Adolescent depression, alcohol and drug abuse. *American Journal of Public Health, 76,* 178–182.

Feinstein, A. R. (1970). The pre-therapeutic classification of comorbidity in chronic disease. *Journal of Chronic Diseases, 23,* 455–468.

Filstead, W. J. (1982). Adolescence and alcohol. In E. M. Pattison & E. Kaufman (Eds.), *Encyclopedic handbook of alcoholism.* New York: Gardner Press.

Friedman, A. (1987). *Adolescent drug abuse diagnosis.* Unpublished manuscript, Philadelphia Psychiatric Center.

Friedman, A. S., & Glickman, N. W. (1986). Program characteristics for successful treatment of adolescent substance abuse. *Journal of Nervous and Mental Disease, 174,* 669–679.

Gittelman, R., Mannuzza, S., Shenker, R., & Bonagura, N. (1985). Hyperactive boys almost grown up: I. Psychiatric status. *Archives of General Psychiatry, 42,* 937–947.

Goodwin, D. W. (1985). Alcoholism and genetics: The sins of the fathers. *Archives of General Psychiatry, 42,* 171–174.

Gossett, J., Lewis, M., & Phillips, V. (1972). Psychological characteristics of adolescent drug abusers and abstainers: Some implications for preventive education. *Bulletin of the Menninger Clinic, 36,* 425–435.

Helzer, J. E., & Pryzbeck, T. R. (1988). The co-occurence of alcoholism with other psychiatric disorders in the general population and its impact on treatment. *Journal of Studies on Alcohol, 49,* 219–224.

Henley, G., & Winters, K. (1988). Development of problem severity scales for the assessment of adolescent alcohol and drug abuse. *International Journal of the Addictions, 23,* 65–85.

Jalali, B., Jalali, M., Crocetti, G., & Turner, F. (1980). Adolescent and drug use: Toward a more comprehensive approach. *American Journal of Orthopsychiatry, 51,* 120–130.

Jessor, R. (1976). Predicting time and onset of marijuana use: A developmental study of high school youth. *Journal of Consulting and Clinical Psychology, 44,* 125–134.

Jessor, R. (1987). Problem-behavior theory, psychosocial development and adolescent problem drinking. *British Journal of Addiction, 82,* 331–342.

Jessor, R., & Jessor, S. L. (1977). *Problem behavior and psychosocial development: A longitudinal study of youth.* New York: Academic Press.

Johnston, L., Bachman, J. G., & O'Malley, P. M. (1987). *National trends in drug use and related factors among American high school students and young adults, 1975–1986* (DHHS Publication No. ADM 87-1535). Washington, DC: U.S. Government Printing Office.

Johnston, L., Bachman, J. G., & O'Malley, P. M. (1988). Details of annual survey. *University of Michigan News and Information Services, 1,* 1–5.

Johnston, L., O'Malley, P. M., & Bachman, J. G. (1989). *Drug use, drinking, and smoking: National survey results from high school, college, and young adult populations, 1975–1988*

(DHHS Publication No. ADM 89-1638). Washington, DC: U.S. Government Printing Office.

Kaminer, Y., Bukstein, O. G., & Tarter, R. E. (1991). The Teen Addiction Severity Index: Rationale and reliability. *International Journal of the Addictions, 26.*

Kaminer, Y., Feingold, M., & Lyons, K. (1988). Bulimia in a pair of monozygotic twins. *Journal of Nervous and Mental Disease, 176,* 246–248.

Kandel, D. B. (1975). Stages in adolescent involvement in drug use. *Science, 190,* 912–914.

Kandel, D. B. (1978). *Longitudinal research on drug use: Empirical findings and methodological issues.* New York: Hemisphere-Wiley.

Kandel, D. B. (1982). Epidemiological and psychosocial perspectives on adolescent drug use. *Journal of the American Academy of Child Psychiatry, 20,* 328–347.

Kashani, J. H., Keller, M. B., Solomon, N., Reid, J. C., & Mazzola, D. (1985). Double depression in adolescent substance users. *Journal of Affective Disorders, 8,* 153–157.

Kozel, N. J., & Adams, E. H. (1986). Epidemiology of drug abuse: An overview. *Science, 234,* 970–974.

Kumpfer, K. L., & Demarsh, J. (1986). Future issues and promising directions in the prevention of substance abuse among youth. *Journal of Children in Contemporary Society, 18,* 49–91.

Lettieri, D. J. (1985). Drug abuse: A review of explanations and models of explanation. *Advances in Substance Abuse, 4,* 9–40.

Longabaugh, R. (1987). Longitudinal outcome studies. In R. M. Rose & J. Barrett (Eds.), *Alcoholism: Origins and outcome.* New York: Raven Press.

Mannuzza, S., Gittelman, R., Konig, P., & Giampino, T. L. (1989). Hyperactive boys almost grown up: IV. Criminality and its relationship to psychiatric status. *Archives of General Psychiatry, 46,* 1073–1079.

McLellan, A. T., Luborsky, L., Woody, G. E., & O'Brien, C. P. (1980). An improved diagnostic evaluation instrument for substance abuse patients. *Journal of Nervous and Mental Disease, 40,* 620–625.

Meyer, R. E. (1986). Old wine, new bottle—the alcohol dependence syndrome. *Psychiatric Clinics of North America, 3,* 435–453.

Miles, C. P. (1977). Conditions predisposing to suicide: A review. *Journal of Nervous and Mental Disease, 164,* 231–246.

Moore, D. (1980). *Client Substance Abuse Index.* Unpublished manuscript, Olympic Counselling Services, Tacoma, WA.

National Institute on Alcohol Abuse and Alcoholism (NIAAA). (1981–1982). *Facts for planning: Alcohol and youth* (No. 1-7). Rockville, MD: Author.

Pandina, R. J. (1986). Problems and trends in studies of adolescent drinking practices. *Annals of Behavioral Medicine, 8,* 20–26.

Remafedi, G. (1987). Adolescent homosexuality: Psychosocial and medical implications. *Pediatrics, 79,* 331–337.

Reichler, B. D., Clement, J. L., & Dunner, D. L. (1983). Chart review of alcohol problems in adolescent psychiatric patients in an emergency room. *Journal of Clinical Psychiatry, 44,* 338–339.

Rich, C. L., Young, D., & Fowler, R. C. (1986). San Diego Suicide Study: I. Young vs. old subjects. *Archives of General Psychiatry, 43,* 577–582.

Rounsaville, B. J., Kosten, T. R., Weissman, M. M., & Kleber, H. D. (1986). Prognostic significance of psychiatric disorders in treated opiate addicts. *Archives of General Psychiatry, 43,* 739–745.

Rounsaville, B. J., Spitzer, R. L., & Williams, J. B. W. (1986). Proposed changes in DSM-III substance use disorders: Description and rationale. *American Journal of Psychiatry, 143,* 463–468.

Rush, T. V. (1979). Predicting treatment outcome for juvenile and young adult clients in the Pennsylvania substance-abuse system. In G. M. Berschner & A. S. Friedman (Eds.), *Youth drug abuse.* Lexington, MA: Lexington Books.

Schuckit, M. A., Zisook, S., & Mortola, J. (1985). Clinical implications of DSM-III diagnoses of alcohol abuse and alcohol dependence. *American Journal of Psychiatry, 142,* 1403–1404.

Siegel, R. K. (1987). *Cocaine: Changing patterns of usage.* Paper presented at the McLean Hospital Symposium on Cocaine, Belmont, MA.

Smart, R., & Jones, D. (1970). Illicit LSD users: Their personality characteristics and psychopathology. *Journal of Abnormal Psychology, 75,* 286–292.

Sobell, L. C., & Sobell, M. B. (1978). Validity of self-reports in three populations of alcoholics. *Journal of Consulting and Clinical Psychology, 46,* 901–907.

Spitzer, R. L., Endicott, J., & Robins, E. (1978). Research Diagnostic Criteria: Rationale and reliability. *Archives of General Psychiatry, 35,* 773–782.

Swaim, R. C., Oetting, E. R., Edwards, R. W., & Beauvais, F. (1989). Links from emotional distress to adolescent drug use: A path model. *Journal of Consulting and Clinical Psychology, 57,* 227–231.

Tarter, R. E. (1990). Evaluation and treatment of adolescent substance abuse: A decision tree method. *American Journal of Drug and Alcohol Abuse, 16,* 1–46.

Tucker, L. A. (1985). Television's role regarding alcohol use among teenagers. *Adolescence, 20,* 593–598.

Weiss, G., & Hechtman, L. (1986). *Hyperactive children grown up.* New York: Guilford Press.

Woody, G. E., McLellan, A. T., Luborsky, L., & O'Brien, C. P. (1985). Sociopathy and psychotherapy outcome. *Archives of General Psychiatry, 42,* 1081–1085.

Zweben, A., & Li, S. (1981). The efficacy of role induction in preventing early dropout from outpatient treatment of drug dependency. *American Journal of Drug and Alcohol Abuse, 8,* 171–83.

15

Geriatric Addictions

ROBERT C. ABRAMS

GEORGE ALEXOPOULOS

Introduction

Although some efforts have been made in recent years to study geriatric alcoholism (Atkinson, 1984; Glynn, Bouchard, LoCastro, & Laird, 1985; Clark & Midanik, 1982), this area has been relatively neglected as a topic of investigation. As a result, the true scope and extent of geriatric alcoholism, whether in patterns of alcohol abuse or of alcohol dependence, remain unknown. This lack of knowledge is compounded in the elderly by particular difficulties in detection; at the same time, the medical and psychiatric consequences of alcohol consumption are probably greatest for older persons. The pervasiveness of alcohol use in our society, coupled with the demographic and political importance of the elderly population, insures an increasing focus on geriatric alcoholism in the future.

That greater attention will be paid to the abuse and misuse of prescription and nonprescription drugs by the elderly is also a certainty. Persons over 65 years of age account for a considerable proportion of *all* medications used in the United States, with a particular emphasis on drugs targeted for the management of chronic conditions. Thus, the addictions that appear in geriatric patients differ from those of younger groups, both in the selection of drugs and in the clinical course of the addictions. As is required for older alcoholics, treatment of geriatric patients with addictions to prescription or over-the-counter drugs requires sensitivity to the life circumstances, physiological changes, and concurrent medical and psychiatric disorders of this population. Following the discussion of geriatric alcoholism, this chapter separately considers geriatric addictions in prescription and nonprescription drugs, reviewing current knowledge and treatment approaches in each area.

Geriatric Alcoholism

Epidemiology

The prevalence of geriatric alcoholism diagnosable by *Diagostic and Statistical Manual of Mental Disorders,* third edition, revised (DSM-III-R) criteria

(American Psychiatric Association, 1987) cannot be asserted with precision. Estimates of problem drinking, generally defined as patterns of abuse or dependence leading to significant social or health consequences, have ranged from 2% to 10% of the general population over the age of 60 and up to 20% of nursing home residents (Bailey, Haberman, & Alksne, 1965; Gaitz & Baer, 1971; Siassi, Crocetti, & Spiro, 1973). These data, however, are mostly derived from community surveys, which base the impression of alcoholism on quantity of intake or presence of alcohol-related problems (Atkinson & Schuckit, 1983). In contrast, studies using clinical diagnosis of elderly medical and psychiatric inpatients have produced prevalence estimates of 18% and 44%, respectively (Schuckit & Miller, 1976; Gaitz & Baer, 1971).

Cross-sectional data suggest that heavy drinking is most frequent in early middle age. Using national survey data, Cahalan, Cisin, and Crossley (1969) found that heavy drinking peaked in the 40- to 49-year age group and declined thereafter. In the same study, Cahalan et al. (1969) reported a particularly sharp decline in the percentage of heavy drinkers among men from the 60- to 64-year age group to the over-65-year age group (from 20% to 7%). A corresponding reduction in the percentage of heavy drinkers among women was also shown, but occurred earlier, at age 50. Abstinence rates for both men and women tend to increase steadily by decade (Barnes, 1979; Cahalan et al., 1969; Christopherson, Escher, & Bainton, 1984).

Closer examination of the over-60 age group reveals small but potentially meaningful deviations from the trends outlined above. For example, some investigators have suggested the possibility of an increase in alcohol abuse after 70 years of age (McCourt, Williams, & Schneider, 1971; Barnes, 1979). In Barnes's data, based on a general population survey in western New York State, heavy drinkers accounted for 24% of males aged 60–69 and 6% of males aged 70–96; among women in the study, heavy drinkers were not represented at all in the 60–69 age group, yet comprised 2% of those aged 70–90. Further investigations are needed to replicate and refine these data. However, there is cross-sectional evidence for the existence of a subpopulation of alcoholics whose problem drinking begins in advanced age, distinct both from younger alcoholics and from similar-age alcoholics having earlier onset. This subgroup may involve women to a greater extent than men.

The apparent decline in alcoholism found in cross-sectional surveys has also been challenged on the basis of differential mortality of alcoholics and nonalcoholics, with particular reference to the higher mortality of alcoholic men (Glynn et al., 1985). Moreover, elderly alcoholics are more likely to be either cognitively impaired or institutionalized and therefore unable to participate in surveys. Cohort differences may also be partially responsible for the reported decline of alcoholism in the elderly (Glynn et al., 1985). For example, the generation that lived through Prohibition and the Depression, when heavy drinking was perhaps less prevalent, might be less likely to produce large numbers of elderly alcoholics than generations that came of age in more permissive times. Data from the investigations by Glynn et al. (1985), which were based on a longitudinal study of aging, showed a decline in problems associated with drinking in successively older cohorts, but no tendency for individuals to decrease their alcohol consumption over time. The tendency for individuals to persist in their drinking habits, health and other conditions permitting, into advanced age was also noted by Christopherson et al. (1984) in their study of drinking patterns among the elderly in rural Arizona, and by Glynn et al. (1985) using data from the Normative Aging Study. Stability of individual drinking patterns, together with the less restrictive attitudes toward drinking in recent generations, may provide the basis for a future increase in geriatric alcoholism. In a recent study, for example, Alexander and Duff (1988) surveyed 260 residents of three retirement communities and found that only 21.5% were abstainers, compared to 45% in the general population (U.S. Bureau of the Census, 1987). Alexander and Duff hypothesized that relatively low rates of abstaining may reflect the middle- and upper-middle-class orientation of retirement communities and the important role of alcohol in their social structure. The cocktail hour appears to be a focal event in the daily life of many retirement communities.

Clinical Features

The division of geriatric alcoholics into clinical subgroups according to age of onset has become generally accepted (Atkinson, 1984; Mishara & Kastenbaum, 1980). The "late-onset" classification in some studies refers to onset of illness after age 60 (Simon, Epstein, & Reynolds, 1968; Rosin & Glatt, 1971) and represents a category of patients who begin to abuse alcohol late in life as a response to the stresses of aging. In other studies, the age of 40 is used as the demarcation between early- and late-onset alcoholism (Schuckit & Miller, 1976; Atkinson, Turner, Kofoed, & Tolson, 1985). The "early-onset" classification represents the category of patients who have established a continuous pattern of abuse in early adulthood. Among patients over the age of 60 who have been hospitalized or come to psychiatric attention for alcoholism, approximately one-third will have become alcoholic after the age of 60 (late-onset), while two-thirds will have had a long history of alcohol abuse (early-onset) (Simon et al., 1968; Rosin & Glatt, 1971). As a rule, the early-onset patients have social and medical histories that reflect the disruption of chronic alcohol abuse, and have more family alcoholism and less current psychological stability than do late-onset patients (Atkinson et al., 1985).

Whether late-onset alcoholism is defined as beginning after age 40 or age 60, it has been asserted that actively drinking older alcoholics probably first became symptomatic in their 40s or 50s (Schuckit, 1982); this seems reasonable because of the greater chance of early death among individuals whose pattern of alcohol abuse begins in late adolescence or young adulthood. According to Schuckit (1982), it therefore follows that geriatric alcoholics as a group tend to have had less criminality, fewer contacts with the mental health system, and more overall stability early in life than younger alcoholics.

Although late-onset alcoholism has been conceptualized as a maladaptive response to recent age-related events rather than the product of long-standing psychosocial problems (Dupree, Broskowski, & Schonfeld, 1984), the relationship between late-onset alcoholism and life events is not straightforward. In a survey of 1,410 noninstitutionalized adults over age 60 living in both retirement and age-integrated communities, LaGreca, Akers, and Dwyer (1988) found that the majority of respondents (73.6%) had experienced at least one importantly stressful life event in the past year, including most frequently the death of a family member or close friend, personal health problems, or family members with health problems. The authors found no association between the occurrence of life events and the frequency, quantity, or negative consequences of drinking. Nevertheless, 5% of this sample had started drinking, increased their drinking, or become heavy drinkers over the preceding year. Social supports, moreover, appeared to have little modifying impact with respect to drinking behavior. These findings, if replicated in a clinical study, would challenge the more conventional view of late-onset alcoholism as having a direct relationship to recent negative life events (Dupree et al., 1984).

The course of geriatric alcoholism has been little studied. One follow-up investigation (Schuckit, Miller, & Berman, 1980) examined the 3-year course of elderly alcoholics. Alcoholism at the outset of the study was associated with the existence of an alcoholic condition 3 years later, although approximately 20% of the subjects had stopped drinking for at least 1 year and 30% developed dementia during the 3-year period. Those subjects originally classified as inactive alcoholics, having had significant alcoholism but not in the recent past, tended to remain symptom-free; only 20% of the inactive group developed recurrence of symptoms during the study period. These longitudinal data further support the persistence of individual drinking patterns over time.

Consequences of Geriatric Alcoholism

The hazards of heavy alcohol consumption in the elderly have been extensively described in the literature (Atkinson, 1984; Mishara & Kastenbaum, 1980). However, the range of alcohol-related problems in the nonalcoholic geriatric population is less well known and deserves mention here. General metabolic changes of aging, including decreased activity of hepatic enzymes and reduction of lean body mass, result in slowed metabolic breakdown and elimination of all drugs. Alcohol, which is water-soluble, is distributed through a smaller mass of lean tissue, and consequently is found in higher concentrations within organs. Blood alcohol levels persist for longer periods of time. In addition, aging is associated with increased sensitivity to all central nervous system (CNS)-depressing agents, including alcohol (Raskind & Eisdorfer, 1976). These factors influence overall tolerance of alcohol, which is usually described as decreasing with age (Bosmann, 1984; Schuckit, 1982). Thus, nonalcoholic elderly patients with pulmonary disease may experience potentially dangerous effects on respiration secondary to CNS responses to alcohol; cardiovascular patients may experience a masking of anginal pain without reduction in the potential for myocardial damage; and in all elderly individuals, relatively small amounts of alcohol are more likely to cause acute confusional states.

Also, the probability of adverse drug interactions is greater in the elderly, since they are likely to be taking more than one prescription or over-the-counter medication at any given time. Alcohol-induced potentiation of CNS depressants such as barbiturates and benzodiazepines often results in confusion, and can cause respiratory depression and death. Alcohol-induced inhibition of the metabolism of many other agents can lead to toxic states (Raskind & Eisdorfer, 1976; Schuckit, 1982); this can occur with both antipsychotic and antidepressant medications, two classes of drugs commonly used by the elderly.

The health implications of chronic alcohol abuse are of course magnified. In addition to the specific metabolic changes of aging outlined here, aging increases the body's sensitivity to stressors and decreases its overall resiliency and efficiency. The effects of aging and habitual heavy drinking can best be regarded as cumulative with respect to the body's capacity to compensate for illness and stress. Some of the health effects of chronic alcoholism may also be attributed to homelessness, negligent hygiene, malnutrition, and poor medical care, all risk factors associated with the alcoholic lifestyle. These factors may be partially responsible for some alcoholic comorbidity. Examples might include the high rates of obstructive pulmonary disease in alcoholics, approximately 90% of whom are also smokers, or the very high rates of esophageal cancer among alcoholics, who represent more than half of all such cases (Mishara & Kastenbaum, 1980).

From the cardiovascular perspective, heavy drinking is specifically linked to the development of cardiomyopathy (McDonald, Burch, & Walsh, 1971) and the exacerbation of already impaired cardiac functioning (Gould, Zahir, & Demartino, 1971). Ingestion of three drinks or more daily has been associated with hypertension and exacerbation of hyperlipidemias (Mendelson & Mello, 1973). Moderate regular use of alcohol may be associated with lower rates of congestive heart disease, and may also exert a protective effect against the development of coronary artery disease by increasing high-density lipoprotein cholesterol (Kannel, 1986). However, the putative cardioprotective effects of moderate drinking have not been established; and chronic heavy drinking has been associated with the development of stroke, arrhythmia, and cardiac failure, as well as having the links to hypertension and hyperlipidemia mentioned previously.

Cognitive impairment is among the most significant clinical consequences of alcoholism. It may occur to some degree in individuals of any age, but the older alcoholic is plainly at greatest risk. Among geriatric alcoholics, the prevalence of full or irreversible dementia has been estimated to be between 25% and 60% (Bienenfeld, 1990). Full dementia involves impaired memory, orientation, calculation, word finding, and abstraction, although some of the dementia in geriatric alcoholics is attributable to Wernicke's encephalopathy, which often presents clinically with isolated memory impairment. Either exacerbation of pre-existing primary degenerative or multi-infarct dementia, or direct CNS alcohol toxicity, is more common than Wernicke's encephalopathy as an etiology of irreversible dementia among geriatric alcoholics. Acute-onset confusion can be brought on by alcohol intoxication or withdrawal (Schuckit, 1982).

Other psychiatric symptoms are often observed in elderly alcoholics. Depression of varying intensity is nearly universal; this may be specifically related to the abrupt drop in blood alcohol levels that follows an episode of heavy drinking (Schuckit, 1979), as well as to the general CNS depressant effects of alcohol or to an underlying depressive syndrome. Auditory hallucinations and paranoid delusions are not infrequently reported (Victor & Hope, 1958). Habitual heavy alcohol consumption leads to erectile and ejaculatory impotence in the male. Although alcohol does not appear to affect total sleep time, rapid eye movement (REM) and δ sleep are both decreased, resulting in irritability and lethargy. Some elderly individuals use alcohol as self-medication for insomnia, particularly for sleep-onset difficulties. However, there is often a rebound wakefulness later in the night in response to falling blood alcohol levels.

Detection and Treatment

Alcoholism is far less likely to be detected and treated in the geriatric population. In part, this is because the impairments in social and occupational functioning that are referable to alcoholism in younger people are not as obvious in the elderly. Losses of jobs, drivers' licenses, and social supports are common experiences for the elderly, whether they are alcoholics or not. Furthermore, the clinical as well as the social consequences of alcoholism are difficult to distinguish from those of aging itself. Sleep and sexual functioning show declines with both normal aging and alcoholism (Hartford & Samorajski, 1982). In particular, the effects of alcohol abuse on cognitive abilities may mimic, if not compound, the deficits associated with primary degenerative dementia. Even occasional social drinking is more likely to be associated with transient cognitive impairment in older than in younger persons.

One problem in the detection of geriatric alcoholism is that the absolute quantities of alcohol consumed are irrelevant, and in fact may be quite small. This is a result of the reduced tolerance for alcohol and CNS-depressing drugs, alluded to earlier in the chapter. The diagnosis of alcohol abuse or dependence must be based on the pattern of alcohol consumption and its medical and social consequences. However, as with all psychiatric diagnoses involving the elderly, DSM-III-R criteria must be interpreted flexibly for each individual, with a view to what would be expectable for the later stages of the life cycle.

Again, criteria for social disruption, such as loss of job or spouse, may not be relevant to someone who is already retired or widowed. Similarly, pre-existing medical problems must be carefully distinguished from those that are demonstrably consequences of alcoholic behavior.

The so-called "enablers" in an elderly alcoholic's social sphere may also contribute to preventing detection. Sometimes referred to as "rescuers," these are individuals who either encourage or passively permit the alcoholic to persist in drinking. Occasionally the enabler is a misguided employer or medical professional, but he or she is more often likely to be a spouse—who may also be an elderly alcoholic (Bienenfeld, 1990). Where physicians are involved, this relaxation of the usual professional vigilance probably represents an insidious age bias, which in turn reflects that of the larger society. Age itself has been identified as a risk factor for inadequate treatment by health care personnel (Wetle, 1987). In a recent study of medical inpatients at Johns Hopkins Hospital, only 37% of elderly individuals identified as alcoholics by standard screening tests were identified in this way by their house officers; in contrast, 60% of screen-positive younger patients were identified as alcoholics by their house officers. Even when correctly diagnosed by their physicians, elderly patients were less likely than younger patients to have treatment for their alcoholism (Curtis, Geller, Stokes, Levine, & Moore, 1989).

What, then, are the circumstances in which geriatric alcoholism *can* be detected? At any age, alcohol dependence or abuse is unlikely to be the chief complaint. In an older person, unexpected or unwarranted reaction to a prescription or over-the-counter drug may be the first indication of habitual heavy drinking. Mental status or behavioral changes, particularly the abrupt onset of confusion, anxiety states, auditory hallucinations, or frank delusions, are also clues to possible alcoholism. It has been noted that depression, while nonspecific, may be linked to drinking as either an underlying condition or a secondary consequence. The presence of clinically significant depression, along with all unexpected drug reactions and behavioral changes, should at least initiate the appropriate history taking regarding possible alcohol abuse. The index of suspicion must necessarily be high, and one should not be misled by individuals' tendency to minimize their levels of anxiety and depression as well as the extent of their drinking. The use of collateral sources of information, such as family members, is typically required. Family members may also report possible alcohol-related behaviors, such as falls, incontinence, memory lapses, arrests, or auto accidents, that a patient may be unable or unwilling to recall. Considerable tact is called for in discussing alcohol problems with an elderly person, but gentleness should not come at the expense of clarity and directness; the older person must inevitably understand and acknowledge that he or she has a drinking problem. Denial, a nearly universal phenomenon in alcoholic patients in the early phases of the illness, can take on a seemingly impenetrable aspect in older persons.

Treatment usually begins with detoxification, which in all but the mildest cases should take place in a hospital setting. Hospitalization is recommended because of the need for careful medical monitoring and the high frequency of concurrent medical problems. Geriatric patients are sensitive to relatively small-dose increments of pharmacological agents, and alcohol detoxification is therefore a lengthier and more hazardous procedure for these patients. To avoid signs and symptoms of withdrawal, Bienenfeld (1990) recommends the preferential use of benzodiazepines having short half-lives, such as oxazepam or lorazepam, over those with longer half-lives, notably diazepam; the incidence of secondary confusion or delirium is substantially greater with the latter. Suggested dosage regimens for the use of benzodiazepines in detoxification vary considerably, but a conservative approach (with hourly monitoring of vital signs if necessary) is probably best suited to the geriatric population.

The rehabilitation aspect of treatment should be tailored to an understanding of the individual's psychological state and motivations for drinking. Most important are the individual circumstances that lead to drinking behavior. These often include concurrent psychiatric syndromes, including depression, anxiety disorder, incipient dementias, and other conditions. Schuckit (1979, 1982) uses the term "secondary alcoholics" to denote the group of patients whose drinking behaviors have arisen only as a consequence of a primary psychiatric disorder. These patients are estimated to account for 5% to 15% of alcoholics of all ages. The practical implication for treatment is that specific psychopharmacological and psychotherapeutic interventions should be directed toward the primary disorder as soon as possible following detoxification. This procedure may also help clarify whether the psychiatric syndrome, usually depression, is pre-existing or secondary to the alcoholism, since a primary syndrome would tend to remain substantially unchanged after detoxification has been completed. It should be understood, however, that any such rules regarding the distinctions between primary and secondary alcoholism may be oversimplifications; for example, some depressive signs and symptoms may be associated with detoxification itself and may persist for varying periods of time.

In the hospital rehabilitation program setting, investigators have proposed a wide variety of therapeutic approaches, including behavioral, supportive, and dynamic psychotherapies, as well as Alcoholics Anonymous (AA) (Schuckit, 1977; Trice, 1959; Zimberg, 1974). Both age-segregated and mixed-age treatment settings have their proponents (Mishara & Kastenbaum, 1980). Some authors note that mixed-age settings have the advantage for both older and younger age groups of the intergenerational perspective encouraged by the age mix. Others prefer the easier atmosphere of similar-age peer groups, and point with concern to the fear and alarm engendered in older people by the harshly confrontational styles adopted, particularly in group therapies, in younger inpatient settings. Also, geriatric patients on mixed-age units may need to be shielded from threatening or other acting-out behaviors of younger substance abuse patients. Many geriatric patients have well-justified fears about their physical safety in such environments. Whether the inpatient unit is mixed-age or age-segregated, whether it treats both primary and secondary alcoholism (the "dual-diagnosis" setting) or focuses its programs specifically on primary alcoholism, or whether it also treats patients having other substance abuse disorders, the critical factors in the treatment milieu appear to be creativity, flexibility, and sensitivity to the needs of the elderly. As an example, disulfiram (Antabuse), a mainstay of treatment in younger patients, is less frequently used in the geriatric population because of the greater possibility of serious medical consequences from adverse reactions. Group work is important, as with younger patients, but family interventions have a particular importance in work with the elderly, since family members are the individuals who may function as enablers. Educational approaches with families often appear to be helpful, perhaps because some family members cannot fathom that a person of advanced age could have a significant drinking problem. Individual psychotherapies are generally present-oriented and supportive in orientation, geared toward clarifying and addressing the life circumstances that have supported drinking. Working with elderly patients in psychotherapy requires sensitivity to the experiences, lifestyle, and outlook of older persons. The depth and extent of losses borne by the elderly persons must be kept in mind particularly; these include losses of spouse, peers, job, health, physical independence, and financial security, among others. However, the efficacy of these approaches for elderly alcoholics has yet to be established in controlled studies.

A point of some controversy in the management of elderly alcoholics is the requirement for strict abstinence. Mishara and Kastenbaum (1980) have argued that abstinence may not be necessary for all geriatric problem drinkers and have accordingly proposed a broader range of criteria for successful treatment outcome—criteria that emphasize improvement in overall functioning rather than duration or completeness of abstinence. Such an approach can be criticized for deemphasizing the individual's adjustment to a life not focused on drinking—an aspect of treatment that most clinicians who work with alcoholics deem essential. AA, in which patients of all ages have found help, is organized around the principle of abstinence and is based on acknowledgment of alcoholism as an ongoing illness. It is reasonable to conclude that abstinence should remain the primary goal of treatment for all alcoholics, with perhaps some degree of flexibility accorded when appropriate in the geriatric population.

There remains a substantial need for well-designed clinical research on the predictors, presentation, course, and outcomes of the various treatment approaches of geriatric alcoholism. Also, data distinguishing the course, outcome, and predictors of outcome for late- versus early-onset alcoholism are needed. The role of various risk factors, including family history, demographic and socioeconomic status, and life events, should be carefully elucidated.

Little is known about prognosis in geriatric alcoholism. Secondary alcoholism as defined by Schuckit (1982) would appear to have a more favorable outlook than primary alcoholism, provided that appropriate treatment is directed toward the pre-existing disorder. Late-onset alcoholism probably has a better prognosis than early-onset geriatric alcoholism. However, there are differences in the literature on the age for designation of late-onset alcoholism, and there is no clear consensus on the requirements for recovery (i.e., length or completeness of abstinence).

Finally, geriatric alcoholism as a public health problem requires increasing efforts at prevention, education, and early identification of individuals at risk. Age specific screening and diagnostic procedures are needed, as well as treatment strategies geared specifically to the elderly population. All of these are the expected fruits of future research.

Prescription Drug Abuse and Misuse in the Elderly

The elderly are the largest users of legal drugs in the national population, accounting for approximately 30% of all prescriptions (Koch & Knapp, 1987). The 1985 National Ambulatory Medical Care Survey of office physicians found that at least one drug was prescribed or given in more than 68% of office visits by patients 65 years of age or older (Baum, Kennedy, & Forbes, 1985). Cardiovascular drugs, sedatives/hypnotics and tranquilizers, and analgesics are the most frequently used medications. It has been estimated that 25% of all persons in the geriatric age range use psychoactive drugs (Finlayson, 1984).

Although the extent of prescription drug problems among the elderly is difficult to determine, the wide use of these drugs, the tendency of older people to be taking multiple medications, and the increased sensitivity of the elderly to toxic effects all enhance the possibility of mishap. Learoyd (1972) reported that almost 20% of the patients admitted to a geriatric unit in a general hospital in Australia had a prescription drug-related disorder. Raskind, Alvarez, Pietrzyk, Westerlund, and Herlin (1976) found that 26% of patients referred to a clinic for dementia workup had had an adverse drug reaction. Whitcup and Miller (1987) reported that more than 20% of patients over 65 years old admitted to a psychiatric hospital in 1 year could be regarded as drug-dependent; of these, half were neither recognized nor detoxified, and some went on to exhibit significant medical complications. In this same study, female benzodiazepine abusers were somewhat less likely to be identified than male alcoholics. Other studies in more representative geriatric populations have produced smaller percentages of drug abuse and dependency. Stephens, Haney, and Underwood (1981), for example, found that of a sample of 1,101 noninstitutionalized residents of Houston over 55 years old, only about 7% could be described as misusers of prescribed psychoactive drugs. However, since 40% of the sample used such drugs, some on a chronic basis, the potential for misuse appears to be considerable.

Problems with prescription drugs may involve intentional abuse, either by erratic use, overuse, or contraindicated use, or unintentional misuse, usually by erroneous underuse or overuse. In either case, the prescribing physician is involved and must assume responsibility for recognizing a patient's capacity to abuse medications intentionally or inability to process instructions accurately. Failure of the physician to take a thorough medication inventory, including both prescription and nonprescription drugs, can easily result in duplication of drugs and an increased possibility of adverse interactions or toxicity. Perfunctory prescribing over the telephone can lead to misjudgment in the selection of medication, failure to take into account the most recent changes in the patient's mental and physical status, and miscommunication of dosing instructions.

There is also evidence that some institutionalized elderly patients are receiving unnecessary, inappropriate, or excessive doses of psychoactive drugs, usually without informed consent. A recent investigation of Massachusetts nursing homes (Beers et al., 1988) revealed that over 50% of residents in 12 representative nursing homes studied over a 1-month period received psychoactive medication; 26% of residents received antipsychotic medication. Many of the antipsychotic drug orders were written on an as-needed (p.r.n.) basis, suggesting that their intended purpose was for behavioral control rather than amelioration of specific psychotic target symptoms. It is likely that the p.r.n. format enhances the potential for inappropriate use by placing the decision to medicate in the hands of multiple staff personnel. Moreover, benzodiazepines were typically given to this group in doses and for time periods sufficient to cause dependency.

For the elderly living independently, analgesics and anxiolytics/sedatives/hypnotics have the greatest potential for prescription drug abuse and misuse. Finlayson (1984) found that elderly individuals who were intentional abusers of prescription drugs primarily abused analgesics, most citing pain as the chief reason for abuse; this group, in contrast to unintentional misusers of prescription drugs, tended to be of high socioeconomic status. A strong trend toward avoidance of stimulants was noted.

Since their introduction in the 1960s, benzodiazepines have been heavily used by elderly populations. One reason may be that these drugs were originally marketed as particularly safe and effective relative to meprobamate, which had previously been widely used and abused by older patients. Also, the elderly have rates of anxiety disorders that, although somewhat lower than those found in younger age groups, are nevertheless considerable. According to a summary by Blazer (1989), based on data from the National Institute of Mental Health (NIMH) Epidemiologic Catchment Area program, the overall rate of anxiety disorders is 5.5% for persons aged 65 or older; the rates for elderly men are lower than for elderly women (3.6% for men overall and 6.8% overall for women). However, these factors alone probably do not explain the extent of benzodiazepine use in the geriatric population.

In one survey, as many as 33% of chronic daily benzodiazepine users were elderly (Mellinger, Bolter, & Uhlenhuth, 1984). Benzodiazepine use in the elderly may appear to be even more disproportionate if usage demographics of benzodiazepine hypnotics are evaluated separately. Schweizer, Case, and Rickels (1989) cite survey data from the National Disease and Therapeutic Index indicating that patients 65 and older account for 26% of prescriptions written for benzodiazepine antianxiety agents, but 40% of prescriptions for hypnotics of this class.

In addition to the relative safety of benzodiazepines, their wide marketing by manufacturers, and the prevalence of anxiety disorders, geriatric use of these drugs may be encouraged by additional factors. One is possible comorbidity with alcohol abuse and dependence. Another factor is potential misuse of antianxiety drugs as self-medication for other conditions, primarily depression. It has been noted that anxiolytics are the medications most frequently prescribed for the elderly by primary care physicians, whereas the drugs most frequently prescribed by psychiatrists for the elderly are antidepressants (Beardsley, Gardocki, Larson, & Hidalgo, 1988). Since primary care physicians account for a higher percentage of patient visits and prescriptions in this age group, their prescribing patterns will have a greater impact and may encourage the tendency of patients to self-medicate depression syndromes with antianxiety agents.

Also involved in geriatric use of benzodiazepines is the ubiquity of sleep disturbances, even among healthy older people. Some of these difficulties reflect age-related changes unrelated to depression or anxiety syndromes. A healthy older person is likely to have more disrupted sleep as well as less total time spent in REM and deeper sleep stages, and will usually be awake for 20% of the night (Miles & Dement, 1980). Consequently, many, if not most, elderly persons complain of insomnia and may well become chronic users of benzodiazepine hypnotics if reassurance or conservative measures are not the physician's first approach.

Relatively little attention has been given to the treatment of prescription drug dependency in the elderly. Hospitalization may be indicated for detoxification or gradual withdrawal from a chronically used drug. Schweizer et al. (1989) have recently shown that gradual tapering of benzodiazepine doses and complete discontinuation of the drugs are at least as well tolerated by hospitalized geriatric patients as by younger patients. In this study, patients had been taking short-half-life benzodiazepines such as lorazepam and alprazolam, as well as long-half-life benzodiazepines such as diazepam and chlorazepate. Although replication and follow-up data are needed, the implications of these data are that older patients may achieve complete abstinence from benzodiazepines with comfort and safety. The other aspects of rehabilitation, as with alcohol disorders, depend primarily on a thorough understanding of the individual circumstances that have led to the problem. With prescription drugs, of course, the chief enabler is likely to be a physician.

In this regard, prevention should focus on conservative use of analgesics and preferential selection of benzodiazepines with short half-lives, as well as attention to the addictive potential of individuals. Reassurance and conservative measures are especially important in sleep problems. For many older patients, the simple advice to go to bed later may reduce the distress caused by lying awake. As with alcoholism, prescription drug abuse, misuse, and dependence should be considered in the evaluation of every geriatric patient, including those who reside in nursing homes, and particularly those presenting with dementia, depression, anxiety, or combined syndromes.

Over-the-Counter and Illegal Drug Abuse in the Elderly

Over-the-Counter Drug Use and Misuse

The prevalence of over-the-counter drug abuse in the geriatric population has never been clearly established, mostly because of difficulties in detecting these behaviors. However, it is well accepted that social, economic, and medical factors all place the elderly at high risk for abuse of, dependence on, or other misuse of over-the-counter preparations. As has been stated, the wide use of medications of all types in this age group increases the possibility of adverse interactions. Over-the-counter drug use in particular increases with age, especially in females, and approximately two-thirds of all persons aged 60 and over consume at least one nonprescription drug on a daily basis (Whitcup & Miller, 1987). This is partially explained by the fact that many age-related conditions, such as arthritis, constipation, and insomnia, can be treated with over-the-counter medications. The inappropriate substitution of over-the-counter preparations for medically prescribed therapies tends to be reinforced by such economic and social factors as reduced income, impaired mobility, and limited access to prescribing physicians. Also contributing to patterns of abuse or dependence are impairments in cognition and judgement, failure to take into account the changes of aging, and the belief that over-the-counter medications are "weak" or harmless. For all of these reasons, medical and social consequences traceable to over-the-counter drugs appear to be of greater significance in the elderly than has previously been acknowledged.

The pharmacokinetic changes associated with aging that tend to increase sensitivity to toxic effects are relevant to over-the-counter drugs as well. Reduced plasma protein binding, reduced activity of major metabolic pathways (particularly hepatic microsomal enzymes), slowed renal excretion, and increased CNS receptor sensitivities, together have the net effect of increasing concentrations of active drugs. For many over-the-counter drugs, such as salicylates, signs and symptoms of toxicity appear at lower doses in older patients. Moreover, older patients more often experience toxic effects associated with long-standing use of nonprescription drugs than do younger patients, chiefly because such drugs are used by elderly patients for symptomatic relief of chronic conditions. For example, elderly patients with chronic arthritis, backaches, or headaches comprise the group at greatest risk for consequences of long-term aspirin or acetaminophen administration (Lamy, 1980). Iron deficiency anemia secondary to gastric bleeding and hypothermia (Lamy & Kitler, 1971) is reported in chronic aspirin takers. As another example, peptic ulcer patients or those with chronic "acid indigestion" who are long-time users of over-the-counter antacids containing calcium carbonate are at risk of developing intractable constipation problems or a paradoxical gastric hypersecretion syndrome (Barreras, 1973). When used chronically, over-the-counter cold preparations containing atropine are associated with anticholinergic toxicity and exacerbation of pre-existing glaucoma. Stimulant laxatives, when taken on a regular basis (as they are by as many as 30% of individuals over 60), can induce a dependent state. Of this group, a conservative estimate is that 3% significantly overuse stimulant laxatives and can be said to be dependent on them (Cummings, 1974). Long-term complications of stimulant laxative dependency or overuse include colonic mucosal changes with diminished tone and motility, sometimes resulting in unpredictable absorption of other drugs, and electrolyte disturbances.

Adverse drug interactions involving over-the-counter medications are frequent in the geriatric age group (Table 15.1). This is perhaps inevitable, considering that 80% of elderly patients taking an over-the-counter drug daily also use alcohol, prescription medications, or both (Whitcup & Miller, 1987). As might be expected, many of these adverse drug interactions involve over-the-counter analgesics. For example, aspirin and acetaminophen both potentiate anticoagulants; aspirin also potentiates methotrexate and oral hypoglycemics, while decreasing the effects of uricosuric agents. Over-the-counter medications having peripheral antihistaminic and anticholinergic properties, such as allergy, sleep, or nasal decongestant products, may compound the anticholinergic effects of antipsychotic or tricyclic antidepressant medications

TABLE 15.1. Some Common Adverse Interactions Involving Over-the-Counter Medications

Over-the-counter drug	Common adverse interactions
Aspirin	Potentiates anticoagulants, methotrexate, and oral hypoglycemics; decreases effect of uricosuric agents
Acetaminophen	Potentiates anticoagulants; may increase alcohol-related hepatotoxicity
Peripheral antihistaminics (allergy and nasal decongestant preparations)	May cause anticholinergic toxicity with concurrent use of antipsychotics or tricyclic antidepressants
Pseudoephedrine and caffeine-containing stimulants	May induce hypertensive crises when used with monoamine oxidase inhibitors or tricyclic antidepressants; decreases effects of antihypertensive, antiarrhythmic, and antianxiety medications
Laxatives	Associated with digitalis toxicity when used chronically
Alcohol-containing products (e.g., cough medications)	Can produce oversedation when used with antihistamines, benzodiazepines, barbiturates, phenothiazines, or tricyclic antidepressants

being taken concurrently. The toxic consequences of such combinations range from oversedation to delirium or central anticholinergic syndrome. Although sympathomimetic amines and stimulant drugs in general are abused less often by older than by younger patients, these drugs are sometimes overused by elderly individuals and can induce hypertensive crises when combined with monoamine oxidase inhibitors or tricyclic antidepressants. As a final example (although many more could be listed here), digitalis toxicity has been associated with prolonged laxative use.

Because some over-the-counter preparations contain alcohol or caffeine, the elderly user may also be at risk for the category of adverse drug reactions related to these substances. For example, oversedation can result from concurrent use of alcohol-containing products and antihistamines, benzodiazepines, or phenothiazines. Caffeine can reduce the therapeutic effects of antihypertensive, antiarrhythmic, or antianxiety medications (Lamy, 1980). Finally, chronic use of over-the-counter products containing alcohol or caffeine can induce physical dependence.

Over-the-counter medications should be included in every medication inventory taken from elderly patients. It will be discovered that some individuals have been medicating themselves by inappropriately substituting over-the-counter drugs for medically indicated treatment. Because the elderly individual may minimize or be unaware of a pattern of over-the-counter drug misuse, it is often helpful to question collateral sources, such as family members or caregivers. Perusal of home medicine cabinets often reveals direct evidence of such behavior in the form of multiple over-the-counter medication containers. Early detection, although it may be difficult, may prevent the development of severe dependence or irreversible toxicity later on. Many problems might be prevented by denying cognitively impaired patients unlimited access to over-the-counter drugs.

For those with well-established patterns of abuse or clinically significant toxicity, there may be no alternative to hospitalization and gradual withdrawal of the over-the-counter medication.

Illegal Drug Use

Illegal drug use, particularly involving substances such as marijuana, heroin, or cocaine, is quite rare in elderly populations. Even older narcotic addicts generally rely on prescription drugs such as codeine, morphine, meperidine (Demerol), or paregoric, obtained legally from physicians (Atkinson & Schuckit, 1983). Winick (1962) developed a "maturing out" hypothesis to explain the disappearance of most narcotics addicts from federal records between the ages of 35 and 45. Possible explanations offered by Winick to explain this phenomenon included reduction of life stresses at this age, selection processes occurring because of death and debilitation of the most severely addicted individuals, and a "burning out" of the addiction. It is possible, moreover, for some addicts to maintain a stable opiate habit for many years without coming to medical or legal attention, or to turn as they become older to more readily available substitutes, such as alcohol. Pascarelli and Fischer (1974) expressed the view that the older narcotic addict population consists mainly of a subset of individuals who have survived into middle or old age without coming into contact with treatment settings; these are the addicts who can manage their habits relatively well on the outside. However, for the same reason, their numbers may be underestimated.

The disinclination of older people to take stimulant drugs may account for the impression of a low incidence of cocaine abuse, particularly the more potent forms of this drug. However, the wide availability of such drugs on urban streets may result in an increase in elderly ·abusers. Eventually, the prospect of an elderly "crack" user may appear less incongruent to health workers, and more cases may be detected.

Treatment of illegal drug use generally requires hospitalization and rehabilitation. Many elderly opiate abusers have obtained their drugs legally and have been self-medicating for underlying depression or anxiety symptoms; they are therefore less likely to present an antisocial profile than younger illegal drug abusers, and may require individualized settings for rehabilitation.

Conclusion

Alcoholism and addictions to prescription drugs and over-the-counter medications are not uncommon disorders in the geriatric population, although their numbers and overall public health significance are probably underestimated. Denial on the part of the elderly patient contributes to low rates of detection, as do the attitudes of family members and health care professionals who minimize or "enable" the problem. This is especially true for substance disorders having onset in old age. In all three areas of addictive behavior discussed in this chapter, the affected elderly patient typically receives medical intervention only after a calamitous event, such as a drug- or alcohol-related accident or a major adverse drug interaction. It is therefore necessary for health care personnel to retain the same index of suspicion regarding substance abuse in an older patient as they would in a younger patient. Age-related differences in the presentation and course of substance abuse must also be borne in mind; in this area, further clinical research is much needed.

Insofar as it is possible to generalize about treatment, it can be said that (1) detoxification is generally a safe procedure in the elderly, but ususally requires hospitalization; (2) abstinence should be the primary treatment goal; and (3) rehabilitation can take place in mixed-age settings, but sensitivity to age differences is crucial. Finally, a note of caution should be sounded regarding the frequently overlooked heterogeneity of the geriatric population. There is wide demographic variability ·within the "over-65" cohort, which encompasses the "young-old" under 75, the "old-old" over 85, and those in between;

considerable individual variation in all aspects of functioning is also seen. We hope that future research in geriatric addictions will take these complexities into account, in order to produce optimally useful clinical information.

References

Alexander, F., & Duff, R. W. (1988). Social interaction and alcohol use in retirement communities. *The Gerontologist, 28,* 632–636.

American Psychiatric Association. (1987). *Diagnostic and statistical manual of mental disorders* (3rd ed., rev.). Washington, DC: Author.

Atkinson, J. H., & Schuckit, M. A. (1983). Geriatric alcohol and drug misuse and abuse. *Advances in Substance Abuse, 3,* 195–237.

Atkinson, R. M. (Ed.). (1984). *Alcohol and drug abuse in old age.* Washington, DC: American Psychiatric Press.

Atkinson, R. M., Turner, J. A., Kofoed, L. L., & Tolson, R. L. (1985). Early versus late onset alcoholism in older persons. *Alcoholism: Clinical and Experimental Research, 9,* 513–515.

Bailey, M. D., Haberman, P. W., & Alksne, H. (1965). The epidemiology of alcoholism in an urban residential area. *Quarterly Journal of Studies on Alcohol, 26,* 20–40.

Barnes, G. M. (1979). Alcohol use among older persons: Findings from a western New York State general population survey. *Journal of the American Geriatric Society, 27,* 244–250.

Barreras, R. F. (1973). Calcium and gastric secretion. *Gastroenterology, 64,* 1168.

Baum, C., Kennedy, D. L., & Forbes, M. B. (1985). Drug utilization in the geriatric age group. In S. R. Moore & T. W. Teal (Eds.), *Geriatric drug use: Clinical and social perspectives* (pp. 63–69). New York: Pergamon Press.

Beardsley, R. S., Gardocki, G. J., Larson, D. B., & Hidalgo, J. (1988). Prescribing of psychotropic medication by primary care physicians and psychiatrists. *Archives of General Psychiatry, 45,* 1117–1119.

Beers, M., Avorn, J. A., Soumerai, S. B., Everitt, D. E., Sherman, D. S., & Salem, S. (1988). Psychoactive medication use in intermediate-care facility residents. *Journal of the American Medical Association, 260,* 3016–3024.

Bienenfeld, D. (1990). Substance abuse in the elderly. In D. Bienenfeld (Ed.), *Verwoerdt's clinical geropsychiatry* (3rd ed.). Balitmore: Williams & Wilkins.

Blazer, D. G. (1989, January 9–10). *Epidemiology and clinical interface.* Paper presented at the Harvard NIMH Conference on Anxiety in the Elderly, Boston.

Bosmann, H. B. (1984). Pharmacology of alcoholism and aging. In J. T. Hartford & T. Samorajski (Eds.), *Alcoholism in the elderly: Social and biomedical issues* (pp. 161–174). New York: Raven Press.

Cahalan, D., Cisin, J. H., & Crossley, H. M. (1969). *American drinking practices.* New Brunswick, NJ: Rutgers Center of Alcohol Studies.

Christopherson, V. A., Escher, M. C., & Bainton, B. R. (1984). Reasons for drinking among the elderly in rural Arizona. *Journal of Studies on Alcohol, 45,* 417–423.

Clark, W. B., & Midanik, L. (1982). Alcohol use and alcohol problems among U.S. adults. In National Institute on Alcohol Abuse and Alcoholism (Ed.), *Alcohol consumption and related problems* (DHHS Publication No. ADM 82-1190, Alcohol and Health Monograph No. 1, pp. 3–52). Washington, DC: U.S. Government Printing Office.

Cummings, J. H. (1974). Progress report: Laxative abuse. *Gut, 15,* 758–766.

Curtis, J. R., Geller, G., Stokes, E. J., Levine, D. M., & Moore, R. D. (1989). Characteristics, diagnosis, and treatment of alcoholism in elderly patients. *Journal of the American Geriatrics Society, 37,* 310–316.

Dupree, L. W., Broskowski, H., & Schonfeld, L. (1984). The Gerontology Alcohol Project: A behavioral treatment program for elderly alcohol abusers. *The Gerontologist, 24,* 510–516.

Finlayson, R. E. (1984). Prescription drug abuse in older persons. In R. M. Atkinson (Ed.), *Alcohol and drug abuse in old age* (pp. 62–69). Washington, DC: American Psychiatric Press.

Gaitz, C. M., & Baer, P. E. (1971). Characteristics of elderly patients with alcoholism. *Archives of General Psychiatry, 24,* 829–836.

Glynn, R. J., Bouchard, G. R., LoCastro, J. S., & Laird, N. M. (1985). Aging and generational effects on drinking behaviors in men: Results from the Normative Aging Study. *American Journal of Public Health, 75,* 1113 1119.

Gould, L., Zahir, M., & Demartino, A. (1971). Cardiac effects of a cocktail. *Journal of the American Medical Association, 218,* 1799–1802.

Hartford, J. T., & Samorajski, T. (1982). Alcoholism in the geriatric population. *Journal of the American Geriatrics Society, 30,* 18–24.

Kannel, W. B. (1986). Nutritional contributors to cardiovascular disease in the elderly. *Journal of the American Geriatrics Society, 34,* 27–36.

Koch, H., & Knapp, D. E. (1987). *Highlights of drug utilization in office practice, National Ambulatory Medical Survey, 1985: Advance data from Vital and Health Statistics No. 134* (DHHS Publication No. PHS 87-1250). Washtington, DC: U.S. Government Printing Office.

LaGreca, A. J., Akers, R. L., & Dwyer, J. W. (1988). Life events and alcohol behavior among older adults. *The Gerontologist, 28,* 552–558.

Lamy, P. P. (1980). *Prescribing for the elderly.* Littleton, MA: PSG.

Lamy, P. P., & Kitler, M. E. (1971). Untoward effects of drugs, part II (including non-prescription drugs). *Diseases of the Nervous System, 32,* 105.

Learoyd, B. M. (1972). Psychotropic drugs and the elderly patient. *Medical Journal of Australia, 1,* 1131–1133.

McCourt, W. F., Williams, A. F., & Schneider, L. (1971). Incidence of alcoholism in a state mental hospital population. *Quarterly Journal of Studies on Alcohol, 32,* 1085.

McDonald, C. D., Burch, G. E., & Walsh, J. J. (1971). Alcohol cardiomyopathy mangaged with bed rest. *Annals of Internal Medicine, 74,* 681–691.

Mellinger, G. D., Bolter, M. B., & Uhlenhuth, E. H. (1984). Prevalence and correlates of the long-term regular use of anxiolytics. *Journal of the American Medical Association, 251,* 375–379.

Mendelson, J. H., & Mello, N. K. (1973). Alcohol-induced hyperlipidemia and beta lipoproteins. *Science, 180,* 1372–1374.

Miles, L., & Dement, W. (1980). Sleep and aging. *Sleep, 3,* 119–220.

Mishara, B. L., & Kastenbaum, R. (1980). *Alcohol and old age.* New York: Grune & Stratton.

Pascarelli, E. F., & Fischer, W. (1974). Drug dependence in the elderly. *International Journal of Aging and Human Development, 5,* 347–356.

Raskind, M. A., Alvarez, C., Pietrzyk, M., Westerlund, K., & Herlin, S. (1976). Helping the elderly psychiatric patient in crisis. *Geriatrics, 31,* 51–56.

Raskind, M. A., & Eisdorfer, C. (1976). Psychopharmacology of the aged. In L. L. Simpson (Ed.), *Drug treatment of mental disorders* (pp. 237–266). New York: Raven Press.

Rosin, A. J., & Glatt, M. M. (1971). Alcohol excess in the elderly. *Quarterly Journal of Studies on Alcohol, 32,* 53–59.

Schuckit, M. A. (1977). Geriatric alcoholism and drug abuse. *The Gerontologist, 17,* 168–174.

Schuckit, M. A. (1979). *Drug and alcohol abuse: A clinical guide to diagnosis and treatment.* New York: Plenum Press.

Schuckit, M. A. (1982). A clinical review of alcohol, alcoholism, and the elderly patient. *Journal of Clinical Psychiatry, 43,* 396–399.

Schuckit, M. A., & Miller, P. (1976). Alcoholism in elderly men: Survey of a general medical ward. *Annals of the New York Academy of Sciences, 273,* 558–571.

Schuckit, M. A., Miller, P. L., & Berman, J. (1980). The three-year-course of psychiatric problems in a geriatric population. *Journal of Clinical Psychiatry, 41,* 27–32.

Schweizer, E., Case, W. G., & Rickels, K. (1989). Benzodiazepine dependence and withdrawal in elderly patients. *American Journal of Psychiatry, 146,* 529–531.

Siassi, I., Crocetti, G., & Spiro, H. R. (1973). Drinking patterns and alcoholism in a blue-collar population. *Quarterly Journal of Studies on Alcohol, 34,* 917–926.

Simon, A., Epstein, L. J., & Reynolds, L. (1968). Alcoholism in the geriatric mentally ill. *Geriatrics, 23,* 125–131.

Stephens, R. C., Haney, C. A., & Underwood, S. (1981). Psychoactive drug use and potential misuse among persons aged 55 years and older. *Journal of Psychoactive Drugs, 13,* 185–193.

Trice, H. M. (1959). The affiliation motive and readiness to join Alcoholics Anonymous. *Quarterly Journal of Studies on Alcohol, 20,* 313–320.

U.S. Bureau of the Census. (1987). *Statistical abstract of the United States: 1986.* Washington, DC: U.S. Government Printing Office.

Victor, M., & Hope, J. M. (1958). The phenomenon of auditory hallucinations in chronic alcoholism. *Journal of Nervous and Mental Disease, 126,* 451–481.

Wetle, T. (1987). Age as a risk factor for inadequate treatment. *Journal of the American Medical Association, 258,* 516.

Witcup, S. M., & Miller, F. (1987). Unrecognized drug dependence in psychiatrically hospitalized elderly patients. *Journal of the American Geriatrics Society, 35,* 297–301.

Winick, C. (1962). Maturing out of narcotic addiction. *Bulletin on Narcotics, 14,* 1–7.

Zimberg, S. (1974). The two types of problem drinkers: Both can be managed. *Geriatrics, 29,* 135–138.

PART FIVE

TREATMENT SELECTION AND MODALITIES

16

Differential Therapeutics for Substance Abuse

ARTHUR I. ALTERMAN
CHARLES P. O'BRIEN
A. THOMAS McLELLAN

Introduction

The objectives of this chapter are to describe the settings of treatment and the major treatment modalities for three of the more significant substance abuse disorders: alcohol abuse/dependence opiate dependence, and cocaine abuse/dependence. In each of these areas, the current state of knowledge concerning the effectiveness of different treatment modalities, including pharmacotherapy, is also reviewed. Although we realize that polydrug abuse is increasingly found in substance abuse patients, to simplify the exposition we deal with each of the disorders in separate sections. The last section of this chapter discusses some general considerations related to the selection of differential treatment strategies for substance abusers.

Alcohol Abuse/Dependence

The treatment of alcohol abuse/dependence (i.e., alcoholism) is currently conceptualized in terms of a three-stage recovery model consisting of detoxification, rehabilitation, and aftercare. Within each of these stages, there is disagreement concerning the provision of treatment on an inpatient or outpatient basis, the most appropriate psychosocial form of treatment, the combination of treatments that should be provided, and the use of and choice of pharmacotherapy.

Detoxification

Detoxification is frequently required following alcohol withdrawal in an alcohol-dependent person. The alcohol withdrawal syndrome consists of eating and sleep disturbances, tremor, paroxysmal sweats, clouding of the sensorium, hallucinations, agitation, temperature elevations, pulse rate changes, and convulsions (Gorelick & Wilkins, 1986; Naranjo & Sellers, 1986). In rare cases, this syndrome can be life-threatening (Gorelick & Wilkins, 1986; Naranjo & Sellers, 1986).

The primary setting for alcohol detoxification continues to be inpatient hospitalization, where detoxification can usually be accomplished within 5 days under medical supervision. This includes the use of medication, usually consisting of a benzodiazepine, vitamin therapy, and, in some cases, measures to correct imbalances in water and electrolytes. Although there is no question that a small number of the presenting cases require inpatient medical attention, a growing literature has described successful alcohol detoxification in the hospital setting with minimal medical supervision (Whitfield et al., 1978); in a nonhospital social setting staffed by paraprofessional personnel (Feldman, Pattison, Sobell, Graham, & Sobell, 1975); or on an ambulatory, outpatient basis under medical supervision (Stinnett, 1982).

Recently, Hayashida and his colleagues (Hayashida et al., 1989) conducted a randomized assignment study comparing the efficacy and costs of inpatient versus outpatient alcohol detoxification. Although successful completion was much higher (95% vs. 72%) for the inpatient treatment, no major group differences were found between the two groups at 1 and 6 months after detoxification. These follow-ups reported on 93% of the patients at 1 month and 85% at 6 months. Costs were found to be at least 10 times greater for inpatient than for outpatient treatment. Another paper by this same group described the safety of ambulatory medical detoxification (Alterman, Hayashida, & O'Brien, 1988).

Although these more recent findings suggest that detoxification can be accomplished on an outpatient basis in the large majority of cases, we have been able to identify a number of variables that individually or in combination suggest a need for inpatient treatment or relatively poor response to ambulatory detoxification. First, patients in immediate need of medical or psychiatric care obviously require inpatient treatment. This can usually be determined in a brief medical examination. In this connection, the Clinical Institute Withdrawal Assessment for Alcohol (CIWA; Shaw, Kolesar, Sellers, Kaplan, & Sandor, 1981) is a useful brief instrument that can be used to assess the severity of the alcohol withdrawal syndrome. Second, patients with no visible housing cannot be treated in ambulatory detoxification, although social setting treatments or nonmedical inpatient treatments would be applicable. In actual practice, most patients can identify at least some minimal housing that is sufficient for ambulatory detoxification to be accomplished. As indicated, patients with no housing usually represent only a small proportion of detoxification candidates. Coexisting drug dependence is also an indicator of poor response to ambulatory detoxification. In a recent study, we found that patients who had three of four symptoms (a history of alcohol-related seizures, a history of delirium tremens, being unemployed, and coming to the initial visit intoxicated) had a 30% chance of completing ambulatory detoxification, as contrasted with a 95% chance if they had none of these symptoms (Volpicelli, Alterman,

Sweeney, & O'Brien, 1990). Linnoila and his colleagues (Linnoila, Mefford, Nutt, & Adinoff, 1987) have recently presented findings suggesting that the failure to medicate the alcohol withdrawal syndrome can lead to a kindling effect, which increases the likelihood of seizures and other serious withdrawal symptoms during future episodes of withdrawal.

Although these findings are preliminary, they point to a need for caution when treating alcoholics who have withdrawal symptoms. A detailed explication of the methods of medical alcohol detoxification is beyond the province of this chapter, but can be found in Gorelick and Wilkins (1986) and Naranjo and Sellers (1986).

Rehabilitation

Completion of detoxification is usually considered to be simply the initial phase of a necessarily long-term treatment for a chronic disorder. Completion of rehabilitation and aftercare treatments, which may take several years, is considered necessary if the objective of achieving an abstinent lifestyle is to be accomplished. A substantial proportion of detoxification patients apparently do not agree with the necessity of continued treatment. A number of writers have reported the discouragement of treatment personnel with the "revolving door" phenomenon of detoxification; this term describes the failure of patients to enter into rehabilitation, their subsequent relapse, and the repeated use of detoxification as a short-term solution (Annis, 1979).

Although there is undoubtedly much validity to the viewpoint that alcoholism treatment is a long-term endeavor, it should be noted that the patient who drops out of treatment is not always wrong. Alterman et al. (1988), for example, found that not all dropouts from outpatient detoxification were doing poorly; some had found what they considered to be more satisfactory treatments. Moreover, these authors found that the 6-month functioning of patients who had sought detoxification was moderately good, despite the fact that a substantial proportion had not entered into further treatment during the 6-month follow-up period (Hayashida et al., 1989). Thus, these findings suggest that although the long-term rehabilitation goal of achieving a satisfactory, abstinent lifestyle is the optimal treatment goal, some patients may internalize less demanding goals that may nevertheless reflect at least some level of improvement. The question of what is the optimum treatment duration remains unanswered.

The primary setting for rehabilitation of alcoholism cointinues to be inpatient treatment, although Miller and Hester (1986a) have reviewed a number of random-assignment studies that found no differences in the effectiveness of inpatient versus outpatient treatments. While there is no systematic evidence to contradict this conclusion, it should be pointed out that all of the random assignment studies reviewed were conducted with middle-class populations. These individuals in large part were still married and held jobs. Thus, for example, Edwards and Guthrie (1967) found a number of years ago that one brief counseling session was as effective for this group of alcoholic patients as more intensive inpatient treatment. Nevertheless, it should be noted that a substantial proportion of alcoholics seeking treatment have fewer social supports and are much less likely to have stable employment than those included in the studies thus far conducted. It is therefore important to determine whether different treatment settings (i.e., inpatient vs. outpatient) are more effective for different kinds of lower-socioeconomic-status individuals. The final section of this chapter discusses patient characteristics that are differentially predictive of treatment success in different settings.

The most common duration of rehabilitation treatment for alcoholism is 17 to 28 days; again, this treatment usually takes place in an inpatient setting. During this period the major goals of treatment are overcoming denial, identifying and learning to cope with obstacles to abstinence, and medical stabilization if necessary. The treatment is usually multimodal and may consist of a number of components, including a relatively structured group therapy that focuses on everyday activities, educational therapy, recreational and vocational therapy, participation in Alcoholics Anonymous, and medical preventive and maintenance treatment. Various other treatments, such as individual counseling, may be included. Recently, efforts to teach patients to identify triggers for craving and ways of coping with these triggers, adopted from relapse prevention methodology (Marlatt & Gordon, 1985), have been incorporated into the group therapy process in many programs. Social skills training and relaxation therapy are other behavioral treatment components that are also found in many programs.

As suggested above, the effectiveness of treatments such as these may vary with the problem levels of the patients that they treat. Thus, some evaluations conducted by private institutions that primarily treat middle- and upper-middle-class alcoholics have reported 1-year abstinence rates on the order of 50% and above (Nathan, 1986). Although these findings may be biased, since they were generally not done by persons independent of the treatment process, there is reason to believe from other sources that they are at least reasonable estimates. The treatment outcome findings for more representative inpatient treatment facilities that serve a wider range of patient types are not as promising. For example, 1-year abstinence rates are 25% or lower for poorly motivated, older, single, unemployed chronic alcoholics with few personal resources seen at public, center-city treatment facilities, such as those in the Armor, Polich, and Stambul (1978) study of 44 federally funded alcoholism treatment facilities. Even for well-motivated, younger, employed subchronic alcoholics with personal resources treated at private treatment facilities, rates of abstinence at and beyond the 3-year mark are typically half or less than 1-year rates (Nathan, 1986).

Miller and Hester (1986b) reviewed the research evidence concerning the effectiveness of different treatments used in alcoholism rehabilitation *for reducing drinking*. They concluded,

As we constructed a list of treatment approaches most clearly supported as effective based on current research, it was apparent that they all had one thing in common as of 1979: they were very rarely used in American treatment programs. The list of elements that are typically included in alcoholism treatment within the United States likewise evidenced a communality: virtually all of them lacked adequate scientific evidence of effectiveness. (p. 121)

Updating their literature review through 1984, the authors concluded that there was little evidence for the effectiveness of psychotherapy or counseling, confrontation, Alcoholics Anonymous, or educational therapy. By contrast, there was some evidence that marital and family therapy, covert sensitization, social skills training, and a broad-spectrum community reinforcement program developed by Azrin (1976) were effective in reducing drinking. Relapse prevention, a treatment focused on identifying potential relapse situations and developing strategies to cope with them, is relatively new, and thus far there are few empirical data concerning its effectiveness (Annis & Davis, 1989; Nathan, 1986).

Outpatient, particularly day hospital, treatment is an alternative form of treatment setting that is being increasingly used. As noted previously, Miller and Hester's (1986a) review paper found no differences between inpatient and outpatient treatments in middle-class alcoholics. One reason for the finding of no differences between inpatient and outpatient alcoholism rehabilitation is that the amount of actual treatment provided in the two settings may not actually differ. Although the expectation is that the 24-hour daily availability of the patient in the inpatient setting results in better treatment, this may not actually be the case. In a recent study performed by our group, using the Treatment Services Review assessment instrument (TSR; McLellan, Alterman, Parikh, Zanis, & Bragg, 1989), inpatients and day hospital patients were not found to differ in the actual amount or types of treatment they reported receiving with respect to substance abuse, legal, psychological, employment, or interpersonal problems; however, inpatients did report receiving more medical care. Inpatient treatment is seen as providing the unstable patient, who is at the nadir of his or her ability to cope, the opportunity to heal and stabilize before going back to a world where alcohol is readily available. On the other hand, outpatient treatment gives the patient the opportunity to deal with and face his or her problems while receiving treatment. There is some indication (McLellan, 1986) that inpatient rehabilitation is more beneficial for patients with poor social stability and greater amounts of psychopathology, but this work was not based on random assignment. Further work is therefore required before it can be determined which kinds of patients do better in inpatient versus outpatient treatment.

Aftercare

As noted, the staged recovery model assumes that alcoholism is a chronic disorder and that recovery requires basic changes in a number of areas of life functioning. This process may take up to 2 years to achieve and is undertaken in aftercare treatment. Because of costs and other practical considerations, aftercare treatment is usually accomplished on an outpatient basis and requires attendance once to three times a week, depending upon the stage of recovery. In the case of older patients considered to have difficulty living independently in the community, or other patients with short term problems of residential/ occupational/social instability, aftercare may take place in a residential setting such as a halfway house or domiciliary program. A focus on relapse-related phenomena and their prevention (i.e., relapse prevention) constitutes possibly the major treatment component in aftercare (Marlatt & Gordon, 1985). Central to the relapse prevention model is the concept that the individual must develop viable and effective alternatives to abusive drinking. These alternatives require both general and specific coping skills, which many alcoholics do not possess. Relapse prevention treatment teaches these skills to the patients (Nathan, 1986). This behavioral–cognitive approach has proven attractive to the alcoholism treatment community, probably because it provides a concrete, tangible methodology with high face validity. Nevertheless, there is still little empirical evidence to support its effectiveness (Annis & Davis, 1989; Nathan, 1986). Helping the patient to deal with life problems concerning family, friends, and employment are other areas of concentration during the aftercare phase. In this regard, the work of Finney and his colleagues (Finney, Moos, & Mewborn, 1980) has shown the importance of the posttreatment environment.

There is currently little knowledge concerning the typical length of stay in aftercare or the proportion of alcoholics who complete the designated program of aftercare treatment. Likewise, little is known concerning whether those who do complete aftercare have accomplished the proposed changes in their coping skills and behavioral repertoire. In most programs, only a small proportion of those who start aftercare complete it. The extent to which failure to complete aftercare is associated with relapse is undetermined. Do patients who complete aftercare treatment have fewer problems and more resources upon entry into treatment than those who drop out? There is presently little information concerning this question, but there are some indications that aftercare is important in maintaining recovery. For example, Billings and Moos (1983) reported that recovering alcoholics experienced significantly fewer environmental stressors and made more consistent and effective use of active cognitive and behavioral coping strategies than relapsed alcoholics. Recovering alcoholics also had a greater number of social and family resources available to them and used them more effectively than relapsed alcoholics.

Pharmacotherapy

Pharmacological treatments for alcoholism fall into two broad categories: antidipsotropics and psychotropic medications. We discuss these in turn.

ANTIDIPSOTROPICS

Antidipsotropics are prescribed with the intention of creating either an adverse physical reaction when the individual consumes alcohol or antagonizing (reducing) the "high" obtained from the drug of choice. All are considered to be auxiliary treatments, to be used in conjunction with existing psychosocial treatments. Disulfiram and citrated calcium carbimide fall into the first category, while naltrexone is in the second.

Both disulfiram and carbimide produce a drug–ethanol reaction by inhibiting the liver enzyme aldehyde dehydrogenase (ALDH), which catalyzes the oxidation of aldehyde (the major metabolic product of ethanol) to acetate (Fuller, 1989). The resulting accumulation of acetaldehyde is responsible for most of the symptoms of the drug–ethanol reaction that occurs following alcohol consumption. The symptoms may include some or all of the following: flushing, rapid or irregular heartbeat, dizziness, nausea, vomiting, difficulty breathing, and headache. Disulfiram also inhibits other enzymes, so that drowsiness and relapse or exacerbation of depression and schizophrenia can be side effects (Fuller, 1989). In comparison with the drug–ethanol reaction to disulfiram, the aversive reaction to carbimide is less severe and shorter-lived. However, this drug is not available in the United States, so that few data exist on its effectiveness. Therefore, the following discussion is limited to disulfiram.

There are a variety of medical and psychiatric contraindications to the use of disulfiram, including severe lung disease, chronic kidney disease, cardiovascular or cerebrovascular disease, and organic brain syndrome (Fuller, 1989). In a recently completed Department of Veterans Affairs (VA) multicenter study (Fuller et al., 1986), which constitutes the largest and most complete study to date, the addition of disulfiram to multimodal treatment programs did not result in significantly more patients maintaining continuous abstinence for 1 year than was achieved without disulfiram. However, a substantial subset of the men who relapsed (i.e., older and more socially stable men) drank significantly less frequently during the year if they had been prescribed disulfiram.

Naltrexone is a long-acting opiate antagonist that has been used effectively for the treatment of opiate dependence (O'Brien & Woody, 1986). For a review, see Volpicelli, Alterman, Hayashida, and O'Brien (1990). Thus, there is some reason to believe that an opiate agonist may also block some of the effects of alcohol (Blum, Futterman, Wallace, & Schwetner, 1977). In a recent pilot study in which naltrexone was used as an auxiliary to standard outpatient treatment for alcoholism (Volpicelli, Alterman, Hayashida, & O'Brien, 1990), it was found that patients randomly assigned to the naltrexone group were much less likely to relapse following a drinking slip.

PSYCHOTROPIC MEDICATION

No psychotropic agent has proven useful as a primary therapeutic tool in alcoholism treatment and rehabilitation. Though several promising lines of evidence have emerged recently, experimental data to support the efficacy of any of these drugs in the reduction of drinking are still lacking or at best equivocal (Miller, Frances, & Holmes, 1989).

Antianxiety Drugs. Overall, controlled research provides no persuasive support for using antianxiety agents with alcoholics, and many physicians caution against their use because of the risks of multiple abuse of alcohol and medication (Miller & Hester, 1986b). It should be pointed out, however, that antianxiety agents would presumably be differentially effective for alcoholics suffering from panic attacks or some of the phobias; however, no systematic research has been conducted on this question.

Antipsychotics. Although early anecdotal and uncontrolled reports were quite optimistic, no evidence has emerged from controlled research to indicate that antipsychotics are of value in treating alcoholism (Miller & Hester, 1986b).

Antidepressants. Although alcoholics entering treatment often manifest considerable depression, most of these are reactive depressions. Antidepressant medication only appears to be effective for treating alcoholics currently experiencing a major depression (Mayfield, 1985).

Lithium. Although a number of early studies showed promising results for lithium in the reduction of alcohol consumption, a more recent, large-scale cooperative study completed by the VA (Dorus et al., 1989) found no evidence that lithium was more effective than placebo. This finding was obtained for both depressed and nondepressed alcoholic patients.

Opioid Dependence

Like alcohol dependence, opiate addiction is seen as a chronic, relapsing disorder (Cooper, 1989). There are four major forms of treatment for this disorder: methadone maintenance (MM) treatment, antagonist drug treatment, residential therapeutic community (TC) treatment, and outpatient drug-free treatment. The last of these, however, has proven to be effective for only a small minority of opiate-dependent patients (Cushman, 1974), and is therefore not considered in this review. Detoxification is often presented as a treatment, but it should only be considered to be a first step in a comprehensive rehabilitation program. The evidence thus far indicates that MM treatment is by far the most effective treatment for the greatest number of patients, although there is still considerable societal opposition to such treatment.

The three-stage recovery model that has been adopted for alcoholism has not been so clearly delineated or separated for opiate dependence. Obviously, many addicts who relapse are in need of detoxification. However, the distinction between rehabilitation and aftercare is not as clear as for alcoholism. Recently, the term "aftercare" has been applied to the treatment of opioid dependence, but its meaning differs from that for alcoholism. That is, "aftercare" has been used to describe a much reduced schedule of treatment for highly stabilized, MM addicts, which could be of value in opening up resources for a greater number of new patients (Cooper, 1989). Below, we discuss the detoxification process for opioid dependence, followed by a discussion of the three major treatment modalities for opioid dependence.

Detoxification

Opiate detoxification is generally implemented in one of two situations. If a patient has been stabilized on methadone for a number of years, appears to have the ability to be drug-free, and communicates this interest, detoxification can be accomplished using a tapered methadone schedule over several months. This process can be implemented on an outpatient basis, although hospitalization is sometimes helpful at the end of detoxification when the dose is less than 20 to 25 mg. Clonidine is often helpful in blocking signs and symptoms of withdrawal related to autonomic hyperactivity. Cushman (1974) has shown, however, that only a small proportion of detoxification candidates are able to remain free of the substance for an extended period of time.

Detoxification is also used as an initial treatment for opiate dependence, usually for heroin addicts who prefer not to participate in MM and wish to enter a drug-free rehabilitation program. As with detoxification alone for alcohol dependence, this treatment is not recommended as the sole approach. Detoxification can be the first step in beginning drug-free outpatient treatment or narcotic antagonist (naltrexone) treatment, and detoxification is a necessary first step for entrance into drug-free rehabilitation programs or TCs.

Numerous detoxification techniques have been proposed. The most commonly used method involves transferring a patient on a short-acting opiate such as heroin to a long-acting opioid such as methadone, which blocks symptoms of withdrawal by cross-tolerance. The dose of methadone can then be gradually reduced according to a predetermined schedule, with adjustments as needed if the patient reports discomfort or shows signs of a withdrawal syndrome. Clonidine (Gold, Pottash, Sweeny, & Kleber, 1980) is a centrally acting antihypertensive medication that lowers blood pressure by central mechanisms, which include α-2 autoreceptor stimulation and therefore inhibition of noradrenergic outflow. Thus clonidine, a nonopioid, is able to block many of the signs and symptoms of opiate withdrawal. This drug can be quite useful in places where opioids for detoxification are not available.

Another option that has recently become available is extended detoxification. This involves giving methadone to block symptoms of withdrawal and then tapering the dose very slowly, without an initial period of stabilization and maintenance. Detoxification using methadone was formerly limited to 21 days, but the new Food and Drug Administration (FDA) regulations permit "long-term detoxification" for up to 180 days. This is really short-term maintenance, and it is likely to be more effective than the usual detoxification, although there are no data yet available on the issue. Still another detoxification technique involves acupuncture or electrostimulation (Patterson, 1984; Ellison et al., 1987) in an effort to ameliorate withdrawal symptoms by stimulation of the endogenous opioid system. One double-blind study (Ellison et al., 1987) has provided evidence that these techniques can reduce symptoms significantly more than placebo; other studies are in progress. However, with all detoxification methods, prompt relapse is likely unless the patient becomes engaged in a long-term aftercare program.

Rehabilitation

MM substitution treatment, antagonist treatment, and inpatient therapeutic community treatment are discussed here in turn.

MAINTENANCE TREATMENT

MM is by far the most commonly used form of narcotic substitution therapy. Levo-α-acetyl methadol (LAAM) is a slower-acting substance with pharmacological effects similar to those of methadone. Studies done to date show that treatment results for those who remain on LAAM compare favorably with those obtained with methadone, although LAAM's slower onset probably contributes to the higher initial dropout rate seen when LAAM is compared with methadone (Woody & O'Brien, 1986). A recent review of the opioid dependence literature concluded that in-treatment performance, as measured by decreased use of narcotics and other illicit drugs, decreased criminal activity, and increased social productivity, improves in a direct linear relationship to the length of time spent in treatment (Cooper, 1989). With respect to length of time in treatment, an average of 40–50% of new patients leave outpatient or residential drug-free treatment within the first 3 months of treatment, compared with an average 14% dropout rate in well-run MM programs (Cooper, 1989).

There is considerable evidence that well-run MM programs are highly effective (Cooper, 1989; Dole, 1989). One of the primary requirements is that a sufficient daily dose of methadone be prescribed. Dole (1989) recently described unpublished data by Ball that revealed an inverse relationship between the percentage of patients who had used heroin during the past month and the dose of methadone hydrochloride prescribed. Daily doses of 60 mg/day and above were associated with virtually no heroin use. That is, a blood level of methadone at concentrations greater than 150 ng/ml is necessary to stop illicit opiate use.

A large body of research thus far has shown that MM is most successful when coupled with a variety of services, including regular client contact and urine drug monitoring (Cooper, 1989). Particularly because many opiate-dependent patients need assistance with vocational and legal problems, and many come to treatment with additional psychiatric symptomatology (Rounsaville, Weissman, Kleber, & Wilber, 1982; McLellan, 1986), there is a need for drug counseling by a certified drug counselor and sometimes a need for psychotherapy or psychotropic medication to combat coexisting psychopathology (Woody & O'Brien, 1986). Research is in progress to determine whether treatment programs that primarily prescribe methadone without additional treatment can be successful. The motivation for using the latter approach is to open up more treatment slots, in the effort to reduce needle sharing that could lead to acquired immune deficiency syndrome (AIDS) (Cooper, 1989).

ANTAGONIST TREATMENT

Opioid antagonists such as naltrexone are substances that bind to opioid receptors but do not produce effects (O'Brien & Woody, 1986). When an antagonist is present in sufficient quantity to occupy all or most opioid receptors, agonist substances such as morphine cannot reach and bind to the receptors. As a result, injection of heroin will have little or no agonist effect, and the pattern of addiction or readdiction will be interrupted. Toxicity data from animal studies and studies of long-term administration indicate that naltrexone has a wide margin of safety. Thus, as long as naltexone is taken by the patient on a regular basis, it will prevent readdiction to opioids.

Naltrexone has been found to be most effective for middle- and upper-class patients (i.e., health care professionals, executives, other professionals), who enter treatment with good jobs to protect, career and family supports, and histories of adequate or above-average functioning (Washton, Pottash, & Gold, 1984). Furthermore, naltrexone represents a meaningful alternative to methadone for those persons whose occupations do not permit them to work while on an MM program. Naltrexone has not been found to be nearly as effective with working-class and street addicts (O'Brien & Woody, 1986). Employment and family supports, which could serve as external motivation for abstinence, are not as intact for these patients. Moreover, many of these patients may be suffering from significant psychopathology (e.g., anxiety and depression), which may be partially medicated by methadone and which also makes it more difficult for the patient to persevere on a course of abstinence.

INPATIENT THERAPEUTIC COMMUNITY TREATMENT

Inpatient drug-free treatment usually takes place in a TC. These TCs are composed of peer groups and staff that constitute the community, or "family," in a residential facility. This peer-to-community structure is seen as strengthening the individual's identification with a perceived, ordered network of others. More importantly, it arranges relationships of mutual responsibility to others at various levels in the program. The operation of the TC itself is the task of the residents, working together under staff supervision. Work assignments, called "job functions," are arranged in a hierarchy, according to seniority, individual progress, and productivity. In the TC, work is seen as mediating essential educational and therapeutic effects. The essential dynamic of the TC is mutual self-help. Thus, the day-to-day activities of a TC are conducted by the residents themselves. In their jobs, groups, meetings, recreation, and personal and social time, the residents are the ones who continually transmit to each other the main messages and expectations of the community.

The TC views the substance-abusing person, rather than the drug, as being the problem. Thus, the commitment to rehabilitation may take several years in a developmental process (DeLeon & Rosenthal, 1989). Evaluations of the effectiveness of TCs reveal dropout rates of about 25% within 2 weeks and about 40% by 3 months. The data indicate that between 15% and 20% graduate from these programs. The findings indicate that a moderate to maximally favorable outcome occurs in about half of the clients followed over a 2-year period, although the rates of total abstinence and elimination of criminal activity are substantially lower (DeLeon, 1985).

Cocaine Dependence

With the recent onset of a cocaine epidemic in this country, associated with the freebase and intravenous forms of use, substance abuse treatment providers were faced with the dilemma of how best to treat this most virulent form of addiction. Lacking a drug substitution method analogous to MM or a specific antagonist similar to naltrexone, treatment providers have initially responded to cocaine dependence by adopting the well-proven methodology of alcoholism rehabilitation treatment. Also, since there is some evidence that high-intensity cocaine use (intravenous or freebase) may induce brain changes that may require biological interventions to reverse and halt the cocaine dependence (Kosten, 1989), a number of pharmacological approaches have been evaluated for their efficacy for improving detoxification from the substance and for subsequent rehabilitation. Not surprisingly, the process of cocaine rehabilitation is also conceptualized in terms of a three-stage model consisting of detoxification, rehabilitation, and aftercare (e.g., "crash," withdrawal, and extinction phases; Gawin & Kleber, 1986), similar to the model advanced for alcoholism. We therefore use this framework in considering the treatment of cocaine dependence.

Detoxification

Although there is no clear evidence that cocaine produces a withdrawal syndrome such as that seen with alcohol, opiates, or sedatives, there is definitely a period of physical and mental instability following continuous use of cocaine, and this has been termed the "withdrawal" period. The withdrawal effects for cocaine are irritability, weakness, a marked reduction in energy, hypersomnia, depression, loss of concentration, increased appetite, and paranoid ideation (hallucinations and delusions). Paranoid effects, if they occur, usually last from 2 to 14 days, but can last longer. Because of limited bed capacities, inpatient detoxification is often limited to cases in need of immediate psychiatric (drug-induced psychosis) or medical (pregnancy, myocardial damage) attention. As a consequence, there has been an intensive effort to evaluate pharmacological agents with some promise of increasing the effectiveness of outpatient detoxification.

Cocaine tends to be used in "runs," in which the user consumes all of the cocaine available and all that he or she can readily acquire. Between "runs," there may be a period of spontaneous detoxification accompanied by fatigue, exhaustion, depression, and episodes of craving. Researchers have postulated that the cocaine "crash" and intense cocaine craving may be linked to dopamine depletion and dopamine autoreceptor hypersensitivity, thus tending to reduce dopaminergic transmission during a "crash" (Gawin & Ellinwood, 1988). Although direct evidence of these changes is lacking, one approach to the pharmacological treatment of the postcocaine state has focused on medications that might restore dopaminergic transmission. Dopamine agonists are one such drug category. Bromocriptine was one of the first dopamine agonists to be investigated. Early reports indicated that bromocriptine could reduce cocaine craving during severe cocaine withdrawal (Dackis & Gold, 1985). Subsequent reports have been less optimistic, and one study using a high dose of bromocriptine reported a very high dropout rate (Tennant & Sagherian, 1987). Amantadine hydrochloride is a direct and indirect dopaminergic agonist that is better tolerated by patients than bromocriptine. Tennant (1986) reported good results with this agent in an open clinical trial. However, no adequate long-term, placebo-controlled, double-blind studies have been done with either bromocriptine or amantadine. Selected benzodiazepines may also possibly be effective as anticraving agents in ameliorating early withdrawal symptoms after cocaine binges, but no controlled research has thus far been conducted with this class of drugs (Kosten, 1989).

Rehabilitation

PSYCHOSOCIAL TREATMENTS

Crowley (1984) has reported moderate levels of success using behavioral contracting techniques with middle-class abusers. Washton (1986) has provided a detailed description of a comprehensive outpatient treatment that has been applied to an employed, middle-class population. The program is modeled after alcoholism treatment and provides up to 2–3 years of treatment. Washton and his colleagues (Washton, Gold, & Pottash, 1986) reported that 59 of 63 patients (94%) completed at least 3 months of treatment and that

67% completed at least 6 months. Follow-up conducted from 7 to 19 months after intake revealed that 81% were abstinent.

Just as for alcoholism treatment and naltrexone or TC treatment of opiate dependence, the treatment outcome findings are not as favorable for working-class and street addicts. As indicated, these patients have fewer employment and family supports, have a poorer history of functioning, and manifest considerably more psychiatric symptomatology than the middle-class patients treated by Washton and his colleagues. For example, we (O'Brien, Alterman, Walter, Childress, & McLellan, 1990) reported the preliminary findings of a comparative study of the effectiveness of day hospital versus inpatient rehabilitation treatment for primarily black, lower-socioeconomic-status males at two VA medical centers. Both programs had been treating alcohol-dependent patients. With the onset of the cocaine epidemic, the programs were expanded to treat cocaine-dependent veterans. The day hospital consisted of 27 hours of weekly structured group therapy, educational therapy, medical care, social work and employment services, and recreational therapy over a 4-week period. The inpatient program provided a similar pattern of services, also over 4 weeks. As indicated previously, the amount of treatment in the two programs differed little, except for a somewhat greater amount of medical care in inpatient treatment (McLellan et al., 1989).

The program completion rate for day hospital alcoholic patients was about 70%, as contrasted with a 90–95% completion rate for inpatient alcoholism treatment. We (O'Brien et al., 1990) found that approximately 43% of the cocaine-dependent patients in the day hospital completed the 4 weeks of treatment, as contrasted with about 86% of the inpatients. The difference between the two groups was statistically significant ($p = .003$). At follow-up 4 months after treatment entry, both groups reported significant reductions in substance use. Seventy-six percent of the patients (79% of the day hospital patients and 73% of the inpatients) reported that they had been cocaine-free during the past month; there were no significant group differences. No data were reported on the proportion of the patients abstinent during the entire 4-month period, but this would clearly be much lower. These results are representative of those obtained by treatment evaluation studies of lower-socioeconomic-status patients that are beginning to be reported.

PHARMACOLOGICAL TREATMENTS

Tricyclic Antidepressants. Desipramine (DMI) is a relatively nonsedating tricyclic antidepressant that produces stimulation in some depressed patients and has some actions similar to cocaine, in that it blocks the reuptake of monoamines released at central synapses. An early double-blind study found no benefit in the treatment of outpatients dependent on cocaine (Tennant & Tarver, 1985). However, more recently, DMI has been tested in a large double-blind trial and compared to placebo and lithium (Gawin et al., 1989). During the 6-week trial, the DMI group had significantly better retention, less reported cocaine use, and longer periods of abstinence than the other two groups. DMI has also been studied in a double-blind trial in methadone patients who were also dependent on cocaine (Arndt, Dorozynski, Woody, McLellan, & O'Brien, 1990). Overall, there was no advantage of DMI over placebo, but if the opiate/cocaine-dependent patients with antisocial personality disorder were excluded, the DMI group showed significant efficacy over the placebo-treated group (Arndt et al., 1990).

Lithium. Neurochemical evidence indicates that lithium has multiple acute effects that counteract those of cocaine (Kleber & Gawin, 1984). Kleber and Gawin (1984) conducted an open 12-week clinical trial with a small number of patients. They found lithium to be effective with patients suffering from a cyclothymic disorder, but it was not effective in discontinuing use in the other patients. In a subsequent large trial (Gawin et al., 1989), lithium was found to be no more effective than placebo in cocaine-dependent outpatients.

Methylphenidate. About 10% of cocaine abusers also qualify for a diagnosis of attention deficit disorder (ADD), residual type (Kleber & Gawin, 1984). A preliminary trial of methylphenidate showed that it temporarily reduced cocaine use, but abstinence from cocaine was not sustained (Kleber & Gawin, 1984). Methylphenidate is generally abused by non-ADD cocaine-dependent patients (Kosten, 1989).

Aftercare

As indicated, the aftercare treatment model has been adopted from alcoholism and has been shown to be effective for middle- and upper-middle-class addicts (Washton et al., 1986). There are thus far no data on its effectiveness for lower-socioeconomic-status patients.

General Considerations

In this section, we discuss patient and treatment factors relevant to determination of differential treatments for substance abusers.

Patient Factors

As has been noted throughout this chapter, middle-class patients presenting with intact employment and familial supports, little psychopathology, and a history of average or above-average functioning are likely to benefit substantially from treatment, whether their problem is alcohol, opiate, or cocaine dependence. As noted previously for alcoholism, minimal treatment may be effective for many of these patients. Can we summarize what we basically know about the patient characteristics associated with a favorable response to treatment? In other words, for a patient just coming into treatment, what may be worth knowing about the patient that will help us determine the most effective treatment for him or her?

As indicated above, intactness of social supports/social stability represents a very positive prognostic indicator. A negative indicator that has emerged in a number of studies is the presence or history of other psychiatric diagnoses, such as major depression, antisocial personality disorder, or other drug dependence disorders (Rounsaville & Kleber, 1986). For example, McLellan (1986) found that a patient's score on the psychiatric section of the Addiction Severity Index (ASI) accounted for about 10% of outcome variance. Using this measure and several other predictors of outcome, McLellan was able to develop an algorithm, which he subsequently used to assign prospective alcohol- and drug-dependent patients to one of six treatment programs in two VA medical centers. A subsequent comparison of the effectiveness of treatment for patients assigned to programs on the basis of the algorithm (i.e., "matched" patients) versus those who, for whatever reasons, were not assigned to treatment according to the algorithm (i.e., "mismatched" patients) indicated 37% greater efficacy of treatment for the matched patients.

The algorithm developed by McLellan (1986) was based largely on psychiatric severity and current psychosocial functioning (i.e. employment and family problems), although the presence of significant legal or medical problems could modify the set of derived decision rules. First, patients were categorized according to psychiatric severity into high, middle, and low groups, consisting of about 30% each in the high and low groups and 40% in the middle group. In general, low-psychiatric-severity patients were assigned to outpatient treatment, except for those with significant family and/or employment problems. Middle-psychiatric-severity patients with more severe family and/or employment problems did better in inpatient treatment. However, middle-psychiatric-severity patients with significant legal problems did poorly in two inpatient alcohol treatment units in the network, and were therefore assigned to either an inpatient combined alcohol/drug inpatient program or an outpatient alcohol program. High-psychiatric-severity patients did poorly in all treatments. However, opiate-dependent patients did somewhat better in MM treatment than in an inpatient TC program, possibly due to the regulatory and weak antipsychotic effects of methadone.

Following up on these findings, McLellan and his colleagues (Woody et al., 1983) conducted a comparative study of the effectiveness of professional therapy plus counseling versus counseling in an MM program. They found that psychotherapy enhanced the treatment gains of both the middle- and high-psychiatric-severity patients, but was not particularly helpful or necessary for low-psychiatric-severity patients. A subsequent paper by this group revealed that patients qualifying for a lifetime diagnosis of major depression in addition to antisocial personality disorder did as well as those with no additional psychiatric diagnoses or those with an additional lifetime diagnosis of depression. On the other hand, "antisocial-only" patients did very poorly

(Woody, McLellan, Luborsky, & O'Brien, 1985). In a recent study, Kadden, Cooney, Getter, and Litt (1989) found that sociopathic alcoholic patients showed greater alcohol-related relapse when treated with interactional therapy than with behavioral coping skills training. These highly interesting findings conflict, however, with those of Woody et al. (1985), who found no differences in the effectiveness of cognitive–behavioral versus supportive–expressive therapies in MM opiate-dependent patients.

A final cautionary note should be included regarding the above-described findings. It is important to recognize that the results of any research may be specific to the interaction of the specific patient–treatment factors that obtain. Thus, as McLellan (1986) suggests, these matching findings many not extend specifically to a different patient sample or different treatment programs.

Other psychosocial patient variables that have at times been shown to be related to treatment outcome are severity of dependence and conceptual level (McLellan, 1989). The data concerning the first variable are mixed and complicated; further knowledge is required to clarify the relation of this variable to treatment response and its relation to other variables. A consistency between the patient's conceptual level and that of his or her counselor has also been found to be associated with a more favorable response to treatment (McLachlan, 1972). Possibly because of practical difficulties in assessing conceptual levels or in obtaining a conceptual fit between counselor and patient, this variable has not been frequently applied in treatment situations. Another psychosocial variable of obvious import to treatment outcome is the patient's motivation/willingness to participate in and commit to treatment. In this connection, the recent work of Miller (1983) in developing procedures to increase patient motivation is of particular interest.

The foregoing pages have also attested to the possibilities for differential pharmacological treatments for some substance abuse patients. Clearly, there is evidence that substance abuse patients suffering from current major depression can benefit from tricyclic antidepressant treatment (Kosten, 1989; Mayfield, 1985). Lithium has also been shown to be effective for cocaine-dependent patients suffering from a cyclothymic disorder (Kleber & Gawin, 1984). In addition, methylphenidate may be effective for the small proportion of cocaine-dependent patients qualifying for a diagnosis of ADD, residual type (Kleber & Gawin, 1984). Research is required to determine whether methylphenidate would be beneficial for the treatment of other substance abusers suffering from ADD. The use of either pharmacotherapy or behavioral treatments for substance abusers suffering from panic attacks or other anxiety disorders in another potential area for differential therapeutics requiring systematic evaluation. Finally, it is important to recognize that the effectiveness of a particular pharmacological treatment cannot be evaluated independently of the psychosocial status of the patient. This naturally makes the determination of drug effectiveness a less than simple matter. That is, as we have seen, the opiate-dependent patient need only take naltrexone regularly to prevent readdiction. This sounds rather straightforward, and it is often the case with high-functioning patients. But naltrexone has not proven to be a viable treatment for lower-class and street addicts who also have fewer social supports, more psychopathology, and a history of poorer functioning.

It goes without saying that the examination of specific patient factors associated with treatment response requires that we can reliably and validly measure these factors. We have employed the ASI (McLellan, 1986) as a general-purpose instrument to assess the substance abuser's level of functioning in seven life areas—alcohol- and drug-related, medical, legal, familial/social, and psychological/psychiatric—prior to, during, and following treatment. Depending upon the interests of the user, it may be helpful to supplement the ASI or related instrument with more detailed items or instruments concerning substance abuse problems, family/social problems, and so on. In addition, the use of structured psychiatric interviews may be necessary for a more detailed diagnostic assessment.

To summarize, the systematic study of the differential effects of treatments for different patients is in its infancy. Such work is costly, time-consuming, and complex. It must necessarily be based on a knowledge of relevant treatment factors, which also only exists in primitive form. The following and final section of this chapter attempts to sketch out some important differentiations concerning substance abuse treatment that are apparent at this time.

Treatment Factors

What are the critical ingredients of treatment? As we have seen, most substance abuse treatments are multifaceted, consisting of a number types of interventions. Thus, even a primarily pharmacological treatment such as MM also includes behavioral contracting, urine screening and contingencies, counseling for personal problems, psychotherapy in some instances, vocational counseling, and so on. Studies thus far show that the combination of treatments is more beneficial than MM alone. Determining the critical features of treatment therefore becomes a difficult task. In considering the dimensions or ingredients of substance abuse treatment, it is important that at least certain distinctions be made concerning treatment factors that are often overlooked.

The features of treatment provided to substance abusers may be described according to a hierarchical framework (McLellan, 1989). At the highest level is the setting (i.e., inpatient vs. outpatient). Receiving treatment in one setting or another implies different patient demands on the patient's psychosocial resources, for example; these demands may be important, depending upon the patient's current status. At the next lower level is the program. We often incorrectly think of programs as being monolithic and uniform. However, distinctly different types of programs such as a day hospital and an evening program encompass a number of distinctive treatment components or elements. What do we learn when we compare a day hospital program with an evening program, if we are unable to specify or measure the components with each? McLellan's (1986) matching findings of nearly a decade ago concerning the effectiveness or ineffectiveness of "certain programs" for patients with significant legal problems reflect this lack of specificity. Without the specification of the different treatment components provided in each of the programs, we are unable to generalize beyond the particular findings. Thus, the next level of treatment specification is the treatment component, such as group therapy or coping skills training. Even at this level, treatments can be quite complex, so that it is most important for any treatment evaluation to provide a detailed specification of the treatment and to insure that this treatment is what is provided to the patient/client. Otherwise, there can be little confidence in what is being evaluated.

Recently, McLellan et al. (1989) developed the TSR (see the discussion of alcohol rehabilitation, above) in an attempt to obtain some assessment of the quantity of different treatments provided by a program. Instead of focusing on specifying the details of the treatment components provided by a program, it uses the patient's weekly report of treatments received in each of the life areas tapped by the ASI (legal, medical, alcohol- and drug-related, etc.). In this way, it is hoped that the quantity of treatments in different life areas provided by different programs or for different individuals can be evaluated in relation to the overall success of these treatments. Thus, the TSR is another approach to quantifying the units and amounts of treatment that a patient or group of patients receive in a program. It is possible also that the TSR can be applied in the future to determining the quantity of life area treatments provided by a specific treatment component.

Finally, at the lowest level of specification, the treatment provider represents a distinctive component of the treatment process. Studies have shown (Cooper, 1989) large differences between the outcomes obtained by different therapists. This seems to be less a question of professional degree or discipline than of approach to the job. Conscientiousness, compassionateness, sensitivity, and responsiveness are various descriptors of counselor behaviors associated with better outcomes. This is a complex but important area that needs to be given increased attention in the future.

Acknowledgments

This work was supported by grants from the National Institute on Drug Abuse, the National Institute on Alcohol Abuse and Alcoholism, and the Department of Veterans Affairs.

References

Alterman, A. I., Hayashida, M., & O'Brien, C. P. (1988). Treatment response and safety of ambulatory medical detoxification. *Journal of Studies on Alcohol, 49,* 160–66

Annis, H. M. (1979). The detoxification alternative to the handling of public inebriates: The Ontario experience. *Journal of Studies on Alcohol, 40,* 196–210.

Annis, H., & Davis, C. (1989). Relapse prevention. In R. K. Hester & W. R. Miller (Eds.), *Handbook of alcoholism treament approaches.* New York: Pergamon Press.

Armor, D. J., Polich, J. M., & Stambul, H. B. (1978). *Alcoholism and treatment.* New York: Wiley.

Arndt, I. O., Dorozynski, L., Woody, G. E., McLellan, A. T., & O'Brien, C. P. (1990). Desipramine treatment for cocaine abuse in methadone-maintained patients. In L. Harris (Ed.), *Problems of drug dependence 1989* (NIDA Research Monograph). Washington, DC: U.S. Government Printing Office.

Azrin, N. H. (1976). Improvements in the community-reinforcement approach to alcoholism. *Behaviour Research and Therapy, 13,* 105–112.

Billings, A. G., & Moos, R. H. (1983). Psychosocial processes of recovery among alcoholics and their families: Implications for clinicians and program evaluators. *Addictive Behavior, 8,* 205–218.

Blum, K., Futterman, S., Wallace, J. E., & Schwetner, H. A. (1977). Naloxone-induced inhibition of ethanol dependence in mice. *Nature, 265,* 49–51.

Cooper, J. R. (1989). Methadone treatment and acquired immunodeficiency syndrome. *Journal of the American Medical Association, 262,* 1664–1668.

Crowley, T. (1984). Contingency contracting treatment of drug abusing physicians, nurses and dentists. In J. Grabowski, M. L. Stitzer, & J. F. Henningfield (Eds.), *Behavioral intervention techniques in drug abuse treatment* (NIDA Research Monograph No. 46). Washington, DC: U.S. Government Printing Office.

Cushman, P. (1974). Detoxification of rehabilitated methadone patients: Frequency and predictors of long-term success. *American Journal of Drug and Alcohol Abuse, 1,* 393–408.

Dackis, C. A., & Gold, M. S. (1985). Bromocriptine as a treatment of cocaine abuse. *Lancet, i,* 1151–1152

DeLeon, G. (1985). The therapeutic community: Status and evolution. *International Journal of the Addictions, 20,* 823–844.

DeLeon, G., & Rosenthal, M. S. (1989). Treatment in residential therapeutic communities. In T. B. Karasu (Ed.), *Treatments of psychiatric disorders* (Vol. 2). Washington, DC: American Psychiatric Press.

Dole, V. P. (1989). Methadone treatment and the acquired immunodeficiency syndrome epidemic. *Journal of the American Medical Association, 262,* 1681–1682.

Dorus, W., Ostrow, D., Anton, R., Cushman, P., Collins, J. F., Schaefer, M., Charles, H. L., Desai, P., Hayashida, M., Malkerneker, U., Willengring, M., Fiscella, R., & Sather, M. R. (1989). Lithium treatment of depressed and nondepressed alcoholics. *Journal of the American Medical Association, 262,* 1646–1652

Edwards, G., & Guthrie, S. (1967). A controlled trial of inpatient and outpatient treatment of alcohol dependency. *Lancet, i,* 555–559.

Ellison, W., Ellison, W., Daulouede, J. P., Daubech, J. F., Pautrizel, B., Bourgeois, M., & Tignol, J. (1987). Opiate withdrawal and electrostimulation: Double-blind experiment. *L'Encephale, 13,* 225–229.

Feldman, D. J., Pattison, E. M., Sobell, L. C., Graham, T., & Sobell, M. B. (1975). Outpatient alcohol detoxification: Initial findings on 564 patients. *American Journal of Psychiatry, 132,* 407–412.

Finney, J. W., Moos, R. H., & Mewborn, C. R. (1980). Posttreatment experiences and treatment outcome of alcoholic patients six months and two years after hospitalization. *Journal of Consulting and Clinical Psychology, 48,* 17–29.

Fuller, R. K. (1989). Antidipsotropic medications. In R. K. Hester & W. R. Miller (Eds.), *Handbook of alcoholism treatment approaches.* New York: Pergamon Press.

Fuller, R. K., Branchey, L., Brightwell, D. R., Derman, R. M., Emrick, C. D., Iber, F. L., James, K. E., Lacoursiere, R. B., Lee, K. K., Lowenstam, I., Maany, I., Neiderheiser, D., Nocks, J. J., & Shaw, S. (1986). Disulfiram treatment of alcoholism: A Veterans Administration cooperative study. *Journal of the American Medical Association, 256,* 1449–1455.

Gawin, F. H., & Ellinwood, E. H. (1988). Cocaine and other stimulants: Actions, abuse and treatment. *New England Journal of Medicine, 318,* 1173–1182.

Gawin, F. H., & Kleber, H. D. (1986). Abstinence symptomatology and psychiatric diagnosis in chronic cocaine abusers. *Archives of General Psychiatry, 43,* 107–113.

Gawin, F. H., Kleber, H. D., Byck, R., Rounsaville, B. J., Kosten, T. R., Jatlow, P. I., & Morgan, C. (1989). Desipramine facilitation of initial cocaine abstinence. *Archives of General Psychiatry, 46,* 117–121.

Gold, M. S., Pottash, A. C., Sweeny, D. R., & Kleber, H. D. (1980). Opiate withdrawal using clonidine. *Journal of the American Medical Association, 243,* 343–346.

Gorelick, D. A., & Wilkins, J. N. (1986). Special aspects of human alcohol withdrawal. In M. Galanter (Ed.), *Recent developments in alcoholism* (Vol. 4). New York: Plenum Press.

Hayashida, M., Alterman, A. I., McLellan, A. T., O'Brien, C. P., Purtell, J. J., Volpicelli, J. R., Raphaelson, A. H., & Hall, C. P. (1989). Comparative effectiveness and costs of inpatient and outpatient detoxification of patients with mild-to-moderate alcohol withdrawal syndrome. *New England Journal of Medicine, 320,* 358–365.

Kadden, R. M., Cooney, N. L., Getter, H., & Litt, M. D. (1989). Matching alcoholics to coping skills or interactional therapies: Posttreatment results. *Journal of Consulting and Clinical Psychology, 57,* 698–704.

Kleber, H. D., & Gawin, F. H. (1984). The spectrum of cocaine abuse and its treatment. *Journal of Clinical Psychiatry, 45,* 18–34.

Kosten, T. (1989). Pharmacotherapeutic interventions for cocaine abuse: Matching patients to treatment. *Journal of Nervous and Mental Disease, 177,* 379–389.

Linnoila, M., Mefford, I., Nutt, D., & Adinoff, B. (1987). Alcohol withdrawal and noradrenergic function. *Annals of Internal Medicine, 107,* 875–889.

Marlatt, G. A., & Gordon, J. R. (Eds.). (1985). *Relapse prevention: Maintenance strategies in the treatment of additive behaviors.* New York: Guilford Press.

Mayfield, D. (1985). Substance abuse in the affective disorders. In A. I. Alterman (Ed.), *Substance abuse and psychopathology.* New York: Plenum Press.

McLachlan, J. F. C. (1972). Benefit from group therapy as a function of patient–therapist match on conceptual level. *Psychotherapy: Theory, Research, and Practice, 9,* 317–323.

McLellan, A. T. (1986). "Psychiatric severity" as a predictor of outcome from substance abuse treatments. In R. E. Meyer (Ed.), *Psychopathology and addictive disorders.* New York: Guilford Press.

McLellan, A. T. (1989). *Patient–treatment matching and outcome improvement in alcohol rehabilitation: Institute of Medicine report on future directions in research and treatment of alcohol dependence.* Washington, DC: National Academy of Sciences.

McLellan, A. T., Alterman, A., Parikh, G., Zanis, D., & Bragg, A. (1989). *A quantitative measure of substance abuse treatment: The Treatment Services Review (TSR).* Unpublished manuscript, University of Pennsylvania.

Miller, S., Frances, R., & Holmes, D. (1989) Psychotropic medications. In R. K. Hester & W. R. Miller (Eds.), *Handbook of alcoholism treatment approaches.* New York: Pergamon Press.

Miller, W. R. (1983). Motivational interviewing with problem drinkers. *Behavioural Psychotherapy, 11,* 142–172.

Miller, W. R., & Hester, R. K. (1986a). Inpatient alcoholism treatment: Who benefits? *American Psychologist, 41,* 794–805.

Miller, W. R., & Hester, R. K. (1986b). The effectiveness of alcoholism treatment methods: What research reveals. In W. R. Miller & N. Heather (Eds.), *Treating addictive behaviors: Processes of change.* New York: Plenum Press.

Naranjo, C. A., & Sellers, E. M. (1986). Clinical assessment and pharmacotherapy of the alcohol withdrawal syndrome. In M. Galanter (Ed.), *Recent developments in alcoholism* (Vol. 4). New York: Plenum Press.

Nathan, P. E. (1986). Outcomes of treatment for alcoholism: Current data. *Annals of Behavioral Medicine, 8,* 40–46.

O'Brien, C. P., Alterman, A. I., Walter, D., Childress, A. R., & McLellan, A. T. (1990). *Evaluation of cocaine dependence treatment* (NIDA Research Monograph No. 95). Washington, DC: U.S. Government Printing Office.

O'Brien, C. P., & Woody, G. E. (1986). The role of naltrexone in the treatment of opioid dependence. In D. Cappell, F. Glaser, Y. Israel, H. Kalant, W. Schmidt, E. M. Sellers, & R. S. Smart (Eds.), *Research advances in alcohol and drug dependence.* New York: Plenum Press.

Patterson, M. A. (1984). Treatment of drug, alcohol and nicotine addiction by neuroelectric therapy. *Journal of Bioelectrics, 3,* 193–221.

Rounsaville, B., & Kleber, H. (1986). Psychiatric disorders in opiate addicts: Preliminary findings on the course and interaction with program type. In R. E. Meyer (Ed.), *Psychopathology and addictive disorders.* New York: Guilford Press.

Rounsaville, B., Weissman, M., Kleber, H., & Wilber, C. (1982). Heterogeneity of psychiatric diagnosis in treated opiate addicts. *Archives of General Psychiatry, 39,* 161–166.

Shaw, J. M., Kolesar, G. S., Sellers, E. M., Kaplan, H. L., & Sandor, P. (1981). Development of optimal treatment tactics for alcohol withdrawal: I. Assessment and effectiveness of supportive care. *Journal of Clinical Psychopharmacology, 1,* 382–389.

Stinnett, J. (1982). Outpatient detoxification of the alcoholic. *International Journal of the Addictions, 17,* 1031–1046.

Tennant, F. S. (1986). *Medical withdrawal from cocaine dependence for cocaine dependent with amantadine and other parkinsonian drugs.* Monograph, Veract Inc.

Tennant, F. S., & Sagherian, A. A. (1987). Double blind comparison of amantadine hydrochloride and bromocriptine mesylate for ambulatory withdrawal from cocaine dependence. *Archives of Internal Medicine, 147,* 109–112.

Tennant, F. S., & Tarver, A. L. (1985). Double blind comparison of desipramine and placebo in withdrawal from cocaine dependence. In L. Harris (Ed.), *Problems of drug dependence 1984* (NIDA Research Monograph No. 55). Washington, DC: U.S. Government Printing Office.

Volpicelli, J., Alterman, A. I., Hayashida, M., & O'Brien, C. P. (1990). *Naltrexone in the treatment of alcohol dependence: Initial findings.* Manuscript submitted for publication.

Volpicelli, J., Alterman, A. I., Sweeney, K., & O'Brien, C. P. (1990). *Prediction of successful completion of ambulatory detoxification.* Manuscript in preparation.

Washton, A. M. (1986). Treatment of cocaine abuse. In L. Harris (Ed.)., *Problems of drug dependence 1985* (NIDA Research Monograph No. 67). Washington, DC: U.S. Government Printing Office.

Washton, A. M., Gold, M. S., & Pottash, A. C. (1986). Treatment outcome in cocaine abusers. In L. Harris (Ed.), *Problems of drug dependence 1985* (NIDA Research Monograph No. 67). Washington, DC: U.S. Government Printing Office.

Washton, A. M., Pottash, A. C., & Gold, M. S. (1984). Naltrexone in addicted business executives and physicians. *Journal of Clinical Psychiatry, 45,* 39–41.

Whitfield, C., Thompson, G., Lamb, A., Spencer, V., Pfeifer, M., & Browing-Ferrando, M. (1978). Detoxification of 1,024 alcoholic patients without psychoactive drugs. *Journal of the American Medical Association, 239,* 1409–1410.

Woody, G. E., Luborsky, L., McLellan, A. T., O'Brien, C. P., Beck, A. T., Blaine, J., Herman, I., & Hole, A. (1983). Psychotherapy for opiate addicts: Does it help? *Archives of General Psychiatry, 40,* 639–645.

Woody, G. E., McLellan, A. T., Luborsky, L., & O'Brien, C. P. (1985). Sociopathy and psychotherapy outcome. *Archives of General Psychiatry, 42,* 1081–1086.

Woody, G. E., & O'Brien, C. P. (1986). Update on methadone maintenance. In D. Cappell, F. Glaser, Y. Israel, H. Kalant, W. Schmidt, E. M. Sellers, & R. S. Smart (Eds.), *Research advances in alcohol and drug dependence.* New York: Plenum Press.

17

Individual Psychodynamic Psychotherapy

LANCE M. DODES
EDWARD J. KHANTZIAN

Individual psychotherapy is widely used in treatment of addicts, though it is perhaps still underappreciated in comparison with group modalities, including self-help groups. Many addicts benefit from a combination of individual and group treatments simultaneously, and some require the individual psychotherapy to be able to remain with other treatments (Khantzian, 1986). Furthermore, a significant number cannot, or choose not to, make use of other treatment and can *only* be treated successfully with individual psychotherapy. In this chapter, we rearticulate and extend ideas that we and others have developed previously, based on our understanding and treatment experience with addicted individuals over many years (Dodes, 1984, 1988; Dodes & Khantzian in press; Khantzian, 1980, 1986).

The rationale for individual psychotherapy with addicts arises from an understanding of the psychological factors that contribute to addiction. Contemporary psychodynamic formulations have stressed, in addition to the role of conflict and the object meaning of alcohol or drugs, deficits and dysfunctions in ego and self or narcissistic functioning as important determinants of a reliance on substances (Dodes & Khantzian, in press). These deficits and dysfunctions have resulted in self-regulation disturbances involving affect life, self-esteem maintenance, the capacity for self-care, and self–other relations. These areas of psychological vulnerability or dysfunction contribute significantly to addictions and are targeted in psychotherapy (Khantzian, 1986).

Although we believe that there are indications for referring addicts to psychotherapy, in practice the reasons why people come to or seek out this treatment are variable. One of them is that many patients, perhaps particularly those who are more psychologically oriented, first seek treatment in psychotherapy. Others begin individual psychotherapy after first seeking treatment through self-help groups or a more educationally based treatment program, such as that offered in many inpatient settings and outpatient clinics. Some of these patients have first achieved abstinence from drug or alcohol use through their prior treatment, and are now seeking treatment for the emotional problems from which they still suffer. Their recognition of these problems is often much clearer now that they are substance-free (although some patients are disappointed to find that their abstinence has brought relief from the troubles caused by substance use, but has not resolved all their emotional difficulties). In exploring these problems, patients come to understand their own psychologies, as well as the place of the abuse of substances in their emotional lives. This understanding not only addresses the reasons for their continued problems when chemical free, but also, by placing the substance problem in the context of their emotional lives, provides a strong internal basis for avoiding relapse.

Another route into individual psychotherapy among addicted patients is via repeated treatment failures in other, less introspective settings. Some of these patients have repeatedly relapsed, despite clear conscious motivation to abstain, because they are unaware of the internal, largely unconscious factors that lead them toward resumed substance use. Their failure to recognize the role of unconscious processes leads them to attribute their behavior to lack of "willpower"; this attribution contributes further to their self-devaluation. Learning about themselves in individual psychotherapy thus contributes not only to a more stable chemical-free state, and to overall general improvement in emotional function, but also to diminished shame concerning their addiction. Likewise, individual psychotherapy may be successfully pursued simultaneously with other treatment, such as Alcoholics Anonymous (AA) or Narcotics Anonymous (NA), or professionally led group therapy. In these cases, the individual work pursues the usual goals of insight and emotional growth, while other modalities focus on support of the patient's chemical-free state.

A number of studies have substantiated the value of individual psychotherapy with addicts. Woody et al. (1983) noted that in seven investigations with methadone-treated patients, where patients were randomly assigned to psychotherapy or a different treatment (most often drug counseling), five of the studies showed better outcome in the psychotherapy group. Woody's own group also found that patients who received psychotherapy and drug counseling had better results than patients receiving drug counseling alone, when measured in terms of number of areas of improvement, less use of illicit opiates, and lower doses of methadone required. Elsewhere (Woody, McLellan, Luborsky, & O'Brien, 1986), this group noted further that the patients with the most disturbed global psychiatric ratings benefited particularly from psychotherapy, in comparison with drug counseling. A number of investigators have documented that there is a high correlation between psychiatric disorders, especially depression, and addiction (Rounsaville, Weissman, Kleber, & Wilber, 1982; Khantzian & Treece, 1985). Brown (1985) found that 45% of a group of abstinent alcoholics in AA had sought psychotherapy, and over 90% of them found it helpful. Rounsaville, Gawin, and Kleber (1985) also reported positive results in a preliminary study treating outpatient cocaine abusers with a modified interpersonal psychotherapy, along with medication trials. Woody et al. (1986) also reported that when psychotherapists were integrated in the treatment team, there was a reduction of stress on the entire staff as a result of their successful management of the most psychiatrically troubled patients. Finally, when psychotherapy was added to paraprofessional drug counseling in an inpatient setting (Rogalski, 1984), patients were found to improve in compliance with treatment, as measured in decreased number of discharges against medical advice, disciplinary discharges, or unauthorized absences.

In addition to these studies that have statistically examined effects of psychotherapy, there is a significant psychodynamic literature reporting on the treatability of addicted patients with psychodynamic or psychoanalytically oriented psychotherapy (Dodes, 1984, 1988, 1990; Frances, Khantzian, & Tamerin, 1989; Khantzian, 1986; Krystal & Raskin, 1970; Silber, 1974; Treece & Khantzian, 1986; Wurmser, 1974; Krystal, 1982; Woody, Luborsky, McLellan, & O'Brien, 1989). The experience of treating addicted individuals in psychodynamic therapy has also provided our best information about the psychology of addiction, which in turn serves as the theoretical basis for technical aspects of the therapy of these patients.

Indications for psychodynamic psychotherapy depend on the patient's capacity to benefit, as well as his or her motivation. Addicted individuals who are able to achieve and maintain sobriety with substance abuse counseling and/or self-help groups, and who are untroubled by conflict, anxiety, depression, or other symptoms, are unlikely to seek psychotherapy. Addicted patients who are able to develop a therapeutic alliance and to be at least moderately introspective, and who have emotional suffering, are candidates for psychotherapy as much as are nonaddicts with similar characteristics. Some of these patients will use psychotherapy to help them to achieve abstinence, whereas others will use it to help them maintain it, and both groups may also use their therapy to help their overall emotional health once they have achieved abstinence.

Psychodynamic Basis for Psychotherapy of Addicted Patients

There have been a number of major contributions to understanding the psychology of the addictions, particularly over the past 20 years (Dodes & Khantzian, in press). The most frequently described function of substance use has been the management of intolerable or overwhelming affects. The idea that certain substances are preferentially chosen on the basis of their specific ability to address (ameliorate, express) certain affective states has been termed the "self-medication hypothesis" (Khantzian, 1985a). Various authors have described connections between certain affects and the use of alcohol or certain drugs—for example, use of narcotics to manage rage or loneliness, and use of cocaine and other stimulants to manage depression, boredom, and emptiness or to provide a sense of grandeur (Khantzian, 1985a; Wurmser, 1974; Milkman & Frosch, 1973). In a more general way, Krystal and Raskin (1970) spoke of a "defective stimulus barrier" in addicts, causing them to be susceptible to flooding with intolerable affective states, which are traumatic. They described a normal process of affective development in which affects are differentiated, desomatized, and verbalized, and pointed to defects in this normal development in addicts. This leaves them with inability to utilize affects as signals, which is a critical capacity in managing them. Without this, drugs may be used to ward off affective experience.

Others have noted the quality of addicts' relatedness to their alcohol or drugs as akin to human object relationships. The chemical becomes a substitute for a longed-for or needed figure—one that has omnipotent properties, or that is completely controllable and available (Krystal & Raskin, 1970; Wieder & Kaplan, 1969; Wurmser, 1974).

Related to the views described above are views of the narcissistic pathology of addicts. Wurmser (1974) described a "narcissistic crisis" in addicts. He noted that for some addicts, collapse of a grandiose self or of an idealized object provides the impetus for substance use in an effort to resolve feelings of narcissistic frustration, shame, and rage. Kohut (1971) also referred to the narcissistic function of alcohol or drugs in addiction as a replacement for defective psychological structure, particularly that arising from an inadequate idealized self-object.

From another perspective, Khantzian (1978) and Khantzian and Mack (1983) have described "self-care" functions—the group of ego functions involved with anticipation of danger, appropriate modulated response to protect oneself, and sufficient positive self-esteem to care about oneself. These appear to be defective in many substance abusers, who characteristically place themselves in danger or fail to protect their health and well-being. This problem may be related to inadequate attention to the protection of the child by the parent, resulting in the failure to internalize these functions. Such self-care deficits should not be overlooked in the process of understanding other bases for self-destructive behavior.

In addition to this ego deficit psychology, several investigators have described a generally defective capacity in addicts to be aware of their affective states. Some addicts appear to be "alexithymic"—that is, unable to name or describe emotions in words. Others have a less clearly definable avoidance of affective states entirely. Krystal (1982) has described substance use in some of these patients as a search for an external agent to soothe them, associated with their lack of sense of ability to soothe themselves. McDougall (1984) has described patients whose use of words and ideas is without affective meaning, and who use alcohol or drugs to disperse emotional arousal and thus to avoid affective flooding. Although the final appearance of this affective intolerance has the quality of an ego deficit, its underlying basis is understood to be a defensive avoidance. Krystal (1982) has described this as arising secondary to psychological trauma in either childhood or adult life.

Finally, addiction may play a central role of seeking restoration of inner control of one's affective state (Dodes, 1990). This need for control in addicts involves a narcissistic vulnerability to being traumatized by the experience of helplessness or powerlessness. The use of substances in these instances is seen as a way of correcting this experience of helplessness. That is, by taking an action (using alcohol or drugs) that can alter one's internal affective state, one may reassert the power to control one's own inner experience. Since the sense of control of inner experience is a central aspect of narcissism, the intense aggressive drive to achieve this control when it is felt to be threatened may appropriately be considered narcissistic rage. This rage is what gives addiction some of its most defining characteristics—namely, its insistent, compulsive, unrelenting qualities, which are relatively unresponsive to realistic factors. And, like narcissistic rage in general, the addictive drive may well overwhelm other aspects of the personality (Dodes, 1990).

Technical Aspects of Psychotherapy with Addicts

There are a number of special considerations in the psychodynamic psychotherapy of addicted individuals (Dodes & Khantzian, in press). From the formulations above, it is clear that various meanings and roles of drugs or alcohol will need to be considered in understanding the patient. In addition, addicts are frequently still abusing substances at the time they are first seen; this poses an immediate threat to their emotional and physical health, their relationships, and their capacity to function. This fact makes it necessary to address the question of abstinence from substance use first, when beginning treatment.

The first step in this process is making the diagnosis of substance abuse or dependence and informing the patient of it. The patient may fail to perceive the extent of the problem, and may present instead with overt denial or minimization. In order to make the diagnosis, and have a basis to present it clearly to the patient, it is necessary to take a careful, detailed history of the problems that have been caused by the patient's use of drugs or alcohol. In taking the history, it is useful to inquire systematically about trouble in the areas of work, medical health, relationships with friends, relationships with family (including small children), legal problems, and intrapsychic problems (depression, shame, anxiety). It is often helpful to ask specifically about what the patient is like when he or she drinks or uses drugs, and the details of what happens at these times, as well as the effects the patient has sought from substance use. Does he or she become more belligerant, moody, withdrawn, sad? Might the patient have had more or better relationships with friends if he or she had never had a drink or a drug? Likewise, patients will often deny trouble in their marriages, but when the matter is explored in detail, they will acknowledge that their spouses would prefer that they drink less, or have asked them on more than one occasion to cut down or stop. Upon reflection, they may recognize that their use of alcohol or drugs has silently become a source of chronic tension in their relationships. Once the areas of difficulties that are due to alcohol or drugs are clarified, and even listed, it is often possible for a patient to acknowledge the global impact of substance abuse on his or her life.

In focusing on the diagnosis of alcoholism or other drug abuse, the patient is not only made cognitively aware of the problem; the realization that he or she is out of control in this area of his or her life is a significant psychological step in itself. It is a blow to the narcissistic potency of the patient; as such, it may be usefully investigated, since it bears on the patient's (frequently important) feelings and issues concerning powerlessness and mastery (Dodes, 1988). From another perspective, Mack (1981) has also underlined that an alcoholic's recognition of failure to be in control of his or her drinking is a first step in the assumption of responsibility.

Through all this early diagnostic and at times confrontational work, as in therapy in general, the therapist's attitude must be exploratory without being judgmental. The patient's denial or minimization is, to begin with, often closely connected with his or her shame. And throughout this initial evaluation, the patient is simultaneously evaluating the therapist—in particular, the therapist's attitude toward the patient and his or her addictive problem. To put it another way, the patient is faced with his or her own projections onto the therapist, and it is important that the therapist not accede to the role of the harsh or punitive superego that is at risk of being invisibly imposed.

Transference issues among addicts arise from a variety of sources, as with patients in general, but often include harsh superego projections, as well as transferences arising from narcissistic deficits leading to idealizing and mirroring relationships, or fearful, guarded positions defensive against being over-controlled or overwhelmed. Countertransference difficulties frequently encountered revolve around frustration, anger, and guilt (Vaillant, 1981), as patients' failures to abstain challenge the therapeutic potency of the treater; at times these difficulties result in withdrawal, inappropriately critical attitudes, or overinvolvement fueled by the therapist's reaction formation. The severe nature of the risks facing addicts makes the work with them both particularly challenging and rewarding. It is important for the therapist to be able to view both the overt behavior and the inner psychopathology of the addict with the same combination of objectivity and compassion that he or she brings to any patient.

The task of developing a therapeutic alliance early in therapy is also made difficult by the patient's ambivalent relationship toward abstention from drinking or drug use, at the same time as the therapist is appropriately concerned with the patient's achieving abstinence. It may be ineffective and even counterproductive to be seen as *requiring* (versus suggesting) something that the patient does not consciously feel is in his or her best interest. Once the patient concurs with the diagnosis, he or she has a necessary, though not always sufficient, basis for an alliance with the therapist to achieve abstinence; in fact, the psychological issues in abstention are complex.

We (Dodes, 1984; Khantzian, 1980) have addressed issues in abstention with alcoholics. Patients' achievement of abstinence hinges in part on the place of substance use in their psychological equilibrium, but also hinges critically on the alliance with and transference to the therapist. For example, many patients quickly achieve abstinence upon beginning psychotherapy, in spite of the evident importance to them of their drugs or alcohol. For others, in whom the substances have not been malignantly out of control (and thus who are not in an immediate emergency situation), and who at first continue to use substances, the threat to successful treatment can be challenging. In a number of these cases we have had the experience of helping patients establish abstinence over time, psychotherapeutically. When the therapist focuses on the patient's failure to perceive the danger to himself or herself, the therapist's caring concern may be internalized by the patient, providing a nucleus for the introjection of a healthy "self-care" function (Dodes, 1984). However, this is not always possible; the patient's ability to perceive the therapist in a benign way that may be internalized depends on aspects of the negative transference either being resolved first, or not being present at the beginning of treatment. For some patients, early achievement of abstinence is possible because of a true therapeutic alliance, whereas in other cases it may arise from unconscious wishes to merge with or be held by a therapist who is idealized, or from compliant identification with the aggressor (Dodes, 1984). In instances where the patient initially does not abstain, a subsequent confrontation of the patient may produce abstention, because the confrontation is finally perceived as the longed-for message of caring about the patient that had been absent or insufficient in the patient's childhood (the kind of parental insufficiency Khantzian and Mack [1983] described in their discussion of the origin of self-care deficits). From a practical standpoint, the clinical choices involved must in the end depend on the immediate risks to the patient. If patients drink only intermittently, and are able to participate genuinely in the process of psychotherapy, we have found that the psychotherapy can continue; it allows an opportunity to explore the issues in the continued drinking, including self-care issues and the transference implications in the failure to abstain. However, when drinking becomes continually destructive, patients are generally unable to participate in the process, requiring early confrontation around the need to be hospitalized or to terminate therapy. Over the course of an ongoing psychotherapy, the capacity for abstinence may vary, depending in part on shifts in the therapeutic relationship (Dodes, 1984). We discuss later the question of relapses in an abstinent patient.

Once abstinence is achieved, the therapy may broaden to explore all areas of the patient's psychological life, as in any psychotherapy. Some authors writing about alcoholism, however, have recommended a kind of staging of the therapy. In this view, the first phase is directed toward helping the patient develop an identity as an alcoholic (Brown, 1985), or spending up to several years focusing on the drinking, on ways to stay sober, and on mourning the losses incurred as a result of drinking (Bean-Bayog, 1985). Although these are unquestionably important issues, and most alcoholics do deal with them to at least some degree, it is unnecessary and potentially counterproductive to attempt to direct the therapeutic process according to a preconceived agenda. As with any patient, imposing one's own focus risks interfering with the free evolution of the patient's thoughts toward deeper and more meaningful understanding of the issues that are important to the patient. In our opinion, while some addicts (like some patients in general) will require a more supportive rather than an exploratory approach, or special approaches based on some of the dynamic factors described above, this decision should be based on an individual assessment of the patient's psychology, rather than on a generalization for all substance abusers. And the approach in treatment may, and should, vary according to the stage of treatment and the status of the patient's abstinence.

The idea of imposing structure in psychotherapy with addicts arises in part from concerns about the ability of the patients to tolerate the process of therapy. At the heart of this is the worry that exploring the important issues in their lives will lead addicts to resume their substance abuse. As noted above, the reverse is often the case: Patients who do not learn about the issues that trouble them may be at much greater risk of continued substance use or relapse. Nonetheless, there have unquestionably been difficulties with pursuing psychotherapy in some instances. As previously summarized (Dodes, 1988), these objections with alcoholics focus on the failure of therapists to attend appropriately to the life-threatening nature of continued substance abuse (Bean-Bayog, 1985), or on failure to make the diagnosis (Brown, 1985). In both cases, therapists may be blindly pursuing therapy while the patients' lives deteriorate. In addition, alcoholics may use therapy to aid their denial of their alcoholism, and some observers have felt that alcoholics may have difficulty with the strong transference feelings of an individual psychotherapy (Vaillant, 1981).

However, all these objections hinge on failures of the therapist, and may be avoided by a therapist who is attentive to these issues (Dodes, 1988). For instance, as described above, attention must be paid initially to achieving abstinence. Likewise, if a patient misuses the treatment to rationalize continued drug or alcohol use, an appropriately responsive therapist would recognize this and bring this misuse into the process of treatment to be identified and dealt with, rather than allowing it to continue. And the therapist should be attentive to the psychology of an addicted patient as to any patient, and should closely monitor the transference and the patient's capacity to observe, tolerate, and understand his or her feelings in the relationship. Addicts have a wide variety of characterological structures, strengths, and weaknesses, and it would be inaccurate to view them as a group as being incapable of dealing with strong transference feelings arising in a psychotherapy. Vaillant's (1981) parallel concern that therapists cannot tolerate their countertransference feelings toward their alcoholic patients also appears too pessimistic, both in our experience and from a reading of the literature.

Finally, in addressing Brown's (1985) concern that the alcoholic patient may be distracted from his or her task of establishing an identity as an alcoholic and maintaining abstinence, this may be taken principally as a reminder to the therapist to attend to the patient's alcoholism (Dodes, 1988).

In fact, in the ongoing therapy of addicts, once abstinence is achie
therapist should always be alert to the meanings and purposes of the pa
substance use as these become clearer. Part of the advantage of psychother
with addicts is that it offers in an ongoing way the opportunity for patients t
take firmer control over their addiction, based on understanding and tolerating
the feelings and issues that contribute to it. This approach by the therapist (i.e.,
being continually attentive to improving understanding of the patient's drug
use) will avoid the problem of distracting the patient from his or her addiction.
Of course, it should be mentioned that any therapist can be fooled: a patient
who denies, minimizes, or distorts the facts about his or her substance use may
render its diagnosis and treatment impossible. This is a limitation to psychotherapy, as it is to other attempted interventions.

Having considered early issues of abstinence and allowing the focus of the
therapy to broaden, we may now consider how the dynamics of addicts
referred to earlier may necessitate a modification of approach. In the case of
patients who have elements of alexithymia, Krystal (1982) and Krystal and
Raskin (1970) proposed certain modifications, particularly early in therapy.
Essentially, they have suggested a preparatory stage that will allow later work
to occur. In this stage, the patient's affects are identified and explained, with
the goal of increasing ego function, including improving the use of affects as
signals and improving affect tolerance. From another perspective, McDougall
(1984) has focused on the countertransference problems produced with such
patients. She described feelings of boredom and helplessness, with consequent
emotional withdrawal by the therapist, and pointed to the need for the therapist to provide a consistent holding environment that may last for years before
the patients are able to acknowledge their emotions. She also offered an
understanding of this process, in terms of the patient creating a "primitive
communication that is intended, in a deeply unconscious fashion, to make the
analyst experience what the distressed and misunderstood infant had once
felt" (p. 399).

A contemporary psychodynamic understanding of addicted patients does
not necessarily suggest modifications of approach, but rather suggests a need
to attend to one or another aspect of the meaning and role of the addiction for
a patient. For instance, for some patients it will be particularly important to
attend to the object meanings of the alcohol or drugs. In some patients,
narcissistic vulnerabilities will be of paramount importance—for instance, the
collapse of idealized objects as described by Wurmser (1974), or the role of
particular affective states in precipitating substance use, mentioned by a number of authors. With some patients, self-care deficits as described by Khantzian
and Mack (1983) are of great significance. From a different perspective, the
active nature of addictive behavior in seizing control of one's affective state as
described by Dodes (1990) may be an important focus in the psychotherapy of
addicts; in such cases, it is important to address patients' experiences of
helplessness and powerlessness as major factors in precipitating substance use.

It is also important for the therapist to be active with patients whose affect management and self-care are seriously impaired (Khantzian, 1986). Excessive passivity with such patients can be dangerous. It is necessary in these cases to empathically draw the patients' attention to ways in which they render themselves vulnerable as a result of their self-care deficits, and to point out how these self-care deficits render them susceptible to addictive behavior. As Krystal (1982) has also said, it is necessary to explore with patients the details of current life situations in order to help them recognize their feelings, and see that these may serve as "guides to appropriate reactions and self-protective behavior rather than signals for impulsive action and the obliteration of feelings with drugs" (Khantzian, 1986, p. 217).

Consistent with the need to maintain an active stance, the therapist may need to serve as a "primary care" physician—especially at the start of treatment, when he or she must often play multiple roles to insure that the patient receives appropriate care from a number of sources (Khantzian, 1985b, 1988). These may include decisions about (and active involvement in arranging) hospitalization and detoxification, involvement with AA or NA, professionally led group treatments, or pharmacological treatment. However, such an active approach, while possibly life-saving, may interfere with the later development of a traditional psychotherapeutic relationship because of the transference and countertransference issues it induces, particularly in regard to the patient's realistic gratitude. If this should become a prominent factor, referral to another therapist for continued psychotherapy may be required (Khantzian, 1985b).

Another consideration in therapy with addicted individuals involves relapses, or the threat of relapses. In either case, just as with the initial attention to abstinence, the therapy must focus on this when it occurs. One reason for this focus is, of course, to attend to the risk to the patient. But relapses (or the patient's awareness that he or she feels a greater urge to use alcohol or drugs) also provide an opportunity to learn about the factors leading to substance use. Frequently patients are unaware of these factors; their lack of awareness contributes to their feelings of frustration and helplessness, and leaves them unprepared for further relapses. A careful, even microscopic, investigation of the feelings, relationships, and events that preceded the relapse will often be revealing. Once these issues and affects are clarified, they frequently contribute to an understanding of the patient's psychology in general, since they center on areas felt to be intolerable by the patient. Often the patient will bring up his or her increased thinking about drugs or alcohol, or certain related behavior, associated with an impending relapse. But at other times the therapist may infer this increased risk, based on what he or she knows of the patient's history and emotional life. Conveying this perception to the patient is one way to help the patient learn to attend to his or her affects (as well as thoughts and behaviors) and utilize them as signals. Dreams may also provide here, as in therapy in general, knowledge of what is currently unconscious. Often, abstinent addicts have dreams about alcohol or drugs that shed light on the meanings of their use, as well as serving as indicators that something current in the patients' lives is reviving the association with alcohol or drugs, and hence warning of the need to attend to risk of relapse.

Finally, a word should be said about organicity. Some treatment providers have viewed addicted patients as too impaired in brain functioning, as a result of drug or alcohol abuse ("wet brain"), to be able to utilize a dynamic psychotherapy until after a lengthy time of abstinence. Certainly there are patients whose memory and capacity for some skilled cognitive functions is impaired immediately after stopping drug or alcohol use. However, in our experience, this limitation is frequently mild or not significant for all but the most severely affected addicts (e.g., alcoholics with hepatic failure and elevated blood ammonia levels). In fact, as inpatient treatment centers regularly observe, patients can do significant and even major work to understand themselves and the dynamic issues in their families, and can also rapidly return to complex tasks, within the span of a few weeks immediately following detoxification. These inpatient programs are usually designed with a first phase for detoxification over 3 to 7 days, following which patients are placed in a therapeutically and educationally intensive rehabilitation phase. It is the rare patient who cannot participate in this, even though inpatient centers nearly always treat patients who have been heavily abusing alcohol or drugs. The implication for psychotherapy is that it is rarely necessary to wait an extended time to begin because of organic factors. Patients who are truly impaired, because their drug or alcohol use is so continuous that they are always either high/drunk or withdrawing, should not be in psychotherapy to begin with, as described above. These patients require hospitalization to break the pattern before they will be able to attend to the work of the treatment.

Psychotherapy and Self-Help Groups

Since psychotherapy and self-help groups are both frequently employed in the treatment of addiction, it is important to consider the issues involved in utilizing both approaches (Dodes, 1988; Dodes & Khantzian, in press). Although psychotherapy is frequently combined with involvement in AA or NA, some authors (Brown, 1985; Bean-Bayog, 1985; Rosen, 1981) have suggested a kind of staging of the therapy. In this view, AA or NA serves as the locus for attending to the patient's addiction and his or her attempts to remain chemical-free, while psychotherapy is either postponed or is assigned an adjunctive role, looking at other areas of the person's life and issues. Rosen's (1981) paper took a closer look at the issues involved in this sequence, and focused on the specific role of the therapy in helping patients to separate from their attachment to AA, which Rosen viewed as having elements of a symbiosis. One aspect of this is the striking fact that AA, quite unlike psychoanalytically oriented psychotherapy, provides no mechanism for termination. In Rosen's view, working through separation and termination is particularly important to many of these patients, and he saw a critical aspect of the role of psychotherapy following AA as permitting this work.

However, as we have described above, there is usually little reason to postpone psychotherapy; consequently, it is important to understand the psychology of engaging simultaneously in psychotherapy and AA or NA. The patient in such a combined treatment will often engage differently with each element; that is, the patient will split his or her transference projections, expectations, and attachments, engaging the therapy and the self-help group at separate psychological levels (Dodes, 1988). Such multiple levels of engagement are always present in any psychotherapy, especially in patients who have significant narcissistic difficulties in addition to their structural conflicts. To put it another way, functions of narcissistic mirroring and valuing are always present in therapy, concurrent with other transferential and intellectual engagements, and concurrent with interpretive work directed toward structural conflicts. Patients' attachment to AA provides opportunity for needed internalization of self-care and self-valuing, with AA serving as a valuing, idealized object (or self-object or transitional object); in this way, important elements of the narcissistic (idealizing and mirroring) transference are assigned to AA (Dodes, 1988). The degree to which the transference is split in this way will vary in different patients. It is critical for the therapist to be aware of this split, since a patient's sobriety may hinge on an idealization of AA or its "Higher Power" concept, and this sobriety may be lost if the idealization is challenged (Dodes, 1988). Consequently, the therapist must first help the patient to increase his or her tolerance of affects and "await internalization of sufficient narcissistic potency" (Dodes, 1988, p. 289), before too closely examining the defenses and functions of AA.

In our opinion, the need for a nondynamic supportive approach through AA may lessen eventually as a consequence of the patient's growth, including that achieved via internalization (either through the therapy or through AA) of a sense of adequate narcissistic potency, as well as growth in ego functions in general. At this point, the patient may be able to remain chemical-free without AA. However, this does not always occur, and this may be understood as the basis for the phenomenon of interminable treatment in AA: "Those individuals who successfully internalize [a self-care] function, may stop attending AA meetings, while those who cannot internalize it, must attend forever" (Dodes, 1984, p. 253). It should be emphasized that this refers to the need to attend AA forever in order to maintain sobriety; clearly, there are many long-term AA members who remain involved because of the important social and interpersonal elements in AA, or because of their interest in helping others. These individuals do not need AA for sobriety, but choose it for other reasons.

As an aside, the fear of disrupting the idealizing transference to AA (and consequently losing the sobriety that is dependent on this transference) may be what underlies the fear of psychotherapy among some patients and some treatment providers (Dodes, 1988). Again, while this is a realistic concern, it is only one aspect of the need for the therapist to be attentive to the technical requirements of addicted patients, and does not contraindicate psychotherapeutic treatment. Overall, the combination of psychodynamic psychotherapy and AA or NA is a highly workable one for the great majority of patients (Dodes, 1988; Khantzian, 1985b, 1988).

Finally, we should comment on the role of the "disease" concept. It is appropriate to consider this here, since this concept is closely linked with the self-help groups and has traditionally been difficult to reconcile with psychoanalytically oriented psychotherapy. Mack (1981) noted that the disease concept has led to "over simplified physiological models and a territorial smugness . . . which . . . precludes a sophisticated psychodynamic understanding of the problems of the individual alcoholic" (p. 129). In addition, the term "disease" itself has not been well or clearly defined, a fact addressed by Shaffer (1985). However, it is both useful and possible to integrate the disease concept into a traditional psychoanalytic psychotherapy (Dodes, 1988). In the first place, focusing on the addictive behavior specifically as an illness is useful, because it helps to avoid the kind of failure to address the problem that some have worried about with psychotherapy. And, as mentioned, acknowledgment of a disease or diagnosis is a narcissistic blow, which can itself be explored in terms of the feelings and issues around it, particularly those of powerlessness in the patient's life (Dodes, 1988, 1990).

Since an illness or disease concept can be useful, it is helpful to have an approach that makes it possible to integrate the concept with a psychoanalytic psychotherapy. Such an approach is to define the "disease" of alcoholism as having two parts: first, the patient's history of alcoholism, and second, the fact that the patient is at permanent risk of repeating this behavior in the future (Dodes, 1988). Clarifying and emphasizing an aspect of the patient's history certainly do not interfere with dynamic work. The risk of repetition of drinking that is so central to the "disease" idea may be troublesome for dynamic exploration, if it has the quality of something that is inexplicable in dynamic terms. However, this risk may be understood as actually the same as the regressive potential of any patient in psychotherapy (Dodes, 1988). Addicts, like all other individuals in psychotherapy, never eliminate totally the potential of resuming old pathological defenses and behaviors. Their risk of resuming substance abuse can be seen as just an example of this general rule. This permanent risk may therefore be understood in traditional regressive terms. Since this is so, the introduction of a "disease" idea defined in this way need not interfere with full exploration of the dynamic issues involved with the addictive behavior.

Conclusion

In this chapter we have presented a description of individual psychodynamic psychotherapy with addicts, based on a contemporary psychoanalytic understanding of their vulnerabilities and disturbances. We have emphasized disturbances in ego function and narcissistic difficulties that affect addicts' capacities to regulate their feeling life, self-esteem, and relationships. A major psychotherapeutic task for addicted patients is to bring into their awareness their emotional difficulties and the way their problems predispose them to relapse into drug/alcohol use and dependence. We have reviewed implications for technique, with regard to characteristic central issues for addicts, and the need in certain cases for active intervention. We have explored strategies for establishing abstinence, including the value of working with self-help groups such as AA and NA. Finally, we have emphasized a flexible approach with regard to the timing, sequencing, and integration of psychotherapy in relation to other interventions and needs, based on patient characteristics and clinical considerations.

References

Bean-Bayog, M. (1985). Alcoholism treatment as an alternative to psychiatric hospitalization. *Psychiatric Clinics of North America, 8,* 501–512.

Brown, S. (1985). *Treating the alcoholic: A developmental model of recovery.* New York: Wiley.

Dodes, L. M. (1984). Abstinence from alcohol in long-term individual psychotherapy with alcoholics. *American Journal of Psychotherapy, 38,* 248–256.

Dodes, L. M. (1988). The psychology of combining dynamic psychotherapy and Alcoholics Anonymous. *Bulletin of the Menninger Clinic, 52,* 283–293.

Dodes, L. M. (1990). Addiction, helplessness, and narcissistic rage. *Psychoanalytic Quarterly, 59,* 398–419.

Dodes, L. M., & Khantzian, E. J. (in press). Psychotherapy of substance abusers. In R. Shader & D. Ciraullo (Eds.), *Clinical manual of chemical dependence.* Washington, DC: American Psychiatric Press

Frances, R. J., Khantzian, E. J., & Tamerin, J. S. (1988). Psychodynamic psychotherapy. In T. B. Karasu (Ed.), *Treatment of psychiatric disorders: A task force report of the American Psychiatric Association* (pp. 1103–1110). Washington, DC: American Psychiatric Press.

Khantzian, E. J. (1978). The ego, the self and opiate addiction: Theoretical and treatment considerations. *International Review of Psychoanalysis, 5,* 189–198.

Khantzian, E. J. (1980). The alcoholic patient: An overview and perspective. *American Journal of Psychotherapy, 34,* 4–19.

Khantzian, E. J. (1985a). The self-medication hypothesis of addictive disorders: Focus on heroin and cocaine dependence. *American Journal of Psychiatry, 142,* 1259–1264.

Khantzian, E. J. (1985b). Psychotherapeutic interventions with substance abusers—the clinical context. *Journal of Substance Abuse Treatment, 2,* 83–88.

Khantzian, E. J. (1986). A contemporary psychodynamic approach to drug abuse treatment. *American Journal of Drug and Alcohol Abuse, 12,* 213–222.

Khantzian, E. J. (1988). The primary care therapist and patient needs in substance abuse treatment. *American Journal of Drug and Alcohol Abuse, 14,* 159–167.

Khantzian, E. J., & Mack, J. (1983). Self-preservation and the care of the self. *Psychoanalytic Study of the Child, 38,* 209–232.

Khantzian, E. J., & Treece, C. (1985). DSM-III psychiatric diagnosis of narcotic addicts. *Archives of General Psychiatry, 42,* 1067–1071.

Kohut, H. (1971). *The analysis of the self.* Madison, CT: International Universities Press.

Krystal, H. (1982). Alexithymia and the effectiveness of psychoanalytic treatment. *International Journal of Psychoanalytic Psychotherapy, 9,* 353–378.

Krystal, H., & Raskin, H. (1970). *Drug dependence: Aspects of ego function.* Detroit: Wayne State University Press.

Mack, J. (1981). Alcoholism, A. A., and the governance of the self. In M. H. Bean & N. E. Zinberg (Eds.), *Dynamic approaches to the understanding and treatment of alcoholism* (pp. 128–162). New York: Free Press.

McDougall, J. (1984). The "dis-affected" patient: reflections on affect pathology. *Psychoanalytic Quarterly, 53,* 386–409.

Milkman, H., & Frosch, W. A. (1973). On the preferential abuse of heroin and amphetamines. *Journal of Nervous and Mental Disease, 156,* 242–248.

Rogalski, C. J. (1984). Professional psychotherapy and Its relationship to compliance in treatment. *International Journal of the Addictions, 19,* 521–539.

Rosen, A. (1981). Psychotherapy and Alcoholics Anonymous: Can they be coordinated? *Bulletin of the Menninger Clinic, 45,* 229–246.

Rounsaville, B. J., Gawin, F., & Kleber, H. (1985). Interpersonal psychotherapy adapted for ambulatory cocaine abusers. *American Journal of Drug and Alcohol Abuse, 11,* 171–191.

Rounsaville, B. J., Weissman, M., Kleber, H., & Wilber, C. (1982). Heterogeneity of psychiatric diagnosis in treated opiate addicts. *Archives of General Psychiatry, 39,* 161–166.

Shaffer, H. J. (1985). The disease controversy: Of metaphors, maps and menus. *Journal of Psychoactive Drugs, 17,* 65–76.

Silber, A. (1974). Rationale for the technique of psychotherapy with alcoholics. *International Journal of Psychoanalytic Psychotherapy, 3,* 28–47.

Treece, C., & Khantzian, E. J. (1986). Psychodynamic factors in the development of drug dependence. *Psychiatric Clinics of North America, 9,* 399–412.

Vaillant, G. E. (1981). Dangers of psychotherapy in the treatment of alcoholism. In M. H. Bean & N. E. Zinberg (Eds.), *Dynamic approaches to the understanding and treatment of alcoholism* (pp. 36–54). New York: Free Press.

Wieder, H., & Kaplan, E. (1969). Drug use in adolescents. *Psychoanalytic Study of the Child, 24,* 399–431.

Woody, G. E., Luborsky, L., McLellan, A. T., & O'Brien, C. P. (1989). Individual psychotherapy for substance abuse. In T. B. Karasu (Ed.), *Treatment of psychiatric disorders: A task force report of the American Psychiatric Association* (pp. 1417–1429). Washington, DC: American Psychiatric Press.

Woody, G. E., Luborsky, L., McLellan, A. T., O'Brien, C. P., Beck, A. T., Blaine, J., Herman, I., & Hole, A. (1983). Psychotherapy for opiate addicts: Does it help? *Archives of General Psychiatry, 40,* 639–645.

Woody, G. E., McLellan, A. T., Luborsky, L., & O'Brien, C. P. (1986). Psychotherapy for substance abuse. *Psychiatric Clinics of North America, 9,* 547–562.

Wurmser, L. (1974). Psychoanalytic considerations of the etiology of compulsive drug use. *Journal of the American Psychoanalytic Association, 22,* 820–843.

18

Family Therapy

ANTHONY W. HEATH

M. DUNCAN STANTON

In a report issued by the National Institute on Alcohol Abuse and Alcoholism in 1974, family therapy was recognized as "one of the outstanding current advances in the area of psychotherapy" for alcoholism (Keller, 1974, p. 116). In 1975, a report prepared for the National Institute on Drug Abuse stated that 69% of surveyed drug treatment programs were providing family therapy for drug addicts and their families, and 74% of the programs considered family treatment "highly important" for the addicts' recovery (Coleman & Davis, 1978). More recently, Liepman, White, and Nirenberg (1986) concluded their review of the clinical and research literature on treatment of children of alcoholics with the comment, "Without family therapy, most families would suffer serious 'side-effects' if the alcoholic were to stop drinking permanently" (p. 53).

By now, the importance of the family in the genesis, maintenance, and alleviation of substance abuse has become well known. Although it is widely acknowledged that genetic and/or other biological components are important in the etiology of many alcohol and drug abuse cases, addiction generally develops within a family context, frequently reflects other family difficulties, and is usually maintained and exacerbated by family interactive processes. Many other factors can also be critical (e.g., environmental, economic, cultural), but family variables have come to assume a position of salience in the arena of addictive symptomatology.

For these reasons, family therapy is recognized as an essential approach to treating the full range of addictive problems in families. Although research in the area of addiction treatment suffers from the usual difficulties of social science outcome research, several reviews have found "overwhelmingly favorable" (Steinglass, Bennett, Wolin, & Reiss, 1987, p. 331) evidence in support of the use of family therapy methods (e.g., Janzen, 1977; O'Farrell, 1989; Olson, Russell, & Sprenkle, 1980; Stanton, 1979, 1985; Steinglass, 1976).

Furthermore, studies comparing the effectiveness of family and nonfamily treatments for addiction lend support to the argument that family therapy is more effective than nonfamily methods. In Stanton's (1979) review of the literature on family treatment for drug abusers, four of six studies that compared family therapy with other treatments showed family therapy to be superior to the other approaches, while the remaining two studies obtained equivalent results. A more recent review of the research on marriage and family treatment for alcoholism (O'Farrell, 1989) concluded that family treatment produces better marital and drinking outcomes than nonfamily methods.

Contemporary family therapy is best understood in the context of the growing societal awareness of the interconnectedness and interdependence of living systems and levels of systems, from cells through individuals, families, and communities to the biosphere. As humanity enters the 1990s, it is increasingly obvious that no man, woman, or child is an "island" and that the rippling affects of every action yield innumerable consequences.

Foundations of Family Therapy

At this point, it seems advantageous to provide an overview of the development of family therapy and ultimately a definition of the term "family therapy" for those unfamiliar with its use. Although family therapy was foreshadowed in the work of psychoanalysts Sigmund Freud (the "Little Hans" case), Alfred Adler, and Harry Stack Sullivan, it is generally considered to have been founded in the 1950s by an eclectic group of researchers, theorists, and psychotherapists, unknown to one another at the time. These individuals, for a variety of reasons, began to interview family members conjointly (i.e., together), usually in order to gain further understanding of the psychiatric problems or symptoms manifested by one member. As anyone who has ever interviewed a family knows, it does not take long to see the myriad ways that family members become involved in a problem; it usually takes only a few moments longer to see the phenomenal resources for change offered by the very same family. Given these eye-opening experiences, the early family therapists began to shift the very focus of treatment from the intrapsychic experiences of the patient to the relational dynamics among the family members, with an eye to the betterment of all. It soon became clear to family therapists that human problems could be conceptualized as existing *between* (or among) people rather than *within* them, and the "patient" became the whole family.

Over the last 20 to 30 years the family therapy field has changed with astonishing fluidity, simultaneously growing, re-evaluating, regressing, and advancing in various quarters around the world. Today, family therapy is considered by many to be an independent profession, with a separate body of scholarly literature, over a dozen family therapy theories, separate licensing in 20 American states, and separate accreditation for master's-degree and doctoral programs in family therapy.

Regardless of one's position on the independence of family therapy, however, it should be emphasized that family therapy is widely considered more than a modality of treatment. Fundamentally, it is a way of construing human problems that dictates certain actions for their alleviation (Stanton, 1988b). Thus, depending on his or her theoretical orientation and other more practical constraints, a family therapist may range from conducting therapy with only the person with the most apparent problem or only the person most concerned with the problem, to conducting therapy with the whole family network, including friends, neighbors, other therapists, social agents, or even systems external to the family. Generally speaking, though, family therapists tend to convene whole families of two or more generations when the presenting problem concerns a child or adolescent, and to see couples or individuals, consulting with other family members, when there is an adult complaint.

Expanding on the thinking of a number of authors in the field, Stanton (1988b) has defined the field of family therapy as follows:

> Family therapy—perhaps more appropriately, systems therapy—is an approach in which a therapist (or a team of therapists), working with varying combinations and configurations of people, devises and introduces interventions designed to alter the interaction (process, workings) of the interpersonal system and context within which one or more psychiatric/behavioral/human problems are imbedded, and thereby also alters the functioning of the individuals within the system, with the goal of alleviating or eliminating the problems. (p. 9)

Many family therapists could prefer Stanton's term "systems therapy" because it corresponds more appropriately to their view of their work. It is the relational, interactional focus of the family therapist's thought and intervention that is characteristic, not the attention to the sociopolitical unit called a "family." Family therapists work with families because the family system is one of the primary systems in which human problems can be most easily understood, and because families often provide leverage for change.

Family Patterns in Addiction

Many studies have shown that addicted people are commonly in close contact with their families of origin or the people that raised them (see Stanton, Todd, & Associates, 1982, for a review). This pattern can even extend to adult alcoholics, as many male alcoholics are observed to be in regular contact with their mothers. These data would indicate that addicted people are often important in their families and that their families important to them. In addition, Stanton et al. (1982) have summarized a number of other characteristics that distinguish drug-abusing families from other seriously dysfunctional families. In brief, the distinguishing qualities include the following:

1. A higher frequency of multigenerational chemical dependency, particularly alcohol, plus a propensity for other addictive behaviors such as gambling (such practices model behavior for children and can develop into family traditions).
2. More primitive and direct expression of conflict in addictive families.
3. More overt alliances—for example, between addict and overinvolved parent.

4. "Conspicuously unschizophrenic" parental behavior.
5. A drug-oriented peer group to which the addict retreats following family conflict, thus gaining an illusion of independence.
6. "Symbiotic" child-rearing practices on the part of addicts' mothers, lasting longer into the addicts' adulthood.
7. A preponderance of death themes and premature, unexpected, and untimely deaths of the addict's family.
8. Pseudoindividuation of the addict across several levels, from the individual–pharmacological level to that of the drug subculture.
9. More frequent acculturation problems and parent–child cultural disparity within families of addicts.

This list should be considered as no more than a sketch of the addictive family. It is necessarily brief, and the reader is referred to Stanton et al. (1982) for references to the original studies on which the outline is based.

Indications for the Use of Family Therapy

The suffering of families in which alcohol and/or drugs are abused is legendary. Parents worry whether their abusing children will come home alive. They rage at their lack of control, they suffer the guilt of the damned, and they grasp at any suggestion that offers hope. Spouses shamefully scurry to hide advancing drinking problems from their neighbors and employers, struggle to maintain their illusions that the drinking is temporary, and wonder what they have done wrong. Children of alcoholics wonder what they have done wrong, assume the burdens of maturity at startlingly young ages, and beg their parents to come home without stopping at the tavern. And grown children of alcoholics find themselves haunted by their pasts—despairing in relationships that inflict only pain. Clearly, substance abuse affects every member of the family, certainly for decades and perhaps for generations.

Family therapy offers every member of these couples and families an opportunity to resolve the problems that plague them. Family therapists believe that family treatment is indicated when any man, woman, or child has a complaint concerning alcohol or drug abuse, whether the individual is the abuser or the "abused." Because they figuratively cast such a large net, family therapists encounter and serve many clients who present themselves for other reasons but also have concerns about substance abuse in their families. These concerns include issues of abuse, addiction, and recovery for adult and adolescent substance abusers, as well as parallel issues for "codependents," children of alcoholics, and adult children of alcoholics for several generations of the family.

Substance abusers themselves, of course, are not the family members most likely to seek the services of a therapist. In fact, the most characteristic feature of substance abuse may be the abuser's denial that the use of the substance is a problem at all. Similarly, it is almost universally accepted that substance abuse is often overlooked by family members; it may even be overtly or covertly encouraged. Recognizing this fact, family therapists offer their services to *anyone* who wants to discuss the substance abuse, and even go so far as to inquire about such an individual's use of alcohol and drugs. Like Al-Anon and related self-help programs, family therapists generally believe that every family member can be helped to survive the abuse, whether the substance abuser stops drinking and/or "drugging" or not.

Family therapy is indicated at the time the problem is initially identified by a family member or a therapist; when the family is mustering its forces to convince the abuser of the extent of the problem and the need for change; during residential treatment for the substance abuse (when it is used); and during recovery, when the family learns new ways to go on in life without chemicals. Guidelines for each of these stages of treatment are offered later in this chapter; however, it is appropriate here to suggest that the lack of some form of family-oriented services in substance abuse treatment may have calamitous consequences.

Without concurrent treatment for nonabusing members, families have been known to attempt to sabotage treatment efforts when those efforts begin to succeed (Stanton, 1979). Examples of this have been commonly reported in the literature; they range from the spouse who gives a bottle of liquor on a holiday to a recovering alcoholic, to the parents who refuse to work together in maintaining rules for their out-of-control adolescent. On the other hand, Steinglass et al. (1987) have asserted, at least regarding alcohol treatment, that the evidence is compelling that "involvement of a nonalcoholic spouse in a treatment program significantly improves the likelihood that the alcoholic individual will participate in treatment as well" (pp. 331–332).

Problems can also occur after residential treatment is completed if families are left out of the treatment process. Sobriety for an individual often has difficult consequences for other family members, who may gain sudden awareness of their own problems or of other problems in their families. Divorce is not uncommon when adult substance abusers "dry out" or "clean up" (Stanton, 1985). Clearly, the family is crucial in determining whether or not someone remains addicted, and the social context of the abuser must be changed if the substance abuser's treatment is to "take hold."

Families can prove to be a highly significant positive influence in recovery as well. In a fascinating observational account of substance abuse among his contemporaries, Auerswald (1980) observed that significant improvements in substance abusers' interpersonal lives often led to a reduction—without professional intervention—in their use of intoxicants. Eldred and Washington (1976) found that heroin addicts rated their families of origin or their in-laws as most likely to be helpful to them in their attempts to give up drugs; their second choice was their opposite-sex partner. Similarly, Levy (1972) found that in a 5-year follow-up of narcotics addicts, patients who successfully overcame drug abuse most often had family support. Family therapists enlist the inherent leverage offered by loving family members.

Like other treatment professionals who have worked with substance-abusing families, family therapists know the difficulty involved in treating substance abuse. Only by working together with extended families, specialists in the field of chemical dependency, physicians monitoring pharmacotherapy, and self-help programs can substance abuse be controlled.

When cooperating in their efforts to help a family, professionals must overcome apparently unfavorable odds and talk to one another if therapy is to succeed. For example, we have found it helpful for outpatient family therapists to visit local treatment centers and get to know the staff. This effort inevitably eases referrals to residential treatment and subsequent referral for continued therapy upon release. It has been our experience that staff members of Twelve-Step treatment programs often suspect, as do many Alcoholics Anonymous (AA) members, that all therapists harbor hostile and ignorant beliefs about addicts. Yet many family therapists would agree with this statement by Davis (1987):

> As a therapist, I operate according to the same presuppositions that operate in self-help groups: that every patient/client already has the resources or the capacity to develop the resources needed, that experts don't have all the answers, and that we are ultimately responsible for our own behaviors. (pp. 138–139)

This is not to say, however, that family therapists universally believe that attendance at AA, Al-Anon, or other self-help groups is necessary for healthy recovery in every case. In those instances when substance abusers and their families are adamantly opposed to involvement in Twelve-Step groups, family therapy may serve as a satisfactory alternative (Heath & Atkinson, 1988).

Clinical Intervention in Family Therapy

Entire books have been written specifically about family therapy with substance abusers, most notably six texts focusing on the problem of alcoholism (Bepko & Krestan, 1985; Elkin, 1984; Kaufman, 1984; Wegscheider, 1981; Davis, 1987; Steinglass et al., 1987), two on drug *and* alcohol abuse (Kaufman & Kaufmann, 1979; Treadway, 1989), one on drug abuse and addiction (Stanton et al., 1982), and one on addicts and other seriously disturbed young adults (Haley, 1980). Similarly, many different modalities of family treatment have been described, including marital therapy; group therapy for parents; concurrent parent and index patient therapy; therapy with individual families, both inpatient and outpatient; sibling-oriented therapy; multiple-family therapy; social network therapy; and family therapy with one person. The purpose of this section is to introduce fundamental methods of family therapy assessment and treatment with substance abusers and their families. Readers interested in studying this area further on their own are referred to the synopses by Heath and Atkinson (1988) and Stanton (1988a), plus the other literature cited below, for a broader understanding of the full range of theoretical and clinical approaches within the overall family therapy community.

Stages of Family Therapy

Our purpose here is to present a selective, integrative model of the stages of family therapy that synthesizes literature on family therapy with alcoholic adults (e.g., Berenson, 1976a, 1976b, 1979, 1986; Davis, 1987; Steinglass et al., 1987) and drug-abusing adolescents and young adults (e.g., Kosten, Jalali, & Kleber, 1982–1983; Piercy & Frankel, 1989; Stanton & Landau-Stanton, 1990; Stanton & Todd, 1979; Stanton et al., 1982), and to emphasize the relatively high degree of consensus among these authors. Although detailed presentation of the techniques of family therapy is beyond the scope of this chapter, the literature cited herein comprises a veritable treasure chest of clear and specific family therapy methods.

STAGE 1: PROBLEM DEFINITION AND CONTRACTING

The first stage of therapy begins when a family member contacts a therapist and requests help. Family therapists work in a wide variety of treatment settings, so they often can be easily located in mental health centers, family service agencies, progressive inpatient and outpatient drug and alcohol treatment centers, employee assistance programs, and private practices. Interestingly, family therapists also are beginning to work in therapeutic communities, where families once were excluded. By making family therapy available, such therapeutic communities are bringing the "real world" into the center and helping families to prepare for reunion.

The therapist's first step is to convene enough of the family to gain adequate leverage to initiate change in family interaction regarding the substance abuse. As previously discussed, this may involve 1, 2, or 30 family members, and may even include other members of the substance abuser's community. Family therapists generally start by working with the most motivated family member or members, convening other family members as necessary (Berenson, cited in Stanton, 1981a).

Next, family therapists attempt to identify and define the problem. When substance abuse is suspected, many begin by asking simple questions, such as "Who drinks?" or "What medications are used in your family?" We ironically refer to these as "loaded" questions, and ask them of all our clients as a matter of course.

To assess the degree of substance abuse, particularly with adult clients, Davis (1987) suggests the use of a standardized questionnaire, such as the Michigan Alcoholism Screening Test (Selzer, 1971) or the National Council on Alcoholism's Major and Minor Criteria for Alcoholism (Criteria Committee, 1972). The history of the abuse, degree of physiological addiction, organic consequences of long-term addiction, prior treatment contacts, family perception of the abuse and its consequences, codependence, and coping behaviors are also topics deserving careful assessment by qualified practitioners (Steinglass et al., 1987). If the therapist is not medically trained, clients are commonly referred to a physician for diagnosis and medical treatment when substance abuse has been chronic and/or when there is any indication of organic impairment due to addiction or disease. Family therapists often suggest that another family member accompany the substance abuser to the physician, partly to offer support and partly to inform the physician of the history of the abuse.

Information gathered during the assessment can then be used by the therapist, when appropriate, to state with confidence that—by some objective standards—the family has a serious drug or alcohol problem. Such confidence is often necessary to overcome denial that a substance abuse problem exists—a defense that can be anticipated in such families (Bepko & Krestan, 1985). It is important to note that many family therapists will avoid becoming personally involved in a debate over whether the substance abuse is really "addiction" or "alcoholism" (e.g., Davis, 1987). In discussing alcoholism, Davis has stated:

> This is not the time to fight over the presence of an "ism." It is enough to establish that there is a serious problem that needs treatment. The drinker and family members can make up their own minds after some success with AA and family therapy as to whether they have been dealing with alcoholism. (p. 53)

Once the problem is defined, the therapist and family identify and prioritize their goals for treatment, starting with the primary goal of helping the substance abuser become "clean and sober," and directly relating each subsequent goal to this primary one. When family members bring up additional issues, the therapist may ask the family to justify them as relevant to the main goal of sobriety (Stanton & Todd, 1979). Considered together, these goals form the basis for determining whether an acceptable treatment contract can be agreed upon with the family (Steinglass et al., 1987).

From the beginning, family therapists work to establish alliances with the senior sober family members. If the abuser is an adolescent or young adult, both parents are involved in these alliances whenever possible. Parents are kept working *together* and are steered away from discussing their marital difficulties, which could divide them and deter them from the primary objective of therapy (Stanton & Todd, 1979). These alliances form the basis for establishing appropriate parental influence in families with substance-abusing adolescents (Stanton et al., 1982; Piercy & Frankel, 1989).

Family therapists' desire for alliances with sober family members and parents of substance abusers gives direction to their approach to motivating clients in therapy. Family members are the most effective motivators known; the most evangelistic therapist cannot do as well. Thus, by forming alliances and encouraging sober family members to step up the pressure, family therapists indirectly work to motivate the substance abuser to pursue and maintain sobriety. Similarly, other professional helpers (e.g., school counselors, teachers, police officers, probation officers) may be enlisted to exert benevolent influence. Here the family therapist serves as coach, initially promoting the effective use of every reasonable threat, promise, and consequence to encourage abstinence, and later encouraging the family to serve as the recovering addict's sponsor to help prevent relapse. For an interesting example of the motivating influence of a family member, we recommend Heard's (1982) rich description of how he used a deathbed wish of a deceased grandfather to promote the recovery of a 23-year-old heroin addict.

Family therapists consider it extremely important during this initial stage to assume a *nonblaming stance* (Stanton & Todd, 1979) toward the entire family. We find that the confronting techniques used in group therapy with substance abusers tend to fan the fires of resistance and to inspire counterattack when dealing with families. Challenges can still be offered to these families, but they must be expressed in nonpejorative ways. Many family therapists use positive interpretation in commenting on family members' behavior. Stanton and Todd (1979) have referred to this as "ascribing noble intentions" or "noble ascriptions" (Stanton et al., 1982). Examples of positive interpretation include statements such as "He's defending the family like any good son would" and "You're trying your best to be a good mother." Such statements tune into both the caring and frustration that most family members experience; they seem to lessen client resistance and promote compliance, thereby allowing therapy to proceed smoothly.

Steinglass et al. (1987) have emphasized that it is essential at this point in therapy to label the substance abuse as a *family* problem and to convince the family members that they are all essential players in the recovery process. Writing about alcoholism, these authors have stated that whenever alcoholism is identified as a problem, the therapist must, in the same session,

> . . . get across to the family that there is no issue more important at this stage of the work than the cessation of drinking, and that the family and the therapist must mobilize all resources toward that goal and that goal alone. (p. 354)

Such an invitation to the family to become part of the solution to substance abuse problems is characteristic of family therapists.

In the characteristic human quest for the answer to the question "Why did this happen to me?", many families seen in treatment have already accepted that genetics and/or a disease process is responsible for their substance abuse, particularly when the problem is alcoholism. At its best, this idea can reduce guilt, blame, and shame in families, and thereby can facilitate entrance into therapy and promote recovery; it is almost always more useful than a moralistic explanation. At its worst, though, it can (1) provoke fear and enable discouraged, wallowing inaction and irresponsible behavior in the family; and (2) engender inaction in a therapist who sees no leeway for change beyond the immutability of genes.

Family therapists do not allow themselves or their clients to become discouraged by the disease explanation of the cause of drug and alcohol addiction; they cannot afford to wait for a pill to cure the disease. Instead, they help their client families to understand that by working together they can overcome all of the disease's symptoms, reverse the ostensible destiny, and lead happy, chemical-free lives.

Of course, there are—and probably will always be—clients who reject the genetic and disease explanations for addiction. Regarding the former, they may be justified, since there is no genetic evidence in a goodly proportion of alcoholics. In any case, these people too can learn to live responsibly and avoid blame and shame. They too can work together with their loved ones to overcome their problems.

STAGE 2: ESTABLISHING THE CONTEXT
FOR A CHEMICAL-FREE LIFE

When substance abuse is identified as a problem, and a therapeutic contract is negotiated, family therapy enters a second stage in which a context for sobriety is established. Berenson has stated that this stage involves "management of an ongoing, serious drinking problem and setting up a context so that the alcoholic will stop drinking" (1976b, p. 33).

Cessation of substance abuse is *generally* accepted by family therapists as a prerequisite for further treatment (e.g., Bepko & Krestan, 1985). Furthermore, many believe that therapists must consistently demonstrate conviction of the importance of abstinence over the course of therapy (e.g., Davis, 1987). In the words of Steinglass et al. (1987).

> Meaningful therapy with an Alcoholic Family cannot proceed if the therapist adopts a laissez-faire attitude about drinking behavior and acquiesces in a decision to allow the identified alcoholic to continue drinking. The therapist must take a firm stand on this issue at the start of therapy, while at the same time acknowledging that it may not be an easy task and that there may be a number of slips before abstinence is achieved. (p. 343)

On the other hand, Berenson, whose innovative work with alcoholics has been described by Stanton (1981a), believes that therapists should concern themselves with achieving substantial changes in drunken behavior instead of abstinence from drinking. Berenson considers it tactically unwise to take a resolute stand in favor of total abstinence, even though abstinence is usually the ultimate goal. This position on abstinence runs counter to the beliefs of several others, including Davis (1987) and Bepko and Krestan (1985). It is consistent, however, with the problem-solving models that have been applied to drug problems by Haley (1976), Stanton and Todd (e.g., 1979), and others (e.g., Heath & Ayers, 1991), who often prefer to leave the decision about the importance of total abstinence to parents or others. These authors believe that therapists who assume a less adamant, less certain position on the necessity of abstinence enjoy more maneuverability (cf. Fisch, Weakland, & Segal, 1982) in therapy. For example, a therapist who states that he or she is not sure whether abstinence will prove necessary may be able to stay out of a couple's argument over the issue long enough to help them try out several new solutions to the problems brought on by the substance abuse.

Independent of the issue of abstinence, Berenson believes that early in therapy the therapist must invest a major effort into getting the family system calmed down, reducing the emotionality, and increasing the distance between family members. Families at this stage of therapy are often overwrought and involved in intense battles and patterns of over- and underresponsibility that lock members together. For a thorough discussion of the therapeutic process of assessing and interrupting overresponsible and underresponsible behaviors, we recommend Bepko and Krestan's (1985) insightful work.

Often family therapists refer family members to Al-Anon, Nar-Anon, Alateen, Alatot, and related self-help programs at this stage, encouraging clients to shop around until they find groups that are "socially compatible and geographically accessible" (Davis, 1987, p. 56). In Bepko and Krestan's (1985) words, the goal of this involvement is to help the family members "shift their role behavior significantly both in the interest of their greatest well-being and with the expectation that a change in their part of the family interaction will eventually lead to the drinker's sobriety" (p. 104). Davis (1987) has suggested that therapists must consistently assign visits to self-help groups, because participation in such groups enhances family therapy in several ways. In addition to encouraging detachment from substance-abusing behavior, Davis (1987) has noted that self-help groups offer validating experiences, provide 24-hour crisis support through sponsors, and emphasize personal responsibility. For a thorough examination of the compatibility of AA and family therapy, we recommend Davis's (1987) detailed exploration of the topic.

Many family therapists supplement the work of self-help groups by working specifically on helping the spouses of substance abusers to achieve a greater degree of emotional detachment. Recognizing that therapists cannot do all the work themselves, Berenson begins by getting the spouse of an alcoholic into a support group, usually Al-Anon or a spouses-of-alcoholics group (Stanton, 1981a). Next, he prepares the spouse for the impending period of pain and depression, perhaps even noting that he or she may have suicidal thoughts as a part of "hitting bottom." Finally, Berenson starts working to help the spouse gain distance from the alcoholic, often by suggesting a brief separation (e.g, a week away from home) in order to promote differentiation. Here Berenson warns the spouse that the alcoholic may try to get him or her back by intensifying the symptom of conflict, usually by increased drinking.

At this point Berenson may involve the alcoholic more in therapy, empathizing with how isolated and alone he or she may feel. Concomitantly, he helps the spouse stick to the plan so that the drunk has a chance to get sober. He tells the spouse that he or she should not expect the alcoholic to improve, but suggests that when he or she realizes that the alcoholic cannot be controlled, the alcoholic may be able to make a change for the better. During this period of disengagement, Berenson does not support any hostile moves against the alcoholic, but only supports moves the spouse makes for himelf or herself.

Berenson has suggested several helpful rules for therapists working through this stage of family therapy (Stanton, 1981a). First, the therapist must have no expectations that the change will occur; rather than "hoping," he or she must be "hopeless." Second, the therapist should want the family members to feel both helpless and hopeless—that is, to "hit bottom," if they have not done so already. Third, the therapist must not look for a single strategic intervention to reverse the multitude of problems in these families, but should work patiently and in a simple, straightforward manner.

Finally, many family therapists move toward getting the substance abuser to attend AA, Narcotics Anonymous, or Cocaine Anonymous as the final step in the second stage of therapy. Bepko and Krestan (1985) have suggested that it is not advisable for therapists to argue with clients about the value of AA, but they should describe AA and its purpose "in a way that is palatable to the particular client" (p. 103). However it is described, most family therapists state clearly that AA is one of the most effective treatments for addiction. Next, we help a substance abuser to find a group with which he or she feels comfortable, then encourage the abuser to attend that group for a period of time before making a decision to continue. We have also recommended the secular sobriety groups described by Christopher (1988) to those individuals who feel uncomfortable with AA's use of the "Higher Power."

STAGE 3: HALTING SUBSTANCE ABUSE

At some point in the family therapy of substance abuse, there always comes a moment of truth. As a result of the changes in their family members' behavior and the probably firm position of the therapist, substance abusers suddenly become aware that they are going to have to choose between their families and their drugs. Substance abusers, when consistently confronted (or abandoned) by parents, spouses, children, friends, employers, and perhaps even by recovering people in self-help groups and/or a therapist, often "hit bottom" and turn to the therapist for help in changing their ways.

At this juncture, Steinglass et al., (1987) suggest that there are basically three possible ways for therapists to proceed. First, a therapist can arrange inpatient detoxification for the addicted substance abuser if this is indicated. A therapist who knows there to be physical dependence on alcohol or drugs should refuse to continue therapy unless this option is selected when needed, since without medical intervention the addict's independent withdrawal is unlikely, if not dangerous. Second, the therapist can agree to let the family attempt detoxification on an outpatient basis, on the condition that if there has been no meaningful progress made toward detoxification in 2 weeks (maximum), then inpatient treatment will be pursued. Third, the therapist can allow outpatient recovery alone, using the family as the "treatment team" if there is evidence that physical addiction is minimal or absent (Scott & Van Deusen, 1982; Stanton & Todd, 1982). Whichever course of action is selected, it is essential for the family therapist to keep all family members involved in the change process, partly so that later they can accept some responsibility for the success of the treatment (Stanton & Todd, 1979). When treatment gets left to the "professionals," family members often seem to fail to realize their responsibility for change. And later, should the recovery process go awry, they may blame the setback on the hospital or treatment program.

STAGE 4: MANAGING THE CRISIS AND STABILIZING THE FAMILY

When the substance abuser becomes "clean and sober," the family therapist should be prepared for a new set of problems. Family members, stunned by the unfamiliar behavior of the "new" family member and often terribly frightened, have been known to make seemingly irrational statements such as "I liked you better when you were drinking." One client we know actually gave a bottle of bourbon to her recently sober husband for his birthday. The potential for relapse is understandably high in this stage.

In discussing alcoholic families, Steinglass et al. (1987) have named an analogous stage "the emotional desert." In their description, families that have been organized around alcohol, especially over many years, experience a profound sense of emptiness when the drinking stops. In the words of Stein-glass et al. (1987), these families "have the sensation of having been cut adrift, loosened from their familiar moorings, lost in a desert without any landmarks upon which to focus to regain their bearings" (p. 344). Instead of experiencing joy over the newfound sobriety, the family members feel empty and depressed. It is not surprising that members of a newly sober family tend to interact in more or less the same way that they did while one member was abusing drugs and/or alcohol.

Couples often experience a feeling of "walking on eggshells" at home and drift into a kind of emotional divorce. Both partners want to preserve the sobriety and the peace, so they interact sparingly and hesitantly, unwittingly re-establishing the same patterns of closeness and distance that they enacted previously. For example, a recently sober alcoholic who wants to talk with his wife about his feelings, may approach her late at night, perhaps even waking her from a sound sleep, just as he did when he was drunk. She, in turn, may rebuff his awkward attempt at communication, leaving him to go off alone to sulk where once he went off to drink. It is not surprising that as recovering couples get to know each other anew, they often find themselves bored, irrationally angry, and unable to resolve or escape from problems that were once avoided with the help of intoxicants.

Where addicted young people are concerned, a family crisis can be anticipated 3 or 4 weeks into this part of treatment (Stanton & Todd, 1979). Most commonly, the crisis occurs in the marital relationship of the parents, with steps being taken toward separation or divorce. Such a crisis puts tremendous pressure on the addict to become "dirty" again in order to reunite his or her family.

Pressure to revert to old ways also can be inadvertently exerted by siblings and children of recovering substance abusers. Gradually these families begin to notice other family problems, long hidden from attention by the magnitude of drug or alcohol problems. As the haze of intoxication clears, children who were once considered helpful may suddenly be seen as withdrawn and depressed; children who were once seen as doing fine in school may be seen to be just getting by; and marijuana-smoking adolescents may be discovered for the first time.

There is some disagreement among family therapists over how quickly to move to resolve family problems in this stage. Berenson has suggested that it is usually advisable to begin this stage with a hiatus from therapy while things calm down, and thus he does not schedule regular appointments, but tells clients, "Get back to me in a month or so" (Stanton, 1981a). Meanwhile, he encourages his clients to continue their AA and/or Al-Anon activities, with the understanding that if this state of distress continues beyond 6 to 12 months, family therapy will resume on a more regular basis. Then, after a period of sobriety, Berenson returns to a more orthodox therapy schedule. Others (e.g., Bepko & Krestan, 1985; Steinglass et al., 1987) believe that regularly scheduled family therapy sessions can be very helpful at these times, especially if they focus on solving the series of problems that hound these families and wear them down.

Therapy in this stage is focused on keeping a family as calm as possible (Bepko & Krestan, 1985), while helping the family establish a new form of stability that is not based on substance abuse (Steinglass et al., 1987). Toward this end, the therapist works to minimize stress and de-escalate conflict; congratulates individuals for their contributions to the family's recovery and encourages them to focus on their own issues; predicts and addresses common difficulties in recovery and fears about relapse; and facilitates minor structural changes in the family to allow adequate parenting (Bepko & Krestan, 1985). Changes in parenting practices are especially vital when the recovering substance abuser is an adolescent (Fishman, Stanton, & Rosman, 1982; Piercy & Frankel, 1989; Stanton & Landau-Stanton, 1990).

Should a relapse into drinking or drug taking occur, the question of responsibility arises. Who is responsible for the relapse? Although conventional drug treatment programs and many individual therapists either thrust the responsibility on the substance abuser or accept it themselves, family therapists tend to assign the responsibility to the abuser's family. As Stanton and Todd (1979) have suggested,

> It should be remembered that the addicted individual was raised by, and in most cases is still being maintained by, his family of origin. It is thus with the family that responsibility rests, and the therapist should help the family either to accept it or to *effectively* disengage from the addict so that he must accept it on his own. (p. 62)

Similarly, the therapist assigns credit to the entire family when credit is due (Stanton, 1981b). Each member, particularly the often neglected spouse, is praised for his or her contribution to the growing "health" of the family. By identifying and rewarding individual contributions, the family therapist spreads out the glory that is usually bestowed on the recovering abuser, and promotes long-lasting changes in family interaction.

STAGE 5: FAMILY REORGANIZATION AND RECOVERY

Whereas in Stage 4 families remain organized around substance abuse and family therapy is focused on resolving difficulties with substance abuse (or the lack thereof), Stage 5 is concerned with helping families to move away from interaction focused on substance abuse issues and toward fundamentally better relationships. Here the substance abuser is stabilized and "clean and sober"; the therapy now focuses on developing a better marriage, establishing more satisfactory parent–child relationships, and perhaps confronting long-standing family-of-origin and codependence issues.

Steinglass et al. (1987) have called this process "family reorganization" (p. 344). Although some families restabilize before reaching this phase and remain organized around alcoholism issues ("dry alcoholic" families), we have observed that for others the previous stages of therapy culminate in a serious family crisis. This crisis then leads to disorganization and ultimately to a fundamentally different organizational pattern, which is coaxed along in this stage of therapy.

With characteristic clarity, Bepko and Krestan (1985) have enumerated four goals for their analogue for this stage, which they have termed "rebalancing" (p. 135). These goals follow:

1. Shift extremes of reciprocal role behavior from rigid complementarity to greater symmetry or more overt complementarity ("correct" complementarity for the specific relationship).
2. Help the couple/family to resolve issues of power and control.
3. Directly address the pride structures of both partners so that new forms of role behavior are permitted without the need for alcohol.
4. Help the couple to achieve whatever level of closeness and intimacy is desirable for them. (pp. 135–136)

For a detailed discussion of the therapeutic methods that Bepko and Krestan (1985) use to implement these goals, the reader is referred to their text.

Davis (1987) has also emphasized that the therapist must help family members to reconsider and redefine the substance abuser's role in the family at this stage of therapy. Old expectations and old behavioral patterns, which were based on living with the addiction, must be replaced by new adaptive ones. For example, a family that has grown used to an alcoholic husband/father may continue to withdraw every time he shows a hint of anger, leave him out of family decisions, and disregard his parenting efforts. family therapy, the father must learn to deal with his anger, making responsible decisions, and to function as a father members must allow him to change.

In the treatment of a family with a young addict during this stage, therapy evolves beyond the crisis management of Stage 4 and toward other issues, such as finding gainful employment and a place to live away from home for the recovering addict (Stanton & Todd, 1979). Parents are often involved in these "launchings" so they can feel part of the addict's eventual success. Over time, it becomes increasingly possible to shift the parents' attention to other siblings, grandchildren, or retirement planning, thereby allowing both the parents and the recovering addict to let go. Should marital issues surface, as they often do, family therapists work to prevent addicts from getting involved in their parents' marriages.

Berenson focuses his work in this stage on the couple's relationship, with the aim of decreasing the emotional distance between the couple without a return either to drinking or to discussions centered on alcohol (Stanton, 1981a). In conjoint sessions with couples and/or multiple-couples groups, Berenson and other family therapists often focus on the severe sexual problems that are common in such marriages (Stanton, 1981a) and teach new skills for dealing with stress and conflict (Bepko & Krestan, 1985). Therapy sessions with the extended family are scheduled if the nuclear family is beset by disruptions from relatives or in-laws (Stanton & Landau-Stanton, 1990).

Finally, it is also during this stage that a number of family therapists (e.g., Coleman, Kaplan, & Downing, 1986; Reilly, 1976; Rosenbaum & Richman, 1972; Stanton, 1977) deal with the often unexpected and unresolved losses and deaths that so many chemically dependent families have experienced. These authors have taken the position that whereas such issues may not need to be covered in order to effect abstinence initially, unresolved grief can "eat away" at progress unless it is brought to terms. The idea is that some sort of family grief work is indicated in order to maintain long-lasting change.

STAGE 6: ENDING THERAPY

In the ideal course of therapy with a substance-abusing family, treatment comes to an end when the clients and therapist(s) agree to stop meeting regularly. Family therapists tend to agree to stop when they believe that serious structural and functional problems that have maintained substance abuse have been replaced with new family rules, roles, and interactional patterns. Optimally, substance abuse has not been replaced with other addictive behaviors; however, sometimes socially acceptable "addictions" (e.g., "workaholism") are tolerated by family therapists when they are tolerated by family members.

Because such abstract concepts as "rules," "roles," "interactional patterns," and even "addictive behaviors" are usually used only by *therapists* to describe families, this description of the ideal changes seen in therapy reflects only the therapist's perspective. The *clients'* view of successful therapy is much more difficult to articulate, partly because their descriptions of success are situation-specific and diverse and partly because of a dearth of qualitative research on the topic. For our purposes here, suffice it to say that from the clients' point of view therapy ends satisfactorily when they believe that family relationships are acceptably harmonious and that major family problems—including substance abuse—have been resolved to the point of becoming tolerable.

The length of therapy and the specific definition of successful treatment vary widely among models of therapy and among individual families. Stanton and Todd (1979), in describing their brief therapy model for treating drug addicts, have broadly stated that therapy is appropriately concluded when "adequate change has occurred and been maintained long enough for the family to feel a sense of real accomplishment" (p. 64). Adherents of other models would not even attempt to reorganize family structure in the ways prescribed in our fifth stage. Instead, they may be content to conclude treatment when family members feel satisfied that the problems originally presented have been resolved (e.g., Heath & Ayers, 1991).

The ending of therapy, often called "termination," need not be thought of as an event or as a process with a distinct endpoint. Elsewhere, one of us has suggested that such a view of termination exposes an assumption that therapy is a lot like surgery, which ideally results in a "cure" of some sort (Heath, 1985). This unintentional metaphor seems terribly inaccurate to the experienced therapist, partly because many client families who have completed therapy to everyone's satisfaction later seek counsel from the same therapist on new, unrelated issues.

For therapists who see therapy as a problem-solving endeavor, it is helpful to use outpatient medical practice as a metaphor to guide outpatient family therapy. In other words, family therapists can be likened to physicians to whom clients ("patients") turn for assistance with a variety of concerns over the decades. Of course, in the treatment of substance abuse, therapy continues on a regularly scheduled basis until the abuse has ceased. But as significant progress occurs, therapists gradually increase the intervals between sessions. Then, when all parties agree to cease regularly scheduled sessions, occasional inoculatory follow-up sessions ("checkups") are scheduled, one at a time, at intervals of 2 to 6 months. It is also made clear to clients that they are welcome to schedule future appointments at any time, and to cancel sessions that seem unnecessary. Therapy clients, like medical patients, are never made permanently "healthy," and the door to the therapist's office remains open, like the physician's.

Finally, it should be noted that family therapy sometimes ends unexpectedly and prematurely, at least as seen from the therapist's perspective. No matter how skilled the therapist, and no matter what the stage of treatment, families generally stop coming to therapy when they want to. In such a circumstance, the responsible therapist makes every reasonable effort to determine whether the family is satisfied or dissatisfied with services rendered, and responds accordingly. Here additional services or referrals for any family member are offered, as are professional opinions about remaining problems, and caveats when appropriate.

In conclusion, the six-stage model presented here is intentionally inclusive. We have made no effort to resolve differences among the many models of family therapy, or to examine the differences between treating drug addicts and alcoholics. Instead, we have broadly sketched a viable course of treatment for the family with a substance-abusing member. Clinicians may wish to emphasize some stages of therapy more than others, depending on their preferred models of treatment.

Special Considerations in Family Therapy

A number of special clinical considerations concern family therapists when they work with substance abusers and their families. Although space does not allow full discussion of all of these issues, several of the more salient considerations are discussed below. The interested reader will find insightful discussions of many of the day-to-day issues that face family therapists in the previously referenced texts, particularly Stanton et al. (1982).

CONVENING DIFFICULTIES

One of the problems that has been identified by therapists working with substance abusers and their families is the difficulty in convening the whole family for therapy (Stanton & Todd, 1981). The families of addicts are particularly difficult to engage in treatment. Fathers, in particular, often appear threatened by treatment and defensive about their contributions to the problem. Since many have drinking problems themselves, they may also fear being blamed for the problem.

Experienced family therapists, recognizing hesitance to participate in therapy, reach out in a concerted effort to recruit families into therapy. They do not rely on other family members to do the recruiting, since this approach often fails. Instead, they work energetically and enthusiastically to extend personal invitations to the reluctant. In less seriously disturbed families, one telephone call may enable a therapist to reassure family members that their contributions are important to the solution of the substance abuse. In more disturbed families, it may be necessary to meet family members on "neutral turf" like a restaurant, to write mutliple letters, or to pay family members for participation in treatment. Stanton and others (Stanton & Todd, 1981; Stanton et al., 1982) have described such engagement procedures in substantial detail, suggesting 21 principles for getting resistant families into therapy.

In order to shift the responsibility for dealing with the substance abuser's problems to the family, a family therapist must have control of the case. The family therapist therefore may wish to direct the overall case management, including the treatment plan, the use of medication and drug tests, and decisions about hospitalization. The family therapist's being the primary therapist also helps to keep substance abusers from manipulating the relationships among a number of therapists.

Stanton et al. (1982) have estimated that approximately 50% of the effectiveness of treatment of drug addicts and their families depends on the efficiency and cohesiveness of the therapeutic system. If family members receive different advice from different professionals, they often end up arguing about the therapy rather than working toward recovery. Cohesion in the treatment system of substance abusers necessarily includes any self-help programs used by their families. Again, it is vital for therapists to know the local self-help groups and to work with them, even if informally, for the sake of their clients.

MEDICATION AND MANAGEMENT

Family therapists who work with substance abusers and their families must have at least a basic knowledge of drug pharmacology. This information aids them during the detoxification process and reduces the tendency toward overcaution that sometimes occurs when a therapist is ignorant of drug effects.

In regard to the use of pharmacotherapy, it is vital that physicians, family therapists, and drug counselors work together as part of a treatment team. Cooperation and open lines of communication are necessary to counteract the manipulative behaviors of many substance abusers. As a part of the team, the family therapist and physician can serve as allies in encouraging family compliance with prescribed medication, and can provide each other with information on patient and family functioning (Woody, Carr, Stanton, & Hargrove, 1982).

Where methadone is concerned, family therapists must have influence over its use. Families tend to believe that their recovering addicts are inherently helpless, fragile, handicapped people, and thus they forgive the most outrageous behavior. For family therapists to argue effectively that addicts can be competent and can function adequately without drugs, they must assert that they are primarily concerned with the addicts' detoxifying and getting off all drugs, including the opioid methadone. To encourage the cessation of methadone use, family therapists and the families themselves must have significant input into how it is dispensed (Woody et al., 1982; Stanton & Todd, 1982).

INVOLVING PARENTS IN DECISIONS

When a substance abuser is an adolescent or a young adult, family therapists consider it vital to involve the parents in all decisions about the treatment of the youth. Thus parents should be involved in decisions about hospitalization, medication, and drug tests. A family therapist will go to some trouble to make the parents part of the treatment team, because it helps to get the couple working together and because the responsibility for the resolution of the problem is rightly theirs. When the parents of the young person are divorced or unmarried, the same holds true; adult caretakers must be encouraged to work together to help their child.

CODEPENDENCE

"Codependence" is a word that is often used to describe the process underlying many problems in the families of substance abusers. At this time there is little consensus over how the term should be precisely defined, but according to Schaef (1986), one of the chemical dependency field's most respected authors, codependence is a disease that parallels the alcoholic disease process and has specific and characteristic symptoms (e.g., external referencing, caretaking, self-centeredness, control issues, dishonesty, frozen feelings, perfectionism, and fear). Codependence has generally replaced the concept of "enabling" and focused attention on the suffering of those who live with, or have lived with, a chemically dependent person.

Family therapists have learned a great deal about addiction and addiction treatment from Schaef and the others (e.g., Beattie, 1987; Wegscheider, 1981) who have bridged the family therapy and chemical dependency professions. They have learned, for example, to address the individual fears and difficulties of the parents, spouses, children, and grown children of alcoholics. They have learned of the many advantages of self-help groups and popular books on codependence for codependents. They have also learned to recognize addictive processes at work in families when individuals express any of the hallmark symptoms of codependence. They already know that the pain of addiction affects everyone in and around these families, often for generations.

TREATMENT DELIVERY SYSTEMS

Conceptualizing substance abuse problems within an interpersonal systems or family framework is not always consonant with the traditional ways in which treatment has been administered. For example, a major residential treatment center for adolescent substance abusers in the midwestern United States offers two sessions of family therapy during a typical 42-day program—an intake staffing and discharge staffing, both of which are informational in nature. The optional multiple-family group, which is attended by a minority of the parents of the center's patients, is used as a forum for psychoeducational programming on addiction and codependence. When the center's administrator was asked why the center did not offer more family therapy, he said that many insurance companies did not consider it a part of necessary medical care and would therefore not pay for family therapy services.

Similarly, many insurance companies will not pay for outpatient family therapy when substance abuse is diagnosed, preferring more expensive inpatient medical treatment services and outpatient services provided by a state-licensed psychiatrist or psychologist. These preferences seem destined to undergo radical change in the United States, given the increasing national awareness of the extraordinary cost of health care, as well as the growing body of knowledge suggesting that there is no overall advantage for long-term, intensive, residential services for alcohol abuse (Miller & Hester, 1986). For whatever reason, the change has begun. Several major insurance companies now limit hospital stays for substance abusers to 22 days, and family therapists are now listed as preferred providers by increasing numbers of health care management companies.

Another disincentive for family therapy in treatment delivery systems concerns the way in which credit is assigned to therapists for their work. Over a decade ago, Coleman and Davis (1978) found that drug counselors and therapists often were not given credit for client contact hours when sessions were held with family members, such as parents or spouses, unless the identified patients were present. They were also not given credit for the additional time required for contacting family members and coordinating sessions with them. Stanton (1979) noted another problem of a different nature: Out of desperation, therapists sometimes have resorted to opening a case for each family member, and to issuing multiple bills for conjoint sessions. This practice is fraudulent and is likely to elicit a harsh response from third-party payers.

To add to the complexity, Schwartzman and Bokos (1979) have observed that ideological dissonance among treatment programs within a community can lead to competition among these programs, resulting in no change or even deterioration in their clients. Schwartzman and Bokos note that such cross-currents recapitulate the kind of tensions that an addict experiences in his or her family.

Although such problems still exist, light is on the horizon. According to the 1989 accreditation standards of the Joint Commission on Accreditation for Healthcare Organizations, residential treatment programs for alcoholism and other drug dependencies must involve family members in the treatment process. This development is being echoed in the growing health care management industry, which is increasingly registering family therapists on its lists of reimbursable providers. In the difficult realm of substance abuse treatment, it seems logical to expect that eventually the entire treatment system will work to facilitate family treatment in every way possible, especially if family therapy proves cost-effective by shortening inpatient stays and reducing repeat admissions.

CONFIDENTIALITY

If substance abuse, especially of the heavy or compulsive variety, is seen as a family phenomenon, many of the existent regulations concerning confidentiality do not make much sense. Although there may be exceptions, such as in emergencies, some of the standing regulations on confidentiality may serve to perpetuate the problem. Shielding a person's drug or alcohol problem from his or her family may even be an exercise in self-delusion—the family members often already know about it—but at the very least, it results in "buying into" the family's denial. Thus confidentiality provisions in law and ethical standards can give license to denial by sanctioning the identified patient as the problem and denying the importance of the family. for these reasons, we believe there is a need to change legal and ethical standards in order to distinguish between confidentiality within the family and confidentiality between the family and others, at least when there is evidence of substance abuse.

THERAPIST SUPPORT

Conducting family therapy with substance-abusing families can be grueling work. Therapists find it to be demanding and draining, and occasionally find that the programs in which they work take on the characteristics of addictive family systems (e.g., "cross-generational" alliances, denial of problems, secrets, "wet" and "dry" behaviors). It is therefore vitally important, for the sake of therapists and clients alike, to establish and maintain healthy administrative policies and procedures that support front-line therapists.

Included in the policies should be protection from unmanageable caseloads. In addition, treatment centers should make ample provision for supervision and consultation on all cases. When appropriate, consultants knowledgeable about family therapy and addiction should be retained. Similarly, continuing education should be made available in order to allow therapists to continue their learning while getting "out of the shop" for a while. Time away from providing services is essential in maintaining one's balance.

Conclusion

A well-dressed, overweight 23-year-old woman walked into a therapist's office and complained of her inability to control her eating. She couldn't understand this problem, she said, because she otherwise had perfect control over her life. In the course of taking a family history, the therapist learned that the client's father was an alcoholic, as was her brother. Her mother was obese.

Two months later, the therapist learned that the young woman and her husband had sexual problems. Three months later, she calmly confessed to having been repeatedly raped as a child by her drunken father. Five months later, the woman casually admitted to having some concern that her husband's drinking and marijuana use were excessive. She hadn't told her husband of her concern. She was afraid he'd get angry with her.

So many people lead lives like this client's. They struggle along, fighting to overcome the horrible emotional scars left by the addictions of their parents.

Many of them succeed, of course, but many also get dragged back into the addictive cycle themselves, unwillingly dragging their children along with them. We wonder how different these lives could have been if the families had been treated by family therapists. And having witnessed the often extraordinary impact of family therapy with addictive families, we wonder why it is not always available in treatment settings, and not always reimbursed by third-party payers, as we enter the 1990s.

Can we really allow this to continue?

References

Auerswald, E. (1980). Drug use and families—in the context of twentieth century science. In B. Ellis (Ed.), *Drug abuse from the family perspective: Coping is a family affair* (DHHS Publication No. ADM 80-910, pp. 117–126). Washington, DC: U.S. Government Printing Office.

Beattie, M. (1987). *Codependent no more.* Center City, MN: Hazelden Educational Materials.

Bepko, C., & Krestan, J. (1985). *The responsibility trap.* New York: Free Press.

Berenson, D. (1976a). A family approach to alcoholism. *Psychiatric Opinion, 13,* 33–38.

Berenson, D. (1976b). Alcohol and the family system. In P. Guerin (Ed.), *Family therapy: Theory and practice* (pp. 284–297). New York: Gardner Press.

Berenson, D. (1979). The therapist's relationship with couples with an alcoholic member. In E. Kaufman & P. Kaufmann (Eds.), *The family therapy of drug and alcohol abuse* (pp. 233–242). New York: Gardner Press.

Berenson, D. (1986). The family treatment of alcoholism. *Family Therapy Today, 1,* 1–2; 6–7.

Christopher, J. (1988). *How to stay sober: Recovery without religion.* Buffalo, NY: Prometheus Books.

Coleman, S., & Davis D. (1978). Family therapy and drug abuse: A national survey. *Family Process, 17,* 21–29.

Coleman, S., Kaplan, J., & Downing, R. (1986). Life cycle and loss: The spiritual vacuum of heroin addiction. *Family Process, 25*(1), 5–23.

Criteria Committee, National Council on Alcoholism. (1972). Criteria for diagnosis of alcoholism. *American Journal of Psychiatry, 128,* 129–135.

Davis, D. (1987). *Alcoholism treatment: An integrative family and individual approach.* New York: Gardner Press.

Eldred, C., & Washington, M. (1976). Interpersonal relationships in heroin use by men and women and their role in treatment outcome. *International Journal of the Addictions, 11,* 117–130.

Elkin, M. (1984). *Families under the influence: Changing alcoholic patterns.* New York: Norton.

Fishman, H. C., Stanton, M. D., & Rosman, B. (1982). Treating families of adolescent drug abusers. In M. D. Stanton, T. C. Todd, & Associates, *The family therapy of drug abuse and addiction* (pp. 335–357). New York: Guilford Press.

Fisch, R., Weakland, J., & Segal, L. (1982). *The tactics of change: Doing therapy briefly.* San Francisco: Jossey-Bass.

Haley, J. (1980). *Leaving home: The therapy of disturbed young people.* New York: McGraw-Hill.

Heard, D. (1982). Death as a motivator: Using crisis induction to break through the denial system. In M. D. Stanton, T. C. Todd, & Associates, *The family therapy of drug abuse and addiction* (pp. 203–234). New York: Guilford Press.

Heath, A. (1985). Some new directions in ending family therapy. In D. Breunlin (Ed.), *Stages: Patterns of change over time* (pp. 33–40). Rockville, MD: Aspen Systems.

Heath, A., & Atkinson, B. (1988). Systematic treatment of substance abuse: A graduate course. *Journal of Marital and Family Therapy, 14*, 411–418.

Heath, A., & Ayers, T. (1991). MRI brief therapy with adolescent substance abusers. In T. Todd & M. Seleckman (Eds.), *Family therapy approaches with adolescent substance abusers* (pp. 49–69). Boston: Allyn & Bacon.

Janzen, C. (1977). Families in the treatment of alcoholism. *Journal of Studies on Alcohol, 38*, 114–130.

Joint Commission on Accreditation for Healthcare Organizations. (1989). *Accreditation manual for hospitals.* Chicago: Author.

Kaufman, E. (Ed) (1984). *Power to change: Family case studies in the treatment of alcoholism.* New York: Gardner Press.

Kaufman, E., & Kaufmann, P. (Eds.). (1979). *Family therapy of drug and alcohol abuse.* New York: Gardner Press.

Keller, M. (1974). Trends in the treatment of alcoholism. In M. Keller (Ed.), *Second special report to the U.S. Congress on alcohol and health* (DHEW Publication No. ADM 75-212, pp. 111–127). Washington, DC: U.S. Government Printing Office.

Kosten, T., Jalali, B., & Kleber, H. (1982–1983). Complementary marital roles of male heroin addicts: Evolution and intervention tactics. *American Journal of Drug and Alcohol Abuse, 9*(2), 155–169.

Levy, B. (1972). Five years later: A follow-up of 50 narcotic addicts. *American Journal of Psychiatry, 7*, 102–106.

Liepman, M., White, W., & Nirenberg, T. (1986). Children of alcoholic families. In D. Lewis & C. Williams (Eds.), *Providing care for children of alcoholics: Clinical and research perspectives* (pp. 39–64). Pompano Beach, FL: Health Communications.

Miller, W. R., & Hester, R. (1986). Inpatient alcoholism treatment: Who benefits? *American Psychologist, 41*(7), 794–805.

O'Farrell, T. (1989). Marital and family therapy in alcoholism treatment. *Journal of Substance Abuse Treatment, 6*(1), 23–29.

Olson, D., Russell, C., & Sprenkle, D. (1980). Marital and family therapy: A decade review. *Journal of Marraige and the Family, 42*(4), 973–993.

Piercy, F., & Frankel, B. (1989). The evolution of an integrative family therapy for substance-abusing adolescents: Toward the mutual enhancement of research and practice. *Journal of Family Psychology, 3*, 5–25.

Reilly, D. (1976). Family factors in the etiology and treatment of youthful drug abuse. *Family Therapy, 2*, 149–171.

Rosenbaum, M., & Richman, J. (1972). Family dynamics and drug overdoses. *Suicide and Life-Threatening Behavior, 2*, 19–25.

Schwartzman, J., & Bokos, P. (1979). Methadone maintenance: The addict's family revisited. *International Journal of Family Therapy, 1*, 338–355.

Schaef, A. (1986). *Codependence misunderstood/mistreated.* New York: Harper & Row.

Scott, S., & Van Deusen, J. (1982). Detoxification at home: A family approach. In M. D. Stanton, T. C. Todd, & Associates, *The family therapy of drug abuse and addiction* (pp. 310–334). New York: Guilford Press.

Selzer, M. (1971). The Michigan Alcoholism Screening Test (MAST): The quest for a diagnostic instrument. *American Journal of Psychiatry, 127*, 89–94.

Stanton, M. D. (1977). The addict as savior: Heroin, death and the family. *Family Process, 16*, 191–197.

Stanton, M. D. (1979). Family treatment approaches to drug abuse problems: A review. *Family Process, 18*, 251–280.

Stanton, M. D. (1981a). Strategic approaches to family therapy. In A. Gurman & D. Kniskern (Eds.), *Handbook of family therapy* (pp. 361–402). New York: Brunner/Mazel.

Stanton, M. D. (1981b). Who should get credit for change which occurs in therapy? In A. S. Gurman (Ed.), *Questions and answers in the practice of family therapy* (pp. 519–522). New York: Brunner/Mazel.

Stanton, M. D. (1985). The family and drug abuse. In T. Bratter & G. Forrest (Eds.), *Alcoholism and substance abuse: Strategies for clinical intervention* (pp. 398–430). New York: Free Press.

Stanton, M. D. (1988a). Coursework and self-study in the family treatment of alcohol and drug abuse: Expanding Heath and Atkinson's curriculum. *Journal of Marital and Family Therapy, 14*(4), 419–427.

Stanton, M. D. (1988b). The lobster quadrille: Issues and dilemmas for family therapy research. In L. Wynne (Ed.), *The state of the art in family therapy research: Controversies and recommendations* (pp. 7–31). New York: Family Process Press.

Stanton, M. D., & Landau-Stanton, J. (1990). Therapy with families of adolescent substance abusers. In H. Milkman & L. Sederer (Eds.), *Treatment choices in substance abuse* (pp. 329–339). Lexington, MA: Lexington Books.

Stanton, M. D., & Todd, T. C. (1979). Structural therapy with drug addicts. In E. Kaufman & P. Kaufmann (Eds.), *Family therapy of drug and alcohol abuse* (pp. 55–69). New York: Gardner Press.

Stanton, M. D., & Todd, T. C. (1981). Engaging resistant families in treatment: II. Principles and techniques in recruitment. *Family Process, 20*(3), 261–280.

Stanton, M. D., & Todd, T. C. (1982). The therapy model. In M. D. Stanton, T. C. Todd, & Associates, *The family therapy of drug abuse and addiction* (pp. 109–153). New York: Guilford Press.

Stanton, M. D., Todd, T. C., & Associates. (1982). *The family therapy of drug abuse and addiction.* New York: Guilford Press.

Steinglass, P. (1976). Experimenting with family treatment approaches to alcoholism, 1950–1975: A review. *Family Process, 15,* 97–123.

Steinglass, P., Bennett, L., Wolin, S., & Reiss, D. (1987). *The alcoholic family.* New York: Basic Books.

Treadway, D. (1989). *Before it's too late: Working with substance abuse in the family.* New York: Norton.

Wegscheider, S. (1981). *Another change: Hope and health for the alcoholic family.* Palo Alto, CA: Science and Behavior Books.

Woody, G., Carr, E., Stanton, M. D., & Hargrove, H. (1982). Program flexibility and support. In M. D. Stanton, T. C. Todd, & Associates, *The family therapy of drug abuse and addiction* (pp. 393–402). New York: Guilford Press.

19

Group Therapy and Self-Help Groups

MARC GALANTER

RICARDO CASTANEDA

HUGO FRANCO

Treatment modalities that employ social networks, such as group therapy and self-help programs, are of particular importance in treating alcoholism and drug abuse. One reason for this is that the addictions are characterized by massive denial of illness, and rehabilitation must begin with a frank acknowledgment of the nature of the patient's addictive process. The consensual validation and influence necessary to achieve such pronounced attitude change are most effectively achieved through group influence. Indeed, for this purpose, a fellow addict carries the greatest amount of credibility. Another reason for employing social networks is that they provide an avenue for maintaining ties to the patient beyond the traditional therapeutic relationship. Furthermore, therapists are not in the position to confront, cajole, support, and express feeling in a manner that can influence the abuser to return to abstinence; a group of fellow addicts or members of the patient's family can do so quite directly.

In this chapter, we explore how the impact of group treatment is effected in a number of disparate settings. We look at therapy groups directed specifically at the treatment of addiction; at Twelve-Step programs, such as Alcoholics Anonymous (AA) and Narcotics Anonymous (NA); and at institution-based self-help for substance abusers. The role of the clinician varies considerably in relation to each of these modalities; in each case, the mental health professional is provided with an unusual opportunity to step out of the traditional role of the psychodynamic therapist or the psychopharmacologist and examine the ways in which social influence is wrought through the group setting.

Group Therapy for Alcoholism and Drug Abuse

A Historical Note

Swinner (1979) has suggested that group therapy constitutes the most commonly applied modality for the treatment of alcoholism and other substance abuse, and many others (Cooper, 1987) regard group therapy as the psychotherapeutic treatment of choice for alcoholics and other drug abusers. The fact that group therapy is less expensive than individual therapy is important as well.

Brandsma and Pattison (1984) have reviewed the topic and have identified numerous group therapy designs that have been utilized in different treatment settings, including ambulatory clinics as well as residential facilities such as hospitals and therapeutic communities. Despite their popularity, however, many group practices can claim neither adequate descriptions of methodology nor supportive outcome studies documenting their efficacy relative to other group and individual treatment approaches (Cartwright, 1987; Castaneda & Galanter, 1987).

Group treatment for alcoholism and other addiction was developed out of general disappointment with the results of attempts at treating alcoholics and other addicted patients in individual treatment (Cooper, 1987). In the case of opiate addicts, for example, group treatment met the need to provide treatment for patients kept in methadone programs. These programs were developed in the face of the overwhelming failure of the early programs for opiate addicts requiring complete detoxification and abstinence (Ben-Yehuda, 1980). Groups for substance abusers have evolved from poorly defined and passive groups with unclear focus, and didactic groups in which all communication flows through the leader, to groups with an interpersonal pattern and focus (Yalom, Bloch, Bond, Zimmerman, & Qualls, 1978) whose leader is trained to interpret psychodynamic issues and is sensitive to interpersonal interactions in the here and now (Kanas, 1982). Substance abusers often are impulsive and have a tendency to act out. Although these characteristics frequently are disruptive of individual treatment, they are more easily managed in the context of a group. Such groups, however, need to be adequately designed to attend to the specific characteristics of substance abusers. Alcoholics, for example, are often uncooperative, have poor attendance, arrive at groups intoxicated, have low tolerance for anxiety, and often monopolize group discussions. Groups provide opportunities for utilizing peer pressure to effect the breaking down of denial of substance abuse and its consequences, and they encourage specific behavioral changes and abstinence. Many practitioners exclude intoxicated patients from the group.

Vannicelli (1982) points out that group treatment offers alcoholics unique opportunities (1) to share and to identify with others with similar problems; (2) to understand their own attitudes toward alcoholism and their defenses against giving up alcohol by confronting similar attitudes and defenses in others; and (3) to learn to communicate needs and feelings more effectively. Kanas (1982) has pointed out that in general, group treatment for the addicted population is not only as effective as any other form of therapy, but also much more economical than individual treatment. Much of the popularity of this modality derives from anecdotal experience of dedicated therapists as well.

How to Refer a Patient to Group Therapy

In referring a patient to group therapy, the clinician should keep in mind the specific characteristics of groups for substance abusers. Psychotherapeutic groups for alcoholics, for example, are most often made up exclusively of alcoholics. The focus of the group is alcoholism and the problems associated with it. Usually each group includes from 5 to 12 members who meet from one to three times a week. Criteria for exclusion include severe sociopathy or lack of motivation for treatment, acute or poorly controlled psychotic disorders, and the presence of transient or permanent severe cognitive deficits. Vannicelli (1982) has observed that often patients are eventually excluded from the group if they are unable to commit themselves to working toward abstinence. Although no specific studies are available to support this, the generally accepted clinical view is that addicts who also are overtly psychotic (actively hallucinating or entertaining delusions) should not be referred to groups whose members are not psychotic. Only recently are attempts being made to study the feasibility of groups composed of so-called "dual-diagnosis" patients (Galanter, Castaneda, & Ferman, 1988).

Group Treatment Modalities

Despite decades of experimenting with groups for substance abusers, no systematic description of treatment modalities is available. At present, a method for classifying group styles still needs to be developed. In addition, systematic comparisons of outcome cannot yet be carried out, since there are no generally agreed-upon outcome variables. Table 19.1 presents brief descriptions of different group modalities for treatment of alcoholics that can be defined at this time.

NOTES ON LEADER AND GROUP STYLE

The optimum style for a leader conducting a group for substance abusers appears to be one in which the focus is group- rather than leader-determined; in which the leader not only is knowledgeable about substance abuse, but also acts as a facilitator of interpersonal process; and in which the group members seek to understand each other from their own perspective.

Groups differ in their aims and the style of their leaders. Some groups allow for discussion of issues other than addiction, in the hope that an association between the addictive behavior and all other problems will be identified by the group members. Other groups focus primarily on relapse prevention through the identification and discussion of all problems, even if unrelated to the addictive behavior. Groups also vary according to the degree of support offered to members—from confrontational groups where support is

TABLE 19.1. Different Group Modalities for Treatment of Alcoholics

Category	Technique	Goals	Curative factors
Interactional	Interpretation of interactional process; promotion of self-disclosure and emotion expression	Promotion of understanding and resolution of interpersonal problems	Increased awareness of own relatedness
Modified interactional	Processing of interactional problems, but strong emphasis on ancillary supports for abstinence such as AA and Antabuse	Promotion of abstinence and improvement of interpersonal difficulties	Incorporation of specific resources to support abstinence, and improvement of interpersonal relatedness
Behavioral	Reinforcement of abstinence-promoting behaviors; punishment of undesirable behaviors	Specific behavior modification	Prevention of specific responses
Insight-oriented psychotherapy	Exploration and interpretation of group and individual processes	Promotion of ability to tolerate distressing feelings without resorting to alcohol	Increased insight and improved ability to tolerate stress
Supportive	Specific support offered to individuals, to enable them to draw on their own resources	Promotion of adaptation to alcohol-free living	Improvement in self-confidence, and incorporation of specific recommendations

given only when a patient espouses the views of the group leader, to supportive groups where individual attitudes and beliefs are accepted and explored.

Despite the obvious importance of group style and the need for clearly described group techniques, very little has been written that provides group leaders with specific group strategies (Vannicelli, Canning, & Griefen, 1984). The question of the group's style (defined as the way in which the group's goals and processes are linked) is not merely one of academic importance. For example, Harticollis (1980) has found that psychoanalytic groups are widely regarded as inadequate, and are not recommended for active substance abusers because of the counterproductive degree of anxiety that they generate. An early study by Ends and Page (1957) demonstrated that the style of a group of alcoholics predicted treatment outcome. In this study alcoholics were assigned to one of several groups of different designs. Group styles varied from one group described as relatively unfocused and "client-centered," whose leader avoided a dominant role and instead promoted interpersonal processes among the group members, to another group based on learning theory, whose leader assumed a dominant role, offered only conditional support, and focused strongly on punishment and reward. At follow-up, those alcoholics treated in the "client-centered" group fared far better than those included in the confrontational group.

EXPLORATORY AND SUPPORTIVE GROUPS

According to Cooper (1987), psychotherapeutic groups based on exploration and interpretation aim at forging an increased ability in their members to tolerate higher levels of distressing feelings without resorting to mood-altering substances. In contrast, purely supportive treatment groups aim at helping addicted group members to tolerate abstinence and assist them in remaining chemical-free without necessarily understanding the determinants of their addiction.

THE INTERACTIONAL GROUP MODEL

An important group style has been described by Yalom et al. (1978), in which therapy is conducted in weekly 90-minute meetings of 8 to 10 members who, under the leadership of two trained group therapists, are encouraged to explore their interpersonal relationships with the group leaders and the other members. An effort is made to create an environment of safety, cohesion, and trust, where members engage in in-depth self-disclosure and affective expression (Yalom et al., 1978). The goal of the group is not abstinence, but the understanding and working through of interpersonal conflicts. (Needless to say, however, "improvement" without abstinence is often illusory.) In fact, groups of alcoholics are oriented away from explicit discussion of drinking. The leaders emphasize that they do not see the group as the main instrument for achieving abstinence, and patients are encouraged to attend AA or seek other forms of treatment for this purpose. Within this format, a group member can be described as "improved" along a series of 19 possible areas of growth, irrespective of the severity of his or her drinking (Yalom et al., 1978).

This interactional model has been further developed by Vannicelli (1982), who, unlike Yalom et al. (1978), recommends that the group leaders strongly support abstinence as essential to the patient's eventual emotional stability. The group leaders firmly endorse simultaneous use of other supports, such as AA and Antabuse (disulfiram) therapy. In contrast to working with neurotics whose anxieties provide motivation and direction for treatment, the leaders of such a group of alcoholics are forced to intervene to provide limits and focus, without generation of more anxiety than necessary. The group therapists resist members' inquiries into the leaders' drinking habits by instead exploring the patients' underlying concerns about whether they will be helped and understood. Patients who miss early group sessions are actively sought out and brought back into the group. Confrontation (particularly of actively drinking

members) is used sparingly and only with the aim of providing better understanding of the behavior, and thus promoting growth and necessary
changes.

OTHER GROUPS USED WITH ADDICTED POPULATIONS

Interpersonal Problem-Solving Skill Groups. According to Jehoda
(1958), interpersonal problem-solving skill groups are based on the premise
that the capacity to solve problems in life determines quality of mental health.
Several empirical studies have lent some support to this assumption, further
suggesting that there is a relation between cognitive interpersonal problem-
solving skills and psychological adjustment. These groups have been applied to
alcoholics (Intagliata, 1978) and heroin addicts (Platt, Scura, & Hannon,
1960) with some degree of success. Usually problem-solving skill groups are
conducted in a limited number of sessions (frequently 10), and are organized to
teach a several-step approach to interpersonal problem solving. Most often,
such steps include the following: (1) Recognize that a problem exists; (2)
define the problem; (3) generate several possible solutions; and (4) select the
best alternative after determining the likely consequences of each of the available possible solutions to the problem. Follow-up studies have determined that
groups with this format have been effective in generating specific skills such as
anticipating and planning ahead for problems, even following discharge from
the treatment, programs. The value of problem-solving skill groups with
respect to other primary modalities of addiction treatment, however, remains
to be determined. It is unclear, for instance, whether these groups contribute to
the overall rates of abstinence achieved in inpatient and outpatient treatment
programs.

Educational Groups. Educational groups represent important ancillary
treatment modalities in substance abuse treatment, not only for addicts but for
their relatives and other social contacts. The obvious purpose of these groups is
to provide information on issues relevant to specific addictions, such as the
natural course and medical consequences of alcoholism, the implications of
intravenous addiction for sexual contacts and the family, the availability of
community resources, and so forth. Often, educational groups provide opportunities for cognitive reframing and behavioral changes along very specific
guidelines. These groups are often welcomed by some treatment-resistant
addicts and alcoholics who are uncooperative with other forms of therapy.
More often than not, educational groups offer structured, group-specific,
didactic material delivered by different means, including videotapes, audiocas-
settes, or lectures; these presentations are followed by discussions led by an
experienced and knowledgeable leader.

Activity Groups. Like educational groups, activity groups constitute another important ancillary modality in the treatment of alcoholics and other

addicts. Unlike educational groups, however, patient participation is the main goal of activity groups, which can evolve around a variety of occupational and recreational avenues. In a safe and sober context, the addict can experience socialization, recreation, and self- and group expression. Activity groups are often the source of valuable insight into patients' deficits and assets, both of which may go undetected by treatment staff members concerned with more narrowly focused treatment interventions, such as psychotherapists and nurses. When appropriately designed, activity groups may constitute invaluable sources of self-discovery, self-esteem, and newly acquired skills that facilitate sober social interactions.

Other groups also promote the acquisition of very specific skills, such as those devoted to reviewing relapse prevention techniques and those aimed at building social skills. These groups are particularly helpful in the early stages of the rehabilitation process of the alcoholic patient.

Relationship of Group Therapy to Individual Treatment

It is not a surprise that group therapists maintain that group treatment is the treatment of choice for alcoholics and other addicts. In support of this, group therapists such as Kanas (1982) invoke not only the difficulty that these patients have in developing an "analyzable transference neurosis" in individual therapy, but also the patients' tendency to display impulsive acting out—both characteristics that are better addressed in the anxiety-diffusing context of a group setting. Alcoholics, for example, are often seen as being orally fixated, with resulting "narcissistic, passive-dependent, and depressive personality traits" (Feibel, 1960). Platt et al. (1960) and Feibel (1960) have pointed out that individual insight-oriented psychotherapy is often said to be contraindicated in addicts, due to the following problems often present in these patients: intolerance of anxiety, episodes of rage and self-destructive behavior as a result of frustrated infantile needs, poor impulse control, and (probably most important) the tendency to develop a primitive transference toward the therapist.

An undeniable advantage of group therapy over individual treatment is that described by Pfeffer, Friedland, and Wortis (1949)—namely, the easily generated peer pressure, which can often promote behavioral changes and a reduction of denial of addiction and interpersonal difficulties. In addition, peer-generated support often serves to satisfy narcissistic and dependency needs. Primitive, intense transferences are often avoided in the group setting because of diffusion among the other members of the group and the "relative transparency of the group leaders" (Kanas, 1982). The tendency to leave treatment prematurely in individual therapy is often countered by the group's ability to promote a reduction of anxiety and to generate a therapeutic alliance, not only with the leader but also with the other group members. As stated above, it is important when deciding between groups and individual therapy to assess the patient's ability to tolerate and benefit from social interactions, as well as his or her level of cognitive and psychological functioning. Patients with moderate cognitive deficits, or paranoid or other psychotic disorders, are likely to become isolated or hostile and to leave the group setting prematurely.

A clinical example of the success of group therapy in a case where individual therapy had no impact follows. At the time of referral, J. M. was a 45-year-old white male, employed as a middle-level administrator in a municipal institution. He had been married for over 15 years and had three children. His chief complaints were frequent mood changes of many years' duration and unprovoked bouts of anger often directed at his wife, children, and coworkers. Although he had no history of psychiatric or medical problems, he reluctantly acknowledged that his wife thought he drank too much and that his boss had strongly demanded that he do something about his angry outbursts and poor job attendance. The patient was referred for individual therapy, but initial attempts at establishing a therapeutic relationship failed. He displayed markedly narcissistic personality traits, which resulted in an often disruptive relationship with the therapist, and he had difficulty in recognizing any interpersonal and mood problems associated with his alcohol consumption. The patient, however, acknowledged drinking more and more often than what was "healthy" for him. His motivation for treatment derived from his determination to maintain his current employment and his interest in "learning how to avoid depressive thinking."

Both the patient and the therapist felt that no progress was being made in individual therapy, and the patient was then referred to alcoholism group treatment. In the group, the patient was exposed to other group members' descriptions of their problems of mood and social relations. On two occasions during the beginning phases of his involvement with the group, he came to the group while intoxicated. The threat of expulsion from the group in the face of these intoxications brought into focus the similar situation he faced at work, where his drinking was also jeopardizing his ability to remain employed. Confronted by group members and therapists alike, he eventually identified a relationship between his drinking and his angry outbursts at home and at work. From the outset, his drinking was interpreted by other group members as a reflection of his alcoholism rather than the expression of psychological conflicts. Following a couple of months in treatment, this patient finally felt that he indeed was an alcoholic. The absence of drinking was associated with a total remission of depressive moods. He eventually made a commitment to abstinence, and he has remained in group treatment for several years.

Other Group Treatment Considerations

A NOTE ON SELF-MEDICATION

Group psychotherapy based on interpersonal and interpretive approaches rests in part on the self-medication hypothesis, which contends that substance abuse should be understood as the outcome of efforts at self-medication of distressing symptoms (Cooper, 1987; Khantzian, 1989). Recent challenges to this theory, however, suggest that drug abuse (particularly abuse of cocaine) may not necessarily be related to attempts at self-medication (Castaneda, Galanter, & Franco, 1989). Accordingly, it is advisable that group leaders be knowledgeable about addiction and be able to anticipate that addicted group members may display drug-seeking behaviors that can best be regarded as conditioned responses (triggered by specific internal or environmental cues, such as the sight of a bottle or feelings of euphoria and celebration), rather than as attempts on the part of the addict at dealing with emotional conflict (Galanter & Castaneda, 1985).

GROUPS WITH METHADONE MAINTENANCE PATIENTS

Groups with methadone maintenance patients experience problems that relate more to the structure of the therapy than to the group content. Encouragement is always needed for patients to participate in these groups. Often, groups for these patients are an efficient way of coping with problems under professional guidance and peers' support (Ben-Yehuda, 1980). These groups generally go through several stages: the development of *esprit de corps,* the division of labor, the establishment of group cohesion, and the development of outside-the-group relations.

DRINKING BY ALCOHOLIC GROUP MEMBERS

Drinking by some group members is to be expected in alcoholic groups. Full-blown slips or covert drinking by any group member interrupts the group process, elicits drinking-related thoughts and behaviors in other members, and requires specific and prompt intervention by the group leader. Often, however, a well-managed drinking episode represents an invaluable learning opportunity for all group members. A slip is not in itself cause for dismissal from the group. A resumption of drinking illustrates to all members the importance of prompt identification and interruption of denial, and the need to constantly assure the effectiveness of selected measures for maintaining abstinence. Responsibility for the slip should be defined to the group as resting entirely on the patient who is drinking, and not on any past event or interaction between other group members.

Drinking can assume different forms, depending on whether it is acknowledged or denied by the person and whether or not, despite the drinking, the group member professes adherence to the group norms regarding abstinence and self-disclosure. Those patients who keep drinking and express no intention to stop should be asked to leave the group. Dismissal from the group is best explained to the patient and to the other group members as justified by the person's present drinking behavior. Readmission into the group once the patient is willing to accept the group norms, including a commitment to achieving abstinence, should always be offered to a patient who is leaving the group. A different approach is to be adopted with patients who express a desire to end the relapse and agree to participate in a discussion within the group of their active drinking. Initially, as soon as there is any information from any source (within or outside of the group) that a group member is drinking, this should be immediately shared with all members. If the patient is intoxicated, he or she needs to be asked to leave the group and return sober the following session. The next meeting should serve as the occasion to explore feelings about drinking behavior and denial. At this point the group norms are reiterated; if necessary, specific contingency contracts are drawn with the drinking member.

Another presentation of the problem is the patient who drinks yet refuses to acknowledge it. It should be part of the group contract that any important information concerning drinking behavior by a group member should be shared with the group. In the face of contrasting versions of a patient's behavior, clarification should be sought from the patient in a way that facilitates "voluntary" disclosure. Eventually, it may be necessary to confront the patient directly; if denial persists, the patient should leave the group.

Outcome Studies

Given the immense popularity of group treatment for alcoholics and other substance abusers, it is surprising to find so few controlled outcome studies. Yalom et al. (1978) reported significant improvement at 8-month and 1-year follow-ups of both alcoholics and neurotics treated in weekly interactional group therapy. Improvement was measured along specific variables, however, and not according to the quality of abstinence eventually attained by the group members. In an early report, Ends and Page (1957) compared the outcome effects on alcoholics of several group therapy designs, including groups based on learning theory, client-centered (supportive) groups, psychoanalytic groups, and nonpsychotherapy discussion groups. They found that both client-centered and psychoanalytic groups yielded better outcomes than did discussion groups and groups based on learning theory, as measured by improvement in self-concept at a 1½-year follow-up. Client-centered groups also were associated with lower rates of readmission than all other groups in this and a subsequent study (Ends & Page, 1959). Mindlin and Belden (1965) studied the attitudes of hospitalized alcoholics before and after participation in either group psychotherapy, occupational groups, or no group treatment, and found that group psychotherapy significantly improved motivation for treatment and attitude toward alcoholism.

The Role of Twelve-Step Groups in the Treatment of Alcoholism and Drug Abuse

Self-help groups represent a widely available resource for the treatment of alcoholism as well as other forms of chemical dependency. AA and other

Twelve-Step organizations such as NA and Cocaine Anonymous (CA) have not only provided a large population of addicts with support and guidance, but have also contributed conceptually to the field of understanding and treating substance abuse. There are, however, important questions for the clinician and for the researcher that need to be answered before the proper role of Twelve-Step programs in the treatment of addicts can be established. In what ways are such self-help programs compatible with professional care? In what ways do these groups achieve their effects? For which patients are they most useful? Familiarity with self-help groups is essential both for the clinician providing care for substance abusers and for the researcher attempting to understand psychosocial factors involved in the outcome of addictions.

History of Self-Help Programs

Self-help groups can be understood as a grassroots response to a perceived need for services and support (Tracy & Gussow, 1976; Levy, 1976). In this sense, AA is the prototypical organization; it provided a model for the other successful groups such as NA and CA, as well as for its more closely related offspring such as Al-Anon, Alateen, and Children of Alcoholics. Levy (1976) proposed a rough division of self-help groups in two types of organizations: Type I groups, which are truly mutual help organizations and include all Twelve-Step programs, and Type II groups, which more frequently operate as foundations and place more emphasis on promoting biomedical research, fund raising, public education, and legislative and lobbying activities (Levy, 1976). Type I and Type II groups are by no means totally exclusive, since Type I associations promote public education and Type II groups sometimes provide direct services.

The development of AA has exerted a major influence on the self-help movement in general. This section of the chapter is concerned only with the development of AA and related Twelve-Step programs for addictions, which are clearly defined as Type I associations.

Origins and Growth of Alcoholics Anonymous

AA's principal founder, referred to as "Bill W." in accordance with the AA tradition of anonymity, was himself an alcoholic. Bill was spiritually influenced by a drinking friend, Edwin Thatcher, who belonged to the Oxford Group, an evangelical religious sect (Kurtz, 1982). Thatcher, usually referred to as "Ebby," attributed his abstinence to his involvement with the Oxford Group, which displayed many of the characteristics to be later shown by AA, such as open confessions and guidance from members of the group. Bill W. coninued to drink despite his encounter with Ebby in 1934, but he felt that there was a kinship of common suffering among alcoholics. During his final hospital detoxification, he experienced an altered state of consciousness characterized by a strong feeling of proximity with God, which gave him a sense of mission to help other alcoholics to achieve sobriety.

Bill's initial efforts to influence other alcoholics were unsuccessful until he met in May 1935 another member of the Oxford Group, "Dr. Bob," who a month later achieved sobriety and became the cofounder of AA. The number of alcoholics who experienced spiritual recovery and achieved sobriety in AA progressively increased; in 1939, when their group membership reached 100, they published *Alcoholics Anonymous,* the book that became the bible for the movement (Galanter, 1989). AA institutionalized practices such as a 90-day induction period, sponsorship relationships, the "Twelve Steps," and recruitment for the fellowship. The expansion and stability of the organization resulted from its "Twelve Traditions," which avoid concentration of power within the organization, prevent involvement of AA with other causes, maintain the anonymity of its membership, and preserve the neutrality of the association in relation to controversial issues. Its membership continued to grow; AA is now a global organization, reported to have over 75,000 informal groups in the United States and 114 other countries, with a membership estimated at 1.5 million. An example of how AA provided a model to other self-help programs for addictions is given by the birth and development of NA.

History and Approach of Narcotics Anonymous

Although the NA program was first applied to drug addiction at the U.S. Public Health Service Hospital at Lexington, Kentucky, in 1947, it was an NA group independent of any institution and formed by AA members who were addicts in Sun Valley, California, in 1953, which expanded and gave NA its current form (Peyrot, 1985). The Sun Valley NA group did not identify itself with a program organized in New York City in 1948 by Dan Carlson, an addict formerly exposed to the Lexington program, because the Sun Valley founders felt that NA should strictly adhere to AA's Twelve Steps and Twelve Traditions by not identifying itself with any specific agency and by not accepting government funds.

There are a few differences between AA and NA. NA members usually use illegal drugs, in contrast to most AA members until recently, who could be described as traditional alcoholics. Also, instead of using the term "alcoholism," NA refers to its problem as "addiction" and addresses the entire range of abusable psychoactive substances. There is, however, a clear overlap of approach and membership between the organizations, despite their complete independence of each other. Following in the footsteps of AA, NA has experienced fast-paced growth. It became an international organization, present in at least 36 countries, with a probable membership of 250,000. According to the NA World Service Office, which publishes NA literature and centralizes information within NA, the growth rate of the organization's membership has been 30–40% a year (Wells, 1987). The growth of NA and other Twelve-Step programs demonstrates the organizational strength and appeal of the AA model.

How Twelve-Step Programs Work

Participation in a Twelve-Step program can start at the moment that the addict meets a member of an organization, reads its literature, or simply attends meetings such as an open meeting or an institutional meeting run by AA or NA speakers (Galanter, 1989). A desire to stop drinking and/or abusing other drugs is the only requirement for membership. Total abstinence becomes a goal from the outset of the participation in the fellowship. Initial participation turns into an induction period, which in the case of AA, for instance, lasts 90 days and encourages daily attendance at meetings. The member is exposed to the Twelve-Step approach to recovery; the First Step consists of admitting powerlessness over the addiction, and consequently breaking with denial. Seeking sponsorship from another member who has been sober for months (preferably, more than a year) is also encouraged. Sponsors are usually of the same sex if the group is large enough, so that emotional entanglements can be avoided to avoid distracting the members from the purpose of attaining and maintaining sobriety. Open meetings usually consist of talks by a leader and two or three speakers who share their experiences of how the Twelve-Step program related to their recovery.

The Twelve-Step program is an attempt to effect changes in the addicts' lives that go beyond just stopping the use of substances—changes in personal values and interpersonal behavior, as well as continued participation in the fellowship. The Twelve Steps are studied and followed with the guidance of a sponsor and participation in meetings focused on each step. Each one involves changes in behavior and attitudes that may profoundly affect the addict's life. The Ninth Step, for instance, involves making amends to people formerly harmed by the addict's behavior. These amends may result in changes in the way in which the person relates to others and interprets the problems that have affected past and present relationships. For instance, an alcoholic man may "talk" to a deceased father whom he formerly hated and attempt a "conciliation" with the image he had of his dead father. The Twelfth Step encourages propagation of the group's philosophy, and consequently fosters the individual's recovery by providing opportunities to others to recover and expand the fellowship.

Traditionally, Twelve-Step meetings are open to all members, but they may be directed to special-interest groups (e.g., gays, women, minority groups, physicians, etc.). Meetings can be of different types, such as discussions, Twelve-Step study, and testimonials; some may be open to nonmembers, and others may be for members only. If the recovery progresses, the member will learn strategies to avoid relapse (e.g., "One day at a time"), will obtain help from other members, and will eventually help fellow addicts in their recovery so that he or she will continue to study the program and how its works. By helping other addicts and by sponsoring newcomers to the program, the individual is helping himself or herself by becoming more involved with the recovery process and the organization's philosophy.

Why Twelve-Step Programs Work

The explanation of why Twelve-Step programs can help people exposed to them is still unclear. From an existential perspective, AA, for instance, encourages acceptance of one's finitude and essential limitation by conveying the idea of powerlessness over alcohol. On the other hand, one can go beyond this limitation be relating to others and sharing some of the painful aspects of human existence. Kurtz (1982) has emphasized that consistency in thought and action is crucial to maintaining a conscious effort to be honest with oneself and others. This effort produces an increased awareness of one's own needs for growth. AA stresses the need for consistency in thought and action in all stages of its recovery program.

From a learning theory perspective, the group selectively reinforces social and cognitive behaviors that usually are incompatible with the addictive behavior. Attendance at meetings is basically incompatible with using the same time to drink or abuse other drugs. Achievements resulting from sobriety are generously praised, and strategies of self-monitoring and self-control are constantly reinforced through constant interactions with others attempting to remain sober. Self-monitoring of emotions and behaviors is enhanced by helping the addict to detect reactions to certain internal and external stimuli (e.g., craving, distress with interpersonal problems, denial in the presence of depressive feelings, unrealistic goals when under pressure, etc.). In addition to self-monitoring, self-control is enhanced by learning a new repertoire of cognitive and social behaviors, such as attending more meetings when craving increases, using the Twelve Steps to cope with stressful life events, and obtaining group support to face painful feelings about oneself and others. Other theoretical perspectives used to understand Twelve-Step programs include operant and social learning views; however, since experimentation with the processes involved in participation in Twelve-Step programs is an almost impossible proposition, the use of learning models remains largely descriptive and speculative.

Self-Help and Treatment Outcome

AA has received more attention from investigators studying outcome variables than other Twelve-Step programs. Consequently, most of our knowledge about the impact of Twelve-Step programs on the lives of addicts is limited to the effects of AA on some samples of alcoholics. The structure of Twelve-Step organizations and their emphasis on anonymity make scientific research on these groups a very difficult task (Glaser & Osborne, 1982). Outcome variables related to participation in AA, such as severity of drinking, personality traits, attendance at meetings, total abstinence versus controlled drinking as a therapeutic goal, and concomitance of AA attendance with professional care, have been studied (Thurstin, Alfano, & Sherer, 1986; Thurstin, Alfano, & Nerviano, 1987; Seixas, Washburn, & Eisen, 1988; Elal-Lawrence, Slade, & Dewey, 1987).

The first variable to deserve attention is that those alcoholics who join AA are not representative of the total population of alcoholics receiving treatment (Emrick, 1987). AA members tend to be, as common sense would indicate, more sociable and affiliative. Studies also suggest that AA members have more severe problems resulting from their drinking and experience more guilt regarding their behavior. Attendance to meetings has been associated in some studies (Emrick, 1987) with better outcome, although the nature of this association remains unclear. Thurstin et al. (1986) found no clear personality traits that might seem to be associated with AA membership, but they reported that success among members appears to be related to less depression, less anxiety, and better sociability. AA seems not to benefit those who can become nonproblem users, and may actually be detrimental to patients who can learn to control their drinking (Emrick, 1987). AA members who receive other forms of treatment concomitantly with their participation in AA meetings probably do better.

As noted above, several problems make it difficult to study outcome factors related to participation in Twelve-Step programs. One is the changing composition of AA membership: More women, younger people, and multiply addicted alcoholics have been joining the organization. The heterogeneity of addictive disorders, the anonymity of membership, the impossibility of experimentation with components of the programs, the self-selection factor in affiliation, and the lack of appropriate group controls all impose serious methodological difficulties in evaluating outcome variables. For clinical purposes, the benefit of membership in self-help groups has to be empirically evaluated for each individual patient.

Self-Help Groups and the Clinician

The relationship between professional treatment and membership in a Twelve-Step group has been less than systematically addressed. Guidelines to orient the clinician have been proposed by Clark (1987). Obviously, acquaintance with Twelve-Step programs is essential in order for the clinician to orient patients regarding their needs, and to respond to possible conflicts between the nature and goals of professional care and the demands of participation in self-help organizations. Clinicians treating addicts can learn about Twelve-Step programs by attending local meetings, by becoming familiar with the fellowships' literature, and by exploring their patients' experiences in the context of their membership in these organizations.

One point deserving emphasis is that physicians should be aware of the danger of prescribing habit-forming substances to addicts, not only because of the inherent dangers involved in the use of these substances, but also because of the goals of programs that demand complete avoidance of chemical solutions for life's problems (Zweben, 1987). When psychotropic medication is strongly recommended, the benefits and risks involved in their use should be carefully discussed with the patient in the context of the goals of Twelve-Step programs. An occasional sponsor may be opposed to any medication, even when a patient clearly needs pharmacological treatment in order to alleviate disabling behavioral or physical conditions. In this situation, the clinician has to address the nature of the conflict involved in the treatment by making the needed medical treatment compatible with the program philosophy. This desirable goal can only be achieved when the clinician is well informed about the nature of Twelve-Step programs and can help the patient to integrate the rationale for medical treatment with the general goals of his or her membership in the self-help program. Avoidance of prescribing drugs with habit-forming potential, willingness to educate patients about the nature of their problems, and a positive attitude toward Twelve-Step organizations make it easier for clinicians to integrate their interventions with the orientation of the fellowship. Candidates for controlled drinking should not be encouraged to participate in abstinence-oriented programs, since the incompatibility of the goals of professional treatment with a Twelve-Step orientation may prove to be very detrimental to therapy (Emrick, 1987).

Clinicians should, in general, encourage their patients to get exposed to Twelve-Step programs, but should remember that a great number of addicts who never participate in these organizations can make good use of professional treatment and successfully recover. Since the composition of the membership of self-help groups has continually changed, it has been possible for patients treated with psychotropic medication, including methadone, to benefit from participation in these groups (Obuchowsky & Zweben, 1987).

Institutional Self-Help Treatment Groups for Substance Abuse

Most ambulatory programs for substance abuse treatment are modeled after ones used in general psychiatric clinics. They rely primarily on professionally conducted individual and small-group therapy. Whether there are more cost-effective options or more potent ones has yet to be fully explored. One alternative approach to conventional institutional treatment is based on psychological influence in a self-help group context, and is designed to allow for decreased staffing. Such an approach to group treatment is designed to draw on the principles of zealous group psychology observed in free-standing self-help approaches to addictive illness, such as those of AA and the drug-free therapeutic communities, but at the same time serves as the primary group-based modality employed in an institutional treatment setting. In other words, it can be employed in institutional settings such as hospitals and clinics and still capture the psychological effect of free-standing self-help groups.

In a study we conducted on this treatment model (Galanter, 1982, 1983), primary therapists were social workers and paraprofessionals experienced in alcoholism treatment, supervised by attending psychiatrists. There were one social worker and one paraprofessional treating patients in the experimental self-help treatment program, and two members of each of the latter disciplines treating the controls; the self-help program therefore operated at half the usual staffing level. The program included an alcohol clinic attached to an inpatient detoxification unit.

The control and the experimental self-help programs illustrate the contrast between institution-based self-help groups and conventional care. In our study, they operated simultaneously and independently in the outpatient department. Therapists in each program were encouraged to perfect their respective clinical approaches, and each group of therapists received clinical supervision appropriate to their own needs and experience. Differences between the two programs are outlined below to illustrate the operation of institutionally grounded self-help group care.

The Orientation Program

In the control (traditional) group setting, two primary therapists served as coleaders of a group for their own patients, and attendance in each session ranged between 8 and 15. In the self-help program the same format was used, but groups were led by patients of the primary therapists who had established sobriety and had demonstrated a measure of social stability over several months. These "senior patients" monitored the progress of patients in the orientation group and were supervised by the primary therapists, who attended the orientation for part of each session, participating in a limited fashion only. A patient in crisis might be invited to return to the orientation group if this was seen as helpful.

Group Therapy

Weekly group meetings were oriented toward practical life issues among controls, but insight was encouraged; progress toward abstinence was a major theme. The two primary therapists served as facilitators for the group, encouraging mutual acceptance and support by their own empathic manner. When confrontation was necessary, it was undertaken by the therapists in a forthright but supportive manner. In the self-help program, groups met with the same frequency, but senior patients assumed the leadership role. Primary therapists attended part of each session and participated intermittently; they served, however, primarily in a coordinating capacity for these groups, and supervised the senior patients. Patients were encouraged to deal with unusual problems by recourse to their peers in the program, either in their therapy group or through senior patients.

Peer Therapy

Self-help program patients were made aware that the primary source of support in the clinic was the peer group. New patients were encouraged to seek out peers and senior patients who would be available to assist them through the program. Senior patients were supervised in assisting with crises, when this was judged clinically appropriate by the primary therapists.

The senior patient program was operated in the self-help modality. Potential senior patients were screened for sobriety and social stability, and assisted in patient management of the program for a time-limited period. Those who served as group leaders met weekly as a group with the primary therapists, focusing on their therapeutic functions in the unit. Under supervision of the therapists, they directed orientation, therapy, and activity groups. Their interventions in more difficult patients' problems were reviewed with the primary therapists, and they referred self-help patients to their respective primary therapists for more troublesome problems. Other senior patients had administrative functions in the program.

Meetings of the full patient complement also took place in the self-help program. A monthly evening meeting open to all patients served as a focus for group spirit and as a context for organizing recreational activities. The meetings were run collaboratively by staff and senior patients, with program-wide activities and patients' progress as the focus. Socialization at the time of these meetings focused on the status of patients' recovery.

Outcome and Comments

In two outcome studies (Galanter, 1982, 1983), we found that the experimental program, with half the staffing of the traditional modality, was quite viable in a municipal hospital alcoholism treatment program. Furthermore, retention of inpatients upon transfer to the alcohol clinic was 38% greater than in the control (non-self-help) program; rates of abstinence in outpatients were no less, and social adjustment over the course of a 12-month follow-up was enhanced. The self-help format appears, therefore, to offer a format for institutional treatment that is less expensive and potentially more effective.

The following case example illustrates the ethos of the self-help program. A 36-year-old outpatient came to the clinic intoxicated, without a scheduled visit, and asked to speak with a senior patient whom he knew well. He had been in outpatient treatment for 8 months, and had been abstinent for the last 4 months. Five days earlier, he had begun drinking subsequent to a crisis in his family, and had missed his group meeting. He gave a history of falling down a staircase earlier in the day, bruising his head. The senior patient he had asked to see and another one were present, and they encouraged him to seek a medical evaluation. The case was then reviewed with the primary therapist, who saw him briefly, wrote a referral for medical assessment, and returned him to the two senior patients' care. After an hour, the senior patients prevailed upon him to go with one of them to the emergency service. The other took him on the following afternoon to a meeting of an AA group that he had previously attended. The patient was able to maintain abstinence until his next weekly group therapy meeting, at which time a group member offered to get together with him during the ensuing week, so as to provide him with some encouragement.

Given a need for increased substance abuse treatment services, it is important to note that counseling staff members (social workers and counselors) comprise 66% of the staffs in all federally assisted alcoholism treatment facilities, which constitute the bulk of publicly supported programs (Vischi, Jones, Shank, & Lima, 1980). The question then arises as to whether these counseling staffers are used in the most cost-effective way. One problematic aspect of this is illustrated by the finding of Paredes and Gregory (1979) that in alcoholism treatment programs, the economic resources invested in alcoholism treatment are not positively correlated with outcome. They concluded that the type and quantity of therapeutic resources invested are related to the characteristics of the agencies themselves, rather than to a treatment strategy conceived for optimal cost-effectiveness.

Two issues common to most small-group therapies for substance abuse in the clinic setting are relevant here. In the first place, whether behavioral, insight-oriented, or directive, they all focus on the concerns of a relatively small number of patients involved in the therapy group (typically 6 to 10), to the exclusion of other program participants. Second, it is generally agreed that such small-group therapy for alcoholics offers a better outcome when conducted in the context of a multimodality program. Such a program may integrate treatment components so as to implement a carefully structured plan, as described by Hunt and Azrin (1973).

These two aspects of small-group therapy may be considered in relation to a self-help-oriented treatment program such as the one described above. With regard to group size, such a program introduces the option of the patients' strong identification with and sense of cohesion in a treatment network of many more than 6 to 10 patients. In fact, it encourages affiliative feelings among the full complement of self-help patients, providing an experience of a large, zealous group (Galanter, 1989). This is promoted by therapeutic contact with a number of senior patients who are involved in the therapy groups; by program-wide patient-run activities, such as the orientation groups open to patients in crisis; and in monthly large-group meetings, also open to all patients. This broader identification forms the bulwark of a self-help orientation.

References

Ben-Yehuda, N. (1980). Group therapy with methadone-maintained patients: Structural problems and solutions. *International Journal of Group Psychotherapy, 30,* 331–345.

Brandsma, J. M., & Pattison, E. M. (1984). Group treatment methods with alcoholics. In M. Galanter & E. M. Pattison (Eds.), *Advances in the psychosocial treatment of alcoholism* (pp. 17–30). Washington, DC: American Psychiatric Press.

Cartwright, A. (1987). Group work with substance abusers: Basic issues and future research. *British Journal of Addiction, 82,* 951–953.

Castaneda, R., & Galanter, M. (1987). A review of treatment modalities for alcoholism and their outcome. *American Journal of Social Psychiatry, 7,* 237–244.

Castaneda, R., Galanter, M., & Franco, H. (1989). Self-medication among addicts with primary psychiatric disorders. *Comprehensive Psychiatry, 30,* 80–83.

Clark, H. W. (1987). On professional therapists and Alcoholics Anonymous. *Journal of Psychoactive Drugs, 19,* 233–242.

Cooper, D. E. (1987). The role of group psychotherapy in the treatment of substance abusers. *American Journal of Psychotherapy, 41,* 55–67.

Elal-Lawrence, G., Slade, P. D., & Dewey, M. E. (1987). Treatment and follow-up variables discriminating abstainers, controlled drinkers and relapsers. *Journal of Studies on Alcohol, 48,* 39–46.

Emrick, C. D. (1987). Alcoholics Anonymous: Affiliation processes and effectiveness as treatment. *Alcoholism: Clinical and Experimental Research, 11,* 416–442.

Ends, E. J., & Page, C. W. (1957). A study of three types of group psychotherapy with hospitalized male inebriates. *Quarterly Journal of Studies on Alcohol, 18,* 263–277.

Ends, E. J., & Page, C. W. (1959). Group psychotherapy and concomitant psychological changes. *Psychological Monograph, 73,* 1–31.

Feibel, C. (1960). The archaic personality structure of alcoholics and its indications for group therapy. *International Journal of Group Psychotherapy, 10,* 39–45.

Galanter, M. (1982). Overview: Charismatic religious sects and psychiatry. *American Journal of Psychiatry, 139,* 1539–1548.

Galanter, M. (1983). Engaged members of the Unification Church: The impact of a charismatic group on adaptation and behavior. *Archives of General Psychiatry, 40,* 1197–1203.

Galanter, M. (1989). *Cults: Faith, healing and coercion.* New York: Oxford University Press.

Galanter, M., & Castaneda, R. (1985). Self-destructive behavior in the substance abuser. *Psychiatric Clinics of North America, 8,* 251–261.

Galanter, M., Castaneda, R., & Ferman, J. (1988). Substance abuse among general psychiatric patients: Place of presentation, diagnosis and treatment. *American Journal of Substance Abuse, 14,* 211–235.

Glaser, F. B., & Osborne, A. (1982). Does AA really work? *British Journal of Addiction, 77,* 123–129.

Harticollis, P. (1980). Alcoholism, borderline and narcissistic disorders: A psychoanalytic overview. In W. Fann (Ed.), *Phenomenology and treatment of alcoholism* (pp. 93–110). New York: Spectrum.

Hunt, G. M., & Azrin, N. H. (1973). A community-reinforcement approach to alcoholism. *Behaviour Research and Therapy, 11,* 91–104.

Intagliata, J. C. (1978). Increasing the interpersonal problem-solving skills of an alcoholic population. *Journal of Consulting and Clinical Psychology, 46,* 489–498.

Jehoda, M. (1958). *Current concepts in positive mental health.* New York: Basic Books.

Kanas, N. (1982). Alcoholism and group psychotherapy. In E. Kauffman & M. Pattison (Eds.), *Comprehensive textbook of alcoholism* (pp. 1011–1021). New York: Gardner Press.

Khantzian, E. J. (1989). The self-medication hypothesis for substance abusers. *American Journal of Psychiatry, 30,* 80–83.

Kurtz, E. (1982). Why AA works. *Journal of Studies on Alcohol, 43,* 38–80.

Levy, L. H. (1976). Self-help health groups: Types and psychological processes. *Journal of Applied Behavioral Science, 12,* 310–322.

Mindlin, D. F., & Belden, E. (1965). Attitude changes with alcoholics in group therapy. *California Mental Health Review Digest, 3,* 102–103.

Obuchowsky, M. A., & Zweben, J. E. (1987). Bridging the gap: The methadone client in 12-step programs. *Journal of Psychoactive Drugs, 19,* 301–302.

Paredes, A., & Gregory, D. (1979). Therapeutic impact and fiscal investment in alcoholism services. In M. Galanter (Ed.), *Currents in alcoholism* (Vol. 4, pp. 441–456). New York: Grune & Stratton.

Peyrot, M. (1985). Narcotics Anonymous: Its history, structure, and approach. *International Journal of the Addictions, 20,* 1509–1522.

Pfeffer, A. Z., Friedland, P., & Wortis, S. B. (1949). Group psychotherapy with alcoholics. *Quarterly Journal of Studies on Alcohol, 10,* 198–216.

Platt, J. J., Scura, W., & Hannon, J. R. (1960). Problem-solving thinking of youthful incarcerated heroin addicts: The archaic personality structure of alcoholics and its indications for group therapy. *International Journal of Group Psychotherapy, 10,* 39–45.

Seixas, F., Washburn, S., & Eisen, S. V. (1988). Alcoholism, Alcoholics Anonymous attendance, and outcome in a prison system. *American Journal of Drug and Alcohol Abuse, 14,* 515–524.

Swinner, P. (1979). Treatment approaches. In M. Grant & P. Swinner (Eds.), *Alcoholism in perspective.* Baltimore: University Park Press.

Thurstin, A. H., Alfano, A. M., & Nerviano, V. J. (1987). The efficacy of AA attendance for aftercare of inpatient alcoholics: Some follow-up data. *International Journal of the Addictions, 22,* 1083–1090.

Thurstin, A. H., Alfano, A. M., Sherer, M. (1986). Pretreatment MMPI profiles of AA members and non-members. *Journal of Studies on Alcohol, 47,* 468–471.

Tracy, G. S., & Gussow, Z. (1976). Self-help health groups: A grass roots response to a need for services. *Journal of Applied Behavioral Science, 12,* 381–396.

Vannicelli, M. (1982). Group psychotherapy with alcoholics: Special techniques. *Journal of Studies on Alcohol, 43,* 17–37.

Vannicelli, M., Canning, D., & Griefen, M. (1984). Group therapy with alcoholics: A group case study. *International Journal of Group Psychotherapy, 34,* 127–147.

Vischi, T. R., Jones, K. R., Shank, E. L., & Lima, L. H. (1980). *The alcohol, drug abuse and mental health national data book* (DHHS Publication No. 80-983). Washington, DC: U.S. Government Printing Office.

Wells, B. (1987). Narcotics Anonymous (NA): The phenomenal growth of an important resource [Editorial]. *British Journal of Addiction, 82,* 581–582.

Yalom, I. D., Bloch, S., Bond, G., Zimmerman, E., & Qualls, B. (1978). Alcoholics in interactional group therapy. *Archives of General Psychiatry, 35,* 419–425.

Zweben, J. E. (1987). Can the patient on medication be sent to 12-step programs? *Journal of Psychoactive Drugs, 19,* 299–300.

20

Cognitive and Behavioral Approaches to Alcohol Abuse

PRISCILLA W. MACKAY
DENNIS M. DONOVAN
G. ALAN MARLATT

Based on our clinical and research experiences, we have found that social learning theory (Bandura, 1977a) provides both a theoretical and practical framework for understanding and treating addictive behaviors. Within this model, addictive behaviors are seen as effective, although maladaptive, coping responses to stressful life events. It is the short-term effectiveness of the addictive behavior that makes it especially difficult to change, even in light of the negative longer-term consequences of engaging in the behavior. In this chapter, we first describe a social learning conceptualization of addictive behaviors. Next, several treatment interventions derived from this theory are discussed. Finally, adopting a stage model of change, we explore a review of maintenance strategies versus change strategies, within a relapse prevention model.

Social Learning Theory of Addiction

Within a social learning framework, three key points about addictive behaviors are important to highlight (George, 1989). First, addictive behaviors are considered learned, socially acquired behaviors with multiple determinants. They are influenced by past learning, situational antecedents, biological makeup, cognitive processes, and reinforcement contingencies. Situational antecedents, or high-risk factors, are factors such as time of day, place, people, or emotional states that increase the likelihood of consuming alcohol. Cognitive processes include anticipation, expectancy and attributions, experience with respect to memory of past events, and modeling.

Reinforcement contingencies are the rewarding aspects of alcohol and of the social setting in which use occurs; these serve to maintain drinking behavior. A number of important principles of reinforcement with respect to alcohol consumption are as follows: (1) The more rewarding or positive an experience is as a consequence of drinking, the greater the likelihood that drinking will be repeated; (2) the greater the frequency of experiencing positive consequences as a result of alcohol consumption, the greater the likelihood of repeating the alcohol consumption; and (3) the more closely in time positive consequences are associated with drinking alcohol, the more likely alcohol is to be consumed. (Conversely, more distally related negative consequences of alcohol consumption will be a less powerful deterrent to continued drinking.) A clinical example illustrates these points. A man who is lonely and socially timid finds that whenever he drinks at the local tavern, he is able to meet and talk to people in a pleasurable way he rarely experiences when sober. His pool game and dancing seem to improve with each beer he drinks. The hangover he experiences the next day as a result of his previous evening's frivolity is less closely associated with his overconsumption than is the social pleasure he derived while drinking. The reinforcing aspects of consuming alcohol will lead to an increased likelihood of his drinking when he feels lonely or socially awkward in the future.

Second, addictive behaviors are seen as occurring along a continuum. In the example of drinking behavior, the two endpoints of the continuum would be problem-free, nondrinking behavior at one end and alcohol dependence with concomitant problems of a severe nature on the other end. It is the interaction among biological influences, situational antecedents, cognitive processes, reinforcement contingencies, and past learning, described above, that determines where on the continuum a person's drinking behavior will fall. Thus, as George (1989) states, the same principles can be used to explain the acquisition and maintenance of both nonaddictive and addictive behaviors.

Third, addictive behaviors are seen as coping attempts, albeit maladaptive ones, in response to stress. Stress can be defined as an "adaptational relationship" between an individual and a situational demand. The individual is seen as having both a particular biological/genetic makeup and a particular social learning history. Situational demands encompass everyday problems such as family and work difficulties, lifestyle imbalances, and emotional states to which the individual must respond. In an "adaptational relationship," the individual strives to achieve a balance between the stressor and his or her ability to cope with the demand. As an individual copes, be it cognitively or behaviorally, he or she is attempting to master, tolerate, or reduce external and internal demands in circumstances that have taxed or exceeded his or her resources (Sanchez-Craig, Wilkinson, & Walker, 1987). If healthy alternatives are lacking, addictive behaviors such as drinking alcohol, restricting food intake or overeating, or using drugs may be the most effective coping ability the individual possesses to restore equilibrium. Or, even if coping skills are possessed, feelings such as anxiety or depression may interfere with the ability to carry out the response. In this case, alcohol use may be a coping response to the anxiety or depression. Hence, addictive behaviors are viewed as a coping strategy within a comprehensive biopsychosocial framework in an attempt to adapt to stress (Monti, Abrams, Kadden, & Cooney, 1989; Shiffman & Wills, 1985).

A social learning view of addictive behaviors has advantages with respect to both conceptualization and treatment alternatives. The first benefit of a social learning approach results from the fact that specific treatment goals can be derived. Thus, the therapist or alcoholic himself or herself can evaluate progress in an ongoing manner, determining the success of goal attainment. A second advantage to this framework is that it becomes more readily apparent whether an intervention is effective. Using the example above of the man who relies on alcohol to alleviate shyness and loneliness, let us assume that an assessment of the individual's high-risk drinking factors indicates that he drinks most frequently and in the greatest quantities when he is in social situations. Thus, a treatment goal may be for this man to develop more effective strategies to interact socially without the use of alcohol. These strategies might include speaking once at each Alcoholics Anonymous meeting, calling a friend to talk on a daily basis, or attending a group where nondrinking acquaintances are likely to be made. Assessment is an ongoing process, thereby allowing an update of goals as new information is acquired. Thus, the individual described above may find that he is having difficulty attaining his goal of speaking in a group because of his anxiety. A new intervention of cognitive restructuring or relaxation training would be advisable at this juncture. Therefore, rather than feeling incapable of achieving sobriety, a difficult and often overwhelming task, the individual can break down the goal of sobriety into several steps and work at achieving them individually or sequentially. A third advantage of a social learning conceptualization is that treatment components can be empirically validated to determine their effectiveness. Later in this chapter, we discuss many of the components used in cognitive–behavioral treatment of alcohol abuse and describe relevant outcome data regarding their treatment efficacy.

Thus far, we have discussed the heuristic value of a social learning framework for understanding and treating addictive behaviors, specifically alcohol abuse. In the following section, specific intervention strategies derived from this conceptualization are presented.

Cognitive and Behavioral Interventions for Alcohol Abuse

Appraisal

An essential aspect of human learning is that we behave not in response to our *actual* environment, but rather to the environment as we *perceive* it to be. This principle leads to an important cognitive intervention—namely, intervention in how we appraise situations. Appraisal occurs when an individual is faced with a situation and must evaluate whether it represents a high-risk event. The importance of appraisal in understanding and treating alcohol abuse has been studied extensively by Sanchez-Craig et al. (1987). They suggest that appraisals, rather than emotions, serve as the mediating link between perception and action. Based on Arnold's (1969) and Lazarus's (1966) formulations, appraisal is defined as "the evaluation of information regarding the relevance of an event to the individual's welfare" (Lazarus, Averill, & Opton, 1974, p. 285). Two types of appraisal are proposed. The first is primary appraisal, in which stimulus events are judged as beneficial, harmful, or irrelevant. Beneficial appraisals typically result in a positive response that may lead to an approach behavior. Harmful appraisals result in negative emotions and lead to avoidance responses.

The second type is secondary appraisal, which refers to the consideration of coping alternatives. Appraisals are highly subjective in nature; they are influenced by previous experience with the event, personality, cultural and personal values, beliefs, preferences, coping characteristics, and demographic features (Sanchez-Craig et al., 1987).

Based on this understanding of the relevance of appraisal, Sanchez-Craig et al. recommend performing a functional analysis of a person's perceptions (i.e., the beliefs, expectations, or opinions held) regarding drinking, with emphasis on the emotions that are generated by the perceptions. This analysis provides information in understanding what may be influencing drinking, as well as providing an opportunity for intervention. As clients are made aware of the events surrounding their drinking episodes, they are instructed to experience as vividly as possible the accompanying emotions. They are informed that although negative emotions, such as fear, anxiety, and hurt, are unpleasant, staying with these feelings will eventually lead to learning to tolerate them and reducing the overwhelming temptation to avoid them by consuming alcohol. Clients are also taught alternatives for appraising situations and encouraged to consider different interpretations for past problematic events. Once a list of alternative cognitive appraisals is generated, clients practice these appraisals while imagining their new self-statements.

The key aspects of reappraisal theory follow the basic tenets of cognitive–behavioral interventions. That is, clients must first become aware of their behavior, or cognitions, by identifying situations in which they occur. More effective strategies are then generated, and finally rehearsal of the new skills is encouraged until the client has achieved a sense of mastery.

Two related therapies of cognitive change are rational–emotive therapy (Ellis, McInerney, DiGiuseppe, & Yeager, 1988) and Meichenbaum's (1971) use of self-statements to control impulsivity, phobias, and schizophrenic behavior. Ellis focuses on the idea of irrational beliefs and suggests that clients can be taught to challenge and correct their faulty thoughts. Meichenbaum incorporates the use of overt verbalization instructions into existing behavior therapy techniques.

Skill Acquisition

An intervention strategy based on the information derived during secondary appraisal is training in skill acquisition. Do individuals have coping alternaves for handling the high-risk situation? If they possess adequate coping skills and are sufficiently motivated, they will respond to the risk in an effective manner and avoid the use of alcohol as a coping alternative. Frequently, however, abusive drinkers are deficient in requisite skills and turn to alcohol as a familiar way to cope with interpersonal and intrapersonal situations (Shiffman & Wills, 1985). Sometimes skills are not lacking, but feelings of anxiety, depression, or anger interfere with the ability to execute the appropriate response. Again, a functional analysis will yield information regarding the kinds of skill deficits a client may have. Alcoholics are not necessarily lacking in general social skills, but rather may be lacking in alcohol-related coping skills (Mackay, 1988; Shiffman, 1989). The extent and type of skill deficits may be functions of parental drinking influences in terms of genetic contributions, as well as of modeling behavior and environmental deprivation (Chaney, 1989). It is not uncommon for problem drinkers to have developmentally missed out on the acquisition of certain skills, because of the interference of early drinking behavior. Thus, age of onset and length of drinking history are important aspects of skill development.

Chaney and his colleagues (Chaney, 1989; Chaney, O'Leary, & Marlatt, 1978) suggest offering skills training to problem drinkers in order to increase the number of active cognitive and behavioral coping alternatives in the drinkers' repertoire. To determine the extent of the client's coping abilities, an instrument (e.g., the Situational Competency Test; Chaney et al., 1978) that assesses coping responses to a variety of alcohol-relevant situations should be administered. In many ways this is comparable to a functional analysis, in that it provides information regarding situations that have been or are likely to be high risks for drinking. Results of this scale can be used to help the clients identify and become aware of areas of potential vulnerability. In keeping with social learning theory, modeling, rehearsal, and feedback are important components in skill acquisition. (See Chaney, 1989, and Chaney et al., 1978, for a description of the skills training program.)

Several studies (Chaney et al., 1978; Freedberg & Johnson, 1981) have supported the efficacy of a skills training component for alcohol treatment, particularly in the context of an inpatient program (Chaney, 1989).

Cue Exposure

A number of investigators (Cooney, Gillespie, Baker, & Kaplan, 1987; Monti et al., 1987; Niaura et al., 1988) have suggested the relevance of cue reactivity in addressing alcohol treatment. Their research suggests that alcoholics develop classical conditioned responses (CRs) to drinking-related stimuli as a consequence of their often long and varied drinking histories. If these CRs are not addressed during treatment, it is not unlikely that a recovering alcoholic will be inadequately prepared, with respect to both anticipation and response, for responses inadvertently triggered by cues in his or her environment. An example was provided by a former intravenous cocaine abuser seen in treatment recently. Despite the fact that approximately 5 months had passed since he had last used cocaine, he reported having experienced an extremely unpleasant reaction both physically and emotionally when he noticed a box of syringes in a hospital room that he was painting as part of his job. Upon his seeing the syringes, a CR of craving occurred. He was startled by the intensity of the reaction, and interpreted the severity of his response as an indication that he still greatly desired drugs and was not adequately committed to abstinence.

Niaura et al. (1988) state that "the presence of alcohol cues disrupts the performance of skills in alcoholics, and the alcoholics with stronger reactions to cues show more impairment in skills" (p. 145). A reasonable treatment strategy, then, would incorporate cue exposure into skills training to enhance the generalizability and effectiveness of outcome (Abrams, Monti, Carey, Pinto, & Jacobus, 1988; Niaura et al., 1988). As alcoholics learn drink refusal skills in the presence of their favorite beverage, for example, extinction to the CR elicited by their beverage should gradually occur upon repeated exposure trials. Although this is a promising area of treatment, further research with controlled groups is necessary.

Aversive Therapies

While cue exposure techniques attempt to deal with cravings by extinction of the CR, an alternative approach is to change the valence of drinking-related cues through counterconditioning. In this paradigm, an aversive unconditioned stimulus (UCS) is paired with a conditioned stimulus (CS)—in this case, alcohol. Once conditioning has occurred, the client will experience an aversive CR to alcohol and hence will try to avoid future contact with it. Thus, an advantage to aversive techniques is that they lessen the client's desire to drink. Two common forms of aversive UCSs that have been shown to be effective in reducing alcohol consumption are electric shock and nausea-inducing drugs (Rimmele, Miller, & Dougher, 1989). Nausea-inducing drugs have been found to be the more effective of the two in reducing alcoholic drinking, possibly due to the greater similarity between modalities.

Traditional aversive therapies, however, pose difficulties. From an ethical standpoint, concerns exist regarding the inducement of stress; from a medical perspective, the procedures are more complicated and require medical supervision. An alternative to *in vivo* pairing of unpleasant events with alcohol, which avoids these drawbacks, is to do so imaginally. In covert sensitization (Rimmele et al., 1989), three phases of imaginal pairings are conditioned. Covert sensitization begins with guiding the client through positive imagery of his or her drinking experience; this is subsequently paired with an aversive response such as vomiting. In the second phase, the escape phase, the aversive response is followed with imagery suggesting nondrinking alternatives, enabling the client to achieve relief from the aversive experience by choosing not to continue drinking. In the third phase, the avoidance phase, nondrinking alternatives are provided prior to the client's experiencing any negative or unpleasant associations, suggesting that any unpleasant events can be avoided altogether by not drinking in the first place.

It is important in generating the scenarios that each guided image be tailored to the individual client. This is best achieved by conducting the sessions individually rather than in groups and by using the client's own experience and words in describing the scenes. Having clients collect self-monitoring data regarding their drinking episodes can provide the rich detail necessary for adequately creating the induction experience. It is important that a variety of settings and situations be covered, including types of beverages consumed, so that effects will generalize. For example, a client may drink beer at home after work, but may choose to drink whiskey when socializing with coworkers after a long day.

Three modalities of aversive sensitization include nausea scenes, in which the client is guided to imagine physically nauseating situations; assisted nausea, in which a noxious odor such as valeric acid is introduced during the sensitization procedure; and emotive scenes, where the aversive images are not of negative physical reactions but include strong feelings such as disgust, humiliation, anxiety, or horror.

With respect to the effectiveness of covert sensitization, results are mixed (Rimmele et al., 1989). One difficulty in interpreting the findings is that there is little consistency across studies regarding the sensitization procedures used. In general, however, results are encouraging and suggest that clearly defined sensitization procedures can be an effective treatment component when combined with methods aimed at teaching more effective coping alternatives to drinking.

A second form af aversive therapy is the use of antidipsotropic medication, which acts as an alcohol-sensitizing agent. Disulfiram (Antabuse) and calcium carbimide are two antidipsotropic medications used in alcohol treatment, although calcium carbimide is not available in the United States (Fuller, 1989; Peachey & Annis, 1984). These drugs are considered under aversive therapies because the consumption of alcohol while taking them results in physically violent reactions, including nausea, vomiting, headache, dizziness, difficulty breathing, and rapid or irregular heartbeat. Both the knowledge about and anticipation of the negative outcome of drinking while on such medications are meant to serve as general deterrents motivating the individual to avoid drinking.

Disulfiram and calcium carbimide produce this alcohol reaction by inhibiting the liver enzyme aldehyde dehydrogenase (ALDH), which catalyzes the oxidation of acetaldehyde to acetate. It is the buildup of acetaldehyde that is responsible for the unpleasant physical symptoms; therefore, if alcohol is not consumed, the reaction is avoided. However, there is a major pharmacological difference between these two drugs, which results in important treatment implications. The inhibition of ALDH is irreversible following disulfiram administration, and therefore at least 4 to 7 days are required after disulfiram is stopped for synthesis of new liver enzyme to take place. With calcium carbimide, the inhibition is not as complete, and only 24 hours are required for adequate enzyme synthesis.

On a treatment level this distinction is important, since much of the effectiveness of antidipsotropic interventions is that they deter drinking because of the patient's desire to avoid the violent physical reaction. Thus a patient must wait a week before he or she can safely resume drinking following disulfiram administration, but only needs to wait 24 hours with calcium carbimide. An advantage to disulfiram, then, is that the latency period allows the patient time for a more thorough consideration of his or her desire to drink (Fuller, 1989). If the drinking temptation is triggered by a crisis situation, it provides an opportunity to address the situation in a more effective way, without using alcohol. One suggestion for the effective use of calcium carbimide is for the client to take it on an as-needed basis, such as when anticipating a high-risk situation. Thus, disulfiram acts more as an aid against impulsive drinking, and calcium carbimide more as a preparation for encountering risky circumstances.

Fuller (1989) provides a thorough discussion of antidipsotropic medications in alcohol treatment. Little outcome research exists regarding the efficacy of calcium carbimide. However, there is more evidence regarding the effectiveness of disulfiram (Fuller, 1989; Fuller et al., 1986; Peachey & Annis, 1984). Because of the possibly severe physical reactions, it is very important to assess patients properly before prescribing disulfiram and to be sure that patients understand the implications of its use. Disulfiram is best used when it is a component of a larger, more comprehensive treatment program and is not the sole intervention provided. Results from a large, controlled clinical trial study (Fuller et al., 1986) suggest that disulfiram did not add additional benefit beyond counseling with respect to achieving continuous abstinence. However, in a subgroup of men who were older and more socially stable, disulfiram was found to reduce the number of drinking days significantly. It is also suggested that disulfiram may be most effective if it is not given as an initial treatment choice, but rather after a patient has attempted sobriety but experienced a relapse (Fuller, 1989). In addition to the pharmacological explanation of antidipsotropic action, patients state that the daily routine of taking the medication serves as a reminder that they cannot drink and must learn new ways to cope without the aid of alcohol. This form of positive expectancy concerning the effectiveness of disulfiram is consistent with the finding of Fuller et al. (1986) that a placebo condition was as effective overall as the active disulfiram condition. Finally, the administration of disulfiram is typically left up to the individual patient; however, there are situations in which monitoring by a counselor, pharmacist, or support person may prove beneficial (see Sisson & Azrin, 1989).

Control Strategies

A final cognitive–behavioral approach to alcohol intervention is that of self-control strategies. The client is seen as having primary responsibility for deciding what changes to make and for making them. The self-control approach includes behavioral techniques and educational information, which can be offered either in a group format with a facilitator or in a self-help manual. This approach is applicable to abstinence-oriented drinkers as well as to problem drinkers who wish to reduce their alcohol consumption.

One of the first decisions is whether the treatment goal is to be abstinence or moderation. This question can be answered as part of the self-control process. The steps as outlined by Hester and Miller (1989) are as follows: (1) setting limits on the number of drinks per day and week and on peak blood alcohol level (BAL); (2) self-monitoring drinking behaviors; (3) changing the rate of drinking; (4) practicing assertiveness in drink refusal; (5) setting up a reward system for achieving goals; (6) identifying which antecedents lead to drinking; and (7) learning coping alternatives to drinking. If there is a question as to whether abstinence is necessary or whether moderation is an acceptable goal, the client can begin at Step 1, setting daily drink and BAL limits. The degree of difficulty that is experienced in reducing alcohol intake in compliance with this goal is a good indication of the severity of the alcohol problem. A goal of abstinence is highly recommended for severely physically dependent individuals.

Self-monitoring involves having clients record information about their drinking just before they consume the alcohol. The information includes date, time, place, emotional state, type of alcohol, alcoholic content, and the person or persons they are with. Providing the client with a card on which to keep this information enhances the likelihood of successful monitoring. It is also helpful to anticipate difficulties clients may encounter as they start keeping this information and to role-play effective strategies for addressing these situations. The goal of monitoring is twofold. First, the clients must focus on their drinking, which brings it to their awareness. Often clients express surprise when they realize how much alcohol they typically consume. Second, the action of monitoring helps to reinforce their treatment goal of moderation as they are reminded of why they are filling out the card.

The next step is to have clients modify their rate of drinking. Instead of quickly gulping drinks down, they are taught to take smaller sips and at a reduced rate. Through a process similar to shaping, the clients are instructed to gradually reduce the strength of the drinks they consume by adding more mixer, switching from hard liquor to wine, and perhaps eventually drinking a nonalcoholic beverage such as "near beer." Clients can also alternate alcoholic beverages with nonalcoholic drinks in an attempt to space their drinks over a longer period of time.

It is beneficial to instruct clients in drink refusal skills, as this will enhance their ability to adhere to their treatment goals. A group format in which tempting scenarios are role-played provides group members with an opportunity to see how others would cope with similar situations. It is helpful to videotape the role plays and allow clients to critique themselves and observe how others see them. A second run-through of the same scenarios allows the clients to incorporate group feedback as well as their own observations.

Positive reinforcement for achievements is an effective way to enhance adherence to treatment goals. The rewards should be individually derived, based on what a client feels are special "treats" for his or her accomplishments. There are a few guidelines for selecting rewards. First, the reward should be realistic. Celebrating a week of abstinence by purchasing a new stereo is unrealistic if the client cannot afford it. A more realistic goal might be to save drinking money and at the end of the week use it to purchase a new compact disc. Second, the reward should be of a value comparable to the accomplishment. A week's worth of abstinence might be rewarded by going to a movie; a year of abstinence might deserve a special vacation. And finally, the reward should be delivered as close in time to the achievement as possible. Delaying the reward reduces the association made between goal attainment and pleasure. Clearly, the valence of rewards is an individual matter, but they should be something enjoyable and special. Making this a concrete exercise by actually writing down what constitutes an accomplishment and the ensuing reward will again serve to remind clients of their commitment, as well as to increase the probability that they will follow through with their plan.

From the self-monitoring data collected in Step 2, clients should be able to recognize patterns in their drinking. What situations, times of day or evening, people, moods, or places represent the biggest threats to their sobriety? Once risky antecedents are identified, new strategies can be generated—from anticipating the risk and better preparing for it, to avoiding the situation altogether.

In summary, self-control strategies include steps to help clients become aware of when, what, where and why they are drinking. With this awareness, they now have the choice to modify their consumption patterns by slowing down their drinking, learning effective ways to refuse drinks, feeling good about not drinking by achieving pleasure in other ways, and anticipating difficult situations and developing more effective coping strategies to conquer these difficulties. The emphasis is on personal responsibility for changing behavior. Kanfer (1986) suggests that rather than emphasizing the evils of alcohol through threats, a more effective strategy is to help clients recognize the advantages of sobriety and to instill a sense of hope and positive anticipation of the benefits of an alcohol-free life.

Stages of Change: Timing Is Important

In keeping with Kanfer's view of effective change strategies, Prochaska and DiClemente (1986) have proposed a comprehensive model for understanding the change process. As in Kanfer's notion, the client is seen as the critical change agent, and the change process is not static but one that evolves in a predictable yet recursive manner. A match should exist between treatment and the natural progression of events the client experiences as he or she considers, attempts, and eventually maintains a change in his or her behavior.

Prochaska and DiClemente (1986) define four stages of change through which an individual progresses: precontemplation, contemplation, action, and maintenance. In the precontemplation stage, the individual is not yet aware that his or her behavior may need modification. Prochaska and DiClemente suggest that environmental or developmental changes may occur to trigger the move from precontemplation to contemplation. For example, behavior that was acceptable in a person's 20s may no longer fit as the individual moves into his or her 30s.

In the contemplation stage, the individual begins to consider whether a behavior change would be beneficial. For example, it may be recognized that heavy drinking is no longer as conducive to a work schedule as it was to a student lifestyle. Thus begins the contemplation of changing behavior. At this point, receptivity to education and self-evaluation are high as the individual considers what would constitute a change, how he or she might benefit, and what are some possible risks or negative consequences of change.

Once the decision to change has been made, the transition to the action stage is begun. Here the client begins to adopt the behavior change strategies derived during the contemplation stage. In the example provided above of heavy drinking, the client may decide to drink only on weekends and limit the number of drinks he or she consumes on such occasions. Instead of going to the bar after work with buddies, the client may switch to going to the gym and working out with new, nondrinking friends.

With a change in behavior, it is essential to consider maintenance of those changes. The methods that are effective in stopping a behavior, such as alcohol consumption, are not necessarily the same strategies employed to maintain those changes (Brownell, Marlatt, Lichtenstein, & Wilson, 1986; Mackay & Marlatt, in press).

As stated previously, a benefit of a stage model of change is that different interventions are more or less appropriate, depending on the client's position in the change process. Strategies used to convince someone of the need to stop or reduce alcohol consumption are different from the strategies employed once a decision to change has been made, and those are different still from the strategies used to maintain the behavior change. In the contemplation stage, individuals are most receptive to consciousness-raising methods such as observations, confrontations, and interpretations (Prochaska & DiClemente, 1983). In this stage the client is often motivated by a desire to avoid the negative consequences of his or her current behavior, such as avoiding hangovers, rather than a desire for the positive consequences resulting from such a change. Kanfer would suggest that an essential part of effective change is that the client begin to recognize and be motivated by the presence of positive change, not just the absence of negative consequences. A self-evaluation process begins in which the client begins to consider the personal consequences of behavior change. This can carry into the next stage, when action is taken.

In the action stage, it is important that a sense of self-determination exist—in other words, that the client see himself or herself as responsible for and capable of making changes. This process is similar to the construct of self-efficacy (Bandura, 1977b), in which the individual evaluates his or her ability to accomplish what he or she intends to. Two additional interventions that facilitate change during the action stage are the presence of supportive relationships in the form of accountability and encouragement, and the receipt of rewards for accomplishments or treatment achievements.

Finally, during the maintenance stage, there is a sense of accomplishment as initial goals have been achieved. With this comes a renewed commitment to stick to changes made. An important consideration at this point is the possibility of relapse. This model of change is cyclical, and an individual who has progressed through all the stages may find himself or herself relapsing. This can be an indication that a visit back to the contemplation stage is necessary as the individual re-evaluates the reasons for and commitment to change. Perhaps new strategies are added, such as beginning disulfiram medication or family therapy. Rather than being an indication of failure, relapse may serve as a signal that reinforcements are needed to the behavior change program.

Relapse Prevention: A Cognitive–Behavioral Model

Overview

Despite the individual's best efforts and commitment to stop drinking, there is a high probability that he or she will return to alcohol use, with the highest period of risk often within the first 90 days after stopping use. Within the cognitive–behavioral perspective, there is an important distinction between taking an initial drink following a period of sobriety and a subsequent return to a pattern or level of consumption comparable to that prior to the decision to stop. The former condition has been described as a "lapse" whereas the latter has been defined as a "relapse." A lapse refers to a single instance in which the individual has violated the decision to change his or her drinking pattern, whether the initial goal was abstinence or self-controlled moderation. Relapse is defined as a more serious breakdown or failure in the person's longer-term attempt to change the target behavior.

A number of important points should be made about relapse. First, in the absence of a commitment to change, drinking behavior even following a period of abstinence should be viewed as neither a lapse nor a relapse. Rather, drinking in the absence of a commitment to change represents a continuation of the typical pattern of behavior. Second, the principles involved in the initial process of getting "clean and sober" appear to be different from those important in the maintenance of these positive gains. Third, a return to drinking for someone who has made a strong commitment to change need not be viewed as an all-or-none phenomenon. Rather, relapse represents a complex, dynamic process, determined by multiple factors and having a number of cognitive, attributional, and affective consequences. However, as a component of a larger process, an initial lapse need not lead necessarily to a more serious relapse. As is implied by the stages-of-change model presented by Prochaska and Di-Clemente (1986), an initial lapse represents a transition point. It may serve to help the person reconsider his or her initial commitment, and may lead to a decision to take additional steps to regain and maintain the desired target goal. On the other hand, it may lead the individual to feel that he or she is a failure for whom there is no future hope, and thus may perpetuate drinking. Related to these possible alternative outcomes, Saunders and Allsop (1987) noted that over 90% of individuals who have attained a goal of abstinence will have used again within a 12-month period; approximately 45–50% will have returned to their pretreatment level of use within this time frame.

A number of different clinical approaches have been developed to help the individual maintain the positive changes brought about through either self-change attempts or formal treatment and to minimze the likelihood of relapse. Despite being based on somewhat different theoretical perspectives of addictions and the underlying determinants of relapse, these relapse prevention approaches share a number of clinical intervention strategies derived from cognitive–behavioral social learning theory (see Donovan & Chaney, 1985, for a more thorough description of the different models of relapse prevention). The model of relapse and its prevention developed by Marlatt and colleagues (George, 1989; Marlatt & George, 1984; Marlatt & Gordon, 1985, 1989) and elaborated by others (e.g., Allsop & Saunders, 1989; Annis & Davis, 1989a; Brownell et al., 1986; Heather & Stallard, 1989; Monti et al., 1989; Shiffman, 1989) has had a major impact on both theory and treatment in the addictions. This section provides a brief overview of this relapse prevention approach, using it as a heuristic model that integrates factors derived from other approaches to relapse prevention and from the specific cognitive–behavioral strategies discussed above.

Relapse prevention consists of a combination of training procedures in behavioral coping skills and cognitive intervention techniques; these have as primary goals the maintenance of positive behavior change, the prevention of relapse, and the development of a more balanced and healthful general lifestyle. The individual is helped to become more aware of those personal, interpersonal, emotional, and situational factors that increase the risk of relapse. An attempt is made to help the individual develop those cognitive and behavioral coping skills necessary to deal with the identified relapse risks effectively and without resorting to drinking. As the intervention process continues, the focus is directed toward the individual's making changes in more general personal habits as a way to gain a more balanced lifestyle and to reduce the level of psychological stress. Finally, individuals are taught about the predictable aftereffects of a lapse if it does occur and the methods to cope with these, in order to keep an initial drinking incident from escalating into a more serious relapse episode. Relapse prevention is a self-control program in which an ultimate goal is to facilitate the individual's ability to self-administer the maintenance techniques that have been learned when confronted with a risk of relapse after the more formal therapy process has been completed.

Relapse Risk

Despite what many alcoholic clients tell us and would want us (and themselves) to believe, relapse is not a random event that "just happens." It appears, on the contrary, that a number of background characteristics of individuals, more general lifestyle characteristics, and more specific circumstances are fairly predictive of an increased likelihood of relapse. Some of these factors are more distant or distal, both in time and in influence on the possibility of relapse (Marlatt & Gordon, 1989; Shiffman, 1989), yet may contribute to a more generalized "relapse proneness." More enduring personal characteristics that have been suggested to fall within this latter category include basic demographic variables, personality factors, degree of alcohol dependence, family-of-origin issues, and familial history of substance use. Somewhat less distal are what Shiffman (1989) describes as "background variables." These factors do not relate specifically to the characteristics of the individual per se, but rather to his or her experiences during the maintenance period. A particularly relevant example in this category is the relative level of stress experienced across time by the individual in his or her personal, professional, and/or interpersonal areas of functioning. This may also reflect the degree of balance between the "shoulds" or demands that the individual is experiencing, relative to the "wants" or ability to engage in more pleasurable and rewarding activities. Often when the individual is under stress as a background context, there is an imbalance in this relationship, leading to feelings of dissatisfaction, frustration, and deprivation.

The final area contributing to relapse risk is that of the more proximal precipitants associated wtih high-risk situations. Cummings, Gordon, and Marlatt (1980) found in one study that although there were a variety of possible relapse precipitants, the greatest number of relapses could be accounted for by three general categories. The first included an interpersonal situation involving peer pressure to use. This pressure was either direct, in which a person was offered a drink by someone, or more subtle and indirect. The latter situation often involved "hanging out" with former drinking buddies (often in a familiar bar or tavern setting, drinking coffee and playing pool) or being at a party where everyone else was drinking. The second category involved negative emotions of an intrapersonal nature. These included feelings of depression, anxiety, loneliness, boredom, and lack of time structure. It is important to note that this situation is in many ways the converse of social pressure as a precipitant. Given that many treatment programs as well as self-control approaches suggest the need to avoid the people, places, and activities associated with drinking, the individual may lose what had been an important (or in many cases the only) source of social and emotional reinforcement and time structure. The result may be an increase in those negative emotional states (e.g., loneliness, boredom) that are associated with relapse risk. The final category was interpersonal in nature, involving anger and resentment that most often was associated with an interpersonal conflict with a person important to the individual (e.g., spouse, family member, boss). These three general categories accounted for over 70% of the relapse situations reviewed by Cummings et al. (1980).

Shiffman (1989) indicates that an understanding of the relapse process requires consideration of factors at all three levels of influence. The more distal personal and background characteristics serve as the backdrop or predisposing factors that produce a vulnerability to relapse; they help explain the "risky" nature of the more specific interpersonal and intrapersonal situations that precipitate drinking. That is, it is the situation as experienced and interpreted by the individual in terms of this backdrop that is important. This helps to explain the individual variability across relapse precipitants.

A number of commonalities can be noted in the more proximal situations associated with a return to use. Each of these has an important bearing on potential areas of assessment and intervention within the relapse prevention model. First, as suggested above, the individual's appraisal of the situation is crucial. In most cases, those situations having a high risk of relapse involve some degree of perceived threat to the individual's sense of control, either of other people and their actions or of the person's own behavior and feelings. Thus, a primary appraisal by relapse-vulnerable individuals is that such situations are threatening them interpersonally or intrapersonally or to their own abilities to remain sober. The individual also evaluates the situation in terms of his or her ability to cope effectively with the demands being experienced in the situation. The outcome of this secondary appraisal process also influences the person's perception of self-efficacy. If through prior experiences with the specific or similar situations, the person believes that he or she both has and can successfully employ the coping skills needed to solve the problem or maintain a sense of control in the situation, it will be perceived as relatively nonthreatening, and the person's self-efficacy will be increased. However, such secondary appraisals often lead to an increased sense of anxiety or concern on the individual's part when either the requisite coping skills are not available or the person is unable to generate or use those coping skills that he or she does have.

A second commonality is that these situations involve a number of cues that may elicit conditioned craving responses. The presence of people, places, activities, and emotional states that have previously been paired with drinking can pull forward urges or cravings on both a physiological and a cognitive–expectational level. Although the exact mechanism underlying the classical conditioning process is still debated, it appears that such cues and the resultant phenomenologically experienced craving play a potentially greater role in relapse than had originally been considered within cognitive–behavioral formulations (e.g., Heather & Stallard, 1989). Heather and Stallard (1989) postulate that interpersonal and intrapersonal situations cannot lead directly to relapse, but must be mediated by an emotional state, either positive or negative. The emotional state in turn leads to a form of craving to drink, either directly, or indirectly by means of social pressure and the presence of drinking-related cues. Under appropriate circumstances, the craving precipitates relapse. Within this perspective, these cues and the conditioned craving represent the most proximal precipitant and the final common pathway through which relapse is mediated.

A third commonality is that the recovering individual does not just stumble into these situations (although, unfortunately, he or she may end up stumbling out of them!). The pathway that may lead ultimately and finally to the strong pull of craving typically began some time previously in a series of what have been described as "apparently irrelevant decisions." These represent a series of decisions that, at the time they were made, appeared to the individual to have no bearing on the ultimate probability of relapse. However, often within the context of the more distal background characteristics of the person's life, these decisions set in motion a chain of events leading the individual closer to a high-risk situation. An actual clinical example is helpful. Following a successful recovery through an inpatient treatment program, an alcoholic patient resumed drinking during the aftercare phase of treatment. When asked what had occurred, he stated that he had "been down at the local tavern, because they serve the best sandwiches in Seattle." After the initial shock of this response wore off (hearing is not always believing!), a more thorough exploration of the relapse precipitants was conducted. In fact, this was a retired individual who prior to treatment had spent most of his waking day drinking and socializing at this tavern, which was located on the same block where he lived. After a period of avoiding the old haunt, he began to feel lonely, isolated, and depressed. He finally began to feel resentful and sorry for himself and his "not being able to do like all the other guys." He went down to the tavern to have lunch and see his old friends. He got caught up in the social life of the group; felt that it was important to be part of the group; and "before I knew it, I was drinking again." The story illustrates the degree to which this man had set himself up to drink by making an apparently irrelevant decision. Others could see what appeared to be his cognitive distortions in the form of rationalizations about going for the food (there are better places in Seattle to get sandwiches, many of which do not serve alcohol!), and his "stinking thinking" in the form of his feelings of resentment about "Others can do it, why can't I?" The example further demonstrates the degree of complexity involved in, and the interactive and dynamic relationship among, relapse precipitants and high-risk situations (Heather & Stallard, 1989).

A final commonality across these situations has to do with the expectancies that people have developed about the effects alcohol will have on them. It is of note that what one expects alcohol to do is not always accurate with respect to its actual results (Donovan & Marlatt, 1980). The primary outcome expectancy involves alcohol's serving as a "magic elixir," enhancing positive feelings and minimizing negative mood states. It is expected that alcohol will enhance social and physical pleasure, enchance sexual performance and responsiveness, increase power and aggressiveness, increase social assertiveness, and reduce tension (Goldman, Brown, & Christiansen, 1987). These beliefs about alcohol's positive effects typically still reside in the individual's "selective memory," are often powerful in nature, and can contribute to the increased risk of relapse. It appears that these expectancies are enhanced and made more salient in those emotional and interpersonal situations previously associated with drinking. Furthermore, it appears that they are associated with, influenced by, and may represent the cognitive manifestations of the conditioned craving elicited by the cues encountered in these situations.

Implications for Assessment

The cognitive–behavioral model of relapse has a number of implications for assessment (Donovan, 1988; Sobell, Sobell, & Nirenberg, 1988). First, assessment represents the first step in the longer process of treatment. Although contemplating change, the individual may initially be ambivalent about giving up drinking. The assessment process can serve to enhance the individual's commitment and motivation to change by "hooking" the side of the client's ambivalence that is inclined toward changing. Miller (1989) has presented a number of interviewing techniques to help motivate the client to move from the contemplation and commitment stage into the action stage. These methods involve increasing the attractiveness of a new behavior and lifestyle associated with the cessation of drinking, and helping to reduce the fears and concerns about change. The general principles involved in this process include a de-emphasis on requiring that the person accept the label of "alcoholic"; a focus on the individual's responsibility for both a thorough self-evaluation of the problem and tentative decisions about the appropriate course of action; an emphasis on the individual's accepting the responsibility for positive changes, attributing them to his or her efforts; and efforts to increase the person's awareness of the discrepancy between continued drinking and important personal beliefs, attitudes, values, and feelings, and then to direct the resultant cognitive dissonance toward an increased motivation for positive change.

Relapse is multiply determined; the factors contributing to a return to drinking are experienced in physiological, cognitive/expectational, emotional/affective, and psychosocial domains. As such, the assessment process needs to be comprehensive and biopsychosocial in nature (Donovan, 1988). As Shiffman (1989) has noted, in order to adequately understand relapse, it is necessary to consider factors from the three levels of personal characteristics, background variables, and more specific high-risk precipitants.

A number of target areas are particularly relevant for assessment in this regard. The first includes the nature, scope, and strength of the individual's coping skills. Chaney (1989) has defined "coping skills" as the ability to use thought, emotion, and action to solve interpersonal and intrapersonal problems. A number of dimensions of coping need to be taken into account (Shiffman, 1989). First, it is important to assess coping skills needed to deal both with general stress (e.g., DeNelsky & Boat, 1986) and with more specific temptations to drink or use again (Wills & Shiffman, 1985). Somewhat different skills appear to be needed to deal with the demands experienced in these two areas, and those skills that the individual has in dealing with general stressors may not generalize to temptation coping situations (e.g., Mackay, 1988).

Second, both behavioral and cognitive coping strategies need to be assessed. It appears that more concrete behavioral coping strategies, such as avoiding drinking friends and settings or engaging in behaviors incompatible with drinking, are more important earlier in recovery, whereas cognitive strategies, such as thinking about the negative consequences of drinking or the positive benefits of sobriety, are more important in the subsequent maintenance phase (Litman, 1986; Litman, Eiser, Rawson, & Oppenheim, 1979). It is also important to determine the individual's tendency to rely more heavily on one or the other of these two forms of coping. Another aspect of this assessment is determining the balance between either having or not having coping skills and either deciding to use them or choosing not to use them in increasing the risk of relapse (Saunders & Allsop, 1987). It is likely that relapse risk is high in the case of either a person who is committed to change but lacks adequate coping skills, or one who is quite skillful but is not firmly resolved and committed to stop drinking. A final dimension to be assessed involves the stages of coping (Shiffman, 1989). These include anticipatory coping, which allows the individual to prevent, avoid, or minimize temptation through planning and stimulus control techniques; immediate coping, which is a response to an immediate threat to abstinence in a high-risk situation or in the face of craving; and restorative coping, which involves the abilities to cope with and overcome the impact of a relapse if it does occur.

Another major area to assess within this model includes the person's level of drinking-specific self-efficacy (Annis & Davis, 1988). Annis and colleagues (Annis & Davis, 1988, 1989a) have developed two assessment procedures that are particularly helpful in this regard. The first is the Inventory of Drinking Situations (IDS). The questionnaire consists of a number of items (versions of different lengths are available) describing situations in which drinking may have occurred in the past. The items fall into eight categories based on those determined by Cummings et al. (1980) to be most highly associated with relapse. These include unpleasant emotions, physical discomfort, pleasant emotions, testing personal control, urges and temptations to drink, interpersonal conflict, social pressure to drink, and pleasant times with others. The individual is asked to rate the frequency with which he or she drank heavily in each of the situations during the past year. The IDS is based on the notion of "habit strength hierarchies" derived from Hullian learning theory; it is assumed that those situations rated most highly with respect to previous drinking represent the greatest risk for relapse. A related measure, the Situational Confidence Questionnaire (SCQ), asks the subject to rate how confident he or she is that it would be possible to resist the temptation to drink in each of the situations. These measures are helpful in determining those situations of greatest concern for the individual and those in which he or she feels the least confident and at greatest risk.

A final point about assessment is that it is a continuous and interactive process (Donovan, 1988; Shiffman, 1989). Brownell et al. (1986) have noted that it is important to consider the interaction of individual, environmental, and physiological factors at each stage of the change process. The target of assessment will change across time, because the individual's skills, perception of self-efficacy, appraisal of the risk involved in different situations, and the extent and nature of social support evolve as the individual implements self-control strategies during maintenance. Assessment at these different stages is helpful both to monitor such changes and to reinforce and further motivate the positive gains the individual has made.

Intervention Strategies

The primary goal of relapse prevention is to minimize the likelihood of the individual's returning to drinking by increasing his or her adaptive coping and problem-solving skills, enhancing the perception of confidence and self-efficacy, and helping him or her to deal more effectively with urges and temptations to drink. Although a number of different intervention strategies may be included in this process (see Marlatt & Gordon, 1985, for a more thorough presentation of these), the cognitive and behavioral methods most frequently used are directed at these three primary target areas.

The first area is helping the individual to develop or enhance both general and temptation-specific coping skills. Monti et al. (1989) have developed a comprehensive coping skills training program that has the prevention of relapse as its primary goal. The specific areas of intervention will depend on the individual and his or her assessed needs. However, potential areas include recognition of personally relevant "warning signs" of high-risk situations, interpersonal communication skills, assertiveness training, relaxation training and more general stress management, anger management and conflict resolution skills, mood management, leisure time structuring, and management techniques. Another important focus is on training the individual in generalized problem-solving skills that can be applied across a wide range of potentially problematic situations. Standard skills training techniques (see Chaney, 1989, for more information on this approach), including modeling, coaching, role playing, instruction, performance feedback, and behavioral rehearsal, are employed in the skill acquisition process. These techniques can be supplemented further by the use of cognitive therapy approaches, such as instructional self-statements (e.g., Meichenbaum, 1977) to help anticipate, prepare for, and maintain coping in high-risk situations, and cognitive restructuring techniques (e.g., Ellis et al., 1988) in which the person is taught to appraise such situations more accurately and to challenge distortions, rationalizations, and irrational beliefs (i.e., "stinking thinking") that contribute to making "apparently irrelevant decisions."

As Allsop and Saunders (1989) note, positive outcome of treatment with alcoholics may be due less to their having coping skills available to them than to their belief that the coping skills they do have will work. This emphasizes the need for interventions that focus on the person's self-efficacy expectancies. Annis and Davis (1989a) outline the use of "homework assignments" within a relapse prevention program; these are meant to increase the individual's beliefs that he or she can cope effectively with high-risk situations. This approach is based on the assumption that the best way of instilling a high level of self-efficacy or confidence in the individual is through actual performance or homework assignments in the "natural environment." The individual is gradually exposed to increasingly challenging risk situations for relapse as these are experienced by the individual in his or her everyday activities and relationships. The homework assignments, as well as the hierarchy of relapse risk on which they are based, are derived from the results of the IDS and the SCQ, administered during the initial assessment.

A number of basic principles are involved in these assignments. First, they must involve some exposure to a drinking situation of sufficient risk that the individual experiences some challenge in maintaining his or her goal (e.g., not drinking). Second, the person should be able to enter the planned drinking risk situation and should be able to experience success in coping with only a moderate degree of effort. Thus, appropriate titration of the "dose" and use of a hierarchy of risk situations are involved. The person should be neither overwhelmed by too great an effort or risk (with the result that he or she becomes discouraged, feels unable to cope, and possibly "fails" by drinking in the situation), nor confronted by a level of risk insufficient to allow the person to feel a sense of personal mastery by successfully coping and "passing" the test. Third, the individual must be able to attribute improved coping skills to his or her efforts rather than to the presence of external aids, such as the therapist, spouse, or alcohol-sensitizing drugs such as disulfiram. Finally, the individual should come to see that the situations involved in the homework are personally relevant, that the success evidenced in coping with these situations along the hierarchy is part of an overall pattern of improved coping, and that this improvement can be attributed to an increase in personal control over drinking behavior. Annis and Davis (1989b) have indicated that such techniques are effective in increasing client's ratings of self-efficacy over the course of treatment and contribute to successful treatment outcome.

A final area of focus within relapse prevention is helping the person deal with the urges and cravings to drink. This represents the more specific area of temptation coping (Wills & Shiffman, 1985). A number of cognitive strategies have been used in this regard (see Marlatt & Gordon, 1985, for a more thorough description). These include instructing the individual that craving is likely to occur; that to experience such feelings does not represent a failure of treatment or of the individual's commitment; that craving typically increases, peaks, and then recedes, much like a cresting wave, and that the individual can successfully "ride out" the urges without falling; and that it is possible to cognitively detach oneself from these feelings (i.e., to separate feeling from action). A number of behavioral intervention strategies have also been employed. One of these involves the very concrete avoidance of high-risk situations and those people, places, and activities previously associated with drinking. A related but somewhat less restrictive approach involves stimulus control procedures that reduce one's exposure to or remove cues associated with drinking (e.g., keeping no beer in the refrigerator, removing beer mugs or wine glasses, etc.). Clients are also helped to verbally label their urges as they become aware of them. In addition, it is useful to help the individual learn to distinguish what are experienced as global, undifferentiated feelings of craving from the emotional, cognitive, and situational cues that elicit such feelings. If such feelings are experienced, the individual is encouraged to perform some activity that breaks the continuity of the urge and the person's focus on it. Litman et al. (1979) indicated that those individuals who were able to avoid relapse often used avoidance and distraction strategies during the initial phases of their recovery, followed over time by an increased reliance on cognitive strategies.

An area in which cognitive–behavioral approaches to relapse prevention have been criticized is their relative lack of attention to other methods to deal with conditioned craving and urges (Heather & Stallard, 1989). It is assumed that those cues that elicit craving are typically positively valenced. It is suggested that an increase in the use of methods designed to specifically counteract conditioned craving would be important. Two approaches are suggested theoretically. The first is counterconditioning, most often exemplified in aversive conditioning techniques. The goal of such approaches is to pair those cues that were previously associated with drinking and that are capable of eliciting craving with aversive consequences, such as pharmacologically or cognitively/imaginally induced nausea. Following treatment along these lines, there will be a shift in the valence of the drinking-related cues; they will come to elicit an aversive CR rather than craving. Of the two possible approaches to counterconditioning, covert sensitization appears to fit better within the context of a self-control strategy: It is more easily generalizable; it allows for the cognitive rehearsal of other methods of avoiding, escaping from, or coping with the risk situation; it is more consistent with modifying one's appraisal of such situations; and it is more likely to allow the attribution of change to personal factors rather than external aids, with a resultant increase in self-efficacy, than is the use of nausea-inducing drugs.

The second theoretical approach to craving involves an extinction paradigm, most often implemented in cue exposure techniques. In this case, the person is exposed to those cues that over the past have been most highly associated with drinking, but without the subsequent use of alcohol. The result over time is an extinction of the CR, with a resultant decrease in the power of these cues to "pull" cravings forward. This approach is consistent with the exposure of individuals to progressively riskier situations in the homework assignments used to increase self-efficacy (Annis & Davis, 1989a). The incorporation of such cue exposure techniques with the cognitive and behavioral coping approaches of relapse prevention has been advocated as a way of increasing the effectiveness of treatment outcome (Heather & Stallard, 1989; Niaura et al., 1988).

The use of alcohol-sensitizing drugs such as disulfiram and calcium carbimide may also be integrated into relapse prevention programs that focus on the goal of abstinence. Their use can be presented within the context of a self-control strategy (e.g., "Each day I take my Antabuse I am making a commitment to myself not to drink"), and may be most useful during the early phases of recovery, when relapse risk is greatest. Peachey and Annis (1986) have suggested that such drugs can also be used before encountering situations that the individual has learned to recognize as having a high risk of relapse associated with them. When using such drugs, the individual may be able to enter high-risk situations without the immediate concern about drinking, given the deterrent influence of the anticipated negative consequences of alcohol's interaction with such medicines. This would allow a shift in the appraisal of the risk associated with such situations, and potentially would allow a reduction in conditioned craving through exposure to and extinction of drinking cues. However, the continued use of such drugs may lead the individual to attribute positive changes to the presence of an external aid rather than to his or her own efforts. In order to allow the person to increase the level of perceived self-efficacy, Peachey and Annis (1984, 1986) have advocated that the use of such drugs be faded out over the latter stages of treatment.

Parameters of Intervention

An advantage of relapse prevention is its versatility, with its ability to be implemented within a number of different settings. Although relapse prevention is based on a cognitive–social learning perspective of addiction and relapse (e.g., Marlatt, Baer, Donovan, & Kivlahan, 1988), it can be used in combination with a number of different approaches. Its primary goal is to maintain positive behavior changes that have been either self-initiated or associated with more formal treatment. Since it appears that different processes and priniciples are involved in the cessation of drinking and the subsequent maintenance of abstinence, relapse prevention may be applied regardless of the theoretical orientation or methods used in treatments aimed at initial drinking cessation and stabilization.

A relapse prevention approach based on coping skills training has been employed as a component of inpatient treatment (e.g., Chaney et al., 1978;

Daley, 1988), as the focus of aftercare following inpatient treatment (e.g., Annis & Davis, 1989a; Ito, Donovan & Hall, 1988; Kadden, Cooney, Getter, & Litt, 1989), and as a free-standing outpatient approach (e.g., Monti et al., 1989). There are still questions about the most appropriate timing of specific components of relapse prevention in the treatment process. A two-phase process has been suggested (Abrams, Niaura, Carey, Monti, & Binkoff, 1986; Brownell et al., 1986), and the need to determine the right mixture of relapse prevention components in both the initial treatment and the maintenance phases has been stressed. Brownell et al. (1986) have suggested that a focus on decision-making and problem-solving skills, cognitive restructuring, and coping skills acquisition should be included in the initial phase, during which the person is becoming sober and stabilized. During the maintenance phase, the emphasis shifts to continued self-monitoring, the development and expansion of social support, and more general lifestyle changes. Annis and Davis (1989a) have noted that the initial assessment, treatment planning, and development and training of coping responses may be accomplished during an inpatient treatment; however, the homework assignments in which the person is exposed to high-risk situations and practices alternative coping strategies are best conducted on an outpatient basis, while the person is functioning in his or her normal living situation.

Both individual and group therapy formats have been employed in delivering relapse prevention (see Monti et al., 1989, for descriptions of both approaches). The individualized nature of the assessment process, the person-specific nature of the high-risk situations, and the development of and work on the individualized drinking risk hierarchy all contribute to an individual therapy format (Annis & Davis, 1989a). However, Chaney (1989) has noted that in the area of coping skills training, important aspects of the treatment—particularly modeling, rehearsal, and feedback—probably occur more powerfully in a group setting. A client model whose skill level is only somewhat greater than that of a peer observer is likely to have a greater impact than a skilled therapist. Rehearsal with and feedback from peers are likely to be more realistic than in individual treatment and may also serve to facilitate generalizability. In addition, the coping skills involved in the relapse prevention approach are meant to provide a means of obtaining social support that is important in maintaining sobriety; the group setting provides a greater opportunity for the development of such support than is found in individual treatment. Annis and Davis (1989a) suggest that if a group format is employed, each client may be seen individually for 5–10 minutes following the group session to formalize and record the homework assignments for the coming week.

Treatment Effectiveness

Relapse prevention has served as a heuristic model that has stimulated considerable clinical activity. It has also led to an increase in treatment outcome evaluations, although these appear to have lagged behind the rate of clinical implementation. Miller and Hester (1986) found in their review of alcoholism treatment approaches that controlled research clearly supports the efficacy of coping skills training. In a more recent review of the cost-effectiveness of treatments for alcohol problems, Holder, Longabaugh, Miller, and Rubonis (in press) found that 10 well-controlled studies supported the superiority of social skills training to control conditions; there were no studies in which the comparison conditions were found to be superior. Of the 35 treatment approaches reviewed, coping skills training had the highest level of overall empirical support and was placed at the top of a category labeled "good evidence of effect." As Chaney (1989) concluded, coping skills training "has received sufficient empirical validation to be ensured a permanent role in alcoholism treatment" (p. 219).

Although the support for skills training is strong, there are fewer data concerning the effectiveness of a more extensive, integrated relapse prevention approach in which skills training is only one of the components (Holder et al., in press). Allsop and Saunder (1989) have presented initial findings from an experimental relapse prevention and management package that was added to a standard inpatient program for problem drinkers. It consisted of a detailed assessment of subjective high-risk situations, the use of motivational interviewing techniques to increase the strength of commitment to change, and problem-solving techniques. Two subjects and a therapist formed treatment teams that met for eight 1-hour sessions. The relapse prevention package relied on action-oriented skills training methods to help patients develop active coping skills. This package was compared to a discussion group focusing on the same topics but without the use of behavioral rehearsal, and a group that received no additional treatment over and above the inpatient program. It was found that the relapse prevention program was superior to the other conditions at the 6-month follow-up in terms of increased ratings of drinking-related self-efficacy and decreased levels of drinking behavior and alcohol-related problems. It was also found that the best predictor of outcome at 6 months was the level of self-efficacy as rated at the end of the initial treatment.

A number of treatment × client interactions have been investigated recently, suggesting that relapse prevention may be more appropriate or effective for some alcoholics than for others. Kadden et al. (1989) compared a broad-spectrum coping skills treatment to an interactional process-oriented approach during aftercare following inpatient rehabilitation. There was no overall difference in drinking outcome measures across the treatment conditions at follow-up, a finding replicating that of Ito et al. (1988). However, patients who were more sociopathic and those who had higher levels of general psychopathology had better outcomes in the structured coping skills group than in the interpersonal groups. Those with lower levels of sociopathy did better in the interactional groups, while those with low levels of psychopathology did comparably well in either group. Annis and Davis (1989b) compared relapse prevention with more traditional counseling during aftercare. No differences were found across conditions among those patients who had "generalized profiles" on the IDS (suggesting similar levels of risk across all the assessed drinking risk situations). However, those with "differentiated profiles" (suggesting greater risk in some types of situation than others) did significantly better with respect to subsequent drinking outcome in the relapse prevention group than in the traditional counseling. It was found that the client–treatment matching effect accounted for over 30% of the outcome variance on the measures of drinking at follow-up.

Summary and Conclusions

The relapse prevention model based on cognitive–social learning theory was derived originally from work with alcohol-dependent individuals (e.g., Chaney et al., 1978; Marlatt & Gordon, 1985; Ito et al., 1988). The goal for treatment of such individuals has been their acquisition and maintenance of abstinence. A future direction, however, is the development and implementation of self-control programs to serve as secondary prevention strategies with individuals who do not meet the diagnostic criteria for alcohol dependence (e.g., Baer, Kivlahan, Fromme, & Marlatt, in press; Kivlahan, Coppel, Fromme, Williams, & Marlatt, 1990). In such an approach, the cognitive–behavioral principles derived from the relapse prevention model are directed toward a goal of moderation in drinking. Individuals are helped to define appropriate drinking goals, to recognize those interpersonal and intrapersonal situations that increase the likelihood of violating the specified goals through excessive drinking, and to develop both general and temptation-specific coping skills to deal with these high-risk situations. Preliminary evidence (e.g., Kivlahan et al., 1990) suggests that the translation of this approach to an earlier-stage prevention strategy for problem drinkers has considerable promise.

An important factor in the evolution of relapse prevention has been the emergence of a biopsychosocial perspective on addictions (e.g., Donovan, 1988; Marlatt et al., 1988). This perspective suggests that in order for us to understand addictions fully, it is necessary to consider those contributions made by the biological domain (including genetic and pharmacological factors), the psychological domain, (including personality features, expectations, self-efficacy, coping skills availability), and the social domain (including cultural and peer group norms, social support) in determining the predisposing vulnerabilites, developmental course, maintaining factors, and areas of intervention (Donovan, 1988). Continued focus on such factors in isolation only contributes to fragmentation within the field (Donovan & Chaney, 1985). In the absence of continued and increased integration of such factors at both a theoretical and a practical level, the likelihood of making advances in treatment is considerably reduced.

An important result of the shift toward a biopsychosocial perspective has been an increased focus on the commonalities across addictive behaviors

(Abrams et al., 1986; Brownell et al., 1986). Although there are important distinctions in the phenomenological experience of addictions to different substances or behavior patterns, there appear to be a number of common features. It appears that comparable biopsychosocial factors may contribute to the maintenance of a wide range of addictive behaviors. There are also a number of similarities in the enduring personal characteristics of individuals involved in addictive behaviors, the background variables associated with their general lifestyle, and the more immediate precipitants leading to their continued involvement in or return to the addictive behavior. This increased focus on the commonalities across addictive behaviors has led to the implementation of relapse prevention strategies to deal with numerous addictions and impulse control disorders (Gossop, 1989). These have included cocaine abuse (Wallace, 1989); opiate dependence (Bradley, 1989; Gossop, Green, Phillips, & Bradley, in press); smoking behavior (Curry, Marlatt, Gordon, & Baer, 1988; Shiffman et al., 1986); eating disorders (Rankin, 1989); compulsive gambling (Brown, 1989); sexual offenses and acting-out behavior (Mackay, 1988; Marques & Nelson, 1989); and the use of intravenous needles among drug users (Stallard & Heather, 1989) and unsafe sexual practices among homosexual males (Marlatt & Gordon, 1989), both of which increase the risks of human immunodeficiency virus (HIV) infection and acquired immune deficiency syndrome (AIDS).

As has often been true in the treatment of the addictions, the implementation of treatment strategies often exceeds the pace of empirical validation of such practices. A number of general areas discussed in this chapter are in need of continued investigation. First, as we have noted previously, a number of the cognitive–behavioral components incorporated into relapse prevention have been found to be effective in reducing drinking behavior. However, it will be necessary to accumulate the results from a number of controlled investigations to determine the clinical efficacy of the larger, more comprehensive relapse prevention model. Second, the best mix and the best timing of the cognitive–behavioral components of relapse prevention still remain to be determined. Third, the most effective interface of these components with the larger stages-of-change process requires further attention. This leads to the final point—that it is necessary to utilize the results of a comprehensive biopsychosocial assessment to facilitate a match between the individual and the most appropriate form of treatment.

The ultimate goal of all treatments for alcohol dependence and other addictive behaviors is to reduce the likelihood of relapse and the negative consequences associated with relapse if it does occur. The cognitive–behavioral methods described in the present chapter provide a series of promising intervention strategies that can be applied systematically to these goals across a broad range of addictive behaviors. Only with continued clinical use and empirical investigation will the utility and effectiveness of the relapse prevention model be determined.

References

Abrams, D. B., Monti, P. M., Carey, K. B., Pinto, R. P., & Jacobus, S. I. (1988). Reactivity to smoking cues and relapse: Two studies of discriminant validity. *Behaviour Research and Therapy, 26,* 225–233.

Abrams, D. B., Niaura, R. S., Carey, K. B., Monti, P. M., & Binkoff, J. A. (1986). Understanding relapse and recovery in alcohol abuse. *Annals of Behavioral Medicine, 8,* 27–32.

Allsop, S., & Saunders, B. (1989). Relapse and alcohol problems. In M. Gossop (Ed.), *Relapse and addictive behavior* (pp. 11–40). New York: Routledge.

Annis, H. M., & Davis, C. S. (1988). Assessment of expectancies. In D. M. Donovan & G. A. Marlatt (Eds.), *Assessment of addictive behaviors* (pp. 84–111). New York: Guilford Press.

Annis, H. M., & Davis, C. S. (1989a). Relapse prevention training: A cognitive–behavioral approach based on self-efficacy theory. *Journal of Chemical Dependency Treatment, 2,* 81–103.

Annis, H. M., & Davis, C. S. (1989b). Relapse prevention. In R. K. Hester & W. R. Miller (Eds.), *Handbook of alcoholism treatment approaches* (pp. 170–182). New York: Pergamon Press.

Arnold, M. B. (1969). Human emotion and action. In J. Mischel (Ed.), *Human action* (pp. 167–197). New York: Academic Press.

Baer, J. S., Kivlahan, D. R., Fromme, K., & Marlatt, G. A. (in press). Secondary prevention of alcohol abuse with college students: A skills-training approach. In N. Heather, W. R. Miller, & J. Greeley (Eds.), *Self control and the addictive behaviors.*

Bandura, A. (1977a). *Social learning theory.* Englewood Cliffs, NJ: Prentice-Hall.

Bandura, A. (1977b). Self-efficacy: Toward a unifying theory of behavior change. *Psychological Review, 84,* 191–215.

Bradley, B. P. (1989). Heroin and the opiates. In M. Gossop (Ed.), *Relapse and addictive behavior* (pp. 73–85). New York: Routledge.

Brown, R. I. F. (1989). Relapses from a gambling perspective. In M. Gossop (Ed.), *Relapse and addictive behavior* (pp. 107–132). New York: Routledge.

Brownell, K. D., Marlatt, G. A., Lichtenstein, E., & Wilson, G. T. (1986). Understanding and preventing relapse. *American Psychologist, 41,* 765–782.

Chaney, E. F. (1989). Social skills training. In R. K. Hester & W. R. Miller (Eds.), *Handbook of alcoholism treatment approaches* (pp. 206–221). New York: Pergamon Press.

Chaney, E. F., O'Leary, M. R., & Marlatt, G. A. (1978). Skill training with alcoholics. *Journal of Consulting and Clinical Psychology, 46,* 1092–1104.

Cooney, N. L., Gillespie, R. A., Baker, L. H., & Kaplan, R. F. (1987). Cognitive changes after alcohol cue exposure. *Journal of Consulting and Clinical Psychology, 2,* 150–155.

Cummings, C., Gordon, J., & Marlatt, G. A. (1980). Relapse: Strategies of prevention and prediction. In W. R. Miller (Ed.), *The addictive behaviors: Treatment of alcoholism, drug abuse, smoking, and obesity* (pp. 291–321). Oxford: Pergamon Press.

Curry, C., Marlatt, G. A., Gordon, J., & Baer, J. (1988). A comparison of health alternative theoretical approaches to smoking cessation and relapse. *Health Psychology, 7,* 545–556.

Daley, D. C. (1988). *Relapse prevention: Treatment alternatives and counseling aids.* Bradenton, FL: Human Services Institute.

DeNelsky, G. Y., & Boat, B. W. (1986). A coping skills model of psychological diagnosis and treatment. *Professional Psychology: Research and Practice, 17,* 322–330.

Donovan, D. M. (1988). Assessment of addictive behaviors: Implications of an emerging biopsychosocial model. In D. M. Donovan & G. A. Marlatt (Eds.), *Assessment of addictive behaviors* (pp. 3–50). New York: Guilford Press.

Donovan, D. M., & Chaney, E. F. (1985). Alcoholic relapse prevention and intervention: Models and methods. In G. A. Marlatt & J. R. Gordon (Eds.), *Relapse prevention: Maintenance strategies in the treatment of addictive behaviors* (pp. 351–416). New York: Guilford Press.

Donovan, D. M., & Marlatt, G. A. (1980). Assessment of expectancies and behaviors associated with alcohol consumption: A cognitive–behavioral approach. *Journal of Studies on Alcohol, 41,* 1153–1185.

Ellis, A., McInerney, J. F., DiGiuseppe, R., & Yeager, R. J. (1988). *Rational–emotive therapy with alcoholics and substance abusers.* New York: Pergamon Press.

Feedberg, E. J., & Johnston, W. E. (1981). Effects of assertion training within context of a mutli-modal alcoholism treatment program for employed alcoholics. *Psychological Reports, 48,* 379–386.

Fuller, R. K. (1989). Antidipsotropic medications. In R. K. Hester & W. R. Miller (Eds.), *Handbook of alcoholism treatment approaches* (pp. 117–127). New York: Pergamon Press.

Fuller, R. K., Branchey, L., Brightwell, D. R., Derman, R. M., Emrick, C. D., Iber, F. L., James, K. E., Lacoursiere, R. B., Lee, K. K., Lowenstam, I., Maany, I., Neiderheiser, D., Nocks, J. J., & Shaw, S. (1986). Disulfiram treatment of alcoholism: A Veterans Administration cooperative study. *Journal of Nervous and Mental Diseases, 256,* 1449–1455.

George, W. (1989). Marlatt and Gordon's relapse prevention model: A cognitive–behavioral approach to understanding and preventing relapse. *Journal of Chemical Dependency Treatment, 2,* 125–152.

Goldman, M. S., Brown, S. A., & Christiansen, B. A. (1987). Expectancy theory: Thinking about drinking. In H. T. Blane & K. E. Leonard (Eds.), *Psychological theories of drinking and alcoholism* (pp. 181–226). New York: Guilford Press.

Gossop, M. (Ed.). (1989). *Relapse and addictive behavior.* New York: Routledge.

Gossop, M., Green, L., Phillips, G., & Bradley, B. P. (in press). Lapse, relapse and survival among opiate addicts after treatment: A prospective follow-up study. *British Journal of Psychiatry.*

Heather, N., & Stallard, A. (1989). Does the Marlatt model underestimate the importance of conditioned craving in the relapse process? In M. Gossop (Ed.), *Relapse and addictive behavior* (pp. 180–208). New York: Routledge.

Hester, R. K., & Miller, W. R. (1989). Self-control training. In R. K. Hester & W. R. Miller (Eds.), *Handbook of alcoholism treatment approaches* (pp. 141–150). New York: Pergamon Press.

Holder, H. D., Longabaugh, R., Miller, W. R., & Rubonis, A. V. (in press). The cost effectiveness of treatment for alcohol problems: A first approximation. *Journal of Studies on Alcohol.*

Ito, J. R., Donovan, D. M., & Hall, J. J. (1988). Relapse prevention in alcohol aftercare: Effects on drinking outcome, change process, and aftercare attendance. *British Journal of Addiction, 83,* 171–181.

Kadden, R. M., Cooney, N. L., Getter, H., & Litt, M. D. (1989). Matching alcoholics to coping skills or interactional therapies: Posttreatment results. *Journal of Consulting and Clinical Psychology, 57,* 698–704.

Kanfer, F. H. (1986). Implications of a self-regulation model of therapy for treatment of addictive behaviors. In W. R. Miller & N. Heather (Eds.), *Treating addicitive behaviors: Processes of change* (pp. 29–47). New York: Plenum Press.

Kivlahan, D. R., Coppel, D., Fromme, K., Williams, E., & Marlatt, G. A. (1990). Secondary prevention of alcohol-related problems in young adults at risk. In K. D. Craig & S. M. Weiss (Eds.), *Health enhancement, disease prevention and early intervention: Biobehavioral perspectives* (pp. 287–300). New York: Springer.

Lazarus, R. S. (1966). *Psychological stress and the coping process.* New York: Mcraw-Hill.

Lazarus, R. S., Averill, J. R., & Opton, E. M. (1974). The psychology of coping: Issues of research and assessment. In G. V. Coelho, D. A. Hamburg, & J. E. Adams (Eds.), *Coping and adaptation* (pp. 249–315). New York: Basic Books.

Litman, G. K. (1986). Alcoholism survival: The prevention of relapse. In W. R. Miller & N. Heather (Eds.), *Treating addictive behaviors: Processes of change* (pp. 391–405). New York: Plenum Press.

Litman, G. K., Eiser, J. R., Rawson, N. S. B., & Oppenheim, A. N. (1979). Towards a typology of relapse: Differences in relapse and coping behaviours between alcoholic relapsers and survivors. *Behaviour Research and Therapy, 17,* 89–94.

Mackay, P. W. (1988). *Alcohol and anger: Coping with conflict.* Unpublished doctoral disserata- tion, State University of New York at Stony Brook.

Mackay, P. W., & Marlatt, G. A. (in press). Cessation versus maintenance: Stopping is starting. *International Journal of the Addictions.*

Marlatt, G. A., Baer, J. S., Donovan, D. M., & Kivlahan, D. R. (1988). Addictive behaviors: Etiology and treatment. *Annual Review of Psychology, 39,* 223–252.

Marlatt, G. A., & George, W. H. (1984). Relapse prevention: Introduction and overview of the model. *British Journal of Addiction, 79,* 261–273.

Marlatt, G. A., & Gordon, J. R. (Eds.). (1985). *Relapse prevention: Maintenance strategies in the treatment of addictive behaviors.* New York: Guilford Press.

Marlatt, G. A., & Gordon, J. R. (1989). Relapse prevention: Future directions. In M. Gossop (Ed.), *Relapse and addictive behavior* (pp. 278–291). New York: Routledge.

Marques, J. K., & Nelson, C. (1989). Understanding and preventing relapse in sex offenders. In M. Gossop (Ed.), *Relapse and addictive behavior* (pp. 96–106). New York: Routledge.

Meichenbaum, D. H. (1971). *Cognitive factors in behavior modification: Modifying what clients say to themselves.* Paper presented at the fifth annual meeting of the Association for Advancement of Behavior Therapy, Washington, DC.

Meichenbaum, D. H. (1977). *Cognitive-behavior modification.* New York: Plenum.

Miller, W. R. (1989). Increasing motivation for change. In R. K. Hester & W. R. Miller (Eds.), *Handbook of alcoholism treatment approaches* (pp. 67–80). New York: Pergamon Press.

Miller, W. R., & Hester, R. K. (1986). The effectiveness of alcoholism treatment: What research reveals. In W. R. Miller & N. Heather (Eds.), *Treating addictive behaviors: Processes of change* (pp. 175–203). New York: Plenum Press.

Monti, P. M., Abrams, D. B., Kadden, R. M., & Cooney, N. L. (1989). *Treating alcohol dependence: A coping skills training guide.* New York: Guilford Press.

Monti, P. M., Binkoff, J. A., Abrams, D. B., Zwick, W. R., Nirenberg, T. D., & Liepman, M. R. (1987). Reactivity of alcoholics and nonalcoholics to drinking cues. *Journal of Abnormal Psychology, 96,* 122–126.

Niaura, R., Rohsenow, D., Binkoff, J., Monti, P., Pedraza, M., & Abrams, D. B. (1988). The relevance of cue reactivity to understanding alcohol and smoking relapse. *Journal of Abnormal Psychology, 2,* 133–152.

Peachey, J. E., & Annis, H. (1984). Pharmacologic treatment of chronic alcoholsim. *Psychiatric Clinics of North America, 7,* 745–756.

Peachey, J. E., & Annis, H. (1986). New strategies for using the alcohol-sensitizing drugs. In C. A. Naranjo & E. M. Sellers (Eds.), *Research advances in new psychopharmacological treat- ments for alcoholism* (pp. 199–216). Amsterdam: Elsevier.

Prochaska, J. O., & DiClemente, C. D. (1983). Stages and processes of self-change of smoking: Toward an integrative model of change. *Journal of consulting and Clinical Psychology, 51,* 390–395.

Prochaska, J. O., & DiClemente, C. D. (1986). Toward a comprehensive model of change. In W. R. Miller & N. Heather (Eds.), *Treating addictive behaviors: Processes of change* (pp. 3–27). New York: Plenum Press.

Rankin, H. (1989). Relapse and eating disorders: The recurring illusion. In M. Gossop (Ed.), *Relapse and addictive behavior* (pp. 86–95). New York: Routledge.

Rimmele, C. T., Miller, W. R., & Dougher, M. J. (1989). Aversion therapies. In R. K. Hester & W. R. Miller (Eds.), *Handbook of alcoholism treatment approaches* (pp. 128–140). New York: Pergamon Press.

Sanchez-Craig, M., Wilkinson, D. A., & Walker, K. (1987). Theory and methods for secondary prevention of alcohol problems: A cognitively based approach. In W. M. Cox (Ed.). *Treatment and prevention of alcohol problems* (pp. 287–331). Orlando, FL: Academic Press.

Saunders, B., & Allsop, S. (1987). Relapse: A psychological perspective. *British Journal of Addiction, 82,* 417–429.

Shiffman, S. (1989). Conceptual issues in the study of relapse. In M. Gossop (Ed.), *Relapse and addictive behavior* (pp. 149–179). New York: Routledge.

Shiffman, S., Shumaker, S. A., Abrams, D. B., Cohen, S., Garvey, A., Grunberg, N. E., & Swan, G. E. (1986). Models of smoking relapse. *Health Psychology, 5,* 13–27.

Shiffman, S., & Wills, T. A. (Eds.). (1985). *Coping and substance use.* Orlando, FL: Academic Press.

Sisson, R. W., & Azrin, N. H. (1989). The community reinforcement approach. In R. K. Hester & W. R. Miller (Eds.), *Handbook of alcoholism treatment approaches* (pp. 242–258). New York: Pergamon Press.

Sobell, L. C., Sobell, M. B., & Nirenberg, T. D. (1988). Behavioral assessment and treatment planning with alcohol and drug abusers: A review with an emphasis on clinical application. *Clinical Psychology Review, 8,* 19–54.

Stallard, A., & Heather, N. (1989). Relapse prevention and AIDS among intravenous drug users. In M. Gossop (Ed.), *Relapse and addictive behavior* (pp. 133–145). New York: Routledge.

Wallace, B. C. (1989). Relapse prevention in psychoeducational groups for compulsive crack cocaine smokers. *Journal of Substance Abuse Treatment, 6,* 229–239.

Wills, T. A., & Shiffman, S. (1985). Coping and substance use: A conceptual framework. In S. Shiffman & T. A. Wills (Eds.), *Coping and substance use* (pp. 3–24). Orlando, FL: Academic Press.

PART SIX

TREATMENT IMPLICATIONS OF NEW ALCOHOL RESEARCH FINDINGS

Advances in prevention and treatment in the addiction field will depend on a widening science base. Although treatment outcome research has been emphasized throughout this clinical textbook, extensive reviews of basic research for each substance are beyond the scope of this volume. However, to give our readers a glimpse of the intellectual challenge and excitement generated by new research, eminent investigators were asked to highlight recent developments in two areas: the genetics and the neurochemical effects of alcohol. No chemical has been more heavily researched than alcohol, and our knowledge of familial transmission of alcohol and alcohol's effects on membranes provides an important biological grounding for efforts at prevention and treatment. These chapters reflect that the search for biological markers and the understanding of genetic influences is more advanced in the area of alcoholism than in other addictive disorders.

21

Alcoholism: A Family Disease

DONALD W. GOODWIN

JULIA K. WARNOCK

A word about the title of this chapter is in order. Several years ago, the National Institute on Alcohol Abuse and Alcoholism published a monograph called *Alcoholism: A Genetic Disease.* We have chosen the word "family" instead of "genetic." We do not believe that alcoholism definitely has been shown to be genetic; no one doubts that it runs in families.

There may also be a need, we feel, to defend the word "disease."[1] In the last several years, a number of books and articles have been published condemning the idea that alcoholism is a disease. Most are written by psychologists, and at least one by a philosopher. It may seem unkind to point this out, but opponents of the disease concept almost always have one thing in common: They rarely treat alcoholics. People who treat alcoholics on a daily basis rarely question the disease concept. Alcoholics are *sick,* and it does not matter what name their sickness is given. They suffer and sometimes die from a process as malignant as any lymphoma.

So the definition of alcoholism becomes a turf war with economic overtones. Philosophers are wonderfully positioned to criticize anything, and psychologists make lower salaries than psychiatrists and naturally resent it. Some of them feel ("unconsciously" might be a good word to use here) that if something is called a disease, the M.D.'s will claim it as their own and exclude non-M.D.'s from the action and the third parties. The truth is that the great majority of M.D.'s avoid treating alcoholism at all costs, and the field is mainly controlled by recovering alcoholics called alcoholism counselors.

In any case, the debate as to whether alcoholism is a disease or "willful misconduct" (to borrow a term used by the Department of Veterans Affairs) is one of the oldest in medicine and, like the wheel, needs constantly to be

---

[1]For that matter, there may be a need to define the word "alcoholism." The *Diagnostic and Statistical Manual of Mental Disorders,* third edition, revised (DSM-III-R; American Psychiatric Association, 1987) prefers "alcohol dependence." We prefer it too; most people would probably rather be called alcohol-dependent than alcoholic. nevertheless, substituting "alcohol-dependent individual" every time one would say "alcoholic" is awkward. Like "schizophrenic" and "diabetic," "alcoholic" is probably here to stay. We recognize this and use the word, although we do not particulary like it.

It might also be a good idea to *define* alcoholism—or alcohol dependence—for the record. We go along with the DSM-III-R criteria, a shortened version of which would be as follows: Alcoholism involves a compulsion to drink alcohol that causes damage to the person and others.

reinvented. Therefore, this chapter begins with a defense of the disease concept. Polemics will end at this point, and the chapter thenceforth deals with studies bearing on the question: Is alcoholism a family disease, and, if so, why? The chapter ends with comments about prevention and about the growing movement for children of alcoholics.

In Defense of the Disease Idea

In defending the disease concept, the first thing we have to remember is that the arguments are purely semantic. "When *I* use a word," as Humpty Dumpty said in *Through the Looking Glass,* "it means just what I choose it to mean—neither more nor less." First, we have to define what *we* mean by "disease."[2]

There is a broad definition of disease and a narrow definition. The broad definition is this: Diseases are what people go to doctors for. They presumably do so because they believe doctors can help them (whether this is true or not). What people go to doctors for changes over time. A hundred years ago, apprehended child molesters saw judges; today they may see psychiatrists as well. Alcoholics see doctors, sometimes for alcoholism. The term "disease" also suggests suffering and sometimes death, and surely no one would deny that these are attributes of alcoholism.

The narrow definition of disease holds that every disease has an underlying biochemical, physiological, or anatomical abnormality, the nature of which may not be known. Alcoholism, in fact, may even meet this narrow definition. Alcoholism runs in families, even when the children are separated from their alcoholic parents and raised by nonalcoholic adoptive parents. This suggests a biological susceptibility (or abnormality, if one prefers). Twin studies also indicate a genetic factor in alcoholism.

If these arguments do not prevail, we can use an analogy: Let us compare alcoholism to chronic lead intoxication. Lead poisoning is characterized by specific signs and symptoms, a more or less predictable course, an uneven demographic spread, and certain complications. Treatment is less than perfect, the best being abstinence from lead. If one changes "lead" to "alcohol," does this description fit alcoholism? It does.

One reason why people, including doctors, have trouble viewing alcoholism as a disease is that alcoholism is associated with having fun, and fun is not usually associated with disease. However, where does this leave syphilis? The point is this: Why or how a person "catches" a disease is not relevant. If some people enjoy lead and eat it like popcorn, this does not change the diagnosis of lead intoxication. Diseases are known by their manifestations as well as their causes, and why alcoholics drink is irrelevant to the diagnosis of alcoholism.

Last, it should be noted that "biological susceptibility" is not necessarily

[2]The dictionary is of little help here. Webster defines "health" as the "absence of disease" and "disease" as the "absence of health."

synonymous with "genetic predisposition." It is possible that an alcoholic's mother drank during pregnancy and that this in some fashion created the vulnerability to alcohol. However, it seems more probable to most of us that genetic factors are involved. Also, like salt in hypertension and obesity in diabetes, habits, conditioning, learning, and availability of alcohol are obviously involved in the development of alcoholism in susceptible individuals.

To summarize, we believe the evidence that alcoholism can properly be called a disease. In particular, the disease of alcoholism fits a pattern of a chronic and relapsing illness similar to many common medical conditions.

Family Studies

The notion that alcoholism runs in families dates back centuries, although reports before 1900 on the familial nature of alcoholism were primarily anectdotal. In the past 90 years, however, more than 100 studies have examined the familial incidence of alcoholism. In reviewing 39 studies conducted over the past four decades, Cotton (1979) summarized statistics on the families of 2,651 alcoholics and 4,083 nonalcoholics. The most striking finding was that, regardless of the nature of the nonalcoholic comparison population, alcoholics were more likely than nonalcoholics to have an alcoholic father, mother, sibling, or distant relative. On the average, almost one-third of any sample of alcoholics had at least one parent with an alcoholism problem. Alcoholic patients were six times more likely than psychiatric patients to report parental alcoholism. Thus, the high rate of parental alcoholism appeared to be not a general characteristic of a disturbed population, but a specific correlate of alcoholism. Alcoholism was more prevalent in male relatives, in the families of female alcoholics, and in near relatives than in distant relatives.

Of course, not everything that runs in families is inherited. Speaking French runs in families, presumably not because of genes. In humans, there are two strategies for identifying possible genetic factors in familial illnesses. One consists of comparing concordance rates of an illness in monozygotic versus dizygotic twins. The second consists of studying adopted individuals who have the illness in their biological families but not in their families of upbringing. Both types of studies have been applied to alcoholism. The findings are briefly reviewed here.

Twin Studies

Several studies have compared identical and fraternal twins with regard to alcohol-drinking practices, alcohol metabolism, and the effect of alcohol on brain waves as measured by electroencephalogram (EEG) (Propping, 1977). A high degree of inheritability is indicated in all three categories.

Alcoholism has been less studied using the twin method, but has been at least addressed in three studies. Swedish investigators (Kaij, 1960) found that monozygotic twins were significantly more concordant for alcoholism than were dizygotic twins; the more severe the alcoholism, the greater the difference. A large Finnish study (Partanen, Bruun, & Markkanen, 1966) found that among younger individuals a difference existed between monozygotic and dizygotic twins with regard to alcohol problems, but there was no difference in older twin pairs. A third study (Murray, Clifford, & Gurlin, 1983), conducted in England, showed no difference at all between fraternal and identical twins. In summary, one twin study produced results consistent with a genetic influence, one did not, and a third was equivocal.

Adoption Studies

The first adoption study of alcoholism was conducted in 1944. It found no difference in drinking behavior between children of alcoholics and children of nonalcoholics, both in their early 20s (Roe, 1944). The sample size was small, and no criteria were presented for the diagnosis of alcoholism; as a result, the finding tends to be discounted. However, one should be cautious about discounting findings that do not correspond to one's bias.

A more recent wave of adoption studies began in the early 1970s, ushered in by a study comparing half siblings of alcoholics with full siblings (Schuckit, Goodwin, & Winokur, 1972). The assumption behind the study was that if genetic factors were important, full siblings would more often be alcoholics than half siblings. This did not prove to be the case. However, the study did find that half siblings, predictably, were from broken families; this presented the opportunity to compare alcoholism in offspring with alcoholism in biological parents as well as parents of upbringing. It was found that having a biological parent who was alcoholic was highly correlated with alcoholism in the sons, but there was no correlation with alcoholism in the surrogate fathers. The study, in short, failed to prove its central hypothesis, but ended up as a kind of adoption study that suggesting biological factors may be more important than environmental factors in producing alcohol problems.

The decade after the studies of half siblings saw the publishing of results from three separate adoption studies conducted in three countries—Denmark, Sweden, and the United States (Iowa) (Bohman, 1978; Bohman, Sigvardsson, & Cloninger, 1981; Cadoret & Gath, 1978; Cadoret, Cain, & Grove, 1980; Cloninger, Bohman, & Sigvardsson, 1981; Goodwin, 1971; Goodwin, Schulsinger, Hermansen, Guze, & Winokur, 1973, 1975). The studies, although involving different methodologies, produced remarkably similar findings: *Children of alcoholics had a high rate of alcoholism even when they were not raised by their alcoholic biological parents, but were raised by adoptive parents whose drinking was light or moderate.*

At first, the findings applied mainly to sons of alcoholics, but later the

Iowa studies indicated similar increased risk in the adopted daughters of alcoholics. The first reports also suggested that alcoholism in the biological parents predicted only alcohol problems in the adopted-away offspring and was not associated with other forms of substance misuse or other psychiatric illnesses. A recent study by Cadoret, Troughton, O'Gorman, and Heywood (1986) reported that a biological background of alcohol problems did predict increased drug abuse in adoptees, so the issue is not completely resolved.

The Danish studies suggested that environmental factors were relatively unimportant in the development of alcoholism. However, recent data from a study by Cadoret, Troughton, and O'Gorman (1987) indicated that alcohol-related problems in an adoptive family also predicted increased alcohol abuse. Beardslee, Son, and Vaillant (1986), in a 40-year follow-up of working-class families, found that exposure to alcoholism in the family environment and a family history of alcoholism independently contributed to the later development of alcoholism.

Two Alcoholisms

Cloninger et al. (1981) have proposed that two types of alcoholism exist. Type 1 is relatively mild, occurs in both sexes, and is influenced by environmental factors (e.g., low socioeconomic status). Individuals with Type 1 alcoholism are more likely to have problems with drinking after the age of 25. Fighting and arrests are not usually associated with the natural history of their disease; however, guilt and fear about dependence on alcohol are typically present. Type 2 affects only men, involves a more severe family history of alcoholism, and is manifested in antisocial features, but is not influenced by social or environmental factors. The two-type hypothesis has attracted a good deal of attention, but has just recently been the subject of replicative studies. Nordstrom and Berglund (1987) found that Type 2 alcoholics, like their biological parents, represented a more severely affected group, with a lower frequency of abstinence and social drinking and a greater tendency to drinking bouts when compared with Type 1 alcoholics. (Some researchers have questioned whether the Type 1 alcoholic would really be considered alcoholic by usual clinical criteria.)

Another typology that has recently become popular involves dividing alcoholics into "familial" and "nonfamilial" alcoholics. Although alcoholism runs in families, it does not run in all families, and there are many alcoholics who do not have a family history of alcoholism. Investigators who have compared alcoholics with a positive family history to those with a negative family history have reported interesting findings. These include an earlier age of onset and a more severe form of alcoholism in the familial alcoholics (Haver, 1987). Penick et al. (1987) recently confirmed the relationship of familial alcoholism to early onset and greater severity, but also found that familial alcoholics had an increased lifetime prevalence of additional psychiatric disorders, and a greater diversity of psychiatric disturbance among biologi-cal relatives. There is some controversy about the latter finding, inasmuch as the children of alcoholics described in the adoption studies (by definition "familial") did not show an increased prevalence of additional psychiatric disorders. Penick et al. (1987) suggest that assortative mating might explain the differences between familial and non familial alcoholics. Possibly their population of Veterans Affairs patients differed in important respects from the subjects in the adoption studies. In any case, whether familial alcoholism involves a greater or lesser risk of additional psychiatric disorders remains unresolved.

There are certain similarities between Cloninger et al.'s (1981) Type 1 and Type 2 alcoholics and familial and nonfamilial alcoholics. For example, both Type 2 alcoholism and familial alcoholism have an early onset and are serious forms of alcoholism (more so than nonfamilial alcoholism). Cloninger et al.'s proposal that heavy-drinking parents and low occupational status have addi-tive effects in increasing alcoholism in the offspring has been supported by a recent study (Parker & Harford, 1987). Another environmental factor that might distinguish Type 1 and Type 2 alcoholism (or familial and nonfamilial alcoholism) may be maltreatment of children by the alcoholic parents. Alco-holics are overrepresented in the population of child abusers (Famularo, Stone, Barnum, & Wharton, 1986), and child abuse may occur more often in familial alcoholics than in nonfamilial alcoholics, although this needs confirmation.

Marker Studies

In light of the evidence that alcoholism is a familial disorder, investigators are searching for biological markers of a predisposition toward alcoholism. Pri-marily, this search has consisted of comparing children of alcoholics (a high-risk group) with children of nonalcoholics (a low-risk group). These studies are conducted before the subjects have had extensive exposure to alcohol, and therefore differences between the two groups may be interpreted as indicators of a possible predisposition rather than as consequences of excessive drinking.

Schuckit (1986), who pioneered what are known as high-risk studies, reviewed major findings in this line of research. He focused primarily on electrophysiological markers and on cognitive and psychomotor markers. The following studies are cited.

Two types of brain waves have been identified as potential markers associated with a predisposition towards alcoholism. The first, event-related potentials (ERPs), are computer-averaged brain waves measuring electrophy-siological brain reactions to stimuli. One part of the ERP, a positive wave observed at 300 milliseconds after a stimulus (P300), occurs in normal in-dividuals after experiencing an anticipated rare event. The P300 reflects an individual's ability to attend selectively to an anticipated stimulus. Alcoholics have been reported to have a flattened amplitude of P300. O'Connor, Hesselbrock, and Tasman (1986) found that preadolescent sons of alcoholics also showed a decrease in size of the P300 wave. However, another laboratory (Polich & Bloom, 1986) failed to document a relationship between family history and P300, leaving the importance of the finding still unresolved.

Schuckit (1986) also cited studies reporting that alcoholics demonstrate less α activity on the EEG than nonalcoholics. Moreover, sons of alcoholics show increased α activity after an alcohol challenge. Schuckit noted that it is possible that alcohol has different reinforcing properties in individuals at high risk for alcoholism. The alcohol may correct for a lower level of α activity, thus producing more feelings of relaxation.

Schuckit (1986) further reviewed studies reporting that high-risk subjects demonstrated decreased verbal IQs, decreased auditory word span performance, lower levels of reading comprehension, and more errors on the Categories test of the Halstead–Reitan Neuropsychological Test Battery, as well as problems with constructional praxis and abstract problem solving.

One consistent finding in Schuckit's own studies has been a lower intensity of reaction to alcohol in the sons of alcoholics. They seem to have an innate tolerance to alcohol. They become less intoxicated when drinking and show lower cortisol and prolactin levels in response to a high-dose ethanol challenge (Schuckit, Gold, & Risch, 1987).

Other differences have been reported between sons of alcoholics and controls. High-risk subjects show a greater cardiovascular reaction to a shock stressor than a moderate-risk group when sober (Finn & Pihl, 1987). That is, alcohol consumption causes a "dramatic" reduction in the degree of reactivity in the high-risk group and leads to increased reactivity in the moderate-risk group. The conclusion is that prealcoholic sons of alcoholics are more sensitive to stress than controls, and that alcohol reduces this sensitivity markedly. This potentially reinforcing effect of alcohol was demonstrated in another study (Levenson, Oyama, & Meek, 1987), where the capacity of alcohol to attenuate physiological responses to stress was more pronounced in high-risk than in low-risk subjects.

Sons of alcoholics possess higher thyrotropin levels than sons of nonalcoholics (Moss, Guthrie, & Linnoila, 1986). This difference was not found in daughters. This is the first report of a male-limited neuroendocrine difference between children of alcoholics and control children.

Perceptual field dependency—that is, an inability to discriminate visually a stimulus from a distracting background—has been reported in alcoholics. However, Tarter, Jacob, Hill, Hegedus, and Carra (1986), using the rod-and-frame test, found no differences in field dependency between sons of alcoholics and sons of depressed fathers and control fathers.

Schuckit (1986) reviewed the literature regarding another type of marker: the possible role of hyperactivity in childhood as a predictor of alcoholism. He described several studies indicating that alcoholics were more likely to report childhood hyperactivity than nonalcoholics, but noted that other studies (including one in his own laboratory) failed to confirm the association. In another paper, Schuckit, Sweeney, and Huey (1987) noted that alcoholics' sons reported more evidence of a hot temper and short attention span than sons of nonalcoholics; however, they found no association between alcoholism in the family and attention deficit disorder (ADD), residual type, in adulthood. Another study (Morton, Fiscella, O'Connor, Jackson, & Slone, 1987), however, identified a "subtype" of alcoholism in which about one-third of young male alcoholic patients displayed symptoms of ADD, beginning in childhood and continuing into adulthood as a residual-type disorder. The relationship between alcoholism and ADD is still poorly understood.

A marker of nonalcoholism has been much studied in recent years. This is the so-called "Oriental flush." About half of all Orientals develop a cutaneous flush and experience unpleasant subjective feelings when drinking even a small amount of alcohol. The reaction is believed to be genetically determined. Recent evidence for this was produced by Japanese investigators (Ohmori et al., 1986). They found that subjects who experienced a flush after drinking were deficient in the enzyme that most efficiently metabolizes acetaldehyde. The flushing is believed to be caused by an increase of acetaldehyde. Orientals with the enzyme deficiency experience unpleasant reactions to alcohol from early infancy. This discourages alcohol consumption and may largely account for the generally low rate of alcoholism in the Orient.

What Is Inherited?

To the extent that a tendency toward alcoholism is inherited, it is biochemical in origin. The chemistry of the brain is still largely a mystery, and even less is known about the effects of alcohol on brain chemistry. Nevertheless, several hypotheses are being pursued and are discussed briefly here.

First, people with a genetic propensity for alcoholism may be deficient in certain forms of biochemical activity required for optimal well-being. These people, given available alcohol, a suitable culture, and an absence of countervailing traits, might discover that alcohol temporarily corrects this hypothetical deficiency, producing an intensity of mood change foreign to those without the deficiency. The model then requires alcohol to have a biphasic effect. That is, there is an initial reinforcing phase followed by a deficit phase, causing subsequent underactivity of the reward system.

There is some evidence that alcohol has a biphasic effect on serotonin metabolism that might correspond to the deficiency model outlined above. Like reserpine, alcohol appears to increase serotonergic activity briefly (during acute intoxication), and then subsequently reduces serotonin activity to subnormal levels. The deficient person then would have two reasons for drinking: He or she would first drink to correct the deficiency, and then would continue to drink to correct the even greater deficiency resulting from the biphasic effect of alcohol on serotonin. Biochemically, this might explain the "addictive cycle" in which a person initially drinks to feel good and then later drinks to stop feeling bad from the substance that originally improved his or her well-being.

The serotonin deficiency hypothesis has gained support from several recent studies, some of which are reviewed by Roy, Virkkunen, and Linnoila (1987). The review concludes that there is a sizeable subgroup of alcoholics with reduced central serotonin turnover, and that drinking may correct this presumed deficiency.

A series of studies of animal and human subjects by Boismare et al. (1987) strongly supports the serotonin deficiency hypothesis. The authors found while studying striatal synaptosomes that alcohol-drinking rats showed an increased serotonin uptake, compared with non-alcohol-drinking rats. The authors also found that antidepressants, which inhibit serotonin uptake, decreased alcohol consumption in alcohol-drinking rats. Pursuing this work with humans, the authors reported that platelet uptake of serotonin was greater in alcoholics and former alcoholics than in controls. The phenomenon could be congenital or induced by previous excessive intake of alcohol. If congenital, it would represent a true biological marker for a predisposition to alcoholism.

Another deficiency hypothesis involves endorphins. There is a theory that alcoholics have decreased levels of endorphins in the nervous system and that alcohol compensates for the deficiency. A paper by Barret, Bourhis, Buffet, Danel, and Debru (1987) is consistent with the hypothesis, showing increased levels of β-endorphins in intoxicated alcoholics. Another recent work (Kotlinska & Langwinski, 1987) suggests that opioid receptors influence the development of ethanol dependence. Opioid antagonists, for example, block the ethanol withdrawal syndrome in rats. On the whole, however, the endorphin theory has fewer data to support it than does the serotonin hypothesis.

A third deficiency hypothesis involves catecholamines. The depletion of central catecholamines by inhibitors of tyrosine hydroxylase or dopamine β-hydroxylase reduces voluntary intake of ethanol in rodents (Pispa, Huttunen, Sarviharju, & Ylikahri, 1986). Furthermore, the activity of tyrosine hydroxlase is higher in the brains of rats that prefer alcohol than in the brains of rats that do not. There is still little work in humans to support this hypothesis. A good review of neurotransmitters, cell receptors, and ethanol was published by Bannister and Losowsky (1986).

In addition to deficiency theories, there is also an "overproduction" theory of alcoholism. This theory holds that a genetic propensity to alcoholism involves the overproduction of substances that in some way facilitate addiction. For example, alcohol produces minute amounts of morphine-like compounds in the brain. One study (Bannister & Losowsky, 1986) found these compounds in greater quantities after alcohol ingestion in the spinal fluid of alcoholics than in that of nonalcoholics. Rats and monkeys drink increased amounts of alcohol when these substances are injected into the brain. Thus, the possibility exists that the genetic defect in alcoholism involves a reduced capacity of the brain to oxidize aldehydes, resulting in the overproduction of morphine-like alkaloid compounds (aldehyde condensation products), which may facilitate alcohol addiction.

Some laboratories are planning deoxyribonucleic acid (DNA) sequencing studies in an attempt to locate a specific gene or genes for alcoholism (the ultimate marker). So far, these studies have not produced data. A report from Japan (Matsushima, 1987) found an elevation of chromosomal aberrations in the lymphocytes of alcoholics compared with those of nonalcoholics. However, when the alcoholics stopped drinking, there was a spontaneous reduction of the aberrations, suggesting that they were caused by alcohol and were reversible.

Implications for Prevention

Education

The evidence for a genetic influence in alcoholism comes entirely from studies conducted in the United States and Northern Europe. Even in these areas, surprisingly few citizens seem aware of the existence of such evidence. A large-scale educational campaign could be justified to alert adolescents with alcoholism in their families of their increased risk of becoming alcoholic. Some adolescents who possess this knowledge have been known to monitor their drinking with special care. The knowledge alone, to some extent, may be preventive.

Similarly, parents should be aware of the familial, if not genetic, basis for at least some alcoholism. For these parents, wisdom probably lies in assuming that *all* alcoholism is familial. The distinction between familial and nonfamilial remains theoretical, and knowledge of one's family is rarely total. To the extent that parents of adolescents can influence their children's drinking behavior (or any behavior), they should be alert to the following warning signals:

1. Any show of secretiveness by the adolescent with regard to drinking.
2. An adolescent's capacity to drink a lot without showing much effect.
3. Oversensitivity shown by the adolescent toward any comment by an adult concerning the adolescent's drinking practices.

The predictive value of these signals is based not on scientific studies, but on clinical judgment, which may or may not be accurate. Predictors of proven value—as we point out next—are scarce indeed.

Antecedents of Alcoholism

The alcoholism literature provides little help in identifying adolescents who will later develop serious drinking problems. There have only been four longitudinal studies of sufficient size and methodological rigor to offer the promise of providing useful information, and they have provided little indeed. What they mainly find is an *absence* of predictors in adolescence (Goodwin, 1988).

Vaillant (1983), who conducted one of the longitudinal studies, was struck by the *healthiness* of his prealcoholic adolescent subjects. They not only had many features identified with "good" mental health, but also came from particularly stable families. They were self-confident, gregarious individuals whose "dependency needs" (if present at all) were marvelously concealed.

Some retrospective studies, but not all, tend to support the idea that antisocial behavior in childhood may predict future alcoholism. In these studies, alcoholics more often give a history of hyperactivity and/or conduct disorder in childhood and early adolescence than do nonalcoholics (Goodwin et al., 1975). These reports need to be confirmed by prospective studies in a variety of populations to be accepted as conclusive.

The strongest predictor of future alcoholism in adolescents is a family history of alcoholism. Every study shows this, including the one by Vaillant (1983). About one in every four or five male offspring of alcoholics (in North America and Western Europe) become alcoholic; about 5–10% of the daughters become alcoholic. In both sexes, the family history of alcoholism increases the risk in the children by a factor of four or five. This information needs to be widely disseminated to the public.

If the child has a family history of alcoholism and is also hyperactive or impulsive ("gets in trouble"), this may increase the chance of future alcoholism; more work needs to be done to establish this definitively.

Another risk factor associated with alcoholism is vocation. Alcoholism is unevenly distributed among occupations. More bartenders and journalists are alcoholics (in the United States) than are, for example, ministers and letter carriers. Perhaps the highest rate of alcoholism reported for any defined group applies to Americans who have won the Nobel Prize for Literature. Of the nine Americans who have won the prize, four were alcoholic and a fifth (John Steinbeck) was a heavy drinker.

There is hope of identifying better predictors in the future. A number of prospective studies of "high-risk" adolescents (i.e., those with alcoholism in their families) are now in progress. Some interesting differences between high-risk and low-risk adolescents have been reported, although their importance as predictors remains to be determined by long-term follow-up (see "What Is Inherited?", above). Biological markers of alcoholism have been the object of many studies in which alcoholics were the subject of investigation. Many genetically controlled traits (colorblindness, blood groups, human leukocyte antigen [HLA] type) have been reported to covary with alcoholism, only to be followed by studies failing to confirm the association. Other presumed markers (e.g., α-aminobutyric acid) probably reflect effects of drinking on the liver, rather than constituting independent markers useful in predicting alcoholism (Goodwin, 1988).

The Children of Alcoholics Movement

Beginning in the early 1980s, a remarkably new movement arose on the medical–social horizon. This movement centered on a sizeable group of people identifying themselves as children of alcoholics (a term that came to be abbreviated during the decade as "COAs").

There were an estimated 28 million COAs in the country; of these, 7 million were children under the age of 18 (Russell, Henderson, & Blume, 1985). Conferences sprang up, well attended by social workers, alcoholism counselors, COAs, and a smattering of psychologists and psychiatrists. A national group, the Children of Alcoholics Foundation, was established. A new lecture circuit came into existence, featuring COA experts, who often were COAs themselves.

The COA movement was mainly promoted by people who adopted environmentalist explanations for alcoholism. Behind the movement is the explicit assumption that children are mainly products of their upbringing. In a sense, the COA movement has been a counterweight to the genetic studies, keeping the nature–nurture controversy in a dynamic equilibrium.

Congress held hearings about COAs, sometimes seeming to elevate the COA problem to the level of the acquired immune deficiency syndrome (AIDS) problem. There was much impassioned testimony. The influential New York lawyer Joseph Califano, in his role as Special Counselor on Alcoholism and Drug Abuse, testified that only heart attacks and strokes come close to alcohol abuse in cost. Califano noted (Woodside, 1982) that at least 10% of the children under 20 years of age in New York State are living with an alcoholic parent. These children, he noted further, frequently display psychological and emotional disorders. They are more likely to fail in school, to abuse drugs or alcohol, and to become truants or delinquents. Even COAs who appear to do well have secret problems. Woodside (1982), founder and president of the Children of Alcoholics Foundation, expressed concern about some children becoming "super copers." These are children who take responsibility for the family by caring for others, cooking meals, and running the household. Later as adults these COAs may become rigidly controlled overachievers, susceptible to serious medical or mental problems.

In parts of the psychiatric community, the COAs became identified as a unique group with specific problems requiring special care. In some hospitals, wards were set aside just for COAs. In 1988 the Children of Alcoholics Foundation identified 235 programs for COAs in 34 states. Still, the new COA experts were concerned that most victims were not being reached. About 75% of the programs had been in operation for 3 years or less; they tended to be small, serving 50 or fewer children a year; and they were concentrated primarily in California, New York, Wisconsin, and Massachusetts. Woodside (1987) laments that "despite their numbers and their overrepresentation in service delivery systems, children of alcoholics are rarely identified or helped" (p. 643).

Is it true that COAs are particularly susceptible to specific disorders requiring specialized care? A review of the large body of literature on the subject suggests that the answer is unknown. Much of the literature consists of testimonial and case reports from patients or from such groups as Al-Anon. Reviewing the literature, one finds that COAs may be poor students or drug abusers; are hyperactive and antisocial; make frequent suicide attempts; have high rates of psychiatric illness; and are often alcoholic. This last statement about being often alcoholic is indisputably true. As noted earlier, the risk of alcoholism in COAs is four or five times that of the risk in the general population.

One common theme emerges from the wealth of anecdotal reports: Alcoholic parents are unpredictable. They sometimes come home and sometimes do not. Their behavior is erratic. The children hate to bring friends over because they cannot be sure how their parents will behave. The family becomes isolated from neighbors and other families, because Mom or Dad would rather drink, and serious drinking is basically a solitary business. So some of the children indeed become "super copers" and often assume the parental role in the ways mentioned by Woodside. While some of these super copers may well end up as super achieving, overstressed adults, a case could be made that assumption of responsibility early in life builds character and prepares children for the coping ahead of them. There are certainly many instances of successful, admired people who as children lost their parents by death and became heads of families at a young age. In previous centuries, when parents commonly died young of illness or in childbirth, 14-year-olds assumed parental responsibility, often without apparent ill effect. Of course, they did not suffer the humiliation of having friends see a mother or father under the influence of drink, but there were many other serious matters to cope with, such as how to survive and how to avoid eviction.

There are only a few empirical studies in which COAs have been compared to other children. While the studies generally show that COAs have more psychological and behavioral problems than children of nonalcoholics, only a minority of these children are rated as severely impaired.

The data from "high-risk" studies raise doubt about the theory that COAs represent a special group. This chapter has reviewed some of these studies, in which children at risk of developing alcoholism are compared to children not known to be at risk. The former sometimes do report more hyperactivity and behavioral problems in school. However, there are no consistent reports that high-risk children differ from low-risk children with regard to mental and emotional problems.

Unfortunately, many studies in this literature are characterized by methodological problems, which render the conclusions tentative. High-risk studies typically involve subjects who are willing to volunteer. Biases may thus enter into the selection process. However, the high-risk study should probably be considered a reasonable methodological technique to add control in the experimental design. The results of many other types of investigations are characteristically ambiguous because of the lack of consistent and valid diagnostic instruments, lack of appropriate control groups, and inadequately measured dependant variables.

Whether or not COAs represent a special psychiatric group, the COA movement has accomplished one worthwhile goal: More COAs are learning that their chances of becoming alcoholics themselves are greater than if they were children of nonalcoholics. Whether or not heredity is the reason, alcoholism clearly runs in families, and families should know about this. Oddly, it seems, many families do not. In 1988, a telephone poll in New York State revealed that only 5% of respondents, including members of alcoholic families, knew that alcoholism runs in families.

This knowledge, we hope, will soon be universal. There are instances of people who watch their drinking very carefully because they have alcoholism in the family. Just as children of diabetics should have their urine checked occasionally for sugar, COAs should be aware of their vulnerability. Let us hope that this knowledge is preventive.

References

American Psychiatric Association. (1987). *Diagnostic and statistical manual of mental disorders* (3rd ed., rev.). Washington, DC: Author.

Bannister, P., & Losowsky, M. S. (1986). Cell receptors and ethanol. *Alcoholism: Clinical and Experimental Research, 10*(Suppl.), 50–54.

Barret, L., Bourhis, F., Buffet, H., Danel, V., & Debru, J. L. (1987). Determination of β-endorphin in alcoholic patients in the acute stage of intoxication: Relation with naloxone therapy. *Drug and Alcohol Dependence, 19,* 71–78.

Beardslee, W. R., Son, L., & Vaillant, G. E. (1986). Exposure to parental alcoholism during childhood and outcome in adulthood: A prospective longitudinal study. *British Journal of Psychiatry, 149,* 584–591.

Bohman, M. (1978). Some genetic aspects of alcoholism and criminality: A population of adoptees. *Archives of General Psychiatry, 35,* 269–276.

Bohman, M., Sigvardsson, S., & Cloninger, C. R. (1981). Maternal inheritance of alcohol abuse: Cross-fostering analysis of adopted women. *Archives of General Psychiatry, 38,* 965–969.

Boismare, F., Lhuintre, J. P., Daoust, M., Moore, N., Saligaut, C., & Hillemand, B. (1987). Platelet affinity for serotonin is increased in alcoholics and former alcoholics: A biological marker for dependence? *Alcohol and Alcoholism, 22,* 155–159.

Cadoret, R. J., Cain, C. A., & Grove, W. M. (1980). Development of alcoholism in adoptees raised apart from alcoholic biologic relatives. *Archives of General Psychiatry, 37,* 561–563.

Cadoret, R. J., & Gath, A. (1978). Inheritance of alcoholism in adoptees. *British Journal of Psychiatry, 132,* 252–258.

Cadoret, R. J., Troughton, E., & O'Gorman, T. W. (1987). Genetic and environmental factors in alcohol abuse and antisocial personality. *Journal of Studies on Alcohol, 48,* 1–8.

Cadoret, R. J., Troughton, E., O'Gorman, T. W., & Heywood, E. (1986). An adoption study of genetic and environmental factors in drug abuse. *Archives of General Psychiatry, 43,* 1131–1136.

Cloninger, C. R., Bohman, M., & Sigvardsson, S. (1981). Inheritance of alcohol abuse: Cross-fostering analysis of adopted men. *Archives of General Psychiatry, 38,* 861–868.

Cotton, N. S. (1979). The familial incidence of alcoholism: A review. *Journal of Studies on Alcohol, 40,* 89–116.

Famularo, R., Stone, K., Barnum, R., & Wharton, R. (1986). Alcoholism and severe child maltreatment. *American Journal of Orthopsychiatry, 56,* 481–485.

Finn, P. R., & Pihl, R. O. (1987). Men at high risk for alcoholism: The effect of alcohol on cardiovascular response to unavoidable shock. *Journal of Abnormal Psychology, 96,* 230–236.

Goodwin, D. W. (1971). Is alcoholism hereditary? A review and critique. *Archives of General Psychiatry, 25,* 545–549.

Goodwin, D. W. (1988). *Is alcoholism hereditary?* New York: Ballantine.

Goodwin, D. W., Schulsinger, F., Hermansen, L., Guze, S. B., & Winokur, G. (1973). Alcohol problems in adoptees raised apart from alcoholic biological parents. *Archives of General Psychiatry, 28,* 238–242.

Goodwin, D. W., Schulsinger, F., Hermansen, L., Guze, S. B., & Winokur, G. (1975). Alcoholism and the hyperactive child syndrome. *Journal of Nervous and Mental Disease, 160,* 349–353.

Haver, B. (1987). Female alcoholics: V. The relationship between family history of alcoholism and outcome 3–10 years after treatment. *Acta Psychiatrica Scandinavica, 76,* 21–27.

Kaij, L. (1960). Alcoholism in twins. In *Studies on the etiology and sequels of abuse of alcohol.* Stockholm: Almqvist & Wiksell.

Kotlinska, J., & Langwinski, R. (1987). Does the blockade of opioid receptors influence the development of ethanal dependence? *Alcohol and Alcoholism, 22,* 117–119.

Levenson, R. W., Oyama, O. N., & Meek, P. S. (1987) Greater reinforcement from alcohol for those at risk: Parental risk, personality risk, and sex. *Journal of Abnormal Psychology, 96,* 242–253.

Matsushima, Y. (1987). Chromosomal aberrations in the lymphocytes of alcoholics and former alcoholics. *Neuropsychobiology, 17,* 24–29.

Morton, A. M., Fiscella, R. A., O'Connor, K., Jackson, M., & Slone, D. G. (1987). Revised criteria for detecting alcoholic patients with attention deficit disorder, residual type. *Journal of Nervous and Mental Disease, 175,* 371–372.

Moss, H. B., Guthrie, S., & Linnoila, M. (1986). Enhanced thyrotropin response to thyrotropin releasing hormone in boys at risk for development of alcoholism. *Archives of General Psychiatry, 43,* 1137–1142.

Murray, R. M., Clifford, C., & Gurlin, H. M. (1983). Twin and alcoholism studies. In M. Galanter (Ed.), *Recent developments in alcoholism* (Vol. 3, pp. 25–46). New York: Gardner Press.

Nordstrom, G., & Berglund, M. (1987). Type-1 and Type-2 alcoholics (Cloninger and Bohman) have different patterns of successful long-term adjustment. *British Journal of Addiction, 82,* 761–769.

O'Connor, S., Hesselbrock, V., & Tasman, A. (1986). Correlates of increased risk for alcoholism in young men. *Progress in Neuropsychopharmacology and Biological Psychiatry, 10,* 211–218.

Ohmori, T., Koyama, T., Chen, C.-C., Yeh, E.-K., Reyes, B. V., Jr., & Yamashita, I. (1986). The role of aldehyde dehydrogenase isozyme variance in alcohol sensitivity, drinking habits formation and the development of alcoholism in Japan, Taiwan and the Philippines. *Progress in Neuropsychopharmacology and Biological Psychiatry, 10,* 229–235.

Partanen, J. K., Bruun, K., & Markkanen, T. (1966). *Inheritance of drinking behavior: A study on intelligence, personality and use of alcohol in adult twins* (Finnish Foundation for Alcohol Studies Publication No. 14). Helsinki: Finnish Foundation for Alcohol Studies.

Parker, D. A., & Harford, T. C. (1987). Alcohol-related problems of children of heavy-drinking parents. *Journal of Studies on Alcohol, 48,* 265–268.

Penick, E. C., Powell, B. J., Bingham, S. F., Liskow, B. I., Miller, N. S., & Read, M. R. (1987). A comparative study of familial alcoholism. *Journal of Studies on Alcohol, 48,* 136–146.

Pispa, J. P., Huttunen, M. O., Sarviharju, M., & Ylikahri, R. (1986). Enzymes of catecholamine metabolism in the brains of rat strains differing in their preference for or tolerance of ethanol. *Alcohol and Alcoholism, 21,* 181–184.

Polich, J., & Bloom, F. E. (1986). P300 and alcohol consumption in normals and individuals at risk for alcoholism: A preliminary report. *Progress in Neuropsychopharmacology and Biological Psychiatry, 10,* 201–210.

Propping, P. (1977). Genetic control of ethanol action on the central nervous system: An EEG study in twins. *Human Genetics, 35,* 309–334.

Roe, A. (1944). The adult adjustment of children and alcoholic parents raised in foster homes. *Journal of Studies on Alcohol, 5,* 378–393.

Roy, A., Virkkunen, M., & Linnoila, M. (1987). Reduced central serotonin turnover in a subgroup of alcoholics? *Progress in Neuropsychopharmacology and Biological Psychiatry, 11,* 173–177.

Russell, M., Henderson, C., & Blume, S. B. (1985). *Children of alcoholics: A review of the literature.* New York: Children of Alcoholics Foundation.

Schuckit, M. A. (1986). Biological markers in alcoholism. *Progress in Neuropsychopharmacology and Biological Psychiatry, 10,* 191–199.

Schuckit, M. A., Gold, E., & Risch, C. (1987). Serum prolactin levels in sons of alcoholics and control subjects. *American Journal of Psychiatry, 144,* 854–859.

Schuckit, M. A., Goodwin, D. W., & Winokur, G. (1972). A study of alcoholism in half siblings. *American Journal of Psychiatry, 128,* 1132–1136.

Schuckit, M. A., Sweeney, S., & Huey, L. (1987). Hyperactivity and the risk for alcoholism. *Journal of Clinical Psychiatry, 48,* 275–277.

Tarter, R. E., Jacob, T., Hill, S., Hegedus, A. M., & Carra, J. (1986). Perceptual field dependency: Predisposing trait or consequence of alcoholism? *Journal of Studies on Alcohol, 47,* 498–499.

Vaillant, G. (1983). *The natural history of alcoholism.* Cambridge, MA: Harvard University Press.

Woodside, M. (1982). *Children of alcoholics: A report to Hugh L. Carey, Governor, State of New York.* New York: New York State Division of Alcoholism and Alcohol Abuse.

Woodside, M. (1987). Children of alcoholics: Helping a vulnerable group. *Public Health Reports, 103,* 643–648.

22

Neurochemical Effects of Alcohol

BORIS TABAKOFF

PAULA L. HOFFMAN

Introduction

Because of its simple molecular structure and its amphipathic properties, ethanol (ethyl alcohol) diffuses easily across biological membranes and is distributed into nearly all tissues and body fluids. Ethanol affects the function of almost every organ in the body; most importantly, by altering the activity of the central nervous system (CNS), ethanol can produce excitation, intoxication, ataxia, incoordination, sedation, and anesthesia in both animals and humans. Most of the CNS-mediated pharmacological effects of ethanol, which are witnessed following acute administration of the drug, will diminish upon prolonged exposure to ethanol (i.e., tolerance develops to ethanol's actions). Furthermore, if ethanol is ingested in substantial amounts during extensive periods of time, an abrupt cessation of ethanol consumption will result in a state of CNS hyperexcitability, characteristic of an ethanol withdrawal syndrome. Restlessness, tremor, diaphoresis, insomnia, and even hallucinations and seizures, which are hallmarks of ethanol withdrawal, indicate that physical dependence on ethanol has developed. It is generally recognized that both acute intake and chronic intake of ethanol influence a number of neurochemical functions, which presumably play a significant role in neuronal conduction and information transmission in the CNS, and thus underlie the behavioral responses to ethanol.

In this chapter, we review the neurochemical events that accompany acute and chronic ethanol administration. Our discussion of the acute effects of ethanol focuses, where possible, on systems that may mediate the anxiolytic and reinforcing effects associated with ethanol ingestion, as well as the systems that may contribute to ethanol-induced sedation and hypnosis. The reinforcing events associated with intake of ethanol are considered as factors promoting continuing use of ethanol. We also emphasize the neurochemical alterations that can be interpreted as adaptive responses of neuronal systems to the presence of ethanol. The adaptive changes may be of importance for the development and expression of tolerance to and physical dependence on ethanol.

Some portions of this chapter have previously appeared in the referenced reviews.

Most of the data presented here were obtained from experiments with animals, but results from human studies are included where available and considered appropriate. The studies with animals and with humans indicate that initial responses to ethanol, as well as adaptive changes, are modulated by both genetic and environmental factors. The concept that genetic factors contribute significantly to individual differences in response to ethanol has allowed for additional means of studying and understanding the pharmacology of ethanol. This concept has also provided prospects for developing markers to identify individuals at risk for alcoholism, as well as organ pathologies associated with chronic ethanol ingestion.

Ethanol Tolerance and Physical Dependence

Studies of individual differences and neuroadaptation in response to the ingestion of ethanol are, in many cases, directed at generating information on why certain individuals consume ethanol in quantities that are injurious to themselves and to those around them. Clearly, "addiction" to a substance such as ethanol may never be adequately defined only by genetically determined differences in sensitivity to ethanol and by the concepts of tolerance and dependence, even though these concepts are currently undergoing a rapid metamorphosis. A host of social, cultural, and personal variables needs to be considered when discussing addictions and considering the reasons why some persons drink alcohol in a self-destructive manner. On the other hand, the concept of an "alcohol dependence syndrome" (Edwards, 1968) has proven to be a valuable tool in beginning to provide operational definitions for substantive portions of the spectrum of alcohol addiction in humans; it has also provided a framework for categorizing various observations regarding pathological drinking behavior and its concomitants. Although the alcohol dependence syndrome contains some elements that are distinctly human, many of the elements (tolerance, withdrawal symptoms, and need-for-relief drinking) are amenable to modeling with infrahuman species. Such models are valuable not only for validating and better describing the components of the syndrome, but also for facilitating assessment of the biological and molecular mechanisms that underlie each particular component.

The development of tolerance to ethanol, following intake of this drug over a period of time, is a well-known phenomenon in both animals and human beings. Operationally, tolerance to ethanol (or to any other pharmacological agent) is present when a diminished response to a particular dose of the drug is observed in an organism, due to the fact that this organism has been exposed to the drug during one or several prior occasions. To state this otherwise, ethanol tolerance can be said to be present if, following acute or chronic ethanol administration, a *larger dose* of ethanol is needed to produce a particular physiological, pharmacological, or behavioral response in an individual, in comparison to the dose needed to produce the same intensity of the response during the initial administration of ethanol. One would conjecture that a neurochemical system responsible for tolerance would also demonstrate a diminished sensitivity to ethanol in the tolerant individual.

In analyses of the development of ethanol tolerance, a distinction between "functional" and "dispositional" tolerance is usually made (see Tabakoff, Melchior, & Hoffman, 1982). Functional tolerance is an adaptive change at the cellular level that leads to resistance to the pharmacological effects of ethanol, whereas dispositional (or metabolic) tolerance is related to the fact that chronic (or occasionally even acute) ethanol exposure results in an increased rate of metabolism of ethanol, which shortens the duration of the action of ethanol. Although a complete conceptual analysis of functional tolerance cannot be incuded here, two important observations concerning this type of tolerance should be emphasized. First, functional tolerance can develop very rapidly; experiments with both animals and humans indicate that tolerance can be demonstrated following a single administration of ethanol. Second, according to recent observations, functional tolerance can be divided into two qualitatively different components: "environment-dependent" and "environment-independent" tolerance.

The development of drug tolerance, at least to some extent, can be explained by the ability of an animal to form learned associations between cues in the experimental situation (environmental cues) and the pharmacological actions of the drug. The establishment of such an association results in the animal's ability to counteract the drug effect by generating a compensatory physiological response. The expression of the compensatory response during the administration of a drug such as ethanol will result in an attenuation of the drug effect, and this event is referred to as environment-dependent tolerance. For instance, when ethanol has been administered in paradigms conducive to development of environment-dependent tolerance, a hyperthermic response to an injection of placebo in the ethanol-associated environment can be noticed as a compensatory (antagonistic) reaction to the well-known ethanol-produced hypothermia. The dependence of this response on environmental cues is revealed by the fact that this type of tolerance is primarily evident in the environment with which ethanol administration has been previously paired, and is not evidenced in a novel, "unconditioned" environment. On the other hand, environment-independent tolerance can be demonstrated regardless of the testing environment and is usually evidenced after more extensive periods of ethanol intoxication. For a more detailed discussion of environment-dependent versus environment-independent drug tolerance, the reader is referred to reviews by Siegel (1979) and Tabakoff et al. (1982).

Physical dependence is operationally defined by the withdrawal symptoms that occur upon abrupt cessation of chronic intake of large doses of ethanol (see Tabakoff & Rothstein, 1983). The withdrawal syndrome is regarded as a manifestation of CNS hyperexcitability, which is created by the sudden abatement of the depressant effects of ethanol. This state of hyperexcitability has been hypothesized to arise from adaptation of various CNS functions that occurs during chronic ethanol exposure. The biological purpose of these adaptive processes is presumably to counteract the effects of ethanol and to "normalize" neuronal functioning in the presence of ethanol. However, an abrupt removal of ethanol from the organism will remove the depressant influence of this drug and reveal the presence of the now "maladapted," excitable CNS. The neuronal hyperexcitability can be manifested in overt withdrawal symptoms, ranging from tremor to seizure activity, and evidence of the propensity for such hyperexcitability should be evident at the neurochemical level as well.

Although both ethanol tolerance and physical dependence have in the past been conceptualized to involve similar CNS adaptive changes, it should be pointed out that these two phenomena cannot at present be reconciled to result from a single, unitary neurochemical mechanism. As a matter of fact, increasing evidence suggests that different central neurochemical processes are involved in the development and expression of ethanol tolerance and physical dependence. The possible cellular actions of ethanol that lead to neuroadaptation include ethanol-induced changes in cell membrane properties and in membrane-bound enzymatic functions; changes of central neurotransmitter metabolism; and alterations in neurotransmitter receptor and ion channel activity. In describing the actions of ethanol, we attempt herein to identify the events responsible for development of tolerance and/or physical dependence.

It should be emphasized that the phenomena of ethanol tolerance and physical dependence may play an important role in promoting ethanol intake, in addition to their importance in the characterization and definition of addiction. If one envisions that the motivation for ethanol intake reflects a balance between the reinforcing and aversive properties of ethanol, it may be postulated that the development of tolerance to the aversive properties, in addition to allowing for intake of larger quantities of ethanol, may also enhance the reinforcing properties of ethanol and thus contribute to excessive ethanol intake. The appearance of withdrawal symptoms in an ethanol-dependent individual has also been suggested to engender further ethanol drinking, in an effort to relieve such symptoms (Edwards, 1968).

Mechanisms of Action of Ethanol

Ethanol Effects on Membrane Properties

In 1901, Meyer proposed that ethanol produces its pharmacological effects (intoxication, sedation, anesthesia) through the perturbation of neuronal membrane lipids. From the time of these experiments, perturbation of biological membranes has been considered as the primary mechanism of action of ethanol. The concept is based upon the observation that ethanol, like many other anesthetic agents, is physically able to dissolve in (partition into) the membrane and produce an expansion of the membrane. This expansion, which is accompanied by increased "fluidity" of the membrane lipids, is postulated to cause disruption of normal processes of neuronal conduction and information processing in the CNS. During the past several years, sensitive physicochemical techniques, including electron paramagnetic resonance (EPR) and fluorescence polarization, have provided evidence that physiologically attainable concentrations of ethanol (25 to 100 mM; approximately 100 to 400 mg%) measurably increase the "fluidity" of cell membrane lipids, and it has been found that these changes in membrane fluidity can be correlated with ethanol-induced sedation (see Tabakoff & Hoffman, 1987). One crucial study involved lines of mice that had been selectively bred for differential sensitivity to the hypnotic effect of ethanol. By use of the EPR technique, neuronal cell membranes obtained from the more sensitive mice (LS mice) were also found to be more sensitive to the lipid-fluidizing effect of ethanol added *in vitro*, compared with membranes from the less sensitive animals (SS mice). These results would appear to support the postulate that ethanol produces some of its pharmacological effects through a relatively nonspecific effect on membrane lipid structure, and that sensitivity to the anesthetic effects of ethanol can be genetically determined.

In addition, using lecithin and cholesterol bilayers, Pang, Braswell, Chang, Sommer, and Miller (1980) showed that, for equal concentrations in the bilayer, ethanol and a wide range of general anesthetics all had similar fluidizing effects, and the ability of ethanol and other anesthetics to fluidize phospholipid bilayers correlated positively with their anesthetic potencies. However, as these and other investigators discuss, such results can lead to erroneous conclusions because such correlations do not demonstrate causal relationships. For example, Franks and Lieb (1984) point out that the interaction of lipid-soluble anesthetics with a hydrophobic site on the enzyme luciferase correlates very well with the solubility of the anesthetics in lipid bilayers. They comment that this correlation is consistent with the hypothesis that membrane *proteins* may be the site of action of anesthetics.

When we consider the "membrane hypothesis" as an explanation of the intoxicating or anesthetic actions of ethanol, we must realize that the ethanol-induced fluidity changes in biological and model membranes are relatively small. If we consider ethanol's actions on synaptosomal membranes, for example, changes of the magnitude produced by ethanol can also be induced by increases in temperature of approximately 0.5°C. Since such variations are normally evident in the daily rhythm of body temperature in humans, a number of investigators have commented that the ethanol-induced increase in lipid fluidity is simply too small to be physiologically relevant. For example, Pringle, Brown, and Miller (1981) state that "until it can be shown either that some bilayer of different lipid composition, or that proteins, very sensitive to small changes in order [fluidity], exist, the disordered lipid hypothesis must be regarded with reservation" (p. 54).

Neural cell membranes are in fact heterogeneous mixtures of lipids and proteins, and areas of differential sensitivity to ethanol within the membrane may result from the presence of microdomains of particular lipid composition. For example, gangliosides, as well as phospholipids and cholesterol, are major components of neuronal membranes and may contribute to increasing the sensitivity of a specific membrane region to ethanol. Gangliosides were recently found to significantly enhance the membrane-fluidizing effect of ethanol when they were added to model phospholipid bilayers (Harris, Groh, Baxter, & Hitzemann, 1984). It is also conceivable that ethanol can produce its effects through a direct action on membrane proteins, or that ethanol may have a particular affinity for the hydrophobic interface between membrane proteins and lipids and may act within this microenvironment.

If, however, ethanol produces its acute intoxicating effects by perturbing the structure of neuronal membranes, it is appropriate to consider that membrane lipid composition may change during chronic ingestion of ethanol, in an attempt by the neuron to resist the ethanol-induced perturbation. One such change may involve the levels of cholesterol in neuronal membranes. In general terms, it appears that cholesterol tends to antagonize ethanol's effects by maintaining optimal membrane fluidity with regard to normal cell functions. Results from several studies have indicated that chronic ethanol exposure produces increased levels of cholesterol in erythrocyte and brain membranes derived from chronically ethanol-treated mice or rats (for review, see Hoffman & Tabakoff, 1985). These observations were initially taken to support the view that development of ethanol tolerance is accompanied by a concomitant increase in cholesterol levels of brain membranes. Later findings, however, weakened the hypothesis of a direct causal relationship between increased synaptosomal cholesterol content and the development of ethanol tolerance, since a different procedure for feeding ethanol to animals produced no change in the levels of membrane cholesterol in whole brains of mice. On the other hand, there is evidence that an interaction between cholesterol and other factors may be necessary for producing the increased membrane resistance to the perturbing actions of ethanol. When cholesterol was removed from the membrane preparations of both control and ethanol-treated animals, it was shown that all the membranes were equally affected by the *in vitro* addition of ethanol (i.e., they displayed no difference in resistance to the effects of ethanol). When equal amounts of cholesterol were added back to the membranes from the two groups of animals, the membranes derived from ethanol-tolerant mice were again found to be more resistant to ethanol. It can therefore be concluded that the presence of cholesterol in membranes is necessary for the expression of the adaptive membrane resistance to ethanol's effects in the ethanol-tolerant animals, but this resistance does not depend on an increase in cholesterol levels.

Results from several investigations imply that membrane fluidity can be modified not only by cholesterol, but also by alterations in the fatty acid composition of membrane phospholipids. A decrease in the proportion of unsaturated fatty acids in synaptosomal phospholipids of mice chronically treated with ethanol has been reported (for review, see Tabakoff & Hoffman, 1989). The changes in the fatty acid substituents in response to chronic ingestion of ethanol may be restricted to a particular class of phospholipids. For instance, resistance of liver microsomal membranes to ethanol-induced perturbation was dependent on the presence of inositol phospholipids in the membranes from ethanol-treated animals (Taraschi, Ellingson, Wu, Zimmerman, & Rubin, 1986). Reconstituted membranes, composed of phospholipids taken from the membranes of control animals, were not resistant to ethanol unless the inositol lipids in these membranes were replaced by inositol lipids from membranes of ethanol-treated animals. This effect was not observed when other classes of phospholipids from ethanol-treated animals were used.

Such changes in the chemical composition of neuronal membranes produced by chronic ingestion of ethanol may in and of themselves produce resistance to ethanol-induced membrane perturbation. Another possibility is that the changes in the chemistry of membranes may alter the ability of ethanol to enter (partition into) the membrane. For example, experiments with synaptosomal membranes prepared from brains of rats chronically treated with ethanol have demonstrated a significant decrease in the ability of lipid-soluble anesthetics to enter such membranes (Rottenberg, Waring, & Rubin, 1981). If, in fact, changes in neuronal membrane lipid composition or properties represent the mechanism underlying ethanol intoxication, tolerance, and/or physical dependence, it is difficult to envision a means by which to pharmacologically manipulate these ethanol-induced responses at their source, since the adult brain is relatively resistant to modification of lipid content.

However, the membrane hypothesis of ethanol's actions has also focused attention on ethanol-induced perturbation of membrane *proteins,* which function as receptors, ionophores, and enzymes. Evidence that specific regions within neuronal membranes can show selective sensitivity to ethanol, and evidence that chronic ethanol ingestion can selectively alter the function of specific membrane constituents, have suggested that various membrane-bound proteins, which are dependent on their immediately surrounding lipids for optimal activity, should also differ in sensitivity to ethanol. As already noted, hydrophobic areas of proteins may also provide an appropriate site for interactions with ethanol. Evidence compiled over the last 10–15 years clearly demonstrates the sensitivity to ethanol of several important neuronal membrane proteins, whereas the functions of other membrane proteins are unaltered by concentrations of ethanol that would be lethal if present in the brains of animals or humans (for reviews, see Tabakoff & Hoffman, 1987, 1989; Hoffman & Tabakoff, 1985; Tabakoff, Hoffman, & McLaughlin, 1988). The selective sensitivity of certain neurochemical systems to ethanol suggests that even though there is no CNS "receptor" for ethanol, as there is for other psychotropic drugs, ethanol may interact selectively with particular "receptive" regions of proteins or neuronal membranes to produce a defined physiological effect (Tabakoff & Hoffman, 1987). Current research has focused attention on the γ-aminobutyric acid (GABA)–benzodiazepine receptor–chloride channel complex, the N-methyl-D-aspartate (NMDA) receptor-regulated ion channels, the voltage-sensitive calcium channels (VSCCs), and the signal transduction systems dependent on the stimulatory guanine nucleotide-binding regulatory protein (G_s) as "receptive" elements for ethanol's actions. As detailed below, ethanol affects these elements at concentrations compatible with those responsible for mild to moderate levels of intoxication (0.05–0.15%; i.e., 10–30 mM), and adaptation of these systems can be related to development of tolerance to and physical dependence on ethanol. However, we need to remember that neuronal systems do not act in isolation and that an action of ethanol on one system may initiate a cascade of events through other neuronal systems. In addition, the activity of systems not substantively affected by ethanol may modulate the acute sensitivity of the affected system or the ability of the affected systems to adapt to the chronic presence of ethanol. Examples of such relationships with regard to serotonergic, noradrenergic, and vasopressin neuronal systems of brain are discussed later in the chapter.

Ethanol Effects on VSCCs

VSCCs are of major importance in altering intracellular calcium levels, and also in coupling signal conduction to transmitter release. A number of VSCCs with different physiological and pharmacological properties have been described (Miller, 1987). These include T-, L-, and N-channels. Little is yet known about T-channels, which are activated by low levels of depolarization and give rise to small, transient calcium currents. L-channels are activated by substantial neuronal membrane depolarization, and their activity is modulated by dihydropyridine (DHP) agonists and antagonists (e.g., nitrendipine, nifedipine, and BAY K 8644). The L-channels are found in neuronal preparations, but do not appear to be linked to neurotransmitter release. N-channels, which are not sensitive to DHPs, have been suggested to be localized in neuron terminals and to mediate neurotransmitter release, whereas L-channels have been postulated to be localized on neuronal cell bodies.

Although controversy had in the past surrounded the question of whether ethanol affected depolarization-induced calcium uptake into synaptosomes, recent work clarified the need to use short depolarization times to study ethanol's actions (see Tabakoff & Hoffman, 1989). Measures of calcium uptake over periods of 1–3 seconds demonstrated that ethanol was a potent inhibitor of synaptosomal depolarization-induced calcium uptake. Interestingly, the acute effects of ethanol and certain other anesthetics on depolarization-dependent calcium uptake were not clearly related to the anesthetics' membrane-disordering effects. The effects of ethanol on calcium influx through VSCCs may, however, be indirect. Studies that demonstrate ethanol-induced release of calcium from mircosomal preparations, from a pool of calcium that is not identical to that influenced by inositol trisphosphate (IP$_3$), can provide an explanation of the inhibition of calcium entry (Shah, Cohen, & Pant, 1987; Rezazadeh, Woodward, & Leslie, 1989; Daniell & Harris, 1989). That is, increases in the levels of intracellular calcium result in an altered equilibrium between calcium inside and calcium outside the cell, even if ethanol does not directly inhibit the activity of the calcium channel protein.

The different possible mechanisms by which ethanol inhibits calcium influx can be assessed by studying the relationship between ethanol's effects on calcium influx and neurotransmitter release (see Tabakoff & Hoffman, 1989). Fast-phase calcium uptake and resulting increases in intracellular calcium concentrations have been reported to be associated with phasic neurotransmitter release. However, while ethanol clearly inhibited calcium uptake, ethanol did not decrease norepinephrine release from a crude synaptosomal preparation. It was suggested that ethanol might alter calcium uptake into neurons that release transmitters other than norepinephrine, since the synaptosomal preparation is heterogeneous. Another possible explanation may be that ethanol, at least in part, alters calcium uptake by L-channels located on nonterminal vesicular elements present in the "synaptosomal" preparation. The most plausible explanation at present is that ethanol is in fact increasing intracellular free calcium by release from microsomes, and this event could decrease calcium influx through VSCCs while leaving transmitter release uninhibited or even increased.

The chronic ingestion of ethanol by rats over a period of several weeks produced resistance to ethanol-induced inhibition of synaptosomal depolarization-dependent calcium uptake (see Tabakoff & Hoffman, 1989). Studies of the binding of [3H]nitrendipine (a DHP) have indicated that the chronic presence of ethanol in the medium bathing cells of neural crest origin (PC12 cells) increases the number of nitrendipine-sensitive calcium channels and increases depolarization-dependent calcium influx. Chronic ethanol administration was also reported to increase the number of [3H]DHP-binding sites in brain membranes. The binding sites for nitrendipine and DHP are believed to represent L-channels, as discussed above, and the characteristics of the increased calcium flux in PC12 cells (e.g., modulation by DHPs) were also consistent with an increased number of L-channels. It is possible that this calcium channel proliferation in cells in culture or in brain promotes neuronal hyperexcitability. The physiological significance of changes in L-channel number is currently being debated. However, it has been reported that administration of DHP-type calcium channel blockers can prevent or reduce ethanol withdrawal seizures in animals (Little, Dolin, & Halsey, 1986). In addition, a calcium channel blocker also reduced ethanol withdrawal symptoms in humans, with few sedative side effects (Koppi, Eberhardt, Haller, & König, 1987). These findings make further investigations of ethanol's effects on various types of VSCCs most important.

Ethanol Effects on GABA-Controlled Chloride Ion Channels

GABA is the major inhibitory neurotransmitter within the CNS of mammals. The actions of this transmitter substance are expressed through its interactions with specific receptors, which are part of a receptor-gated chloride channel. This complex also includes binding sites for benzodiazepines and barbiturates

(GABA-A receptors). GABA also interacts with receptors coupled to a class of calcium and potassium channels, and, in an inhibitory manner, to adenylate cyclase (GABA-B receptors) (Olsen, 1987). Although earlier studies of ethanol's actions focused on alterations in the metabolism or release of GABA, more current work has demonstrated a selective and potent effect of ethanol on GABA A receptor-gated chloride conductance. There is little evidence for an effect of ethanol on GABA-B receptors.

The GABA-A receptor-gated channel has been cloned and shown to consist of three polymorphic subunits (Schofield et al., 1987). These subunits have been labeled α, β, and γ, and the GABA recognition site has been proposed to reside on the β subunit, while the α subunit has been proposed as the site for binding of and modulation by benzodiazepines. The activity of this complex is also modulated by barbiturates, and the γ subunit is necessary for expression of this modulatory activity. Several α subunits have recently been cloned, and the characteristics of various subtypes of GABA-A receptors have been related to the type of α subunit being expressed in a cell. Given the similarities in the pharmacology of benzodiazepines, barbiturates, and ethanol, significant attention has been focused on assessing the actions of ethanol on the GABA-A receptor-gated chloride channel (see Allan & Harris, 1987; Harris & Allan, 1989). Electrophysiological studies on spinal cord neurons of frogs demonstrated that ethanol could significantly potentiate GABA's inhibitory activity, but similar studies with brain tissue produced conflicting data. Attempts to demonstrate an effect of ethanol on the binding of GABA or benzodiazepines to their receptors, or on modulation of GABA binding by the benzodiazepines or barbiturates, produced data indicating that even anesthetic levels of ethanol had little effect on the interaction of GABA with its receptor site. An examination of the binding of the compound t-butylbicyclophosphorothionate (TBS) to the GABA–benzodiazepine receptor–chloride channel complex, however, demonstrated that ethanol could produce a perturbation of this system. TBPS binds within the chloride channel formed by the α and β subunits of the receptor complex, and it was proposed that ethanol may interact with GABA indirectly by actions at the chloride channel.

More direct demonstrations of GABA receptor–ethanol interactions were made possible by use of microsacs of neuronal membranes called "synaptoneurosomes" (see Allan & Harris, 1987; Harris & Allan, 1989) With such preparations from brain tissue of animals, ethanol, at concentrations of 10–30 mM, was shown to potentiate the ability of GABA to increase the uptake of radioactively labeled chloride into the synaptoneurosomes (chloride conductance). Such a potentiation of GABA's actions and chloride conductance would be expected to increase neuronal hyperpolarization and to inhibit information transmission within the CNS. The physiological significance of ethanol's actions at the GABA receptor-gated chloride channel was established through experiments with animals selectively bred for sensitivity to ethanol's hypnotic effects (the LS and SS mice described above) and through the use of an imidazobenzodiazepine partial inverse agonist (i.e., a compound that has effects opposite to benzodiazepines), RO 15-4513, acting at the benzodiazepine receptor. When brain tissue, and particularly cerebellar tissue, from SS and LS mice was used to prepare synaptoneurosomes, the preparations from the ethanol-resistant SS mice were found to be insensitive to ethanol-induced potentiation of GABA-stimulated chloride uptake. On the other hand, GABA-stimulated chloride uptake in tissue preparations from the ethanol-sensitive LS mice was shown to be significantly potentiated by addition of ethanol to the assay mixtures (Harris & Allan, 1989). RO 15-4513 was able to reverse ethanol's potentiation of GABA-stimulated chloride conductance in synaptoneurosome preparations from rat brain. Furthermore, when RO 15-4513 was administered to animals that subsequently received ethanol, the benzodiazepine inverse agonist diminished the sedative and anxiolytic effects of ethanol (Suzdak et al., 1986). It should, however, be stressed that not all actions of ethanol are diminished or reversed by RO 15-4513 (see Lister & Nutt, 1988). For instance, neither the behavior-activating effects of low doses of ethanol, nor the respiratory depression produced by high doses of ethanol, is altered by RO 15-4513. The compound is also an anxiogenic and proconvulsant agent, and the exact mode of its antagonism of a select spectrum of ethanol's actions is still being debated. However, the data do support the hypothesis that certain actions of ethanol are mediated by the GABA–benzodiazepine receptor complex.

Evidence has also accumulated that tolerance to the sedative effects of ethanol may be a result of adaptation of the GABA receptor-gated chloride channels to the chronic presence of ethanol in the CNS. When GABA-activated chloride conductance was assayed in synaptoneurosomes prepared from brain tissue of mice or rats that were chronically fed ethanol, a reduced response to ethanol added to the *in vitro* assay was found (Allan & Harris, 1987).

Ethanol Actions at the NMDA Receptor

The major *excitatory* neurotransmitter in the brain is the amino acid glutamate. An inhibitory effect of ethanol on the function of this transmitter would be complementary to the reported potentiation by ethanol of the response to GABA, and might be expected to contribute to the pharmacological effects of ethanol. The actions of glutamate are mediated by at least three subtypes of receptor, designated on the basis of ligand-binding and electrophysiological studies as kainate, quisqualate, and NMDA receptors (McLennan, 1988). All of these receptor subtypes are coupled to cation channels. NMDA receptor-gated channels, when open, are permeable to monovalent cations and calcium, and the actions of NMDA are blocked selectively and noncompetitively by phencyclidine (PCP) and magnesium ions, in a voltage-dependent manner (suggesting sites of action of PCP and magnesium within the ion channel). Glycine enhances the actions of NMDA, but not kainate or quisqualate, and the function of NMDA receptors is also modulated by zinc and polyamines.

The properties of the NMDA receptor-gated channel have been studied in some detail because of the implicated role of the channel complex in neuronal plasticity (long-term synaptic potentiation), hypoxic damage, epileptiform seizure activity, and neuronal development. Thus, *a priori,* a role of the NMDA receptor could be suggested in the cognitive deficits produced by ethanol intake, as well as in the teratogenic effects of ethanol and in the seizures that accompany ethanol withdrawal.

Studies measuring NMDA-stimulated calcium uptake by neural cells grown in culture have demonstrated that calcium influx is potently inhibited by ethanol, with significant inhibition observed at 10 mM ethanol (Hoffman, Rabe, Moses, & Tabakoff, 1989). The response to kainate is much less effectively blocked by ethanol. In addition to these biochemical findings, electrophysiological studies using whole-cell patch clamp preparations of dissociated hippocampal neurons in culture have demonstrated that ethanol selectively inhibits NMDA-induced ion currents (Lovinger, White, & Weight, 1989). Higher ethanol concentrations were necessary to inhibit the response to kainate or quisqualate. In addition to the selective sensitivity to ethanol of the NMDA receptor-gated ion channel (as opposed to the kainate or quisqualate receptor-coupled channels), it is important to note that the concentrations of ethanol that alter the responses to NMDA are those found in the brains of humans who have consumed moderate amounts of alcohol.

Because the NMDA receptor has been shown to be involved in epileptiform seizure activity, adaptation and increased sensitivity of this receptor during chronic intoxication with ethanol could contribute to ethanol withdrawal seizures. "Up-regulation" of the NMDA receptor complex has been observed by ligand-binding studies (Grant, Valverius, Hudspith, & Tabakoff, 1990). MK-801 is a noncompetitive antagonist of NMDA and binds within the open channel of the NMDA receptor-gated ion channel complex. [^{3}H]MK-801 binding was shown to be significantly increased in hippocampal membranes of ethanol-fed mice at the time of ethanol withdrawal. The hippocampus, among other areas, has previously been shown to be involved in ethanol withdrawal seizure activity. An increase in hippocampal NMDA receptors would be expected to result in increased sensitivity to endogenous glutamate, and to contribute to the CNS hyperexcitability that is characteristic of ethanol withdrawal. In fact, the increased number of NMDA receptors in the ethanol-withdrawn animals was demonstrated to alter the sensitivity of the animals to agents acting at the NMDA receptor. When ethanol-withdrawn mice were injected with NMDA itself, ethanol withdrawal seizure severity increased, and a higher proportion of lethal seizures occurred in the NMDA-treated mice than in vehicle-injected animals (NMDA at the dose used did not produce seizures in control mice). Administration of NMDA receptor-gated channel antagonists (e.g., MK-801) reduced withdrawal seizure severity in the ethanol-withdrawn animals. These results suggest a new pharmacological approach to the treatment of certain symptoms of alcohol withdrawal.

The pattern of events observed for the NMDA receptor (i.e., up-regulation of the receptor-gated channel after chronic ethanol exposure) is reminiscent of responses noted with VSCCs, described above. The precise contribution to ethanol withdrawal symptomatology of changes in each of these types of calcium channel needs further elucidation. It is, however, becoming evident that alterations in neuronal calcium homeostasis may be responsible for the more severe aspects of the ethanol withdrawal syndrome, whereas adaptive responses in the GABA receptor-gated chloride channels may be primary contributors to the development of tolerance to the sedative and incoordinating effects of alcohol.

Effects of Ethanol on Neurotransmitter Turnover

Changes that occur in the release and metabolism of neurotransmitters after the administration of ethanol to animals and humans have been the subject of numerous reports (for reviews, see Hoffman & Tabakoff, 1985; Tabakoff & Hoffman, 1989). The reported neurotransmitter changes probably result from ethanol-induced perturbation of the ion channels that control the excitability of the neurons under investigation, and/or may be secondary to alterations in input from connecting neurons that are being affected by ethanol. Although we consider various neurotransmitter systems separately, it should be kept in mind that these rather well-defined transmitter systems interact, often making if difficult to dissociate primary from secondary effects of ethanol on neurotransmitter metabolism. Whether the effects of ethanol on the various neurotransmitter systems are direct or indirect, knowledge of the actions of ethanol may allow for selective and rational intervention in a segment of ethanol's actions. For instance, serotonin (5-HT) uptake inhibitors (zimelidine, fluoxetine) have been shown to reduce alcohol consumption by animals and humans, but these agents do not modify the anesthetic actions of ethanol. Given the evidence for acute effects of ethanol on serotonergic systems (see below), one might predict that 5-HT uptake inhibitors could substitute for ethanol in certain individuals.

SEROTONIN

A significant quantity of data has been generated in attempts to define the acute and chronic actions of ethanol on the serotonergic systems of brain. These data indicate that results are dependent on a multitude of factors related to experimental design (e.g., dose, time, species, etc.; see Hoffman & Tabakoff, 1985; Nutt & Glue, 1986). A selective assessment of available work does indicate that acute administration of large doses of ethanol to rodents increases the quantity of the major 5-HT metabolite, 5-hydroxyindoleacetic acid (5-HIAA), in brain. This increase in 5-HIAA is accompanied by a reduction or no change in 5-HT levels, and the results, taken in concert, would lead one to conclude that acute ingestion of ethanol can increase the release and/or turnover of 5-HT. An examination of animals after they have been chronically treated with ethanol, so that they are physically dependent on ethanol, indicates that 5-HT turnover is decreased during the early stages of withdrawal (Nutt & Glue, 1986; Tabakoff, Hoffman, & Moses, 1977). This process of neuroadaptation to chronic exposure of the brain to ethanol is, however, reversible, since 5-HT turnover is normalized several days after the chronic administration of ethanol is terminated. Data on serotonergic activity in brains of human alcoholics provides some parallels to observations with inbred animals, but adds the complexity of individual variability, which may reflect inherent, genetically determined differences in brain function and behavioral patterns.

The literature in biological psychiatry is replete with examples of decreased serotonergic function associated with antisocial personality disorders, violence, and impulsive behavior. A subtype of alcoholism (Type 2) that includes individuals characterized by violent, impulsive behavior has also been described by Cloninger (1987). Measurement of cerebrospinal fluid (CSF) 5-HIAA levels in alcoholic violent offenders (when sober) has shown these individuals to have low 5-HIAA levels (Roy, Virkkunen, & Linnoila, 1988). It was concluded that lowered serotonergic neuron activity may be an inherent characteristic of the violent, impulsive subtype of alcoholic.

If one assumes that acute ingestion of alcohol can increase 5-HT turnover in human brain, as demonstrated with animals, one can speculate that alcohol intoxication may "normalize" serotonergic activity in individuals who are inherently hyposerotonergic. A study of intoxicated and withdrawn alcoholics by Ballenger, Goodwin, Major, and Brown (1979) demonstrated that CSF 5-HIAA levels in these individuals were within the normal range during the time that alcohol was present in their systems, but that 5-HIAA levels were significantly below normal several days after withdrawal. The low CSF 5-HIAA levels may be a result of alcohol withdrawal, the inherent low activity of serotonergic neurons in these individuals, or both of these factors. In any case, one can consider that individuals may learn to use ethanol to treat the results of serotonergic hypoactivity, whether this is inherent or a result of neuroadaptive mechanisms associated with chronic ethanol ingestion.

It is the possibility that alcohol is being used in a self-medication attempt that provides justification for use of 5-HT uptake inhibitors and other serotonergic drugs to reduce alcohol ingestion in humans and animals. Earlier work with zimelidine and more recent studies with ditalopram and fluoxetine indicate that these 5-HT uptake inhibitors can reduce alcohol intake in human heavy drinkers, and in animals selectively bred to consume large quantities of alcohol (Murphy et al., 1988; Naranjo et al., 1984, 1987). The reduction in alcohol intake by human beings treated with 5-HT uptake inhibitors is modest, but provides evidence that neurobiological mechanisms (the 5-HT systems of the hypothalamus) that control ingestive behaviors in general may be amenable to modulation for the purpose of controlling alcohol intake. It is not as yet clear which postsynaptic 5-HT receptor systems are of primary importance in mediating the actions of released 5-HT on alcohol ingestion. Recent work has demonstrated a selective action of ethanol on the function of 5-HT$_3$ receptors, and little effect on the agonist- and antagonist-binding characteristics of 5-HT$_{1A}$ and 5-HT$_2$ receptors (Buckholtz, Zhou, & Tabakoff, 1989; Grant, Lovinger, White, & Barrett, 1990); it is also of interest that selective 5-HT$_3$ receptor antagonists can block the discriminative stimulus properties of ethanol in animals trained to distinguish ethanol from other fluids (Grant, Lovinger, et al., 1990). In the future, direct stimulation of the appropriate 5-HT receptor system by specific agonists may provide a more efficacious alternative to the 5-HT uptake inhibitors in reducing alcohol intake in humans.

NOREPINEPHRINE

A number of studies have shown that both acute doses of ethanol and chronic ethanol administration influence the rate of synthesis, release, and catabolism (turnover) of norepinephrine (NE) (see Hoffman & Tabakoff, 1985). Acute administration of low to moderate doses of ethanol enhances the rate of catecholamine synthesis in both mice and rats, but the endogenous steady-state levels of NE are apparently not affected. In human studies, Borg, Kvande, Mossberg, Valverius, and Sedvall (1983) observed an elevated formation of the NE metabolite 3-methoxy-4-hydroxyphenylglycol (MHPG) in CSF after acute administration of 1.0–1.5 g/kg ethanol to healthy male volunteers. A cautious interpretation of the sum of findings would be that lower ethanol doses increase the rate of NE synthesis and turnover. Suppression of NE neuron activity and NE turnover is observed following higher, anesthetic doses of ethanol.

An increase in NE turnover has been reported following chronic ethanol exposure (see Hoffman & Tabakoff, 1985). The NE metabolism was elevated both at the time of withdrawal and throughout the period during which overt withdrawal signs were witnessed, and remained elevated even following the disappearance of observable, acute withdrawal symptoms. This time course indicates that increased NE neuronal activity following withdrawal of animals from chronic treatment with ethanol cannot be regarded as a response to the stress produced by the withdrawal of ethanol, nor as a determinant factor for the overt signs of ethanol withdrawal.

DOPAMINE

Acute administration of high doses of ethanol causes an increase in the rate of tyrosine hydroxylation—an effect that is especially apparent in dopamine (DA)-rich brain areas (e.g., striatum) of both mice and rats. Although one exception exists, the enhancement of DA synthesis has consistently been reported to be accompanied by a corresponding increase in the formation of dihydroxyphenylacetic acid (DOPAC), one of the major metabolites of DA (see Hoffman & Tabakoff, 1985). These results could be indicative of the fact that an acute dose of ethanol stimulates the release of DA from DA neuron terminals, resulting in a compensatory increase in the rate of DA synthesis. This view is supported by electrophysiological findings showing that acute doses of ethanol increase the firing of DA neurons in the nigrostriatal and mesolimbic pathways in the brain of rats (Mereu, Fadda, & Gessa, 1984).

During chronic administration of ethanol, tolerance develops to the ethanol-induced enhancement of DA turnover; this tolerance appears to be fully developed after approximately 7 days of daily injections of ethanol, or oral ethanol ingestion, in both mice and rats (see Hoffman & Tabakoff, 1985). In human alcoholics undergoing withdrawal, CSF levels of homovanillic acid (HVA), a DA metabolite, were reduced, indicating decreased turnover of DA, in comparison to DA turnover in those individuals not showing withdrawal symptoms (Major, Ballenger, Goodwin, & Brown, 1977). These results may indicate that in humans as well as in other animals, decreased dopaminergic activity may contribute to withdrawal symptomatology. The administration of DA agonists has been reported to ameliorate certain ethanol withdrawal symptoms in humans (Borg & Weinholdt, 1982).

ACETYLCHOLINE

A decreased release of acetylcholine (ACh) has been measured, both *in vitro* and *in vivo*, after administration of an acute dose of ethanol (see Hoffman & Tabakoff, 1985). The observation that an acute dose of ethanol increased endogenous ACh levels in rat brain may also be interpreted as an indication of a decreased release of this transmitter. It should, however, be noted that the amount of ethanol administered, as well as the brain area studied, greatly influenced the obtained results.

A series of adaptive changes in cholinergic function appears to occur following chronic ethanol treatment. Thus, an increased *in vitro* release of ACh in cortical slices from rats chronically treated with ethanol has been reported. Decreased brain levels of ACh, which could reflect increased neuronal release, were found during and after chronic ethanol treatment. As with the acute effects of ethanol, the changes appeared to be restricted to particular brain regions (see Hoffman & Tabakoff, 1985).

It has also been found that acute ethanol administration increases high-affinity choline uptake (necessary for ACh synthesis) in certain brain areas, whereas choline uptake was reduced in other brain regions. Upon withdrawal of ethanol, high-affinity choline uptake in striatum was elevated for about 3 days, indicating an increased activity of cholinergic neurons in this brain region during the withdrawal period (see Hoffman & Tabakoff, 1985). This change was suggested to result from decreased dopaminergic input. Results from receptor-binding studies lend additional support to the contention that adaptive changes in central cholinergic function may occur as a response to chronic ethanol exposure. Although no differences in [³H]quinuclidinyl-ben-zylate ([³H]QNB, an ACh receptor antagonist) binding to muscarinic cholinergic receptors were present when *striatal* tissue from control and ethanol-withdrawn mice was compared, there was a significant but transient increase in the number of [³H]QNB-binding sites in hippocampus and cortex of ethanol-withdrawn animals (see Hoffman & Tabakoff, 1985). This effect dissipated by the second day of withdrawal. Thus, in rodent models, chronic ethanol administration appears to result in a general increase in activity of brain cholinergic neuronal systems. The time course of the changes in cholinergic receptors suggests that the ethanol-induced "supersensitivity" to ACh in certain brain areas may be related to symptoms of ethanol withdrawal, including seizures. Interestingly, other procedures (e.g., kindling) that result in CNS hyperexcitability similar to that observed in ethanol withdrawal have also been reported to produce supersensitivity to ACh in certain brain areas. Based on the brain region-specific changes in the ACh receptor in ethanol-withdrawn animals, it seems possible that administration of cholinergic antagonists might be useful in ameliorating some specific ethanol withdrawal symptoms.

Alterations in the binding of [³H]nicotine to rat brain membranes, following 150 days of ethanol administration, have been observed (Yoshida, Engel, & Liljequist, 1982). The direction of the changes depended on the brain region being examined. The number of [³H]nicotine-binding sites was decreased in the hippocampus, but increased in hypothalamus and thalamus. The significance of [³H]nicotine binding in the brain is not known at present, and will need further elucidation.

Effect of Ethanol on Signal Transduction in the Central Nervous System

The interaction of a number of hormones and neurotransmitters with their membrane-bound receptors leads to activation of adenylate cyclase (AC) and increased production of the intracellular messenger, cyclic adenosine 3',5'-monophosphate (cAMP) (Freissmuth, Casey, & Gilman, 1989). cAMP activates protein kinase A, which leads to phosphorylation of various soluble and membrane-bound proteins and results in the physiological effects of the hormones and neurotransmitters. The action of cAMP is terminated by its metabolism by cyclic nucleotide phosphodiesterase. Guanine nucleotide-binding proteins (G proteins) couple AC to various membrane-bound receptors. The G proteins associated with receptors for agonists that stimulate AC activity are designated G_s. In some instances, hormones or neurotransmitters inhibit AC activity, and the G proteins that couple the receptors for these agonists to the enzyme are called G_i. Several other guanosine triphosphate-binding proteins that are similar in structure to G_s and G_i have been described; these proteins couple receptors to effectors other than AC, or, in some cases, their function is not yet known.

Both G_s and G_i consist of three subunits, α, β, and γ (Freissmuth et al.,

1989). The β and γ subunits of G_s and G_i appear to be very similar, whereas their α subunits are unique. The mechanism by which agonists stimulate AC activity, and the role of G_s in this process, have been studied in great detail (Freissmuth et al., 1989). Ethanol *in vitro* increases basal guanine nucleotide- and agonist (isoproterenol)-stimulated AC activity in cortical tissue (see Tabakoff et al., 1988). Ethanol also increases the rate of activation of AC by the guanine nucleotide analogue, Gpp(NH)p. These findings are consistent with the postulate that G_s plays an important role in the effect of ethanol on cerebral cortical AC activity, a possibility supported by ligand-binding studies. Ethanol *in vitro* has little effect on antagonist (iodocyanopindolol) binding to cortical β-adrenergic receptors, but agonist (isoproterenol) binding is very sensitive to ethanol's effects. At low concentrations (10 to 20 mM), ethanol decreased the affinity for isoproterenol of the high-affinity form of the receptor (which reflects formation of the agonist–receptor–G_s complex). Thus, in cerebral cortical membranes, ethanol appears to interact with G_s, perhaps altering its conformation and rate of activation, and promoting the interaction of guanine nucleotides with G_s.

Ethanol also increases DA-stimulated AC activity in striatal membranes (see Tabakoff et al., 1988). Ethanol does not effect either dopamine binding to its striatal (D_1) receptor or guanine nucleotide binding to G_s. However, the stimulation of Gpp(NH)p-activated AC activity suggested that ethanol could enhance DA-induced activation of G_s in the presence of Gpp(NH)p.

The heterogeneity of brain membrane preparations, even when derived from circumscribed brain areas, has led a number of investigators to assess the effect of ethanol on AC activity or cAMP production in more homogeneous populations of intact cells in culture and in membrane preparations derived from these cells (see Tabakoff et al., 1988). Results in cell culture systems have been quite similar to those in brain. Ethanol was reported to increase prostaglandin E_1 (PGE)-stimulated AC activity in N1E-115 cells, a murine neuroblastoma clone. The effect of ethanol was observed only during the first few minutes of PGE stimulation, suggesting that ethanol increased the initial rate of AC activation. In NG108-15 cells, a neuroblastoma–glioma cell line, ethanol was reported to enhance cAMP production (measured by radioimmunoassay) in response to an adenosine analogue, PIA. Quite similar results have been found in rat pineal cells in culture, where ethanol significantly increased cAMP accumulation in response to isoproterenol or vasoactive intestinal peptide. In rat pineal glands in organ culture, ethanol enhanced the cAMP response to low doses of isoproterenol. The effect of ethanol on agonist-stimulated AC activity in these studies again suggests a primary site of action for ethanol within the receptor–AC coupling system—that is, at G_s or the G_s-AC interaction.

G_s and G_i are quite similar in structure, mechanism of action, and membrane localization. If ethanol affects G_s and AC via its membrane-perturbing effects, an effect on G_i might also be reasonably postulated. However, very little or no effect of ethanol on hormone or neurotransmitter-induced inhibition of AC activity has been reported (see Tabakoff et al., 1988). In striatal tissue, ethanol *in vitro* had no effect on opiate (morphine or enkephalin) inhibition of AC activity, even though ethanol at high concentrations does alter ligand binding to opiate receptors in striatal tissue and other preparations. Similarly, ethanol did not alter inhibition of striatal AC activity by acetylcholine.

The selective sensitivity of G_s to ethanol, and the changes in receptor-coupled brain AC activity following chronic ethanol ingestion by animals, suggest that the AC system in accessible tissues of humans may represent a marker of ethanol intake. Such a biochemical measure would be useful clinically as an objective monitor of ethanol drinking behavior. It has been found that receptor- and G-protein-coupled AC activity is, in fact, lower in platelets and lymphocytes of alcoholics than in control subjects (see Tabakoff & Hoffman, 1988). However, in the study using platelets, some of the lowest AC activity was observed in cells obtained from subjects who reported that they had been abstinent from alcohol for periods of 1 to 4 years. These findings suggest either that the alteration in platelet AC activity reverses very slowly (unlike the changes in brains of animals), or that the lower platelet AC activity is an inherent characteristic of alcoholics, and thus may be useful as a marker of a genetically determined predisposition to alcoholism (Tabakoff & Hoffman, 1988). The development of such a biochemical marker would be of significant value in allowing for early intervention with the aim of prevention of alcohol abuse and alcoholism.

Systems That Modulate Neuroadaptation to Ethanol

The information presented above has been focused on the neurochemical systems that may be directly affected by acute ingestion of ethanol and on systems that may be part of a cascade of events initiated by these direct effects of ethanol. A number of the systems directly affected by ethanol have been noted to develop a resistance to ethanol's actions over the course of chronic treatment of animals with ethanol, or to alter their intrinsic activity during the course of such treatment. It is postulated that the witnessed neuroadaptive changes in neuronal structure or activity are the determinants of alcohol tolerance and physical dependence.

A concept that has been applied to the neurobiology of both learning and tolerance is that of "extrinsic" and "intrinsic" neural systems. Intrinsic systems encode specific information, such as tolerance to a particular effect of ethanol, by changes in their structure or function. An example of such a change would be the alteration in the sensitivity of the GABA receptor-gated chloride channel to the effect of ethanol. Extrinsic systems, on the other hand, can influence the development, maintenance, or expression of tolerance and/or dependence, but do not encode tolerance or dependence in themselves. A number of studies indicate that both intrinsic characteristics of certain neurons and extrinsic neurochemical events modulate the rates and extents of development of various forms of tolerance and of physical dependence. Underlying the propensity of an animal to develop tolerance to or dependence on ethanol are genetic variables, which may control both the intrinsic and extrinsic determinants of tolerance and dependence.

Extrinsic Systems: Neurotransmitter Effects on Tolerance

Two candidates for the extrinsic systems modulating ethanol tolerance are the noradrenergic and serotonergic neuronal pathways of brain. As discussed, the activity of both of these systems is affected by ethanol, but a more direct approach to studying the roles of these neurotransmitter systems in tolerance has been to specifically modify the activity of the neurotransmitter systems, and to determine the effect of the modification on the development or maintenance of ethanol tolerance. In rats, depletion of brain 5-HT was shown to delay the development of tolerance to the hypothermic and motor-impairing effects of ethanol (see Hoffman & Tabakoff, 1985). The specific serotonergic pathway involved was the one connecting the median raphe nucleus to the hippocampus. In mice, partial destruction of catecholaminergic neurons by 6-hydroxydopamine (6-OHDA) blocked the development of tolerance to the hypnotic and hypothermic effects of ethanol (see Hoffman & Tabakoff, 1985). In animals treated with desmethylimipramine prior to administration of 6-OHDA, noradrenergic systems were protected, and tolerance developed as usual. Recent data indicate that interaction of NE with β-adrenergic receptors coupled to AC may be important for the development of tolerance in mice. Although partial depletion of brain NE by 6-OHDA blocked the development of tolerance, daily intracerebroventricular treatment with forskolin, an activator of AC, overcame this blockade (Szabó, Hoffman, & Tabakoff, 1988).

In rats, depletion of NE did not block the development of tolerance to the hypnotic effects of ethanol, although it altered the initial response of the animals to ethanol. On the other hand, development of tolerance to the *hypothermic* effects of ethanol in rats was blocked by administration of the NE neurotoxin DSP-4 (Trzaskowska, Pucilowski, Dyr, Kostowski, & Hauptmann, 1986). It was also found that, although partial destruction of brain noradrenergic neurons did not block the development of tolerance to the hypnotic effect of ethanol in rats, combined destruction of both NE and 5-HT systems could completely block tolerance development, whereas destruction of serotonergic neurons only delayed tolerance development (see Hoffman & Tabakoff, 1985; Tabakoff et al., 1988).

In certain studies described above, neurotransmitters were depleted prior to ingestion of ethanol, but the animals ingested equivalent amounts of ethanol during the period of chronic ethanol intoxication. An important conclusion that can be drawn, therefore, is that the presence of ethanol in the CNS is necessary but not sufficient to produce ethanol tolerance. In addition to the presence of ethanol, the activity of certain neuronal pathways seems to be required in order for tolerance to be manifest. This requirement was also quite clearly demonstrated using a model system of an identified synapse in *Aplysia* (see Hoffman & Tabakoff, 1985). Ethanol accelerated the decay of posttetanic potentiation at this synapse, and, with repeated exposure, the ethanol effect diminished (i.e., tolerance developed). However, the development of tolerance was strictly dependent on adequate stimulation of the presynaptic terminal in the presence of ethanol. Such invertebrate model systems of synaptic plasticity have been used to great advantage in studies of the biochemistry and electrophysiology of learning, and may provide further insights into mechanisms of ethanol tolerance.

Extrinsic Systems: Neuropeptide Effects on Tolerance

Arginine vasopressin (AVP) is another compound that has been found to be important for expression or maintenance of ethanol tolerance (see Hoffman, 1987). Mice made functionally tolerant to various physiological effects of ethanol were found to remain tolerant, even without further ethanol ingestion, for as long as they received once-daily subcutaneous or intracerebroventricular injections of AVP. In mice, depletion of brain NE prevented the maintenance of tolerance by AVP, suggesting a role for noradrenergic systems in this action of the hormone. An analogue of AVP (des-9-glycinamide AVP [DGAVP]) also maintained tolerance to the motor-incoordinating effect of ethanol in rats. In these animals, depletion of brain 5-HT prevented the action of DGAVP. Specifically, DGAVP could no longer maintain tolerance after chemical denervation of the dorsal serotonergic afferent pathways to the hippocampus. Thus, AVP appears to modulate the activity of the extrinsic neurotransmitter systems that influence ethanol tolerance development; this illustrates the complex nature of neuronal interactions that contribute to neuroadaptation.

Recently, AVP receptors have been identified in lateral septum, hippocampus, and other brain areas (see Tribollet, Barberis, Jard, Dubois-Dauphin, & Dreifuss, 1988). Septal and hippocampal AVP receptors appear to have characteristics in common with V_1 vasopressin receptors as defined in peripheral tissues. A study using agonists and antagonists selective for V_1 or V_2 receptors has demonstrated that the ability of vasopressin to maintain ethanol tolerance is mediated by a CNS receptor with V_1 characteristics (Szabó, Tabakoff, & Hoffman, 1988).

Pittman, Rogers, and Bloom (1982) reported that ethanol tolerance did not develop in Brattleboro rats given ethanol chronically, in contrast to control animals. Brattleboro rats do not produce active AVP because of a mutation that interferes with the translation of messenger ribonucleic acid for the vasopressin precursor molecule. These findings suggest a mechanism by which genetic variablity can also influence ethanol tolerance.

Summary and Conclusions

It should be clear from this overview that ethanol, although it is a relatively small and chemically simple molecule, is capable of selective influences on basic mechanisms of information transmission in the CNS. The earlier concept—namely, that ethanol is a nonspecific drug that produces its pharmacological effects via generalized perturbation of the structure of neuronal membranes—has given way to a realization that there are specific "receptive sites" that are especially sensitive to ethanol. These sites may include particular lipid microdomains, lipid–protein interfaces, or hydrophobic regions within particular proteins. As an example, the neuronal receptor systems that are selectively sensitive to ethanol include the GABA receptor-coupled chloride channel, the NMDA receptor-gated ion channel, the 5-HT$_3$ receptor-coupled potassium channels, and the G$_s$ protein. Interestingly, these systems appear to undergo adaptive changes in response to chronic ethanol ingestion, and may thus be implicated in the development of certain aspects of ethanol "craving," tolerance, and physical dependence. Furthermore, certain neurotransmitters and neuropeptide systems have been identified that are essential for the modulation of the rate of development or dissipation of ethanol tolerance.

The identification of the neuronal pathways that are sensitive to ethanol, and that adapt to the chronic presence of ethanol in the brain, has allowed at least a tentative linkage to be proposed between specific neurochemical and behavioral responses to ethanol. It is of some interest that alcohol withdrawal symptomatology may be a collage of effects generated by malfunction of several neurotransmitter systems. For instance, blockade of up-regulated NMDA receptors in an alcohol-dependent animal will significantly diminish withdrawal seizures, but will have little effect on tremor of the limbs. Knowledge of such specific relationships within the spectrum of acute and chronic effects of ethanol opens new avenues for the development of more effective and specific therapies for various deleterious effects of alcohol. These observations also provide a focus for examination of genetic factors that contribute to individual variability in susceptibility to alcoholism.

References

Allan, A. A., & Harris, R. A. (1987). Involvement of neuronal chloride channels in ethanol intoxication, tolerance and dependence. In M. Galanter (Ed.), *Recent developments in alcoholism* (Vol. 5, pp. 313–325). New York: Plenum Press.

Ballenger, J. C., Goodwin, F. K., Major, L. F., & Brown, G. L. (1979). Alcohol and central serotonin metabolism in man. *Archives of General Psychiatry, 36,* 224–227.

Borg, S., Kvande, H., Mossberg, D., Valverius, P., & Sedvall, G. (1983). Central nervous system noradrenaline metabolism and alcohol consumption in man. *Pharmacology, Biochemistry and Behavior, 18,* 375–378.

Borg, S., & Weinholdt, T. (1982). Bromocriptine in the treatment of the alcohol withdrawal syndrome. *Acta Psychiatrica Scandinavica, 65,* 101–111.

Buckholtz, N. S., Zhou, D., & Tabakoff, B. (1989). Ethanol does not affect serotonin receptor binding in rodent brain. *Alcohol, 6,* 277–280.

Cloninger, C. R. (1987). Neurogenetic adaptive mechanisms in alcoholism. *Science, 236,* 410–416.

Daniell, L. C., & Harris, R. A. (1989). Ethanol and inositol 1,4,5-trisphosphate release calcium from separate stores of brain microsomes. *Journal of Pharmacology and Experimental Therapeutics, 250,* 875–881.

Edwards, G. (1968). The alcohol dependence syndrome: A concept as stimulus to inquiry. *British Journal of Addiction, 81,* 171–183.

Franks, N. P., & Lieb, W. R. (1984). Do general anesthetics act by competitive binding to specific receptors? *Nature, 310,* 599–601.

Freissmuth, M., Casey, P. J., & Gilman, A. G. (1989). G proteins control diverse pathways of transmembrane signaling. *Federation of American Societies for Experimental Biology Journal, 3,* 2125–2131.

Grant, K. A., Lovinger, D. M., White, G., & Barrett, J. E. (1990). Blockade of the discriminative stimulus properties of ethanol by 5-HT$_3$ receptor antagonists. *Federation of American Societies for Experimental Biology Journal, 4,* A989.

Grant, K. A., Valverius, P., Hudspith, M., & Tabakoff, B. (1990). Ethanol withdrawal seizures and the NMDA receptor complex. *European Journal of Pharmacology, 176,* 289–296.

Harris, R. A., & Allan, A. A. (1989). Alcohol intoxication: Ion channels and genetics. *Federation of American Societies for Experimental Biology Journal, 3,* 1689–1695.

Harris, R. A., Groh, G. I., Baxter, D. M., & Hitzemann, R. J. (1984). Gangliosides enhance the membrane actions of ethanol and pentobarbital. *Molecular Pharmacology, 25,* 410–417.

Hoffman, P. L. (1987). Central nervous system effects of neurohypophyseal peptides. In C. W. Smith (Ed.), *The peptides* (pp. 239–295). New York: Academic Press.

Hoffman, P. L., Rabe, C. S., Moses, F., & Tabakoff, B. (1989). N-methyl-D-aspartate receptors and ethanol: Inhibition of calcium flux and cyclic GMP production. *Journal of Neurochemistry, 52,* 1937–1940.

Hoffman, P. L., & Tabakoff, B. (1985). Ethanol's action on brain biochemistry. In R. E. Tarter, D. H. van Thiel, & K. L. Edwards (Eds.), *Alcohol and the brain: Chronic effects* (pp. 19–68). New York: Plenum.

Koppi, S., Eberhardt, G., Haller, R., & König, H. P. (1987). Calcium-channel-blocking agent in the treatment of acute alcohol withdrawal: Caroverine versus meprobamate in a randomized double-blind study. *Neuropsychobiology, 17,* 49–52.

Lister, R. G., & Nutt, D. J. (1988). Alcohol antagonists: The continuing quest. *Alcoholism: Clinical and Experimental Research, 12,* 566–569.

Little, H. J., Dolin, S. J., & Halsey, M. J. (1986). Calcium channel antagonists decrease the ethanol withdrawal syndrome. *Life Sciences, 39,* 2059–2065.

Lovinger, D. M., White, G., & Weight, F. F. (1989). Ethanol inhibits NMDA-activated ion current in hippocampal neurons. *Science, 243,* 1721–1724.

Major, L. F., Ballenger, J. C., Goodwin, F. K., & Brown, G. L. (1977). Cerebrospinal fluid homovanillic acid in male alcoholics: Effects of disulfiram. *Biological Psychiatry, 12,* 635–642.

McLennan, H. (1988). The pharmacological characterization of excitatory amino acid receptors. In D. Lodge (Ed.), *Excitatory amino acids in health and disease* (pp. 1–12). Chichester, England: Wiley.

Mereu, G., Fadda, F., & Gessa, G. L. (1984). Ethanol stimulates the firing rate of nigral dopaminergic neurons in unanesthetized rats. *Brain Research, 292,* 63–69.

Meyer, H. H. (1901). Zur Theorie der Alkoholnarkose: III. Der Einfluss wechselnder Temperatur auf Wirkungesstarke und Teilungskoeffizient der Narkotica. *Naunyn-Schmiedeberg's Archives of Experimental Pathology and Pharmacology, 46,* 338–346.

Miller, R. J. (1987). Multiple calcium channels and neuronal function. *Science, 235,* 46–52.

Murphy, J. M., Waller, M. B., Gatto, G. J., McBride, W. J., Lumeng, L., & Li, T. -K. (1988).

Effects of fluoxetine on the intragastric self-administration of ethanol in the alcohol preferring P line of rats. *Alcohol, 5,* 283–286.

Naranjo, C. A., Sellers, E. M., Roach, C. A., Woodley, D. V., Sanchez-Craig, M., & Sykora, K. (1984). Zimelidine-induced variations in alcohol intake by nondepressed heavy drinkers. *Clinical Pharmacology and Therapeutics, 35,* 374–381.

Naranjo, C. A., Sellers, E. M., Sullivan, J. T., Woodley, D. V., Kadlec, K., & Sykora, K. (1987). The serotonin uptake inhibitor citalopram attenuates ethanol intake. *Clinical Pharmacology and Therapeutics, 41,* 266–274.

Nutt, D., & Glue, P. (1986). Monoamines and alcohol. *British Journal of Addiction, 81,* 327–338.

Olsen, R. W. (1987). The gamma-aminobutyric acid/benzodiazepine/barbiturate receptor–chloride ion channel complex of brain. In G. W. Edelman, W. E. Gall, & W. M. Cowan (Eds.), *Synaptic function* (pp. 257–271). New York: Wiley.

Pang, K. Y., Braswell, L. M., Chang, L., Sommer, T. J., & Miller, K. W. (1980). The perturbation of lipid bilayers by general anesthetics: A quantitative test of the disordered lipid hypothesis. *Molecular Pharmacology, 18,* 84–90.

Pittman, Q. J., Rogers, J., & Bloom, F. E. (1982). Arginine vasopressin deficient Brattleboro rats fail to develop tolerance to the hypothermic effects of ethanol. *Regulatory Peptides, 4,* 33–41.

Pringle, M. J., Brown, K. B., & Miller, K. W. (1981). Can the lipid theories of anesthesia account for the cutoff in anesthetic potency in homologous series of alcoholics? *Molecular Pharmacology, 19,* 49–55.

Rezazadeh, S. M., Woodward, J. J., & Leslie, S. W. (1989). Fura-2 measurement of cytosolic fee calcium in rat brain cortical synaptosomes and the influence of ethanol. *Alcohol, 6,* 341–345.

Rottenberg, H., Waring, A., & Rubin, E. (1981). Tolerance and cross-tolerance in chronic alcoholics: Reduced membrane binding of ethanol and other drugs. *Science, 213,* 583–585.

Roy, A., Virkkunen, M., & Linnoila, M. (1988). Monoamines, glucose metabolism, aggression towards self and others. *International Journal of Neuroscience, 41,* 261–264.

Schofield, P. R., Darlison, M. G., Fujita, N., Burt, D. R., Stephenson, F. A., Rodriguez, H., Rhee, L. M., Ramachandran, J., Reale, V., Glencorse, T. A., Seeburg, P. H., & Barnard, E. (1987). Sequence and functional expression of the $GABA_A$ receptor shows a ligand-gated receptor super-family. *Nature, 238,* 221–227.

Shah, J., Cohen, R. S., & Pant, H. C. (1987). Inositol trisphosphate-induced calcium release in brain microsomes. *Brain Research, 419,* 1–6.

Siegel, S. (1979). The role of conditioning in drug tolerance and addiction. In J. D. Keehn (Ed.), *Psychopathology in animals: Research and treatment implications* (pp. 143–168). New York: Academic Press.

Suzdak, P. D., Glowa, J. R., Crawley, J. N., Schwartz, R. D., Skolnick, P., & Paul, S. M. (1986). A selective imidazobenzodiazepine antagonist of ethanol in the rat. *Science, 234,* 1243–1247.

Szabó, G., Hoffman, P. L., & Tabakoff, B. (1988). Forskolin promotes the development of ethanol tolerance in 6-hydroxydopamine-treated mice. *Life Sciences, 42,* 615–621.

Szabó, G., Tabakoff, B., & Hoffman, P. L. (1988). Receptors with V_1 characteristics mediate the maintenance of ethanol tolerance by vasopressin. *Journal of Pharmacology and Experimental Therapeutics, 247,* 536–541.

Tabakoff, B., & Hoffman, P. L. (1987). Biochemical pharmacology of alcohol. In H. Y. Meltzer (Ed.), *Psychopharmacology: The third generation of progress* (pp. 1521–1526). New York: Raven Press.

Tabakoff, B., & Hoffman, P. L. (1988). Genetics and biological markers of risk for alcoholism. *Public Health Reports, 103,* 690–698.

Tabakoff, B., & Hoffman, P. L. (1989). Adaptive responses to ethanol in the central nervous system. In H. W. Goedde & D. P. Agarwal (Eds.), *Alcoholism: Biomedical and genetic aspects* (pp. 99–112). New York: Pergamon Press.

Tabakoff, B., Hoffman, P. L., & McLaughlin, A. (1988). Is ethanol a discriminating substance? *Seminars in Liver Disease, 8,* 26–35.

Tabakoff, B., Hoffman, P. L., & Moses, F. (1977). Neurochemical correlates of ethanol withdrawal: Alterations in serotonergic function. *Journal of Pharmacy and Pharmacology, 29,* 471–476.

Tabakoff, B., Melchior, C. L., & Hoffman, P. L. (1982). Commentary on ethanol tolerance. *Alcoholism: Clinical and Experimental Research, 6,* 252–259.

Tabakoff, B., & Rothstein, J. D. (1983). Biology of tolerance and dependence. In B. Tabakoff, P. B. Sutker, & C. L. Randall (Eds.), *Medical and social aspects of alcohol abuse* (pp. 187–220). New York: Plenum Press.

Taraschi, R. F., Ellingson, J. S., Wu, A., Zimmerman, R., & Rubin, E. (1986). Phosphatidylinositol from ethanol-fed rats confers membrane tolerance to ethanol. *Proceedings of the National Academy of Sciences of the United States of America, 83,* 9398–9402.

Tribollet, E., Barberis, C., Jard, S., Dubois-Dauphin, M., & Dreifuss, J. J. (1988). Localization and pharmacological characterization of high affinity binding sites for vasopressin and oxytocin in the rat brain by light microscopic autoradiography. *Brain Research, 442,* 105–118.

Trzaskowska, E., Pucilowski, O., Dyr, W., Kostowski, W., & Hauptmann, M. (1986). Suppression of ethanol tolerance and dependence in rats treated with DSP-4, a noradrenergic neurotoxin. *Drug and Alcohol Dependence, 18,* 349–353.

Yoshida, K., Engle, J., & Liljequist, S. (1982). The effect of chronic ethanol administration on high affinity ^{3}H-nicotinic binding in rat brain. *Naunyn-Schmiedeberg's Archives of Pharmacology, 321,* 74–76.

Index